W9-CDB-945

BUSINESS AND GOVERNMENT IN AMERICA SINCE 1870

A Twelve-Volume Anthology
of Scholarly Articles

Series Editor

ROBERT F. HIMMELBERG

Fordham University

A GARLAND SERIES

131314

SERIES CONTENTS

VOLUME

4

ANTITRUST AND REGULATION DURING WORLD WAR I AND THE REPUBLICAN ERA 1917-1932

Edited with introductions by

ROBERT F. HIMMELBERG

GARLAND PUBLISHING, Inc.
New York & London
1994

Library of Congress Cataloging-in-Publication Data

Antitrust and regulation during World War I and the Republican era,
1917–1932 / edited with introductions by Robert F. Himmelberg.
    p.   cm. — (Business and government in America since
1870 ; v. 4)
    A collection of articles that were originally published from 1962
to 1990.
    ISBN 0–8153–1406–X (alk. paper)
    1. Antitrust law—United States—History. 2. Restraint of
trade—United States—History. 3. Trusts, Industrial—Government policy—United States—History. 4. United States—Economic policy—To 1933. I. Himmelberg, Robert F. II. Series.
KF1649.A2A414 1994
343.73'0721'09042—dc20
[347.30372109042]   93–47671
                                                     CIP

Printed on acid-free, 250-year-life paper
Manufactured in the United States of America

CONTENTS

SERIES INTRODUCTION

This compilation of articles provides a very broad and representative selection of the scholarly literature found in learned journals on the subject of government-business relations in the age of industry, the period since 1870. The scope of this collection is wide, covering all the arenas of business-government interaction. Sectorially, the focus is on manufacturing and transportation, upon whose rapid expansion after the Civil War the modern industrial economy was founded.

For the volumes covering the years from 1870 to 1965 (Volumes I through IX) it has been possible, while exercising selectivity, to include a very high proportion of everything published within the past thirty years. This literature is found largely in historical journals. More selectivity had to be employed for Volumes X through XII, which cover the period since 1965. Historians have not yet trodden much on the ground of the very recent past but social scientists and legal scholars have offered abundant materials, so abundant as to require a relatively severe selectivity. By choosing articles that appear to have a long-term analytical value and by excluding those too narrow in scope, too preoccupied with methodological questions or otherwise unsuitable for a non-specialized audience, an extensive and accessible body of writing has, however, been assembled for the post-1965 period, mainly from economics and legal periodicals.

The volumes are designed to contain articles relating to a particular period and to one or more topics within a period. The literature of business-government relations has four logically distinct major topics: antitrust, regulation, promotion, and cooperation. These topics define distinctive aspects of the relationship. Yet, the distinctions sometimes in practice blur, the ostensible, publicly proclaimed purposes of policy sometimes differing from the actually intended purposes or the actual outcomes.

Antitrust policy emerges in Volume I, which covers the era 1870–1900 when big business appeared, and figures prominently throughout the series. Several volumes are devoted entirely to it. Uniquely American, at least until relatively recently, antitrust policy has a complex history and much of what scholars have discovered about its origin and evolution is recorded only in the articles gathered in this collection. The literature reproduced here makes clear that the intent and impact of antitrust policy has varied enormously during its one-hundred-year history, which dates from the Sherman Act of 1890. Tension between competing objectives has existed from the outset. Should the "trusts" be broken up on the grounds that super-corporations inevitably conflict with democratic government and entrepreneurial opportunity? Or should only "bad trusts", those guilty of crushing competitors through unfair methods, suffer dissolution? Is cartelistic behavior always an illegal restraint of trade, or should it sometimes be tolerated if it helps small business to survive? Put most broadly, should the aim of antitrust policy be simply promoting competition, or should other conflicting social and economic values be recognized?

Business regulation also arose during the early stages of industrialization, appearing at the federal level with the enactment of the Interstate Commerce Act in 1887. The term "regulation" is used here to denote government policies intended, not to promote or restore competition, but to require specific behavior from business. The classic justification for regulation was the argument that in some situations the public interest could be served only through governmental prescription, that in some instances a remedy simply could not be obtained through the workings of the marketplace. Theoretically there are two such instances. The first occurs in the case of "natural monopoly," market situations in which competition would be wasteful and competing firms do not and should not exist. Railroads and public utilities were early identified as industries of this sort and were the first targets of government regulation. Would-be regulators early discovered a second justification for applying the regulatory approach, the situation in which competition fails to provide rival firms with incentives to avoid methods that may injure public health or well being. The argument found early expression in regulation of the meat-packing industry and has over the course of the twentieth century created a remarkable body of federal regulatory practices. The history of regulation, however, has not unfolded, any more than the history of antitrust, according to the logic of theory. It has been determined by the interplay between many factors, including the ideas of reformers, the complaints of those who have felt injured, policy rivalries among businessmen themselves, and the capacity or incapacity of government to execute planned reform. A major focus of recent literature on regulation, and to an extent on antitrust also, is the thesis of capture, the notion that regulatory efforts have often fallen captive to the interests they were intended to oppose.

The third theme of relations between government and business, promotion and encouragement, also emerged during the initial stages of the industrial era. Railroad subsidies abounded during the age of building the transcontinentals, of course, and protective tariffs were almost as old as the Republic itself. In the early twentieth century government support of trade expansion abroad enlarged and gradually became a major thread of government policy. Resembling promotion but logically distinct in many respects is the fourth category of business-government interaction, the area of cooperative relationships. Few scholars, even those who believe ongoing conflict has chiefly characterized business-government relations, would deny that cooperation has occurred at certain points, as during American participation in the major wars of the twentieth century. But in recent years many writers who conceive of business-government relations as taking place within a "corporatist" framework have perceived the scope and continuity of cooperative tendencies as very broad.

These four categories describe the subjects or topics around which scholarly investigation of business-government relations has revolved. There is, however, another approach to analyzing the literature of this relationship, one in which we ask about a writer's interpretive perspective, the conceptualizations the writer brings to the subject. All historians and social scientists, including those who created the literature collected here, adopt an interpretive standpoint from which to view society and its workings. An interpretive standpoint is a way of understanding the structure of society and the way those structural elements relate and interact; in other words, it is a "model" of society. Several rival models have competed for acceptance among scholars in recent times. Readers will be better equipped for informed reading of the literature assembled in these volumes if they are knowledgeable about these interpretive standpoints and the aim here therefore is to define the most important of these and give them appropriate labels.

Until the 1950s the prevailing interpretation of business-government relations—indeed, of American history generally—was the progressive viewpoint. The term progressive refers in the first place to the reform ideology and activity of the early twentieth century, the period before World War I. The perspective of the progressive generation continued for many years to dominate historical writing, not only on the period itself but on the whole of American history. According to the progressive perspective, the rise of big business during the late nineteenth and early twentieth centuries created a radical shift in the balance of economic and political power in America in favor of concentrated wealth. The rise of the "trusts", the powerful firms that came to predominate in many industries in the years after 1880, and the creation of cartels and other arrangements for suppressing competition, threatened independent capitalists and consumers with raw economic exploitation. This concentration of economic power threatened to utterly suborn representative political institutions as well and reduce American democracy to a plutocracy. In the progressive view the predominating tone of business-government relations was therefore necessarily antagonistic and conflictual.

The progressive paradigm became deeply embedded in the American consciousness. Reformist politicians have often reverted to it in shaping their ideological and rhetorical appeals. Franklin D. Roosevelt's attack in the campaign of 1936 upon "economic royalists" and John Kennedy's denunciation in 1962 of Big Steel during the controversy over price guidelines as "utterly contemptuous of the public interest" are vivid examples. The progressive outlook is evidently a persistent element in the popular historical consciousness. The power of the progressive conception of American history is in fact readily confirmed by reference to the way twentieth-century history is periodized, in textbooks and popular histories, into epochs of reform (the Progressive, New Deal, Fair Deal and Great Society periods) and of reaction (the Twenties, the Eisenhower and Reagan eras).

But if the progressive interpretation of business government relations retains some force among some historians and in the consciousness of liberal opinion makers and the public, its hold on much of the academic mind has long since weakened. A reaction among historians and other academics against the progressive paradigm emerged soon after the end of the Second World War and gathered force during the 1950s. The reaction was especially sharp among historians writing business history. Writing at a time when a reinvigorated American economy appeared to have overcome the doldrums of the 1930s and to be demonstrating the superiority of capitalism over other systems, energetic business and economic historians completely revised the progressive interpretation of the founders of American big business. The revisionists interpreted the founders not as greedy robber barons but as heroes of the entrepreneurial spirit, the spirit of enterprise and productivity. This revisionist interpretation proved too one-dimensional and celebratory to be maintained without modification. Revisionism, however, did succeed in thoroughly discrediting the progressive point of view. This circumstance, together with the impact of interpretive concepts emanating from post-war social science, moved historians to replace the progressive paradigm with a new and more sophisticated framework for understanding American political economy, the pluralist framework.

Pluralism as the dominant interpretive mode replaced progressivism in the 1950s and 60s. Speaking broadly, the pluralist model understands public policy as the result of struggle between economic and social groups. A major by-product of industrialization is the sharpening of differences between groups playing distinctive economic roles and a heightened articulation of self-interested goals and purposes on the part of such groups. Thus, government-business relations, that is, the shape of government policies towards business, are the result of rivalries among the major interest groups, business, labor, consumers, and so on. But the nature of the struggle is complex because the major groups are themselves divided into more or less rivalrous sub-groups. Business itself is divided; both intra- and inter-industry rivalries exist, sometimes in acute forms. Government policy is not merely the result of nonbusiness groups seeking to shape that policy but also of some business interests seeking to impose their own wishes on others.

During the 1960s pluralist interpretation became more complex. One important source of this heightened complexity was what some commentators have called the "organizational" outlook. Again influenced by currents in American social science, this time sociology, practitioners employing the organizational perspective are struck by the ever-increasing importance of large bureaucratic organizations in American life since the onset of industrialization. Business has continuously evolved in terms of an ever larger role for the large corporation, but other spheres, including government and the professions, also are organized in terms of large hierarchical bureaucracies. Borrowing from Weberian sociological traditions, writers impressed by the organizational perspective have explored the thesis that large bureaucracies wherever situated have similar requirements and tend to develop in those who manage them similar values and expectations. Thus, this brand of pluralism stresses the extent to which group leaders, including the managers and technicians who run the large corporations, developed accommodative as well as merely self-seeking motives. Business leaders, many of them at least, came to share certain values, such as respect for stability in the overall economy, which leads them to seek harmonious and cooperative relationships between interest groups and between them and the government. Government is assigned the role, in this construct, of facilitating and stimulating cooperative modes of behavior and umpiring conflicts. In the literature on business and government, figures who have advocated this kind of polity are often dubbed "corporatists" or "corporate liberals." Broadly defined, corporatism is the practice of cooperation between government and the corporate world to resolve economic issues. The existence and the importance of corporatist relationships has been one of the major emphases of recent scholarship but there is much disagreement as to the intentions of its practitioners and its impact. Some scholars have interpreted corporatism in a more or less positive light, as an ideology and a practice entailing cooperation rather than conflict between government and business, as an alternative to an adversarial relationship, a way of obtaining desirable economic performance from business without resorting to governmental coercion.

But others, especially but not only those writing in the vein of the "New Left", have argued that members of the corporate elite have frequently pursued their own narrow interests under the cover of ostensibly cooperative endeavors. The New Leftists emerged in the 1960s, expounding a more radical criticism of business than the progressive-liberal historians had advanced. The New Leftists doubted or denied outright that the American system was pluralist at all in any meaningful sense. Control of public policy might appear as a contest between social groups, but in fact one group, or rather class, those who controlled big business, enjoyed such lopsided power that the contest was apparently not real. Behind the facade of political infighting over government policy toward business, the masters of the corporate world quietly steered events toward outcomes which cemented in place control of the economy by monopoly capital.

These four conceptualizations, the progressive, the pluralist, the corporatist, and the New Leftist, are essentially theories of the structure and process of American political economy. However, rarely are researchers slavishly devoted to a theoretical perspective. Thus, those who see, in the progressive vein, an ongoing conflictual relationship between the people and business sometimes argue against the reformers and in favor of the businessmen. Even more significant and widespread is the conclusion of many writers using the pluralist or corporatist modes of interpretation, that regulation has not fostered equity and economic progress but rather has hardened the economy's vital arteries. Pluralists initially assumed that policies arising from a political arena to which all organized interests have access will inevitably achieve benign results, that the policy outputs will construct a system of "countervailing power" among organized interest groups. The assumption of acceptable outcomes is still prevalent, but a skeptical version of the results of interest group rivalries became manifest in the late

1960s, holding that both in origin and ongoing impact, business regulation was too often subject to "capture." In this view, regulatory measures and agencies and other policies seeking to guide business behavior toward balanced and generally acceptable outcomes readily fall under the control of the very interests they were intended to regulate.

There has emerged in recent years still another approach to the origin and process of social-economic policy that has been applied to the business-government connection. In this interpretation of the connection, a few examples of which will be found in articles collected here, emphasis is placed on the relative autonomy of government administrators and regulators. Seen by the pluralists as merely the creatures of the organizational struggles that result in public policies, in this new view regulators are seen as possessing substantial room for independent action. Thus the state is not merely to be seen as a passive receptor and executor of outcomes that social forces determine but as having a partially autonomous role which the officers of the state presumably will use to extend their own interests rather than the interests articulated by social groups.

These categories, progressivism, pluralism, corporatism, Leftism and the "autonomous officialdom" viewpoint, represent the major schools of thought and interpretation that readers will discover in the literature reproduced in these volumes. Writers investigating specific historical incidents, trends or problems have, in most cases, written through the framework provided by one or another of these interpretive models. As an alert reader will discover, most writers do have certain assumptions about the structure and dynamics of social relationships, and these assumptions stem from one of the models that have been described.

Interpretation of the relationship between business and government in the age of industry has given rise to a literature that is large and complex. It presents a stimulating intellectual challenge and is certainly relevant for anyone seeking understanding of contemporary business-government relations and endeavoring to predict, or to shape, their future course.

INTRODUCTION

This period is remarkable for the range of economic and political circumstances it contains. It begins with the entry of the United States into World War I under the leadership of Woodrow Wilson and a Democratic Congress. Industrial mobilization in 1917–1918 generated full employment of resources, but demobilization produced a sharp postwar depression in 1920. Hard times, as well as disaffection over Wilson's wartime economic policies and disillusionment with the results of his diplomacy, produced an overwhelming wave of voter resentment against the Democrats and a landslide vote for the Republicans. Warren G. Harding and a Republican-controlled Congress promised to take the country back to "normalcy." The decade of the twenties became the decade of Republican prosperity and political supremacy, but the party's luck ran out in 1929, shortly after Herbert Hoover, the most progressive and reformist Republican leader of his era, became president in 1929. The Great Depression, its beginning signalled by the Great Crash of the stock market in October, 1929, pitilessly enveloped the nation in a unceasing wave of unemployment, foreclosures and business failures. Hoover struggled but failed to reverse the downward path of the economy. The result was the political upheaval of 1932, which installed Franklin D. Roosevelt in the White House and initiated an epoch of Democratic control lasting until Eisenhower's election in 1952.

Though remarkably varied in terms of economic, political and social conditions, the era from 1917 to 1932 contains at least one strong unifying theme, the strengthening and broadening of contact between business and government. The most important element in this closer relationship is the growing practice of cooperation. Cooperation took the traditional form of government support for business endeavors as, for example, in the growing assistance Washington gave to American exporters. But it also took a more complex form as some government and business leaders sought to link their two realms in efforts to solve endemic economic and social problems. These "corporatist" activities are taken up, however, in Volume V of this series. In this volume articles are collected that illuminate another side of business-government relations, a side that indicates that despite the corporatist trend of the period, there remained something of the adversarial in business-government relations as well. As many writers have shown, and they are well-represented in the next volume, the Wilson administration endeavored as much as possible to mobilize the economy for war through cooperative rather than command methods. The great wartime agencies such as the War Industries Board sought to implement priorities and price-fixing policies through agreement rather than dictate. But, as some of the articles reproduced in this volume indicate, controversy remained, as the Democrats were reluctant to concede every decision to business or to allow the wartime suspension of antitrust to continue into the post-Armistice period. Again, after the Republican return to power in 1921, businessmen were gratified by a friendlier taxation and regulatory atmosphere, but conflict nonetheless broke out, particularly regarding antitrust policy, where many business elements wanted to go much further toward a cartelized economy than the government was ready to permit. Herbert Hoover, both while secretary of commerce and president, strongly supported industrial organization and trade association cooperative activities, but his vision of their purposes and limitations prevented him from supporting the demand from businessmen for virtual elimination of traditional antitrust limitations. During the Depression years, business dissatisfaction with Republican unwillingness to let antitrust lapse became more severe as more and more industries and key leaders became convinced that wholesale cartelization was the way to stabilize the economy and promote recovery.

Newton D. Baker and the Genesis of the War Industries Board, 1917-1918

Daniel R. Beaver

D URING two and one half critical months from late March to mid-June 1917, Secretary of War Newton D. Baker helped make three high policy decisions that in a substantial way shaped American industry's part in World War I. The first decision, made on March 28, called for an army of one million men to be raised by selected draft and trained by June 1918. The second, made on May 14, after the arrival of British and French military missions in Washington, directed that an expeditionary force of undetermined size be dispatched to France. The third, made on June 14, declared that those troops should be on the French battle line by the end of July 1918. This army would have to be supplied and equipped, and the country faced a host of difficult if not insurmountable problems in meeting the challenge. Except for government arsenals, usable plant capacity was already committed to producing munitions for the Allies and could not be freed for four to six months. Existing civilian plants had to be converted to war production and new plants had to be built. There was no lead time; weapons had to be approved, in some cases even designed, after American entrance into the war. Traditional military supply procedures also had to be modernized.[1] Finally, and this is the question toward which this discussion is directed, the business community and the War Department had to be brought together in such a way as to assure prompt delivery of materiel and to avoid unnecessary disruption of civilian production. Just what was Secretary Baker's role in shaping the early policies of the War Industries Board and why after ten months of war were his powers over economic

Daniel R. Beaver is assistant professor of history in the University of Cincinnati.

[1] Prior to the war, the U.S. Army was not supplied through a single agency. The Quartermaster and Ordnance departments did the bulk of the buying, but the Office of the Surgeon General, the Office of Chief of Engineers, and the Office of the Chief Signal Officer purchased considerable material. Although the bureau system was economical in peacetime, it was ineffective in wartime because there was no way to establish priorities between bureaus or to regulate interbureau competition.

mobilization sharply curtailed? Answers to these queries show how personal beliefs, institutional loyalties, and party politics interacted when Americans for the first time made total war at long range.

It was ironic that Baker should preside over a massive war effort, for he was known over the nation as an antimilitarist.[2] Short, slightly built, and youthful looking, few men could have been less a picture of a warrior than he. Some of those closest to him in the administration believed he lacked personal force. Yet in his way he was effective. Baker had learned early the advantages of the indirect approach. He was adept at concealing his thoughts, and despite a reputation for graciousness and accommodation he could be so quietly ruthless if occasion demanded he was accused during the war of untruthfulness, deviousness, and hypocrisy. Writing afterward of Baker's work one of his assistants, former dean of Columbia University, Frederick P. Keppel, stated (not for publication) that Baker was the kind of person who let unimportant matters and people take his time and that he operated on the theory that if left alone many things "settle themselves." But Keppel added that Baker tended to do many things that might better have been done by subordinates and in turn he let subordinates "handle and botch matters which he should have dealt with personally."[3]

One of the more complex members of the Wilson circle, Baker had made his reputation as reform mayor of Cleveland, Ohio. As the heir of Tom L. Johnson in the Ohio Progressive movement, the Secretary of War might have been expected to be something of a political evangelist. But he had little use for crusaders or zealots and preferred to follow a moderate line on most issues. For example, in 1916 President Woodrow Wilson, knowing of Baker's long interest in child labor legislation, asked him for an opinion about a certain amendment to the Keating-Owen Child Labor Act. Baker replied:

The problem is in part at least the old puzzle of favoring the limitation of State authority and State adequacy as against National intervention. Things which 20 years ago seemed to me exclusively matters of State concern have come with the passing years to be obviously appropriate subjects for National legislation because of the changed character of the things themselves, and so I do not know that I have reached any clear conclusion as to where the Federal Government ought to stop . . . police regulation, but for practical purposes I am entirely clear that at present we ought not to do anything more than we have done.[4]

[2] Oswald Garrison Villard, *Fighting Years: Memoirs of a Liberal Editor* (New York, 1939), 248-49.
[3] Frederick P. Keppel, "Newton D. Baker" [March 1919?], Ralph Hayes Papers (Manuscript Division, Library of Congress).
[4] Baker to Wilson, Nov. 27, 1916, Newton D. Baker Papers (Manuscript Division, Library of Congress).

Localism and voluntarism were the cornerstones of his creed. "I have long believed," he wrote in 1916 to his friend Judge John H. Clarke of Cleveland, "that the problems of democracy have to be worked out in experiment stations rather than by universal applications, so that I regard Cleveland and Ohio as a more hopeful place to do things than any national station whatsoever."[5] Baker was not among those who saw the war as an opportunity to increase the power of the federal government in the life of the nation, and he opposed the creation of new agencies that might place more power permanently in federal hands.

Shortly after the struggle with Germany began Baker revealed the deep crosscurrents of his thought. He was determined that the conflict should not change traditional relationships between national, local, and private power to any marked degree. On May 2, 1917 he addressed a meeting of state and local councils of national defense and insisted that the best method of organizing the country was through voluntary associations formed at the local level. Given the choice between initial delay and regimentation, he stated he would prefer delay.[6] His influence pervaded the War Department and the Council of National Defense of which he was chairman. The latter group with its advisory committee of business experts was intended to bring the military into contact with industry in just such an emergency. If Baker had been so inclined he might have been able to fuse those two agencies into one powerful defense unit.[7] But he agreed with Major General Hugh L. Scott, then Chief of Staff, that the War Department must

[5] Baker to John H. Clarke, March 13, 1916, *ibid.* This letter gives significant insight into Baker's political philosophy. Like his friends Brand Whitlock, former mayor of Toledo, Ohio, and his old college roommate Frederick C. Howe, the pioneer city planner, Baker opposed extension of federal power. As Mayor Tom Johnson's Law Director in Cleveland, Baker fought for municipal home rule for over a decade. The experience convinced him that power must remain close to the people; the farther removed it was from that source the more danger there was that it would be corrupted either by ignorance or through design. For a discussion of Baker's early career see Clarence H. Cramer, *Newton D. Baker, A Biography* (Cleveland, 1961), 13-63.

[6] Transcript of proceedings of the National Defense Conference, held under the auspices of the Council of National Defense, May 2, 3, 1917, Josephus Daniels Papers (Manuscript Division, Library of Congress). Unlike President Wilson and some of his advisers, Baker had little fear of the business community. In Cleveland he had been able to work closely with certain business leaders in social reform, especially in creating lake front parks and playgrounds. If Wilson and some members of the administration were unwilling to be too much dominated by business interests who had formerly opposed them, Baker was much more alarmed about expansion of federal power than he was about alleged business influence.

[7] Baker insisted that after the United States entered the war all the authority any agency needed was available either directly or indirectly through delegation of presidential emergency power. Thus the Secretary of War never hesitated to act because he thought that he, or anyone else for that matter, lacked power. See for example Baker's letter to Wilson of Nov. 17, 1917, quoted at length later in this article.

3

have final authority to determine type, amount, and production priority of military equipment.[8] Thus civilians on the advisory board were largely overruled on policy questions by the military. A munitions board was formed in late April to expedite certain kinds of armaments, but the pleas of its chairman, industrialist Frank A. Scott, for real power were ignored. At the end of June 1917 a jerry-built array of 150 committees was associated helter-skelter with various army bureaus.[9] It appeared that Baker, motivated in part by deep personal reservations and in part by his desire to protect War Department prerogatives, would neither use all the potential power that he possessed nor allow anyone else to use it.

If the Secretary of War seemed unconcerned about the proliferation of boards, another member of the administration was much troubled. Secretary of the Treasury William G. McAdoo insisted that one man must be given independent control of industrial mobilization with power independent of the military. McAdoo was very close to Bernard M. Baruch who at that time was chairman of the raw materials committee of the advisory board, and in May 1917, on Baruch's recommendation, he advised Wilson that one person should be appointed with full power to control and direct purchasing by the military and for the Allies.[10]

Wilson was impressed with McAdoo's advice, but when the President asked Baker about the desirability of having a director of purchases the Secretary of War would have nothing to do with the idea. Baker asserted that the task was too big for any man and suggested instead a more limited advisory council that would include members of the Munitions Board, the Supply Committee of the Council of National Defense, and representatives of the State and Treasury departments, through which the regular executive agencies, in cooperation with the Allies, might purchase supplies in the United States.[11] On June 13 Baker sent to the President a plan which he suggested would make the Council of National Defense more effective in meeting the needs of the government through a War Industries Board. This plan contemplated "an immediate subordination of all committees to the Council of National Defense with the Advisory Commission acting in a purely advisory capacity." The War Industries Board would take the place of the former munitions board and would consist "of a civilian chairman, with Army and Navy representatives, and the proposed purchasing

[8] Hugh Scott to W. J. Nicholson, April 5, 1917, Hugh Scott Papers (Manuscript Division, Library of Congress).
[9] New York *Times*, July 11, 1917.
[10] McAdoo to Wilson, May 16, 1917. William G. McAdoo Papers (Manuscript Division, Library of Congress).
[11] Baker to Wilson, May 28, 1917, Baker Papers.

agent of the Allies with such additions to its membership as might be appropriate for the consideration of special subjects." The War Industries Board chairman would be one of five "official representatives of the government." The others would be a chief of raw materials, a chief of priorities, a chief of finished products, and a purchasing agent for the Allies, and all five would be subordinate to the Council of National Defense.[12]

Baker consulted none of the Advisory Commission, except Gifford, about the proposed reorganization. Baruch continued, as he had done since May, to suggest that a single individual be appointed to control all purchasing. On July 11 Baruch wrote the President that "Yesterday the Advisory Commission was shown for the first time the plan of reorganization as proposed by the Council of National Defense. I do not agree with the reorganization as being a wise one or an improvement on the present plan."[13] Doubt about the effectiveness of the plan was widespread within the Advisory Commission and among members of the Council of National Defense. Like Baruch, Julius Rosenwald, Director of the Committee on Supply, Secretary McAdoo, and Secretary of the Navy Josephus Daniels all believed that it did not provide the central control necessary to make the war effort effective.[14] But Baker would not be moved. Writing to the President on July 14 the Secretary of War stated that "Mr. Baruch and Mr. Rosenwald did not believe the plan effective. . . . Mr. [David F.] Houston, Mr. [Daniel] Willard, Mr. [William C.] Redfield, Mr. [Franklin K.] Lane, and I all took the other view and we had an earnest discussion." Baker added, "I understand what Mr. Baruch's feeling about it is, although I do not share his feeling and I do not know what remedy he would suggest if any."[15]

Disturbed by the difference of opinion among his advisers and moved by the weight of opinion against the "Baker Plan" the President wrote his Secretary of War a few days later:

I have, as you know, been giving a great deal of thought to the plan of reorganization submitted to me some time ago by the Council of National Defense. The more I think of it the more it seems to me that the the organization can be still more simplified greatly to its advantage. My suggestion—a suggestion which I hope you will be kind enough to lay before the Council,—

[12] Baker to Wilson, June 13, 1917, *ibid.* The plan was prepared by Walter S. Gifford, Director of the Advisory Commission, who apparently suggested the name "War Industries Board."

[13] Baruch to Wilson, July 11, 1917, Woodrow Wilson Papers (Manuscript Division, Library of Congress), File II, Box 122.

[14] Diary of Josephus Daniels, July 9, 1917, Daniels Papers.

[15] Baker to Wilson, July 14, 1917, Wilson Papers, File II, Box 122.

is that the three persons to whom will be entrusted the direction of purchases of raw materials, the purchases of finished products, and the arrangement of priorities of purchase and of shipment shall themselves be members of the War Industries Board together with . . . representatives of the War and Navy Departments, under the chairmanship of Mr. Scott; that the War Industries Board serve as a clearing house for the determination of the immediate needs of the Government and the sequence of those needs; and that the three officials I have named, those charged, namely, with the purchase of raw materials, with the purchase of finished products, and with the determination of priorities, shall in association with Mr. [Herbert C.] Hoover in the matter of the purchase of foodstuffs be the executive agency through which all our purchases are arranged for.[16]

The President's solution brought supervision of the more important aspects of the industrial effort together in one committee yet kept the WIB in an advisory or at most consultative relationship with the War Department.[17] It associated the supply committees of the Council of National Defense with the proper sections of the WIB. The duties of the new board were officially defined as follows:

The Board will act as a clearing-house for the war-industry needs of the Government, determine the most effective ways of meeting them, and the best means and methods of increasing production, including the creation or extension of industries demanded by the emergency, the sequence and relative urgency of the needs of the different Government services, and consider price factors and, in the first instance, the industrial and labor aspects of problems involved and the general questions affecting the purchase of commodities.[18]

The new agency represented a victory for Baker and the Army who desired a board to coordinate rather than to direct the industrial efforts of the United States. After publication of the reorganization plan on July 28 McAdoo wrote the President that he was "genuinely discouraged that such a complicated piece of machinery has been set up" and again advocated that executive authority be invested in one man rather than in a board where the military could exert undue influence. On the other hand, Baker, his fears of economic regimentation at rest and his defense of the War Department supply program successful, wrote to Wilson that he was confident and happy about the new board and sure that in a very little while its harmony would be complete.[19]

During the late summer and autumn there was a tug of war within the

---

[16] Wilson to Baker, July 17, 1917, Baker Papers.

[17] Daniels Diary, July 28, 1917.

[18] Grosvenor B. Clarkson, *Industrial America in the World War: The Strategy Behind the Line, 1917-1918* (Boston, 1923), 37.

[19] McAdoo to Wilson, July 30, 1917, Wilson Papers, File II, Box 123; Baker to Wilson, Aug. 1, 1917, Baker Papers.

WIB to determine whether soldiers or business leaders would dominate it. In mid-September Chairman Frank Scott, harassed by lack of authority and his health broken by strain, said he would have to resign, and it seems that the President was under immediate pressure from McAdoo in particular to name Baruch as chairman.[20] It was no secret that Baker considered Baruch nothing more than a daring speculator, and many members of the WIB felt the same way. On September 18 Robert S. Lovett told Wilson that he would resign if Baruch were named. To avoid trouble Wilson suggested that Baker select Lovett to replace Scott.[21] Baker replied that he was aware that "the Judge had some feeling of the kind suggested" but added that Scott had promised not to resign formally until "a suitable person could be found."[22] A little later Baker did name Lovett to serve unofficially until he could find a permanent replacement for Scott. No businessman appeared interested in the post unless he was assured an immediate grant of power. On November 6, 1917 Baker met with Homer L. Ferguson of the Newport News Shipyards and begged him to assume the task. Secretary Daniels, who accompanied Baker, wrote in his diary that Baker exclaimed, "You cannot leave until you accept," but Ferguson refused unless given broad authority to carry his plans into effect.[23] Unwilling to give such assurances Baker then turned to Daniel Willard, president of the Baltimore and Ohio Railroad and chairman of the Committee on Transportation of the Advisory Commission. In a letter to the President Baker told of the circumstances surrounding Willard's appointment:

I had a talk with Mr. Willard a day or two ago about the Chairmanship of the War Industries Board. His first remark to me on the subject was: "My son is fighting in France, and I cannot of course decline to do anything on this side which I am asked to do." He was, however, much concerned to solve for himself the question as to whether he could make a success of the task. The embarrassment in his mind arose from the fact that the War Industries Board as such has no power conferred by statute, and he felt that decisions which he might make would need to be very fully backed up by the Secretary of the Navy and by me, or indeed even by you, in order to be sure of getting them executed with speed and firmness.

Baker further related that inasmuch as the President had set up the WIB "with the idea of all of us co-operating through it," Willard should have no concern over the matter of power. Baker concluded by saying that after

[20] Baker to Wilson, Sept. 21, 1917, Wilson Papers, File II, Box 127; Clarkson, *Industrial America in the World War*, 82-85.
[21] Wilson to Baker, Sept. 18, 1917, Baker Papers.
[22] Baker to Wilson, Sept. 21, 1917, Wilson Papers, File II, Box 127.
[23] Daniels Diary, Nov. 7, 12, 1917.

taking the matter under advisement Willard accepted the appointment.[24] But even as he forwarded Willard's acceptance to the President, Baker was turning to another solution, one that he hoped would coordinate the war effort effectively without creating a national industrial czar or removing ultimate control of priority and procurement from the War Department.

Baker's attempt at an independent solution resulted from the virtual collapse of the war effort in the late fall and winter of 1917-1918. If Baker had been lucky he might have been able to withstand the storm of criticism that was sure to rise over inevitable equipment shortages, but the most severe weather in years struck the country that winter. In the heavily industrialized East only enough coke remained by mid-December to keep the blast furnaces going for a few more weeks. Autumn gales slowed the passage of both cargo and troopships on the North Atlantic, while trainloads of military supplies continued to pour into the northeastern ports where the army was scheduled to embark. Ships could not find berthing facilities in New York harbor, and the congestion made it virtually impossible to provision ships ready to sail. Major General Leonard Wood wrote a friend that it seemed the War Department was a victim of a brand of noisy inertia, like "a green man in an automobile, with one foot pushing down on the clutch and the other on the acclerator [sic]."[25]

In December the Congress, alarmed at the growing paralysis of the war effort, began a series of investigations into all its aspects, thus casting party politics in a most disturbing way into the controversy. Republicans were after Baker's scalp for his tactless handling of General Wood and Theodore Roosevelt earlier in the year.[26] Democratic Senator George E. Chamberlain of Oregon, chairman of the Senate Military Affairs Committee, was convinced that Baker lacked the personal force to conduct a successful mobilization. As the investigation continued it became clear that Chamberlain and his colleagues were sincerely alarmed and favored the creation of a powerful munitions office, similar to the English Ministry of Munitions, to control and allocate war materials. Republicans indicated that they would be satisfied only if control over production were placed in their hands

---

[24] Baker to Wilson, Nov. 17, 1917, quoted in Frederick Palmer, *Newton D. Baker: America at War* (2 vols., New York, 1931), I, 379.

[25] Hermann Hagedorn, *Leonard Wood: A Biography* (2 vols., New York, 1931), II, 236.

[26] Baker had refused in April 1917 to allow Theodore Roosevelt to raise a volunteer division to fight in France. A short time later he had passed over Leonard Wood, the senior officer in the Army, to appoint John J. Pershing Commander of the AEF. In August Wood had been relegated to the command of a training division at Camp Funston, Kansas.

through the choice of Roosevelt, Wood, or Elihu Root to head such an agency.

Baker was forced to reexamine his approach to supply problems in an atmosphere of crisis. During the first part of November he appointed Benedict Crowell, a Cleveland businessman, Assistant Secretary of War for quartermaster supplies. On December 5, to sidetrack possible strengthening of the WIB, he suggested that an "entirely informal" group consisting of the Council of National Defense, the Secretary of the Treasury, and the heads of the war agencies, be formed to discuss and coordinate all government purchasing.[27] In that way the WIB would continue to serve as a clearing house for orders and might even set priority, but it could not determine in any way the requirements of the army. He announced a little later that he had decided to agree to a plan "under consideration for some weeks" and form "a war council within the war department" to act as his personal advisers on purchase and supply.[28] To put his plan into effect he freed Major General William I. Crozier, Chief of Ordnance, and Major General Henry G. Sharpe, Quartermaster General, from administrative duties and made them permanent members of the War Council. He then named Major General George W. Goethals Acting Quartermaster General and Brigadier General Charles B. Wheeler as Acting Chief of Ordnance.[29]

Baker's own work was interrupted in early December by the arrival in Washington of a report from Thomas N. Perkins, representative of the WIB at the Inter-Allied Conference that met in Paris and London, November 29 to December 3, 1917. Perkins' recommendations, similar to plans already bruited about in Congress, were as follows:

The United States should at once organize a supply department, preferably a munitions department or ministry, with complete statutory powers; or, failing that, a board acting with delegated powers from the heads of the several services . . . charged with the duty of filling the requirements of the several services of our own Government and . . . of the Allies. This supply department should have the best possible man at its head and the best organizing and executive ability in the country on its staff. It should organize the industrial resources of the country.[30]

On December 21, 1917, Colonel P. D. Lochridge, Acting President of the War College, informed the Chief of Staff, Major General Tasker H.

[27] Baker to McAdoo, Dec. 5, 1917, McAdoo Papers, Letterbook 56.
[28] Chicago *Daily Tribune*, Dec. 16, 1917.
[29] New York *Times*, Dec. 17, 18, 19, 1917.
[30] Report of the Representative of the War Industries Board [Perkins], Dec. 11, 1917, *Papers Relating to the Foreign Relations of the United States, 1917, Supplement 2, The World War* (2 vols., Washington, 1932), I, 441-42.

Bliss,[31] who had just returned from France, that the WIB's plan would make it necessary to go to Congress for new legislation that might contain compromises as harmful as the faults they were intended to correct. Lochridge advised that the General Staff undertake immediately a reorganization that would meet the demands of the war without completely destroying the system under which the army operated during normal times. The War College recommended the creation of two new assistant chiefs of staff, to be called the Director of Purchases and the Director of Storage and Traffic, assisted by a civilian Surveyor General of Supply. Through those agencies the work of the supply bureaus would be coordinated, and the Surveyor General, acting in concert with the Director of Purchases, could establish intimate relations between the army and the business community. Thus there would be no need to strengthen the WIB, which would continue to serve in an advisory capacity and as a clearing house for supplies. The Chief of Staff was to be freed from all routine duties, allowing him to give his entire attention to the various agencies of the War Department, while the bureaus were to be brought under the control of the General Staff for the duration of the war.[32]

The report that Perkins had sent from London electrified Baker as much as it did Bliss and Lochridge. Suspending his own project, the Secretary of War moved to implement the War College Plan. He selected Palmer E. Pierce, former liaison man between the War Department and the WIB, as Director of Purchases, while he named Goethals as Director of Storage and Traffic, combining in Goethals the most vital supply responsibilities in the War Department. Baker followed up those appointments in the first weeks of January by bringing a number of businessmen, led by the new Surveyor General of Supply, Edward R. Stettinius, a partner in J. P. Morgan and Company, and Samuel McRoberts, former manager of the National City Bank of New York, into the War Department to work closely with Goethals and Pierce.[33] Finally, he reshaped his own office to fit the new pro-

[31] Bliss was appointed Chief of Staff upon the retirement of General Scott in Sept. 1917. During Bliss' absence in November his duties were performed after a fashion by Acting Chief of Staff Major General John Biddle.

[32] Memorandum from the War College to the Chief of Staff, Dec. 21, 1917, War College Records, Record Group 165, War Department Records, World War I Section (National Archives). Although select committees of the General Staff had been working on Bureau reorganization since July 1917, the evidence indicates that the WIB report of Dec. 11, 1917 influenced the timing of the War College recommendations as much as internal War Department problems.

[33] New York *Times,* Jan. 3, 1918; Hayes to Baker, Jan. 26, 1918, Hayes Papers. The announcement of Stettinius' appointment caused a flurry of excitement in the press. Although he named Stettinius at approximately the same time as McRoberts, Baker did not

gram by sending a bill to Senator Chamberlain authorizing the appointment of two new assistant secretaries of war to lighten the burdens of supervising the various bureaus.[34] Baker's War Council, now little more than an appendix, lingered until the late spring of 1918, when its personnel were either retired or assigned to other duties.

Meanwhile the congressional investigation of the war effort moved toward a climax. Baker's announcement on December 19 that the changes he was making in the War Department were not connected with the hearings then in progress did not impress the newspapers. A New York *Times* editorial declared: "Making General Crozier a scapegoat for the delays, omissions, and futilities of the War Department is the wrong way to reform a bad business."[35] The radical reform of the military establishment, made public on January 15, 1918, merely increased demands for housecleaning in the Washington administration.[36] Some members of the WIB guessed that Baker was attempting, particularly by the Stettinius appointment, to circumvent them and make unnecessary any further delegation of power.[37]

The strongest indictment of Baker occurred when members of the Advisory Commission of the Council of National Defense testified. Chamberlain and his colleagues probably had been receiving information from some members of the WIB and the Advisory Commission for some time. Willard and Baruch appeared before the committee, indicted the War Department, and demanded that authority to purchase all supplies for the United States and its allies be vested in one man. Willard averred that the War Department had exhibited no distinct disposition to help the WIB, while Gifford claimed, "If the Government during the next eighteen months is not better prepared to use its vast resources than it is now we are going to fall down on running the war."[38] Waddill Catchings, director of the War Service Committee of the United States Chamber of Commerce, told the senators that he had been informed in September that the WIB was not working properly and termed Baker's direction of the supply program "most pernicious." "The view of the American businessman," Catchings

want the appointment publicized. One Colonel Osborn told the newspapers that Stettinius was to be the new Director of Supply. Such an appointment would have given the country the impression that a Morgan partner was to control all the vast purchases of the War Department. Baker caught the newspapermen before they had sent their stories and explained to them that Stettinius was to be Goethals' associate rather than his superior.

[34] Baker to Chamberlain, Jan. 24, 1918, Records of the Office of Secretary of War, Record Group 107, War Department Records, World War I Section (National Archives).

[35] New York *Times*, Dec. 20, 1917.

[36] *Ibid.*, Jan. 18, 1918.

[37] Clarkson, *Industrial America in the World War*, 52-54.

[38] New York *Times*, Jan. 15, 16, 1918.

concluded, "is that the war program is not properly balanced. . . . The conviction has obtained for a long time that things are not being done in the right way. . . . We are at sea without a chart."[39]

A few days later Chamberlain introduced a bill in the Senate to create a war cabinet of "three distinguished citizens of demonstrated executive ability." The new body would include no members of the official cabinet, would be superior to the Secretary of War and the Secretary of the Navy in the direction of the war effort, and would be responsible only to the President. The measure received bipartisan support in both houses of Congress. Republican James W. Wadsworth, Jr., stated: "This is no time for partisanship. We need men of vision, ability, and courage to handle our war problems," while Democrat Gilbert M. Hitchcock explained that the bill was "not to embarrass the Administration, but to help it."[40] Willard's resignation as chairman of the WIB on January 15 did little to reestablish national confidence.

Baker took the accusations deeply and personally. His concern was best shown in two letters. The first was written to his friend and law partner Thomas Sidlo on December 25, 1917, in which he stated:

I have not allowed myself to be disturbed about the newspaper comment or the Congressional investigation. I know nothing easier than to be a Secretary of War until you've tried it. Undoubtedly there are people in this country who would find my job easier than I find it. To me it is a heavy, hard task and full of responsibility but I am quite certain that many of those who criticize would find themselves in deep water if they tried to wrestle from day to day with the perplexities which arise here. My comfortable state of mind and my confidence arise from the fact that my Army and other associates here are as loyal and hardworking and intelligent a set of men as I've seen anywhere. That they may make mistakes goes without saying; but that there has been any conscious wrong doing, I know is impossible, at least in high places. The people of the United States do not expect us to be perfect,—they only expect us to try to be,—and that we're doing, with all the shortcomings which normally attend such attempts.[41]

But by mid-January he was convinced that he could no longer help the administration and that he must resign. He wrote the President:

As I know the impersonal quality of your purpose I know you will not keep me here a moment longer than is wise and I can well imagine that a time may come when you find it possible to advance the cause and consolidate the sentiment of the country by making a change either by sending me to other service or to none.

[39] *Ibid.*, Jan. 17, 1918.
[40] *Ibid.*, Jan. 21, 1918.
[41] Baker to Thomas Sidlo, Dec. 25, 1917, Baker Papers.

As my whole desire is to serve, not in my way but in yours, I shall neither question nor misunderstand what you think best to have me do.[42]

A note in Secretary of the Navy Daniels' diary revealed the effect of the crisis on the Secretary of War:

Newton Baker came over to confer about a letter he had written to the President saying that he had but one purpose—to have the country united to win the war— and that in view of the criticism, he was ready to [submit?] his resignation so the President could name a man as Secy. of War who would unite the country. I told him the President would not permit it. That the opposition would be satisfied with nobody except T.R., Root or Wood and the President would not name either [sic] and instead of compromising or uniting, his resignation would have the opposite effect. Looks 5 years older. I told him that within a few months his critics would see how unjust they were.[43]

Intervention by President Wilson ultimately saved his Secretary of War, but this is not the place to tell that story. It is best to concentrate on the events that led to the curtailment of Baker's powers over the civilian sector of the war effort. Wilson opposed a munitions board on the English ministry model, especially if it meant being saddled with Republicans Roosevelt, Root, or Wood, but he knew that it would be politically disastrous to muddle along in the way the administration had been doing for the previous six months. And there was at least one man who seemed to know a way out. Since July McAdoo had been lying in wait to scalp Baker. Around the first of the year McAdoo, according to Baruch, said that Baruch was being thought of as a possible replacement for Baker.[44] When Wilson made it clear that he would not have Baker sacrificed, McAdoo moved to have Baruch made chairman of the WIB with independent power. The struggle between McAdoo and Baker began on January 24, 1918 when the Council of National Defense met to consider a replacement for Willard. When Daniels suggested Baruch's name, he thought that Baker was inclined to agree that the choice of Baruch would be a good one, but the war secretary was merely avoiding an argument and was keeping his own counsel.[45] On the same day Baker submitted a report to President Wilson that contained his recollection of what had occurred at the meeting and his own ideas about a chairman. He indicated that Daniels favored Baruch but emphasized that Secretary of Agriculture Houston, Secretary of Commerce Redfield, and Vance C. McCormick of the War Trade Board believed that Baruch did

[42] Baker to Wilson, Jan. 21, 1918, Wilson Papers, File II, Box 134.
[43] Daniels Diary, Jan. 23, 1918.
[44] Bernard M. Baruch, *The Public Years* (New York, 1960), 46; Margaret L. Coit, *Mr. Baruch* (Boston, 1957), 166-72.
[45] Daniels Diary, Jan. 24, 1918.

not possess the executive ability to fill the post. Baker favored John D. Ryan, President of Amalgamated Copper, suggesting that his appointment "would be more acceptable in the eastern part of the country, and perhaps would carry the greatest assurance of strong business, executive capacity." Although he admitted that Baruch was politically "the most absolutely loyal man in sight," he claimed that he did not "know enough about his executive capacity to recommend him."[46]

McAdoo was up in arms when he heard of Baker's proposal and immediately wrote an angry letter to the President condemning not only Ryan but also many of Baker's other appointments. McAdoo asserted that Stettinius in particular was not completely loyal to the administration and warned Wilson: "As I have been going over the country I have been impressed with the suspicion of and feeling against the big interests—and J. P. Morgan and Co.—as they are believed (and justly I think) to have made enormous sums through financing and purchasing for the Allies prior to our entrance into the war." Baruch, he continued, was the "ablest man for the place. . . . Absolutely loyal and dependable," while the only reason Baker had for opposing him was Baruch's "reputation as a Wall Street speculator." McAdoo indignantly concluded, "I do not believe it wise or sound policy to put ourselves too fully in the hands of our enemies and the 'interests' and take the unnecessary risk of losing the confidence of the masses of the people as well."[47]

Wilson decided to strengthen the WIB while Baker was still hopefully juggling the organization of the War Department in an effort to make such a step unnecessary. The President listened to both Baker and McAdoo and also cast about for the view of others less involved. He agreed with Justice Louis D. Brandeis that only by freeing Baker from civilian responsibilities could the country get the "full benefit of his great ability and fine qualities."[48] For a short time he considered Stettinius for WIB chairmanship, but Colonel Edward M. House, who was probably told by McAdoo, wrote: "I hear that Stetinius [sic] is being thought of as head of the War Industries Board. McAdoo and [Joseph P.] Tumulty think it would be a mistake and I am inclined to agree with them. I am afraid it will look too much like the Morgans are running things."[49] Still officially uncommitted, the President on February 1, 1918 requested that Baker and Baruch meet

[46] Baker to Wilson, Jan. 24, 1918, Wilson Papers, File II, Box 134. Baker later brought Ryan into the War Department to head the army's air program.
[47] McAdoo to Wilson, Jan. 27, 1918, *ibid.*, File II, Box 134.
[48] Alpheus Thomas Mason, *Brandeis: A Free Man's Life* (New York, 1946), 524.
[49] House to Wilson, Feb. 6, 1918, Wilson Papers, File II, Box 135.

and agree to some mutually acceptable arrangement to make the WIB an effective agency to coordinate the war effort. Baker sent him the results of the conference on the following day:

The conference summarized in the attached letter was had without committing you in any way as to the person to be chosen as Chairman. Yesterday I discussed the matter with Secretaries Houston, Lane (who was not present before) and Daniels. Houston was still very sure that Baruch had not the organizing facility. Lane was doubtful and said that he would like thinking it over. I confess I do not know where to look for a better suggestion.

The plan agreed to by Baker and Baruch was quite comprehensive. At the beginning of the conference Baker insisted that the power to set specifications must rest with the army and suggested that the WIB ought to continue as a coordinating rather than a directing agency. But apparently Baruch convinced Baker that congressional criticism could only be quieted by forthright reform of the civilian sector of the war effort. Baker agreed that the WIB should become a "legal, authoritative, responsible, centralized agency" to expedite the demands of the military. Moreover, it should have power, subject to the approval of the President, "to commandeer plants, products, equipment, manufacturing facilities, mines and materials," and the additional power of "distributing materials thus commandeered." Most important it was agreed further that the Board should procure military supplies, control the industry of the country, and determine prices and compensation, thus assuring that *"single representatives of War, Navy, Allied, and Shipping Boards could meet, clear the difficulties, coördinate their needs, and in consultation with the chairman of the War Industries Board submit their programme for his [the Chairman's] final allocation, distribution, and judgment."*[50]

Baker was so reluctant to accept Baruch that the President reached his decision without taking the war secretary any further into his confidence. It is not clear just when Wilson made his choice final, but when McAdoo wrote him asking that Baruch become his assistant in the Railroad Administration, Wilson replied that he had decided to appoint Baruch chairman of the WIB as soon as he could do so "without risking new issues on the Hill."[51] Baker never revealed what he thought about Baruch's appointment. When the presidential letter announcing Baruch's selection and calling for "the fullest possible co-operation of your department" arrived,

[50] Baker to Wilson, Feb. 2, 1918, with memorandum of the meeting with Baruch, *ibid.* Italics added.
[51] Wilson to McAdoo, Feb. 26, 1918, *ibid.*, Box 136.

15

Baker had left Washington on a tour of the fighting front in France to see
the AEF and to study the military, logistical, and diplomatic problems that
the army was facing overseas.[52]

The administration's decision seemed so obvious that Grosvenor B.
Clarkson later declared that the same thing could have been accomplished
as easily in July 1917 as it was in February 1918. All that was necessary
was to appoint a chairman like Baruch who could "look any man in the eye
and tell him to go to hell."[53] But it was not so simple a matter to lead a
democracy into war. Nor is it now so simple a matter to judge critically the
men and issues involved in that situation. Officially a nation may be at
peace one day and at war the next, but the men and women who make up
that nation and its government go through a period of transition before
they will face war's all-consuming demands.

One can understand Baker's dilemma. The struggle had forced him into
an incongruous role. No amount of administrative juggling could solve the
technological and industrial questions involved in meeting such a massive
challenge in a short time. It was not that he was unaware of the need for
strong executive control. Indeed, he understood perhaps too well the axiom
that the War Department must have primary authority to set equipment
requirements and specifications. But for the first eight months of the
conflict, he was as much concerned with safeguarding traditional political
and economic institutions as he was in getting on with the war. Grave fall
and winter events swept away his preconceptions and confronted him with
unpleasant realities. He began to throw aside old dogmas and to seek new
answers for immediate problems. After December 1917 the issue became
more than one of institutional adjustment. It became a battle to keep the
control of the war effort in the hands of the War Department in particular
and of the Wilson administration generally. And Baker simply could not
move quickly enough to avert a political crisis. Interparty and intraparty
politics played a vital part in bringing the struggle to a climax, and Baruch
was chosen to chair the WIB as much because he was the only available
Democrat as for his drive and business ability. Ultimately Wilson made the
decision that helped spur lagging industrial mobilization and Baker, to his
credit, remained on at the War Department and did not complicate matters
further by resigning. In months to come the Secretary of War would fulfill
in his own way Justice Brandeis' confidence in his "great ability and fine
qualities."

[52] Wilson to Baker, March 4, 1918, Baker Papers.
[53] Clarkson, *Industrial America in the World War,* 44.

Joseph Brandes

Product Diplomacy: Herbert Hoover's Anti-Monopoly Campaign at Home and Abroad

Editor's Introductory Note

Joseph Brandes, currently professor of history at the William Paterson College of New Jersey, was an early student of Hoover's economic diplomacy and a pioneer in seeking to understand the mixture of nationalism and internationalism that Hoover espoused. His *Herbert Hoover and Economic Diplomacy,* published in 1962, was both a perceptive study of Hooverian ideology and a detailed examination of how this ideology was applied in the programs of the Bureau of Foreign and Domestic Commerce. As such, the book became both a stimulus to new inquiry and a key work in an emerging revisionist scholarship, with which Brandes has maintained contact and to which he has continued to contribute. He is also an authority on American Jewish history and the author of *Immigrants to Freedom* (1971).

In the paper published here, Brandes traces and analyzes Hoover's actions against foreign economic combinations and especially against the British rubber cartel that threatened America's expanding automobile industry. There are numerous parallels, he notes, between this situation and the raw material and fuel crises of recent years, parallels that make the subject more interesting and more relevant than it was once thought to be. And having pointed these out, he examines not only the development and nature of the threat but also Hoover's perceptions of it, the ideology and political factors shaping his responses, his arguments during the debate over American protectionism, and the impact of his campaigns on foreign and domestic behavior. Hoover, he concludes, was more than a politician responding to pressures from industrial groups. His concerns were with protecting an economy geared to mass production and consumption, an economy that was conceived of as the key to progress and harmony, both at home and abroad. And while his prescriptions for doing this called for market restoration, they also recognized the limitations and weaknesses of this remedy and would supplement it with constructive forms of trade control and cooperative action. Within the prescriptions were tensions and contradictions that Hoover never fully resolved.

Here as elsewhere, Brandes joins with those who have seen Hoover as a practical idealist yet have denied that the ideals to which he subscribed were those of laissez-faire capitalism. Although he attacked the rubber cartel and similar institutions as leading inevitably to irrational and exploitive forms of market control, he supported other forms of national protection and cooperative action as being rational and progressive. And while these rational and progressive forms tended to be those in which Americans were engaged, thus lending credence to charges that Hooverism was little more than the pursuit of national advantage, there were also areas in which he granted significant roles to foreign governments and transnational organizations. Of these Brandes tells us relatively little. But they have been explored in other recent scholarship. And taken in conjunction with this, Brandes's work seems to point to an engineering ideal of harmony through rational structures and relationships as being more important than the ideals of unfettered competition or national power.

Product Diplomacy:
Herbert Hoover's Anti-Monopoly Campaign
at Home and Abroad

Though history may not repeat itself, there are some interesting echoes in the 1970s of the struggle against foreign combinations of raw materials in the 1920s. As secretary of commerce, Herbert Hoover fought the cartel-like price-fixing of rubber, potash, sisal, and even coffee. Then, as now, the world's most affluent and advanced industrial nation represented the political economy of continued expansion. Real growth was the key to stability and social progress at home, to power abroad, and growth was seen as depending to some extent on access to and competitive markets in key raw materials.

Conditioned by a heritage of limitless resources and productive ingenuity, Americans tended to assume a mastery of their own fate (especially in the 1920s). They seemed unwilling to face the nation's growing dependence on various foreign supplies and on an effective functioning of the international economy. Yet, some policy makers did perceive dangers that would become an overriding national concern by the mid-1970s.

It was a crisis long in the making, traceable to America's mass production industries. In the 1920s, the automobile industry in particular seemed threatened by foreign restrictions of the rubber supply and sharply rising rubber prices. Then, as now with oil or bauxite or a score of other commodities, a wide range of "solutions" was offered —including measures to achieve national self-sufficiency and to retaliate in kind. Anti-foreign attitudes also rose to the fore, as pressures were brought to bear against the officially-sponsored cartels and this issue became commingled with such other economic foreign policy issues as inter-allied war debts. Naively, perhaps, then as now, Americans sought to ascertain which of their erstwhile allies could still qualify as their friends.

During the Republican ascendancy of the 1920s, the grand marshal of economic policy at home as abroad was Herbert Hoover, a competent and willing leader in the anti-cartel struggle. Among his more moderate weapons was a strikingly contemporaneous public relations campaign for conservation, featuring such slogans as "Economize on Rubber" and "Help Hoover Against the English Rubber Trust," and accompanied by the patriotic appeal of "1776-1925."[1] In addition, he was able to bring a wide range of other weapons to bear in the spheres of public and intergovernmental pressure.

Indeed, many of the issues and responses of the 1920s are echoed within the raw materials crises (not oil alone) of the 1970s, as if reflecting a kind of repetitive aspect of industrial America's political economy. In an approach not unlike Hoover's, a senior fellow of the Brookings Institution advises that "only unity among consumers can effectively counter unity among producers." Without a revision of international trade rules, he warns, the problem could become just as acute for raw materials dominated by "several other commodity cartels," including copper, bauxite, and coffee.[2] Brazil's "coffee cartel" (Hoover's old nemesis, the Coffee Institute) also announced steep price increases for 1974, labeling its decision an "A-Bomb."[3]

As always, it seems, public policy has had to consider diverse economic interest groups, not to mention the ever-elusive concept of the national interest encompassing the American consumer. Yet, the clashing pressures have always been complex. In the coffee trade, for example, the concerns of roasters were not identical with those of the distributors, and among the consumers of rubber from British Malaya were such politically influential manufacturers as Goodyear, Goodrich, and U.S. Rubber as well as their ultimate customers for tires or hot water bags. Behind the Big Three of rubber manufacturing, moreover, were such Wall Street firms as Dillon, Read and Kuhn, Loeb, and Company, involved with foreign investments. Consequently, financial considerations cutting across international boundaries clashed with the notion of safeguarding America from the foreign monopolies' grip.

Assessing the "morals" of "multinational" oil corporations, Leonard Silk inquired recently whether they could ever be expected to pursue other goals than short-term profit maximization, or display greater obedience now to the demands of the United States than to those of Saudi Arabia.[4] Ironically, federal policies encouraging foreign investment, justified for decades on the grounds of national security, culminated in Senator Henry M. Jackson's charges of "corporate disloyalty" against the Arabian American Oil Company. It had refused to supply U.S. military forces during the Arab-Israeli War of 1973. In this light, Hoover's early insistence (1922) that "America should have at least a quarter interest in this [oil] business [as] a matter of national pride . . ." seems a bit quaint. He was appealing at the time for the broadest possible participation by American firms in the Mesopotamian oil fields and, as he frequently did, was offering advice "from the point of view of American commercial interests."[5]

Perennially, it seems, Americans have disagreed among themselves on issues of private profit and governmental intervention, production quotas and import controls, tax and tariff policies, corporate and social responsibilities, enforcement of anti-trust laws, divestiture, and even nationalization. A mingling of populist and progressive impulses, with a dose of *petit bourgeois,* gave rise periodically to skepticism directed against domestic as well as international big business. Congressional investigations and pressure for more vigilant scrutiny by the Justice Department or regulatory agencies have been the outcome. In this vein were the past complaints of some farm-state congressmen, in the course of 1926 hearings, that profiteering by tire manufacturers had gone far beyond the actual price increases of crude rubber. New York's fiery Fiorello H. La Guardia, as well as southern and western congressmen, remained unconvinced that governmental efforts to combat raw materials cartels would benefit anyone except the large corporations. And American industry's defensive efforts—encouraged by Hoover—to create a rubber buying pool were condemned by others as violating the anti-trust laws.[6]

In a somewhat parallel mood perhaps, Senator Frank Church of Idaho, chairman of the Subcommittee on Multinational Corporations early in 1974, found that "Wall Street lawyers were sent to the Middle East . . ." and had worked out an "arrangement . . . to abruptly reduce the taxes paid by the companies to the United States Treasury while dramatically increasing the tax revenues accruing to the oil producing governments." Others have noted the interlocking directorates among the oil companies, including a number of investment bankers serving on the boards of two or more oil companies, as cause for potential actions by the Justice Department, Federal Trade Commission, and the Securities and Exchange Commission.[7] Above all, perhaps, these charges of Clayton Act violation have been intended to mobilize public reproach, always a potent weapon in a democratic society. In brief, echoes of the 1920s persisted into the economic foreign policy debates of the later era.

Hoover's Attack on Foreign Combinations: the 1920s Ideology

The Hoover policies were based on an ideological amalgam of nineteenth-century classical economics with the needs of twentieth-century business in the United States. A "free" economy was revered by Hoover as the democratic force on which depended the continued progress of all the American people. Not merely the advancement of entrepreneurial interests or material progress, but all the things which made America great stemmed from the competitive business tradition modified by changing circumstances.

In practice, the application of these principles was shaped by the fact that Hoover preferred a pragmatic approach to specific issues. On the one hand, for example, he fought bitterly for free international access to raw materials, especially those the United States did not possess. Relying on nineteenth-century theories of free trade and "comparative advantage," he assailed the resort to "monopoly" control of such products as rubber, coffee, potash, and others. International amity was threatened, Hoover asserted, by foreign combinations to restrict prices and production. On the other hand, he defended American tariff protectionism as essential to continued national prosperity, minimizing the opposition aroused at home and abroad by the Republican trade policies. And American prosperity, he believed, was the cornerstone upon which world-wide recovery and prosperity must rest.

In combating foreign "monopolies," Hoover appealed to American national feeling and kept himself in the forefront as the champion of American economic rights abroad. Against such foreign interests, he mobilized a counter-offensive which in some respects exerted greater pressure than the offending "monopolies." The Commerce Department, for example, effectively blocked loans to the Brazilian coffee interests and to the Franco-German potash cartel, and British rubber interests were threatened with a well-financed American buying pool.

Efficient service to private American interests became the keynote of the Commerce Department's widespread operations. Yet Hoover had accepted the cabinet position in Harding's administration partly because of a desire to put into practice his own economic and social principles. His experience as relief administrator in Europe had convinced him more firmly than before that the ways of "American individualism" were superior to any other system, that unlike some of European capitalism, private enterprise in the United States fostered opportunity for all individuals and was thus an expression of equality and "social justice." Belief in these traditional American ideals was the truly "liberal" approach, Hoover maintained, although he was himself attacked often by self-styled progressive and internationalist groups.

It would be misleading to imply that Hoover's concept of the voluntary partnership between government and business was intended to serve the interests of business alone. The Commerce Department was no passive partner sacrificing its own initiative either to Wall Street or Main Street. Thus, in spite of the opposition of many investment houses, Hoover promoted a program of governmental supervision over foreign lending so that the diplomatic and economic interests of America would be given due consideration. Hoover insisted on adequate loan standards, as a governmental responsibility, to prevent "unproductive" uses and eventual loss to American investors or consumers.

Surely, as concluded by Peri Arnold, Hoover was "no simple *laissez-faire* ideologue."[8] Hoover attempted to coordinate governmental actions with private economic interests in the name of the public good. He was well aware of the instabilities and losses resulting from the business cycle, the striving for profit through economies of scale and technological efficiency. Competition was hardly synonymous with productivity. Moreover, he believed, American individualism was uniquely tempered by the necessary cooperativeness of the frontier heritage and its social concerns. By contrast with the still-festering problems of Europe, the actual accomplishments of American society represented "the one great moral reserve in the world today."[9]

These virtues could be extended by a judicious partnership of free enterprise "voluntarism" with the benevolent supervision of the state. "Regulations to prevent domination and unfair trade practices, yet preserving rightful initiative, are in keeping with our social foundations," Hoover maintained.[10] When the Department of Commerce responded to the needs of American business, whether surveying alternate sources of crude rubber or finding export markets for the finished product, it was going beyond mere service to a limited constituency or clientele. It was, as Hoover saw it, serving the nation by providing aid to its "most creative and beneficial element,"[11] especially when the latter was threatened from abroad.

Thus, the effects of artificially high rubber prices were painted by Hoover on a broad canvas. Not only were domestic distributors and manufacturers hurt by fluctuating inventory values, but the cartel's actions caused an "arousal of national feeling" and even a determination by the whole "consuming world to fight militantly for its existence." We of the wealthy United States "could take care of ourselves," Hoover proclaimed aggressively, "we have it within our powers to retaliate." And a strong national response had become necessary because the normal "higgling of merchants [was] lifted to the plane of international relations, with all its spawn of criticism and hate." The international monopolies of raw materials ran counter to the cherished "belief that economic progress must depend upon the driving force of competition."

Their interference with the "inalienable right" of buyers to bargain with sellers threatened the basis of international commerce and well-being, "for no single nation can dissociate its prosperity from the prosperity and good will of all of them." None could boast the right to monopolize a product which other nations required "for their standards of living and comfort," especially when prices were raised "far beyond [a] reasonable profit" because "no voice at all" was granted to consumers. As such restrictions spread and were backed by governmental patronage or direct legislation, they could "only lead to mutual disaster."[12]

With his first-hand knowledge of world affairs, Hoover knew how distant were the ideals of economic equilibrium and cooperation in the aftermath of World War I. His wartime commander-in-chief, President Wilson, saw little cause for optimism after peace was achieved. "It is evident to me that we are on the eve of a commercial war of the worst sort," he warned in 1920, "and I am afraid that Great Britain will prove capable of as great commercial savagery as Germany has displayed for so many years in her competitive methods."[13]

Friction had begun during the war when the British, controlling three-fourths of the world's plantation supply in their southeast Asian colonies, had listed crude rubber as contraband. American manufacturers had been "greatly exercised over [the] embargoes." And foreshadowing the tensions of the 1920s, Secretary of State William Jennings Bryan had threatened: "If American manufacturers are not to obtain necessary supplies, prices of American goods which [Britain] may desire will be greatly increased, if, indeed the exportations from this country be not ultimately prevented."[14] It was a case of nationalism and neutral rights on the part of the Great Commoner, and an issue that had been painstakingly resolved through American reassurances that the finished product would not reach Britain's foes.

With the war over and wartime controls largely scrapped, Hoover saw a "world rapidly gaining stability." But he still feared the snowballing effect of new restrictions abroad leading to protectionist pleas at home "every time some industry fell into trouble." Fortunately, the United States had not yet followed the example set by foreign combinations. Even the farm relief bills being considered in Congress were characterized by a basic generosity. They offered "the benevolent aspect of proposing to fix a higher price to our home consumers than to foreigners and to thus bless the foreigner with cheaper food."[15] But "we" would have to protect our interests, and the British and other sponsors of price-fixing combinations should realize that their actions were threatening those competitive commitments which were the key to economic progress.

As the world's major agricultural exporting nation, America could not be counted upon for unlimited generosity or patience in the face of provocation. On the other hand, Britain was a foremost importer of foodstuffs and raw materials, Hoover liked to note, vulnerable to the threat of an American *cotton* producers' combination, for example. Although distasteful ideologically, retaliation might nonetheless be required "from a national point of view." This was a reality which the British government should be urged to consider in a "comprehensive"

24

manner, recognizing that "they" might suffer more than the United States from the same "currents which they have been to some degree responsible for putting in motion."

In short, Hoover hoped that the British Government could be persuaded diplomatically to desist from the harmful effects of price fixing on "the whole fabric of international commerce and of wholesome international relations . . . [even] world welfare. . . ."[16] Such was Hoover's explicit advice to Secretary of State Kellogg, to be transmitted through our ambassador in London, Alanson B. Houghton, toward the end of 1925. But Britain did not yield.

Nor were Hoover's ideas without detractors at home. His opposition to loan flotation on behalf of the accused cartels inspired a *Wall Street Journal* plea "begging him not to overburden himself." Could not the nation count on a capable secretary of the treasury, Andrew Mellon, and his equally effective colleague, Frank Kellogg, to conduct economic foreign policy? "Mr. Hoover's Helpfulness" in aborting a $40,000,000 flotation for the German Potash Syndicate—"something of a monopoly in its way"—was a disappointment to Lee Higginson & Co. and to other financiers. The journal claimed that potash was used mainly in cotton and truck farming, but little in the major wheat and corn belts where substitutes were available.

Moreover, Hoover might "wisely let the Brazilian coffee industry alone," and discontinue his persistent tie-in between foreign pricing policies and access to American financial markets. The combinations were able to obtain their loans in London, anyway. Worse still was Hoover's use of loan restrictions as "a club for the collection of foreign debts." Generally, the journal found, Wall Street might need "Washington's advice but not Washington's control." "Mr. Hoover is not really necessary in such councils," concluded its New Year's editorial of 1926.

Hoover did not shrink from such blunt challenges. In a press release marked specifically for the western farm papers, the secretary of commerce relished the role of America's progressive conscience, speaking out against Wall Street opportunism. When the time of reckoning came for "the American banking community," Hoover predicted, "the commissions which might be collected on floating such loans would be no compensation." There would be a "justifiable criticism . . . from the American potash and coffee consumers when [they] become aware that American capital was being placed at the disposal of these agencies through which prices were held against our own people and which if located upon our own soil would be a violation of our laws."[17]

In an official memorandum, Hoover acknowledged the availability of European funding for the Brazilian coffee valorization program. It only confirmed his view of the occasionally irresponsible Europeans willing to "enter into a gamble to hold the price of coffee." Still, "it was better that it be done by some outsider than done by American bankers against the interests of the American public." If the government was responsible for the welfare of farmers requiring potash, at least equal care was demanded by the "numerical importance of the coffee consumer." It was, he said "wholly impossible for the American Government to be either directly or indirectly a party to further conspiracies against the American consumer," and hence imperative that loans to Sao Paulo or similar foreign combinations be disapproved.[18]

While Hoover's acceptance of classical economics included at least a limited recognition of comparative advantage in international trade, it did not extend to the totally free flow of capital across national boundaries. The national interest, defined as the greatest good for the nation's greatest numbers, sometimes required that the "invisible hand" of the world's market places be superseded. Millions of jobs, after all, were tied to the continued prosperity of the American automobile industry, now threatened by British rubber restrictions. And because of this, the federal government was justified in launching an intensive search for alternate sources. Whether plantations "under American control" in the Philippines, or encouragement to Firestone's mammoth projects in Liberia, or synthetic production at home, there was a need for engineering developments that the "invisible hand" had not brought forth.

"It may be that Mr. Hoover has an exaggerated idea of government help," was the significant plaint of some of his opponents.[19] At times, his hard line on loans and the "sensational speeches" of his antimonopoly allies in Congress (such as House Majority Leader John Q. Tilson) caused diplomatic repercussions in Latin America as well. Even the *Times* of Argentina was cited as predicting a "come-back" of British economic influence because Hoover "interfered so very definitely in the matter of lending money to the Brazilians." Insensitive to "South American dignity," he had failed to seek the tactful screen of a bland rejection by Wall Street intermediaries, preferring a blunt statement of official policy.[20]

Hoover's disclaimer was a model of statesmanlike rectitude:

No one wishes to maintain the good will of foreign nations more than I do, but I would be serving the American people badly if I did not bespeak their interest as consumers against the monstrous imposition which has been imposed upon them in many directions. Furthermore, unless the growth of foreign monopolies directed against consuming countries can be halted, we shall all be confronted with an era of international friction such as we have never hitherto conceived.[21]

Further, in a typical display of national confidence, Hoover warned that the United States was "strong enough" to take the lead in combating foreign monopolies. The diplomatic pressures of those "few" governments fostering such restrictions would be more than outweighed by the gratitude of fifty-odd consuming nations. And in separate advisory letters to Kellogg, he urged continuing counter-pressures against Britain to "shift their policy," not only on rubber but also on the financing of potash and coffee restrictions. Through such financing, he concluded, the "British become parties to further impositions upon our consumers."[22]

Classic ideals of economic growth mingled with consumer protection and moral indignation. In a little over a year, from the Spring of 1924 to Summer 1925, coffee prices rose from thirteen to thirty cents a pound through artificial restrictions, a condition condemned by Hoover for "mulcting the American people at the rate of $200,000,000 annually." With profits of 65% and higher, the managers of the Brazilian valorization scheme—"nothing but a group of speculators"—grew fearful of declining consumption. For American resistance ultimately proved effective, creating unmanageable surpluses. Having realized the "folly of their program," the Brazilians vainly sought loans to prevent "general disaster." They could not have these, Hoover maintained, nor "any contract entered into for restraint of trade and plunder of the American people."

Only if direct participation were granted to "American consumers . . . a strong hand in the control of the valorization scheme itself," could a loan to Sao Paulo be considered. And it would be much better if there were a complete abandonment of such foreign combination schemes. If allowed to fail, their collapse "might be one of the best lessons the world has had that the American people cannot be perpetually held up."[23]

As if to amend Harding's classic statement, Hoover pronounced that "it is the business of the Administration to give such protection to the American consumer as it can" in the face of foreign conspiracies, even if Wall Street preferred to finance them.[24] To a degree, this was consistent with his definition of American individualism as the motor for profitable efficiency but also as a "constant militant check upon capital becoming a thing to be feared."[25] Government-supported cartels stifled consumption as well as competition. Consequently, through 1928, Hoover continued a wary opposition to funding for Brazil's Coffee Institute, refinancing proposals included.[26]

By 1928, Hoover and Julius Klein, his hard-working director of the Bureau of Foreign and Domestic Commerce, had managed to mobilize the American industry into a defensive National Coffee Council. The latter could eventually advise "Candidate Hoover" that having "become the dread of Brazilian Coffee Interests" he might well relent in his new role as presidential nominee and assure Latin Americans that no hostility was intended except for the monopoly's "excessive and artificially maintained prices."[27] Eventually, of course, Hoover would tour Latin America and seek to establish a more cordial relationship.

The Struggle Over Rubber

Fence mending would also be required for the relationship between the United States and Britain. For here the growing dependence of the United States on rubber imports, the efforts of British plantation owners and their political allies to control the supply and price of rubber, and Hoover's attacks on this British cartel all worked to create much ill feeling.

The plantation rubber industry's growth was a twentieth-century phenomenon paralleling the dynamic American automobile industry which it supplied. Rubber production, concentrated in Britain's Asian colonies, was subject to the uncertainties of colonial investment and fluctuating markets. World War I caused further trading instabilities, and wartime price inflation had then yielded to sharp declines during the depression of 1920–21. Plantation interests suffered, as did the American manufacturers caught with high-priced inventories. For the latter, including Goodyear, U.S. Rubber, and Goodrich, the strains of depression brought closer dependence on such investment banking houses as Morgan and Dillon, Read. Only the Firestone Company was able to avoid a degree of control by financiers.

Faced with surpluses and further price declines—from a high of

over sixty cents a pound in 1918 to twenty-eight cents by October 1921
—the British Rubber Growers' Association appealed for governmental
aid. Winston Churchill, secretary of state for the colonies, appointed
a special committee consisting mainly of growers and headed by Sir
James Stevenson (who was also chairman of the influential Committee for Demobilization and Reconstruction). With rubber down to
twelve and a half cents by August 1922, and Dutch growers refusing
cooperation, the British decided to go it alone with a plan of production quotas to maintain prices. They were frankly suspicious of American proposals for cooperation between growers and consumers or for
a joint investment program leading to greater profitability, some even
fearing a "plot to bankrupt our rubber producing concerns so that the
people in America could have bought up the whole lot."[28]

The British were not impressed, apparently, with appeals on behalf
of business and consumers or with other American "free trade" shib-
boleths when these were accompanied by protectionist tariffs. Confronted with a war debt obligation to Washington of about $4.6
billions, many Englishmen (including Winston Churchill as the new
chancellor of the exchequer) could see one means of repayment in
higher prices for British rubber. Moreover, it was "impossible," in
Churchill's words, for the government "to witness the financial ruin
of the rubber-producing colonies."[29]

Subsequently, the British legislation formalized as the Stevenson
Act was denounced by Secretary of Commerce Hoover for placing a
"super-charge upon the American consumer of from $625 to $675
millions per annum." Later, looking back on the 1920s through the
medium of his *Memoirs,* Hoover upbraided Winston Churchill for the
part he played, when, as secretary of state for the colonies, he initiated
this "worst example" of foreign price controls. The Stevenson Act,
Hoover recalled, "forced up" rubber prices from a "highly profitable" 20 cents per pound (in 1922) to a $1.21 by 1925, "and the extra
dollar was mulcting the United States at the rate of $900,000,000 per
annum." [The damage estimate apparently had grown with the
passage of time.][30]

Under the terms of the Stevenson Act or "Plan," which was enforced by colonial legislation in British Malaya and Ceylon, the actual
production of each rubber plantation for the year ending October 31,
1920, was fixed as the "standard output." When the Plan went into
effect, in November 1922, rubber exports were limited to only 60% of
"standard." If a planter chose to ship 65% of his "standard output,"

the usual duty of one penny per pound was raised to four pence on the entire shipment, not merely on the excess. Beyond 65% of "standard," each 5% increase added a penny's tax to the total shipment. In a none-too-successful attempt to adjust the Plan to changing market conditions, a cumbersome system was set up whereby the permitted percentage of "standard" production could be raised or lowered.[31] In practice, this lack of elasticity contributed to charges of greedy profiteering and exploitation of consumers.

In tackling the problem, Hoover and the Department of Commerce did not await an initiative from the industry. They led rather than followed. Thus, when the "Big Three" in control of the Rubber Association of America were persuaded by a growers' delegation to accept the Stevenson Plan on a trial basis in 1923—after all, "stabilization" might benefit both protagonists—Hoover was skeptical. He doubted that British governmental supervision could provide a sufficiently flexible supply at "fair" prices, bluntly warning the delegation of American intentions to survey alternative sources.

By contrast with the conciliatory efforts of U.S. Rubber Company Director John W. Davis, former ambassador to Britain, and of the Morgan interests, Hoover encouraged an independent search for new sources at both the governmental and private levels. Specifically, Harvey Firestone's determinations for a "head-on attack" against the British rubber controls found an ever-responsive ally in the Department of Commerce.[32]

Congressional adherents of Department of Commerce policy were influential, providing budgetary increases at a time when other governmental funding was slashed. Included among them were such Anglophobes as Senator Medill McCormick, chairman of the Foreign Relations Committee, and a man strongly supportive of achieving economic independence from "British colonial restrictions . . . stifling American consumers." By March 1923, Congress had responded to Hoover's calls for a "National Defense against this price control" with a half-million-dollar appropriation to finance both a world-wide search for alternative sources and rubber-producing experiments within the Western Hemisphere. In addition, the Commerce Department received a mandate to ascertain "whether these controls were being used to the detriment of the American consumer."[33] If necessary, it was also indicated, the Webb-Pomerene Act could be amended so as to permit import buying pools that could reinforce the demand side of the equation.

30

The ensuing survey explored investment opportunities and generated debates over the virtues of growing rubber in the Philippines—under the American flag—as compared to new Latin American plantations. Firestone's ambitions in Liberia were also encouraged. There, it was thought, ample lands and cheap labor would facilitate an American development to rival those of European possessions. Before the Rubber Survey ended, Department of Commerce agents had been sent to the tropical wilderness of Central America, the Philippines, Ecuador, and the bargaining tables of London and The Hague.

Though less dramatic and less publicized than the exploratory expeditions, the Commerce Department's negotiations with the Netherlands government and the Dutch growers may have been a more influential factor in weakening the British controls. In spite of official British pleas for cooperation with their restriction scheme, the Dutch producers remained outside the system, and their decision to compete made the Stevenson Plan less effective.

In February 1923, Hoover discussed with the Netherlands minister in Washington (A. C. de Graeff) "the apprehensions of American capital" concerning the possibility that Holland might join forces with the British rubber controllers. This possibility was subsequently denied by an official telegram from The Hague, transmitted to Hoover in the expectation that it would (according to de Graeff) "remove the apprehension which till now seems to have withheld American capital from investing on a larger scale in rubber plantations in . . . the Netherlands East Indies." Replying for Hoover, Dr. Klein agreed that this could be expected and expressed the Department's gratification.[34]

Until the end of 1924, the campaign continued to appear as more of a governmental crusade than a project of the Rubber Association of America. Except for the Firestone Company, the major manufacturers were wary of the risks involved in plantation rubber and of the joint financial ventures being proposed to reduce such risks. Even with price increases to twenty-four cents a pound, the industry preferred to place its faith in the "free" forces of international trade and finance, an attitude encouraged by the bankers' Anglophilism. Within limits, moreover, they expected to pass the higher costs along to the consumer. On March 6, 1924, Hoover again urged the legalization of a buying pool, using as his vehicle a well-publicized letter to Senator Arthur Capper of Kansas. But this proved premature. Although the senator presented the proposal, it failed to win sufficient backing.

In his letter Hoover argued that "if by an extension of the Webb Pomerene Act . . . our consumers were allowed to set up common purchasing agencies for these imported raw materials where there is a positive combination in control, I am confident that our people could hold their own." Pooled buying he continued, would be particularly effective in an industry where there were so few primary purchasers of raw materials.[35] Nor did he give up on efforts to secure it. From 1925 through 1927, as prices rose, the needs of a booming economy became more acute, and changes took place in the rubber companies' boards of directors; Hoover's campaign gained new momentum, and in 1928 Congress would debate the Newton Bill to legalize an American buying pool. Ironically, by this time, its opponents could claim that other measures had already broken the back of the British combination.

Slaying the Dragon of Foreign Monopoly

In the spring of 1925, rubber prices reached seventy cents per pound, and during that summer they climbed to $1.10. Under these circumstances, Hoover and the Department of Commerce found it much easier to awaken the militancy of the Rubber Association of America. Clearly, the British growers had not delivered on their promise to maintain adequate supplies within a reasonable price range. It was a situation that required the fuller mobilization of both the Commerce and State departments.

On one front, Hoover expressed "gratification" with the Firestone Company's aid in the department's world-wide Crude Rubber Survey. There would, he pledged, be further "cooperation between the Department and [Firestone's] representatives," including those charged with the vast Liberian investments.[36] On another, Hoover sympathized with the concerns expressed by Senator Walter Edge of New Jersey. The latter had received "timely and logical" reports from the Department of Commerce, and he wondered now whether the price-gouging planters might "make more money than is necessary almost for the discharge of the British debt." Even though this could be the case, he felt, "some of our own interests seem to be protecting them," and there was merit, he thought, in retaliating with higher American cotton prices through a special tax on exports to Britain.[37] Otherwise, Senator Edge feared, New Jersey's tire manufacturers would face extinction.

If there was any advantage to the high prices, Hoover noted publicly, it consisted of an inducement to greater domestic self-sufficiency through "chemical reclamation." Previous estimates that 20% of American supplies might be derived from this source were now doubled, this coming at a press conference that followed a meeting with industry leaders. Until this potential could be realized, however, the great concern was with inadequate releases of rubber, in violation of "assurances by Lord Stevenson."[38] An industrial delegation also met with Secretary of State Kellogg, who gave them a "sympathetic but naturally indefinite" reply to their request for pressure on London. Apparently, no such action would be taken without due guidance from Commerce.[39]

Higher prices also gave new life to proposals for an American buying pool. Again, in August 1925, Hoover urged Congress to review the limitations of the Sherman Anti-Trust Act placing "our people" at a disadvantage on the world's market places. Overseas buyers, he noted, enjoyed the protection of our antimonopoly laws, and on top of this we prevented "combinations of our consumers . . . to protect themselves against combinations of foreign producers."[40] Nor was Hoover happy about journalistic reports linking the discomforts of the American consumer with the necessary repayment of British war debts, as if one justified the other.

In the public relations field, the Commerce Department's Editorial Division recognized that "sky-rocketing" prices made rubber "one of the hottest new subjects."[41] The result was a continuing flood of press releases, departmental surveys, reports, and exhortations, as well as the secretary's usual monthly meetings with the editors of trade papers. Opinion leaders such as publishers and bankers were cautioned, however, against presuming that American firms were profiting "by this [foreign] manipulation." Such price rises had almost bankrupted the industry in the depression of 1920. He also counselled patience. To those who pressed for quick retaliation, he pointed out the "difficulty of inaugurating international trade wars . . . involving many thousands of innocent exporters and others." Admittedly, the situation was so grave that "nothing can stop the demand for reprisals." But he "earnestly hoped that such a national boycott could be avoided."[42]

On December 10, 1925, as rubber prices peaked at over $1.20 per pound, the press received another major policy statement in the form of another letter to Senator Capper. "It is inherent in all unregulated monopolies everywhere," Hoover wrote, "that they can never be content with reasonable returns but must sooner or later undertake extortion." The British controls of East Indies rubber were "a sufficient illustration of where these things carry." While denying approval of "trade reprisals," Hoover advocated an urgent list of "wholly defensive" measures. Among these were the "discouraging" of loans to such combinations, voluntary conservation measures, the development of alternate sources and of substitutes, and cooperative "bidding" on the buyers's side.[43]

The glare of publicity was to some degree essential and inevitable. Yet, it brought curious political overtones at home and abroad. The foreign combinations being opposed were, after all, primarily those administered by British authorities, and the *Journal of Commerce,* with its own set of economic biases, tended to be critical editorially. Hoover, it charged, had begun a "War on British Rubber Trade Restriction." Ironically, the images appearing there were almost diametrically opposed to the label of "British sympathizer" that the Hearst press kept trying to pin on Hoover. For a time, at least, the Hearst chain preferred to ignore some of the campaign against British rubber controls rather than change its views, and this it continued to do even as P. J. Croghan of Commerce's Editorial Division accumulated a file of anti-Hoover protests from British newspapers.[44]

Indeed, diplomatic officials were hard put to keep up with their reports on the anti-Hoover and anti-American material in the British press. From Belfast, for example, Consul Henry P. Starrett reported widespread hostility on the "rubber question," an hostility, he felt, that was exacerbated by American attitudes on tariff protection and the payment of inter-allied war debts. As the Belfast *Northern Whig* (December 24, 1925) put it, "Great Britain, Brazil, and other powers are simply retaliating now . . . on account of the nonsensical, outrageous and damnable rates of the Fordney-McCumber Tariff Law." The "composite view," Starrett concluded, "wears an ugly aspect."[45]

The embassy in London also collected clippings of "ill natured comment" aroused by what the *Outlook* called Hoover's "diatribe" against the Stevenson Plan. The latter, according to this periodical, had saved the rubber industry and even increased the world's production. Consequently, Hoover's "assumption of moral superiority" was unjustified, especially in view of American tariff policies and attempts by the United States to raise prices on cotton, copper, corn, and the products of "infant industries." Nor was the United States acting unselfishly when, having almost achieved a corner on gold, it undertook "energetic measures" against the export of American capital. The kind of "laissez-faire which Mr. Hoover advocates," added the *New Leader,* "can only mean . . . the triumph of the Trust.'"[46]

Even the staid London *Times,* quoted by the United States embassy in "strictly confidential" dispatches, considered the attack on British rubber controls to be "inaccurate, unwise, and calculated to arouse ill feeling on the part of Americans imperfectly familiar with the facts." Its editors feared that "Hoover's laments may . . . serve to check a world-wide movement for the amicable adjustment of difficulties between the nations by mutual concession and agreement.'"[47]

In addition, the embassy anxiously informed the State Department that Prime Minister Stanley Baldwin (Conservative) intended to make political capital out of the American threats to retaliate with controls on cotton and wheat. Baldwin, it was feared, would use these threats to obtain government subsidies for the expansion of cotton and wheat resources within the empire, thus decreasing the need for American supplies. Left unsettled, the Stevenson Plan controversy could lead to a full-scale trade war and autarchic national policies.[48]

Other segments of the British press concentrated on invidious estimates of American wealth, coupled with personal attacks on Secretary Hoover. The *Manchester Guardian* expounded on the prosperity of the typical American motorist and the high profits of the tire manufacturers. It concluded that "Mr. Hoover . . . has been making himself a little ridiculous" in fighting the Stevenson Plan at a time when American "monopolies" operated as they pleased. In support of its contention, the newspaper quoted Congressman Loring M. Black's (D., N.Y.) statement that it made no sense "to legislate for the British when we cannot legislate for ourselves.'"[49]

The London *Daily Telegraph* also advised Hoover to look to the American rubber manufacturers if he honestly wished to find those who "fleeced" the American motorist. In spite of their wealth, continued the editorial, American companies unwilling to assume the risks of developing plantation rubber were now finding fault with the justifiable profits of British capital. Nor was it logical for Hoover to charge the Stevenson Plan with monopoly when Harvey S. Firestone possessed the resources to start his own 100,000-acre rubber-growing project in Liberia.[50]

In a similar lead editorial titled "Hooverism," the *Yorkshire Post* censured the Department of Commerce for having replaced "the Anglo-American sentimental attachment" of the war years with a crude debtor-creditor relationship. Attacking the Hoover letters to

Senator Capper, the *Post* concluded bitterly that "in the United States abuse of Great Britain is always a good political move."[51]

Understandably, such sentiments were amplified in the *Rangoon Gazette,* a journal described by Consul Charles J. Pisar (Burma) as closely connected with the Colonial Office. The *Gazette* saw in "Mr. Hoover . . . one of those political economists who would like [to see his country] . . . prosperous while all others are either poverty stricken or struggling with second rate conditions." Its editorial, captioned "America versus Europe," predicted a combination of aggrieved European debtors and raw material producers united in "an economic Pact of Locarno directed against America."[52]

Eventually, a British protest delegation descended upon the State Department, consisting of Envoy Extra-ordinary and Minister Plenipotentiary Sir Henry G. Chilton (in Washington through the years of the Stevenson Plan crisis, 1924–28) and Sir John Broderick, commercial counselor of the British Embassy. The two Englishmen demanded that the American Government should "either permit them to put their own views forward [to the American public] or . . . stop the Department of Commerce from making its attacks on the policies of the British Government." They declared it "inconceivable" for a corresponding official of the British Board of Trade ever to make similar accusations in public against the official trade policies of another government.[53]

An exchange of confidential telegrams between Kellogg and Ambassador Alanson B. Houghton in London shed light on the diplomatic problems raised by the Stevenson Plan. In July 1925, after "consulting fully with Rutherford, Vice President of [the] Goodyear Company," Houghton conferred with Foreign Secretary Sir Austen Chamberlain regarding the gravity of the rubber situation. He warned Chamberlain that the United States was fully prepared to encourage the use of rubber substitutes, and to seek independent sources of supply.[54]

If American manufacturers were forced out of business because of high rubber prices, with consequent unemployment in the United States, Houghton continued, the "effect on public opinion at home would be unfavorable, and [would] tend to bring up our position on free exports." There was no telling then what counter-measures might be considered by an aroused Congress.[55] All this was a rather thinly veiled threat of retaliatory American controls on cotton and wheat, which probably did not surprise Chamberlain. Previously, on several occasions, Hoover and the congressional investigators of raw material "monopolies" had commented bluntly on the availability of this weapon and pointedly reminded the British that the value of their exports to the United States had increased by 74% between 1913 and 1925.[56]

Houghton finally explained his lack of success with the Foreign Ministry by declaring that "relief can be obtained" only through a broad settlement of differences "on general grounds of high policy."[57] Kellogg's telegraphed response repeated the demands of the Rubber Association of America, which had urged "further representations to the British Government" with insistence "that the restriction plan should be entirely suspended November first [1925]." This also coincided with "Secretary Hoover's views." But as Kellogg saw it, the virulence of the American anti-Stevenson campaign "might make it more difficult for the British Government to modify its policy," especially if the news of State Department pressure on the British were "to leak out into the press."[58]

Confronted with American pressures, the British held out the prospect of increased standard production allowances as well as the release of an additional 6,000 tons by early 1926. Sir Austen Chamberlain, foreign secretary, personally assured Ambassador Houghton that "His Majesty's Government regret that they cannot go further than this." They were, he said, sympathetic to the complaints of American consumers. But meager financial reserves, labor problems, and high risks had put British producers in a difficult position. And American manufacturers, he thought, were partly at fault. They had operated as speculators and failed to build up adequate inventories. The embassy viewed Chamberlain's response as a "great concession," and Hoover, after receiving the relevant position papers from Acting Secretary of State Joseph E. Grew, acknowledged the British action as "helpful." He doubted, however, that an early and substantial increase in production was feasible.[59]

Hoover's goal was not concessions, even if they resulted in substantially greater supplies. It was elimination of the Stevenson Plan with its official restrictions and future uncertainties. "The whole question of governmental control of prices," he noted, "fills me with grave misgivings for the future of world relations."[60] His attitude was in tune with his vision of a dynamic international community derived from equal access to resources, markets, and investments. Under a kind of world-wide Open Door, American business could flourish.

Yet significantly, he was far less ready to attack U.S. advantages in Latin America than to complain about "closed doors" in the Far East or Middle East.[61]

Criticizing the Stevenson Plan's use of an average-price concept which incorporated the fluctuations of many years, the Department of Commerce persisted in its complaint that "the just price mentioned by the British Government . . . is just 35% of that now being charged us." America was thus being overcharged far beyond the theoretical free market equilibrium price. In the past American manufacturers who had accumulated rubber inventories had suffered serious losses. They had been "tricked" and "held up by price manipulation." And if the peak prices declined again as a result of the new concessions, the American manufacturer would have to slash his own prices and "write off great losses upon his inventories."[62]

In the fall of 1925 the Rubber Association warned Kellogg and Hoover that the promised release of additional supplies was being delayed through "circumstances probably not understood by the British Foreign Office." The result was an "increased measure of danger confronting a great American industry," which necessitated further pressures in London.[63] Kellogg's response was to consult Hoover on "the taking of formal action by the Government of the United States." Initially, he was told to hold off until the situation in regard to rubber shipments became clearer. But as prices continued to rise, Hoover not only counseled Kellogg to "be perfectly firm" but also renewed his campaign to deny American credit to foreign combinations. Legislation might be passed, he suggested, under which uncooperative bankers could be charged with complicity to violate the Sherman Anti-Trust Act.[64]

Subsequently, the investment firm of Dillon, Read and the Big Three rubber manufacturers undertook their own negotiations with London seeking to replace the Stevenson Plan with a new syndicate controlled by Wall Street. Churchill, as chancellor of the exchequer, seemed intrigued by the proposal and by its potential for easing Britain's balance-of-payments problem. But the plan was quashed by Washington. In an "urgent and confidential" message, Kellogg reiterated Hoover's principles: "This Government cannot countenance any plan to fix the price of rubber or any other commodity. Furthermore, participation by American citizens would certainly be a violation of the spirit if not the letter of our anti-trust laws." If consummated, such a scheme would threaten "the whole fabric of international commerce and even of wholesome international relations." It would justifiably earn the opprobrium of all responsible world powers. And as one of these powers, the American government had "a primary duty to discourage international combinations . . . from becoming interlocked with international finance." It seemed as if the Clayton Act were writ large for the world's acceptance!

Seemingly contrite, Sir Austen Chamberlain disclaimed a knowledge of American law and provided assurances of even greater allowable rubber exports, up to 100% of standard production, by February 1, 1926. The British foreign secretary regarded this "maximum measure of relief" as equivalent to virtually suspended controls, with a likelihood that the Stevenson Plan itself would be subject to substantial "modification" in line with American interests.

Houghton, however, remained suspicious, especially in view of the continuing high prices and of Churchill's "very clever" maneuvers with the American financial delegation. And, indeed, on the intrinsic issue of governmental controls, Churchill informed Sir Esme Howard (ambassador to Washington) that His Majesty's Government was hardly "in a position to enforce upon the colonies concerned [Malaya and Ceylon] the abolition of control."[66] Thus the diplomatic struggle continued to build.

The next initiative came from Harvey Firestone, who, bolder than the Big Three of the Rubber Association, now proclaimed bellicosely that although "we are trapped by a maneuver for British imperial advantage . . . we can minimize the immediate cost to America." This could be done "by meeting an invading nationalism with a defending nationalsim,"[67] one that would have as its goal an independent American control of rubber sources. Although Secretary of State Charles Evans Hughes had once warned Firestone that the age of gunboat diplomacy was over, he now moved, with the aid of Hoover and Kellogg to acquire "extensive control" over the administration of Liberia, including (by the end of 1926) a lease for up to 1,000,000 acres of rubber plantation land.[68]

Suspecting that the larger, well-financed American manufacturers sought to preserve the Stevenson Plan as a means of protecting their own high-priced stockpiles, Firestone requested Hoover to affirm his stand for outright abolition. And unconcerned "that a sudden drop would cause the large manufacturers tremendous losses," he insisted that "stable prices can only be reached by the unrestricted workings of the law of supply and demand." In any case, the supply of reclaimed rubber was expected to double to 200,000 tons in 1926.[69]

Hoover's friendly response emphasized that he was still "unalterably opposed" to any kind of arrangement with London's restriction authorities. In turn, Firestone praised Hoover's anti-monopoly campaign for the downward pressure it had created on prices. Even as the exchange took place, Hoover continued to alert the public to the alarming prospects for the coming year. At present prices, the 900,000,000 tons of needed rubber would cost the nation $666,000,000 more than it would if sold at what the price-fixing body itself had declared to be a "fair" price.[70]

Hoover, though, must have doubted that such predictions would come to pass. On the one hand now, he received confirmation that British exports from Ceylon and Malaya would, indeed, rise to 100% of standard production by the promised date of February 1, 1926. On the other, he was encouraged by new prospects for American rubber manufacturers "collectively establishing and financing some organization to stimulate production through providing capital, guaranteeing future prices, establishing purchasing and collecting agencies [etc.]." In Brazil especially, inquiries were made regarding assurances against export duties, abstention from joining governments which restricted free production, and other attitudes toward large-scale American rubber development. And before the end of 1925, Hoover had received affirmative responses from Rio de Janeiro, including a promise that combinations would be eschewed as "wholly injurious to Brazilian interests."[71]

Summation

Throughout 1925 Hoover had marshaled his forces against foreign combinations, and by early 1926 he was scoring a number of successes. The House Committee on Interstate and Foreign Commerce endorsed his wide-ranging program for independent rubber sources, recommending governmental aid to obtain such concessions. Conservation measures, the use of reclaimed rubber, and relentless pressures against the Stevenson Plan also had their effects. By May, rubber prices were down to fifty cents a pound and continuing to decline.

The battle against scarce and high-priced rubber had apparently been won. Yet throughout, Hoover's concerns had been far more fundamental. He was striving somehow to transfer to a world level the values which he considered uniquely American. These were not necessarily reflected in the policies of all big businesses. For the initiative and efficiency which Hoover so much admired were found more often in enterprises of medium magnitude. These were still striving for growth, still competitive, not yet the giants secure in their control of entire industries, not yet above requiring productive governmental aid. Beyond business, however, Hoover proclaimed also a concern for the countless Americans whose jobs and living standards he saw intertwined with its economic fortunes.

It was good politics, of course, to urge an Open Door policy on behalf of American business and for the protection of American consumers. This was especially true in view of America's postwar nationalism and the further disillusionment with Europe. Such a policy embraced the mood of the era, and it was far from isolationist.

Yet what Hoover was attempting can also be seen as an extension of the peculiar relationship between the emergence of the United States as a world power and its progressive reform movement. Thus, Hoover spoke out fervently on behalf of jobs for American workers and safeguards for consumers, as well as opposing wasteful loans to military dictatorships. The personality of Theodore Roosevelt epitomized this paradox of the big stick abroad and benevolent public policy at home —a contradiction wrapped within the elusive and changing concepts of national interest. In the 1920s, Hoover opposed demands that the government of the Philippines modify its immigration and land policies in favor of plantation development, while at the same time he backed Firestone in Liberia. The former, he feared, verged on the stifling of economic opportunity through official bureaucratic restrictions and monopolistic advantages to larger firms.

Among the forces shaping Hoover's ideology there was, inevitably, the impact of that latter-day progressive and wartime chief, Woodrow Wilson. A strong sense of morality, a faith in the Puritan ethic and in the unique values of America, a commitment to democratic government as a means of implementing such ideals—these were undoubtedly crystallized by the experience of volunteer public service in World War I and beyond.

Individualism and group cooperation could blend, as they had in the idealized image of the frontier. In an age of revolution and social upheaval, such as the postwar world, the goals of material advancement seemed as urgent as ever. In the 1920s, when American economic policy was shaped so much by Hoover, perhaps the nation's Department of Commerce sought even to adapt that old frontier shibboleth of "internal improvements" to the newer world-wide opportunities and frontiers transcending national lines. Through trade channels, at least, American values as well as American products would be exported abroad.

41

New opportunities could be developed best, in Hoover's view, by channeling the efficient individualism of American enterprise into the international economy. While governments could advise, inform, and provide safeguards for the free play of market forces, they could not displace them without risk to economic progress itself. Thus, the government-sponsored combinations controlling vital foreign resources were viewed as major impediments to be overcome if America's dynamic capitalism was to serve the nation and the cause of world progress.

NOTES

1 *New York Times,* December 27, 1925.

2 C. Fred Bergsten, "Some Vital Commodities Are Subject to 'Resource Diplomacy,' " *New York Times,* Sunday, January 27, 1974; Eric Sevareid's T.V. editorial, "The Era of Product Diplomacy," February 20, 1974.

3 "Brazil Is Raising Prices of Coffee," *New York Times,* December 24, 1973; for Brazil's governmental Coffee Institute in the 1920 struggle, see Joseph Brandes, *Herbert Hoover and Economic Diplomacy: Department of Commerce Policy, 1921–1928* (Pittsburgh, 1962), pp. 133, 137, passim (available in reprint edition, Westport, Conn., 1975: Greenwood Press).

4 Leonard Silk, "Multinational Morals," *New York Times,* March 5, 1974.

5 "Aramco Concedes Denying Oil To U.S. Military Since October," *ibid.,* January 26, 1974; Hughes to Hoover, "Confidential," August 17, 1922; Hoover to Hughes, August 19, 1922, Herbert Hoover Papers (Herbert Hoover Presidential Library, West Branch, Iowa), Commerce Section, Hughes.

6 United States Congress, House, Committee on Interstate and Foreign Commerce, *Hearings on Crude Rubber, Coffee, Etc.,* 69 Cong., 1 Sess. (Washington, 1926), 55–56, 273; La Guardia and others, in *Congressional Record,* 70 Cong., 1 Sess. (April 5, 1928), 5971, 5983–84, 5996.

7 Senator Church hearings, *New York Times,* January 31, 1974; "25 on Boards of Oil Companies Scrutinized in Antitrust Inquiry," *ibid.,* March 12, 1974.

8 Peri Ethan Arnold, "Herbert Hoover and the Department of Commerce: A Study of Ideology and Policy," Ph.D. Diss. (U. of Chicago, 1972), 22.

9 Herbert Hoover to Woodrow Wilson, in Hoover, *Memoirs,* 3 vols. (New York, 1951–52), 1:457.

10 Herbert Hoover, *American Individualism* (Garden City, 1922), p. 55.

11 Arnold, "Hoover and Commerce," 81.

12 Herbert Hoover, "Foreign Combinations Now Fixing Prices of Raw Materials Imported Into the United States" (Washington, 1925), pp. 3–4, 6, 8–9, 11.

13 Woodrow Wilson to Undersecretary of State Franklin L. Polk, March 4, 1920 (Polk Mss, Yale University Library), in John A. De Novo, "The Movement for an Aggressive American Oil Policy Abroad, 1918-1920," *American Historical Review,* 61 (July 1956), 858-59; Frank R. Chalk, "The United States and the International Struggle for Rubber, 1914-1941," Ph.D. Diss. (U. of Wisconsin, 1970), 33.

14 Bryan to Ambassador Walter Hines Page, November 12, December 2, 1914, in *Munitions Industry, Report on Existing Legislation,* 74 Cong., 2 Sess., Senate Report No. 944, Part 5 (1935), 99-100, cited in Chalk, "Struggle for Rubber," 11-12.

15 Hoover, October 31, 1925, in *Munitions Industry, Report,* cited in Chalk, "Struggle for Rubber."

16 Hoover to Kellogg, letter and memorandum, November 28, 1925, Hoover Papers, Commerce Section, Secretary of State Kellogg.

17 "Mr. Hoover's Helpfulness," *Wall Street Journal,* January 1, 1926, and "Statement by Secretary Hoover Regarding Foreign Monopolies," January 4, 1926, Hoover Papers, Commerce Section, Foreign Comb., Misc.

18 Hoover Memorandum, August 25, 1925, Hoover Papers, Commerce Section, Foreign Loans.

19 *Wall Street Journal,* January 1, 1926.

20 *The Times of Argentina,* November 16, 1925, article enclosed by H. F. McCreery of Hard & Rand Inc., December 22, 1925, Hoover Papers, Commerce Section, Foreign Loans, Sao Paulo. For additional background on Hoover's anti-monopoly stand, as well as a fresh, comprehensive, scholarly treatment of related themes, see Joan Hoff Wilson's, *American Business & Foreign Policy, 1920-1933* (Lexington, 1971), esp. 171-75.

21 Hoover to McCreery, January 5, 1926, Hoover Papers, Commerce Section, Foreign Loans, Sao Paulo.

22 Hoover to Kellogg, November 28, 1925, Hoover Papers, Commerce Section, Secretary of State Kellogg.

23 Hoover memorandum, August 25, 1925, Hoover Papers, Commerce Section, Foreign Loans.

24 *Ibid.*

25 Hoover, *American Individualism,* p. 38.

26 Hoover to Charles Evans Hughes, February 8, 1928, Hoover Papers, Commerce Section, Foreign Loans.

27 Berent Friele, National Coffee Council (U.S.), to Julius Klein, June 25, 1928; Klein to Friele, July 6, 1928, Bureau of Foreign and Domestic Commerce Records (National Archives, RG 151), 640 (Brazil).

28 James H. Thomas speech to Parliament, July 27, 1925, *Parliamentary Debates,* 187:104, quoted in Chalk, "Struggle for Rubber," 31.

29 Churchill, quoted in Howard and Ralph Wolf, *Rubber: A Story of Glory and Greed* (New York, 1936), pp. 220-21.

30 *Fourteenth Annual Report of the Secretary of Commerce,* 39; Hoover, *Memoirs,* 2:82.

31   A factual report on the operations of the Stevenson Plan was presented by Representative Walter H. Newton (Minnesota) during the congressional debate on his bill to legalize American pools for the purchase of rubber and other raw materials. *Congressional Record,* 70 Cong., 1 Sess. (April 5, 1928), 5974–80.

32   Chalk, "Struggle for Rubber," 44–45, 52, 62; Brandes, *Hoover,* chapter 4, "Rubber in the Political Economy of Britain and America."

33   U.S. Congress, House of Representatives, Committee on Appropriations, *Third Deficiency Appropriations Bill, 1923,* 67 Cong., 4 Sess. (Washington, 1923), p. 496; also the later *Preliminary Report on Crude Rubber, Coffee, Etc.,* of the House Committee on Interstate and Foreign Commerce, 69 Cong., 1 Sess. (Washington, 1926), p. 1, passim.

34   A. C. de Graeff to Hoover, February 12, 1923; Julius Klein to de Graeff, February 21, 1923, BFDC Records, 254 (Dutch East Indies); see also Ervin Hexner, *International Cartels* (Chapel Hill, 1945), p. 285, and Wolf, *Rubber,* p. 231.

35   Hoover to Capper, March 6, 1924, quoted fully in Charles R. Whittlesey, *Government Control of Crude Rubber* (Princeton, 1931), Appendix D, p. 216. Hoover's letter was distributed through the major Department of Commerce offices to numerous newspapers; see Chalk, "Struggle for Rubber," 67, 291.

36   Hoover to Mark Felber, Firestone Tire & Rubber Co., March 18, 1925, Hoover Papers, Commerce Section, Foreign Comb.—Rubber.

37   Walter E. Edge to Hoover, May 27, 1925; Hoover to Edge, May 28, 1925, Hoover Papers, Commerce Section, Foreign Comb.—Rubber.

38   Statement by Secretary Hoover at Press Conference, June 2, 1925; A. L. Viles, General Manager, The Rubber Association of America, to E. G. Holt, Acting Chief, Rubber Division, "For the information of the Secretary," June 4, 5, 1925, Hoover Papers, Commerce Section, Foreign Comb.—Rubber.

39   P. L. Palmerton, Chief, Rubber Division, to Harold Phelps Stokes, Secretary's Office, July 18, 1925, Hoover Papers, Commerce Section, Foreign Comb.—Rubber.

40   Hoover to Representative Clarence Mac Gregor (New York), August 5, 1925, with enclosures, Hoover Papers, Commerce Section, Foreign Comb.—Rubber.

41   See, for example, P. J. Croghan, Editorial Division, August 6, 1925, Hoover Papers, Commerce Section, Foreign Comb.—Rubber.

42   Hoover to Justus Collins, Kanawha Banking & Trust, Charleston, W. Va., September 19, 1925, and copy of memorandum, Hoover Papers, Commerce Section, Foreign Comb.—Rubber.

43   Hoover to Capper, December 10, 1925 (released for morning papers December 15, 1925), Hoover Papers, Commerce Section, Foreign Combinations: Statements of H. H.

44   Croghan to Stokes, May 26, 1925; *Journal of Commerce,* editorial, May 25, 1925; London's *Morning Post* editorials as cited in the *New York Times,* December 27, 1925, all in Hoover Papers, Commerce Section, Foreign Comb.—Rubber.

45   Henry P. Starrett (U.S. Consul, Belfast), January 4, 1926, State Department Records (National Archives, RG 59), 841.6176/69.

46   *The Outlook* (London), November 7, 1925, the *New Leader* (London), November

6, 1925, and other clippings contained in the reports of Ray Atherton (first secretary, U.S. Embassy, London), November 13, 1925, State Dept. Records, 841.6176/37.

47   U.S. Embassy (London) to the State Department, "Strictly Confidential" Dispatch #681, January 6, 1926, State Dept. Records, 841.6176/67, including editorial from the London *Times,* January 5, 1926.

48   *Ibid.*

49   U.S. Embassy (London) to the State Department, January 21, 1926, State Dept. Records, 841.6176/72, including editorials from the *Manchester Guardian,* January 12, 1926, and the *Daily Telegraph,* January 9, 1926.

50   *Ibid.*

51   *Yorkshire Post,* January 6, 1926, quoted by Stillman W. Eels (U.S. Consul, Leeds), January 6, 1926, State Dept. Records, 841.6176/68.

52   Clippings from the *Rangoon Gazette,* dispatch of Consul Charles J. Pisar (Burma), February 1, 1926, State Dept. Records, 841.6176/77.

53   Memorandum by William R. Castle, assistant secretary of state, November 3, 1926, State Dept. Records, 841.6176/123.

54   Houghton to Kellogg, July 23, 1925, State Dept. Records, 841.6176/6.

55   *Ibid.*

56   *Preliminary Report,* 5. Part of this increase was the result of an intensified demand for rubber in the United States, and inflated prices.

57   Houghton to Kellogg, July 23, 1925, State Dept. Records, 841.6176/6.

58   *Ibid.;* Kellogg to Houghton, July 27, and October 10, 1925, State Dept. Records, 841.6176/26, 27.

59   Aide-Memoire, U.S. Embassy, London, July 22; Chamberlain to Houghton, August 15; F. A. Sterling, counselor of embassy, to the secretary of state, August 17, 18; Grew to Hoover, September 8; Hoover to the secretary of state, September 14, 1925, all in Hoover Papers, Commerce Section, Foreign Comb.—Correspondence, Sec'y of State.

60   Hoover to Kellogg, September 25, 1925, Hoover Papers, Commerce Section, Foreign Comb.—Correspondence, Sec'y of State.

61   For a definition of the Open Door, see Joan Hoff Wilson's insightful discussion in *American Business,* p. 9, passim.

62   Department of Commerce, "Memorandum On Dispatches From The American Embassy In London Relative To The Rubber Situation," with Hoover letter to Kellogg, September 25, 1925, Hoover Papers, Commerce Section, Foreign Comb.—Correspondence, Sec'y of State.

63   Viles letter and memorandum to Kellogg, October 7, 1925, Hoover Papers, Commerce Section, Foreign Comb.—Correspondence, Sec'y of State.

64   Kellogg to Hoover, October 10; Hoover to Kellogg, October 13, November 13, 1925, all in *ibid.*

65 Houghton to Kellogg, November 25, Kellogg to Houghton, December 1, with covering letter to Hoover, December 2, 1925, all in *ibid.*

66 Houghton to Kellogg, December 4, with Kellogg's covering letter to Hoover, December 4; Chamberlain to Howard, December 3, 1925, all in *ibid.*

67 Firestone, quoted in James C. Lawrence, *The World's Struggle With Rubber* (New York, 1931), p. 46.

68 Chalk, "Struggle for Rubber," 89-90; see also 95-97, 132-34, 146-47, passim.

69 Firestone to Hoover, "Confidential," December 12, Hoover to Firestone, December 14, confirming a personal conference, Firestone to Hoover, December 16, 1925, Hoover Papers, Commerce Section, Foreign Comb.—Rubber.

70 Harold Phelps Stokes, assistant to Mr. Hoover, To the Editor of the *New York Times,* December 31, 1925, including passage from letter to Senator Capper, Hoover Papers, Commerce Section, Foreign Comb.—Rubber.

71 Kellogg to Hoover, December 23, incl. reports from Houghton, Hoover to Kellogg, December 17, incl. wording of instructions to embassy in Rio de Janeiro; Leland Harrison, assistant secretary of state, to Hoover, December 24, 1925, Hoover Papers, Commerce Section, Foreign Comb.—Rubber.

SUMMARY OF COMMENTARY BY DISCUSSANTS AND CONFEREES

Discussion of the paper began with formal commentaries by Professor Ellis W. Hawley of the University of Iowa and Professor Joan Hoff Wilson, who was at the time affiliated with California State University, Sacramento. Both commentators were impressed with the parallels that Brandes had drawn between the situation of the 1920s and that of recent years, and both praised the way in which he had reconstructed and documented the rubber controversy. Each, however, raised questions about the paper's conceptual framework, noting, in particular, its tendency to slight the managerial and cooperative ideals with which Hoover was associated elsewhere and therefore to make him more of an anti-monopolist and free trader than he actually was. The anti-monopoly campaigns, Hawley suggested, are better understood as a rationalizer's attack on managerial malpractice than as drives to create the world envisioned in classical economics. Had they been more successful, they might well have been followed by campaigns to build new managerial institutions. But given the structural peculiarities of the rubber industry and the power of those being attacked, they failed to develop much beyond efforts to displace the malpractitioners through appeals to nationalist and competitive ideals. Wilson also thought that Hoover's use of free trade, anti-monopoly, and consumerist rhetoric could not be taken as reflective of his real goals and intentions. But unlike Hawley, she was inclined to see Hoover and his associates as practitioners of a diplomatic "realism" that used whatever was expedient and feasible to advance national interests. Elaborating upon this point later, she suggested that New Era diplomats, Hoover included, were disposed to build American monopolies where they could, to share markets where they had to, and to accept competition where it was unavoidable.

In addition, the commentators made several other points. Hawley agreed with Brandes that Hoover's programs envisioned a coordinated amalgam of public and private activities; but he did not see this as justifying the label of "neo-mercantilist." Wilson was more inclined than Brandes to see both the rubber and coffee campaigns as failures. And in both commentaries, there were questions raised about divisions within the American business community, about the different courses taken by rubber and oil diplomacy, and about the relationship of the events described to such matters as political ambition, European stability, and Latin American development.

The subsequent discussion from the floor began with a series of remarks by Michael Hogan, author of *Informal Entente: The Private Structure of Cooperation in Anglo-American Economic Diplomacy, 1918–1928.* In these Hogan argued that there was an Open Door ideology at work in the American diplomacy of the 1920s. The latter was not neo-mercantilist in the sense of accepting trade warfare as the normal state. Nor could it all be reduced to mere expediency, as Wilson seemed to be suggesting. But the Open Door conception of the period was no longer identical with the free trade conception of classical economics. It had been redefined to recognize the need for managerial coordination and investment safeguards, and in a number of areas its proponents seemed willing to settle for a kind of Anglo-American partnership institutionalized at both the governmental and private levels. That such institutions failed to develop in rubber, Hogan thought, was due partly to the resentment aroused by Hoover's charges and partly to the uncompromising positions taken on American tariffs and the workings of the Stevenson Plan.

Given an opportunity to respond, Professor Brandes then made several points. The British, he suspected, entered partnerships where they felt compelled to, and not because policy was being made by the cooperative-minded. In oil such a partnership had seemed preferable to continued conflict. But in rubber, which was grown chiefly within the

British Empire, they were much more resistant to calls for open doors or shared development. He also suspected that the neo-mercantilist label as applied to American policy had some justification, at least in effect if not in intention. Hoover and his supporters, after all, had worked to enhance the nation's favorable balance of trade, keep gold within the country, and restrict outward investment flows; and they had persisted in this despite the criticism of economic internationalists and the warnings of international financiers. Finally, Brandes suspected that the commentators were seeking a degree of consistency in Hoover that did not exist. Like other politicians, he could at times embrace contradictory lines of policy and simply ignore or paper over the inconsistencies in his economic and social thought.

As the session drew to a close, several other items were also brought into the discussion. There were comments, both from the floor and from the panel, concerning how foreign cartels threatened not only American living standards but groups interested in foreign investment opportunities. There were observations, especially from Melvyn Leffler, concerning Hoover's perceptions of a future in which America was likely to become increasingly dependent on raw material imports and would therefore have to become more of an exporting nation. There was further discussion of how Hoover's political ambitions may have led him to assume the role of monopoly fighter, especially in the period from 1926 to 1928. And in response to questions from Francis O'Brien, there was some speculation about the relationship between Hoover and Louis Brandeis and what this may have contributed to Hoover's anti-monopoly stance. On this, Neil Basen volunteered the information that the two men had drunk sherry together and discussed public issues. But neither he nor others had any knowledge of specific influences.

WILLIAM R. CHILDS

Origins of the Texas Railroad Commission's Power to Control Production of Petroleum: Regulatory Strategies in the 1920s

The "Railroad Commission of Texas" conjures up visions of oil and gas and power politics and perhaps the question, What does "railroad" have to do with petroleum?[1] The Railroad Commission (RCT) also brings to mind modern America between 1930 and the 1970s, when the Texas agency controlled from 35 to 45 percent of the oil and gas produced in the United States. These images come from cultural myths of the Lone Star State, from Americans' fascination with conspiracies, and, most telling, from the lack of historical analyses of the commission, its staff, and its regulatory strategies.[2] The prevailing views of the commission are unfortunate ones, for they not only neglect the agency's regulation of railroads, natural-gas utilities, and buses and trucks but also skew the understanding of how the state commission came to regulate petroleum in the first place, how it devised policies for doing so, and how it legitimized itself and defended that legitimacy under the weight of the East Texas crisis between 1930 and 1935.

In this article I will focus on the lesser-known portion of the story: developing petroleum regulatory strategies in Texas in the 1920s. Taking the point of view of the commission itself will enrich our understanding of why and how petroleum production came to be controlled in the following decade by statewide "proration" orders, a system for allocating monthly production allowables for each oil field in the state. The Texas story in the 1920s was moving in a direction different from that taken in the 1930s in Texas and the nation, but the legitimacy established in the earlier decade proved important in the latter. Texas became an important cog in the national proration machinery of the 1930s not only because of its large petroleum reserves but also because its oil conservation agency,

JOURNAL OF POLICY HISTORY, Vol. 2, No. 4, 1990.
Copyright © 1990 The Pennsylvania State University Press, University Park, PA.

the Oil and Gas Division of the Railroad Commission, had legitimized itself in the eyes of many industry members during the preceding decade.

The story offers the opportunity to sustain and to question several themes and conclusions in the historiography of big business, regulation, and policymaking in modern America. Affected somewhat by post–World War I fears of an oil shortage, the story in Texas nonetheless occurred during a time of constant but relatively slow-paced change in the modern petroleum industry and thus offers a clear contrast in policymaking with the more compressed and contentious 1930s. The story also questions current historical scholarship that maintains the economic structure of an industry, more than any other force, determines the context in which management and regulators operate.[3] How the regulators and regulated in Texas understood the law and acted upon that understanding permeates the story as much as their learning more each year about the economic (and geological) forces of the petroleum industry.[4]

Petroleum conservation in Texas in the 1920s occurred within the larger context of business-government relations in the United States in the twentieth century. That context included industrywide associational activities, continuities in Progressive Era ideals and practices, elements of southern business progressivism, and of course the Texas political economy.[5] These subtexts combined with the economic and legal forces to shape a regulatory culture in which the Texas regulators and oil operators made policy choices in the 1920s. Thus, the narrative-analytical approach employed in this article pushes the organizational synthesis[6] to embrace points of view being developed by cultural and social historians and social behaviorists.[7]

This article is divided into six sections. The first summarizes the historiography; the second describes the agency, explains why it began to regulate petroleum production, and introduces the commissioner who would guide the implementation of conservation policy. The third section recounts a crisis in 1919 that not only anticipated the crisis of the 1930s but also set the agenda for regulation in the 1920s. The fourth section lays out the strategies of regulation the Texas regulators and operators implemented and notes how the process legitimated the Texas agency in the eyes of industry leaders. The fifth section discusses why and how proration agreements appeared in Texas before 1930. The final section highlights the significance of the story, notes how it affected the 1930s, and relates it to the prevailing historiography.

I will argue contrary to prevailing scholarship, that the RCT actively pursued regulatory strategies in the 1920s to conserve the state's petroleum resources; that its commissioners, one in particular, worked cooperatively with industry executives, within a Progressive Era approach, to reconcile conflicts between prevailing legal doctrines and the economic structure of the industry; and that through a dual private-public management approach to rationalizing the industry, the regulators not only made headway in conservation but also legitimized the agency in the eyes of industry leaders. Though attacked often during the production crisis after 1930, that legitimacy survived and became central to national efforts to rationalize oil production in the 1930s.

Historiography

In brief, the scholarship reveals this basic outline of petroleum regulation in America before 1940: Even though several states in the 1910s enacted conservation statutes, effective conservation methods did not materialize until fields in Oklahoma and the East Texas Field had flooded the market with oil from 1929 to 1931. From the crisis-management of these fields, there issued forth in the mid-1930s a national consensus on how to control the production of oil. Since Texas held by far the majority of proven reserves, it fell upon the RC Texas to establish monthly statewide proration schedules if the industry were to be stabilized. Once the courts sustained the commission's methods of allocation, once the Connally Hot Oil Act of 1935 was implemented, and once the Interstate Oil Compact Commission was in operation, the RCT, it has been argued, effectively became the locus of control over the production, and therefore the price, of petroleum.[8]

The accepted story, however, has a peculiarly post-1930 slant that has slighted important activity occurring in the federal and state arenas in the 1920s.[9] Federal efforts to control production in the 1920s have drawn some attention, especially the work of the Federal Oil Conservation Board and the Bureau of Mines.[10] Those scholars who have chronicled the private sector's attempts to foster controls of production tend to locate the impetus for and experimentation in this reform with the subject of their histories—the operators and executives of the integrated firms. They include the associational work of the American Petroleum Institute (API) and state and national efforts in both the 1920s and 1930s, but mention state agencies like the RCT only in passing.[11]

State policies in the 1920s to conserve petroleum resources have drawn even less attention than federal or industry efforts. A few policy historians have noted that conservation statutes existed in the key producing states of Oklahoma, Texas, and California.[12] Some include brief mention of early attempts to force proration in Oklahoma, and some allude to private efforts in Texas to control production before 1931. But for Texas specifically, most seem to agree with one scholar, who maintained that in the 1920s "there was little interest in the part of the industry, and considerable apathy on the part of the regulatory agency, toward the enforcement of the conservation statutes."[13]

The origin of this misleading conclusion appears to be the first and apparently only study of the Oil and Gas Division of the RCI in the 1920s, a master's thesis written in 1931 by Robert Conrod, a student in the Political Science Department at the University of Texas at Austin. Reflecting the usual foibles found in most master's theses, Conrod's work paradoxically exhibited an understanding of the complexities of the petroleum industry and a presentist, ahistorical orientation. According to Conrod, the agency in the 1920s had "ignored or half-heartedly enforced" its own rules and had not established a uniform statewide enforcement of the rules. In addition, it allowed for a great amount of waste and became so closely connected to industry interests that it had failed to defend the public interest.[14]

Conrod's thesis tells a story and offers analyses very different from the ones I offer here, which have been developed after studying the correspondence of the Oil and Gas Division between 1917 and the early 1930s.[15]

The Railroad Commission, the Oil Field Problem, and Commissioner Gilmore

In 1916, one year before the RCI began regulating the petroleum industry, its three elected commissioners were served by an administrative staff of twelve employees. (The original commissioners in 1891 had begun with only three.) For the first twenty-five years of its existence, the agency had been exclusively male and Democratic in its staff makeup; in 1916 the first woman was hired. All employees worked on railway-related matters, such as shipper complaints, requests from the railways to construct or abandon sections of track, and, ceaselessly it seemed, rate investigations. Most of the day-to-day routine work took place in offices scattered throughout the Austin capitol building and in various hearings rooms and courtrooms throughout Texas and the nation.[16]

The working culture of the commission in 1916 was remarkably little different from that established by the first chair, John H. Reagan. Despite the election of some commissioners who were more interested in personal political advancement than in regulation, the agency had maintained

Progressive Era strategies of public policymaking that embraced cooperative exchanges of ideas among private-sector businesses, expert engineers and accountants, and disinterested public servants. The small-scale staff and the hiring of experts had sustained the progressive approach to regulation.[17] With duties associated with an industry different in structure from railroading, however, the culture of the commission would necessarily change.

The agency's old and new activities, moreover, included a prominent subtext of southern-style business progressivism.[18] Business progressivism in Texas and the South incorporated the belief that a "New South," an ideal established in the late nineteenth century by southern journalists, should be based on cooperative business-government initiatives to industrialize the region. Boosterism (awarding tax breaks and touting a low-wage labor market) and attempts to bring efficiency and honesty to government animated local and state efforts to attract industrial enterprise to the South. The appearance of oil in some of the southern states (Texas, Louisiana, Oklahoma, and Arkansas) seemed for many to be a prayer answered, but as with so much of southern business history after the Civil War up to the mid-twentieth century, business and political leaders ironically failed to capitalize on the opportunity to create a truly progressive "New South."[19] Countering the boosterism, moreover, was a peculiarly southern aversion to monopoly, a legacy of the populist agitation of the late nineteenth century. In Texas, particularly, the antitrust actions against Standard in 1899 sustained a widespread hatred for Standard and the "major" oil firms and support for the "independents" well into the twentieth century.[20]

The movement for petroleum conservation reflected in the more immediate context of the late 1910s' policymakers' favorable reaction to government control of production during the Great War, as well as legislative responses to waste and economic instability in the state's oil fields. On the national level, the war experience marked a radical shift in the history of the petroleum industry. World War I revealed that petroleum production was a necessity of the modern machines of war and therefore held elements of a public utility, which made it subject to government controls. In addition, conservation became a leading political issue because national government officials believed another war might catch the United States without sufficient supplies of petroleum. The war also highlighted the industry's complex makeup of economic forces: With an already growing automobile population and the new fuel demands from the nascent airline industry and fuel-oil-propelled U.S. Navy, oil firms naturally focused on the gasoline market. The geology of oil, however, presented some difficulties in meeting this market. Natural gas often appeared along with the oil, and because there existed only a small market for natural gas at this time (as fuel for cooking and heating in urban areas), drillers vented the gas into the air.[21]

In Texas, petroleum conservation had been an issue sporadically since the 1890s; legislation in 1899, 1905, and 1913, which was not enforced, had ordered drillers to case off their wells not only to prevent loss of natural gas associated with the oil but also to forestall saltwater encroachment into oil sands and agricultural lands. In the late 1910s, however, waste of gas became a key political issue when Texans suffered shortages of coal and natural gas during the cold winter of 1917–18, even as the state's oil wells vented billions of cubic feet of gas into the air. The oil-well drillers and operators were unhappy also because the market for their product was unstable: new pools of oil inevitably led to lower prices, which did not return enough money to pay off loans for drilling.[22]

When the oil operators' pleas for state control of production peaked between 1917 and 1919, along with public outcry over the lack of stable supplies, the lawmakers gave enforcement powers of the new conservation statutes to the RCT for essentially two reasons. First, the administrative tasks involved transportation regulation (pipelines in a 1917 act), with which the commissioners were already familiar. Second, the agency's track record since its inception in 1891—it had maintained a profile of efficiency in administration and enthusiastic promotion of the entire Texas economy—made it a popular institution in which to lodge important administrative tasks.[23]

Two statutes in particular, An Act Regulating Pipelines in 1917 and the Oil and Gas Conservation Act of 1919, outlined the commission's duties. The 1917 law instructed the RCT to devise rules and rates for the transportation of petroleum pipeline and to make sure, when production levels exceeded the pipeline's capacity, that the pipeline companies took "ratably," or proportionately, from each producer in a field. This action was intended to protect the small-scale producer from discrimination by integrated pipeline firms who, if not regulated, would transport only oil from their production units. The 1919 law instructed the RCT to monitor oil- and gas-drilling practices and filing of production reports, and to make rules to carry out the laws' provisions against wasteful practices. The petroleum companies would pay the costs of regulation through a tax on crude production (at first, 1/20 of 1 percent of the *market* value). Unlike earlier railway legislation, however, the petroleum laws did not give the commission the authority to establish prices. Indeed, the Texas laws specifically avoided economic regulation per se: The Texas regulators were to prevent physical waste but were not to be concerned with economic waste, or production above market demand.[24]

Significantly, regulation of petroleum in Texas followed in the wake of earlier and ongoing administrative control over production in Oklahoma. The Oklahoma petroleum conservation laws, which the Corporation Commission began enforcing in 1915, from the beginning tied conservation of resources to economic waste rather than to physical waste. The Oklahoma lawmakers had been persuaded by the operators that to allow oil to be sold at a price so low that it would not furnish a return to investors and drillers would be wasteful and therefore impede conservation of the state's resources. Although Oklahoma administrated the laws more directly than did the RCI and perhaps met more success in controlling total production, that state was just as stymied as Texas by some important legal restraints, which will be introduced in the next section.[25]

The 1919 Texas law contained rather specific provisions designed to eliminate waste in the oil fields of Texas. Certificates of compliance with the law and with RCT rules and regulations were required before a pipeline company could connect its lines to an oil producer's well. The law also required operators to maintain records on the history of each well drilled (through well "logs," which detailed each stratum the drill bit passed through) and on the well's production levels. The RCT could shut down wells, but only after waste had occurred and only through a tedious process in the courts. Given that the new regulatory statute required new knowledge and effort from the commissioners, they were given a $1,000-per-year increase in salary, which now totaled $5,000 per year.[26]

In the spring of 1919 the three elected commissioners were Allison Mayfield, who had served since January 1897; Earl B. Mayfield, who had come on board in January 1913; and Clarence E. Gilmore, who took his position in January 1919. As with most of their predecessors, these three men were lawyers. While they were capable regulators and not indifferent to their job on the RCT, the Mayfields, especially during election campaigns, seemed more interested in the state's politics.[27]

Gilmore was different. Although in 1919 he possessed no experience in government regulation, more than any other commissioner (there would be several changes in the 1920s) he emerged as the guiding force in the agency's attempts to conserve petroleum in the 1920s. Born in October 1872 on a farm in Van Zandt County (east-southeast of Dallas), Gilmore studied law at home and at the University of Texas. He had been a farmer, clerk, and teacher before pursuing a journalist's career in the mid-1890s. An editor and owner of two small-town papers, he became president of and general attorney for the Texas Press Association in the early 1900s. Meanwhile, he served as state representative for three terms, from 1906 to 1910. Elected to the RCT in 1918, he was relected in 1924 and was chair of the agency from 1923 until his death. As a regulator, he was licensed in 1921 to argue before the U.S. Supreme Court and became active in cooperative activities between the Interstate Commerce Commission (ICC) and the state regulatory agencies.[28]

Gilmore's professional life, then, included ties to the southern business and national progressive movements. Underscoring the value the Progressive Era placed on the disinterested expert, Gilmore refused to "invest one cent" in the oil and gas industries. But that did not diminish his fascination with "the game" and from promoting the industry for the Texas economy, much as previous commissioners had attempted for railways. Given his talents, the Mayfields' inadequacies, and several changes in the commissioners' ranks during the decade, Gilmore would emerge as the leading authoritative figure on conservation of petroleum at the RCT.[29] In fact, Gilmore would find himself immersed in the modern petroleum industry just a few months after taking office.

Prologue to Petroleum Conservation Policy: The Burkburnett Field, 1919

Located in North Texas, northwest of Fort Worth near the Red River boundary with Oklahoma, the Burkburnett field had opened up even before the 1919 law had gone into effect in June. The immediate problem was insufficient pipeline capacity to carry away flush production. The rational response, of course, was to stop the drilling until enough pipe could be laid to syphon off production.[30]

As Gilmore and the Mayfields discovered, however, the nineteenth-century legal precedent, the "rule-of-capture," forestalled rational economic responses. Essentially, the rule-of-capture decreed that what was beneath a property owner's surface holdings belonged to him if he captured it. Since oil usually flowed toward wells already drilled, property owners scrambled to drill wells before their neighbors did in order to get not only "their" oil but also as much of their neighbor's as possible. A clear case of the law encouraging unfettered capitalistic production, the rule-of-capture lay at the root of the chaos and waste in all flush fields. Ironically, the Texas 1917 pipeline law underscored the drilling madness in Burkburnett. Reflecting the doctrine of correlative rights, which somewhat contradicted the rule-of-capture,[31] the 1917 statute ordered the

RCT to ensure that pipelines took proportionately from all producers; thus, more producers appeared than would have been the case had they not had that assurance. (Oklahoma attempted to avoid this problem by focusing its control on production, not transportation.)[32]

Gilmore leaped to the forefront to manage the crisis, but was embarrassed by predicting success too early. At first, he believed that more pipeline connections would suffice and predicted the new pipe would be in by October 1. That did not happen. Meanwhile, he and the other commissioners, at the suggestion of more established operators in the field, took bold action in July when they ordered a shutdown of production for five days. But the attorney general, C. M. Cureton, declared the order invalid and issued one of his own. The new order required the pipelines to take oil from everyone in the field; if the available capacity could not take all of the oil, then the pipeline companies were required to take proportionately from each well. Thus was born the first proration order in Texas.[33]

All the while, however, the commissioners understood that they were treading on new and unknown ground and needed more time to work out correct solutions. A crisis situation was not the best atmosphere in which to develop expert testimony and well-conceived policies. Not only did the regulators not know the extent of the problems at hand, they were not sure which firms were under their jurisdiction. The commissioners, believers in the Progressive Era approach of rational investigation and response to technical problems, could not respond quickly enough. Given the political atmosphere surrounding passage of the 1919 conservation law, the extent of detail work involved in proration, and the tedious procedures attending court suits, the regulators *encouraged* cooperative experimentation among the operators to relieve the production crisis.[34]

Gilmore and the other commissioners made several errors in judgment in the summer and autumn of 1919, but they learned some valuable lessons from the crisis management. Neither the 1917 nor the 1919 law gave them *direct* control over wasteful production, but, by combining the enforcement powers of both laws, they could exert *some* control. On the basis of the 1917 pipeline law, for example, when the oil exceeded the pipelines' capacity, the RCT could have the pipeline companies, through proration agreements, take proportionately from each producer. The 1917 law also furnished power to the regulatory agency to demand pipeline run reports; then, using the 1919 law, the RCT could prosecute operators for wasteful production when the pipeline runs exceeded prorated levels. Nonetheless, the regulators remained unsure in 1919 of their authority and only tentatively sponsored private proration agreements in Burk-

burnett (and also simultaneously in South Texas). These private agreements, however, could be and were disrupted when one or more operators
chose not to cooperate. The gaps in authority prevented the regulators
from reconciling the controversy between the economic need for conservation and the legal constraints of the rule-of-capture and correlative rights.
Thus, there was a "regulatory failure" in Burkburnett.[35]

The Burkburnett proration scheme represented an experiment in industry self-regulation in which the RCT lent only tentative public support.
The plan relied heavily on private-sector "umpires," who mediated controversies among the operators in the field. The umpires determined how
much oil would flow, which wells would produce how much oil per day,
and which wells would be connected to the pipelines before others. (Control over the drilling of new wells, however, was not included in the
private-sector plan.) The operators hired gaugers to measure the flow of
crude from each well, but rumors that some oil gaugers accepted bribes to
falsify the readings undermined the experiment in self-regulation. If the
measurements were faulty, then the *daily* pipeline reports to the RCT
were of little use. In fact, the commissioners could do little to stop
offenders, for they could act only *after* waste had occurred. Their authority to act in any case was in doubt as well. Some questions remained: were
all pipeline firms common carriers? Could a state agency control interstate
pipelines?

Despite Gilmore's efforts to cajole operators into compliance, proration
failed to control the situation; by October there was no proration scheme
in operation. In the event, the crisis abated on its own as drilling activity
slackened and oil prices stabilized; the operators saw no reason for continuing the proration program.[36]

Gilmore realized during the crisis that if a *common purchaser act* were
enacted, giving the RCT authority over the proration of *purchases* of oil,
production could be controlled and waste prevented. There would be
less pressure to drill unnecessary wells in order to capitalize on the rule-
of-capture.[37] Oklahoma had some success using this approach,[38] but such
a strategy would not emerge in Texas until more knowledge existed of
how oil fields functioned, until the idea of "unitization" of fields had
filtered through the industry, until the Texas regulators had sponsored
proration experiments later in the 1920s, and until the East Texas fiasco, 1930–35, had forced the Texas lawmakers to give the commission
adequate authority.[39]

Notwithstanding the failed management of the Burkburnett crisis, the
commissioners established rules and regulations under the recently enacted conservation statute even as the crisis continued. They solicited

information and advice from ,established and experienced operators through public hearings and communications to the commission; they also consulted other state agencies, most notably the Oklahoma Corporation Commission.[40]

The regulators then promulgated a list of more than forty rules that outlined how an oil field should be exploited in order to minimize waste. The list included rules for placement of slush pits and storage tanks; for casing-off the drilled hole in order to prevent saltwater and gas from fouling surrounding strata or rising to the surface to contaminate agricultural resources; for "shooting" a well hole (using nitroglycerin to clear a clogged hole); for plugging a dry hole; and for connecting to a pipeline carrier. The regulators required permits to be issued before any of these operations could take place (at least a dozen different forms were involved) and made provisions for on-site inspection by employees of the commission. In Rule 37, promulgated in part to minimize fire dangers and in part to prevent landowners from taking their neighbors' oil, the commissioners established the minimum distances to be maintained between oil wells in a common pool.[41]

With these rules, the RCT became part of a dual management team (the oil operators comprised the other half) to manage an orderly development of the industry in Texas. Despite the detailed rules and regulations, the regulators' strategies from the beginning opted for less direct and strong commission oversight in favor of more cooperative approaches to preventing wasteful practices. More direct regulation was not possible in 1919, given the lack of knowledge of how oil fields operated, the position of most oil operators, including the so-called major firms, whose managers ideologically opposed government interference, and the lack of clear authority to force the operators to follow conservation rules. During this formative period, the populist antitrust heritage in Texas surfaced only occasionally to criticize the commissioners for serving the interests of the major integrated companies.[42] For the most part, then, the program established in 1919 and the early 1920s reflected a cooperative endeavor between business and government to learn together how to manage wisely the state's resources.

The failure to manage the Burkburnett crisis did not prevent the Texas regulators from attempting to enforce the conservation laws. They simply had to find other methods with which to balance the conflict between economic forces (control of production, price regulation, conservation) and legal forces (rule-of-capture, correlative rights, antitrust). The oil-field rules and the relative calm of the 1920s would offer them the chance to do so.

Establishing Legitimacy: Strategies of Oil Conservation, 1919–1929

As the Burkburnett crisis unfolded, Clarence Gilmore and the other commissioners realized that, in the absence of crisis conditions, their new duties in oil conservation would be implemented better through decentralizing the commission and creating a separate department designed to foster cooperative activities with the industry. They hired George Butte, a law professor at the University of Texas, to establish an administrative force. The first Republican ever hired knowingly by the RCT, Butte was forty-two in 1919 and had lived a life that many could not have duplicated in three lifetimes; and his work for one year on the RCT would not be the highlight of his career. Butte held many qualities that signified he was a servant of the people, dedicated to honest and efficient government and to cooperative business-government enterprises.[43] After he showed up for one year of work on 1 October 1919, Chief Supervisor Butte skillfully integrated his ideas with those Gilmore and the staff had been implementing since June. Much of the Oil and Gas Division's staff structure and many of its bureaucratic forms drew from the Oklahoma experience.[44]

Butte, and by extension the RCT, implemented the conservation laws on the basis of an "intensive" definition of conservation. Butte believed "a wise use of natural resources" involved "bringing about a slow, wise and economical exhaustion so as to insure continuity of service for the future.[45] From the beginning, and because the laws forbade considerations of market demand, the Texas regulators viewed themselves strictly as conservation agents charged with preventing the physical waste of the state's resources.

To enforce the conservation laws, Butte and Gilmore developed three strategies: (1) educating the oil operators in sound field practices and regulatory procedures, (2) the gathering and analysis of statistics, and (3) the development of cooperative activities among the oil operators and between the operators and the commission. These three strategies were inextricably intertwined: the RCT staff would educate the operators in proper drilling procedures and in filling out regulatory forms; the reports would comprise the statistics that would become, after proper analysis, the basis for informed cooperative activities. Although the analysis of statistics was less successful than had been hoped, education, statistics gathering, and cooperation proceeded apace throughout the decade.[46]

Butte implemented these strategies through the decentralized portion of the RCT, the Pipeline and Conservation Department (later, the Oil and Gas Division), which was established shortly after he arrived. During his year at the RCT, Butte fostered a sense of pride and professionalism in the work of the Oil and Gas Division, especially in the field force, which consisted of a fluctuating number of "deputy oil and gas supervisors" assigned to specific geographic areas of the state. Butte, as Gilmore had done during the summer, instructed the men in the field on how to educate the operators in sound oil-field operations, in following the rules of the commission, and in reporting statistics carefully and in a timely matter. The Chief Deputy Supervisor patiently explained to his deputy supervisors why they should emphasize fire prevention, be tactful in their dealings with the operators, and keep track of their expenses in an entirely open manner. He established the tradition of having the field force come to Austin once a year for a conference, during which the deputy supervisors could mingle, meet one another, and exchange information and "war stories" from the fields.[47] In this manner, Butte established an agency culture based on professional, efficient public service that underscored the RCT's commitment to conservation of petroleum resources throughout the decade. That the thousands of operators filed the required reports, if not completely filled out and if not always on time, suggests the strategy of education had worked.[48]

Butte's efforts during 1919–20 seemed prescient indeed. Despite the advanced age of the oil industry (begun in the United States in the mid-nineteenth century), its modern era had begun only in 1901 with the Spindletop discovery in Southeast Texas. Not enough was known about how oil pools worked, too many oil drillers were inexperienced, and wasteful gushers still fascinated. Butte's efforts to enforce the state's petroleum conservation laws prepared the RCT for a decade of expansion in drilling activity; the battle to prevent waste would take place in all sections of the largest state in the union during a decade that seemed to have a major discovery every year. In addition, the changing makeup of the industry in Texas would present difficulties. While only half a dozen major firms produced over half the petroleum in 1918–19, another 2,500 firms competed with thin investment resources. That number would soar to more than 12,000 by mid-decade.[49]

The discoveries in Burkburnett had been only a part of widespread activity in North Texas in the late 1910s. Then, in 1921–23, several fields opened up in the Corsicana area (southeast of Dallas–Fort Worth); none was spared the horror of fires and the waste of natural gas. Drillers then moved south into the "boot toe" of the state, into the so-called Laredo district, where once again unthinking overdrilling depleted the gas, thus diminishing the flow of oil. Such wasteful practices, tempered by an increasing presence of RCT personnel in the fields throughout the decade, were nonetheless overshadowed by the state's overall production picture.

Production increases after 1925 came steadily: 22 million barrels more were produced in 1926 than in 1925; 50 million barrels more in 1927; 40 million more in 1928; and 39 million more in 1929. Much of the increase came from discoveries in West Texas (1923–25 and after) and new discoveries in older producing areas. Gas discoveries in the Panhandle (1925 and after) troubled the commission because the market for gas was still underdeveloped and waste was a foregone conclusion as producers vented the gas into the air or built inefficient gasoline and carbon black plants. Meanwhile, discoveries in other states—Oklahoma, Arkansas, Louisiana, and Kansas—led to periodic price declines when supply overreached demand. Despite increasing drilling costs (because new oil was found usually much deeper than previously discovered oil), waste remained a key problem. Rising imports added to the production problems as the share of national production in Texas increased from about 22 percent in 1920 to about 30 percent in 1930.[50] This, then, was the changing context in which the Oil and Gas Division pursued its conservation strategies.

While Butte's tone of administration remained important in enforcing the conservation laws throughout the 1920s,[51] it was in the work of the deputy supervisors in the field that we discover how the strategies of education and statistics gathering led to cooperative experiments in a variety of areas, from drilling practices to proration agreements. Essentially the deputy supervisor was to prevent waste from occurring below and above the ground. The commission tried to hire only men who had "practical" oil experience, preferably in oil-well drilling. The first deputy supervisor, J. L. Mildren, was in many ways one of the best hired during the 1920s. His previous experience in the industry and with the Oklahoma regulatory agency gave him more expertise than anyone else at the commission. A few deputy supervisors hired later were less professional and less able than Mildren, but most labored hard for little pay ($2,400 to $3,600 per year) often under severe conditions.[52]

Depending on his location, a deputy supervisor would have to travel hundreds of miles in order to inspect operations. One deputy supervisor found it easier to live out of his car, rather than maintain a permanent residence. Another reported he had used the railway, stage, jitney, saddle horse, and auto in order to make his rounds. Since many of the supervisors were assigned to flush or boomtown fields, they faced many of the same problems the oil operators did such as inflationary prices for food and lodging, inadequate lodging and office space, and difficulty in securing supplies. For much of the decade, town chambers of commerce offered the deputy supervisor free office space in the chambers' offices; when other higher-paying customers (lawyers and royalty salesmen) appeared, however, the town's boosterism gave way to monetary rewards and the deputy supervisor had to fend for himself. Despite the hardships, many deputy supervisors took pride in their job and worked hard to make the conservation laws work.[53]

Through the work of the deputy supervisors in the field and the coordination of their work from the Austin office, the RCT encountered and overcame many problems in oil production and conservation during the 1920s. As mentioned above, there *was* waste attending oil production in the 1920s, but the deputy supervisors prevented even more waste than would have been the case in an unfettered market. Simply suggesting better ways in which to run a drilling platform made the field man indispensible in meeting the goals of conservation. Inspection of, and sometimes direction in, the plugging and casing of abandoned wells by the deputy supervisors helped prevent pollution of oil sands by encroaching water and pollution of water sources by encroaching oil. In the Panhandle, to cite another example, operators identified the problem of using the wrong drilling equipment for the existing subsurface strata; the chief deputy supervisor in Austin promoted discussion and the commissioners issued an order prohibiting the use of rotary tools when cable methods would better protect the various gas, oil, and water strata beneath the field. Similar guidance from a deputy supervisor helped inexperienced operators in the Laredo field.

The deputy supervisors attended industry conferences (sometimes at their own expense), reported to the chief supervisor what had been discussed, and in this manner fostered exchange of information between the industry and the regulatory agency. In at least two instances, a deputy supervisor sponsored dinners to promote discussion among the operators. Through the work of the deputy supervisors, then, and through the coordination of the information in the chief supervisor's office, the Oil and Gas Division strove to establish a cooperative atmosphere between all interest groups in the Texas petroleum industry. In so doing, the commissioners sidestepped their own doubts about their statutory authority. The RCT thus emerged as a legitimizing force in the twin movements of petroleum conservation and industry self-regulation.[54]

As the American oil industry expanded throughout the 1920s, so did the Oil and Gas Division, but the growth of the division occurred in a measured way and was not proportional to the growth in the number of oil firms subject to RCT regulation. The increasing number of firms—12,000 by 1925—not only strained existing staff but also affected monies available for administration. More competitors meant more oil was produced and that led to lower oil prices; and because the division's appropriations (until 1929) were tied to the market price for crude (not the number of barrels produced), lower prices meant less monies for administering the conservation laws. In effect, the Oil and Gas Division found itself operating like any business, matching expenses to revenues. In 1922 Chief Deputy Supervisor J. W. Hassell explained to an oil operator in Wichita Falls that "we have to treat the State as a unit, just as it is treated as a unit by the Highway Department, for instance. If each county received back all of the tax paid by automobile owners, there would necessarily be large territories of the State that would go without any attention whatever as far as this tax is concerned." Fluctuating receipts led to fluctuating numbers of deputy supervisors, and that led to administrative inefficiencies.[55]

The growth in the number of new oil firms, coupled with occasional crises in new oil fields, strained the division's effectiveness. Attempts to continue the annual get-together of the deputy supervisors helped maintain morale somewhat, but constant attention to the spending of state monies for supplies, car repairs, new cars, and living expenses in inflation-ridden boomtowns took its toll on the field force. Throughout the decade, deputy supervisors opted for the more lucrative private-sector jobs in which they could earn much more money with their expertise. What is remarkable, really, is that despite these problems, the Oil and Gas Division continued to foster cooperative action among the operators.[56] Each new oil field became safer and more organized more quickly than had been the case before 1919.[57]

The Early Proration Agreements, 1927–1929

What is not surprising is that by the mid- to late-1920s cooperation to foster safer production techniques had moved regulator and regulated toward efforts to control the amount of oil produced. Throughout the industry, and including the Bureau of Mines in Washington, D.C., discussions on how to control production, derived from practical experience in the fields, continued during the decade.[58] In Texas, private operators came to the RCT for help in developing proration plans in order to keep prices from dropping to ruinous levels. The commissioners, concerned with their lack of authority,[59] encouraged the operators to devise their own plans; meanwhile, the regulators investigated whether or not they could sanction the private agreements on the basis of physical waste.

By 1927, the commissioners had concluded that proration could be utilized to prevent physical waste. In October, they sanctioned a proration plan in the Yates oil field in West Texas; other plans followed in the Winkler and Howard fields, also in West Texas, and in the Van field in East Texas. Gilmore described the commission's approach toward proration in 1928 through allusion to the state's mythic past: "In the language of a distinguished Texas patriot, [Davy Crockett] we want to be sure we are right, then go ahead." Gilmore explained in 1929: "Proration is a new thing. We have gone into it slowly, for we had to convince ourselves that the law made it our duty to undertake this as the only means of preventing waste. . . . We consulted [the attorney general]. . . . We did not undertake proration until we had had numerous hearings and from sworn testimony developed the fact that such action on our part was necessary to preserve this field [Yates] from actual physical waste."[60] Clearly, as in the enforcement of the field rules, the commissioners had to devise regulatory strategies that reconciled the economic and geological forces with existing legal constraints.

It should be emphasized here that private-sector oil-firm executives, mostly from the integrated majors, initiated discussions of proration and that company employees performed much of the experimentation with proration before 1930. The Yates proration plans, for example, came about after company engineers had investigated the extent of the pool and the patterns in which the wells had been drilled and after discussions among the operators. Investigation and consultation, of course, continued after the first proration order was made, for the "experts" did not know all there was to know about how oil fields operated. The improvements in Yates were significant for the entire petroleum industry, for before the East Texas field was discovered, Yates was the largest field in the United States: 20,000 acres, with 392 wells producing potentially 5,250,000 barrels per day.[61]

Evidence suggests that these early proration orders did work within the limited geographic region of each oil pool (they were not coordinated on a statewide basis). They worked in part because the major oil companies dominated operations in most of the prorated fields, which made negotiations simpler, if not speedier. As one chronicler of the industry noted about the Van field in 1929, ". . . the Pure, Sun, Shell, Texas, and Humble companies unitized their leases and developed the new field in an orderly process." But also important to the success of these early proration orders was the presence of the RCT as the legitimizing agency for the experiments. Chairman Gilmore, especially, had studied the new engineering and geological information that came from the investigations; his expertise and the prestige of his office underscored the successful proration experiments.[62]

Certainly the investigations, the legal opinions of the attorney general, and the generally cooperative atmosphere enveloping the Oil and Gas Division and the operators lent a sense of legitimacy to the proration orders in the late 1920s. The fact remained, however, that any one operator could refuse to obey an "order" of the RCT and get away with it. The cooperative approach had not reconciled completely the imperatives of the rule-of-capture with the economic structure of the industry because the RCT still lacked authority to tie conservation to market demand.[63] Nonetheless, as long as a "big pool" did not appear, as long as someone like Clarence Gilmore remained on the commission, and as long as the deputy supervisors were experienced (of the eleven I have identified of the fifteen deputy supervisors in 1930, at least eight had previous drilling experience),[64] the cooperative business-government experiments in prorating oil production seemed to be moving the industry in Texas toward a more stable future. Beginning in early 1929, however, the cooperation of the previous ten years came under immense strains as crisis after crisis rocked the RCT.

Summary and Conclusions

In summary, the strategies of regulation the Oil and Gas Division developed in the 1920s hinged on several related issues. First, from the beginning, Gilmore and Butte had understood that the oil operators were inexperienced not only in dealing with a government agency but also in the business of oil-well drilling and production. They devised a program of education and hired knowledgeable deputy supervisors to be the teachers in the field. Second, the commissioners had learned from the Burkburnett crisis in 1919 that the details of prorationing would swamp its staff if the oil operators did not police themselves. Such duties would prevent the agency from pursuing its major task of preventing waste—from policing the fields for rules violations to exchanging information on substrata conditions and new drilling methods. The regulators, then, encouraged the private operators to establish proration plans on their own. Third, the commissioners continuously sought accommodations between economic and legal imperatives. That effective conservation of petroleum through proration was inextricably tied to the price of crude oil concerned them, for they did not want to be associated with price-fixing, which ran afoul of antitrust and personal-property law; their job was conservation. The regulators issued the proration orders in the late 1920s on the basis of legitimate conservation issues, even if the private operators had developed the plans more to match production to market demand than to serve conservation. Both public and private interests were being served, if imperfectly and quasi-legally.

Meanwhile, in early 1929 the commissioners sponsored a bill in the Texas legislature that would allow them to do what they had been doing anyway through the proration orders. Probably because Humble Oil supported the change, the concept was dropped from the final bill. The legislature, moreover, expressing continued Texan populist fears of monopoly, defined "waste" as not being "economic waste" but only "physical" waste. This so-called Anti-Market Demand Law was the first in a series of events during 1929 and into the early 1930s that challenged the accommodations achieved between the private and public sectors in the 1920s.[65]

Clarence Gilmore died unexpectedly on 10 October 1929 while attending a railway hearing in San Antonio. Gilmore's comprehension of the economic and geologial aspects of pretroleum conservation was not matched by either of the other two commissioners; his presence would be sorely missed in the crises to come, for the Progressive Era style of investigation and consultation would give way to internecine politics within the RCT.[66]

As the Stock Market crashed and the nation slid into a deep economic depression, Texas lawmakers steadfastly refused to allow the commission to prorate production on the basis of market demand. In late summer 1930 the commission faced an injunction suit, filed by a reputable operator in the Panhandle, that challenged directly the proration program. Then, in October 1930, an obscure oil operator struck an oil sand on a farm in East Texas where the geologists of the major companies had unequivocally announced there would be no oil. This new pool equaled in size the combined area of the eight biggest pools that had been discovered in the United States. The price of oil dropped from $1.10 in October 1930 to 25 cents per barrel in January 1931.[67]

The new East Texas pool, challenging as it was to the admittedly shaky authority of proration, was not the only problem the RCT faced. Simultaneously, the agency was dealing with new duties under the recently enacted motor carrier legislation and with the growing national railway transportation problem. Internal changes also undermined the Progressive Era style of regulation that had survived for nearly forty years: A staff that numbered 69 in 1930 would grow to nearly 500 by 1932; commission offices would be scattered throughout the capital city and the state, and the three commissioners would not get along with one another.[68] From outside the commission, moreover, independent oil operators, Texas law-makers, and other states' and federal officials attacked the regulators for not reacting quickly enough to the crisis in the East Texas field. Because Texas held the largest petroleum reserves, the other states' and federal officials saw its conservation program as the key to controlling national production.

Attempts to remove petroleum regulation from the commission were turned back three times,[69] however, as the lawmakers and the various interest groups of majors, independents, and royalty owners in Texas slowly realized what Gilmore had known throughout the 1920s—that the agency required more authority. Significantly, a longtime employee of the RCT, an engineer dedicated to Progressive Era strategies, was prominent in sustaining the strategies during the tumultuous early 1930s, although he was summarily fired in 1934.[70] Meanwhile, and this has been underem-phasized in the scholarship, operators in oil fields other than East Texas continued to abide by the RCT's monthly proration orders. Finally, in November 1932, the legislature passed the Market Demand Act, and, by 1935, the state's authority to control production of petroleum had been defined through accommodating the economic and geological forces, on the one hand, within the parameters of state and national laws, on the other. The commission's legitimacy in the national program had built upon the legitimacy established on the state level in the 1920s.[71]

The story and analyses offered in this essay lead to several historical and historiographical conclusions. First, the pattern of government-business relations in Texas mirrored similar federal efforts in the 1920s to coax a variety of industries to solve their own problems through cooperative exchange of ideas and planning of supplies and prices. But just as the Justice Department in 1930 began to crack down on associational activity across the nation as contrary to antitrust laws, so too did the Texas legislature prevent the RCT from joining with oil operators to form a public-private trust.[72] Second, the antitrust legal tradition, the rule-of-capture and correlative rights emerged as equally strong determinants with the economic and geologic forces of the petroleum industry to shape the context within which the regulators and regulated operated.[73]

Third, dedicated public servants, such as Gilmore and Butte and the deputy supervisors, and the private-sector engineers and executives be-lieved in what they were attempting to do. To them, the economic and legal issues were malleable and subject to rational controls, even as those forces were changing. Using the decentralized management structure of the Oil and Gas Division, much as managers of some large-scale business enterprises were doing in the 1920s to meet changing needs of the consumer market, reflected the regulators' passion for Progressive Era reform strategies and structures.[74] The story in Texas became not just a rehearsal for the 1930s but a necessary experimental phase during which the legitimacy of the RCT was established.[75] The positive heritage of the RCT, established early in the 1890s, was sustained through the 1920s in a very different industry environment than earlier railway regulation. Contrary to existing scholarship, then, the commission was not apathetic to conservation, but instead actively pursued the state's and industry's interests. Its failure to eliminate all wasteful practices cannot be traced to apathetic regulators, but rather to inadequate statutory authority and inadequate administrative monies.

Fourth, because of the nature of American regulation in general and because of the southern progressive approach to business-government promotion of industrial development, RCT commissioners imposed on their regulatory duties a dual-management approach in which private and public worked together to plan the industry's development. This worked fairly well in the 1920s because the crises were fewer and smaller in scope; there was time to work out difficult issues of economic markets and legal constraints. The East Texas crisis did not lend itself to such slow-paced policymaking, but the work that had come before in the calmer period contributed in tone and in substance to the final conclusion to the East Texas crisis.

Other business-government stories from the 1920s contributed to the outcomes of the 1930s. What had taken place within the industry, on the federal level, and in Oklahoma and California combined with the Texas story to bring about the accommodations of the mid-1930s. Because most observers believed the control of the Texas fields was necessary to make proration work across the nation, the story in Texas takes on special significance. But the origins of the RCT's power to prorate production of oil lay not in the crisis management of the 1930s, but rather in the calmer times of the 1920s.[76]

The Ohio State University

Notes

1. Research for this article was funded in part by a 1988 NEH Summer Stipend and the Ohio State University. Individuals who offered helpful suggestions on earlier drafts include

Mansel Blackford, Ed Constant, Michael Green, Austin Kerr, Diana Olien, Edwin Perkins, and two anonymous readers for *JPH*.

2. For one example of the view that the RCT controlled world oil prices, see Richard H. K. Vietor, *Energy Policy in America Since 1945: A Study of Business-Government Relations* (Cambridge, 1984), 6, 22–23, 193. Only one book exists on the RCT, and it covers only a few selected petroleum topics from 1930 to the 1970s: David F. Prindle, *Petroleum Politics and the Texas Railroad Commission* (Austin, 1981).

3. Thomas K. McCraw, "Introduction: The Intellectual Odyssey of Alfred D. Chandler, Jr.," in McCraw, ed., *The Essential Alfred Chandler: Essays Toward a Historical Theory of Big Business* (Boston, 1988), 17: "As with *Strategy and Structure*, the argument [in *The Visible Hand* (1977)] contains a fair amount of economic and technological determinism"; McCraw, *Prophets of Regulation Charles Francis Adams, Louis D. Brandeis, James M. Landis, Alfred E. Kahn* (Cambridge, Mass., 1984), 305; "*More than any other single factor, this underlying structure of the particular industry being regulated has defined the context in which regulatory agencies have operated*" (emphasis in the original). As McCraw's biographical approach showed clearly, while structural forces (technologies and markets) determine whether a business will be big or a particular regulation effective, it is left to perceptive individuals to understand those structural forces and to implement appropriate strategies and management structures. For an example of another historian who believes individuals can and do make a difference within the political-economic context, see Michael B. Stoff, *Oil, War, and American Security: The Search for a National Policy on Oil, 1941–1947* (New Haven, 1980).

4. The long-range story, moreover, reflects a general state-to-federal pattern found in regulatory history, for in the 1920s Texas law limited the context of action, while in the 1930s the tensions of federalism characterized much of the debate over petroleum controls. See McCraw, *Prophets of Regulation*, esp. chap. 2.

5. For associational activities, see Ellis W. Hawley, "Three Facets of Hooverian Associationalism: Lumber, Aviation, and Movies, 1921–1930," in Thomas K. McCraw, ed., *Regulation in Perspective* (Boston, 1981), 95–123. For examples of the continuity between progressivism and the 1930s, see Ellis W. Hawley, *The New Deal and the Problem of Monopoly: A Study in Economic Ambivalence* (Princeton, 1966); Robert F. Himmelberg, *The Origins of the National Recovery Administration: Business, Government, and the Trade Association Movement, 1921–1933* (New York, 1976); Bruce E. Seely, *Building the American Highway System Engineers as Policy Makers* (Philadelphia, 1987); and William R. Childs, *Trucking and the Public Interest: The Emergence of Federal Regulation, 1914–1940* (Knoxville, 1985). While the degree to which government agencies were involved in associational activities in the 1920s differed from one industry to the next, in general the activities formed the groundwork for further experimentation in cooperative activities in the 1930s. For works on southern business progressivism, see George B. Tindall, *The Emergence of the New South, 1913–1945* (Baton Rouge, 1967), and Dewey W. Grantham, *Southern Progressivism: The Reconciliation of Progress and Tradition* (Knoxville, 1983). Norman D. Brown, *Hood, Bonnet, and Little Brown Jug: Texas Politics 1921–1928* (College Station, Tex., 1984), furnishes the subtext of the Texas political economy, as well as that of southern progressivism, Texas-style.

6. Louis Galambos, "The Emerging Organizational Synthesis in Modern American History," *Business History Review* 54 (Autumn 1970): 279–90, and "Technology, Political Economy, and Professionalization: Central Themes of the Organizational Synthesis," *BHR* 57 (Winter 1983): 471–93. For criticisms of the organizational synthesis, see Alan Brinkley, "Writing the History of Contemporary America: Dilemmas and Challenges," *Daedalus* (Summer 1984): 132–34.

7. For examples of works using cultural approaches to understand institutional behavior, see Charles Dellheim, "The Creation of a Company Culture: Cadburys, 1861–1931," *American Historical Review* 92 (February 1987): 13–44, and "Business in Time: The Histo-

rian and Corporate Culture," *The Public Historian* 8 (Spring 1986): 9–22; Susan Porter Benson, *Counter Cultures: Saleswomen, Managers, and Customers in American Department Stores, 1890–1940* (Urbana, 1986). For a convenient collection of essays on organizational culture, see the special issue of *Administrative Science Quarterly* 28 (1983).

For related discussions, see Thomas Bender, "Wholes and Parts: The Need for Synthesis in American History," *Journal of American History* 73 (June 1986): 120–36, and "A Round Table: Synthesis in American History," *JAH* 74 (June 1987): 107–30. Although not tagging their work as "cultural," the following focus on some of the same aspects of agency culture as found in the works cited above: Robert A. Katzmann, "Federal Trade Commission," and Suzanne Weaver, "Antitrust Division of the Department of Justice," both in James Q. Wilson, ed., *The Politics of Regulation* (New York, 1980).

8. Support for this summary can be found in this note and in notes 9–13 below. Erich W. Zimmermann, *Conservation in the Production of Petroleum: A Study in Industrial Control* (New Haven, 1967), 140–160, esp. 146–47 n. 4, wherein Zimmermann, citing Joseph E. Pogue, suggests proration's origins lay in the interaction between economic necessity to stabilize prices and the legal difficulty presented by the rule-of-capture (which will be introduced in the third section of this article). This article will describe specifically how and when and why the interaction took place. The best narrative of the political story in Texas in the 1930s is Barbara Sue Thompson Day, "The Oil and Gas Industry and Texas Politics, 1930–1935" (Ph.D. diss., Rice University, Houston, 1973).

9. A qualified exception is Harold F. Williamson et al., *The American Petroleum Industry: The Age of Energy, 1899–1959* (Evanston, Ill., 1963), 321–38. The authors give credit to state efforts in the 1920s for laying the groundwork for the 1930s, yet they focus on Oklahoma's efforts, and mention those in Texas only in passing.

Most historians have been drawn to the drama of the East Texas Field, the "hot oil" controversy, the petroleum code, the doomed efforts of Secretary of Interior Harold Ickes to garner federal control of petroleum production, and the evolution of the Interstate Oil Compact Commission—all events that took place in the 1930s. See especially Robert E. Hardwicke, "Legal History of Conservation of Oil in Texas," 214–68, and Maurice Cheek, "Legal History of Conservation of Gas in Texas," 269–86, both in *Legal History of Conservation of Oil and Gas: A Symposium* (Chicago: The Section of Mineral Law of the American Bar Association, December 1938); Hardwicke, "Texas, 1938–1948," in Blakely M. Murphy, ed., *Conservation of Oil and Gas: A Legal History, 1948* (Chicago: The Section of Mineral of the Law American Bar Association, 1949), 447–516; James P. Hart, "Oil, The Courts, and the Railroad Commission," *Southwestern Historical Quarterly* 44 (January 1941): 303–20.

10. For overviews of federal policies in the 1920s, see Gerald D. Nash, *United States Oil Policy, 1890–1964* (Pittsburgh, 1968), chaps. 4, 5, and John G. Clark, *Energy and the Federal Government: Fossil Fuel Policies, 1900–1946* (Chicago, 1987), chaps. 4, 6, 7. For a good overview of the controversies in the 1930s, see Hawley, *New Deal and Problem of Monopoly*, 212–20.

11. Henrietta M. Larson and Kenneth W. Porter, *History of Humble Oil & Refining Company: A Study in Industrial Growth* (New York, 1959), 257–63, and chap. 13, nicely complements the Day dissertation; Kendall Beaton, *Enterprise in Oil: A History of Shell in the United States* (New York, 1957), 337, 380–83; John G. McLean and Robert W. Haigh, *The Growth of Integrated Oil Companies* (Boston, 1954), 101. As will be shown in the text, the impetus for proration in Texas did come from the private sector, but the RCT played a role in sponsoring such endeavors, thus lending a sense of legitimacy that the private operators seemed to believe was necessary for proration schemes to work. As with so many associational schemes in the 1920s, fears of antitrust prosecutions were assuaged when government agents sanctioned industrial cooperative agreements. Of course, as it turned out, government sanctions did not get around the antitrust laws. For material on how the American Petroleum Institute (API), the major trade association of the petroleum industry, worked

to rationalize production, see Joseph A. Pratt, "Creating Coordination in the Modern Petroleum Industry: The American Petroleum Institute and the Emergence of Secondary Organizations in Oil," *Research in Economic History* 8 (1983): 179–215.

12. California presents a curious aspect to the story. Its petroleum fields were not tied economically to the so-called Mid-Continent area of Kansas, Oklahoma, Texas, and Louisiana. But the private and public leadership concerned with conservation in California exchanged experiences and information with their counterparts in the Mid-Continent area, thus facilitating progress toward control of production. For the economic market situation, see Zimmermann, *Conservation of Petroleum*, 159–60, and for the exchange of information, see, for example, the articles in the 1931 volume of *Transactions* (American Institute of Mining and Metallurgical Engineers). See also Mansel G. Blackford, *The Politics of Business in California, 1890–1920* (Columbus, Ohio, 1977), chaps. 3, 5.

13. Zimmerman, *Conservation in the Production of Petroleum*, 145 (quotation); W. P. Z. German, "Legal History of Conservation of Oil and Gas in Oklahoma," in *Legal History of Conservation of Oil and Gas*, 110–213; Nash, *United States Oil Policy*, 113–14, mentions Texas controls in the 1920s, but he focuses on Rule 37, the well-spacing rule, moves on quickly to the post-1929 period, and appears to rely heavily (113 n. 1) on the Robert Conrod's M.A. thesis (see note 14 below). See also Wallace F. Lovejoy and Paul T. Homan, *Economic Aspects of Oil Conservation Regulation* (Baltimore, 1967), 33–35. Most of the scholars cite Hardwicke (see note 9 above). Edward W. Constant II, "State Management of Petroleum Resources, Texas, 1910–1940," in George H. Daniels and Mark H. Rose, eds., *Energy and Transport: Historical Perspectives on Policy Issues* (Beverly Hills, 1982), 157–75. Despite the title, the essay does not focus on state regulatory activities in the 1920s. Instead, the author presents a cogent survey of the federal courts' acceptance of proration on the basis of scientific enquiry and the recognition that due process had been followed by the RCT in judging a great amount of conflicting evidence.

Clark's recent book, *Energy and the Federal Government*, 146–52, continues to misrepresent the Texas story: "But neither Oklahoma nor Texas seriously enforced their laws until after 1926, when a series of enormously productive oil fields were discovered. Political opposition, especially by the smaller producers, and the decisions of federal courts during the 1930s stymied conservation efforts in Texas. In short, the regulatory efforts of these states failed to modify the rule of capture or to compel the application of the best technology and scientific knowledge to the exploitation of particular pools" (152). Clark cites here Zimmermann, Nash, and Constant noted above, and two other works. Clark's book was concerned mainly with federal policy and he simply did not check out the state stories carefully enough. He is correct that the rule-of-capture held up reform, as will be noted later in the text. His assertion that the state agencies did not apply technology and science in the fields needs to be modified: as the text will show, the regulators in Texas tried to stay on top of breaking developments and in some cases effected change in oil drilling based on new knowledge.

14. The responsibility for this omission in the historiography lies less with Conrod's flawed dismissal of the RCT's actions and more with those scholars following him who failed to examine his work closely. Robert Lucas Conrod, "State Regulation of the Oil and Gas Industry in Texas," M.A. thesis, Political Science, University of Texas, Austin, 1931), iv–v, 110–15, 115 (quotation). Conrod seemed too influenced by ongoing events in East Texas, for too often he charged the regulators with lack of action when in fact the regulators lacked the knowledge and, significantly, the authority to act responsibly during the East Texas fiasco. He carried this orientation backward into the 1920s to argue that the RCT's strategy of cooperation with oil industry operators had led the commission down the path of regulatory failure. My reading of Conrod's thesis reveals a young student enamored by the "progressive" or "conflict" approach to political economy and dedicated to an ideal, scientific approach to regulation. Thus, his thesis contains occasionally insightful analyses that are undermined by assertions that reveal a lack of comprehension of what actually had

occurred in the preceding decade and what was possible given the context of the times. Even though he had access to the people who worked at the Oil and Gas Division, he apparently did not check their oral interviews with the correspondence available in their offices. Conrod, who began his study in November 1930, had access to the files of the division, but he apparently made little use of them. This is not surprising, given the difficulty the staff had in using its own disorganized files. See, for only one example of the chaos, H. E. Bell, Memorandum to the Railroad Commission, 31 July 1924, Box 4–3/391, wallet 1926, Record Group 455, Texas State Archives, Austin (hereafter cited as RG 455, TSA). Note: the archivists at the Texas State Archives are in the process of renumbering the boxes, Michael Green to Childs, 3 April 1990, copy in Childs's possession. When the longer work is completed, I will send to the Archives all the letters I photocopied for research purposes.

15. I found the eighty-two boxes of Oil and Gas Division correspondence at the Texas State Archives very disorganized; some railroad and motor carrier materials were scattered throughout, and there was little sense of chronological or thematic organization to the materials.

16. *Twenty-Fifth Annual Report of the Railroad Commission of Texas for the Year 1916* (Austin, 1917), xxxii [hereafter cited as –th Annual Report of RCT (date)]. The positions included a secretary, a civil engineer, an expert rate clerk and assistant, an expert accountant and two assistant accountants, a rate clerk, a traveling inspector, two general clerks, and the porter; "Railroad Commission. Report of Subcommittee No. 5," *Reports of Subcommittees of the Central Investigating Committees of the House and Senate Third Called Session of the Thirty-Fifth Legislature of Texas Including Audits* (Austin, n.d.), 606–39. Since 1910, numerous part-time workers had been hired to help with the rate investigations and the appeals of the *Shreveport* case of 1914, which effectively gave ratemaking authority over intrastate rates to the Interstate Commerce Commission.

17. As I will show in a book-length study, the RCT came into existence in 1891 as the result of political agitation in Texas for control over the alleged discriminatory practices of the railroads. Although late in its inception relative to many other railway regulatory commissions, including the Interstate Commerce Commission, the Texas agency, under the leadership of John H. Reagan, one of the authors of the Interstate Commerce Act in 1887, quickly came to the forefront in the development of railway regulatory strategies.

18. Another aspect, a dark-side progressivism that encompassed Ku Klux Klan activities, Jim Crow segregation laws, and the prohibition issue, would affect the story later and tangentially in the 1930s, when political personalities on opposite sides of the social issues clashed over the economic and legal issues.

19. See C. Vann Woodward, *Origins of the New South, 1877–1913* (Baton Rouge, 1951, 1971), chap. 6; Tindall, *Emergence of the New South,* 219–25ff.; Grantham, *Southern Progressivism,* esp. xv–xxii; and Brown, *Hood, Bonnet, and Little Brown Jug,* 4–8. For incisive critical appraisals of the origins and results of boosterism and business progressivism in the South, see James C. Cobb, *The Selling of the South: The Southern Crusade for Industrial Development, 1936–1980* (Baton Rouge, 1982), 5ff., and *Industrialization and Southern Society, 1877–1984* (Chicago, 1984), chaps. 2, 6. For an intriguing and probably correct overview that has influenced the southern perspective in this article, see Gavin Wright, *Old South, New South: Revolutions in the Southern Economy Since the Civil War* (New York, 1986). Given the racial and class orientations of the New South program (black and poor white Southerners were stuck in a low-wage cycle that was underscored by unwillingness to spend monies for progressive educational institutions), the South held fast to its tragic burden of history. Despite the opportunities offered by petroleum, Texans did not break the southern pattern. The irony was that southern businessmen and politicians, in trying to industrialize their region, attempted to attract the very kind of business that discouraged industrial and urban development: peripheral-style firms that focused on extraction and low-wage manufacturing industries (lumber, petroleum, textiles).

20. Joseph A. Pratt, "The Petroleum Industry in Transition: Antitrust and the Decline of Monopoly Control in Oil," *Journal of Economic History* 4 (December 1980): 819–20, traces the Texan hatred of Standard to the so-called Waters-Pierce case and the political personality of Joe Bailey. Carl Coke Rister, *Oil! Titan of the Southwest* (Norman, Okla., 1949), 187–89.

"Major" oil firms include corporations that had integrated at least two of the operations involved in the industry—production, transportation, refining, and marketing. "Independents" were firms engaged in only one of the operations. Of course, as the oil industry expanded in the 1920s, many "independents" became integrated, either by internal expansion or through merger.

21. Conrod, "Regulation of Oil and Gas in Texas," 3–11; Nash, *U.S. Oil Policy*, chap. 1. Unclear during this time was what in just a few years (1923 and after) would become more widely accepted as fact: gas was a key element of the "drive" that brought the oil to the surface through the oil well; allowing the gas to escape diminished the drive and thereby reduced the total amount of oil recovered. See Harry Pennington to R. D. Parker, 30 October 1929, Box 2–10/560, wallet 1929–31, RG 455, TSA, wherein Pennington explained that he theorized in 1919 about gas lift and that in 1923 the industry became aware of methods through which to conserve the gas lift.

22. Hardwicke, "Legal History of Conservation of Oil in Texas," 217 n. 4; Earl B. Mayfield to Frank M. Smith, 13 June 1919, Railroad Commission of Texas Letter Press, Record group 455, Texas State Archives, Austin (hereafter cited as RCTLP). The RCTLP is a series of 255 volumes, each with 700 to 1,000 onionskin copies of outgoing letters from the RCT, 1891 to the 1930s. Some letters found in the RCTLP were not located in the division records. Conrod, "Regulation of Oil and Gas in Texas," 19–24. The 1913 law ordering casing-off of natural gas pertained only to gas wells, not oil wells.

23. In 1917, the state legislators, in an attempt to expose corruption and to streamline state government along southern progressive lines, ordered an internal audit and investigation of each state agency. The RCT passed its examination with only one minor indiscretion exposed (the pipeline expert was not an expert). Indeed, in early 1918, the investigatory committee concluded that while the commissioners were highly capable, they had been *underworked* because the so-called *Shreveport* rate case had turned over to the interstate Commerce Commission (ICC) most railway ratemaking duties. Meanwhile, discussions about general state utility regulation had been taking place in the legislature. See "Report of Subcommittee No. 5," 603–4. Indeed, the committee noted that the *Shreveport* case of 1914 had eliminated state control of most railway operations; consequently, the commissioners had very little to do. Despite *Shreveport*, however, the commission still dealt with railroad-related matters, only now in cooperation with the ICC. In the 1920s, moreover, the commission would have to deal with the new motor buses' and trucks' effects on railway competition. "Efficiency" here alludes to administrative efficiency, not whether the results of RCT regulatory strategies helped the railways and the Texas economy; Hart, "Oil, Courts, and Railroad Commission," 307–8, notes a general confidence in the state had developed from the RCT's record in railway regulation. In 1920, natural-gas utilities were placed under the RCT as well, *29th Annual Report of RCT* (1920), 5–6.

24. Hardwicke, "Legal History of Conservation of Oil in Texas," 217–18; Conrod, "Regulation of Oil and Gas in Texas," 22–30, wherein he outlines the RCT's responsibilities; Clarence Gilmore to Department of Conservation, State of Louisiana, 13 September 1919, RCTLP. The tax increased in 1919 to 1½% and in 1923 to 2% of value of production; see Chief Supervisor to Miller Walker, 19 March 1927, Box 4–33/395, wallet 1927, RG 455, TSA.

25. For the story in Oklahoma, see German, "Legal History of Conservation of Oil and Gas in Oklahoma," and Williamson (note 9 above). The Oklahoma commission had been established in 1907, but its duties with regard to petroleum were not clearly spelled out until 1914–15. The next state to follow suit was Kansas in 1931; Texas would not incorpo-

rate market-demand regulation until 1932. The curious twist in this story is this: Fears of trustlike activity by the integrated majors in Oklahoma furnished the basis for including price-fixing power for the commission; if the commission could regulate production on the basis of a minimum price, then the small-scale operators would be protected from underselling by the large-scale integrated firms. In Texas, however, antitrust fears forestalled the use of market demand regulation until 1932 because Texans believed the majors would direct any regulatory scheme that controlled prices.

26. Conrod, "Regulation of Oil and Gas in Texas," 25–30; Gilmore to Mildren, 20 August 1919, Box 4–3/382, wallet 1919–20, RG 455, TSA; RRC to Mildren, 20 August 1919, RCTLP.

27. The Mayfields were cousins and active in the Texas Democratic party. Allison Mayfield, while a highly respected railway regulator and jealous guardian of states rights, twice had tried unsuccessfully to swing a coveted appointment to the ICC. Earle Mayfield, using his experience and connections with the RCT and courting Ku Klux Klan support, won election to the U.S. Senate in 1923. For Earl B. Mayfield, see Brown, *Hood, Bonnet, and Little Brown Jug*, 7, 99ff., 106; for Allison Mayfield, see Vertical File, Biographical, Barker Texas History Center, Austin (hereafter cited as BTHC); A. Mayfield to E. M. House, 6 October 1906, and to C. H. Lockhart, 21 June 1916, both in RCTLP.

28. "Clarence Gilmore Victim of Heart Attack," *Austin American Statesman*, 11 October 1929, 1; Vertical File, Biographical, BTHC; Gilmore to S. H. Huston, 2 August 1919, RCTLP, for reference to public service.

29. For examples of the disinterested progressive public servant, see Childs and Seely (note 5 above); for the legacy of efficient public administration, see Thomas K. McCraw, "The Progressive Legacy," in Lewis L. Gould, ed., *The Progressive Era* (Syracuse, 1974), 184–85, 187–90. For Gilmore's expressed enthusiasm for the petroleum industry, see Gilmore to Marshall, 16 September 1919, RCTLP.

Walter Splawn, who later became a member of the ICC, was appointed to succeed Earle Mayfield in March 1923, Gilmore to John E. Benton, 11 May 1923, RCTLP. C. V. Terrell succeeded Splawn in August 1924; W. A. Nabors succeeded Allison Mayfield in March 1923 and would be succeeded by Lon Smith in January 1925. No other changes occurred until Gilmore died in 1929.

30. Allison Mayfield to C. M. Cureton, 11 July 1919, RCTLP; Gilmore to J. L. Mildren, 20 August 1919, Box 4–3/382, wallet 1919–20, RG 455, TSA.

31. Correlative rights came from the 1900 U.S. Supreme Court case, *Ohio Oil Company v. Indiana*, 177 U.S. 190. In this case, Indiana had enacted a law preventing waste in order to serve not only the public's interests but also the interests of *all* owners of an oil field. No one individual could have the freedom to act in a manner that would injure the property rights of other landowners in the field. Thus, prorating pipeline runs assured that every producer in the field would have some of his oil taken to market when there was too much production for the market to absorb. See German and Zimmermann citations in note 32 and Williamson et al., *Age of Energy*, 322, wherein the authors note that the Oklahoma situation brought into conflict property rights and the rule-of-capture. Alas, the authors do not use the term "correlative rights," but the German article furnishes a solid analysis of correlative rights. As Williamson et al. point out (322–23), the reason the Oklahoma legislation did not work well, even though it included consideration of market demand, was the lack of control over drilling.

32. Zimmermann, *Conservation in the Production of Petroleum*, 96–100, for the effects of the rule-of-capture; RCT to Lionel Adams, 20 October 1923, Box 2–10/544, wallet 1923, RG 455, TSA; German, "Oil and Gas Conservation in Oklahoma," 122–33.

33. Gilmore to J. A. Germany, 24 July 1919, RCTLP, wherein Gilmore noted that not all drillers and operators were willing to cooperate and abide by the shutdown order; Gilmore to J. L. Mildren, July 1919, RCTLP, noted that there was uncertainty as to whether or not a shutdown would injure the wells; Gilmore to C. H. Clark, 20 October

1919, Box 2–10/539, wallet 1922, RG 455, TSA; A. Mayfield to C. M. Cureton, 11 July 1919, RCTLP. Conrod, "Regulation of Oil and Gas in Texas," 31–43, presents an account of Burkburnett. That he misspelled Gilmore's name ("Gilman") suggests the reader use caution. Conrod's description of Burkburnett relied heavily on articles from the *National Petroleum News.*

34. Gilmore to C. H. Hurdleston, 1 February 1919; Gilmore to Empire Petroleum Company, 16 August 1919; Gilmore to Ellis Campbell, 25 August 1919; RRC to Mildren, 19 August 1919, all in RCTLP. A related problem was the lack of control over the railways, which remained under federal control from the war period. Much of the crude was transported by tank car, but the railroads could not furnish enough extra cars; see Gilmore to D. C. Ernest, 17 September 1919, RCTLP.

35. Gilmore to C. H. Clark, 20 October 1919, Box 2–10/539, wallet 1922, RG 455, TSA; Gilmore to J. A. Germany, 24 July 1919; Gilmore to D. C. Earnest, 11 August and 17 September 1919, all in RCTLP; C. H. Clark to RCT, 11 October, and Gilmore to Clark, 14 October 1919, Box 4–3/384, wallet 1920–29; Gilmore to L. H. Moss, 29 March 1920, Box 2–10/534, wallet 1920, all in RG 455, TSA.

McCraw, *Prophets of Regulation,* 308: "Even though much of regulatory history is tinged with apparent failure, regulation cannot properly be said either to have 'failed' or 'succeeded' in an overall historical sense." Yet as McCraw notes, general perceptions of failure in regulatory policies have dominated public thinking. The Burkburnett and later East Texas situations lend support to this generalization.

36. Gilmore to Cureton, 17 July 1919 (two letters); Gilmore to S. H. Huston, 2 August 1919; Gilmore to Earnest, 17 September 1919 (re oil gauger graft); RRC to Mildren, 19 August 1919; Gilmore to Prairie Pipe Line Company, 30 August 1919, all in RCTLP; Clark to RCT, 11 October and Gilmore to Clark, 14 October 1919, Box 4–3/384, wallet 1920–29, RG 455, TSA; Conrod, "Oil and Gas Regulation in Texas," 43.

37. Gilmore to Clark, 14 October 1919, Box 4–3/384, wallet 1920–29, RG 455, TSA; Gilmore to L. H. Moss, 29 March 1920, Box 2–10/534, wallet 1920, RG 455, TSA. Gilmore's ideas about common purchaser legislation built upon—quite logically—the by then well-known approach to railway regulation. The chaos in the oil fields matched the chaos of the railway systems in the late nineteenth century; as price of crude and legal considerations drove the movement for controls in the 1920s, so too had the rates of transportation and legal constraints driven the movement toward state and federal regulation of railways. That pipelines were a form of transportation underscored the continuity in thinking between railway and petroleum regulations. Others in the 1920s would suggest similar approaches, but the final solution would not mirror the clearheaded reasoning Gilmore developed in 1919–20, for changes within the RCT, disagreement among experts as to what the law allowed, and culturally-based politics and symbols in Texas (states rights and antitrust) would impede rational development of petroleum controls. For suggestions similar to Gilmore's, see Major F. Bryce, 18 May 1927, Box 2–10/553, wallet 1927, RG 455, TSA; for the Oklahoma law, see J. T. Elliott, Conservation Agent's Daily Report, 30 July 1929, Box 2–10/582, wallet letters, RG 455, TSA.

38. German, "Conservation of Oil and Gas in Oklahoma," 113–33. I suspect Gilmore developed his ideas from the experience in Oklahoma, but I found only circumstantial evidence in the records to support this.

39. Zimmermann, *Conservation in the Production of Petroleum,* 76 (". . . during the twenties unitization was viewed by some as a more or less universal remedy for the ills that beset the petroleum industry. However, for reasons inherent in the situation, a different solution was adopted—state regulation, including prorating . . .") and 122–23, including n. 20. Zimmermann is sensitive to the complexities in the story of petroleum conservation, 109–13, but he does not offer a detailed history of how the "reasons inherent in the situation" actually emerged. While the East Texas field would be accorded its own peculiar proration scheme, the other fields would be based at least in part on unitization. The Texas legisla-

ture passed a common purchaser law in 1930, but the RCT did not use it because (1) there was still the problem of not being able to control production through controlling drilling, and (2) the pipeline firms generally prorated their runs anyway.

40. On 12 November 1919, the commission sent out letters to numerous states asking for information that might aid its attempts to conserve petroleum. Replies came from Kansas, Illinois, Kentucky, and Pennsylvania. Louisiana, Wyoming, New York, West Virginia, Ohio, and Indiana were contacted, but I could not find their replies. See Box 4–3/375, wallet 9–23, RG 455, TSA.

41. Art Walker to Allison Mayfield, 28 February, Campbell Russell to RCT, 20 June, and Chair to Russell, 25 June 1919, all in Box 2–10/532, wallet 1917–20, RG 455, TSA; Earl B. Mayfield to Frank M. Smith, 13 June 1919, RCTLP; Conrod, "Regulation of Oil and Gas in Texas," 43–56, summarizes the rules, lists the forms, and criticizes the RCT for listening to the operators and for promulgating rules that had vague language; the result, according to Conrod, was easy circumvention of the law. The one exception was Rule 37, which Conrod noted was not vague, but specific; ironically, this rule was abrogated often as exceptions were granted liberally (Conrod, 68–70: during the first eleven years an average of 437 waivers to Rule 37 were granted and only 61 were denied). Scholars and devotees of petroleum regulation have overemphasized the importance of Rule 37 relative to the numerous other rules that encouraged safer oil-field operations. Rule 37 established 300 feet between each well and no closer than 150 feet to the nearest property line as the minimum distances to be kept. Butte to Elliott and Amen, 3 February 1920, Box 2–10/535, wallet 1921, RG 455, TSA (re shooting); "How to Plug a Well by Mud-Laden Fluid Process," Office of RCT (n.d.), Box 4–3/382, wallet 1919–20, RG 455, TSA. Operators had to file a form (Rule 9) as notice of intention to plug a well twenty-four hours before actual plugging, along with a complete well log; then, after the operation was completed, the operator had to file another form listing plugging materials and procedure followed. Form 12 was an application for Form 5 (pipeline certificate).

42. I. F. Shaw to Texas RRC, 6 November 1919, Box 4–3/386, wallet 1921–31, RG 455, TSA, for populist complaints re Rule 37; A. H. McCarty to Allison Mayfield, 10 November 1919, Box 2–10/567, wallet 1931, RG 455, TSA, for defense of the "small fellows."

43. Born in San Francisco in 1877, Butte moved with his family to Texas ten years later. After receiving a B.A. in 1895 from Sherman College, Texas, he taught school and studied law before entering the University of Texas in 1902. He received a B.A. and M.A. at UT and then left for Oklahoma, where he practiced law from 1904 to 1911. From Oklahoma, Butte took his family to Europe. After studies at the University of Berlin, the University of Heidelberg, and the University of Paris, Butte returned to teach at the UT Law School. His knowledge of Germany landed him a commission as a Major in the U.S. Army in 1918 and he headed the foreign intelligence department of the general staff. He returned to the UT Law School after the armistice. After his year with the RCT, Butte in 1920 drafted a general public utilities bill, which the legislature did not pass, and in 1924 ran an impressive race for governor against "Ma and Pa" Ferguson; his strong showing based on the campaign strategy of honest and efficient government underlay the Lone Star State's voting for Hoover in 1928. In succession, Butte became attorney general for Puerto Rico (1925–28), an assistant to the U.S. attorney general, and associate justice of the insular Supreme Court of the Philippines. The only flaw in this makeup, and it apparently escaped contemporary observers, was that Butte held interests in oil leases for his land in Oklahoma while he worked with the RCT. See the George C. Butte Papers (esp. Boxes 2B163, 2B169, 2B172, and 2B173) and Vertical Files, BTHC; Norman D. Brown, *Hood Bonnet, and Little Brown Jug,* 247–51; George McMillan to Butte, 28 April 1920, Box 2B169, folder 1897–1921, Butte Papers, BTHC. Butte died in Mexico City in 1940. Texas would not pass a general utilities regulatory bill until 1975; the first Republican commissioner would be appointed in 1987.

The "Republican" label for Butte is a bit misleading, as it is for Herbert Hoover. Both were "independent" public servants who believed "politics" should focus not on party as much as on the man and his ethics. See Brown, *Hood, Bonnet, and Little Brown Jug*, 247.

44. Art L. Walker to Allison Mayfield, 28 February 1919, Campbell Russell to RCT, 20 June 1919, Chair to Russell, 25 June 1919, all in Box 2–10/532, wallet 1917–20, RG 455, TSA; Conrod, "Regulation of Oil and Gas in Texas," 43–51. See RRC to Mildren, 19 August 1919, RCTLP, for an early example of the cooperative approach. The RCT filed some suits for noncompliance with its rules, but only after the agency had given the operators one full year to learn the ropes of regulation; Butte to Wortham, 20 September 1920, Box 3–4/364, wallet 1919–22, RG 455, TSA.

45. Butte, Memorandum for the Commission, 27 April 1920, Box 2–10/584, wallet Fuel Co. Case, RG 455, TSA.

46. Butte to Editor, *Texas Monthly Review*, 7 February 1920, Box 2–10/534, wallet 1920; Butte to T. L. Coplin, 13 February 1920, Box 4–3/385, wallet 1920–29, both in RG 455, TSA. In the latter, Butte suggests "the idea of a wholesale Spring clean-up in the Burkburnett field, to be conducted under the direction, and at the instance, of the Railroad Commission"; Butte to Herman Walker, 9 June 1920, Box 4–3/381, wallet 1919–20, RG 455, TSA. For examples of the problems encountered in developing statistical sources, see H. E. Bell, Memorandum to the Railroad Commission, 9 and 15 January 1926, Box 4–3/391, wallet 1926, RG 455, TSA, wherein Bell notes that the operators are filling out and filing the required forms, but the office staff had been unable to keep up with the avalanche ("almost twice as many completion and plugging records as were reported to us a year ago"—Jan. 91); Auditor, Sinclair Pipe Line Company to RCT, 9 August 1926, Box 2–10/548, wallet 1925–31, RG 455, TSA.

47. J. W. Hassell to Jack Morehouse, 20 December 1922, Box 2–10/545, wallet 1923–23, for example of fluctuating numbers of deputy supervisors; RCT to R. P. McLaughlin, 11 November 1919, Box 2–10/567, wallet 1931; Chief Supervisor to J. L. Mildren, 26 October 1919, Box 4–3/364, wallet 1919–22; Butte to W. B. Wortham, 12 and 30 March and 1 July 1920, Box 4–3/364, wallet 1919–22; R. D. Parker to Hoffer, 7 June 1928, Box 2–10/556, wallet 1928, for example of continuation of annual meeting, all in RG 455, TSA; Gilmore to Ellis Campbell, 25 August 1919, RCTLP, indicates Gilmore, before Butte arrived, had established that the deputy supervisors had to be diplomatic in their dealings with oil-field operators. The close monitoring of expense accounts reflected the close audits of the 1917 investigations of state agencies and the progressive concern for efficient government.

48. One of Butte's special concerns was the danger of fire in the oil fields. Such accidents not only killed workers and wasted valuable resources but could be prevented. The fire problem reflected once again the consequences of the rule-of-capture. The more wells drilled on an operator's lease, the more quickly could he get "his" oil out of the ground. The close proximity of wells, open-air storage pits, and closely spaced steel storage tanks (to hold the overproduction), as well as electric motors and careless oil-well drillers, all added up to a dangerous situation in the fields. Prompted by Butte's letters, the deputy supervisors focused on the fire problem; and fires in the fields became less common later in the 1920s. Meanwhile, Rule 37 helped alleviate somewhat the problem of fires, but that rule was often abrogated in practice; reduction in fires can be attributed to the hands-on and personal contacts initiated by the deputy supervisors. See Arnold to Walthall, 25 August 1923, Box 4–3/373, wallet 1923–23; RCT to A. H. McCarty, 12 November 1919, Box 2–10/567, wallet 1931; Bell to R. C. Lomax, 1 November 1926, Box 4–3/391, wallet 1926; Butte (for the Commission) to Robert H. Hoffman, 15 September 1920, Box 4–3/371, wallet 1920–23, all in RG 455, TSA; Conrod, "Regulation of Oil and Gas in Texas," 17, 68–70.

49. Secretary to T. H. Gilmour & Co., 20 October 1919, Box 2–10/533, wallet 1916–21; Clerk, Memorandum to Chief Supervisor, n.d., Box 2–10/551, wallet 1926, all in RG 455, TSA; Rister, *Oil!*, 185–86.

50. Rister, *Oil!*, 171–86, 220–21, chaps. 18–21; the percentages of national production from Texas were estimates taken from C. A. Warner, *Texas Oil and Gas Since 1543* (Houston, 1939), 106. The increase was not sustained throughout the decade: 1925 saw a drop to about 19 percent of national production.

51. For examples of the continuation of Butte's approach to administration, see Chief Supervisor to John Lock, 14 November 1923, Box 2–10/542, wallet 1923–24, RG 455, TSA, wherein the Chief Supervisor suggests writing a letter to the operators to encourage them to plug the wells properly: "We believe that a personal letter in these instances is much better than a circular letter"; Chief Supervisor to *Dallas News*, 30 December 1925, Box 4–3/388, wallet 1924; Assistant to Chief Supervisor to Morehouse, 17 December 1928, Box 2–10/555, wallet 1928, wherein it is suggested that the deputy supervisor experiment with a new method for preventing water encroachment during drilling, all in RG 455, TSA. A good example of the camaraderie established through the annual meeting is R. C. Lomax, "The Deputy Supervisor," address at Annual Meeting of Deputy Supervisors, Austin, 29 and 30 July 1927, Box 2–10/557, wallet 1926–27, RG 455, TSA.

52. Conrod, "Regulation of Oil and Gas in Texas," 48, complained about the lack of training of the deputy supervisors; Gilmore to Ellis Campbell, 9 September 1919, Box 4–3/387, wallet 1921–31; Mildren to Gilmore, 12 May 1919, Box 4–3/364, wallet 1919–22, both in RG 455, TSA; Gilmore to Mildren, 9 August 1919, RCTLP. For examples of less professional deputy supervisors, see Sadler to Allison Mayfield, 4 May 1921, Box 44–3/382, wallet 1919–20 (deputy supervisor carrying a gun), Morris to Sadler, 15 May 1921, Box 2–10/535, wallet 1921 (reports of drunken driving), both in RG 455, TSA. See W. F. Arnold to Hassell, 20 September 1922, Box 4–3/386, wallet 1921–31, for an example of the deputy supervisor helping with drilling methods. See Hassell to H. W. Bell, 21 September 1922, Box 2–10/536, wallet 1922, which was labeled "Personal and Confidential," for an example of the RCT trying to circumvent civil service employees in order to find experts for jobs in the fields, both in RG 455, TSA.

53. For a representative example of the daily activities of a deputy supervisor, see H. H. Fitzpatrick, Conservation Agent's Daily Reports, for January 1926, Box 4–3/387, wallet, 1924–26; D. C. Morris to D. E. Woods, 2 November 1920, Box 4–3/359, wallet, 1933; ? to Butte, 17 April 1920, Box 4–3/382, wallet 1919–20; Morris to Woods, 11 and 25 November 1920, Morris to RRC, 13 and 28 November, 10 December 1920, and Morris to Woods, 16 November 1920, all in Box 4–3/359, wallet 1933; Morehouse to Bell, 1 February 1926, Box 3–4/387, wallet 1924–26; all in RG 455, TSA. For examples of the local chamber of commerce of offering or taking away office space, see Morris to Woods, 16 November 1920, Box 4–3/359, wallet 1933; Morris to J. P. Sadler, 10 December 1920, Box 2–10/536, wallet 1920–23; Jack Morehouse to Laten Stanberry, 3 February 1923, Box 2–10/542, wallet 1923–24; Chief Deputy Supervisor to W. J. Carden, 23 February 1923, Box 2–10/543, wallet 1923, all in RG 455, TSA.

54. All of the following are found in RG 455, TSA: W. F. Arnold, "General Report on My Trip to the Laredo Fields," 16 December 1922, Box 4–3/348, wallet 1920–22, reports on problems and cooperation: "Operators, who less than one year ago felt antagonistic toward us, have come to us for help, now realizing that we are of actual value to them"; Chief Deputy Supervisor to John Brownlee, 18 October 1923, Box 10/543, wallet 1923; Coplin to Bell, 20 August and 6 September, and Bell to Coplin, 27 August and 15 September 1924, Box 2–10/539, wallet 1922; Omar Burkett to Bell, 19 August 1925, Box 2–10/585, wallet misc.; Morehouse to Earl Calloway, 12 March 1926, Box 4–3/387, wallet 1924–26. In the latter, Morehouse noted that "after I got the movement well under way I worked pretty well under cover, so as not in any way to have it appear as being instigated by the Department"; B. C. Clardy, Memorandum to H. E. Bell 13 December 1926, Box 2–10/551, wallet 1926; J. T. Elliott to Parker, 30 April 1928, and Parker to Elliott, 4 May 1928, Box 2–10/556, wallet 1928; Underwood, Johnson, Dolley & Simpson to Parker, 11 September 1928, Parker to Underwood et al., 13 September 1928, and "Order Restricting the

Use of Rotary Tools in Lefors Field in Gray County," 29 September 1928, all in Box 2–10/555, wallet 1928. R. G. Barnum to Bell, 27 January 1927, Box 2–10/553, wallet 1927, gives a detailed report of a meeting of operators that had been suggested by the commission's staff. J. M. McDonald to Parker, 25 July 1929, Box 2–10/557, wallet 1929, and Chief Deputy Supervisor to Frank Fouch, 24 April 1929, Box 2–10/558, wallet 1929, reflect the continuation of the cooperative approach, necessitated in part by the imprecise nature of the commission's authority.

55. Hassell to W. M. Priddy, ? April 1922, Box 2–10/540, wallet 1922, RG 455, TSA (quotation). In June 1920, the division had fifteen employees, including nine deputy supervisors. The number of deputy supervisors dropped from twelve in 1921 to nine in 1923 and rose to fourteen in 1926 and seventeen in 1927. By November 1929, the Oil and Gas Division held twenty-five employees (fifteen deputy supervisors) comprising nearly half of the entire RCT staff (which included now a Motor Transportation Division along with railroad rate and engineering sections); Butte to W. A. Nabors, 24 June 1920, Box 2–10/534, wallet 1920; Hassell to Morehouse, 20 December 1922, Box 2–10/545, wallet 1923–24; Chief Supervisor to J. T. Elliott, 19 October 1926, Box 3–4/387, wallet 1924–29; Bell to R. A. Smith, 4 April 1927, Box 4–3/394, wallet 1927, all in RG 455, TSA; Commissioners to Moore Lynn, 16 November 1929, RCTLP. In 1929, the legislature changed the method of appropriating monies for the division by placing it on a regular budget (still another instance of concern for efficiency in government); Gilmore to Walter Cline, 18 March 1929, RCTLP.

56. All of the following are found in RG 455, TSA, except where noted: Chair to Lon A. Smith, 13 September 1923, Box 4–3/361, wallet 1931–35, wherein the RCT complains to the Comptroller that the plunge in oil prices has cut funds to where the commission cannot perform all of the "police work" necessary. Indeed, lack of monies postponed the annual meeting of deputy supervisors in 1929; Leslie McKay to Homer Pierson, 11 July 1929, Box 2–10/559; H. H. Fitzpatrick to RCT, 27 June, 1922, Box 4–3/384, wallet 1920–29; Arnold to Bell, 2 May 1924, Box 4–3/388, wallet 1924; Bell to R. C. Lomax, 1 November 1926, Box 4–3/391; wallet 1926; S. W. Blount to Parker, 25 June 1931, Box 2–10/560, wallet 1929–31 (in this case Blount asked to be rehired after working in the private sector); John Hoffer to Parker, 7 June 1929, Box 2–10/558, wallet 1929.

A curious barrier to effective enforcement emerged in 1926. Bell to S. W. Blount, 11 February 1926, Box 2–10/550, wallet 1925, explains that "the New Revised Statutes [1925] did not carry forward that part of the Conservation Law that assesses a penalty for the violation of a rule or order of the Commission"!

57. For examples of continuing cooperation and safer development of the oil and gas fields later in the 1920s, see (all in RG 455, TSA): R. G. Barnum to Bell, 27 January 1927, Box 2–10/553, wallet 1927 (president of West Texas Oil and Gas Association reports on exchange of ideas with RCT deputy supervisors); Memo, B. C. Clardy, n.d., probably March 1927, Box 4–3/381, wallet 1927–31, folder Clardy correspondence (re informal conference between RCT officials and representatives from the Church and Fields district); Chief Supervisor to J. W. Carden, 27 July 1928, Box 2–10, wallet 1928 (re journalist wanting to write a positive article of RCT efforts); J. M. McDonald to Parker, 25 July 1929, Box 2–10/557, wallet 1929 (operators want RCT to encourage association); Coplin, Conservation Agent's Daily Report, 8 October 1929, Box 2–10/584, wallet letters (followup meeting of operators from Nacona field and report that gas waste has been reduced).

58. Parker to Harry Pennington, 30 October 1929, Box 2–10/560, wallet 1929–31, RG 455, TSA; F. H. Lahee, "Unit Operation and Unitization in Arkansas, Louisiana, Texas and New Mexico," *Transactions of the American Institute of Mining and Metallurgical Engineers* (New York, 1930), 34–42; W. P. Z. German, "Compulsory Unit Operation of Oil Pools," 11–37, H. C. Hardison, "Proration of Yates Pool, Pecos County, Texas," 74–79, and David Donoghue, "Proration in Texas," 67–79, all three in *Transactions* (New York, 1931). For private-sector support of self-regulation of production and an overview of federal

efforts to encourage conservation, see Larson and Porter, *History of Humble*, chaps. 11, 13. The authors note (298) that Humble executives were especially active between 1927 and 1930 in encouraging proration and unitization of production in Texas. For an overview of the activities of the American Petroleum Institute, the industry's most important trade association during this period, see Pratt, "Creating Coordination in the Modern Petroleum Industry." Pratt shows that the API focused on the gathering of statistics, promoted standardization of drilling tools, and stayed away from the conservation and price-fixing issues.

59. The Chief Supervisor in 1927, H. H. Bell, avoided considering the marketing problem because the laws did not allow him to; Bell to George S. Marshall, 16 May 1927, and Bell to W. H. Holmes, 18 May 1927, Box 2–10/551, wallet 1926.

60. The Hendricks field in West Texas apparently initiated a proration plan before the larger Yates field; Rister, *Oil!*, 299. For references to proration in the Oil and Gas Division records before 1930, see (all in RG 455, TSA, except where noted): C. D. Neff to Gilmore, 12 March 1928, Box 4–3/384, wallet 1920–29; ? to Morehouse, 9 April 1928, McKay to Morehouse, 26 May 1928, both in Box 2–10/552, wallet 1928; Gilmore to W. B. Hamilton, 4 May 1928 (first quotation), and Gilmore to John W. McGee, 18 March 1929 (second quotation), both RCTLP; W. H. Holmes to RCT, 17 May 1928, Box 2–10/541, wallet 1928; Gilmore to Charles R. Groff, 18 August 1928, Box 2–10/560, wallet 1929–31; Parker to Fitzpatrick, 2 November 1929, Box 2–10/448, wallet 1929. While Gilmore presents the position that all of this was aboveboard, the absence of direct references in the records to "numerous hearings and from sworn testimony" suggests otherwise. Larson and Porter, *History of Humble*, 319, mentions RCT hearings on the Winkler field. Of course, the possibility exists that the records have been missfiled; I found some motor-carrier and railway material in oil and gas boxes. The articles from *Transactions* cited above fail to mention the RCT, except in its sanctioning role.

61. Hardison, "Proration of Yates Pool," passim; Larson and Porter, *History of Humble*, 316–21. First, well potential (the amount of oil the geologists and engineers thought lay beneath the well), then acreage allotments (again, a unit with which to estimate the amount of oil beneath the owner's land) formed the basis of proration in Yates.

Primary evidence in the Oil and Gas Division correspondence seems to sustain Larson's and Porter's assertions that Humble was less selfish and more interested in the common good than any other major firm; C. D. Neff to C. Hansen, 12 March 1928, Box 4–3/384, wallet 1920–29, RG 455, TSA (this letter also notes how the "experts" were inconsistent in estimating reserves).

62. Rister, *Oil!*, 306 (quotation); Larson and Porter, *History of Humble*, chap. 13, and for Gilmore's role, 312, 451; Conrod, "State Regulation of Oil and Gas in Texas," 72–79.

63. Larson and Porter, *History of Humble*, 451, for the weakened position of the RCT, c. 1931.

64. *29th Annual Report of the RCT* (1930), 64; in late 1929, Moore Lynn, acting state auditor, ran a biographical and employment survey of all state employees. Most of the replies from the employees of the Oil and Gas Division can be found in Box 2–10/565, RG 455, TSA. Of the eleven I located, only two lacked previous oil-drilling experience, but one of those had five years and the other four and one-half years experience with the division. The Chief Deputy Supervisor had previous drilling experience.

65. Humble Oil was associated in the Texan mind with Standard Oil; see note 20 above. "Moody Measures Still Wait Action," *Austin American Statesman*, 10 February 1929; Parker to E. G. Allen, 11 January 1929, Box 2–10/561, wallet 129–30, RG 455, TSA; Day, "Oil and Gas and Texas Politics," 68; Larson and Porter, *History of Humble*, 312–15, chap. 13.

66. "In Memory of Clarence Gilmore," *28th Annual Report of the RCT* (1929), 3–4; "Neff Rail Member," *Austin American Statesman*, 14 October 1929; Parker to Tilly, 16 October 1929, Box 2–10/558, wallet 1929, RG 455, TSA. C. V. Terrell and Lon Smith were commissioners when Gilmore died. Terrell seemed more comfortable with railway

81

regulation. He constantly referred to R. D. Parker, the Chief Deputy Supervisor, on oil and gas matters during legislative hearings in 1932, "Solons' Rights Challenged by Pope," *Austin American Statesman*, 5 November 1932, 1. Former governor Pat Neff was appointed to replace Gilmore; Neff did not get along with Terrell or Smith; "Terrell and Smith Tell House Version of Split with Neff," *Austin American Statesman*, 19 July 1931, 1.

67. *Danciger Oil & Refining Co. of Texas et al. v. Smith et al.* 4 *Federal Supplement* 236 (1933), 236–7 n. 1; Hart, "Oil, Courts, and the Commission," 312; Day, "Oil and Gas and Texas Politics," 83–87. For a description of the RCT's good relations with the Danciger firm, see Parker to J. P. Lightfoot, 6 June 1928, Box 4–1/395, wallet 1928, RG 455, TSA.

68. *39th Annual Report of the RCT* (1930), 63–65; *41st Annual Report of the RCT* (1932), 85–91.

69. "Texas Topics," *Austin American Statesman*, 7 May 1931, 4; "Oil Board Plan Killed," *Austin American Statesman*, 5 August 1931, 1; Day, "Oil and Gas and Texas Politics," 204–6 (April–May 1932).

70. R. D. Parker represented the continuity in Progressive Era approaches. Born on 2 February 1878, Parker received an engineering degree from the University of Texas at Austin in 1898. After serving with the U.S. Geological Survey, teaching at UT, and working for two railways, Parker became chief engineer of the RCT in 1908 and held that position until 1920. He then joined the Natural Gas Utilities Division of the RCT and in 1927 took over as Chief Oil and Gas Supervisor. After Leaving the RCT in 1934, he worked for the Texas Petroleum Council and later entered private practice in engineering until he retired in 1948. He died in September 1958. See "R. D. Parker," Vertical File, Biographical, BTHC, and *Time Magazine*, 2 July 1934, 50, for the story behind Parker's firing. See "Lawmakers Forgetting Politics and Trying to Aid Oil Industry," *Austin American Statesman*, 19 July 1931, 12, wherein Raymond Brooks, a longtime observer of Texas politics, noted that the explanation of the facts behind the RCT's problems, much of which Parker brought before the lawmakers, had restored the legitimacy of the RCT.

71. The story in the 1930s will be developed in more detail in my forthcoming book. The distinctive features of the East Texas field, particularly its numerous operators, led to a different kind of proration system than had been developing in the 1920s. Unitization as found in Yates was not adopted in East Texas; instead, each well was rated for bottom-hole pressure and potential and on that basis given a production quota based on the entire field's quota. The sheer number of operators, the populist tradition in the area, and the inability to control the giant field from the beginning explain why proration developed differently there than elsewhere.

72. For a convenient listing of the pertinent literature, see McCraw, *Prophets of Regulation*, 147–52 and 342nn. 9, 13, 343 nn. 14, 18.

73. In the East Texas field, the legal and political forces blocked rational, unitized development; thus one could argue that in this case, the legal forces were stronger than the economic ones.

74. Alfred D. Chandler, Jr., *Strategy and Structure: Chapters in the History of the American Industrial Enterprise* (Cambridge, Mass., (1962).

75. Williamson et al., *Age of Energy*, 327–28, makes a similar argument, but in the immediate context of the book, the reference is to Oklahoma specifically and/or other states' efforts generally. No significance is given to the efforts in Texas.

76. Thomas K. McCraw, "Business and Government: The Origins of the Adversary Relationship," *California Management Review* 26 (Winter 1984): 33–52, suggests that "the conditions of legitimacy [in business-government relations] seem to be a complex amalgam of efficiency, fairness, and shared power" (47). He goes on to suggest six categories that might explain successful business-government policymaking: (1) a sense of crisis, (2) opportunity for a positive-sum game, (3) a coherent strategy implemented by first-rate talent, (4) high-percentage initial steps, (5) an identifiable measure of success other than profit, and (b) some means of controlling the agenda and limiting the number of players. The story in

this essay supports some but not all of McCraw's speculations. A sense of crisis was absent in the 1920s story, but creative approaches still emerged to develop conservation in the oil fields. (McCraw suggested crises were not essential but often were helpful in forging creative policymaking.) Throughout the 1920s, the RCT attempted to help all players achieve something positive from government intervention: Small-scale, nonintegrated oil operators as well as the major integrated firms were given fair hearing. Gilmore and Butte represent the first-rate talent with a coherent strategy; Parker represents the continuity after 1929. The RCT eschewed high-percentage first steps because of the lack of authority in the statutes; the Oklahoma agency, however, with the authority, took strong action early. Identifying success other than profit in the story has to rest upon the growing legitimacy of the agency in the eyes of industry leaders. The proration agreements in the fields other than East Texas brought a measure of stability and thus the chance for steadier profits. Finally, despite the lack of market-demand legislation, the RCT and the industry controlled the agenda of conservation and made headway in stabilization of production until the East Texas crisis shattered temporarily that stability.

The Transformation of the Federal Trade Commission, 1914-1929

By G. Cullom Davis

During the presidential campaign of 1920, Republican candidate Warren G. Harding sought the support of the American electorate in inaugurating an era of "less government in business and more business in government."[1] In the years that followed, this campaign pledge was fulfilled to such an extraordinary degree that historians of the 1920's have constructed as one of the central pillars of "normalcy" the pro-business orientation of the federal government. A related phenomenon was the mounting hostility with which progressive reformers viewed this rapprochement between government and the business community.

At the focal point of government-business relations was the Federal Trade Commission. Still relatively untested when the decade began, the Commission underwent a severe trial when confronted with the sweeping transition from progressivism to "normalcy." After a few years of stubborn resistance, it sharply if belatedly altered its activities in 1925 to conform more closely to prevailing views in Congress and the White House. As a consequence, the attitudes of those two opposing groups—progressives and businessmen—which had been, respectively, its warmest defenders and its sharpest critics before 1925 were suddenly reversed. A close study of its behavior and stature during the years from 1914 to 1929 should produce insights into the nature of the Commission and into the temper of American politics in the 1920's.

The passage of the Federal Trade Commission Act in September, 1914, had been considered by many observers of the political scene as the final solution of a long-standing controversy over methods of

EDITOR'S NOTE:—This article received the Mississippi Valley Historical Association's Pelzer Award for 1962.
[1] Warren G. Harding, "Less Government in Business and More Business in Government," *World's Work* (New York), XLI (November, 1920), 25.

regulating business. The dispute, which had puzzled and divided reformers since the turn of the century, had centered on the question of whether business could be regulated more effectively by stringent legislation to reinforce the Sherman Anti-Trust Act, or by an administrative commission vested with far-reaching powers. Exponents of the latter view had argued that the ideal instrument of regulation was a small, independent commission, composed of carefully selected experts and isolated from the corrupting and fluctuating influences of everyday politics. Originating chiefly within the ranks of progressive reformers, the controversy had quickly spread to the two major political parties and had served as a prominent issue in the heated presidential campaign of 1912. Now, in 1914, the issue had seemingly been settled by the creation of the Federal Trade Commission. That agency, vested with unprecedented powers to investigate, publicize, and prohibit all "unfair methods of competition," represented a crowning triumph for advocates of the commission concept of regulation. Its five members, appointed by the President, would presumably administer an impartial and consistent policy in accordance with the progressive ideals of strict regulation and vigorous antitrust activity.[2]

General agreement on the importance of the Federal Trade Commission Act did not, however, mean general approval of its provisions. The public was sharply divided on the wisdom and potential benefits of the law. Among progressives the reaction was generally enthusiastic. The bill had been passed by a comfortable majority, with the outcome in the Senate determined largely by the co-operation of the reform-minded senators of both parties. Theodore Roosevelt, still reigning as the patriarch of progressivism, asserted that its enactment meant that the Democrats had adopted "a little of the Progressive Platform," while President Wilson, who had exerted strong pressure for its passage, was proud to claim it as a major accomplishment of his "New Freedom" program.[3] The atti-

[2] "The Newest Part of the Government," *World's Work*, XXX (May, 1915), 24; "An Unseen Reversal," *New Republic* (New York), I (January 9, 1915), 8. Among the best general accounts of progressivism and the Federal Trade Commission are Arthur S. Link, *Woodrow Wilson and the Progressive Era, 1910-1917* (New York, 1954); Eric F. Goldman, *Rendezvous with Destiny: A History of Modern American Reform* (New York, 1952); and Robert Cushman, *The Independent Regulatory Commissions* (New York, 1941).

[3] Theodore Roosevelt to Dwight B. Heard, January 29, 1915, Elting E. Morison (ed.), *The Letters of Theodore Roosevelt* (8 vols., Cambridge, 1951-1954), VIII, 885; Arthur S. Link, *Wilson: The New Freedom* (Princeton, 1956), 440-42; Alfred

tude of the Republican progressives was summed up tersely in the following statement by Senator Albert B. Cummins of Iowa: "I am not half-hearted in my support of this measure. I believe in it thoroughly. I look forward to its enforcement with a high degree of confidence."[4] Similar expressions of approval also came from some of the leading reform journals of the period. The *New Republic*, for example, in one of its early issues, commended the establishment of a regulatory commission and hopefully predicted that it would produce "historic political and constitutional reform"; and in his weekly journal, *La Follette's Magazine*, Senator Robert M. La Follette contributed an editorial praising the law and anticipating "much relief to the public and to honest business."[5]

In contrast to the united support offered it by progressives, the Federal Trade Commission received a divided reaction from the business world. As the *Outlook* observed, many businessmen hoped that the law would produce "genuine co-operation" between business and government, but there were others who viewed the new agency "with foreboding." The former group, whose attitude might have been described as cautious optimism, included the powerful United States Chamber of Commerce. Through its official publication, *The Nation's Business*, the Chamber observed that the Commission's value would have to be judged on the basis of its future course of action. So long as it acted as a "constructive and timely aid to business," rather than as an enemy, it would enjoy the businessman's support. But it would lose that support, the Chamber warned, if it undertook "investigations of no constructive significance" or if it acted as "a court of inquisition."[6]

Less optimistic business interests viewed the Commission with apprehension and hostility. They feared that it would become an all-powerful agency, combining the functions of all three branches of government and endeavoring to dissolve free enterprise into small, unprofitable units. Illustrative of this position was the attitude of Senator Frank B. Brandegee of Connecticut, who had stubbornly op-

Lief, *Democracy's Norris: The Biography of a Lonely Crusade* (New York, 1939), 139; Belle C. and Fola La Follette, *Robert M. La Follette* (2 vols., New York, 1953), I, 487.

[4] Quoted in Link, *New Freedom*, 442.

[5] "An Unseen Reversal," *New Republic*, I (January 9, 1915), 8; *La Follette's Magazine* (Madison), VII (May, 1915), 2.

[6] "The Federal Trade Commission Begins Work," *Outlook* (New York), CIX (March 31, 1915), 746; "Opportunity of the Federal Trade Commission," *The Nation's Business* (Washington), III (March 15, 1915), 1.

posed the Trade Commission bill, and who warned that the Commission would be "a burden upon the varied business interests of the land" and, even worse, the first fatal step toward a "socialistic program of government."[7] Although this extreme point of view was relatively rare among businessmen in 1915, it was an accurate forecast of the conservative attitude that was to evolve in the next ten years.

In its first decade of activity, the Federal Trade Commission proved a disappointment to many of its original supporters. Progressives generally placed the blame for this failure outside the Commission itself. They correctly judged that its poor record was due to a combination of three damaging factors: a series of adverse court decisions, the active opposition of many congressmen, and an uncooperative attitude on the part of many businessmen. The commissioners themselves, or at least a majority of them, worked hard to fulfill the original purpose of the Federal Trade Commission Act. Consequently, in spite of its disappointing record, the Commission continued up to 1925 to enjoy the support of progressives.

It would probably be accurate to say that before 1925 a majority of the commissioners desired to execute a strict regulatory policy in accordance with the progressive ideals of economic reform. Most of President Wilson's appointees shared this progressive view, and because commissioners were appointed for seven-year terms the progressive majority remained intact for a few years following Wilson's departure from office. Consequently, it was not until 1925 that the remaining Wilson appointees faced a majority selected by Warren G. Harding and Calvin Coolidge. Up to a point, then, the Commission was able to operate independently and to maintain a consistent policy in spite of the changing complexion and policies of the White House.

The work of the Federal Trade Commission was just beginning when the United States entered the First World War. During the conflict its regulatory activities were necessarily curtailed in the interest of the war effort, and the Commission functioned chiefly as a fact-finding bureau for the War Industries Board and other temporary agencies.[8] Thus, the duties which it was created to perform did

[7] *Congressional Record*, 63 Cong., 2 Sess., 12799-801 (July 27, 1914).

[8] Nelson B. Gaskill, *The Regulation of Competition* (New York, 1936), 66; Federal Trade Commission, *World War Activities, 1917-1918: A Memorandum by Henry*

not really begin until after 1918, but as soon as conditions permitted it initiated a program of vigorous investigation. Its first target was the meat-packing industry, where it undertook an extensive investigation of the five largest firms. In a lengthy report, issued late in 1919, it pointed out that the major meat packers were engaged in profiteering activities that constituted unlawful restraints of trade.[9] This revelation, and the broad punitive recommendations which accompanied it, provoked a sharp congressional controversy which resulted in the first major setback for the Commission. Led by Senator James E. Watson of Indiana, a leading right-wing Republican, conservatives in Congress condemned the investigatory methods and findings of the Commission. The outcry had a damaging effect, both direct and indirect, upon the stature and effectiveness of the Commission. The clamor served to stall proceedings in the case to such an extent that formal action was never taken against the defendants, and the Commission was rebuked in the Republican platform of 1920 for "unfair persecution of honest business." And in 1921 Congress added its own reproach in the Packers and Stockyards Act, which transferred jurisdiction over meat packers to the Department of Agriculture.[10]

Not only in Congress but also in the courts, the Federal Trade Commission encountered crippling obstacles. The most serious blow, delivered in a series of judicial decisions, was denial of the Commission's right to define the specific meaning of "unfair methods of competition." Instead, this power was assumed by the courts, which generally defined it in such narrow terms that many Commission rulings were reversed. The courts also insisted on the right to review not only the Commission's procedure in cases, but its findings of fact as well. In other words, factual evidence gathered by the Commission was not accepted *prima facie,* but became subject to review and hence to possible dismissal by the courts. According to Nelson B. Gaskill, who served as one of the more active and conscientious members of the Commission from 1920 to 1925, these adverse rulings "com-

Miller (Washington, 1919), 15; Federal Trade Commission, *Annual Report* (1919), 3.
    ' E. Pendleton Herring, *Public Administration and the Public Interest* (New York, 1936), 118-20; George Odell, "The Federal Trade Commission Yields to Pressure," *The Nation* (New York), CXII (January 12, 1921), 36.
    [10] Odell, "Commission Yields to Pressure," *Nation,* CXII (January 12, 1921), 37; Kirk H. Porter (comp.), *National Party Platforms* (New York, 1924), 459; David B. Truman, *The Governmental Process: Political Interests and Public Opinion* (New York, 1951), 420; Federal Trade Commission, *Annual Report* (1918), 5, 22-25.

pletely devitalized" the Commission and "reduced it to terms of a futile gesture."[11]

In its contacts with businessmen, the Federal Trade Commission met with increasing defiance and animosity. Its investigators were denied access to company records or were permitted to examine only selected materials. In some cases its rulings were actually ignored or defied, the most notable instance being in the case against the Aluminum Company of America. Following an intensive investigation, the Commission in 1924 ordered the company to halt certain illegal practices. Reports that this ruling had not been obeyed led to a second investigation, but by that time the Commission membership had changed, and the case was eventually dropped.[12] Thus hampered by the unfriendliness of Congress, the courts, and the business community, members of the Commission experienced the futility and frustration of striving to carry out a vigorous regulatory policy in an environment which was decidedly hostile to such action.

The commissioners' disappointment over their record contrasted sharply, however, with the unswerving and heartening loyalty expressed by leading progressives. Up to 1925 progressives looked with confidence to the Federal Trade Commission as their most effective weapon in the war against monopoly and unfair business practices. The very failures of the Commission served to reinforce the arguments in favor of its existence, for so long as the commissioners themselves remained dedicated to the principles of progressivism, the Commission appeared to be the only potentially effective regulator of business. The fact that its work had been sabotaged by the exponents of a pro-business viewpoint merely emphasized the virtues of a strong, independent commission. This continuing loyalty of progressives to the Commission was accurately expressed in *La Follette's Magazine*: "The Federal Trade Commission was intended by Congress to do exactly the things it has done, as an independent body, non-partisan in its personnel and unhampered by intereference from other branches of the government."[13]

That progressives continued to rely upon the Federal Trade Com-

[11] Carl McFarland, *Judicial Control of the Federal Trade Commission and the Interstate Commerce Commission, 1920-1930* (Cambridge, 1933), 45-62; Gaskill, *Regulation of Competition*, 6.

[12] Thomas C. Blaisdell, *The Federal Trade Commission: An Experiment in the Control of Business* (New York, 1932), 89-90.

[13] "Coolidge Slaughters the Federal Trade Commission," *La Follette's Magazine*, XVII (May, 1925), 66.

mission up to 1925 is also indicated by the fact that they frequently sought aid and information from it. Many of its investigations of business activities were initiated at the request of liberal reformers in Congress. A noteworthy example was the investigation of the utilities industry. In 1924 a number of leading progressives, including Senators George W. Norris and Thomas J. Walsh and Governor Gifford Pinchot of Pennsylvania, expressed their alarm at the expanding network of interconnected utility corporations, which they called the "power trust." Certain large companies were suspected of monopolistic control over many other utilities representing an aggregate capital investment of hundreds of millions of dollars. Progressives urged that the federal government take action, and they unhesitatingly selected the Federal Trade Commission as the proper agency to direct an investigation. Senator Norris' resolution embodying these demands was finally passed in February, 1925. Thus, until the early months of 1925 progressives were willing and even eager to intrust important investigative and regulatory tasks to the Commission.[14]

Probably the most frequent and consistent favorable publicity for the work of the Commission during the early years of its activity appeared in *La Follette's Magazine*. Senator La Follette utilized the journal to publicize attempts in Congress to "hamstring the Federal Trade Commission" by cutting its appropriation, and he was also quick to praise the Commission's accomplishments, which he considered numerous and important.[15] After his death in 1925, this policy was continued, and in 1926 an editorial reviewing the Commission's achievements prior to 1925 made the statement that "the Federal Trade Commission during the past ten years has not only restrained the greed of the steel trust, but it has investigated the packers, the harvester trust, grain exchanges, lumber trusts, aluminum trust, fertilizer trust, and other great organizations." In short, the editorial concluded, "the Commission was the friend of labor, of the farmers, of cooperative organizations, and of the small business men."[16]

Another progressive, Senator William H. King of Utah, also summarizing the accomplishments of the Commission before 1925,

[14] Carl D. Thompson, *Confessions of the Power Trust: A Summary of the Testimony Given in the Hearings of the Federal Trade Commission on Utility Corporations* (New York, 1928), xvii; *Cong. Record*, 68 Cong., 2 Sess., 910 (December 29, 1924).
[15] See, for example, "On Guard for the People," *La Follette's Magazine*, XIV (February, 1922), 22; *ibid.*, XVII (February, 1925), 20.
[16] "The Senate and the Federal Trade Commission," *ibid.*, XVIII (January, 1926), 2.

argued that it "performed service of the very highest character, and did much to protect honest business from unfair practices." This view was echoed by Josephus Daniels, who had served as secretary of the navy under President Wilson. Daniels observed that the Commission had "done much good and proved . . . a deterrent to unfair practices in business," in spite of the heavy opposition which it had encountered.[17] Progressives were of course disappointed that the Commission had not completely fulfilled its original aims, but they nevertheless continued to support it on the grounds that its short-comings were the result of a hostile environment rather than of any inherent defects. This unbroken loyalty bolstered the Commission against the increasing attacks being made upon it by representatives of business.

During the same ten-year period the attitude of businessmen to-ward the Commission had shifted from their initially divided and un-certain reaction of 1915 to a steadily increasing united opposition to its work. Their criticism ranged from mild displeasure and vexation at the Commission's investigations to sharp attacks upon its very foundations. Viewed collectively, the businessmen's attacks called for either a radical transformation or the outright abolition of the Com-mission.

Those voices which expressed displeasure in subdued language in-cluded prominent individuals and publications in the business world. The *Nation's Business*, which had hopefully adopted a "wait and see" policy in 1915, revealed a growing exasperation in the years that followed by publishing articles criticizing the Commission's activi-ties. One of these essays, contributed by a New York banker, attacked the alleged tendency of regulatory commissions to become "prosecut-ing functionaries" and concluded that the very principles of investi-gation and regulation, which of course formed the basis for the Com-mission's existence, "instead of simplifying a complex situation . . . tended to make it more complicated and obscure."[18] This view was reiterated in other articles in the same journal. Writing in 1925, former Secretary of Commerce William C. Redfield warned that "after ten years of endurance, the business world is rebelling against the unjust methods of the Federal Trade Commission." He added that the Commission had wrongly assumed the functions of "accuser,

[17] *Cong. Record*, 69 Cong., 1 Sess., 5944 (March 20, 1926) ; Josephus Daniels, "To Strangle the Trade Commission," *La Follette's Magazine*, XVII (June, 1925), 86.
[18] George E. Roberts, "The Illusion of Federal Commissions," *Nation's Business*, XII (January, 1924), 42, 46.

judge, and jury," thereby becoming "a disappointment and a scourge to the business world." Another article in the same issue charged that instead of helping business as it was originally intended to do, the Commission had placed "every possible obstacle in its way and . . . condemned and maligned businessmen for practices of which they were innocent."[19] Another business publication, the *Wall Street Journal*, bluntly depicted the Federal Trade Commission as "a crusading, muck-raking body."[20]

A more extreme form of attack by businessmen was forcefully expressed by William E. Humphrey, the man who was to play the key role in the Commission's transformation in 1925. Humphrey was a former congressman from the state of Washington, an active Republican party regular, and one of President Coolidge's campaign managers in the 1924 election. His close connection with northwestern lumber interests, which had suffered the unfavorable publicity of a Federal Trade Commission investigation, made him a particularly bitter foe of its work. He charged that the pre-1925 Commission was "an instrument of oppression and disturbance and injury instead of a help to business," and asserted that "No other governmental agency ever had a practice so tyrannical and so repugnant to every sense of justice."[21] Although Humphrey's views were probably more extreme than the typical businessman's attitude, they nevertheless revealed the extent to which many business spokesmen had become hostile to the Commission by 1925.

Thus if the Federal Trade Commission had not lived up to its initial promise prior to 1925, the blame for this failure clearly lay in circumstances beyond that agency's control. This conclusion is indicated not only by the record of the Commission itself, but also by the conflict between the views of progressives and businessmen toward it. An organization which continued to enjoy the support of progressive reformers, and which at the same time incurred the mounting hostility of business interests, was plainly still directed toward the progressive ideals which had given it birth. The Commission's survival thus constituted by 1925 one of the last remaining bulwarks of progressivism against the rising tide of reaction and conservatism in the federal government. Its continued existence, how-

---

[19] William C. Redfield, "Where the Federal Trade Commission Failed," *ibid.*, XIII (May, 1925), 29-30; Jack Underwood, "Don't Shoot—We're Coming Down," *ibid.*, 30.

[20] Quoted in *Literary Digest* (New York), LXXXV (May 16, 1925), 11.

[21] Quoted in Herring, *Public Administration*, 125. See also William E. Humphrey, "A Friend of Honest Business," *Nation's Business*, XVI (June 5, 1928), 31.

ever, was precarious. With a total membership of five men, the Commission was destined eventually to come under the control of a conservative majority. Opponents of the Commission, who had attacked it frontally in Congress and in the courts, had also succeeded in quietly placing two staunch conservatives on its board by 1925. In that year they were able, as one progressive journal angrily observed, to "destroy it from the inside" by appointing a third and pivotal conservative to its membership. That development, with its important repercussions, quickly elevated the Commission to new heights of controversy and criticism.[22]

The year 1925 stands out, therefore, as a critical turning point in the early history of the Federal Trade Commission. As a result of the vital change in its membership and leadership from a progressive to a conservative majority in that year, it experienced a far-reaching transformation of its fundamental purpose and practices. And in consequence of this transformation, it became the subject of serious concern, re-evaluation, and controversy among government officials and professional students of politics. This controversy revealed a remarkable reversal in the roles of the Commission's former allies and enemies as progressives and businessmen exchanged their positions with regard to the Commission itself. Businessmen overnight became loyal defenders of the Commission, while progressives united in attacking it and even in demanding its abolition. On one point, however, everyone agreed after 1925: the Federal Trade Commission had now broken with its progressive origins and ideals and had completely if belatedly reoriented its activities to conform to the prevailing pattern of "normalcy."

To place responsibility for these changes upon a single person is to invite disbelief and a charge of oversimplification. With minor qualifications, however, the general conclusion is inescapable that the appointment of William E. Humphrey as a member of the Federal Trade Commission in February, 1925, set off a chain reaction which eventually included all of the developments summarized above. Under these circumstances, a careful study of the man and his appointment is warranted.

It has been noted that Humphrey was one of the Commission's more formidable opponents before 1925. During his career as a congressman he was known as a sincere and staunch exponent of the business viewpoint. This reputation was further substantiated after 1917,

[22] *La Follette's Magazine*, XVII (May, 1925), 66.

when he became a lawyer and vigorous lobbyist for northwestern lumber interests. There was nothing secretive about Humphrey's work; he was proud of his business associations. An article in *The Nation* in 1925 paid him the supreme compliment when it pointed out that "big business has no warmer friend or defender," and Senator Norris, who had served with Humphrey in the House, characterized him as "a fearless advocate of big business" and "one of the greatest reactionaries."[23] The most revealing evidence of this conservative viewpoint, however, was provided by Humphrey himself. He once declared, for example, that many years of experience in Washington had given him "a profound distrust of the reformer."[24] Such language was scarcely calculated to endear its author to the progressives.

Up to the time of Humphrey's appointment, the Federal Trade Commission was controlled by a progressive-minded majority. Early in 1924, four Wilson appointees remained to direct the activities of the five-man Commission. These were Huston Thompson, who had served as assistant attorney general under Wilson; Victor Murdock, who prior to his 1917 appointment was a progressive congressman from Kansas; Nelson B. Gaskill, who later wrote a book lamenting the disappearance of the progressively oriented Commission; and John F. Nugent, who resigned from the Senate in 1921 to become a commissioner. Gradually, however, the Harding and Coolidge appointees gained in number. Vernon W. Van Fleet, a friend of Indiana's Senator Watson and a former lobbyist for the National Association of Manufacturers, was appointed in 1922. Victor Murdock was replaced in 1924 by Charles W. Hunt, whom *La Follette's Magazine* briefly characterized as a "reactionary Republican of Iowa."[25] Thus with the appointment of Humphrey to succeed Nelson Gaskill in February, 1925, majority control over the Federal Trade Commission passed into the hands of the more recent appointees.

Progressives sharply but unsuccessfully opposed Humphrey's appointment. Its effect was "to set the country back more than twenty-

[23] "Mr. Coolidge Makes Good," *Nation*, CXX (February 25, 1925), 202; George W. Norris, "Boring from Within," *ibid.*, CXXI (September 16, 1925), 297-98; *Cong. Record*, 68 Cong., 2 Sess., 3053 (February 5, 1925).
[24] William E. Humphrey, "Not Guilty until Proved," *System: The Magazine of Business* (Chicago), LI (February, 1927), 153.
[25] Herring, *Public Administration*, 122; Blaisdell, *Federal Trade Commission*, 76; *La Follette's Magazine*, XVII (May, 1925), 66.

five years," according to Senator Norris, who pictured the Commission as now standing "three to two in favor of the big-business idea." *La Follette's Magazine* asserted that the Commission consisted of "three reactionaries and two Progressives," and *The Nation* charged the Coolidge administration with the "deliberate breaking down of governmental safeguards against the evils of big business." In spite of these attacks, however, and of the obvious implications of Coolidge's selection, Humphrey's appointment was easily confirmed in the Senate by a vote of 45 to 10.[26]

This controversial change in the personnel of the Federal Trade Commission was but the prelude to a still more significant transformation of its rules of policy and procedure. The Commission adopted the first three of a new set of rules of procedure in March, 1925. In the first of these it specified that henceforth its investigations were to be confined strictly to those cases which included definite allegations of unfair practices detrimental to the public interest. This restricting rule was designed to end the congressional practice of authorizing the Commission to undertake sweeping economic studies of a general nature. A second change was the announcement that in the future the Commission would strive to settle most of its cases by "stipulation," or informal agreement, rather than through the costlier and more time-consuming process of formal action by either the Commission or some other government agency. Settlement by stipulation was considered desirable because it would give defendants the benefits of reduced legal expenses, less public exposure of their misdeeds, and a friendlier relationship with the government.

A third new rule gave defendants the opportunity to present their arguments informally and confidentially in a preliminary hearing before a board of review. The record of those hearings was not to be printed or given any publicity, so that defendants could speak freely without fear of being held responsible at some later date for their informal testimony. In insisting upon the adoption of this rule, Commissioner Humphrey charged that in the past the Commission had been employed all too often as "a publicity bureau to spread socialistic propaganda." A fourth rule change, adopted a few weeks later, providing that stipulation agreements were to be made confidentially without any public announcement of the settlements, further empha-

[26] *Nation*, CXX (February 25, 1925), 202; CXXI (September 16, 1925), 297-99; *La Follette's Magazine*, XVII (February, 1925), 20; *Cong. Record*, 68 Cong., 2 Sess., 4416 (February 23, 1925).

sized a determination to curtail the Commission's ability to publicize its actions. Thus stipulation now became all the more attractive to defendants, because it offered them a means of avoiding altogether any unfavorable or damaging publicity.[27]

The guiding influence behind this transformation was the newly appointed commissioner, William E. Humphrey, who had immediately assumed vigorous leadership of the conservative majority. His virtual domination of the Commission served, as one writer has observed, "to inaugurate a 'new era' in its activities." Humphrey himself freely and proudly acknowledged his responsibility for the new era. "I certainly did make a revolutionary change in the method and policies of the commission," he was quoted as saying in 1928. "If it was going east before, it is going west now."[28] Humphrey's influence was also decisive in other important developments within the Federal Trade Commission. He was chiefly responsible, for example, for the decision against reopening the earlier case against the Aluminum Company of America, thus thwarting the demands of progressives who charged that the original Commission order had been disobeyed by the company. He also succeeded in enlarging the Commission's board of review—which conducted the informal preliminary hearings—frankly admitting that his purpose was to "stack" the board with a compliant majority. "What of it?" he asked brazenly in answer to criticism. "Do you think I would have a body of men working here under me that did not share my ideas about these matters? Not on your life. I would not hesitate a minute to cut their heads off if they disagreed with me. What in hell do you think I am here for?"[29]

Humphrey's pro-business attitudes also led him to encourage more extensive use of a procedure through which the Commission had permitted industry-wide meetings, or "trade practice conferences," to formulate their own rules of behavior. If these rules fell within the Commission's jurisdiction, they could be approved by that agency and given the force of law. Despite their appealing informality and sense of co-operative effort, such conferences had been infre-

[27] Federal Trade Commission, *Rules of Practice and Procedure and Statements of Policy* (Washington, 1927), 13-17; Federal Trade Commission, *Annual Report* (1925), 111; Blaisdell, *Federal Trade Commission*, 81-83; Herring, *Public Administration*, 125-29.

[28] Herring, *Public Administration*, 125; William E. Humphrey, quoted in *Cong. Record*, 70 Cong., 1 Sess., 2956 (February 14, 1928).

[29] Humphrey, quoted in *Cong. Record*, 70 Cong., 1 Sess., 2956. See also Blaisdell, *Federal Trade Commission*, 89.

quent prior to 1926. In that year, however, Humphrey brought about the creation within the Commission of a new department, the trade practice conference division, whose purpose was to encourage industrial self-regulation. The new procedure, it was pointed out, "permits an industry to make its own rules of business conduct . . . in co-operation with the commission." The plan was effective, for after 1926 the average number of trade practice conferences jumped from less than three to about sixteen per year. The general effect was to introduce an atmosphere of co-operation and common effort into relations between business and the Commission and to promote a tendency toward less governmental interference on the one hand and more corporate independence on the other.[30]

Viewed together, these procedural changes constituted a sharp departure from earlier Commission policy and from the progressive ideal of strict regulation. Essentially, the new policy was friendlier, more trusting, and more co-operative toward business. In the first place, the Commission had now expressed a strong preference for settling cases by informal, confidential agreement rather than by formal Commission order. Second, it had taken steps to curtail its powers of publicity and investigation, thereby shielding defendants from public embarrassment and criticism. Finally, it now exhibited such confidence in the ability and willingness of business to regulate itself that its own function in the regulatory process was being performed more as partner than as overseer. The members themselves summarized the new viewpoint in 1927, when they declared that "helping business to help itself wherever and whenever it can be done . . . is the principle of this new policy." In that same year they asserted that "the legitimate interests of business are in perfect harmony with the true interests of the public."[31] In other words, after 1925 the majority of the Commission no longer viewed business as an actual or even potential enemy to be investigated suspiciously and regulated stringently, but rather as a friend and partner to be assisted and encouraged in pursuit of common aims.

Within a period of one year, therefore, the Federal Trade Commission had undergone a radical transformation of its fundamental purpose and policy, and it was only natural that the two groups most

[30] Federal Trade Commission, *Annual Report* (1927), 1; Federal Trade Commission, *Trade Practice Conferences* (1929), v; Blaisdell, *Federal Trade Commission*, 92; Gaskill, *Regulation of Competition*, 115.

[31] Federal Trade Commission, *Annual Report* (1927), 1; Federal Trade Commission, *Trade Practice Conferences* (1927), 2.

directly concerned should mirror this change in their attitudes toward the Commission. Progressives and businessmen continued as before to view the Commission from opposite positions, but their respective attitudes were completely reversed. Instead of criticizing and attempting to weaken the Commission, businessmen after 1925 began to defend its activities. Conversely, progressives ceased supporting what had once been a vital part of their reform program and began to attack the Commission and even to demand its abolition.

The attitude of the business community toward the new policy of the Commission was perhaps most revealingly expressed by Humphrey himself. He observed in 1927 that "the businessmen who have come in contact with the Commission during the last year realize this change in attitude, and I know that they fully endorse it." In 1926 the Commission itself testified to this response of businessmen when it noted "an increasing degree of cooperation on the part of business." Humphrey dismissed the critics as "the vocal and beatific fringe, the pink edges that border both of the old parties." "No longer," he noted with satisfaction, would the Commission serve "as a means of gratifying demagogues."[32]

Other voices from the business world expressed these same sentiments. A prominent New York banker wrote in the *Nation's Business* that the Commission was finally coming to the correct conclusion that "the only way to regulate business effectively is to let it regulate itself," and the United States Chamber of Commerce expressed its formal approval of the Commission's course of action. In its annual meetings of 1925 and 1926 the Chamber passed resolutions endorsing the new rules of those two years. One resolution happily predicted that the changes would make the Commission "increasingly constructive, effective, and helpful to American business." The *Magazine of Wall Street*, a trade periodical of banking and finance, lauded the new rules as "an encouraging development" in the campaign to end the Commission's "legalized persecution of business." Thanks to the work of Humphrey, it added, the Commission had been converted from a "hectoring, tyrannical and . . . tireless snooper" into "an instrument of protection," thus heralding a "new trend toward making government the fair and understanding arbiter of business."[33]

---

[32] Humphrey, "Not Guilty until Proved," *System*, LI (February, 1927), 154; Federal Trade Commission, *Annual Report* (1926), 1; Humphrey, "Evidence, Not Suspicion, to Govern," *Nation's Business*, XIII (June 5, 1925), 18.

[33] O. H. Cheney, "The Answer to the New Competition," *Nation's Business*, XV

Progressives, shocked by the rapid and disastrous transformation of the Federal Trade Commission, were vociferous critics of the new policy. The progressive reaction, both spontaneous and sharp, appeared in the remarks and activities of politicians and in leading news publications. One of the first to complain was Commissioner Huston Thompson, whose experience enabled him to anticipate the probable outcome of Humphrey's rules changes. Thompson attacked those changes which curtailed the Commission's publicity power as "wholly dangerous and subversive to the public welfare," paving the way for "a new system of government by secrecy." Thompson was joined by John F. Nugent, the other progressive remaining on the Commission, and in vain the two men warned that the revised rules would convert the Commission into a "star-chamber."[34] Progressives in Congress were equally critical. Senator Thomas J. Walsh charged that Commissioner Humphrey's changes were intended "to limit, if not utterly destroy, the usefulness of the commission." William E. Borah of Idaho claimed that the Commission could no longer fulfill its original purpose, and Senator Norris, who had accurately predicted the probable effect of Humphrey's appointment, also joined in the attack.[35]

Among progressive publications, the sharpest reaction came from *La Follette's Magazine*. In what proved to be his final editorial contribution, the ailing Senator La Follette wrote a bitter epitaph for the Federal Trade Commission. "The last of the Commissions at Washington to be taken over by the forces it was intended to regulate," he said, "the Federal Trade Commission has been packed with its worst enemies, its rules have been perverted, the law under which it was created has been emasculated, and its usefulness has been destroyed." The finishing blow, according to La Follette, had been dealt by the three conservative commissioners, and he concluded that pro-business control of the Commission had done much more to subject the public to business exploitation "than was accomplished by [Secretary of In-

(October, 1927), 16; *ibid.*, XIII (June 5, 1925), 42; *ibid.*, XIV (June 5, 1926), 38; *Proceedings of the Academy of Political Science* (New York), XI (January, 1926), 655, 659, 686; "Making an End to Legalized Persecution of Business," *Magazine of Wall Street* (New York), XXXIX (April 9, 1927), 1064-66.

[34] Huston Thompson, quoted in *Literary Digest*, LXXXV (May 16, 1925), 11; George Soule, "Rules and Men: The Quarrel in the Federal Trade Commission," *New Republic*, XLIII (June 24, 1925), 119; Huston Thompson, "Secrecy Strangles Trade Commission," *La Follette's Magazine*, XVIII (December, 1926), 182.

[35] *Cong. Record*, 70 Cong., 1 Sess., 2899 (February 13, 1928); "Federal Trade Commission," *Outlook*, CXL (June 3, 1925), 176; Norris, "Boring from Within," *Nation*, CXXI (September 16, 1925), 299.

terior Albert B.] Fall when he turned the naval reserves over to the oil monopoly."[36] Similar criticism appeared in other progressive magazines. George Soule, co-editor of the *New Republic*, warned that the new rules refusing to publicize certain types of cases might enable "business malefactors" who enjoyed influence with the Commission to "get away with murder." An editorial in *The Nation* complained that the Commission had lost its real power, and that its probable future course of action would be "to do only what business desires."[37]

Following their initial reaction of surprise and bitter criticism, progressives became even more convinced of the uselessness and actual disservice of the Federal Trade Commission as it was now constituted. Fearful that the Commission might begin to do more harm than good, they attempted in Congress either to restrict its activities or to abolish it altogether. The possibility that a regulatory commission could serve the interests it was designed to control was not new to the progressives of the 1920's. As early as 1892 Richard Olney, who later became President Cleveland's attorney general, had observed that the Interstate Commerce Commission could be "of great use to . . . railroads" by serving as "a sort of protection against hasty and crude legislation hostile to railroad interests."[38] This possibility appeared to have been dramatically verified by the recent policy changes of the Federal Trade Commission. Progressives therefore publicized the process in their mounting attacks upon the Commission.

Within a year following the first rules changes a serious movement, championed by leading reformers and progressive publications, was under way to abolish the Federal Trade Commission. One of the first to take up the proposal was Representative Tom Connally of Texas, who remarked that the Commission was "suffering from pernicious anemia" and charged that it had become "a city of refuge to which the guilty may flee, a sanctuary for those who violate and defy the laws of the United States." The original sponsor of the bill to abolish the Commission was Senator William H. King of Utah. In explaining the need for such action King asserted that the Commission had become "not only a useless appendage, but . . . a real men-

[36] *La Follette's Magazine*, XVII (May, 1925), 65-66.
[37] Soule, "Rules and Men," *New Republic*, XLIII (June 24, 1925), 118-19; *Nation*, CXX (May 20, 1925), 563.
[38] Richard Olney, quoted in Marver H. Bernstein, *Regulating Business by Independent Commission* (Princeton, 1955), 264-65. For another statement of this notion, see Thurman Arnold, *The Folklore of Capitalism* (New Haven, 1937), 212, 215, 217.

ace." King's bill was fated to die in committee, but in the course of the debate other progressives spoke in its behalf. One of these was Senator Norris, who denounced the Commission as "the refuge for monopoly, unfair competition, and unfair business methods." Norris was joined by his Nebraska colleague in the Senate, Robert B. Howell, who described the Commission as "the sanctuary of utility corporations," and Senators Borah of Idaho and Carter Glass of Virginia also supported the proposal for dissolution.[39]

Frustrated in their efforts to abolish the Commission, progressives next attempted to relieve it of any duties which could be more satisfactorily handled by some other government agency. They believed that even if it should remain under the control of pro-business commissioners, its evil influence might still be minimized, and it was this argument that prompted Senators Walsh and Norris to urge in 1928 a new investigation of the utilities industry, to be conducted by a Senate committee rather than by the Federal Trade Commission.

Progressives were especially dissatisfied with the results of an investigation which had recently been made by the Commission at their insistence, and whose findings, published in 1927, had reported no evidence either of illegal activities in the utilities industry or of the existence of the alleged "power trust." In February, 1928, therefore, Walsh introduced a resolution calling for a new investigation by a special committee of five senators. He insisted that the task should not be given to the Commission because, he said, any investigation by that agency would "not be . . . of any value." During a three-day debate on this resolution Walsh was supported by Norris and Senator William J. Harris of Georgia. An alternative motion, designating the Commission as the investigating agency, was attacked by the progressives as a sinister maneuver engineered by big business. Senator Harris, who had served on the Federal Trade Commission from 1915 to 1918, warned that the defeat of Walsh's motion "would be a great victory for the Water Power Trust."[40] Such progressive publications as *La Follette's Magazine* and the *New Republic* also sup-

[39] *Cong. Record*, 69 Cong., 1 Sess., 481 (December 8, 1925); 3630-31 (February 9, 1926); 5966 (March 20, 1926); *ibid.*, 70 Cong., 1 Sess., 2899 (February 13, 1928); Herring, *Public Administration*, 116-17; Robert B. Howell, "Competition Lowers Utility Rates," *La Follette's Magazine*, XVIII (January, 1926), 6.

[40] *Cong. Record*, 70 Cong., 1 Sess., 2891, 2899, 2952, 2958 (February 13, 14, 1928). See also Thompson, *Confessions of the Power Trust*, 5; Lief, *Norris*, 307.

ported Walsh's demand for a Senate investigation,[41] but once again the efforts of a handful of progressives against an essentially conservative majority in Congress were doomed to failure. The Walsh motion was defeated, and the alternative resolution passed easily.[42]

Thus, within a startlingly brief period of time, the Federal Trade Commission experienced a radical transformation of its functions as well as its friends and foes. As a result of the important policy changes promoted by Commissioner Humphrey, businessmen abruptly halted their campaign against the Commission and became its loyal supporters. Progressives, on the other hand, reacted bitterly against the change and now attacked the Commission with the same scorn that they had directed against the other conservative institutions of the period. It was ironic that this agency, which had been one of the most important and auspicious products of the progressive program, should have been transformed after 1925 into a pro-business institution which threatened not only to weaken but even to subvert the entire regulatory process. Under these circumstances, it is not surprising that the progressive estrangement from the Federal Trade Commission was bitter, almost vengeful. Disillusioned and disaffected, liberals experienced the frustrations of a thoroughly hostile political environment from 1925 until changing economic conditions made possible their resurgence after 1929.

[41] See, for example, "First Blood in the Power War," *New Republic*, LIV (February 29, 1928), 56; and "The Issue of Electric Power," *La Follette's Magazine*, XX (March, 1928), 34.

[42] *Cong. Record*, 70 Cong., 1 Sess., 3028 (February 15, 1928).

The Great Freight Rate Fight

By Sam Hall Flint

At the stroke of midnight Thursday [May 29, 1952] *the Southland emerged from a phase of industrial bondage to the North dating back to the War Between the States. . . . The bondage, under which Dixie industry has suffered for nearly 90 years, was freight rate discrimination against Southern shippers. Under provisions of an Interstate Commerce Commission order . . . rates ending that discrimination, became effective as of 12:01 a.m. Friday.*

That evening in an Atlanta home Albert Riley, chief capitol reporter for the *Atlanta Constitution*, read from his story that would run on page one the next morning. He continued: "Walter R. McDonald, Georgia Public Service Commissioner, who led a 15 year Southern struggle to end this discrimination, has estimated the new rates will save Dixie shippers $28,000,000 a year."

Seated in the center of the semicircle of listeners, his unseeing eyes glued on Riley, Walter McDonald held in his lap Uniform Classification Number 1, the result of many years' effort and the final cog in the complex machinery to eliminate discrimination. The classification and the new rates became effective on "Yankee" Memorial Day. To symbolize the bringing together of North and South rate structures and to dramatize the good relations which prevailed among former adversaries, the classification book was designed with a gray cover imprinted in blue.

Seated on either side of McDonald were Joseph G. Kerr, chairman, and R. E. Boyle, vice-chairman, of the Southern Freight Association which represented all the railroads in the South. Stalwart member G. Arthur Austin and Chairman of the Board John W. Cooper were there to celebrate the major role that the Atlanta Freight Bureau had played from the very beginning of the struggle. Not present, but often mentioned that evening, was the late Eugene L. Hart, for twenty years traffic manager of the Atlanta Freight Bureau and perhaps the foremost transportation rate expert in the nation. He had walked with Walter McDonald every step except this final victorious one.

Riley concluded his account: "But for the first time since Appomatox the South is now on an equal basis with the North in rate schedules, and uniform class rates are the same everywhere in the nation, east of the Rockies, on a pound-for-pound and mile-for-mile basis."[1]

Truly, it was a great moment. Now, thirty-two years later, most of the principals in this siege on economic discrimination which began fifty years ago are no longer here. Memories of those remaining are fuzzy. Records are scattered and incomplete.

Consequently, there are vast misunderstandings about the origin and nature of the discrimination, its effect on the South's economy, how the fight was really won, and what has happened since victory was signaled at midnight, May 30, 1952.

Perhaps it is most surprising that confusion persists about how the discrimination worked to the disadvantage of Southerners. Ask today's well-informed person how the old freight-rate system damaged the South, and the most likely answer is: "The rates were higher in one direction than the other." But generally this was not true, and, where true, it was largely irrelevant to the problem. The next most-harbored opinion is that rates in the South were higher than in the North. This was true, but it was only part of the cause of the economic mischief.

The real damage was inflicted in three ways. First, over a long period of time, and with general acceptance of southern producers, low rates were established from South to North on raw and semi-finished materials, while higher, often prohibitive, rates were maintained on products manufactured from those materials. Second, a three-part rate scheme (applying mostly to manufactured articles) had a diabolical effect on the southern manufacturer's ability to compete either in northern markets or in his own southern backyard. Third, as the railroads operating in the South became aware that often their interests would be best served by establishing lower northbound rates to make Southern manufacturers competitive, they found themselves unable to do so. Northern rails insisted on maintaining rates from the South higher than for equal distances in the North.[2]

There are many illustrations of how these three discriminatory patterns operated. For example, in 1939 there were but sixteen commodity groups on which the rate level in southern territory was lower than in the North. These accounted for one-third of the South's rail tonnage and 10 percent of the North's. But what were the commodities? Sand and gravel, lumber, pulpwood, phosphate rock, fertilizer, and iron ore accounted for 75 percent. Not one of the sixteen groups included a genuine manufactured article. These lower rates encouraged export of raw materials from the deep South to border points and beyond to northern manufacturing centers.[3]

More damaging to Dixie were the favorable South-to-North rates on raw materials contrasted with the highly prejudicial rates on the manufactured products made from those same materials. For instance, rates on bales of cotton going from South to North were about the same as rates within the North, but on unfinished cotton fabrics, bleached cotton fabrics, and oil cloth, the South-to-North rates were 10, 11, and 54 percent higher, respectively. For crude cottonseed oil the South-to-North charge was only 7 percent higher than rates in the North, but for salad oil the rate was 24 percent higher, and for oleomargarine it was 35 percent more. Rates on ceramic clay transported from South to North were actually 5 percent *lower* than within the North, but they were 37 and 55 percent *higher* on the plumbers' goods and chinaware made from such clay.

Pig iron, for another example, could be shipped from Alabama, Georgia, or Tennessee to northern states at rates 10 percent below what northern steel mills paid to ship this primary product within their own territory. But if the pig iron were converted into steel plates, the southern manufacturer was at a 27 percent disadvantage, and if it were further fabricated into hand tools, there was a 51 percent rate disadvantage.[4]

Thus the South through such artificial means was maintained as an extractive and agricultural economy.

The second discriminatory rate scheme—the class rate colossus that was not subdued until 1952—was even more widespread and damaging in its effect. Mile for mile, the basic class rates between points in the South were much higher than within the North. Several studies concluded that the southern class rates were, on the average, 39 percent higher than northern rates (table 1).[5]

But even this major handicap was not the most serious problem.

TABLE 1

Basic Class Rates—1945
(In cents per 100 pounds)

	100 Miles	300 Miles	600 Miles	1,000 Miles
Northern Point to Northern Point	62	96	135	182
Southern Point to Southern Point	84	134	189	249
Percent Southern Rate Higher	35%	40%	40%	37%

Source: 262 I.C.C. 447, 745 (1945)

When deciding how to make rates between the North and South, the ICC came up with the ingenious plan of "laminating the scales." Essentially, this meant that for a haul in either direction between North and South the cost would be lower than for the same distance within the South, but higher than for the same distance within the North (the differences being generally dependent upon the distance traveled in each territory).[6]

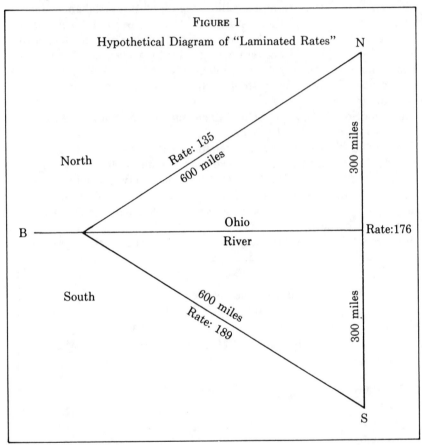

FIGURE 1

Hypothetical Diagram of "Laminated Rates"

Figure 1 illustrates the tri-dimensional discrimination resulting from the so-called lamination of the disparate rate levels. A hypothetical example has been chosen so that the interterritorial movement is equally divided between northern and southern mileage. A southern manufacturer at point S (South) trying to reach the northern market at point N (North) would have had to pay a rate 30 percent higher than his equidistant competitor at point B (Border). If S tried to compete in the market at border point B, shipping entirely at the southern rate level, he would pay fully 40 percent more than a manufacturer at N shipping the same distance. And this is not all. The point N shipper could also have reached a market at southern point S paying a rate about 7 percent lower than a competitor at point B or anywhere else in the South 600 miles away.

A frequently used illustration, which was not hypothetical, involved Atlanta and New York competing in the Chicago market. On a 40,000-pound shipment rated class 35 (a rating applying to a wide range of manufactured goods) Atlanta's shipper paid $296 for the 731-mile haul. New York, 896 miles away, paid only $232. Had Atlanta been permitted to ship at the northern rate level, it would have had not a $64 handicap but instead a $24 advantage.[7]

Throughout this discussion the terms "class rates" and "commodity rates" will recur, and differentiation may often be elusive. Class rates constitute a general system which provides a rate from any origin to any destination on any article which conceivably might be shipped. All articles are "classified" and assigned a percentage of first class. First-class rates are established for various mileage blocks. So within each of the different territories (southern, northern, western, and southwestern) the class rates for any given distance would be the same for all articles bearing the same ratings, without regard for origin, destination, or direction of movement.

Commodity rates, which moved the preponderance of the tonnage, were designed to meet special situations, often involving competition between producing points, ports, and raw materials having the same end uses, and between transportation companies. Unlike class rates, they were not always the same for like distances, but, while the pattern of commodity rates departed from the rigid class rate structure, their level was generally made in relation to the class rates of the territory in which they applied. So when the ICC dealt with South-to-North commodity rates on manufactured articles, it would cite differences in "transportation conditions" and generally prescribe rates higher than those paid by northern manufacturers for shipping the same products the same distances.[8]

Moreover, as was the case with the interterritorial laminated class rate structure, ICC-prescribed commodity rates usually inflicted a double penalty on the southern manufacturer. When the rates were made the same in both directions, northern-produced commodities would move into the South at rates lower, distance considered, then the southern manufacturer was charged.[9]

The railroads in the South frequently tried earnestly to help the manufacturers on their lines reach northern markets, but often they were frustrated when their northern connections vetoed the proposed rate reductions.

Partial view of Southern Railway's Inman transfer and classification yard, Marietta Road. This view looking southwest shows the residential area on the hills beyond the tracks, once known as Rockdale Park. Inman Yard has grown, and Rockdale Park is now the site of a housing project known as Perry Homes. (A.H.S.)

As suggested in the lead paragraph of Albert Riley's front-page story, there has been a popular belief that transportation discrimination against the South was another lingering result of the North's vindictiveness following the War Between the States. This colorful theory, however, is not well supported by facts. The ICC did not come along until twenty-two years after Appomatox, and it was more than forty years later before the disparate and hurtful rate systems were formally ordered into effect. But this is not to say the Civil War was unrelated to twentieth-century freight discrimination. The post-war railroads of the South, faced with huge rebuilding costs and little traffic, relied on higher rates to pay their bills and assuage their absentee owners. Several levels and systems of rates evolved in different parts of the South, and the resultant intramural discrimination became the major concern of southern manufacturers. Thus the ICC's 1926-27 decision which brought near-uniformity to intra-South rates and which "rationalized" charges on freight moving between the South and North was generally accepted as desirable progress.[10]

History has been fairly comfortable with describing the freight rate controversy as a "fifteen-year" or "two-decade" fight, but accounts tend to be silent on the details of when, where, and how there first developed the impetus to free the South of its economic shackles.

The *where* is very likely Warm Springs, Georgia, and the *when* is shortly after Franklin D. Roosevelt became president in 1933. FDR spent considerable time in Georgia and was intensely aware of and concerned about the economic plight of his adopted state and the remainder of the South. In a 1938 presentation he explained to the whole nation some of the policies and programs he had already adopted and undertaken: "It is my conviction that the South presents now the nation's Number One economic problem — the nation's problem — not merely the South's. For we have an economic imbalance that can and must be righted, for the sake of the South and of the nation."[11]

Well before he made that statement, Roosevelt, perceiving the absence of cohesive effort by southern leaders to solve the region's problems, began urging southern governors to form an association or conference. In 1934, eight states formed the Southeastern Governors' Conference, primarily to provide a united front to combat "freight rate discrimination against the South." In 1939, the membership expanded and the name was changed to the Southern Governors' Conference.[12] After consultation with Southern manufacturers and others, a subcommittee consisting of Governors Bibb Graves of Alabama, Olin D. Johnston of South Carolina, and Eurith Dickson Rivers of Georgia was authorized to proceed with litigation before the Interstate Commerce Commission.

Although strong sentiment — voiced most loudly by the Georgians, Governor Rivers and Walter McDonald — was expressed for a "broad, frontal attack," pragmatism prevailed. It was necessary to muster not only financial assistance but also knowledgeable commercial testimony to convince the ICC that the rates it had sanctioned were inflicting tangible harm on real people.

Gene Hart promptly identified a list of southern manufactured products most severely handicapped by the rate structure. Boots and shoes, canned goods, cordage, drugs and medicines, electrical supplies, fire hydrants, metal furniture, pipe fittings and other plumbers' goods, soapstone and talc, stoves and stone were all in the original complaint. For various reasons, some were dropped, but it was not difficult to demonstrate the oppressive rate handicap imposed upon southern producers of the remaining commodities.[13]

Two examples, stoves and stone, illustrate the problem. Chattanooga, Tennessee, and Erie, Pennsylvania, are equidistant from Cincinnati, yet a Chattanooga stove manufacturer was at a 43 percent disadvantage. Similarly, a Birmingham, Alabama, stove works, the same distance from

Baltimore as Joliet, Illinois, paid rates 33 percent higher than its Joliet competitor.

Despite superior qualities, granite and marble quarried in Elberton, Tate, and other North Georgia locations had serious problems competing with Vermont quarries. To thirty central state destinations the average distance from Elberton was lower by more than a hundred miles, but the average Elberton rate was 12 to 17 percent higher.[14] A stream of witnesses testified how, in those depression times, their businesses and the jobs they provided were jeopardized by inequitable rates. A producer of granite monuments in Elberton tried to compete in Chicago with a Barre, Vermont, producer 130 miles further distant, but he had to overcome a rate penalty of almost 7 percent of his selling price. Further east at Detroit nearly 10 percent of the sales price would be eroded by the freight penalty. An even worse plight was described by a witness for the Georgia Marble Company which began encountering freight disadvantages vis-a-vis Vermont before it even got out of the South. The testimony showed that the line of equality was in the Carolinas. North of there Vermont always had an advantage.

And so it went, as, for the first time, the ICC had before it a mosaic depiction of the effect its actions and inaction had on the economy of an entire region. This time, the pieces making up the picture were not just sterile numbers. The commission heard stories of crippled southern business, of underpaid and unemployed southern workers, and of railroads in the South deprived of business by refusal of northern lines to join in rate reductions.

Governor Rivers eloquently testified of the South's determination to achieve equality of economic opportunity:

> I have reached the conclusion that economically as well as politically, this country should be regarded as one nation, and that our railroad systems should serve national rather than territorial interests. . . . a just rate relationship which will enable the South to ship her goods to Official territory in competition with those in Official territory will permit a rapid and large development of Southern industry; will add to the demand for labor, thus giving employment to labor that could not find employment if the present rate system continues. . . . The problem will be better solved by permitting a parity of rates from any one point in the country to any other point in the country on the same commodity.

Earlier Alabama's Governor Graves had also spoken in favor of "parity of rates." He demanded that rates be "made on the same level, distance considered." In conclusion Graves said, "In this case we present to the Commission the question of the right of all people in these States to have a full and fair opportunity to participate in the commerce of the entire nation."[15]

The governors enunciated two themes to which, during the long years ahead, the South would carefully adhere. First, the region sought only parity—not an advantage nor erasure of its distance handicap. Second, benefits sought from rate equalization were not just sectional but indeed national.

Despite the preponderance of evidence and the right of their cause, the southern complainants faced powerful opposition from northern manufacturers, railroads, and governors. Two entrenched dogmas were even more formidable. First, for twenty years the ICC in twenty different cases had soberly found that "transportation conditions" in the North were more favorable than in the South, and, therefore, lower northern rates were justified. Somehow this vague term had eluded demands for definition, but clearly it implied cost justification. The South responded to the challenge with a persuasive cost analysis that showed that rail costs in the South were actually much lower than in New England and no higher than those in other parts of the North.[16]

The second tenet to be dislodged was even more anomalous. With straight-faced seriousness the North argued that the South had many advantages in climate, water, natural resources, lower labor rates, and lower taxes. So, the argument went, it was like a handicapped horse race in which the best horses must carry the most weight or like a golf tournament in which the par-shooters give strokes to duffers. It was only right, they said, that the South should be similarly handicapped with higher freight rates.[17]

With the two sections pitted state versus state and manufacturer versus manufacturer, and with the northern railroads defending their preferential rates, the position of the southern rail lines became critical. Joe Kerr, chairman of the Southern Freight Association, spoke for all the southern lines when he argued that the southern shippers "have made a showing which justifies and requires the establishment of rates from the South to Official Territory [which are] either the same or approximately the same as the level within Official Territory." He endorsed the national interest theme of the southern governors, saying, "We believe that the making of competitive rates from the South to Official Territory on the basis which we advocate is not only in the interest of Southern railroads and Southern shippers, but is likewise in the interest of the great mass of consumers in Northern territory and, therefore, in the general public interest."[18]

On November 22, 1939, the ICC by a five-to-four decision ruled in favor of the South on all fundamental points. At the time, some southerners expressed disappointment at the relatively small immediate financial benefit of rail rate equality on a limited number of articles, many of which by then were being hauled by trucks. But to those who had never let the big picture fade, the precedents set were priceless.

On the issue of "transportation conditions" the ICC said, "the cost of transporting the articles . . . from producing points in the South into the North, compared with that of transporting like articles within the North, does not justify . . . higher levels of rates than . . . within the North."

On the issue of handicapping the South because of its so-called natural advantages, the ICC ruled, "it is not our province so to prescribe rates as to enable shippers in any section to neutralize, through differences in transportation charges, higher production costs or other economic or natural disadvantages."[19]

Now it was time for the "broad frontal attack." Already in 1939 the ICC had initiated an enormous investigation of all classifications and class rates applying east of the Rocky Mountains.[20] By any measurement this was to be a magnum leap in scope, area, economics, and time from the just-completed Governors' Case. This study involved ten thousand commodities instead of nine and covered the entire nation except for the Mountain-Pacific states. It would be six years before an initial decision in this Class Rate Case, and the final victory dinner was twelve and a half years away. Yet it is reasonable to treat this case briefly, not because it was not important, not because it was not a truly arduous struggle, but because the South's victory was foreordained by the commodity case decision and by subtle changes in transport economics and regulatory philosophy which were just becoming apparent.

Aside from scope and importance, the Class Rate Case placed new demands on the governors and others in the South determined to see the equalization fight through. This time the railroads of the South would be tenacious opponents rather than allies. The northern states, having found that they could lose their cherished rate advantage, mustered the strength of their governors' conferences and state and quasi-public agencies to fight with intensified fury. At the same time, within the South there emerged considerable opposition from interests oriented to extractive and heavy manufacturing industries. These shippers and associations, mostly in Alabama and Tennessee, ostensibly feared that their already-favorable rates might be increased to compensate for reductions in the general level of Southern rates might be increased to compensate for reductions in the general level of Southern rates.[21] However, there is reasonable suspicion they were also heavily influenced by their mostly northern owners.[22]

On the positive side, the South would no longer have the heavy burden of proving the relative cost of railroad service. The staff of the ICC would assume this responsibility. In addition, this time the South was joined by the western and southwestern states which suffered from even more discriminatory rates. Encouraged by the South's initial victory, they became enthusiastic crusaders for equality.

View from Peters Street bridge. Nelson Street bridge, center. Terminal Station and
Atlanta Gas Light Company storage tanks, rear. Madison Avenue (Spring Street)
freight facility of Southern Railway, foreground. (A.H.S.)

Off and on for five years the ICC conducted hearings in the most
mammoth rate investigation it had ever undertaken. Hundreds of weary
witnesses punished by the rigors of wartime travel testified for days on
end presenting thousands of pages of charts, statistics and arguments.
Two major surprises produced by the evidence both worked to the
South's advantage. It had long been contended that the South's class
rate handicap was partially offset by classification ratings which were,
on the average, lower. A careful study irrefutably showed that the opposite was true; the southern rate handicap was, in fact, compounded by
relatively *higher* classifications.[23]

The other revelation was even more compelling. The first truly scientific cost-finding effort completely blasted the age-old assumptions of
more favorable "transportation conditions" in the North. Research
showed that railroad costs in the South were actually consistently
lower.[24]

It now seemed to the Southerners who had long toiled in this vine-
yard that victory was inevitable. The question was "when." Indeed, the

opposition forces must have seen it the same way because their efforts were more and more concentrated on obstruction and delay. They asked for postponements at every turn and filed a barrage of petitions asking the ICC to drop the entire investigation because it diverted attention from the war effort.[25] But, however slowly, the mills did grind. In May 1945 the ICC came forth with its order.

All classifications of freight in the United States were to be uniform. There would be one scale of class rates applying between all points east of the Rocky Mountains. Realizing that much time would be required to develop the new classification, the ICC ordered prompt interim relief for the South and West by reducing their rates 10 percent and increasing the northern rates the same amount. Between the several territories the rates were also reduced 10 percent.[26]

But the northern opposition was not finished. Joined by the western railroads, they secured a restraining order from the District Court of the United States for the Northern District of New York. It was not until a year later that the court ruled against them.[27] They appealed to the United States Supreme Court, and again a year passed. Finally, on May 12, 1947, the ICC decision was upheld, and on August 22 the temporary relief became effective.[28]

It had been ten years since the South had begun its fight for equality, and five more years lay ahead before complete victory would be claimed. Because the freight rate fight was a popular cause throughout the South, it was quickly espoused by literally hundreds of people—mostly those involved in or oriented to politics.

It was a huge project which produced enormous economic benefit, so there is ample credit to share among the many who served as strategists, technicians, persuaders, toilers, and leaders. A few names stand out as those having the greatest impact. Governors Graves, Rivers, and Johnston were foremost in the 1937 beginning, and a long line of governors thereafter kept the fight alive. Gordon Browning of Tennessee had the unique experience of contributing at the beginning and end. Governor in 1937, he completed his terms and years later again was elected. He was chairman of the Southern Governors' Conference when the culmination came in 1952. Mentioning others would serve only to accent the omissions. But in the political arena there is one more who must be recognized. Georgia's fifth district congressman, Robert B. Ramspeck, was largely responsible for a significant change in the law, without which the ICC might have justified ruling against the South. The Ramspeck Resolution, later incorporated in the Transportation Act of 1940, outlawed discrimination against a "region" as well as against individual transportation users.[29]

Playing a dual role was J. Haden Alldredge of Alabama, who, as chief economist for the Tennessee Valley Authority, wrote a scholarly but lucid report entitled *The Interterritorial Freight Problem of the United States*. The report was issued in 1937, almost concurrent with the governors' first attack on the rate structure.[30] Subsequently, President Roosevelt appointed Alldredge to be a member of the ICC, where he served with great distinction. Without impugning his judicial outlook, it is fair to say he served as the conscience of the ICC during its consideration of the class rate investigation and as a counter-balance to certain northern commissioners intent upon preserving the advantages of their homeland.

The value of Dr. Ford Edwards's breakthrough in rail cost-finding far transcends the South-North fight, but it was likely the one most critical evidentiary element in the outcome of the Class Rate Case. The South benefited from the counsel and advocacy of highly talented attorneys, principal among them Edgar Watkins of Atlanta and J. Van Norman of Louisville, Kentucky.

Though respected adversaries, the railroads of the South also deserve credit. When the 1945 decision went against them, the southern carriers, resisting great pressure from railroads and shippers outside the South to join in court action, announced that, while not agreeing with the ICC decision, they would do everything possible to make it work.[31] And make it work they did. Joe Kerr and Jack Boyle led, cajoled, and finally drove all of the nation's other railroads into completion of the huge task of developing the uniform classification.

Finally, the focus should be on two who clearly merit distinctive recognition. During the long ICC hearings Gene Hart, traffic manager of the Atlanta Freight Bureau, and Walter McDonald, Georgia Public Service Commission chairman, were often described as the "Gold Dust Twins" because they were inseparable in their strategy and prosecution of the South's cause as well as in their travel to and from the seemingly interminable meetings. Not only to Gene Hart, the transport expert *non pareil* but to the Atlanta Freight Bureau must go much credit. Most large cities had counterparts to the Atlanta Freight Bureau, but generally they were absorbed in mundane activities and were provincial in their outlook. Georgia and the South have been benefited by a bureau which, to this day, not only has the big picture in mind, but also is willing to invest in improving it. (The name of the Atlanta Freight Bureau was changed to Georgia Freight Bureau in 1976 to symbolize its expanded service to firms outside Atlanta. Currently it has 450 members in all parts of Georgia.)

The accomplishments of Walter McDonald would have been extraordinary for anyone, but they are especially impressive for a person who was totally blind. He served as a member of the Georgia Public Service Commission for three decades. Throughout the freight rate campaign he was director of the freight rate section of the Southern

Walter McDonald
(Photograph courtesy of
Sam Hall Flint)

Governors' Conference and was president of the organization of southern regulatory commissions, which was also involved in the fight. But, much more, he was the strategist, organizer, fund raiser, spokesman, and motivator. When others faltered, he shouldered more. He never compromised the objective. His was the victory.

The downplaying of one name often associated with the South's freight rate fight requires some explanation. Ellis Gibbs Arnall, governor of Georgia, 1943-47, conceived and initiated in 1944 a conspiracy case against the railroads which is often described in the press as the "Georgia Freight Rate Case."

First, what the Georgia case was *not*. It was not a freight rate case. The report of the Supreme Court's special master states: "The amended complaint, on which the present suit is based, sought no relief against rates as such. It was directed solely against the practices and set-up of the defendants' rate associations."

Had Georgia won the case, not a single freight rate would have been changed, but Georgia did not win. It was *not* a victory. The report of the special master recommended against Georgia on every issue the suit raised, and on November 27, 1950, the Supreme Court dismissed the suit.[32]

It was *not* an integral part of the South's successful effort to end rate discrimination. All the southern states, including Georgia, were banded together in the long fights before the ICC. No southern state joined Georgia in the approach through the court.[33]

Second, what the Georgia case *was*. It was a great personal accomplishment for Governor Arnall, who himself brilliantly argued the case and won a five-to-four decision by the Supreme Court to accept original jurisdiction and to permit the state to sue on behalf of its citizens. The suit served also to focus attention on the freight rate issue and on Georgia after the ICC administrative battles were largely over.

Third, what the Georgia case *might* have been. There are those who, while conceding the suit by Governor Arnall did not directly achieve anything, insist its pendency goaded the ICC to a faster and favorable decision.[34] The sequence of significant dates refutes this contention. The key precedent-setting decision in the Governors' Commodity Rate Case came in 1939. In the same year the ICC began the class rate investigation. It was decided in 1945, before any evidence was taken in the Georgia case.[35] Clearly, Governor Arnall's tactics did result in enactment, over a presidential veto, of the Reed-Bullwinkle bill, providing the railroads with anti-trust immunity for the very conspiratorial behavior he alleged.[36] When this story began in the mid-1930s, the marks of economic subjugation lay heavy on the South. One need not resort to statistics, but only recall the dusty roads, unpainted homes, barefoot children, primitive schoolhouses, and fields of cotton stubble and broomsedge. Paved streets, inside plumbing, telephones, electric appliances, parks and playgrounds, and even jobs, were commonplace in the industrial North but were luxuries in much of the South. As late as 1940, more than one-third of the South's gainfully employed worked in the extractive industries—removing natural resources largely for processing and consumption in the North. And in every southern state per capita income was lower than the national average.[37]

Virtually every economic condition which once plagued the South has been reversed. "Transportation conditions" in the North so deteriorated that a huge segment of its rail system bankrupted and is just now recovering under the skilled management of a former Southern Railway executive. Other northern lines have merged with the major railroads of the South. And most of the very rates which once handicapped southern industry are now actually lower within and from the South than in the North.

Today there is little quarrel with the proposition that discriminatory freight rates once retarded the economic development of the South. But there is little agreement about the extent to which the South has benefited from removal of the discrimination. This discussion makes no attempt to deal broadly with the South's overall economy. It can be demonstrated statistically that since the 1930s the South has indeed risen in value added by manufacture, plant investments, employees and wages, and all the generally accepted measurements of economic activity.

No longer the despised "Nation's Number One Economic Problem," the southern states are now part of the envied and not entirely loved "Sunbelt." Rep. Robert W. Edgar (D.-Pa. 7th) declared, "Now the North Needs Federal Help." He described the economic plight of the South in the thirties and then stated: "Fifty years later the South has surpassed the North in virtually every indicator of economic growth. But this economic miracle owes a debt to one of the Depression's greatest ironies; that a Northern President, only 70 years after the Civil War split the regions apart, chose to lift the South from poverty."[38]

The improvements in the South's relative position stem from many changes. The demography of the region has been altered by, first, outward and then inward migration; government spending programs have had a major effect; and improved economic opportunity for blacks constitutes a major factor. So where do freight rates enter the picture? Skeptics might credit the progress to the South's natural advantages of climate, water, forest, and other resources, and to not-so-natural advantages such as "good business climate" and lower taxes. But all these advantages have always been there. Their value relative to the major and tangible disadvantage of transportation cost was simply inadequate to attract to the South any industry or investment except that directly dependent on its extractive resources. The discriminatory rate structure acted as a virtually insurmountable barrier to the South's economic development and to the opportunity of its people to share fairly in the nation's wealth. The triumphs of thirty years ago removed the barrier, and, once permitted to flex the muscles of its natural and human strengths, the South began to flourish.

Children will continue to be most impressed by "The Great Locomotive Chase"; they love the story of how Georgians thwarted the daring try of Andrews' Raiders to destroy the Western & Atlantic Railway, "The Lifeline of the Confederacy." But someday they should be told of another North-South railroad battle, and that one of Atlanta's and the Southland's most important and lasting victories was in the great freight rate fight.

Notes

An attorney, Mr. Flint represented the Southern Governors' Conference in the freight rate controversy during the late 1940s and early 1950s. He resides on St. Simons Island and is retired from the Quaker Oats Company. He is a member of the board of directors of Conrail and is a former transportation director of the Georgia Public Service Commission.

1. *Atlanta Constitution*, May 30, 1952.

2. William H. Joubert, *Southern Freight Rates in Transition* (Gainesville: University of Florida Press, 1949), 355-57, 361-62, 333-34.

3. ICC Dockets 28300 and 28310. Exhibit No. 164 (Witness Charles E. Bell) *Statement of Commodities on which Rate Level in Southern Region is Lower than in Eastern District, 1939.* (1941)

4. Henry B. Kline, *Freight Rates—The Interregional Tariff Issue.* Papers of the Institute of Re-

search and Training in the Social Sciences, Vanderbilt University, Number Three (April 1942).

5. J. H. Alldredge. *The Interterritorial Freight Rate Problem of the United States*, 75th Congress, 1st Session (1937), House Document No. 264. Also, *State of Alabama et al. v. New York Central Railroad Company et al.*, 235 ICC 255, 273.

6. Joubert, *Southern Freight Rates*, 298-309. Also 128 ICC 567.

7. 235 ICC 255. Calculated, and based in part, on table of distances and rates at p. 272.

8. *Blue Ridge Glass Corporation v. Akron, Barberton Belt Railroad Co.*, 201 ICC 421 (1934).

9. Joubert, *Southern Freight Rates*, 363.

10. Ibid., 16-24, 310-11.

11. Roosevelt's frequently cited quotation appeared in the National Emergency Council's *Report on the Economic Conditions of the South* (Washington, D.C.: Government Printing Office, 1938), 1.

12. *Newsletter, Southern Governors' Association*, Vol. 1, No. 2 (February 1981).

13. ICC Docket 27746, *Brief and Argument for Complainants*.

14. *State of Alabama v. New York Central R. Co.* 235 ICC 255, table A, p. 279. (1939)

15. ICC Docket 27746, *Brief and Argument for Complainants*.

16. ICC Docket 27746, II, 47; I, 8. (Lists twenty cases decided between 1916 and 1936.)

17. ICC Docket No. 27746, *Brief on Behalf of New England Governors' Freight Rate Committee*.

18. ICC Docket No. 27746, *Brief for Southern Railroads*.

19. *State of Alabama et al. v. New York Central Railroad Co. et al.*, 235 ICC 255 (1939), 326, 321.

20. ICC Dockets Nos. 28300 and 28310, *Class Rate Investigation, 1939*.

21. Ibid., *Testimony of C.E. Widell*, Witness for Southern States Industrial Council. November 1942.

22. Walter R. McDonald, *Southern Territorial Freight Rates* (Atlanta, Georgia: 1942 Southern Governors' Conference), 4.

23. *Class Rate Investigation, 1939*, 262 ICC 447, 494-96 (1945).

24. Joubert, *Southern Freight Rates*, 352-55.

25. ICC Dockets 28300 and 28310, *Petitions of National Industrial Traffic League (June 9, 1942); Evaporated Milk Association (July 16, 1942); Anheuser Busch, Inc. (September 21, 1942), inter alia, for Indefinite Postponement of Hearings and Consideration of Termination of Proceedings.*

26. *Class Rate Investigation, 1939* 262 ICC 447 (1945), 702.

27. *State of New York et al. v. United States Atchison, T. & S.F. Ry. Co. et al. v. Same*, 65 F. Supp. 856 (May 9, 1946).

28. *New York v. United States*, 331 U.S. 284 (1947). The "first" shipment under the new rates was a metal drum of dressed Georgia poultry, which Walter McDonald sent at 12:01 a.m., May 30, 1952, to Governor Browning, routed over the state-owned W&A Railway (then operated by the NC&StL), *Atlanta Constitution*, May 30, 1952.

29. Public Law No. 785, 76th Congress, 3rd Sess. (1940).

30. Alldredge, *The Interterritorial Freight Rate Problem*.

31. Press release "Phoned Associated Press, June 15, 1945, 5:40 p.m."

32. Report of Special Master Lloyd K. Garrison, 9, 206. Received by Supreme Court, June 5, 1950, 339 U.S. 975. Georgia's standing to file bill of complaint was established in *Georgia v. Pennsylvania R.R. Co. et al.*, 324 U.S. 439 (1945). The final decision was 340 U.S. 889 (1950).

33. The state of Alabama did file motion to intervene on February 10, 1947, but on May 12, 1947, the motion was denied.

34. This seems to be the position taken by Arnall in his 1946 book, *The Shore Dimly Seen* (Philadelphia: J.B. Lippincott, 1946). See Editor's Note below.

35. 235 ICC 255 (1939) and 262 ICC 447 (1945).

36. June 17, 1948, 62 Stat. 472. For sources that overstate the role of Governor Arnall see James F. Cook, *Governors of Georgia* (Huntsville, Ala.: Strode Publishers, Inc., 1979), 257; Zell Miller, *Great Georgians* (Franklin Springs, Ga.: Advocate Press, 1983), 22; Celestine Sibley, "Southern as a Cotton Patch," *Atlanta Weekly*, October 30, 1983; and *Atlanta Constitution*, January 5, 1981, 1.

37. ICC Docket 28300, W.H.S. Stevens, *A Statistical Summary of Selected Data on the Economic Development of the U.S. by Freight Rate Territories* (1941).

38. *Philadelphia Inquirer*, December 27, 1981.

Editor's Note: Governor Arnall's version of his role does not differ from Mr. Flint's in fact, but it does in emphasis. The former governor explained his view in "The South's Readmission to the Union," a Franklin Forum Lecture to the Atlanta Historical Society on February 2, 1982 (typescript provided to the Society by Governor Arnall). Arnall stressed his role as a publicist for the southern position speaking to various groups in the North and West. The refusal of other states to join Georgia's conspiracy case was called a "defeatist attitude." He declared that "long years of waiting for Interstate Commerce Commission action had become a habit." Arnall clarified, as did Mr. Flint, "this was not a freight rate case; . . . we were not asking the Supreme Court to consider rates." The Supreme Court's acceptance of jurisdiction in the case shocked the railroads. The opinion of Justice William O. Douglas did not change any rates, but it accepted Georgia's contention that discriminatory rates were harmful. Douglas wrote: "They may stifle, impede or cripple old industries and prevent the establishment of new ones. They may arrest the development of a state or put it at a decided disadvantage in competitive markets." After quoting Douglas, Governor Arnall made his point that the Georgia suit stimulated rate action. "About this time, the Interstate Commerce Commission, like Rip Van Winkle, began to bestir itself. . . . A few weeks later, on May 15, 1945, out came the commission's decision in the freight rate case that had been before the deliberate body since before the beginning of the Second World War. . . . The Interstate Commerce Commission agreed with nearly everything the advocates of equal freight rates for the South and West had been contending." A. G. Mezrik and Stephens Mitchell were quoted in praise of Arnall's efforts.

Mr. Flint's intentions are not so much to denigrate the efforts of Governor Arnall as to highlight the critical role played by the Atlanta Freight Rate Bureau. In fact, he regards the Arnall administration as "one of the most beneficial Georgia has ever had." An article about Walter McDonald in the *Atlanta Journal-Constitution*, February 3, 1963 (supplied to the editor by Mr. Flint), gives a balanced view:

"During the freight rate fight, [Walter McDonald] came at one point into disagreement with then-Governor Ellis Arnall, when the governor proposed suing transportation facilities in the courts. Mr. McDonald demurred because he held the case was a matter of statute law, to be approached via the Interstate Commerce Commission. He was right. So was Gov. Arnall, for Arnall appreciated the publicity value of a governor suing in the courts."

Bradley R. Rice

The Trade Association Movement in Cotton Textiles, 1900-1935[1]

Louis Galambos

I

Despite the advances made in business and economic history during recent years, scholars have yet to produce an adequate historical appraisal of the trade association movement of the twentieth century. In the 1920's and 1930's the associations attracted considerable academic interest, but the resulting books and articles were, for the most part, narrow in scope; they suffered from a lack of perspective and a paucity of reliable information about a contemporary subject.[2] In subsequent years economists and economic historians have marched off to conquer new fields—of late, the field of economic growth—and little has been done to improve our understanding of the trade organization. Although the associations have played an important role in the evolution of our twentieth-century business system, they have become a sort of white whale in our economic past. Like Moby Dick, the associations are frequently seen, often mentioned, repeatedly attacked, but never really captured—at least not by the historian.[3]

The following article approaches this elusive quarry by means of a case study of the regional and national associations in a major manufacturing industry, cotton textiles, during the years between 1900 and 1935. Hopefully, an examination of the manner in which associations have evolved in this industry will enable us to understand more fully: 1) the origins of the modern trade association movement; 2) the nature and functions of the institutions it created; and 3) the direct and some of the indirect effects that these institutions have had on America's capitalistic system.

II

Around the turn of the century when the association movement began in cotton textiles, management was already supporting a fairly elaborate structure of local, state and regional associations. The most important of these were the regional groups: in the South, the American Cotton Manfacturers Association; in New England, the Arkwright Club of Boston and the National Association of Cotton Manufacturers.[4] All three of these regional associations were cut from the same cloth. They were rudimentary organizations with a relatively small income from dues and at best a tiny staff. Most of their work was done by committees, some of them ad hoc, some permanent, selected from the association's membership. Of the three groups, only the Arkwright Club could draw funds directly from the corporations represented by its members, and it was the only one that could occasionally deploy substantial amounts of money in political campaigns.[5]

There was very little need for more high-powered organizations. Lobbying, one of the major activities of the Arkwright Club and the American Association, was done in a very informal manner. The association's main contribution was to provide a place for the manufacturers to meet and discuss the tactics to be used and the goals to be sought in political action.[6] In the economic sphere, the association dinners were convenient occasions for consummating price and production agreements. But, again, this activity was usually informal and personal; only on rare occasions did the associations attempt to control production on a regional basis.[7] The dissemination of technical information was another customary function, but this task could also be performed without a large staff.[8]

As should be apparent, the regional trade groups which already existed when the association movement began were not very formidable organizations. Only occasionally did they demand any attention or support from their members. This type of organization sufficed primarily because the industry's politico-economic environment was so favorable during the nineteenth century.

III

In the early years of the twentieth century, however, management in this industry began to experience new difficulties. Out of these troubles arose that marked increase in the intensity and volume of associative activity which is referred to in this article as the trade association movement. One of the problems which gave rise to the association movement was political. Management was unnerved when progressive reformers sent a host of new reform organizations to challenge business in the legislatures. On many occasions the old techniques of lobbying no longer sufficed to control events in either Washington or the state capitals.[9] Haphazard, personal methods had been effective in the past but the officers of the southern and northern associations began to recognize at this time that they needed improved lobbying techniques and stronger trade organizations.[10] This was especially true after the Wilson Administration took office in 1913. They needed organizations that could constantly be in touch with the legislatures, that could gather supporting statistics, that could prepare impressive briefs substantiating their claims and countering their enemy's charges. The changing political environment of the twentieth century thus created a special need for new forms of trade association activity.[11]

During these same years, the general organizational revolution which was sweeping America also stimulated the cotton manufacturers to alter their trade associations. As this revolution progressed, it surrounded the manufacturer with a growing number of new organizations which he could not afford to ignore. Some of these groups were hostile, others friendly, but all of them demanded his attention. For instance, the National Industrial Conference Board, which was founded in 1916, was decidedly pro-business. Nevertheless, it was desirable to keep in touch with the Conference Board, even to keep representatives on the Board. In this way the cotton manufacturer could learn what other trade organizations were doing and insure that the interests of the cotton textile industry were protected whenever the Board took any action. The National Association of Manufacturers (established in 1895, but especially active after 1903), the American Society for Testing Materials (1898), and the U.S. Chamber of Commerce (1913) were all friendly to the businessman. But in order to take advantage of the potentiality offered by these several associations, it was necessary to maintain an effective liaison organization.[12]

This new and challenging milieu also contained many hostile organizations. The labor unions were enemies. There were government commissions and agencies (especially in New England) which began to investigate, and in some cases to regulate, aspects of business behavior which heretofore had been the exclusive concern of the manufacturer himself. Even agencies which regulated other industries— the Interstate Commerce Commission, for example—created special problems for the cotton manufacturer. In 1906 the ICC began to exercise effective control over railroad rates. Since the mills depended upon interstate shipments of cotton, coal, mill supplies, and finished products, decisions affecting freight rates were of vital importance to the manufacturer. It was essential, then, to be represented when the Commission was considering these questions.[13]

But the individual businessman had neither the time nor the special skills necessary to negotiate with these various agencies, commissions and associations. He had, in short, a special need for effective and watchful representatives, for an associational middleman. And as soon as the cotton manufacturer set up a new association to protect his interests, it was necessary for his friends and foes to establish contacts with this organization or perhaps even to form additional associations to defend their own position. Thus, as the organizational environment became more complex, the association movement fed on itself—with new institutions creating the need for new institutions and for an elaborate network of inter-associational committees and councils.

A third force behind the association movement in cotton textiles grew out of the effort throughout American industry to impose rational or systematic controls upon business activities. Within American industry the interest in rationalization increased tremendously around the turn of the century. Although systems of rational control were introduced primarily by big business, executives in the atomistic textile industry were aware that they too might realize increased profits through rationalization. They were handicapped by the small size of their firms. But they sought to offset this disadvantage by sponsoring cooperative programs directed by their trade associations. Interest was expressed in standard rules for the cotton trade,[14] standard specifications for cloth and yarn,[15] and uniform principles of cost accounting.[16] Of course, before this work could be done it was necessary to strengthen the trade organizations so they could handle the complex technical problems of rationalization. In this way the widespread interest in improved systems of control helped to convince management that the old style of trade association could no longer satisfy their demands for inter-firm cooperation.

The economic problems of the industry produced a similar desire for new forms of cooperative action. By 1911 rapid expansion in New England and the South had brought cotton textiles to the brink of a serious problem of excess capacity (or, as the manufacturers referred to it, overcapacity).[17] As the profit margin narrowed, the growth rate in New England tailed off. But the southern industry continued to expand.[18] Despite the threat of excess capacity and intense competition, the advantages of producing in the low-cost South stimulated continued entry and growth.[19] The results were cutthroat competition and, in turn, a strong interest in any program that promised to "stabilize" the cotton textile market.

One means of achieving stability was through production control. But in cotton textiles it was unlikely that production could be controlled on a long-range basis unless a new kind of trade organization was created. Management in such highly concentrated industries as iron and steel had been able to control production through the old style of loose combination, but they had the advantage that only a small number of competitors was involved.[20] In cotton textiles it would be no small accomplishment just to bring the representatives of all the mills together; it would be even more difficult to persuade all of them to adopt a common policy, especially when some of the producers were in the North, some in the Southern Piedmont; and finally, the job of "policing" such an agreement could hardly be done by a trade association which did not have a substantial permanent staff. To achieve even partial success in production control, it was obvious that the industry would have to establish stronger trade organizations.

Around 1911 management in cotton textiles began to develop an especially strong interest in forming the kind of trade association that would prevent "uncertainty and loss" by means of curtailment in a "general or cooperative way." This desire to control production on an industry-wide basis was only one of the driving forces behind the trade association movement, but it was a force that accounted in subsequent years for some of the most important innovations in the industry's structure of associations.[21]

In cotton textiles the association movement was thus a direct product of four fundamental problems which were created for management by a series of decisive changes within and without their industry. The new environment produced within the managerial group a strong desire to prevent further erosion of its political position, to protect the industry's interests in a new and demanding organizational milieu, to reap the fruits of rationalization, and to escape the cutthroat competition which resulted from excess capacity. These problems could not, it seemed, be solved by individual action. Cooperation was essential. Consequently, the institutions of inter-firm cooperation had to be strengthened to satisfy the special needs imposed upon management by a rapidly changing environment.[22]

IV

In an attempt to cope with these new conditions, management revamped the existing trade organizations: the regional associations were given additional income, more staff members, new committees and new functions. In New England the mill treasurers broadened the scope of the National Association in the early 1900's.[23] In 1907 they also found it necessary to add to the duties performed by the Arkwright Club.[24] Finally, in 1916-17, they completely re-organized NACM. Heretofore, persons had joined the association and paid dues as individuals, not as representatives of the firm with which they were associated. Now, a form of corporate membership was established so that the association could draw upon companies instead of individuals for financial support.[25] In the South the American Association grew rapidly, both in membership and in breadth of activities during the early 1900's; and in 1917 the southerners thoroughly reorganized their association.[26]

In addition to strengthening the regional institutions, management in cotton textiles created several new trade organizations. One of these was the Textile Bureau (1913), which sought to protect the domestic market from the competition of foreign goods by "preventing undervaluations and the fraudulent practices of some importers."[27] Another, the Textile Alliance (1913), attempted to guard the mills against misrepresentation or other shady practices engaged in by some of the companies which sold supplies to the mills.[28] After several years of negotiations, an inter-associational committee, the National Council of American Cotton Manufacturers, was formed in 1913 to coordinate the efforts of the northern and southern regional associations.[29] Other new organizations included the small groups established to facilitate the exchange of statistical data among manufacturers; these statistical or "open-price" groups were set up by the mills producing cotton blankets, print cloth, duck, gingham and yarns.[30] Finally, in the mid-twenties the industry at last organized a national association, the Cotton-Textile Institute, with the aim of "stabilizing" the entire market for cotton textiles.[31]

V

Through these new and reorganized associations, management in cotton textiles attempted to adjust to the new environment, to regain, for instance, its old political power. The regional associations, assisted after 1913 by the National Council, greatly improved the industry's lobbying techniques. These improvements were not achieved by merely pouring more money into political action (although this was done); the changes were, for the most part, a result of a more methodical, well-organized approach to political problems. When the Underwood tariff bill came before Congress in 1913, the new techniques were beginning to be adopted. By 1921, when tariff next became an issue, the transition from the old to the new style of lobbying was completed.

The new style of pressure group politics was, above all, systematic. The First World War was barely over before the associations had begun to prepare for their coming battle for a hightr tariff.[32] First, a special consolidated tariff committee was formed in order to line up as many organizations as possible behind a single tariff proposal. In addition to the representatives from the regional associations, this consolidated committee was supported by the Association of Cotton Textile Merchants of New York. For the actual work of lobbying, the consolidated committee was broken into sub-committees which gathered essential statistics and determined what rates the industry would request. Through the sub-committees, the industry established contact with the Committee on Ways and Means and the Tariff Commission. The sub-committees also prepared schedules and charts to present at the conferences and hearings. Several meetings were held in Washington, and representatives were sent to the hearing before the Committee on Ways and Means. After the public hearings, more meetings were held with members of the House Committee. New schedules and demonstrations were prepared. Out of this carefully organized campaign came the cotton schedule that was approved by the House of Representatives. And this was only half the job. The entire process was repeated when the Senate handled the measure. The high tariff on cotton goods imposed by the resulting Fordney-McCumber Act, was in one sense, a tribute to effective group action in a Congress that was no longer dominated by stalwarts like Uncle Joe Cannon and Nelson Aldrich.

The advantages of operating from a strong organizational base and of employing systematic methods of lobbying were apparent in the industry's political activities throughout the 1920's and early 1930's. During the first phase of the New Deal, for instance, the industry was no longer dealing with a friendly Republican administration. Nevertheless, the associations in cotton textiles were extremely effective spokesmen for their philosophy and their specific programs for economic recovery. The Cotton-Textile Institute and its association leaders worked closely with the other business groups which were advocating industrial control by trade associations. Together, these various groups constituted a strong coalition favoring industrial self-regulation. The inclusion in the N.I.R.A. of provision for self-regulation can be seen, I believe, as a measure of the successful manner in which the associations in cotton textiles and other leading industries had adjusted their operations to the new system of pressure-group politics that characterized American government in the twentieth century.[33]

VI

The associations were even more successful in coping with the new organizational environment which surrounded the cotton textile manufacturer in modern America. One of the major jobs of the associations was that of dealing with governmental agencies and commissions. The burden of maintaining relations with the ICC and the railroads became so great in 1907 that the Arkwright Club found it necessary to set up a special transportation bureau.[34] Later, the American Association, NACM, and several of the state associations established similar transportation departments.[35] By employing lawyers experienced in transportation work these agencies took a great burden off the shoulders of the manufacturers; the association provided management with both skillful representation and countervailing power in the highly regulated market for transportation services.

The ICC was. only one of the government organizations with which the associations kept in close contact. The Department of Agriculture was the scene of prolonged negotiations after the government began (1909) to issue standard grades of cotton. And the associations were of course concerned when the Department's crop reports influenced the price of raw cotton.[36]

After the United States entered the First World War, the associations' services as organizational middlemen were of vital importance to the industry. New government agencies were sprouting up overnight. As the web of controls became more complex, effective association work was increasingly important. When, for instance, government began to fix prices on cotton goods, the National Council represented the industry before the Price Fixing Committee of the War Industries Board.[37] The National Council's Foreign Trade Committee also cooperated with the War Trade and Shipping Boards in supervising cotton shipments, compiling trade statistics, and facilitating financial arrangements in foreign trade.[38]

Following the war there were fewer government controls to worry about, but the associations now found it highly profitable to cooperate with the Department of Commerce. Under Herbert Hoover's direction, the Department sponsored a variety of programs designed to help the businessman. In all of these programs the trade associations in cotton textiles represented their industry. The regional associations and the National Council cooperated with the Department's Bureau of Standards and the Federal Specifications Board (which was established in 1921) in devising government specifications for textile products. In the Department's extensive campaign to encourage standardization, the associations again played a vital role as liaison between the government and the individual businessman.[39]

After 1927 the Cotton-Textile Institute gradually took over the job of maintaining the industry's relations with the federal government. The Institute kept in close contact with the Department of Commerce; and when the Bureau of Internal Revenue began to revise tax policies in regard to depreciation rates, CTI presented the industry's case in a long and complex series of negotiations.[40] In 1933 the tempo of governmental activity rapidly increased, and in Washington's complex administrative environment, the Institute's skillful representation was an extremely valuable asset. It was the Institute that directed the industry's operations under the N.R.A. and that defended the cotton manufacturer's interests before the myriad organizations established in the 1930's to revive and reform our economic system.[41]

The associations in cotton textiles also maintained diplomatic relations with other trade organizations. In a typical associative program aimed at increasing consumption of cotton goods, the Institute cooperated with some twenty other trade associations, ranging from the National Association of Purchasing Agents to the Architectural League of New York.[42] The individual company, especially in this industry, could not maintain the extensive contacts essential to this sort of operation. In almost every activity it became necessary to muster group support, and every year there were more groups with which to contend. The trade association movement in cotton textiles provided management with effective means for coping with this particular problem and thus with America's twentieth-century Organizational Revolution.

VII

Although the association movement was not very successful in equipping the industry to harvest the fruits of rationalization, there were, nevertheless, certain positive accomplishments. Both the southern and northern mills were able to devise and introduce standard rules and specifications for the cotton trade. The "Carolina Mill Rules" were issued in 1904 for the southern trade, and northern cotton buyers accepted the "New England Terms" in 1911. These standard rules imposed order on a market which heretofore had been controlled only by the traditions of the trade. Under the rules, specific standards were established for classifying cotton, for determining when excess bagging and ties had been added to the bales, and for filing claims based upon sub-standard shipments. Almost every aspect of the contract between cotton buyer and cotton merchant was explicitly defined. There was still some room for differences of opinion, but this too was controlled by providing for arbitration of disputes.[43]

During these same years, the cotton manufacturers would have liked to impose a similar set of rules upon the market for finished products. In 1907 and 1908 the National Association and ACMA worked out standard specifications and a standard sales note for the cotton goods market. But before they could introduce the rules, they ran into opposition from the commission merchants who normally sold their goods. The manufacturers themselves were unable to proceed without the support of the merchants—especially after the industry began to feel the effects of excess capacity.[44] Not until 1934 were the "Worth Street Rules"—which included a standard sales note and specifications—adopted in the dry goods market; the initiative in this case came primarily from the merchants themselves.[45]

The codes of business behavior which became popular in the 1920's were also a means of rationalizing inter-firm relations. Cotton textiles did not experiment with business codes so extensively as did some other industries, but the Institute sponsored codes which were adopted by the manufacturers of carded yard (1927) and wrapping twine (1928). Each of these codes imposed a rudimentary kind of planning and control upon areas of business behavior which had thus far been entrusted to the "invisible hand."[46]

Another form of rationalization involved the standardization of industrial products. Management's interest in standardizing goods and equipment had been aroused before the First World War, but the pace of standardization in cotton textiles accelerated tremendously in post-war America. This was primarily a result of cooperation between firms and between the associations and the government. After a five-year trial period, the National Association adopted in 1920 the "Standard General Methods for Testing Cotton Fabrics" devised by the American Society for Testing Materials.[47] Further progress was made during the early twenties, when the regional associations embarked on a formidable campaign to reduce the number of styles and sizes of various commercial products. Assisted by the Department of Commerce, the members of the regional associations decided, for instance, that it was wasteful to manufacture so many different varieties of cotton blankets. With fewer "unnecessary" sizes and grades, production would be more efficient, unit costs lower, and both the manufacturer and the public could benefit. Before this time it had been assumed that the market would take care of this. But in the 1920's, standardization of products became the subject of extensive planning on the part of the businessman and government officials. This sort of planning was actively promoted by the regional trade associations in cotton textiles.[48]

The associations also contributed to the development of improved and standardized cost accounting techniques, another aspect of the rationalization movement. As early as 1893, the National Association had undertaken a study of unit cost accounting. In 1894 the organization had produced a simple guide for the New England mills to follow in determining costs.[49] In subsequent years both NACM and the American Association sponsored discussions of accounting problems, and in 1920 the National Association again attempted (rather unsuccessfully) to introduce a standard method of determining unit costs.[50] A more significant step toward improved and standardized methods of cost accounting was taken after the Cotton-Textile Institute was formed. Under the Institute, the cost accounting program was part of a three-pronged attack upon the problem of cutthroat competition; the Institute hoped that better cost accounting would stiffen the industry's resistance to price cutting. At meetings sponsored by the association, accountants from the various mills worked with the Institute's staff to develop basic principles of cost accounting which could be applied to all of the mills throughout the country. As a result of these conferences, the association was able to issue in 1928 a manual of cost accounting principles "for Guidance as to Sales Policies."[51]

The Cotton-Textile Institute relentlessly campaigned for the adoption of its system or a similar plan, for anything in fact that would give management a clear idea of unit costs. In 1930 the association began to supervise the installation of accounting systems in the mills, and by 1932 CTI was satisfied that the program had significantly altered accounting techniques in the industry. A survey of southern mills at this time indicated that the number of mills with adequate cost systems had increased from 25% to 61% since 1925.[52]

These various cost accounting programs accelerated the adoption of rational techniques of control, although ultimately they seem to have done nothing to prevent price declines. Even when the mills adopted uniform principles of cost accounting, the hoped-for uniformity of cost estimates was not achieved. Better cost accounting could help the firm control its own operations, but if offered no escape from cutthroat competition.[53]

The cost accounting programs, the codes, standardization—all of these were involved in the industry's attempt to garner through the trade association the blessings of rationalization. Some progress was made, some benefits indeed realized. But when placed beside the systems of control developed by such industrial giants as Standard Oil or General Motors, it becomes apparent that the corporation was a strong, the association a weak, platform from which to systematize economic activity. Without the iron hand of centralized authority, thoroughgoing controls could not be imposed. Measured as a reaction to the need for rationalization, the trade association movement in cotton textiles was, at best, only a moderately successful response.

VIII

Even less successful, ultimately, were the efforts to use the trade association to eliminate cutthroat competition by controlling production. The first significant attack upon the problems of production control started when management began (in 1914 and subsequent years) to form "open-price" associations. These groups were organized by the manufacturers of blankets, print cloth, gingham, duck, yarn, and various fine goods. Under the open-price plan, manufacturers or their selling agents submitted reports on production, stocks on hand, unfilled orders and in some cases, prices (hence the name, open-price) to their association; the association's staff processed the data and sent reports back to the contributing members. Each participant thus had an intimate knowledge of what was happening in his particular market and of what his competitors were doing.[54]

In theory, the exchange of information might have created a more competitive market by removing frictions. In fact, the plan was designed and introduced for the purpose of preventing, not improving, competition. The goal was stability. It was intended that participating companies, guided by the figures, would avoid price cuts and thus would maintain fairly stable shares of the market. And initially, at least, some of the executives in cotton textiles seem to have felt that the open-price groups were helpful in preventing cutthroat competition.[55]

Such a plan perforce operated in the shadow of the Sherman Anti-Trust Act. With competitors exchanging and discussing statistics, there was always the danger that open-price would become price fixing, that an agreement to share statistics would become an agreement to share the market. For a number of years, however, the government seemed satisfied that the exchange of statistical information was not a violation of the anti-trust statutes. As a result, the open-price idea was firmly entrenched before the Justice Department even sought a decision from the courts.[56]

In February, 1920, however, the government brought a suit against the American Hardwood Manufacturers' Association, an organization of southern lumber manufacturers who were operating an open-price plan.[57] Armed with a lower court decision which condemned open-price competition as an illegal restraint, the Justice Department threatened in March, 1920, to take legal action against the statistical groups in other industries, including cotton textiles.[58] In 1921 the Supreme Court strengthened the government's threat by supporting the lower court. The open-price plan of the Hardwood Association was denounced "as an old evil in a new dress and with a new name."[59]

Buffeted by these adverse legal decisions, several of the open-price groups in cotton textiles collapsed. A few of the associations had apparently already begun to fall apart during the war when large profits made the exchange of statistics unnecessary. But whatever their immediate reasons for disbanding, the new legal environment prevented a resurgence of the open-price groups after the war.[60]

In the mid-twenties, however, two important developments brought about a revival of the open-price plan in cotton textiles. First, the industry's economic ailments became especially acute. Excess capacity, magnified now by the adoption of two-shift operations, produced a severe depression, with substantial losses to companies in the South and an awesome wave of liquidations and bankruptcies in the North.[61] At the same time, the Supreme Court reversed its field, giving the stamp of legality to the open-price plans of the Maple Flooring Manufacturers' Association (1925) and the Cement Manufacturers' Protective Association (also 1925).[62] Although the earlier *Hardwood* decision was not actually overruled, the Court's new attitude toward the exchange of statistical information encouraged associations to undertake open-price activities.

These decisions flashed a green light for the cotton textile industry, and in the fall of 1926, management organized the Cotton-Textile Institute. Through the Institute the manufacturers inaugurated a statistical program that was intended to "stabilize" the market. First, the association's members were divided into "product groups" which brought together all of the manufacturers of a single product such as wide sheeting; the product groups operated like the earlier open-price associations. The members submitted and received statistical reports on production, stocks on hand and unfilled orders. There was some exchange of price information, but, for the most part, CTI focused upon the central problem of production, not price.[63] At the meetings of the various product groups, the members discussed the statistics; and, as might be expected, the leitmotif of these discussions was the need for less production, especially when inventories were mounting and the price level sagged.[64] The Institute also built its cost-accounting plan around the product groups. The third part of CTI's attack upon cutthroat competition was aimed at the demand side of the market. By advertising and promoting new applications for the industry's standard products, CTI's "New Uses" division tried to enlarge the demand for cotton textiles.[65]

Although the Institute resembled in several ways the associations of the previous century, there was one very important difference: this new type of trade association was designed to serve as a permanent form of industrial organization. No longer was cooperation a means of riding out brief flurries of stormy competition. The twentieth-century association, like the modern corporation, embodied a long-range view of the economy, the industry, the individual firm, and the association itself. This new outlook was reflected in the Institute's complex and substantial administrative framework, in its large annual income (over $400,000 in 1929), and in its skillful association leaders. Membership in CTI was for a three-year period, and this too pointed up the fact that management had established an association to weld together all of the mills on a permanent basis.[66]

The principles that underlaid CTI were almost identical to the new concept of competition arising in oligopolistic industries such as copper or iron and steel. There was, furthermore, some direct cross-fertilization, as the association drew ideas from the business practices characteristic of the more concentrated industries. When the Institute's staff and officers extolled the new cooperative outlook, they frequently cited as praiseworthy the attitude of executives in big steel or copper. The cotton textile manufacturer, they said, must learn to think like Judge Gary of U.S. Steel. Although cotton textiles were as yet hardly touched by the concentration movement, the association sought to influence the industry's market behavior by persuading management to accept the business philosophy usually associated with oligopolistic industries.[67]

A significant number of the manufacturers in cotton textiles found the new outlook very appealing. In New England where the mills were being driven to the wall by low-cost southern competition, it is not hard to understand why cooperation was acceptable to management. But in the South, too, many executives agreed with H. R. Fitzgerald, of Danville, Virginia, who felt that the industry had to cultivate "the Institute spirit."[68]

There were, nevertheless, manufacturers who were hesitant, uncertain, and, as yet, unwilling to turn their backs on the old style of rough and tumble competition. As William D. Anderson of Macon, Georgia observed:

> My personal preference would be to stay out of the Institute. My choice always will be to have a free hand to run our own business as we see fit to run it, and regardless of what anybody else does.
>
> However . . . the question in my mind is whether or not we have not come on to a different day, whether or not we are facing conditions that call for a different type of treatment from that to which difficulties have heretofore yielded.[69]

While Anderson and others could not decide whether to accept the new ideas, there was a hard core of cotton textile manufacturers who decisively rejected the cooperative ideology. Executives like the young, exuberant Colonel Elliot White Springs of Lancaster, South Carolina, were not at all attracted by the association's promise of industrial stability. Springs was unwilling to get entangled in any cooperative programs. He later described the kind of textile manufacturer who was, he said, a

> Bastard, First Class. He runs his mills twenty-four hours a day, six days in the week, fifty-two weeks in the year. When he goes to New York he lunches along at the Automat . . . He makes the finest cloth in the market, because if he did not, the customers would reject every yard of it. He has never curtailed for the good of the industry. . . . Join me [Springs added] at the Automat for lunch someday.[70]

Since CTI could bring into the fold neither the dedicated competitors (like Springs) nor those who were uncertain about cooperation (like Anderson), it was impossible for the association to control production. In fact, the Institute had barely gotten underway in 1927 before a period of declining prices indicated with authority that the program, as originally designed, would not "stabilize" the market.[71]

For the next five years the association continued to search for an effective means of achieving this elusive goal. The quest gradually led the Institute to impinge more and more upon the individual decisions that members made about their production schedules. First, CTI experimented with short, "emergency curtailments." When the statistical reports indicated that orders were falling off, stocks building up, and prices declining, the association announced to the members that certain mills were curtailing operations. The members were then asked to notify the Institute whether they were taking similar action and whether the association could so inform the other companies. The association thus suggested a means of reducing production a specific amount and provided each mill with information about the schedule adopted by its competitors.[72]

These "emergency curtailments" were merely stopgap measures, and when the general industrial depression of the thirties began, it was obvious that more forceful and systematic curtailment was needed. In 1930 the association recommended that all of the mills adopt a maximum operating schedule of 55 hours a week on the day shift, 50 hours at night.[73] This was followed by an intensive campaign to eliminate women and minors from the night shift. Since it was assumed that this latter program would restrict the available labor supply (forcing a cutback in production), the night-work plan combined a humanitarian goal with the association's fundamental objective of production control. By 1932 the night-work proposal had been adopted by almost ninety percent of the industry, but the association was still unable to stabilize prices.[74]

With CTI falling short of its mark, many cotton textile manufacturers had decided by late 1932 that voluntary plans for production control would never work. Like Donald Comer of Birmingham, they felt that "if the Federal Trade Commission or if a National Defense Committee could be set up that would under some constitutional provision give all industry including owner and worker the right to organize itself for its best protection, I think it would be an advance."[75] The opportunity to make this "advance" came after the new administration was elected in 1932. And at that time, the Cotton-Textile Institute's leaders lent their support to the varied forces pressing the New Deal to set up a government-sponsored program of production control. The result of this pressure was Title I of the National Industrial Recovery Act.

Even before the N.I.R.A. was through Congress, the Institute was working with the government officials who were slated to take charge of the new agency.[76] Cotton textiles was, consequently, the first industry to adopt code under N.R.A.[77] From 1933 through 1935, Code No. 1 was in force, and the Institute had primary responsibility for directing a program of compulsory production control. Indeed, the association was involved in every aspect of the N.R.A.'s system of economic controls, including the particularly sensitive area of labor-management relations.[78]

Unfortunately for CTI, the machine-hour limitations of the N.R.A. were not much more successful in stabilizing prices than the earlier, voluntary programs. Under the cotton textile code, the mills were limited to a production schedule of two forty-hour shifts a week, but this restricted schedule still left the industry with excess capacity and the inevitable downward pressure upon prices.[79] The Institute attempted to work out a program of flexible production controls, but the National Industrial Recovery Act was invalidated by the Supreme Court before the new plan could be put into operation.[80]

Neither the Cotton-Textile Institute nor the earlier open-price associations were able to stabilize the market for cotton goods. Competition gradually eliminated much of the industry's excess capacity, but this was a process which the associations learned to live with, not one which they actively supported. Of the four basic "needs" which gave rise to the association movement, the modern trade organization in this industry was least successful in satisfying the desire to escape the pressure of intense competition.

IX

The association movement in cotton textiles was thus both a failure and a success. Measured as an alternative to oligopoly, the associations obviously failed to stabilize the industry's market; even with the backing of the federal government, the trade associations never achieved their goal of price stability. Somewhat more successful were the associative programs which rationalized various aspects of business behavior. Although unable to match the accomplishments of the large corporation, the associations made some progress in standardizing products, in improving cost accounting techniques and in establishing uniform rules for the cotton trade. It was, however, as political representatives and organizational middlemen that the associations were most successful. The trade associations enabled the cotton textile manufacturer to protect his interests in a society dominated by large-scale organizations. Working through their associations, the businessmen in cotton textiles were able to master the arts of pressure-group politics.

Once firmly established, the new style of trade organization became itself an active agent in the creation of a new ideological climate for business enterprise. The associations and their professional staff members were constant advocates of a particular business philosophy. Whether in the short term the manufacturers accepted this philosophy or not, the associations continued to preach and practice; in the long run they could not help but shape management's outlook. The associative ideology demanded from the manufacturer the kind of responses which, according to Joseph A. Schumpeter's brilliant prognosis, would inevitably lead to the demise of the capitalistic system.[81] This new gospel replaced the individualistic, competitive concepts of the nineteenth century with an ideal of rationalized, cooperative behavior; it made stability a key goal of economic activity.

In the long run the creation of this new ideological environment—a secondary effect of the movement—was undoubtedly as significant as the more direct, more obvious, results such as better political representation. And one does not have to be a Schumpeterian pessimist about this change in ideology. By helping to erode the foundations of the nineteenth-century business philosophy, the association movement merely prepared the cotton manufacturer to accept the realities of a more stable society in which the businessman could no longer ignore the social and political implications of his actions.

The Johns Hopkins University

NOTES

1. This project was begun as a dissertation at Yale University and carried forward at Harvard's Graduate School of Business Administration, where I was Business History Fellow. I am indebted to both of these institutions for financial assistance and direction, particularly for the help that was given to me by David M. Potter, who was my thesis director. I have also received research funds from Rice University and the American Philosophical Society, and I appreciate their support. Furthermore, I am obligated to William T. Heyck, Arthur M. Johnson, Leonard M. Marsak, Sydney H. Nathans, Gaston V. Rimlinger, and Frank E. Vandiver—all of whom have read parts of this manuscript and have given me valuable suggestions.

2. For a sampling, the reader might see the following: Emmett H. Naylor, *Trade Associations: Their Organization and Management* (New York, 1921), or the same author's article on the "History of Trade Associations in America," in U.S. Department of Commerce, *Trade Association Activities* (Washington, D.C., 1923), pp. 301-307; Franklin D. Jones, *Trade Association Activities and the Law* (New York, 1922); F. Stuart Fitzpatrick, *A Study of Business Men's Associations* (Orlean, New York, 1925); The National Industrial Conference Board, *Trade Associations: Their Economic Significance and Legal Status* (New York, 1925); I. L. Sharfman, "The Trade Association Movement," *American Economic Review*,

16:203-218 (March, 1926); Benjamin S. Kirsh, *Trade Associations: The Legal Aspects* (New York, 1928); Joseph H. Foth, *Trade Associations: Their Services to Industry* (New York, 1930); Simon N. Whitney, *Trade Associations and Industrial Control* (New York, 1934); Benjamin S. Kirsh and Harold R. Shapiro, *Trade Associations in Law and Business* (New York, 1938).

3. The most useful accounts of the trade association movement can be found in Thomas C. Cochran and William Miller, *The Age of Enterprise* (New York, 1942), *passim*; Arthur R. Burns, *The Decline of Competition* (New York, 1936), pp. 43-75; Charles A. Pearce, *Trade Association Survey* (Washington: Temporary National Economic Committee, Monograph No. 18, 1941); and George W. Stocking and Myron W. Watkins, *Monopoly and Free Enterprise* (New York, 1951), pp. 231-255.

4. The American Cotton Manufacturers Association was first organized under the name Southern Cotton Spinners' Association; in 1903 the name was changed and to avoid confusion, I have used ACMA throughout this article (except in the footnotes). American Cotton Manufacturers Association, *Proceedings*, XXV (1921), 121, 150; Southern Cotton Spinners' Association, *Proceedings*, VII (1903), 54-55, 163. Evelyn H. Knowlton, *Pepperell's Progress* (Cambridge, 1948), p. 128, discusses the origins of the Arkwright Club, as does *By-Laws of the Arkwright Club and List of Officers and Members, Together with a Brief Account of Its Origins* . . . (Boston, 1924), pp. 16-19. NACM was first organized as the New England Cotton Manufacturers' Association; it changed its name to National Association in 1906, and throughout this article (again, except in the footnotes), I have referred to the association as NACM. NACM, *Transactions*, LXXX (1906), 93-97.

5. The annual and semi-annual volumes of NACM, *Transactions*, and ACMA, *Proceedings*, must be used with caution, but they are nevertheless the best available sources on the general activities and organization of these associations. For general information pertaining to the Arkwright Club, consult Evelyn H. Knowlton, *Pepperell's Progress*, p. 128; Melvin T. Copeland, *The Cotton Manufacturing Industry of the United States* (Cambridge, Mass., 1917), pp. 157-158; and the letters of the treasurer (Treasurer to Selling Agent, and Treasurer to Miscellaneous) in the records of the Lawrence Manufacturing Company, Baker Library, Harvard University.

6. C. P. Baker to Townsend & Yale, April 28, 1894; C. P. Baker to C. F. North, June 5, 1894; C. P. Baker to Nelson W. Aldrich, April 9, 1894; C. P. Baker to Robert Pilling, April 12, 1897; C. P. Baker to Samuel Townsend, January 11, 1900; Lawrence MSS; Southern Cotton Spinners' Association, *Proc.*, V & VI (1901), 44.

7. Victor S. Clark, *History of Manufactures in the United States*, II (New York, 1929), 720-721; Evelyn H. Knowlton, *Pepperell's Progress*, p. 128; Melvin T. Copeland, *The Cotton Manufacturing Industry*, p. 157. When the southern association was organized in 1897, it had a Committee on Curtailment of Production of Warps and Other Yarns. ACMA, *Proc.*, XXV (1921), 150. Also see: "Statement of Edward Stanwood before the Committee on Expenditures in the Department of Justice," June 28, 1911, Northern Textile Association MSS. This statement by the Secretary of the Arkwright Club and other papers subsequently cited as NTA MSS. are in the office of the association in Boston, Mass. I am deeply indebted to William F. Sullivan, Jessie E. Vint, and Josephine A. Loughry for mak-

ing these papers available to me and for assisting me in countless ways during my study of these materials.

8. See, for instance, NACM, *Trans.*, LXIX (1900), 212-225, 327-339, 341-348.

9. NECMA, *Trans.*, LXXVIII (1905), 78-79, 81-96; NACM, *Trans.*, LXXXVI (1909), 99-100; NACM, *Trans.*, LXXXVIII (1910), 128-129; NACM, *Trans.*, XC (1911), 238; NACM, *Trans.*, XCII (1912), 250; NACM, *Trans.*, XCVI (1914), 411; NACM, *Trans.*, XCVII (1914), 40; NACM, *Trans.*, XCVIII (1915), 120A-120E, 120H; "Preliminary Report, Joint Meeting, New York City," January 17, 1917, NTA MSS; Cotton Manufacturers Association of Georgia, *Report*, XXX (1930), 45-47, 58.

10. ACMA, *Tariff Bulletin No. 2*, pp. 3-4. ACMA, *Proc.*, 16 (1912), 91. Mr. F. S. Love, Executive-Secretary of the American Cotton Manufacturers Institute, allowed me to examine this tariff bulletin and other materials in the association's library in Charlotte, N.C. I am grateful to Mr. Love and his staff for helping me while I was visiting their office.

11. ACMA, *Proc.*, XV (1911) 212; ACMA, *Proc.*, XVI (1912), 90-91; NACM, *Trans.*, XC (1911), 320; NACM, *Trans.*, XCI (1911), 46-47; NACM, *Trans.*, XCII (1912), 127-128; "Preliminary Report, Joint Meeting, New York City," January 17, 1917, NTA MSS.

12. *Ibid.*; NACM, *Trans.*, CI (1916), 87-88, 92.

13. C. P. Baker to George Dexter, April 14, 1903, Lawrence, MSS. David Clark, "Organization of Cotton Manufacturers Association of North Carolina," Typewritten MS. in the office of the association, Charlotte, N.C. I would like to thank Mr. Hunter Marshall and Mr. Tom Ingram for allowing me to inspect certain of their records. Cotton Manufacturers Association of Georgia, *Report*, XXX (1930), 59; NACM, *Trans.*, LXXXII (1907), 334-335; NACM, *Trans.*, XC (1911), 238. Albert G. Duncan, president of NACM, complained in 1914 that: "The history of the last few years of national and state legislation has witnessed a development of commissions never before dreamed of in any country under a republican form of government." NACM, *Trans.*, XCVII (1914), 40.

14. NACM, *Trans.*, XCII (1912), 303-304, 422; ACMA, *Proc.*, IX (1905), 241; C. P. Baker to A. N. Mayo & Co., April 16, 1906, Lawrence MSS.

15. NACM, *Trans.*, LXXXV (1908), 48-63; ACMA, *Proc.*, XIII (1909), 167-177.

16. NECMA, *Trans.*, LXXIII (1902), 116; ACMA, *Proc.*, VIII (1904), 67.

17. Lloyd G. Reynolds, "Cutthroat Competition," *American Economic Review*, 30:736-747 (December, 1940). Reynolds discusses the cotton textile industry (pp. 739-744), and while in general I am following his definition of terms, I do not agree with him that excess capacity appeared in the industry in 1923. It seems more likely that the industry had excess capacity as early as 1911, although the period of declining profits was interrupted by the First World War. Gordon Donald, "The Depression in Cotton Textiles, 1924 to 1940" (Ph.D. dissertation, The University of Chicago, 1951), p. 6, supports this view, as does Stephen J. Kennedy, *Profits and Losses in Textiles* (New York, 1936), pp. 9-10, 126-128. The most careful study of profits in cotton textiles indicates that the industry's period of subnormal earnings began before the War. U.S. Bureau of Internal Revenue, Excess Profits Tax Council, *The Cotton Textile Industry: An Economic Analysis of the Industry with Reference to the Investigation of Claims for Relief Under*

Section 722 of the Internal Revenue Code (Washington, D.C., 1948), especially p. 38.

18. U.S. Bureau of the Census, *Cotton Production and Distribution, Bulletin 134* (1916), pp. 33-34.

19. Chen-Han Chen, "The Location of the Cotton Manufacturing Industry in the United States, 1880-1910" (Ph.D. dissertation, Harvard University, 1940), pp. 145-148, 165-168, 196, 211-212, 407-408; Richard A. Lester, "Trends in Southern Wage Differentials Since 1899," *Southern Economic Journal*, 11:317-344 (April, 1945); Ben F. Lemert, *The Cotton Textile Industry of the Southern Appalachian Piedmont* (Chapel Hill, N.C., 1933), pp. 99-102, 105-111. The best general account of the expansion of the southern industry is in Jack Blicksilver, *Cotton Manufacturing in the Southeast: An Historical Analysis* (Atlanta, Ga., 1959), pp. 1-88.

20. In 1909 there were 1,324 separate establishments (as defined in the census report) in the cotton textile industry. Only 12 per cent of these establishments produced goods valued over $1,000,000 per annum, and this group of mills manufactured only about one-half of the industry's total product. U.S. Bureau of the Census, *Thirteenth Census*, X (1909), 37, 44.

21. ACMA, *Proc.*, XIV (1910), 113, 200-201; "Statement of Edward Stanwood," June 28, 1911, NTA MSS; ACMA, *Proc.*, XVIII (1914), 94-96; NACM, *Trans.*, XCIV (1913), 243-250.

22. For some different views of the origins of the general association movement see: Simon N. Whitney, *Trade Associations*, p. 38; and Kenneth E. Boulding, *The Organizational Revolution* (New York, 1953), p. 21.

23. NACM, *Trans.*, LXXXIV (1908), 100-103, 131-132, 352, 423; NACM, *Trans.*, LXXVI (1909), 324-327.

24. *By-Laws of the Arkwright Club and List of Officers and Members*, p. 19.

25. NACM, *Trans.*, CI (1916), 82-113, 250; NACM, *Trans.*, CII (1917), 417-421.

26. Southern Cotton Spinners' Association, *Proc.*, VII (1903), 54-55, 163; ACMA, *Proc.*, IX (1905), 247-248; ACMA, *Proc.*, X (1906), 91-92, 315-316; ACMA, *Proc.*, XI (1907), 98, 302; ACMA, *Proc.*, XXI (1917), 56-63.

27. NACM, *Trans.*, XCVI (1914), 115-116.

28. NACM, *Trans.*, C (1916), 409.

29. ACMA, *Proc.*, XVII (1913), 160-161; NACM, *Trans.*, XCIV (1913), 87-89, 140-142.

30. "Minutes of Meeting of Certain Selling Representatives of Manufacturers of Cotton Blankets." December 4, 1918, Nashua Manufacturing Company Records, Baker Library, Harvard University; "Preliminary Report, Joint Meeting, New York City," January 17, 1917, NTA MSS; *The (New York) Journal of Commerce and Commercial Bulletin*, November 11, 1915 and March 19, 1920.

31. Cotton-Textile Institute, "Minutes, Organization Meeting," October 20, 1926, NTA MSS.

32. For the following account of the industry's lobbying efforts in 1919-1921, see: National Council, "Minutes," March 11, 1920, December 14, 1920, and March 8, 1921, NTA MSS; NACM, *Trans.*, CVI (1919), 216; NACM, *Trans.*, CXII (1922), 207-218; NACM, *Trans.*, CXIII (1922), 50; ACMA, *Proc.*, XXV (1921), 177-178.

33. The efforts of CTI's officers and their associates to make industrial self-

regulation a public policy are recounted by the author in some detail in "The Cotton-Textile Institute and the Government," *Business History Review*, 38:186-213 (Summer, 1964).

34. Charles Storrow, *et al.*, "Circular Letter," September 30, 1907, NTA MSS. By 1908 the Transportation Agency had, according to C. P. Baker, already been able to get a reduced rate on knit goods sent from Lowell, Mass., to Philadelphia and Baltimore. C. P. Baker to E. M. Townsend & Co., June 25, 1908, Lawrence MSS.

35. Cotton Manufacturers Association of Georgia, *Report*, XXX (1930), 59; Cotton Manufacturers Association of North Carolina, *Proc.*, XI (1917), 65-69; ACMA, *Proc.*, XXIII (1919), 132-137; NACM, "Outline of Enlarged Activities," July 12, 1917, Nashua MSS.

36. NACM, *Trans.*, LXXX (1906), 134, 381; NACM, *Trans.*, LXXXVII (1909), 35-36; NACM, *Trans.*, XCVII (1914), 215-222.

37. NACM, *Trans.*, CIII (1917), 36-39; NACM, *Trans.*, CIV (1918), 245-248; National Council, "Minutes," May 22 and 23, 1917, and January 11, 1918; National Council, "Statement from the War Service Committee," July 30, 1918, NTA MSS.

38. ACMA, *Proc.*, XXII (1918), 75.

39. NACM, *Bulletin No. 14* (June 15, 1921), *No. 25* (May 15, 1922), *No. 29* (September 15, 1922); Russell T. Fisher to E. T. Pickard, March 11, 1925, NTA MSS: NACM, *Trans.*, CXI (1921), 374-383; NACM, *Trans.*, CXII (1922), 49-54; NACM, *Trans.*, CXVIII (1925), 57-59; ACMA, *Proc.*, XXVIII (1924), 183-184.

40. George A. Sloan, *Fourth Annual Report of the Cotton-Textile Institute, Inc.* (1930), pp. 22-24.

41. The annual reports of NACM and ACMA provide some information on CTI's activities from 1933 through 1935, but the best guide to the Institute's NRA experience is the "Minutes of the Cotton Textile Industry Code Authority, 1933-1935," Goldthwaite H. Dorr MSS. I am grateful to Mr. Dorr and to Mr. John K. Watson for allowing me to examine these records and other papers which I have subsequently cited as Dorr MSS.

42. NACM, *Trans.*, CXXIII (1927), 192-196; Cotton Manufacturers Association of North Carolina, *Proc.*, XXII (1928), 56-57, 86-87.

43. ACMA, *Proc.*, IX (1905), 241; NACM, *Trans.*, XCI (1911), 47. In 1911 the "New England Terms for Buying and Selling Cotton" were issued in pamphlet form.

44. ACMA, *Proc.*, XIII (1909), 167-177; ACMA, *Proc.*, XIX (1915), 138; NACM, *Trans.*, LXXXVII (1909), 48; NACM, *Trans.*, LXXXVIII (1910), 175-176.

45. Association of Cotton Textile Merchants of New York, *Twenty-Five Years, 1918-1943* (New York, 1944), pp. 38-44.

46. W. D. Anderson, *et al.*, "Code of Trade Practices for the Cotton Wrapping Twine Industry," November 20, 1928; and "Draft of Letter," December 6, 1927, Dorr MSS; Mary G. Conner, "Memorandum Re: Carded Yarn Trade Practices Code," June 21, 1927; and William J. Donovan to G. W. [sic] Dorr, June 21, 1927, Records of the Department of Justice, RG 60, File 147, National Archives (hereafter NA).

47. NACM, *Trans.*, CX (1921), 115.

48. NACM, *Bulletin No. 25* (May 15, 1922), *No. 29* (September 15, 1923),

and *No. 56* (December 15, 1924), NTA MSS; NACM, *Trans.*, CXI (1921), 374-383; NACM, *Trans.*, CXVII (1924), 260; NACM, *Trans.*, CXVIII (1925), 57-59.

49. NECMA, *Trans.*, LIV (1893), 22-25, 36; NECMA, *Trans.*, LVI (1894), 50-73.

50. ACMA, *Proc.*, VIII (1904), 67; ACMA, *Proc.*, XIX (1915), 100; ACMA, *Proc.*, XX (1916), 119-120; NECMA, *Trans.*, LXXIII (1902), 116; NACM, *Trans.*, LXXXIV (1908), 136-151; NACM, *Trans.*, XCV (1913), 234-254; *Trans.*, CX (1921), 36-39; NACM, *Trans.*, CXII (1922), 58-113, 270-271; NACM, *Trans.*, CXIII (1922), 46.

51. ACMA, *Proc.*, XXXI (1927), 106-107; CTI, "Minutes of Narrow Sheetings' Cost Accountants' Meeting," August 9, 1927, Dorr MSS; Walker D. Hines, *First Annual Report of the President, The Cotton-Textile Institute, Inc.* (1927), p. 16; CTI, *An Outline of Bases to be Used in Predetermining Costs for Guidance as to Sales Policies* (New York, 1928).

52. Cotton Manufacturers Association of North Carolina, *Proc.*, XXIII (1929), 73; Walker D. Hines, *Third Annual Report of the President of the Cotton-Textile Institute, Inc.* (1929), pp. 15-16; Sydney P. Munroe to Donald Comer, January 6, 1931, Donald Comer MSS. These papers were made available for my study by the late Donald Comer of Birmingham, Alabama. When I began working on the collection, the papers were in Birmingham, but since that time they have been placed in the Baker Library, Harvard University. I am very grateful to Mr. Comer for giving me access to these papers. George A. Sloan, *Fourth Annual Report of the Cotton-Textile Institute, Inc.* (1930), pp. 16-17; George A. Sloan, *Sixth Annual Report of the Cotton-Textile Institute, Inc.* (1932), pp. 3-4.

53. *Ibid.*, pp. 22-23; Simon N. Whitney, *Trade Associations*, pp. 68-69.

54. H. E. Danner, "Statement of National Association of Finishers of Cotton Fabrics, as per letter of transmittal," March 17, 1921, RG 60, File 147, NA; Blanket Association, "Minutes," February 4, 1919; "Report to Members," February 5, 1919, and May 22, 1919, Nashua MSS; ACMA, *Proc.*, XX (1916), 94; ACMA, *Proc.*, XXI (1917), 39-40; NACM, *Trans.*, CXI (1921), 378; *The Journal of Commerce*, November 11, 1915; Milton N. Nelson, *Open Price Associations* (Urbana, Illinois, 1923), pp. 16-17.

55. "Minutes of Meeting of Certain Selling Representatives of Manufacturers of Cotton Blankets," December 4, 1918, Nashua MSS.

56. "Statement of National Association of Finishers of Cotton Fabrics: [ca. 1920], RG 60, File 147-0, NA.

57. James W. Silver, "The Hardwood Producers Come of Age," *Journal of Southern History*, 23:439 (November, 1957).

58. *Journal of Commerce*, March 19, 1920.

59. *American Column & Lumber Company v. United States*, 257 U.S. 410 (1921).

60. H. E. Danner to E. E. Gann, November 20, 1920; William R. Benham to Edward E. Gann, August 23, 1920; C. Stanley Thompson, "Memorandum for Colonel Goff," March 2, 1922; all in RG 60, File 147, NA; *Textile World*, 67:43 (April 18, 1925); U.S. Federal Trade Commission, *Open-Price Trade Associations* (U.S. Senate, Document No. 226, 1929), pp. 381-382, lists only the National Association of Finishers of Cotton Fabrics and the Southern Yarn Spinners' Association among the open-price groups active in the mid-twenties.

61. Gordon Donald, "The Depression in Cotton Textiles," contains an excellent discussion of the industry's economic difficulties. Also see: Stephen J. Kennedy, *Profits and Losses*, pp. 195-200; and Lloyd G. Reynolds, "Cutthroat Competition," pp. 739-744.

62. *Maple Flooring Manufacturers' Association* v. *United States*, 268 U.S. 563 (1925); *Cement Manufacturers' Protective Association* v. *United States*, 268 U.S. 588 (1925).

63. Cotton-Textile Institute, "Minutes, Executive Committee," October 4, 1926, and "Minutes, Organization Meeting," October 20, 1926, NTA MSS; Walker D. Hines, *First Annual Report*, p. 6; G. Sloan, "Memorandum for Mr. Hines," October 18, 1927, Dorr MSS. In some cases the product groups were used to set minimum prices, but this apparently was the exception, not the rule. Robert S. Smith, *Mill on the Dan: A History of Dan River Mills, 1882-1950* (Durham, N.C., 1960), pp. 215-219. W. D. Hines to B. B. Comer, June 16, 1927, Comer MSS., contains a description of the statistical plan used by the print cloth group.

64. G. A. Sloan to G. H. Dorr, December 12, 1927; G. H. Dorr, "Draft of letter to be sent to members of Wide Sheeting Group," November 29, 1927; "The Situation in Print Cloths," April 1928, Dorr MSS.

65. G. A. Sloan to Donald Comer, September 30, 1928, Comer MSS; Cotton Manufacturers Association of North Carolina, *Proc.*, XXIII (1929), 50, 71.

66. CTI, "Minutes, Board of Directors," September 30, 1926, Dorr MSS; CTI, "Minutes, Organization Meeting," October 20, 1926, NTA MSS.

67. Cotton Manufacturers Association of Georgia, *Report*, XXVI (1926), 27, 61, 63; NACM, *Trans.*, CXXI (1926), 148, 150; NACM, *Trans.*, CXXVIII (1930), 99; Cotton Manufacturers Association of North Carolina, *Proc.*, XX (1926), 87, 89.

68. CTI, "Minutes, Board of Directors," October 20, 1926, NTA MSS.

69. W. D. Anderson to Donald Comer, January 16, 1928, Comer MSS.

70. *Fortune*, 41:66 (January, 1950).

71. The following materials provide information on the Institute's difficulties in 1927-1929; CTI, "Print Cloth and Narrow Sheetings Weekly Production Statistics," and "The Situation in Print Cloths" (April, 1928), Dorr MSS; W. D. Hines, "To Executives of Chambray Mills," February 14, 1929; W. D. Hines to W. D. Anderson, June 25, 1929, Comer MSS. Simon N. Whitney, *Trade Associations*, pp. 73-75, correctly concludes that CTI's program failed to stabilize either prices or profits. The average manufacturing margin on grey goods was 21.8 cents in 1927; 19.7 cents in 1928, and 18.1 cents in 1929. Stephen J. Kennedy, *Profits and Losses*, p. 248.

72. W. J. Vereen, "To Narrow Sheetings Manufacturers," December 9 and 14, 1927; W. D. Hines to D. Comer, December 20, 1927, and May 31, 1929, Comer MSS; CTI, "Steps taken by the industry . . . to bring the production of cotton into line with the demand therefore," Dorr MSS.

73. George A. Sloan, *Fourth Annual Report*, p. 14.

74. CTI formally adopted the night work plan at the annual convention, October 15, 1930, and continued to support the program through 1931 and 1932. CTI, "Minutes, Annual Meeting," October 15, 1930; G. A. Sloan to D. Comer, December 4, 1931; G. A. Sloan, "Memorandum to Cotton Mill Executives," March 1, 1932; CTI, "Minutes, Executive Committee," June 16, 1932, Comer MSS; George A. Sloan, *Sixth Annual Report*, pp. 4, 11, 24-25. The average manufactur-

ing margin on grey goods was 15.8 cents in May 1930 and 10.8 cents by May 1932. Stephen J. Kennedy, *Profits and Losses*, p. 249.

75. Donald Comer to Hugo Black, December 24, 1932. Also see, B. B. Gossett, "To Our Members," June 3, 1932; CTI, "Minutes, Executive Committee," October 18, 1932; CTI, "Minutes of the Annual Meeting," October 19, 1932, Comer MSS; George A. Sloan, *Sixth Annual Report*, p. 10.

76. G. A. Sloan, telegram to D. Comer, May 21, 1933, Comer MSS; "Minutes, Cotton Textile Industry Committee," May 24, 1933, Dorr MSS.

77. Franklin D. Roosevelt, "Code Approval No. 1," July 9, 1933, Records of the National Recovery Administration, RG 9, 1809, NA.

78. "Minutes, Cotton Textile Industry Committee," May 1933 through May 1935, Dorr MSS.

79. Even CTI's officers recognized that the Code had not really solved their basic problem of cutthroat competition. The Cotton Textile Industry Committee and the Cotton-Textile Institute, "In the Matter of Survey of Cotton Textile Industry . . ." (Pamphlet available at the office of the American Cotton Manufacturers Institute), pp. 8, 10, 50.

80. National Industrial Recovery Board, "Minutes," March 6, 21, and 23, 1935, RG 9, Central Record Section, NIRB, 8449, NA; "Minutes, Cotton Textile Industry Committee," March 15, 1935, Dorr MSS.

81. Joseph A. Schumpeter, *Capitalism, Socialism, and Democracy* (3rd ed.; New York, 1950), pp. 131-163.

Wilson Progressives vs. DuPont:
Controversy in Building the Nitro Plant

by R. Eugene Harper

When the Great War broke out in Europe in August 1914, few Americans seriously believed the United States would become involved in such folly. Nevertheless, inexorably, the United States was drawn into the conflict, and gradually came to realize the massive requirements of its commitment. The war bogged down into stalemated trench warfare early on, characterized by a series of indecisive but bloody engagements. Much American public opinion came to view the German side as evil because of its invasion of neutral Belgium, the use of poison gas, and numerous alleged atrocities. Certain American banks and munitions makers were soon reaping the benefits of large Allied war orders. The administration of President Woodrow Wilson proclaimed American neutrality in the war, but ultimately had difficulty remaining evenhanded. As Germany stepped up its use of the new submarine weapon, the Wilson administration, particularly after the May 1915 sinking of the passenger ship *Lusitania*, found itself deeply involved in diplomatic negotiations to protect American neutrality threatened by German submarine warfare.[1]

As war continued and the nation found itself more deeply involved, opponents of the Wilson administration demanded that steps be taken to prepare the nation for possible war. Wilson and his advisors adamantly opposed any large escalation of American military might, but they did undertake sufficient preliminary steps to blunt the "preparedness" issue in time for the 1916 election. Wilson's diplomacy also brought a German agreement in 1916 to respect American neutrality. Thus, the president was able to win reelection as the candidate of Progressivism, for his popular domestic reform program; as a candidate of Peace, for his successful diplomacy; and as a candidate of Preparedness, for his initial steps toward military readiness. Unfortunately, Germany decided to risk American hostility and began unrestricted submarine warfare in early 1917. Wilson delayed, searched for alternatives, but reluctantly asked Congress for a Declaration of War on April 2, 1917 and received it four days later.[2]

R. Eugene Harper is Professor of History at the University of Charleston, Charleston, West Virginia, and has published articles in the *Western Pennsylvania Historical Magazine*, *Journal of the West Virginia Historical Association*, and the *Proceedings of the First National Conference on American Planning History*. He earned M.A. and Ph.D. degrees from the University of Pittsburgh, and a masters degree in City and Regional Planning from Ohio State in 1985. His upcoming book, *The Social Structure of the Western Pennsylvania Frontier*, is under contract with the University of Pittsburgh Press.

---

1. Standard works on the events leading to United States participation in World War I include: Arthur S. Link, *Woodrow Wilson and the Progressive Era* (New York: Harper & Brothers, 1954); John M. Blum, *Woodrow Wilson and the Politics of Morality* (Boston: Little, Brown and Company, 1962); John A. Garraty, *Woodrow Wilson* (Westport, CT: Greenwood Press, 1977). Arthur S. Link, *Wilson the Diplomatist* (Baltimore: The Johns Hopkins Press, 1957) is a particularly insightful study of Wilson's foreign policy by his great biographer.
2. Wilson accepted war more in order to gain the status of a beligerent so as to be able to continue to influence Allied and German policy rather than to apply military might to defeat Germany. *See* Link, *Wilson the Diplomatist*, 85-88.

When the United States entered the war in 1917, the Wilson administration had little idea of what that entry would entail. At the highest levels it was felt that America's role "would be largely one of moral support."[3] The military needs of the Allies and America's role in the war were not fully understood until the fall of 1917, following the trip to the battlefront by Colonel Edward House, Wilson's personal advisor, and Chief of Staff Tasker Bliss.[4] By then even the limited American role imposed severe strains on the War Department's inadequate organization. During the difficult winter of 1917-18, shortages of strategic materials and basic implements of war, disease in army camps, and transportation and shipping bottlenecks plagued the War Department. "The American war effort was faltering and in a brief time might crumble completely." Criticism of the administration was widespread. Congress conducted its own investigation of the war effort, and Secretary of War Newton D. Baker seriously considered resigning.[5] Gradually, the situation improved and many problems were resolved by spring 1918. Internal reforms were carried out in the War Department. Bernard Baruch accepted leadership of the War Industries Board and brought strong direction to that planning body that had been leaderless for three months. The Overman Act, passed in 1918, also gave the administration broad powers of executive reorganization. Nevertheless, Secretary Baker, the administration and much of the nation "had been only half at war" for the better part of a year.[6]

The reluctance of the Wilson administration to gear up for war reflected a strong desire to avoid conflict and to find alternative means to achieve peace. The appointment of Newton Baker as Secretary of War in March 1916 had been made in order to temper "the demands of the army for military expansion and diminish the agitation for preparedness that threatened to disrupt the President's own circle."[7] Baker had outspoken pacifist views and excellent credentials as a Progressive reformer attacking the power of large monopolistic business. "Localism and voluntarism were the cornerstones of his creed." Not surprisingly, he fought against many of the increases of governmental power and centralization that the war effort came to demand.[8] Likewise, Secretary of the Navy Josephus Daniels brought an anti-business reform background with him to the Navy Department. Both men served as the focus of rage for administration critics of the war effort, and both reflected the strong predilection that Woodrow Wilson personally had to avoid or minimize the war issue.[9]

The demands of war mobilization threatened the fundamental power relationships between government and the economy. Much of the administration's apparent ambiguity regarding the war effort resulted from trying to find a middle political ground between those who demanded major alterations in the traditional structure of power and those

3. Quoted in Alfred D. Chandler, Jr. and Stephen Salsbury, *Pierre S. DuPont and the Making of the Modern Corporation* (New York: Harper & Row, Publishers, 1971), 401.
4. *Ibid.*; Daniel R. Beaver, *Newton D. Baker and the American War Effort 1917-1919* (Lincoln: University of Nebraska Press, 1966), 79.
5. Beaver, *Baker*, 87, 89-93, 101-02.
6. *Ibid.*, 93-97, 104-07; quotation, 108; David M. Kennedy, *Over Here: The First World War and American Society* (New York: Oxford University Press, 1980), 128-31.
7. Beaver, *Baker*, 4.
8. Kennedy, *Over Here*, 96; Beaver, *Baker*, 1-8, quotation, 6, 75, 104.
9. Kennedy, *Over Here*, 96-97. A good statement of Wilson's philosophy of government and foreign policy may be found in Link, *Wilson the Diplomatist*, 1-16. Link summarized Wilson's views: "Thus America's mission in the World War was not to attain wealth and power, but to fulfill the divine plan by service to mankind, by leadership in moral purposes, and above all by advancing peace and world brotherhood," 15-16.

Controversy in Building

who viewed any such attempt with strong skepticism, if not outright horror.[10] This ambiguity within the Wilson administration had a direct impact on the decisions surrounding the building of Explosives Plant "C" at Nitro.[11]

The question of powder for this greatly expanding American role was a small part of the total war demand, but obviously a crucial part. The primary propellant for bullets and artillery shells was smokeless powder, which had largely replaced the old standard black powder. Benedict Crowell, the Assistant Secretary of War who jointly authored what might be termed a semi-official history of the war effort, wrote:

> In 1914, the total producing capacity of all the powder mills in the United States was approximately 1,500,000 pounds of smokeless powder every month. Under the stimulation of war orders from Europe, this capacity had grown until, by the spring of 1917, when we came into the affair, it had increased perhaps thirty times. Once our officers understood the situation in Europe and struck the agreement with the Allies that put upon us the burden of supplying a great part of the explosives to be used by the anti-German forces on the western front, the early 1917 capacity of America for producing smokeless powder, great as it had seemed to be, looked small indeed compared to what we should have to attain.[12]

As the war dragged on into late spring and summer 1918, the War Department studied plans that would double or triple the thirty-division army then being mobilized. After studying options calling for sixty, eighty and one hundred divisions, the War Department decided in July to field and equip an eighty-division army, over two million men, by the summer of 1919. Equipping that many divisions would be a major task; there were those in the department who felt the nation's munitions industry might not be able to fulfill the needs of the thirty-division program, let alone eighty divisions. To meet the goal for 1919 would have required the "production of one billion pounds of smokeless powder in the year 1919," an amount, according to Assistant Secretary Crowell, that would have required the munitions industry "to double the rate of output reached just before the Armistice."[13]

There were five major companies supplying the American munitions market who might be called upon to help meet this burgeoning demand: DuPont, Atlas, Hercules, Aetna and Canadian Explosives, Ltd. The army also had some small facilities like those at Newport and Indian Head, Maryland. Among these, E. I. DuPont de Nemours & Company of Wilmington, Delaware, was the preeminent firm, and in fact had close ties to the other three American firms. Hercules Powder Company and Atlas Powder Company were separated from DuPont by a 1912 anti-trust action. Both Pierre DuPont, president of the firm, and his brother, Irenee, first vice president and chairman of the executive committee, held large blocks of stock in Hercules and Atlas as did a number of other members of the DuPont family. Aetna Explosives Company was also in the hands of DuPont in-laws,

10. Kennedy, *Over Here*, 137. Kennedy's book is an excellent account of the ways the war effort fundamentally altered the political economy and social relationships of the United States.
11. For a concise account of the construction of Explosive Plant "C," Nitro, see William D. Wintz, *Nitro the World War I Boom Town: An illustrated history of Nitro, West Virginia and the land on which it stands* (South Charleston: Jalamap Publications, 1985), especially pages 39-86.
12. Benedict Crowell and Robert Forrest Wilson, *The Armies of Industry*, vol. 1, *Our Nation's Manufacture of Munitions for a World in Arms, 1917-1918* (New Haven: Yale University Press, 1921), 164.
13. Beaver, *Baker*, 157-61; Crowell and Wilson, *Manufacture of Munitions*, 168. Signing the Armistice on November 11, 1918, of course, obviated this extensive buildup.

but was run so poorly that the DuPont brothers refused to aid the company. Their testimony to this effect was so convincing to army officials that the army did not seriously use Aetna in any major way.[14] Aetna suffered the worst disaster of the war effort when an explosion at its TNT plant in Oakdale, Pennsylvania, outside Pittsburgh, killed approximately two hundred people.[15] DuPont's preeminent role in the field is evidenced by the fact that the DuPont Company paid 90 percent of the receipts from the "munitions tax" levied solely on the powder industry.[16]

The war allowed all the companies to do well and make very large profits. DuPont expanded its operations early to meet the demands of European orders. It built a major guncotton plant (guncotton was the basic source of nitrocellulose used to produce smokeless powder) in Hopewell, Virginia in 1915 and expanded other existing facilities at Pennsgrove and Carney's Point, New Jersey, across the river from Wilmington. The facilities at Carney's Point expanded from one plant to four plants with a total capacity of 625,000 pounds of powder per day. By the end of the war, DuPont's assets had grown from $83.4 million in 1914 to $308 million in 1918. Net earnings peaked at $82 million in 1916 which provided, after taxes, a return on investment of 100 percent. Net earnings in 1917 and 1918 were $49 million and $47 million. The company expanded into a number of new chemical fields and purchased a very large block of General Motors stock, which paved the way for DuPont executives, especially Pierre S. DuPont, to play a major role in the subsequent emergence of this auto giant.[17]

DuPont was, in fact, contracted to build the Nitro facility, but the contract was quickly cancelled by Secretary of War Baker. The cancellation of the contract and the subsequent delay in beginning the Nitro project illustrated the internal ambivalence of the Wilsonian war effort and may well have influenced the future history of the Nitro community.

There were several threads intertwined in the cancellation of the DuPont contract. First, there were the powder needs of the European Allies and the United States, and the gross underestimation by the administration of America's role. Then there was the past relationship between the Army Ordnance Department and DuPont which had developed a tradition of competence and trust that convinced the Ordnance people that DuPont was the only company capable of meeting their needs. Finally, many political leaders in Congress and the administration, coming from strong Progressive political backgrounds of fighting against big business monopolies, distrusted much of the business community and DuPont specifically. Many believed DuPont's war profits were indefensible if not obscene. Thus, the resulting conflicts pitted the military against the civilian leadership

14. Merle Crowell, "Eight Months ago a Cornfield: Today a City of 27,000," The American Magazine, vol. 80, no. 6 (December 1915), 20, 95; "Munitions Industry," Hearings before the Special Committee Investigating the Munitions Industry, United States Senate, Seventy-third Congress, Pursuant to S. Res. 206, Part 13, December 13, 1934 (Washington: United States Government Printing Office, 1935), 2934, 2936; Chandler and Salsbury, Pierre S. DuPont, 396, 402-03.

15. Crowell and Wilson, Manufacture of Munitions, 172; The Charleston Gazette, May 19 and 21, 1918.

16. Chandler and Salsbury, Pierre S. DuPont, 396.

17. Merle Crowell, "Eight Months Ago," 20, 95; Chandler and Salsbury, Pierre S. DuPont, 427-30, 397. Much of the attention of the Senate Committee hearings of 1934, chaired by Senator Gerald Nye, focused on the alleged excess profits made by the whole munitions industry during the war and their economic power afterward. See details of the DuPont holdings in Senate Reports on Public Bills, etc., Seventy-fourth Congress, second session, January 3-June 20, 1936, Senate Report, 944, Part 3, vol. 1, Munitions Industry Report on Activities and Sales of Munitions Companies (Washington: United States Government Printing Office, 1936), 21-27.

Controversy in Building

within the administration, and pitted a large segment of the Wilson administration against DuPont.

An early view shows the construction of houses at Nitro. [courtesy William D. Wintz].

DuPont's earliest inquiry of the government came in June 1916 when Pierre DuPont informed the government of the company's capacity and the extent to which it was thoroughly committed to Allied war orders. He had hoped to elicit some government response as to possible needs for the war effort and potential postwar uses for the plants. However, the administration made no response, and passage of the "munitions tax" shortly afterward, which in effect singled out DuPont as the primary corporation to be taxed, incensed, rightly or wrongly, Pierre DuPont. Concern for possible interruptions of nitrate supplies from Chile led DuPont to propose that his company be allowed to develop a nitrate facility at Muscle Shoals, Alabama. Again he was rebuffed when Congress directed that only a government-owned and -operated plant be built there. Navy Secretary Daniels "openly attacked private military powder manufacturers and advocated more government-built and -operated plants." Pierre DuPont, rankled by what he believed were unfair attacks on his company, was indiscrete enough to suggest publicly during the 1916 election campaign that thinking persons might believe a change of administration desirable.[18] Thus, as the Wilson administration won reelection to a second term on its Progressivism, Preparedness and Peace platform, there appeared to be no room for DuPont in the administration's future plans.

Nevertheless, the war situation deteriorated rapidly, and one month after his March 1917 inauguration, Wilson asked Congress for a Declaration of War. This new situation

18. Chandler and Salsbury, *Pierre S. DuPont*, 395-98, quotation, 397.

The Nitro Plant 97

elicited another exchange between the government and DuPont. In March, Bernard Baruch, then a member of the Advisory Commission of the Council of National Defense, predecessor organization to the War Industries Board, requested information on the status of raw materials necessary to make explosives. DuPont's reply of March 22 indicated a rated capacity of its plants for 27.5 million pounds of powder each month, 98.5 percent of which was contracted for by the Allied governments. Some minor additional capacity was being added and, under very favorable conditions, rated capacity might be exceeded by 3 million pounds per month. Not stated but clearly implied was the fact that if the American government contemplated any need for powder approximating the European demand, new facilities would be needed.[19] Again the official reaction was silence. The army went on to procure its modest needs through the normal bidding process. Of the four bids received, that of DuPont was the lowest and the only one that could meet the Ordnance Department's time frame. The military's demands could still be met by the excess capacities of the industry, and DuPont was recommended for the contract because DuPont's prices were "lower than the present cost of manufacturing this powder at the Army powder factory." As a result, DuPont's capacity was now fully pledged through May 1918.[20]

By fall 1917 the government's basic early spring premise that its major contribution would be moral support had changed drastically. The Ordnance Department began projecting needs that doubled DuPont's already committed 1917 capacity. To meet such unprecedented demands, the Ordnance Department turned to DuPont, and the negotiators soon reached an agreement. Pierre DuPont brought four basic demands to the bargaining table. They were: (1) that his company should have complete control over the building and the operation of the plant—he wanted no responsibility for others' mistakes; (2) that his company should be paid a fair rate of return for work done even though the size of the project might result in a dollar amount some would consider too large; (3) because he believed in incentives for success, DuPont insisted that the agreement allow the company, as part of long-standing policy, to reward key executives and department heads with bonuses for exceptional work; and (4) that the company be given an incentive to do better than meet minimal expectations, namely, that the company share fifty-fifty with the government any savings it could achieve below the contract price. The Army insisted that any plant be an army facility but otherwise was willing to accept the terms. On October 25, 1917, a contract was signed employing DuPont as agent for the government to build and operate new factories that would produce one million pounds of smokeless powder each day. The cost of construction was expected to be approximately $90 million and initial orders for powder were placed for an additional $155 million. The $245 million contract was the largest offered any company during the war.[21]

The contract called for DuPont to receive a construction fee equal to 15 percent of the cost of construction and 5 cents for each pound of powder produced. Contingency fees existed if the contract were terminated in less than six months. The agreed-upon price was 44.5 cents per pound, and any savings below that figure were to be shared equally with the government.[22]

19. *Ibid.*, 400-01; "Munitions Industry," Hearings, Part 13: 2952, 2934, 2944-45 and Exhibit no. 1118, 3125. There also had been a preliminary December 1916 meeting of a DuPont representative with Washington officials. *Ibid.*, 2952.

20. Quoted in Chandler and Salsbury, *Pierre S. DuPont*, 402. The words are those of Colonel Jay E. Hoffer of the Ordnance Department.

21. *Ibid.*, 405-08. Terms of the contract are discussed also in "Munitions Industry," Hearings, Part 13: 2954-59.

22. "Munitions Industry," Hearings, Part 13: 2957; Chandler and Salsbury, *Pierre S. DuPont*, 407-08.

Wade Bennett used thirty-two oxen to pull heavy equipment to the construction site. [courtesy William D. Wintz].

During the first several months of the United States' involvement in the war, while the Wilson administration struggled with decisions, Pierre DuPont had not been idle. He had been convinced earlier that additional capacity was likely to be built, but the company could not offer to build such plants without specific contracts either from abroad or from the American government.[23] Once the United States became involved in the war, Du-Pont undertook its own preliminary investigation to locate new plant sites. Between April 25 and July 12, 1917, company engineers toured sites in seven states and evaluated their data. By August 3, "a definite recommendation was made for the selection of the Charleston [Nitro] site."[24] DuPont began taking options on the property October 4, stopped October 5, but resumed on October 23. On October 31, surveys were begun on portions of the optioned land.[25] The same day, just six days after the contract agreement had been reached, Secretary of War Baker telegraphed DuPont officials, cancelling the contract: "Do nothing about it until you hear further from me." DuPont officials assumed there were only minor technical problems to be ironed out and continued preliminary activity. By November 13, topographical maps were complete enough to locate the plant, and by

23. Chandler and Salsbury, *Pierre S. DuPont*, 401; "Munitions Industry," Hearings, Part 13: 2942-43. Powder plants would be essentially useless after the war. Thus, private industry could not invest its capital in assets that would soon be worthless unless the price paid for the powder included the cost of amortizing the new plants. This is what occurred with the European orders. The other option would be for the government to pay fully for the plants as a cost of war. This the United States government did.

24. "Munitions Industry," Hearings, Part 13, Exhibit no. 1117, Wilmington, Delaware, December 13, 1917, "MEMORANDUM, INVESTIGATIONS AND SECURING SITES FOR SMOKELESS POWDER PLANTS BY E. I. DUPONT DE NEMOURS AND COMPANY IN THE INTERESTS OF THE UNITED STATES GOVERNMENT," 3124. Nitro (the name selected by the Ordnance Department and derived from the chemical term nitrocellulose for the type of gunpowder manufactured) was selected as a site because it met security requirements of being sufficiently inland to be safe from attack, adequate transportation connections by rail and river, available raw materials and land, and the necessary climate (Wintz, *Nitro*, 3-4, 39-42).

25. "Munitions Industry," Hearings, Part 13: 3124.

The Nitro Plant   **99**

November 24, all options were completed and DuPont was ready to start actual construction work.[26] Construction did not start, and DuPont did not build the Nitro plant. The differences were not minor technical matters; they were deep and fundamental.

The cancellation of the contract came from the War Industries Board with the approval of Secretary of War Baker. Although negotiations continued for nearly two months, no agreement could be reached. Chief opponents on the War Industries Board were Leland L. Summers, a consulting engineer and Robert Brookings, a manufacturer and philanthropist who later founded the Brookings Institution. Secretary Baker as well as other Wilsonian appointees shared continued distrust of DuPont. The crux of the controversy was the belief that the contract was too costly, and DuPont would make an excessive profit. The army negotiators, who had mistakenly assumed the board would treat the matter in a routine fashion, argued to no avail that the contract was reasonable.[27] In subsequent meetings, DuPont made minor modifications, which proved inadequate to satisfy Brookings. In a letter of November 14, 1917, to Secretary of War Baker, Brookings, the main protagonist in this dispute, expressed his concerns on the contract.

MY DEAR MR. SECRETARY: You have doubtless heard that the War Industries Board by invitation of General Crozier had a long conference today with General Crozier, Col. Hoffer and Mr. McRoberts, representing the Ordnance Department, and Col. Butler and Mr. du Pont, representing the du Pont Company. I wish to say to you confidentially that while our protest has produced changes in the contract which will probably save the Government $5,000,000 or $6,000,000, and has modified one or two other conditions of the contract in the Government's interest, it still remains in shape where those who expressed themselves, Judge Lovett, Mr. Baruch, and myself, declined to approve it. While upon the one hand Col. Hoffer devoted himself to criticising the Indian Head cost submitted to you as compared with the cost of several kinds of material today, upon the other hand the du Pont people frankly admitted that they expected to make 10¢ per lb. under the contract. In other words, that they expected to produce the powder at 10¢ less than the fixed price mentioned in the contract. Practically the only changes offered were to rebate 6 ½¢ [sic] of the 15% charged on construction out of the profits they would make on operation, to be paid, however, in installments which would require 16 or 18 months operation of the plant in order to secure it. The other change, as I remember it, reduced their compensation from 5¢ to 3½¢ per lb. under certain conditions where the powder cost more to produce than the price named in the contract.

My only purpose in sending you this communication is to emphasize the conviction which I think we all have in the War Industries Board that, when a large sum of money like this is to be expended, unless we participate in the first stages of the conference and are able to mold it along lines which we feel to be fair and equitable, it is almost impossible to do anything with it. General Crozier, Col. Hoffer, and Mr. McRoberts had recommended in the most unqualified way this original contract, and, in our interviews with General Crozier and Col. Hoffer, no amount of arguments made any impression upon them, as they still insisted that the contract was not only a reasonable one, but one which evidenced the greatest generosity upon the part of the du Ponts. You can readily see how difficult it is to get men who have so conclusively passed upon a proposition to admit that they have made a mistake. I may be wrong, but I have the feeling that if we had participated in this negotiation from the beginning we could have just about reduced it one-half, i. e. 7½% on construction and probably 2½¢ per lb. for operation. Even this would have given them an absolutely secured profit of 7½ million dollars per year for nothing on earth but directing the policy of the company from their main office, as, of course, everything else was chargeable to the cost of powder and the Government furnished absolutely all the capital, and, by the terms of the contract, assumed risk of every kind and character.

26. *Ibid.*, 2959, 2961, Exhibit no. 1117, 3124.
27. Chandler and Salsbury, *Pierre S. DuPont*, 411-13.

Controversy in Building

On leaving the conference, General Crozier announced that he felt that, regardless of the price the Government must have immediate action on this, and immediate action could only be had through the du Ponts, and therefore he would urge upon you the emergency necessity which, in his judgement, overshadowed all question of cost.

It was suggested to the du Ponts that they go ahead and construct the plant and operate it after construction, charging all cost of every kind and character to the Government, and, after they had demonstrated the great service rendered the Government, to leave to the Secretary of War the question of their compensation, assuring them that the Secretary of War could not do other than treat them fairly—in fact liberally—if he assumed the responsibility of paying them a fair price for their service. They may consider this, although I do not think it was received very favorably.

It seemed to me that you should have from the War Industries Board as quickly as possible our interpretation of this interview, and, not wishing to intrude upon your much occupied time, I concluded it was better to send you this communication at once by bearer.

Yours very respectfully.[28]

Brookings believed he had evidence that powder could be produced by the army at its Indian Head facility for approximately 33 to 35 cents a pound, not the 44.5 cents contract figure. He contended DuPont had a 10 cents profit margin built in and no risk in the venture. Army personnel disputed Brookings's estimates of the Indian Head costs, and Pierre DuPont also disputed Brookings's charges during the Nye Committee Investigations of the 1930s. Among DuPont's criticisms were the pre-war cost figures for raw materials which did not represent actual inflated prices of 1917-18.[29] Pierre DuPont further noted that DuPont would have built Nitro at less expense than it ultimately cost the government. He concluded his testimony:

I think it is very pertinent here to bring in this letter which will go in the record as the opinion of a man, and probably not worth anything; he made a bad guess, in other words. They hired somebody else to do the work [meaning the Thompson-Starrett Company that built Nitro] who did not have the knowledge, and the consequence was they paid more than if they had taken us up on the original proposition. That is the record and the story.[30]

Irenee DuPont, who was the "Mr. du Pont" at the meeting with Brookings and the War Industries Board, was more contemptuous in the 1930s in dismissing Brookings's allegations. Irenee DuPont testified:

I think I was the Mr. DuPont there at that time, because I had an interview with Mr. Brookings. I could not say if this is the one. But at that interview he told me he would rather pay a dollar a pound for powder for the United States in a state of war if there was no profit in it rather than pay the DuPont Company 50 cents a pound for powder if they had 10 cents profit in it. That is what he told me. I think that is where the 10 cents came from; I do not suppose I denied it. I plainly recall that I put down Mr. Brookings as a woodenware manufacturer in St. Louis or somewhere. He evidently did not appreciate that we might have a war on the east coast of the United States. I was fearful of war. Apparently he thought that he was far enough inland so that it did not matter much.[31]

28. "Munitions Industry," Hearings, Part 14, December 14, 1934, Exhibit no. 1142: 3269-70.
29. Ibid., 3173-76; Chandler and Salsbury, 412-13.
30. "Munitions Industry," Hearings, Part 14: 3176-77.
31. Ibid., Chandler and Salsbury note this exchange, Pierre S. DuPont, 411. DuPont officials long had been concerned that their Delaware River facilities were vulnerable to German submarine attack.

The Nitro Plant 101

The issue might not have come up if Secretary Baker had not shared the same distrust of DuPont. It was his suggestion that the board scrutinize the DuPont contract.[32] In a subsequent conference, Baker angered the DuPont president by telling him that he "could not conceive of services of anyone being worth such a price" as DuPont's potential profit could be. Fundamentally, Baker felt that "since the United States faced a war emergency, private companies should be willing to accept nominal profits." Since Pierre DuPont obviously did not agree and stuck to his initial demand, Baker began the search for other contractors. Meanwhile, the War Industries Board made a counteroffer to DuPont of one million dollars profit on the contract with any additional profit to be negotiated after the plant began operation. Calculating this to be a return of one-quarter of one percent, DuPont refused.[33]

Turning to others, Baker offered the New York engineering firm of Thompson-Starrett one million dollars for doing one hundred million dollars of work. Thompson-Starrett initially protested it had no experience with powder plants, but Baker responded, as L.J. Horowitz, the company president recalled, by saying that he and President Wilson had made up their minds "that we will win the war without DuPont." As the delay extended into weeks and DuPont stood poised to begin actual construction, Pierre DuPont wrote Secretary Baker asking, in effect, for a decision one way or the other, but Baker was still trying to find alternatives despite the military's insistence that DuPont was the logical choice.[34]

The general store at the corner of First Avenue and 41st Street provided all the supplies needed by the Nitro workers. [courtesy William D. Wintz].

32. Chandler and Salsbury, *Pierre S. DuPont*, 411. In Beaver's study of Baker's war leadership, the DuPont munitions contract is not mentioned. The older study by Palmer very briefly outlines the dispute stating Baker found the terms and cost too high. Frederick Palmer, *Newton D. Baker: America at War.*, vol. 2, (New York: Dodd, Mead & Co., 1931), 327.
33. Chandler and Salsbury, *Pierre S. DuPont*, 415-18.
34. *Ibid.*, 418, 414, 415-17; "Munitions Industry," Hearings, Part 14, Exhibit no. 1146, 3272-73.

102   *Controversy in Building*

In mid-December, Baker decided to have the government create its own entity to build and operate powder plants. To head the new agency, Baker recruited Daniel C. Jackling of American Smelting and Refining Company, one of many "dollar-a-year" men who came to government service during the war. Jackling held discussions with Thompson-Starrett who agreed to build facilities with only half the capacity the government wanted and made it clear they did not have the expertise to do even that without DuPont assistance. Final discussions with DuPont yielded no significant change in terms. DuPont agreed to give Thompson-Starrett all their preliminary engineering reports and drawings and technical information, but refused to divert manpower to the project.[35]

The controversy boiled down to two contradictory views of the role of private enterprise in a national emergency. The Progressive views prevailing in the Wilson administration were that patriotic duty ought to be the primary motive of wealthy corporations to undertake essential government service. Pierre DuPont just as firmly believed that his company was entitled to a fair return on the sale of its experience and technical knowledge. Secretary Baker, with his belief in localism and voluntarism, had a vision of the war effort he was striving to attain. On July 11, 1918, he expressed that vision to the workers building the plant at Nitro:

> I take a good deal of pride in this enterprise. It would not be right for me to say that I was the first who believed in its possibility, but I was one of the first who even thought that it would be possible for us by an appeal to the labor and intelligence of the American people in a short space of time to construct this great enterprise successfully and operate it. My faith has now been vindicated and it has been vindicated by your work.[36]

Pierre DuPont's position was just as clearly presented in the December 19, 1917 memorandum summarizing the final failed negotiations:

> Mr. DuPont laid great stress in the conversation upon the fact that his proposition was based, in principle and terms, upon other similar contracts that the Government was awarding, that the terms of compensation were approximately the same as had been accorded in such other contracts, and he stated that he thought he was entitled to know why the Government was not willing to pay him the same rate of compensation that it was paying the others.[37]

---

35. Chandler and Salsbury, *Pierre S. DuPont*, 419; DuPont's final terms and the final offer Jackling was authorized to make may be read in the December 19, 1917 memorandum: "MEMORANDUM OF CONVERSATION HELD (BY TELEPHONE) IN MR. BARUCH'S OFFICE BETWEEN MR. PIERRE DUPONT OF WILMINGTON AND MR. JACKLING WITH MR. EUGENE MEYER JR. PRESENT," December 19, 1917, Record Group 156, Office of the Chief of Ordnance, U.S. Government Explosive Plants. Correspondence Relating to the Nitro, West Virginia Powder Plant, 1918-1919, Box No. 5, File "Nitro Operations," Modern Military Field Branch, Washington National Records Center, Suitland, MD, National Archives and Records Service, Washington, DC. Hereafter cited as R.G. 156, Correspondence. (The words "by telephone" are penciled in on the original typed copy.).
36. ADDRESS OF THE SECRETARY OF WAR, NITRO, W. VA., JULY 11, 1918, R.G. 156, Correspondence, Box 6, File "Nitro Secretary's Visit," 3.
37. MEMORANDUM OF CONVERSATION . . . , R.G. 156. Correspondence, Box 5, File "Nitro Operation," 3.

In July 1918 construction of the plant to manufacture powder needed by the United States and Allied troops began after months of delays and arguments between the government and DuPont. This inspection tour of the Nitro plant included Daniel G. Jackling, hired by the government to oversee construction, Secretary of War Newton D. Baker, U.S. Army Chief of Staff General Peyton C. March, and Milo Smith Ketchum, assistant director in charge of construction at Nitro. [courtesy William D. Wintz].

104   Controversy in Building

The government formally signed a contract with Thompson-Starrett on January 18, 1918, to build facilities capable of producing 500,000 pounds of powder daily—later increased to 625,000 pounds.[38] To fulfill the other half of the government's need, Jackling again turned to DuPont. Both sides backed down from previous positions. Pierre DuPont was frankly fearful that if a powder shortage developed, he and his company would be blamed. Baker, too, had come to accept the fact that DuPont's involvement was necessary. Thus, a contract was signed with DuPont on January 29, 1918 to build facilities that became the Old Hickory plant on land near Nashville, Tennessee, that DuPont had also optioned as the second choice site. The capacity of this plant was also 500,000 pounds of powder originally, but was later expanded to 900,000 pounds daily. DuPont accepted $500,000, one-half the original offer, as the fee to construct the plant. He agreed to operate the plant for 3.5 cents, not 5 cents, per pound commission. The incentive to split any savings below the 44.5 cents price remained. Later, to free himself of government interference in the construction process, Pierre DuPont offered, and the government accepted, a March 23 contract revision, that DuPont would build the plant for a one dollar fee in return for the company's absolute control over the construction process. The Old Hickory plant was built by a specially created subsidiary company, Du-Pont Engineering Company. Pierre DuPont, fearful that the legal position of the War Industries Board was weak and that the Ordnance Department might exceed its authority in a contract, used the subsidiary to insulate his company from a subsequent finding that the contracts were invalid. He had proposed such an arrangement for the Nitro contract and his prudence was vindicated for there was a subsequent questioning by auditors of the Old Hickory contract.[40]

Barracks to house construction workers were the first buildings at the site; eventually there were twenty-eight with two hundred beds apiece. [courtesy William D. Wintz].

38. Contract, January 18, 1918, R.G. 156 Nitrate Division (T) Appraisal Report of U.S. Government Explosives Plant at Nitro, W. Va., January 15, 1919, Box 1, entry 392. The contract may also be found in U.S. "GOVERNMENT EXPLOSIVES PLANT, Daniel C. Jackling, Director, REPORT ON THE CONSTRUCTION OF U.S. GOVERNMENT EXPLOSIVES PLANT "C," NITRO, WEST VIRGINIA, In Six Parts" (Nitro, West Virginia, 1919), Typescript, 1:10-18. The first two volumes of this report contain the history of the plant and are in typescript. The other four volumes are photographic. These volumes are housed in The Modern Military Field Branch in Suitland, MD, and a copy is owned by Mr. William Wintz of St. Albans, WV who graciously allowed the author to have access to the volumes. Hereafter cited as Report on Construction.
39. Chandler and Salsbury, Pierre S. DuPont, 419-21, 425; "Munitions Industry," Hearings, Part 14: 3226.
40. Chandler and Salsbury, Pierre S. DuPont, 408; "Munitions Industry," Hearings, Part 13: 2947, 2953-54.

The Nitro Plant   105

After the war, DuPont officials compared cost figures of the two plants. "Had Jackling constructed Old Hickory, it would have cost $109,320,000 instead of $90,000,000 . . . ; had DuPont built Nitro the cost would have approximated $63,000,000 instead of the $76,525,000 it did cost."[41] Either way, taxpayers' savings would have amounted to $13 million to $19 million. In their written report, investigators for the Nye Committee in the 1930s criticized DuPont's role:

> The Government threatened to build the plant itself but it had no real alternative to accepting the terms of the DuPonts. A man was appointed to undertake the work who apparently had no prior experience in powder manufacture. The DuPont Co. refused to cooperate in assisting the government effort. Finally, a contract was signed under which the DuPont Engineering Co., a wholly owned subsidiary of the DuPont Co., built the Old Hickory powder factory without risk to itself and made a profit on operation of the plant amounting to $1,961,560.[42]

This interpretation of these events is at least overzealous in its criticisms. Whatever other wrongs the investigators believed DuPont may have committed, it stretches any candid reading of the record to lay all the blame on DuPont and charge it with a failure to assist the government. Hearing testimony,[43] the memorandum of Jackling's December 19, 1917 conversation with Pierre DuPont,[44] and the government's own official history of the building of the plant,[45] all of which were available to the investigators, deny any such simplistic reading of these events.

This proved to be the first and only shipment of powder from the Nitro plant. [courtesy William D. Wintz].

41. Chandler and Salsbury, *Pierre S. DuPont*, 427; "Munitions Industry," Hearings, Part 14: 3176.
42. Senate Report 944, Part 4, vol. II, *Munitions Industry Report Relating to Industrial Mobilization in Wartime*, 36.
43. "Munitions Industry," Hearings, Part 14: 3176-79.
44. MEMORANDUM OF CONVERSATION . . . , R.G. 156, Correspondence, Box 5, File "Nitro Operation."
45. *Report on Construction*, Part 1, 6.

Controversy in Building

As for the impact these events had on the future development of Nitro, one can only speculate. DuPont signed the Old Hickory contract January 29, began surveying February 6 and broke ground March 8. By June 9, the Charleston newspapers were reporting the Nashville plant was expected to produce its first powder in early July. The June start-up of the first sulfuric acid unit assured the production date, and the first powder was processed on July 2, 1918, 116 days after ground breaking.[46] Had a similar timetable been applied to the original October 25 contract, powder might have been produced at Nitro by April 1, 1918. Instead the first powder came from the Nitro plant just at the Armistice. Since the original contract called for the full one million pounds of powder, a second plant may have been started at Nashville, but it would have been the unfinished and smaller plant. Would this reversal of situations have helped the development of Nitro after the war? Had Nitro been the essentially completed plant at the Armistice, would the army have changed any of its postwar plans and kept Nitro rather than Old Hickory? Would the village which grew from nothing to approximately twenty-five thousand population, then dropped suddenly to a few thousand, have had a chance to become more stable than it did? Would DuPont have built a fibersilk plant after the war at Nitro rather than at Old Hickory as they did? Would that have had any impact on the postwar economic development of the Nitro area? The dispute between DuPont and the Wilson administration over the Nitro contract and the resulting delay in construction insured that the answers will never be known.

Employees of the plant received their pay from this pay wagon at the work site. [courtesy William D. Wintz].

46. *The Charleston Gazette*, June 9, 1918; "Munitions Industry," Hearings, Part 13: 2956.

47. Robert E. Corlew. *Tennessee: A Short History*, 2nd ed. (Knoxville: The University of Tennessee Press, 1981), 517; "Munitions Industry," Hearings, Part 17 (December 20, 1934), 4222.

The Nitro Plant   107

Herbert Hoover and the Sherman Act, 1921-1933: An Early Phase of a Continuing Issue

*Ellis W. Hawley**

I.

In the history of American antitrust law, Herbert Hoover has never had a prominent place. His name has not been associated with any major innovation; partly, one suspects, because he cannot be fitted easily into the conventional categories of antitrust advocate or opponent, his ideas and positions have received relatively little attention. Yet, for a dozen years, from 1921 to 1933, Hoover was a major participant in debates about the role of antitrust law in American economic regulation and development.[1] During this period, he was involved centrally in efforts both to modify the Sherman Act and to preserve it. Consequently, a fuller knowledge and understanding of this aspect of his career can shed light both on his place in modern American history and on historical forerunners of current debates about antitrust revision. In important respects, his efforts to reconcile cooperative stabilization and developmental mechanisms with antitrust objectives resemble current efforts associated with the "industrial policy" and "national competitiveness" movements. An exploration of these efforts can add perspective to current policy concerns.[2]

With these purposes in mind, this Essay attempts to reconstruct and seeks to understand Hoover's participation in the antitrust debates and the policy decisions of the 1921-1933 period. It focuses initially on the Hooverian regulatory design that emerged from his wartime and immediate postwar experience and that he attempted to implement as Secretary of Commerce. Hoover's design for regulation, I shall argue, is basic to understanding why he could be viewed both as a "trustbuilder" and an "antitruster." Second, the Essay explores in detail two contrasting phases of his involvement with antitrust questions. During the first phase, from 1921 to 1927, Hoover sought revisions that would make the law compatible with

---

*Professor of History, University of Iowa.

1. For the best account of Hoover and antitrust, see R. HIMMELBERG, THE ORIGINS OF THE NATIONAL RECOVERY ADMINISTRATION: BUSINESS, GOVERNMENT, AND THE TRADE ASSOCIATION ISSUE, 1921-1933 (1976). Himmelberg, however, focuses on the movement for legalization of cartels rather than on Hooverian regulatory designs and their interaction with the antitrust tradition.

2. For a discussion of recent and current debates, see O. GRAHAM, THE INDUSTRIAL POLICY DEBATE (forthcoming); THE INDUSTRIAL POLICY DEBATE (C. Johnson ed. 1984); THE POLITICS OF INDUSTRIAL POLICY (C. Barfield & W. Schambra eds. 1986); R. REICH, TALES OF A NEW AMERICA (1987); R. REICH, THE NEXT AMERICAN FRONTIER (1983); TOWARD A NEW U.S. INDUSTRIAL POLICY? (M. Wachter & S. Wachter eds. 1981); L. Schuppener, The Rehabilitation of the Corporatist Model (Ph.D. Diss., U. of Iowa, 1987).

his regulatory designs, and during the second phase, from 1928 to 1933, he became a defender of the Sherman Act against those who would repeal, suspend, or eviscerate it. These two phases, I shall argue, are best seen not as manifestations of confusion or vacillation, but as two facets of a larger and generally coherent and consistent outlook. Third, the Essay focuses briefly on several "Hooverian" organizations developed to deal with the problems of particular industries, noting especially how the histories of these organizations illustrate the difficulties inherent in what Hoover was attempting. Finally, the Essay returns to the relevance of Hoover's experience for current concerns, noting, among other things, the persistence of the issue of how to reconcile cooperative mechanisms with antitrust objectives, the significance of his successes and failures, and the implications for policy choices yet to be made. His encounters with and battles over the Sherman Act, the Essay concludes, merit greater attention than either antitrust studies or Hoover studies heretofore have given them.

II.

Hoover's first encounter with the Sherman Act came during World War I, when as Federal Food Administrator, he preached both the necessity and the desirability of making business organizations a part of the wartime administrative apparatus. Markets alone, he argued, could not do the job. Because the United States lacked and wished to avoid the creation of a centralized national bureaucracy, Hoover further argued, it must draw much of the needed machinery from the organizational life of the private sector. Doing so, he acknowledged, would produce combinations that normally would be subject to prosecution under the Sherman Act. But because these were needed and could be made to serve national ends, it was the law that must give way.[3] In practice, moreover, the law did give way. Both President Woodrow Wilson and Attorney General Thomas Gregory accepted Hoover's line of argument, and an appropriate interpretation of the Food Administration's Enabling Act followed; antitrust ceased to be an obstacle to administrative syndicalism, both in Hoover's domain and in those of the other major war managers.[4] In the words of one of Hoover's

---

3. *See* H. Hoover, Preliminary Note on the Organization of the Food Administration (June 1, 1917) (available at Hoover Presidential Library, Pre-Commerce Papers, Box 18, Wilson File); H. Hoover, Statement to Food Administration Organization Meeting (July 26, 1917) (available at Hoover Institution, Food Administration Collection, Box 1); H. Hoover, Memorandum on Organization of Commodity Controls (June 12, 1917) (contained in Letter from Herbert Hoover to President Woodrow Wilson) (available at Hoover Presidential Library, Pre-Commerce Papers, Box 18, Wilson File); Letter from Herbert Hoover to President Woodrow Wilson (May 31, 1917) (available at Hoover Presidential Library, Pre-Commerce Papers, Box 18, Wilson File); Letter from Herbert Hoover to President Woodrow Wilson (June 29, 1917) (available at Hoover Presidential Library, Pre-Commerce Papers, Box 18, Wilson File); Letter from Herbert Hoover to Thomas Gregory (Aug. 22, 1917) (available at National Archives, Food Administration Records, Record Group 4, Boxes 1 & 2); Letter from Herbert Hoover to President Woodrow Wilson (Aug. 22, 1917) (available at National Archives, Food Administration Records, Record Group 4, Boxes 1 & 2).

4. Letter from Thomas Gregory to President Woodrow Wilson (Aug. 23, 1917) (available at National Archives, Food Administration Records, Boxes 1 & 2); Letter from President Woodrow Wilson to Herbert Hoover (Aug. 23, 1917) (available at National Archives, Food Administration Records, Boxes 1 & 2); *see also* Rothbard, *War Collectivism in World War I*, in A

assistants, action by the trades "to regulate and police themselves" became "one of the fundamental principles" of wartime economic control.[5]

Unlike some advocates of antitrust suspension, however, Hoover did express concern that the war system could destroy the competitive arrangements necessary for postwar progress. The combinations necessary for wartime economic control could be turned to repressive ends or could provoke a shift of power to political managers, both of which would mean protection of inefficiency and backwardness. Furthermore, in the case of the meat-packing industry, Hoover had to concede that the very combinations that were essential to his program were not only "very difficult to deal with" but had the potential to generate a "monstrous growth" of monopoly, exploit suppliers and consumers, and put politicians and their appointees into the meat-packing business.[6] In September 1918, Hoover responded to an investigation of the meat-packing industry by the Federal Trade Commission (FTC), which had charged the industry with "profiteering" and proposed remedies that would decentralize its corporate structure and introduce public ownership and operation into portions of it. Hoover, sounding much like a "trustbuilder," defended the existing system of negotiated profit limitations and excess profit taxes and argued against using war powers for reform purposes.[7] But he also sounded like an "antitruster" as he accepted the FTC's findings of "a growing and dangerous domination" and proposed an "ultimate solution" that called for divorcing meat "manufacturing" from the other phases of the industry and encouraging "decentralized" slaughter houses to the extent that technology would permit.[8] In Hoover's response, his ideas about the industrial structure that would best serve peacetime purposes did not differ greatly from the ideas of the "antitrusters" who would subsequently help to shape the Packers and Stockyards Act of 1921.[9]

NEW HISTORY OF LEVIATHAN (M. Rothbard & R. Radosh eds. 1972) (discussing the syndicalist and corporatist features of the wartime administrative apparatus).

5. A. Merritt, Memorandum on War Time Control of Distribution of Foods (Feb. 1, 1918) (available at National Archives, Food Administration Records, Box 621). For a discussion of self-regulation, see 1918 U.S. FOOD ADMIN. ANN. REP. 6-8; 1917 U.S. FOOD ADMIN. ANN. REP. 10-11.

6. Letter from Herbert Hoover to President Woodrow Wilson (Feb. 21, 1918) (available at Hoover Presidential Library, Pre-Commerce Papers, Box 18, Wilson File); Letter from Herbert Hoover to President Woodrow Wilson (with accompanying memoranda) (July 8, 1918) (available at Hoover Presidential Library, Pre-Commerce Papers, Box 19, Wilson File) (responding to FTC report of June 28, 1918). For further elaboration of Hoover's views, see Letter from Herbert Hoover to President Woodrow Wilson (Mar. 26, 1918) (available at Hoover Presidential Library, Pre-Commerce Papers, Box 18, Wilson File) (reviewing the deteriorating situation in meat industry); Letter from Herbert Hoover to President Woodrow Wilson (May 13, 1918) (available at Hoover Presidential Library, Pre-Commerce Papers, Box 18, Wilson File); and Letter from Herbert Hoover to President Woodrow Wilson (May 21, 1918) (available at Hoover Presidential Library, Pre-Commerce Papers, Box 18, Wilson File). See also Cuff, The Dilemma of Voluntarism: Hoover and the Pork-Packing Agreement of 1917-1919, 53 AGRICULTURAL HIST. 727, 728-47 (1979) (stressing Hoover's dilemma in being dependent on a business group that had acquired a generally negative public image).

7. Letter from Herbert Hoover to President Woodrow Wilson (Sept. 11, 1918) (available at Hoover Presidential Library, Pre-Commerce Papers, Box 19, Wilson File).

8. Id.

9. See Cuff, supra note 6, at 745-46 (Act reflected antitrust views of Farm Bloc congressmen and their allies in antitrust agencies).

In the immediate postwar period, moreover, Hoover did not associate himself with the business-based movement to legalize cartels on a permanent basis. Unlike a number of former war administrators, he devised no plan for a "peace industries board" empowered to grant antitrust exemptions, and in 1919 he kept his distance from the controversial efforts of Secretary William Redfield's Commerce Department to establish "socially responsible" price minima through industrial agreements. In this case, Hoover seemed to agree with Attorney General A. Mitchell Palmer's ruling that Redfield's plan could not be implemented without violating the Sherman Act.[10] Nor was Hoover unsympathetic with those who criticized business "bigness" and wanted to use the Sherman Act to curb "overgrowth." Speaking in late December of 1919, he agreed that the "combination of capital for larger unit production" was—up to a point—"economically sound." But it was not sufficiently recognized, he said, that "overgrowth of [larger] units" led to "bureaucratic administration," rendered growing units in time "less efficient than small units," and induced larger units to try "to dominate the community" and to violate the "primary principle of equality of opportunity."[11] Hoover concluded that the Sherman Act's capacity to check the effects of large combinations must be retained. In early 1921, as he prepared to take over the Commerce Department, he assured President-elect Warren Harding that his plans for rebuilding and strengthening the agency did not include efforts to change the Sherman Act in the way that some business groups and leaders were proposing.[12]

Even as he rejected business arguments for cartelization and further consolidation, Secretary Hoover embraced the strand of postwar managerialism that drew on the war system's machinery for standardization, statistical analysis, and conflict resolution. Hoover saw in managerialism the potential for a "new economic order" that could turn "drift" into "mastery" and use "applied science" to enhance national economic welfare. Initially, the proposals for realizing this potential typically urged the retention of agencies established during the war. But when Congress rejected these proposals, the adherents of managerialism offered an array of designs for coaxing the appropriate regulatory machinery from the private sector and

---

10. *See* Himmelberg, *Business, Antitrust Policy and the Industrial Board of the Department of Commerce, 1919*, 42 Bus. Hist. Rev. 1, 1-23 (1968) (same); Himmelberg, *The War Industries Board and the Antitrust Question in November, 1918*, 52 J. Am. Hist. 59, 59-74 (1965) (recounting these efforts). Hoover's attitude is described in E.E. Hunt, *America and Food*, at 78-81 (available at Hoover Institution, Hunt Papers, Box 19). Hunt was Hoover's associate and right-hand man from 1919 to 1933. In 1934 he wrote a series of accounts about this experience; the accounts were intended to become a book. *America and Food* is one of these.

11. Memorandum to Herbert Hoover, Excerpts on Combinations: Some Notes on Industrial Readjustment—Control of Corporations (undated) (available at Hoover Presidential Library, Commerce Papers, Box 19, Combinations File) (containing excerpts from Hoover's address of Dec. 27, 1919).

12. *See* Telegram from Herbert Hoover to President-elect Warren G. Harding (Feb. 23, 1921) (available at Hoover Presidential Library, Pre-Commerce Papers, Box 6, Harding File). Hoover remembered in his memoirs that he regarded the Sherman Act as unique to the United States and as being one of the reasons that the United States economy was more progressive than the European economies. *See* 2 H. Hoover, Memoirs of Herbert Hoover: the Cabinet and the Presidency, 1920-1933, at 168 (1952).

building a managerial capacity into society itself. Falling into this pattern, for example, were the projects being pushed by activist elements in the managerial and economics professions, by the promoters of a variety of private-sector "institutes" and "surveys," and especially by a "reform wing" of the engineering societies. Following Hoover's return from Europe in 1919, Hoover quickly forged connections with many of these groups and accepted their view that the postwar economic gyrations and accompanying labor and social turmoil constituted strong evidence of the need for management of economic forces. He then used his standing in the engineering profession to develop his own design for action. In 1920, as president of the new Federated American Engineering Societies, Hoover persuaded his fellow professionals to support a much publicized *Waste Survey* intended both to demonstrate the need for management and to stimulate appropriate institutional formation.[13]

In Hoover's design for reducing "waste," which he defined to include unemployment and faulty investment as well as operational inefficiencies and misuse of resources, "information" and "cooperation" were to play key roles. The market, he believed, did not produce enough of either, at least not for the stage of development into which American economic life had now entered. This explained why economic decision makers often lacked the knowledge needed for rational choices and why wastes that would yield only to collective action remained a part of the system. Hence, continued progress required that leaders imbued with a system consciousness and ethic of service, in other words, leaders like himself, become builders of new informational services and of needed forms of associational action. In effect, they had to equip a competitive economic order with some of the intelligence and coordinating machinery envisioned by advocates of economic planning, a task that in Hoover's view could be done without losing the impulse for progress that came from competitive enterprise and a carefully delimited state.[14] They had to implement, as Hoover would put it

---

13. Various sources discuss manifestations of this postwar managerialism. *See* G. ALCHON, THE INVISIBLE HAND OF PLANNING: CAPITALISM, SOCIAL SCIENCE, AND THE STATE IN THE 1920s, at 43-47, 63-67 (1985); M. GREEN, THE NATIONAL CIVIC FEDERATION AND THE AMERICAN LABOR MOVEMENT, 1900-1925, at 394, 413, 436-49 (1956); E. LAYTON, THE REVOLT OF THE ENGINEERS 172-204 (1971); Andrews, *Unemployment Prevention and Insurance*, 10 AM. LAB. LEGIS. REV. 233, 233-39 (1920); Eakins, *The Origins of Corporate Liberal Policy Research, 1917-1922*, in BUILDING THE ORGANIZATIONAL SOCIETY 163-79 (J. Israel ed. 1972); Hawley, *"Industrial Policy" in the 1920s and 1930s*, in THE POLITICS OF INDUSTRIAL POLICY 64-66 (C. Barfield & W. Schambra eds. 1986); *see also* FEDERATED AMERICAN ENGINEERING SOCIETIES, WASTE IN INDUSTRY (1921) (an example of such thinking); Abstract of Address by Herbert Hoover before the American Engineering Council's Executive Board and Convention of Engineers at Syracuse, N.Y. (Feb. 14, 1921) (available at Hoover Presidential Library, Public Statements File (PS 128)) (outlining Hoover's plans and hopes for Waste Survey); E. Hunt, Between Two Worlds 5-10 (unpublished manuscript) (discussing Hoover's postwar thinking) (available at Hoover Institution, Hunt Papers, Boxes 19 & 20); E. Hunt, Reconstruction 11-13 (unpublished manuscript) (available at Hoover Institution, Hunt Papers, Boxes 19 & 20) (discussing Hoover's postwar designs); E. Hunt, Notes on the Hoover Creed (unpublished manuscript) (available at Hoover Institution, Hunt Papers, Boxes 19 & 20) (discussing the emergence of Hoover's postwar program).

14. H. Hoover, Address before the Chamber of Commerce (May 8, 1923), *reprinted in* N.Y. Times, May 9, 1923, at 7, col. 1; E. Hunt, American Individualism (unpublished manuscript) (available at Hoover Institution, Hunt Papers, Boxes 19 & 20); E. Hunt, Notes on the Hoover Creed, *supra* note 13; *see also* W. BARBER, FROM NEW ERA TO NEW DEAL: HERBERT HOOVER, THE

a few years later, a "plan of individualism and associational activities" that would "preserve the initiative, the inventiveness . . . the character of man" and yet would "enable us to socially and economically synchronize this gigantic machine that we have built out of applied science."[15]

In Hoover's scheme, the rise of managerial leadership within the large business corporation was important. Such leaders, Hoover believed, could take a larger and broader view of what constituted good business and, therefore, could act as builders of the needed organizational machinery.[16] But even more important to the scheme was the notion that the trade associations, which had developed to protect the shared interests of competitors and had been temporarily used as units of war administration, could now serve as a key component of the envisioned intelligence and coordinating apparatus. The trade associations, in Hoover's plan, would become important components of the new informational services and would educate businessmen to use these services properly. Trade associations also would serve as vehicles for the cooperative endeavor that was necessary to devise and implement waste elimination plans, and they would work to give the conception of good business practice a broader social content and to enable their members to fulfill these social obligations. Hoover believed these kinds of associational activities were clearly in the public interest and legal under any reasonable reading of the Sherman Act. Far from restraining trade, the proper kind of associational activities would mean larger markets, greater economic opportunity, a firmer base for healthy and constructive competition, and a spur for initiative and inventiveness.[17]

The problem, of course, was that the informational services, standardization, and "better business" activities that were to be a part of the Hoover system could also be used for anticompetitive purposes. Not surprisingly, those with anticompetitive motives were quick to seize upon Secretary Hoover's call for "information" and "cooperation" as a cover for what they had in mind. In particular, promoters of "open price plans," under which competitors exchanged price information through a bureau of their trade

---

ECONOMISTS, AND AMERICAN ECONOMIC POLICY, 1921-1933, at 8-41 (1985) (relating these ideas to the emergence of a "new ecomomics" to which Hoover and his associates subscribed).

15. H. Hoover, Address before the American Engineering Council, Washington, D.C., on the Engineer's Place in the World (Jan. 10, 1924) (available at Hoover Presidential Library, Public Statement File, vol. 14, no. 345A).

16. *See* Cheney, *We Can Cooperate and Yet Compete*, 14 NATION'S BUS. 13 (June 1926), (describing the benefits of the shift to managerial leadership); Letter from Herbert Hoover to Harvey Ingham, editor of *Des Moines Register* (Sept. 19, 1925) (available at Hoover Presidential Library, Commerce Papers, Box 5, Agriculture—Department of Agriculture and Department of Commerce File) (describing broader outlook and larger economic understanding resulting from tendency to divorce ownership from management).

17. *See* H. Hoover, The Value of Trade Associations (Jan. 1925) (available at Hoover Presidential Library, Commerce Papers, Box 602, Trade Associations File) (tentative manuscript draft prepared by Domestic Commerce Division containing excerpts from Hoover's statements about trade associations); H. Hoover, Address before the Penn College Commencement, Oskaloosa, Iowa (June 12, 1925) (available at Hoover Presidential Library, Public Statements File, vol. 20, no. 496); H. Hoover, Address before the National Distribution Conference (Jan. 14, 1925) (available at Library of Congress, Harlan Stone Papers, Hoover File, Box 47).

association, were quick to insist that their goal was rational pricing to eliminate waste, not the facilitation of price-fixing conspiracies as was being alleged by antitrust lawyers. These alleged trustbuilders were soon hailing Hoover as one of them and invoking his name in their clashes with antitrust authorities.[18] This development led antitrusters to denounce him for his encouragement of "industrial piracy."[19] But Hoover believed his critics' interpretation of the law amounted to an unjust and irrational "perversion" of the Sherman Act that could block the institution building essential to economic progress.[20]

III.

The event that would turn Hoover into a Sherman Act revisionist despite his promise to Harding[21] came in December of 1921, when the Supreme Court ruled that the "open price plan" of the Hardwood Manufacturers Association was indeed a device for illegal restraint of trade.[22] In July 1921, Hoover had started his new *Survey of Current Business*, which advertised itself as a first step toward building the informational services needed for the elimination of waste and as an exercise in "cooperation" because the statistical data would come primarily from cooperating trade associations.[23] But it was possible to interpret the *Hardwood* decision as saying that any kind of statistical work by a trade association constituted a violation of antitrust law. Fear that it would be so interpreted not only caused consternation in the trade associations but posed a challenge to Hoover's whole prescription for economic progress. Association executives reported a "panicky feeling" and wondered if further statistical reporting to the *Survey of Current Business* was now "proper."[24] To resolve the issue, Hoover quickly arranged for conferences with Attorney General Harry Daugherty and other Justice Department officials.[25]

---

18. *See Untermyer Warns Trade Association*, N.Y. Times, June 11, 1921, at 6, col. 1-2; C. McKercher, Future of the Open Price Policy (undated address) (available at Hoover Institution, Commerce Papers, Box 1, Feiker File); Letter from A.A. Ainsworth to Herbert Hoover (June 1, 1921) (available at National Archives, Commerce Department Records, Record Group 40, File 76850/1, Box 436); Letter from Samuel Untermyer to Attorney General Harry Daugherty (June 12, 1921) (available at National Archives, Justice Department Records, Record Group 60, File 60-10-2-115x); *see also* W. Barber, *supra* note 14, at 42-46 (pointing out the same problem).

19. *See* S. Untermyer, Honest and Dishonest Trade Associations: An Address at Temple Beth-el 4, 9-10 (1922) (pamphlet) (available at Hoover Presidential Library, Commerce Papers, Box 604, Trade Association File).

20. *See* 2 H. Hoover, *supra* note 12, at 169.

21. *See supra* text accompanying note 12.

22. American Column & Lumber Co. v. United States, 257 U.S. 377, 412 (1921).

23. 1922 Sec'y of Comm. Ann. Rep. 88-89.

24. Letter from D.S. Hunger to Herbert Hoover (Dec. 21, 1921) (available at National Archives, Commerce Department Records, File 81288, Box 505); Letter from George McIlvaine, President of American Trade Association Executives, to Herbert Hoover (Feb. 4, 1922) (available at Hoover Presidential Library, Commerce Papers, Box 602, Trade Associations File) (enclosing Letter from George McIlvaine to Attorney General Harry Daugherty (Dec. 29, 1921)).

25. *See* Telegram from Herbert Hoover to Solicitor William Lamb (Jan. 3, 1922) (available at Hoover Presidential Library, Commerce Papers, Box 603, Trade Associations—Attorney

At these meetings, Secretary Hoover and Commerce Department Solicitor William Lamb tried to get Daugherty to say that the mere collection and publication of statistics through trade association machinery was not illegal and that this should be distinguished from what had been done by the Hardwood Manufacturers Association.[26] The Commerce Department also hoped to get a similar statement of opinion about standardization work, ethical promotion, and various other associational activities. But Daugherty said that his department was always suspicious of trade association programs.[27] The best that Hoover could get was an exchange of letters, released to the press in February 1922, in which he asked questions about eleven kinds of activity. Daugherty agreed that most of the activities could be legal but that each would have to be examined to see whether it restrained trade or suppressed competition.[28] Some trade association lawyers and executives saw this as an "important step forward,"[29] but others insisted that Daugherty had for all practical purposes "said nothing" and that their "people," therefore, were still highly reluctant to begin the kind of activities outlined in Hoover's letter.[30] Nor were Hoover and Lamb satisfied, especially when they were subjected to a wave of inquiries asking whether particular plans and programs came within their definition of legal and constructive activities that contributed to "progressive economic organization" and enhanced "public welfare."[31]

Hoover's official reply to these inquiries was that his department had no authority to interpret the antitrust laws or the statements made by the Department of Justice.[32] Behind the scenes, however, Secretary Hoover

General File) (notifying Lamb of conference with Attorney General); Memorandum from Solicitor William Lamb to Herbert Hoover (Jan. 16, 1922) (available at Hoover Presidential Library, Commerce Papers, Box 603, Trade Associations—Attorney General File) (containing statement of permissible activities issued after consultation between Secretary of Commerce and Attorney General).

26. Memorandum from Solicitor William Lamb to Herbert Hoover (Jan. 16, 1922) (available at Hoover Presidential Library, Commerce Papers, Box 603, Trade Associations —Attorney General File); Letter from Herbert Hoover to Attorney General Harry Daugherty (Feb. 3, 1922) (available at Hoover Presidential Library, Commerce Papers, Box 603, Trade Associations—Attorney General File).

27. Letter from Attorney General Harry Daugherty to Herbert Hoover (Feb. 8, 1922) (available at Hoover Presidential Library, Commerce Papers, Box 603, Trade Associations —Attorney General File).

28. *See* Commerce Department Press Release (Feb. 16, 1922) (available at Hoover Presidential Library, Commerce Papers, Box 603, Trade Associations–Attorney General File) (consisting of whole correspondence between Department of Justice and Department of Commerce from Feb. 3 to Feb. 9, 1922); *see also* L. GALAMBOS, COMPETITION AND COOPERATION: THE EMERGENCE OF A NATIONAL TRADE ASSOCIATION 93-94 (1966) (recounting this episode).

29. Letter from Gilbert Montague to Herbert Hoover (Feb. 15, 1922) (available at Hoover Presidential Library, Commerce Papers, Box 602, Trade Associations File).

30. Letter from Charles R. White, Secretary of Eastern Paperboard Manufacturers Association, to Herbert Hoover (Feb. 13, 1922) (available at Hoover Presidential Library, Commerce Papers, Box 603, Trade Association—Correspondence on Press Releases and Proceedings—Daugherty-Hoover Correspondence File).

31. Letter from Herbert Hoover to Attorney General Harry Daugherty (Feb. 3, 1922) (available at Hoover Presidential Library, Commerce Papers, Box 603, Trade Association—Attorney General file); *see* Letter from Solicitor William Lamb to Herbert Hoover (Mar. 13, 1922) (available at National Archives, Commerce Department Records, File 81288, Box 505) (expressing disgust with pleas to rule on one plan or another).

32. *See, e.g.,* Letter from Herbert Hoover to Charles R. White, Secretary of Eastern

moved to bring public opinion into line with his thinking and to find ways of keeping the statistical activity associated with the *Survey of Current Business* in operation. The *New York Evening Post*, with which Hoover had connections, ran a series of articles on the subject, most of which stressed the positive side of trade association work. The *Post* subsequently published the articles in a booklet entitled *Cooperative Competition*.[33] Further, in a step designed to explore just how much of the statistical machinery could be associational and how much had to be governmental, Hoover convened a Trade Association Conference in April 1922[34] that brought over five hundred associational representatives and other interested parties to Washington, D.C.[35] There, Hoover tried to commit the representatives to continued statistical reporting, to educate them about proper collection and reporting procedures, and to ease their fears that participation without further assurances from the Attorney General would eventually lead to "government control of business."[36] "One of our constant national problems," Hoover told the conferees, was how to obtain beneficial "cooperation without creating dominations of groups that would stifle equality of opportunity" or losing the benefits of competition.[37] But he did not see this as an unsolvable problem, particularly if government and business worked together to develop appropriate organizational forms; he did not believe that misuse of potentially beneficial forms of cooperation justified the prohibition of them. People, he said, "have been murdered with brickbats but that is no reason for prohibiting brick houses."[38]

Paperboard Manufacturers Association (Feb. 16, 1922) (available at Hoover Presidential Library, Commerce Papers, Box 603, Trade Association—Correspondence on Press Releases and Proceedings—Daugherty-Hoover Correspondence File); Letter from Herbert Hoover to Homer Jackson, Associate Editor of *Reliable Poultry Journal* (Feb. 20, 1922) (available at Hoover Presidential Library, Commerce Papers, Box 602, Trade Associations File); Letter from Herbert Hoover to A.F. Allison, General Secretary of International Association of Garment Manufacturers (Feb. 16, 1922) (available at Hoover Presidential Library, Commerce Papers, Box 602, Trade Associations File).

33. New York Evening Post, Cooperative Competition (1922) (pamphlet containing selected articles from Mar. 18 to Apr. 7, 1922).

34. *See* Department of Commerce Press Release (Mar. 17, 1922) (available at Hoover Presidential Library, Commerce Papers, Box 603, Trade Association Conference File) (notifying trade associations of Apr. 12, 1922 conference; *see also* Department of Commerce, Official Summary of Proceedings of the Conference of Trade Associations, Washington, D.C., Apr. 12, 1922 (Apr. 15, 1922) (available at Hoover Presidential Library, Commerce Papers, Box 602, Trade Associations Conference File) (containing Hoover's opening remarks); Letter from Solicitor William Lamb to Herbert Hoover (Apr. 1, 1922) (available at Hoover Presidential Library, Commerce Papers, Box 603, Trade Association Conference File) (discussing dissemination of press release).

35. Shidle, *Hoover on Trade Associations*, 46 Chilton's Automotive Industries 847, 847 (1922) (reporting on conference attendance).

36. *See* R. Emmet, Memorandum on Handling of Trade Association Reports (Apr. 5, 1922) (available at Hoover Presidential Library, Commerce Papers, Box 603, Trade Associations File); F. Surface, Memorandum on Trade Association Reports (undated) (available at Hoover Presidential Library, Commerce Papers, Box 603, Trade Associations File); *see also* Shidle, *supra* note 35, at 847 (containing excerpts from Hoover's address to conference).

37. H. Hoover, Address before the Trade Association Conference (Apr. 12, 1922) (available at Hoover Presidential Library, Commerce Papers, Box 603, Trade Associations Conference Correspondence File).

38. *Id.* at 4.

Not all of the conferees were satisfied by the conference,[39] but the sentiments expressed there were encouraging enough that Hoover proceeded with plans for revamping the *Survey of Current Business*. The new *Survey* included services under which associations might have plans for statistical report preparation approved, submit the reports to the Commerce Department, and have the Department distribute the reports to association members and other interested parties. The details for the service were worked out and implemented by special assistant David Wing,[40] to whom Hoover assigned a departmental function labeled "cooperation with trade associations."[41]

In addition, two significant decisions were made. One was to produce a book on "trade association activities," that in theory would help to give the trade associations a "sense of direction" and steer them into "constructive" channels.[42] The book was to be produced by the Commerce Department with input from an advisory committee drawn from business organizations.[43] The second decision was to work with sympathetic Federal Trade Commissioners, especially FTC Chairman Nelson Gaskill, to establish what amounted to a friendly advisory service to examine doubtful

---

39. One conferee expressed disappointment over the narrowness and shortsightedness of the people assembled. *See* Letter from Hugh F. Fox to E.E. Hunt (Apr. 13, 1922) (available at Hoover Presidential Library, Commerce Papers, Box 287, Hunt File).

40. Memorandum from Herbert Hoover to William Steuart (May 3, 1922) (available at Hoover Presidential Library, Commerce Papers, Box 148, Commerce Department—Trade Associations Statistics File) (notifying Steuart of Wing's "work in connection with the statistical questions arising out of the Trade Association Conference").

41. *See* D. Wing, Report on Work Covering Cooperation with Trade Associations week ending May 13, 1922 (May 13, 1922) (available at Hoover Presidential Library, Commerce Papers, Box 148, Commerce Department—Trade Associations Statistics File); D. Wing, Report on Work Covering Cooperation with Trade Associations week ending May 20, 1922 (May 23, 1922) (available at Hoover Presidential Library, Commerce Papers, Box 148, Commerce Department—Trade Associations Statistics File); D. Wing, Report on Work Covering Cooperation with Trade Associations week ending May 27, 1922 (May 27, 1922) (available at Hoover Presidential Library, Commerce Papers, Box 148, Commerce Department—Trade Associations Statistics File). After consultation with trade association representatives, Wing recommended measures to ensure that the distribution of information a trade association collected from its members was fair, efficient, and legal. *See* Letter from David Wing to R. Emmet (June 7, 1922) (available at Hoover Presidential Library, Commerce Papers, Box 148, Commerce Department—Trade Associations Statistics File) (requesting Hoover's views about his plan); D. Wing, Memorandum on Methods of Cooperation with Associations in Distributing Trade Information (May 27, 1922) (available at Hoover Presidential Library, Commerce Papers, Box 148, Commerce Department—Trade Associations Statistics File) (containing preliminary plan for collecting and distributing trade information and identifying expenses of distribution); *see also* Department of Commerce, The Department's Cooperation for Distribution of Trade Statistics Gathered by Trade Associations (undated) (available at Hoover Presidential Library, Commerce Papers, Box 603, Trade Associations File) (adopting, in large part, Wing's plan); Letter from W. Mullendore to Roy Cheney (Sept. 7, 1922) (available at Commerce Department Records, File 81288, Box 505) (outlining the plan of statistical cooperation being worked out).

42. Letter from Frederick Feiker to Julius Klein (Dec. 8, 1922) (available at National Archives, Bureau of Foreign and Domestic Commerce (BFDC) Records, Record Group 151, File 712.1).

43. *See* Department of Commerce, Trade Association Activities vii (1923). The members of the committee are listed in a report entitled *General Committee Cooperating on Trade Association Activities* (available at Hoover Presidential Library, Commerce Papers, Box 604, Trade Association Activities File).

projects and practices. In response to letters from Wing, Gaskill began writing opinions expressing his "personal views and analyses,"[44] and these were passed along to business inquirers. As Wing put it, the arrangement made it possible "to give the inquirer a friendly criticism of his project."[45]

Hoover used his *Annual Report* in 1922 to reassert his arguments about the need for "cooperative action" in the "public interest" if America was to have a "progressive economic system."[46] Both in the report and elsewhere, he began advocating legislation that would allow a government agency to extend antitrust immunity to approved forms of associational action.[47] Initially, he had resisted this idea, refusing in particular to endorse the version of it embodied in a bill introduced by Senator Walter Edge of New Jersey.[48] But, at the Trade Association Conference, he supported another Edge bill that called for a congressional study committee,[49] and by May 10, 1922, Hoover was prepared to go further. When he discussed the subject of antitrust exemptions at a meeting of the National Association of Manufacturers, he was ready to recommend modification of the Clayton Act[50] with an amendment that allegedly would accomplish the purposes of Edge's first bill.[51] Wing, Gaskill, Edge, and others then began work to produce suitable legislation, initially in the form of an amendment to the Clayton Act,[52] but later conceived of as a law analogous to the Capper-Volstead[53] and Webb-Pomerene[54] Acts that had granted antitrust exemptions to agricultural cooperatives and export combinations. Under proposed regulation, a

---

44. D. Wing, Summary of Reports on Cooperation Work for Distribution of Association Statistics 3 (Aug. 5, 1922) (available at Hoover Presidential Library, Commerce Papers, Box 148, Commerce Department—Trade Associations Statistics File).

45. D. Wing, Report on Work Covering Cooperation with Trade Association ending June 17, 1922 (June 19, 1922) (available at Hoover Presidential Library, Commerce Papers, Box 148, Commerce Department—Trade Associations Statistics File).

46. 1922 SEC'Y OF COMM. ANN. REP. 2, 29-30.

47. *Id.* at 30-31.

48. *See* Letter from Herbert Hoover to Senator Wesley Jones (Apr. 7, 1922) (available at Hoover Presidential Library, Commerce Papers, Box 604, Trade Associations Legislation File); Letter from Senator Walter Edge to Herbert Hoover (Apr. 22, 1922) (available at Hoover Presidential Library, Commerce Papers, Box 604, Trade Associations Legislation File); Letter from Senator Walter Edge to Herbert Hoover (May 5, 1922) (available at Hoover Presidential Library, Commerce Papers, Box 604, Trade Associations Legislation File); *see also* S. 3385, 67th Cong., 2d Sess., 62 CONG. REC. 54,901 (1922) (bill introduced by Senator Edge).

49. *See* H. Hoover, Address before the Trade Association Conference (Apr. 12, 1922) (available at Hoover Presidential Library, Commerce Papers, Box 603, Trade Associations File); *see also* S.J. Res. 188, 67th Cong., 2d Sess., 62 CONG. REC. 54,901 (1922) (introduced by Senator Edge and Representive McArthur).

50. Act of Oct. 15, 1914, ch. 323, § 1, 38 Stat. 730 (1914) (codified at 15 U.S.C. §§ 12-27 (1982)).

51. H. Hoover, Address before the National Association of Manufacturers, New York, N.Y. (May 10, 1922) (available at Hoover Presidential Library, Commerce Papers, Box 427, NAM File).

52. *See* Letter from Herbert Hoover to Senator Walter Edge (June 12, 1922) (available at Hoover Presidential Library, Commerce Papers, Box 545, Senate File); Letter from Senator Walter Edge to Herbert Hoover (June 14, 1922) (available at Hoover Presidential Library, Commerce Papers, Box 545, Senate File).

53. Act of Feb. 18, 1922, ch. 57, § 1, 42 Stat. 388 (1922) (codified at 7 U.S.C. §§ 291, 292 (1982)).

54. Act of Apr. 10, 1918, ch. 50, § 1, 40 Stat. 516 (1918) (codified at 15 U.S.C. §§ 61-65 (1982)).

government agency, to be established either in the Federal Trade Commission or the Department of Commerce, could exempt trade information programs that in its judgment did not restrain trade or serve as instruments for price-fixing.[55]

Secretary Hoover's statements and actions were not without their critics. In April and May of 1922, Hoover became involved in heated and much publicized exchanges with Samuel Untermyer,[56] counsel for a New York State committee engaged in exposing trade restraints in the building and housing industries and an exponent of the view that most trade associations "ought to be exterminated instead of being encouraged to further exploitation of the public."[57] Hoover's programs, Untermyer charged, were being used as covers for a "new form of industrial piracy" seeking to "entrench itself" in the American economy; the programs were evidence of how "naive" and "credulous" Hoover could be; and the programs failed to recognize that if murder by brickbats did not justify their prohibition, one should certainly keep them out of the hands of those with a "predisposition to commit murder."[58] Moreover, Untermyer was not alone. Other antitrusters offered similar though less colorful critiques, and equally worrisome to Hoover were some businesses' charges that the likely consequences of his organizational and legislative efforts would be a further intrusion of government into business decision making. This was the view, for example, of the influential *Manufacturers' News*, which chided entrepreneurs for thinking that any good could come of the congressional study advocated by Hoover and Edge.[59] This view also was echoed by some trade association papers and in some of the lobbying focused on the legal changes that Edge was proposing. Edge sometimes thought, he told Hoover in June 1922, that a good many business groups preferred "to try to evade or circumvent the Sherman Act rather than put themselves under even semi-jurisdiction of the Federal Trade Commission or for that matter any governmental tribunal."[60]

---

55. D. Wing, Summary of Report on Cooperation Work for Distribution of Association Statistics (Aug. 5, 1922) (available at Hoover Presidential Library, Commerce Papers, Box 148, Commerce Department—Trade Associations Statistics File); Letter from David Wing to R. Emmet (June 19, 1922) (available at Hoover Presidential Library, Commerce Papers, Box 148, Commerce Department—Trade Associations Statistics File).

56. *See* N.Y. Times, Apr. 13, 1922, at 4, col. 3; N.Y. Times, Apr. 14, 1922, at 14, col. 2; N.Y. Times, Apr. 17, 1922, at 19, col. 4; Commerce Department Press Release (Apr. 13, 1922) (available at Hoover Presidential Library, Commerce Papers, Box 604, Trade Associations File). The published letters included: Letter from Samuel Untermyer to Herbert Hoover (Apr. 8, 1922) (available at Hoover Presidential Library, Commerce Papers, Box 604, Trade Associations File); Letter from Herbert Hoover to Samuel Untermyer (Apr. 11, 1922) (available at Hoover Presidential Library, Commerce Papers, Box 604, Trade Associations File); and Letter from Samuel Untermyer to Herbert Hoover (Apr. 13, 1922) (available at Hoover Presidential Library, Commerce Papers, Box 604, Trade Associations File).

57. N.Y. Times, Apr. 13, 1922, at 4, col. 3.

58. S. UNTERMYER, *supra* note 19, at 4, 10-15; Letter from Samuel Untermyer to Herbert Hoover (Apr. 16, 1922) (available at Hoover Presidential Library, Commerce Papers, Box 604, Trade Associations File); *see also* S. UNTERMYER, LAW ENFORCEMENT AGAINST BIG AND LITTLE CRIMINALS: ADDRESS BEFORE DUNWOODIE MASONIC LODGE 8-10 (1922).

59. *Pure Bunk*, 21 MANUFACTURERS' NEWS, no. 16, at 14 (Apr. 20, 1922).

60. Letter from Senator Walter Edge to Herbert Hoover (June 14, 1922) (available at Hoover Presidential Library, Commerce Papers, Box 545, Senate File).

Given the less than fully supportive business attitudes, Edge was inclined to let the legislative project "drift."[61] Even after Hoover and he agreed to have "another go" at it in late 1922, they found neither Congress nor business responsive enough to keep the project alive.[62] Hoover's other initiatives, however, did seem relatively successful through much of 1923. The book *Trade Association Activities*[63] was prepared, published, and hailed as ascertaining and illuminating the "constructive" side of trade associations. It offered still another product of the collaboration with Nelson Gaskill, a chapter on the "legal phases" of trade association activities that was finally included despite the belief of the book's preparers that the matter was a "touchy" subject.[64] At the same time, despite some friction over procedures and departmental reluctance to endorse all statistics in given categories, the revamped informational service continued to add new associational cooperators.[65] And in the Gypsum Industries Association consent decree of January 1923, denounced by Untermyer as a "virtual repeal of the antitrust laws,"[66] the Department of Justice seemed to be moving closer to Hoover's position. In the decree, it expressly accepted educational work and various other associational activities as legal and permissible.[67]

In the case of the Justice Department, though, appearances were deceptive. In 1922 Attorney General Daugherty had flirted with the idea of advisory opinions on associational projects. But he had also come under attack in Congress and the press for lax law enforcement and other misdeeds, which had led him to back away from the idea of advisory opinions when special antitrust prosecutor James Fowler argued against it. In the Gypsum case, moreover, the Justice Department's attorneys did not see the decree as being compatible with the kind of price reporting that Hoover was promoting,[68] a position that quickly became clearer in the decrees that followed *United States v. Linseed Oil Company* in June 1923.[69] In this case the Armstrong open-price system used by the linseed oil industry met the same fate as that of the hardwood manufacturers, and in its wake

---

61. *Id.*

62. *See* Letter from Senator Walter Edge to Herbert Hoover (Oct. 2, 1922) (available at Hoover Presidential Library, Commerce Papers, Box 604, Trade Associations Legislation File); Letter from Herbert Hoover to Senator Walter Edge (Oct. 4, 1922) (available at Hoover Presidential Library, Commerce Papers, Box 604, Trade Associations Legislation File); *see also* R. HIMMELBERG, *supra* note 1, at 32-33 (discussing Senate's refusal to act on Edge's resolution).

63. DEPARTMENT OF COMMERCE, *supra* note 43.

64. Letter from Frederick Feiker to Julius Klein (Dec. 8, 1922) (available at National Archives, BFDC Records, File 712.1); Letter from Julius Klein to Frederick Feiker (Dec. 11, 1922) (available at National Archives, BFDC Records, File 712.1).

65. *See* DEPARTMENT OF COMMERCE, *supra* note 43, at 20; Letter from Herbert Hoover to E.W. McCullough (Sept. 20, 1922) (available at Chamber of Commerce Records, General Files); E.W. McCullough, Memorandum of September 28, 1922 (available at Chamber of Commerce Records, General Files).

66. N.Y. Times, Jan. 4, 1923, at 1, col. 6; N.Y. Times, Jan. 5, 1923, at 17, col. 1.

67. *See* NATIONAL INDUSTRIAL CONFERENCE BOARD, TRADE ASSOCIATIONS: THEIR ECONOMIC SIGNIFI-CANCE AND LEGAL STATUS 350-53 (1925) (containing text of Gypsum decree).

68. *See* Letter from Roscoe Mitchell to Attorney General Harry Daugherty (Oct. 5, 1922) (available at National Archives, Justice Department Records, File 60-0, Sect. 11); *see also* R. HIMMELBERG, *supra* note 1, at 33-38 (discussing Justice Department activities during 1923).

69. 262 U.S. 371 (1923).

the Justice Department's disapproval of the work that David Wing was doing for Hoover became clear and explicit. In a decree finally promulgated on November 26, the Tile Manufacturers Credit Association agreed to refrain from all statistical collection not officially requested by a governmental agency,[70] and in an even more stringent decree promulgated on December 13, the Cement Manufacturers Protective Association was barred from all statistical activity.[71] Once again the trade association world and Hoover's interconnections with it were in consternation, and again it seemed that his designs for progress could not be squared with antitrust law enforcement.

On December 11, 1923, Hoover asked for another exchange of opinion with the Attorney General. His cooperative plan, he said, had been developed in the light of the correspondence in early 1922. Yet the *Tile Manufacturers* decree seemed to indicate that the plan was now in conflict with Justice Department policy; if this was so, vital work for meeting the nation's informational needs would be greatly impaired.[72] In response, Daugherty denied that the Justice Department's position had changed. What had happened, he implied, was that the Commerce Department had used a misreading of the earlier correspondence to develop an improper program and to offer improper legal advice; Daugherty now was not disposed to accept this misreading. He did not agree with Hoover's view that the collection and distribution of unidentified price statistics on closed transactions should be permissible when the information was made available to all. Nor did Daugherty think it proper for the secretary of an association to distribute statistical reports to its members, even if this were done under the auspices of a governmental department. Daugherty believed that information should be distributed "strictly through a responsible medium," which meant a government agency.[73] Daugherty's opinions, when released to the press on January 10, 1924, brought intense criticism

---

70. *See* United States v. Tile Mfrs. Credit Ass'n, Equity No. 201 (S.D. Ohio, final decree filed Nov. 26, 1923), *reprinted in* 1 T. LINDSTROM & K. TINGE, ANTITRUST CONSENT DECREES 75-76 (1974) (available at National Archives, Justice Department Records, File 60-55-14); *see also* Justice Department Press Release (Nov. 26, 1923) (available at National Archives, Justice Department Records, File 60-55-14) (describing association and practices now prohibited); Letter from Charles Cheney to A. Seymour (Nov. 26, 1923) (available at National Archives, Justice Department Records, File 60-55-14) (protesting crippling effects of decree on trade association work); Letter from David Wing to Herbert Hoover (Dec. 10, 1923) (available at Hoover Presidential Library, Commerce Papers, Box 713, Wing File) (describing Justice Department's attitudes since *Linseed Oil*).

71. United States v. Cement Mfrs. Protective Ass'n, Equity No. E 22-25 (S.D.N.Y., final decree entered Dec. 13, 1923) (available at National Archives, Justice Department Records, File 60-10-2), *rev'd*, 268 U.S. 588 (1925); *see* Cement Mfrs. Protective Ass'n v. United States, 268 U.S. 588, 592 (1925) (trade association activities alone are not restraints of commerce prohibited by Sherman Act); *see also* Letter from Shale to Attorney General Harry Daugherty (Dec. 13, 1923) (available at National Archives, Justice Department Records, File 60-10-2) (noting Judge Knox's action in signing final decree).

72. Letter from Herbert Hoover to Attorney General Harry Daugherty (Dec. 11, 1923) (available at Hoover Presidential Library, Commerce Papers, Box 602, Trade Associations File).

73. Letter from Attorney General Harry Daugherty to Herbert Hoover (Dec. 19, 1923) (available at Hoover Presidential Library, Commerce Papers, Box 604, Trade Associations Press Release File).

from business.[74] Yet initially, Hoover bowed to the opinions. On February 16, the Commerce Department announced that it would continue the *Survey of Current Business*, but it also announced that it would distribute information only through its own publications, would no longer receive and redistribute material on behalf of cooperating associations, and would express no views on the legal status of trade associations.[75]

Under the circumstances created by Daugherty's stand, Hoover was even willing to consider legislation that would equip his fact-gathering operation with compulsory powers.[76] But the real need, he continued to believe, was to change the interpretation of the Sherman Act that the Justice Department now had embraced and was convincing the courts to accept. Legislative revision, Hoover thought, was still a possibility; when Nelson Gaskill urged revision on President Calvin Coolidge,[77] Hoover seconded the effort and expressed his willingness to work with Gaskill and "such people as are like minded in the Administration" to produce "a real analysis and a proposition for an entire revision of the restraint of trade laws."[78] In addition, through speeches and departmental publications, Hoover continued trying to educate public opinion on the matter, arguing anew that the very arrangements and activities now under a legal cloud could become the basis of a great "transformation in the whole super-organization of our economic life."[79] Because these arrangements and activities could save the nation from the twin evils of monopoly and "socialism,"[80] new legislative definitions of proper and improper forms of

---

74. Department of Commerce Press Release (Jan. 10, 1924) (available at Hoover Presidential Library, Commerce Papers, Box 604, Trade Associations Press Release File) (containing letters cited *supra* notes 72-73). For criticism of Daugherty's opinions, see N.Y. Times, Jan. 10, 1924, at 36, col. 2; N.Y Times, Jan. 20, 1924, § II, at 8, col. 1; N.Y. Times, Feb. 3, 1924, § II, at 13, col. 3.

75. Department of Commerce Press Release (Feb. 16, 1924) (available at Hoover Presidential Library, Commerce Papers, Box 604, Trade Associations Press Release File). For reaction to the Commerce Department's decision, see N.Y. Times, Feb. 17, 1924, at 3, col. 3. For a subsequent explanation of the policy to an inquirer, see Letter from Stephen Davis to Arthur Macruahan (Apr. 1, 1924) (available at National Archives, Commerce Department Records, Box 505, File 81288).

76. *See* Draft of a bill, An Act Authorizing and Directing the Director of Census to Collect and Publish Certain Statistics (undated) (available at Hoover Presidential Library, Commerce Papers, Box 127, Commerce Department—Bureau of the Census File); Memorandum from Herbert Hoover to William Steuart (Nov. 7, 1923) (available at Hoover Presidential Library, Commerce Papers, Box 127, Commerce Department—Bureau of the Census File); Memorandum from Herbert Hoover to Stephen Davis (Nov. 14, 1923) (available at Hoover Presidential Library, Commerce Papers, Box 127, Commerce Department—Bureau of the Census File); Memorandum from F. Murphy to William Steuart (Feb. 20, 1924) (available at Hoover Presidential Library, Commerce Papers, Box 127, Commerce Department—Bureau of the Census File); Letter from J. Nevins to Herbert Hoover (Feb. 16, 1924) (available at Hoover Presidential Library, Commerce Papers, Box 127, Commerce Department—Bureau of the Census File).

77. Letter from Nelson Gaskill to President Coolidge (Feb. 1, 1924) (available at Hoover Presidential Library, Commerce Papers, Box 199, Federal Trade Commission File).

78. Letter from Herbert Hoover to Nelson Gaskill (Feb. 8, 1924) (available at Hoover Presidential Library, Commerce Papers, Box 199, Federal Trade Commission File).

79. H. Hoover, Address before the Annual Meeting of the United States Chamber of Commerce, Cleveland, Ohio (May 7, 1924) (available at Hoover Presidential Library, Commerce Papers, Box 84, Chamber of Commerce—United States File).

80. *Id.*

cooperative action had become imperative, particularly in "the interest of maintaining the small business unit."[81] Yet, neither legislation nor education promised a quick solution, especially in an election year when politicians would try to win votes by "baiting industry."[82] Although much of Hoover's position finally would prevail, victory would come not through legislation or education, but through the less direct method of putting "like minded" people in the key administrative and judicial positions.

More than any other individual, the agent of change in overthrowing the Daugherty interpretation was Harlan F. Stone, a noted corporate lawyer who had become Dean of the Columbia University Law School. A close friend of both Coolidge and Hoover's, Stone's views on associational activity and the Sherman Act clearly qualified him as "like minded." When Coolidge demanded Daugherty's resignation in late March of 1924, perhaps partly because of his troubles with business, but mostly because of his apparent involvement in the Harding scandals, Stone became the new attorney general. Within four months he was regarded as having no desire to upset the "business advancement plans" of the Department of Commerce, as Daugherty had done, and as having views that were leading some associations to resume previously suspended statistical work.[83] Subsequent developments, moreover, made it even clearer that Hooverism now was replacing the doctrine that had shaped the tile and cement decrees. Cooperation between business and government was becoming the new watchword, pushed particularly by Stone's new assistant attorney general, William J. Donovan.[84] The Justice Department became a participant in Hoover's legislative project now being spearheaded by a committee of the United States Chamber of Commerce.[85] While legislation was being discussed, Stone and his lawyers also were working on an alternative in the form of a "test case" that Hoover and he hoped would elicit from the Supreme Court the interpretation of the Sherman Act they wanted.[86] Their choice was a case involving the statistical program of the Maple Flooring Manufacturers' Association, a case framed to turn on the lower court's decision that statistical interchange programs of any consequence must necessarily restrain trade and, therefore, are illegal per se.[87]

When he selected the case, Stone did not know that he would be appointed in early 1925 by President Coolidge to fill a vacancy on the

---

81. 1924 SEC'Y OF COMM. ANN. REP. 22-24.

82. Wooton, *Legality of Trade Statistics a Vital Issue as Keen Competition Looms Ahead*, 25 COAL AGE, no. 4, at 399 (1924). Wooton was one of the publicists who helped Hoover to get his messages into the business and trade press.

83. *See* 26 COAL AGE, no. 24, at 107, 122 (1924); *see also* R. HIMMELBERG, *supra* note 1, at 45-47.

84. Letter from Harlan Stone to Charles Warren (Jan. 19, 1925) (available at Library of Congress, Stone Papers, Box 30) (describing Donovan and his contributions).

85. The new initiative is discussed in N.Y. Times, Sept. 23, 1924, at 27, col. 2; N.Y. Times, Nov. 17, 1924, at 1, col. 1; and 61 AM. MACHINIST 560c (1924).

86. R. HIMMELBERG, *supra* note 1, at 46-48.

87. United States v. Maple Flooring Mfrs. Ass'n (W.D. Mich., final decree entered Jan. 4, 1924) (available at National Archives, Justice Department Records, File 60-160-9-124), *rev'd*, 268 U.S. 563 (1925); *see* Maple Flooring Mfrs. Ass'n v. United States, 268 U.S. 563, 586 (1925) (holding that trade associations that "openly and fairly" engage in trade activities without agreement or concerted action do not violate Sherman Act).

Supreme Court, but it was as an associate justice that he again considered the facts and issues in *Maple Flooring Manufacturers Association v. United States*.[88] By April, trade papers were expressing the view that Justice Stone's "sympathetic and profound study of the whole question [now would] stand him in good stead."[89] Hoover, moreover, clearly expected to see his position vindicated. On April 3 he sent a large package of relevant materials for Stone's "edification."[90] Hoover also responded to requests for additional information. He could not have been too surprised when the opinion handed down on June 1, authored by Stone and joined by five of his colleagues, held that there had been no proof of restraint of trade in the maple flooring industry and that, because the kind of information-gathering and exchange under attack was different from the type held illegal in the *Hardwood* and *Linseed Oil* cases, these practices were not illegal per se.[91] Taken in conjunction with *Cement Manufacturers Protective Association v. United States*,[92] decided in the same way and handed down at the same time, *Maple Flooring* provided a comprehensive and positive statement of which forms of statistical exchange were legal.

In Hoover's view, Stone's opinion was not only good law, but a "great economic document" amounting to a charter for "progressive economic organization."[93] A variety of businesses also hailed it as such and proceeded to thank Hoover for his role in bringing it about.[94] Furthermore, in the two years following the decision, the Commerce Department again expanded its work in building new informational services and "constructive" forms of cooperative action. A revised version of *Trade Association Activities* was produced and published, and again it spelled out how the "national interest" could be served by furthering this new and "fundamental step in

---

88. 268 U.S. 563 (1925).

89. 27 COAL AGE, no. 15, at 545 (1925).

90. Letter from Herbert Hoover to Harlan Stone (Apr. 3, 1925) (available at Library of Congress, Stone Papers, Box 17) (including excerpts from his annual reports, his leading speeches, his correspondence with Daugherty, report on trade association activities, and a study of business cycles completed under auspices of President's Conference on Unemployment).

91. *Maple Flooring Mfrs. Ass'n*, 268 U.S. at 586-87; *see also* Letter from Harlan Stone to Herbert Hoover (Apr. 20, 1925) (available at Library of Congress, Stone Papers, Box 17) (requesting additional information).

92. 268 U.S. 588 (1925).

93. *See* Letter from Herbert Hoover to Harlan Stone (June 3, 1925) (available at Library of Congress, Stone Papers, Box 17); *see also* H. Hoover, Statement at Press Conference (June 4, 1925) (available at Hoover Presidential Library, Commerce Papers, Box 602, Trade Associations File).

94. Letter from E.H. Gaunt to Herbert Hoover (June 5, 1925) (available at National Archives, Commerce Department Records, Box 505, File 81288); Letter from Jacob Newman to Herbert Hoover (June 10, 1925) (available at National Archives, Commerce Department Records, Box 505, File 81288); Letter from C.H. Sherrill to Herbert Hoover (June 22, 1925) (available at National Archives, Commerce Department Records, Box 505, File 81288); *see also* Letter from Nathan Williams to Stephen Davis (June 16, 1925) (available at National Archives, Commerce Department Records, Box 505, File 81288); L. Bell, Memorandum on Maple Flooring and Cement Decisions (June 7, 1925) (available at Hoover Presidential Library, Commerce Papers, Box 602, Trade Associations File); *see also* 115 IRON AGE 1725-26 (1925) (discussing significance of decisions); Jones, *Trade Statistics and Public Policy*, 3 HARV. BUS. REV. 394 (1925) (viewing decisions as victory for economists and economic knowledge).

the gradual evolution of our whole economic life."[95] The statistical, standardization, and "better business" programs were also expanded, each with a large and growing associational component.

In conjunction with this expansion, a number of industry-specific programs were started.[96] In a variety of "problem" industries, departmental officials worked to build cooperative structures that in theory could provide needed elements of planning and controls over "destructive competition" without giving up healthy forms of competitive freedom and incentive.[97] In the Department's relations with the antitrust agencies, moreover, conflict was superseded by harmony and cooperation, at least to the extent that the antitrust agencies were now using Hooverian rhetoric to justify their own efforts to promote "self-regulation."[98] Hoover also endorsed these efforts, especially the Justice Department's new procedure for obtaining an advisory opinion and the FTC's new machinery for producing and approving trade practice agreements.[99] He viewed them as constructive extensions of his own regulatory design.

As for amendments to the Sherman Act, Hoover continued to believe that a formal grant of limited discretionary power to an administrative agency, a grant that would allow it to make some of the distinctions currently being made by the courts, would be desirable. But he doubted that such legislation had any chance of passing.[100] For the most part, he

95. DEPARTMENT OF COMMERCE, TRADE ASSOCIATION ACTIVITIES viii (1927). For the decision to produce the book, see Letter from J. Walter Drake to John Matthews (Mar. 26, 1926) (available at National Archives, Commerce Department Records, File 81288).

96. DEPARTMENT OF COMMERCE, *supra* note 95, at 20-51, 75-90, 108-12; Clark, *Industry Is Setting Up Its Own Government*, N.Y. Times, Mar. 21, 1926, § XX, at 5.

97. H. Hoover, Address before the Chamber of Commerce of the United States—Fourteenth Annual Meeting, Washington, D.C. (May 12, 1926) (available at Hoover Presidential Library, Public Statements File, vol. 24, no. 579).

98. On the "change of attitude" in the Department of Justice and the Federal Trade Commission, see R. HIMMELBERG, *supra* note 1, at 48-51, 54-67; 1926 FTC ANN. REP. 5, 47-48; 1927 FTC ANN. REP. 1, 7; FEDERAL TRADE COMMISSION, TRADE PRACTICE CONFERENCES v-vii (1929); Shepherd, *Today's Trust Busters*, 83 COLLIER'S 8, 8-9, 44 (Feb. 23, 1929); 123 COMMERCIAL AND FIN. CHRONICLE 1059 (1926) (quoting Samuel Untermyer); W. Donovan, Address before the Association of Attorneys General, Detroit, Mich. (Sept. 1, 1925) (available at Hoover Presidential Library, Commerce Papers, Box 604, Trade Associations—Press Releases File) (statements of assistant attorney general); Letter from William Donovan to Messers. Furst, Schwartz, and Schwager (May 22, 1926) (available at National Archives, Justice Department Records, Section 13, File 60-0); Letter from William Donovan to William Cobb (June 17, 1927) (available at National Archives, Justice Department Records, Section 13, File 60-0).

99. For examples of and testimony about Hoover's endorsements and encouragement, see Letter from Herbert Hoover to President Calvin Coolidge (Sept. 22, 1926) (available at Hoover Presidential Library, Commerce Papers, Box 199, Federal Trade Commission File); Letter from S. Davis to O. Stafford (Nov. 5, 1926) (available at National Archives, Commerce Department Records, File 81288); Letter from Herbert Hoover to W.A. Vincent (Oct. 31, 1927) (available at Hoover Presidential Library, Commerce Papers, Box 602, Trade Associations File); Letter from Herbert Hoover to William Humphrey (May 19, 1928) (available at National Archives, Commerce Department Records, File 82245/39); Letter from Abram Myers to Herbert Hoover (July 6, 1931) (available at Hoover Presidential Library, Presidential Papers, Box 154, FTC File). Ironically, Nelson Gaskill, who had earlier championed the kind of relationships with business that were adopted after 1925, was not reappointed to the FTC in 1925, apparently because of bad personal and political relations with Senator Walter Edge. *See* R. HIMMELBERG, *supra* note 1, at 52 n.12.

100. *See* Letter from Herbert Hoover to James F. Burke (Jan. 24, 1927) (available at Hoover

kept his distance from the resurgent business movement that advocated extending the principles enunciated in *Maple Flooring*, overthrowing the per se ban against price-fixing laid down in *United States v. Trenton Potteries Co.*,[101] also written by Stone, and dealing with "destructive competition" through the legalization and formation of full-fledged industrial cartels. Encouraged by the post-1925 developments, this movement took on new life and kept trying to involve Hoover in its activities, but these efforts were mostly without success.[102] Ironically, the movement's supporters in government were found mostly among the new advocates of "self regulation" in the antitrust agencies. In the debates over the kind of antitrust law that was appropriate to a modern organizational society and the kind of conduct the antitrust agencies could properly permit and encourage,[103] Hoover eventually would take a position on the other side. In the second phase of his twelve-year involvement in the controversies surrounding antitrust law, he would function much more as a defender seeking to preserve the Sherman Act than as a critic seeking to revise it.

IV.

As Hoover moved from the Commerce Department to the White House, advocates of using cartels to curb "destructive competition" took some encouragement from his talk about antitrust modernization, cooperative solutions, and the need for better regulatory structures in the natural resource industries.[104] Some antitrusters also were afraid that he was about to mount "a grand offensive" against the Sherman Act.[105] But these hopes

---

Presidential Library, Commerce Papers, Box 69, Burke File); Draft of Letter to Samuel Lindsay (Sept. 11, 1925) (unsent) (available at Hoover Presidential Library, Commerce Papers, Box 269, Hoover, Herbert—Membership, Academy of Political Science File).

101. 273 U.S. 392, 395-402 (1927).

102. The standard response to requests for advice and support was to say that it was not a "function" of the Commerce Department to interpret antitrust law or offer advice on what it permitted or should permit. *See* Letter from S. Davis to Clancey Lewis (Mar. 16, 1926) (available at National Archives, Commerce Department Records, File 81288); Letter from S. Davis to Charles Murphy (Sept. 10, 1926) (available at National Archives, Commerce Department Records, File 81288).

103. For examples of the proposals being made, see L. BOFFEY, HOW TO MEET PRESENT COMPETITIVE CONDITIONS (1928); Montague, *Lawful Combination in Industry*, MINING CONGRESS J. 23-25 (Jan. 1928); Podell & Kirsch, *The Problem of Trade Association Law*, 2 ST. JOHN'S L. REV. 1, 12-18 (1928); Williams, *The Sherman Act To-Day*, 141 ATLANTIC MONTHLY 412, 420-24 (1928); Williams, *The Sherman Act To-Morrow*, 141 ATLANTIC MONTHLY 845-52 (1928); Letter from W.A. Vincent to Herbert Hoover (Oct. 24, 1927) (available at Hoover Presidential Library, Commerce Papers, Box 602, Trade Associations File); Letter from Ralph Easley to William Donovan (Mar. 26, 1928) (available at National Archives, Justice Department Records, File 60-0); S.P. Bush, Competition, Cooperation, and the Law (available at National Archives, Justice Department Records, File 60-126-13).

104. *See* Letter from B.C. Forbes to Owen Young (Jan. 7, 1929) (Owen D. Young Archives, Van Hornesville, New York, File 1-181); Letter from Rush Butler to George Akerson (Apr. 20, 1929) (enclosing text of radio broadcast of Apr. 16, 1929) (available at Hoover Presidential Library, Presidential Papers, Box 63, Antitrust Laws File); Iden, *Business Leaders Voice Their Sentiments on the Anti-Trust Laws*, 43 MAG. OF WALL STREET 636, 638 (1929) (Hoover's willingness, as Secretary of Commerce, to modify antitrust regulations of lumber industry to eliminate waste seen as indication of government's willingness to modify Sherman Act).

105. Pinchot, *Hoover and the "Big Lift,"* 127 NATION 706, 706-08 (1928).

and fears had no real basis in Hoover's thinking or intentions at the time. As he considered the problem areas in antitrust, he worried not about the effects of an allegedly outmoded law, but rather about the lack of sufficient economic analysis in antitrust decision making, the need to keep the growing wave of business mergers within reasonable bounds, and the checks needed to keep some business groups from misusing their associational programs and thereby discrediting associational action in general.[106] Only in the case of the natural resource industries was he willing to endorse a portion of an argument for cartels, and even there, he felt, the regulatory structure should have a considerable public component.[107]

During the initial phases of his presidency, Hoover's efforts to perfect his "cooperative system" and to use it to organize recovery from the stock market crash were not accompanied by calls for antitrust relief to make the desired cooperation possible.[108] On the contrary, the new leadership in the Department of Justice, apparently with Hoover's strong support, not only rejected the arguments for antitrust relief, but began to reconsider and question the schemes for "self-regulation" that had been encouraged during the 1926-1928 period.[109] Attorney General William D. Mitchell proceeded to scrap most of the advisory opinion procedure and to make it clear, particularly in a major policy address delivered at a meeting of the American Bar Association in October 1929, that his department would

---

106. *See* Letter from Frederick Feiker to George Akerson (Aug. 14, 1929) (available at Hoover Presidential Library, Presidential Papers, Box 196, Mergers File); Letter from Herbert Hoover to John Lord O'Brian (Aug. 30, 1929) (available at Hoover Presidential Library, Presidential Papers—Cabinet Offices, Box 21, Justice—Correspondence File); Letter from John Lord O'Brian to Herbert Hoover (Sept. 4, 1929) (available at Hoover Presidential Library, Presidential Papers—Cabinet Offices, Box 21, Justice—Correspondence File); *see also* R. HIMMELBERG, *supra* note 1, at 89-90.

107. *See* R. HIMMELBERG, *supra* note 1, at 88-89, 114 (discussing unitary operation of oil pools and eradication of destructive competition in bituminous coal and timber industries).

108. Hoover's efforts to stabilize the economy and secure an appropriate flow of spending took the form of calling for and securing elaborations and extensions of the conference and committee system that he had built as Secretary of Commerce. *See Business to the Rescue*, NATION 651-52 (Dec. 4, 1929) (Hoover holds White House conference of nation's business leaders to discuss steps to stabilize the economy); *Mobilizing Business Stability*, BUS. WK. 30-31 (Dec. 4, 1929) ("The Hoover conferences . . . are a logical part of a general program Mr. Hoover has been developing for eight years, intended to help stabilize and balance industrial growth...."); *President Leads Movement for Stabilization*, BUS. WK. 33-34 (Nov. 27, 1929) (Hoover's conferences are a "continuation and direct application" of his past efforts to promote greater stability of business); H. Hoover, Address before Annual Meeting of the Chamber of Commerce of the United States, Washington, D.C. (May 1, 1930) (available at Hoover Presidential Library, Public Statements File, vol. 46, no. 1279); H. Hoover, Address before the Business Conference (Dec. 5, 1929) (available at Hoover Presidential Library, Presidential Papers, Box 92, Business Conference File); White House Press Release (Nov. 22, 1929) (available at Hoover Presidential Library, Presidential Papers, Box 92, Business Conference File); Telegram from Herbert Hoover to Julius Barnes (Nov. 15, 1929) (available at Hoover Presidential Library, Presidential Papers—President's Personal File, Box 5, Barnes File); Letter from Herbert Hoover to Robert Lamont (May 17, 1929) (available at Hoover Presidential Library, Presidential Papers-Cabinet Offices, Box 8, Commerce—Correspondence File); *see also* W. BARBER, *supra* note 14, at 78-86 (discussing theory of recovery program and the steps taken to implement it).

109. On the actions of the Justice Department, see *Trade Associations under Investigation*, BUS. WK. 22-23 (Feb. 19, 1930); R. HIMMELBERG, *supra* note 1, at 90-95; 2 H. HOOVER, *supra* note 12, at 302.

"deal vigorously" with every violation of antitrust law coming to its attention.[110] He also declared that Congress, not the Department of Justice, was the place in which to amend the antitrust laws,[111] and in John Lord O'Brian he had an antitrust chief of similar views. While O'Brian denied that any general campaign of a "sensational" or "crusading" character was in the offing,[112] he now was ready to hear critics of what his predecessor had encouraged and condoned, to open official investigations of the programs being criticized, and to move against cartelistic price and production agreements.[113] Eventually, cases would be filed against groups such as the Bolt, Nut, and Rivet Manufacturers Association,[114] the Wool Institute,[115] the Sugar Institute,[116] and the Asphalt Shingle and Roofing

---

110. Mitchell, *How the Department of Justice Views Mergers*, 149 PRINTER'S INK 153, 153-54 (1929) (containing Mitchell's address to the American Bar Association). The preface to the article also places the message in context. The reaction is discussed in *Mitchell's Ax Out for the Trusts*, 103 THE LITERARY DIG. 13 (Nov. 23, 1929) (Attorney General Mitchell warns American Bar Association that he intends to "deal vigorously" with antitrust violations unless Congress directs otherwise); *Trade Associations under Investigation*, BUS. WK. 22-24 (Feb. 15, 1930) ("The Department of Justice is not the place in which to amend the anti-trust laws or any other Acts of Congress.").

111. *Trade Associations under Investigation*, BUS. WK. 23 (Feb. 15, 1930).

112. *See* Letter from John Lord O'Brian to William Mitchell (Jan. 17, 1930) (available at National Archives, Justice Department Records, File 60-0, Section 16) (reporting his statements to *New York Journal of Commerce* reporter); *see also* Justice Department Press Release (May 15, 1930) (available at National Archives, Justice Department Records, File 60-0, Section 16).

113. *See* J. O'Brian, Address before the Annual Meeting of U.S. Chamber of Commerce (May 1, 1930) (available at Hoover Presidential Library, Presidential Papers—Cabinet Offices, Box 22, Justice Department File); *see also Trade Associations under Investigation*, BUS. WK. 22-23 (Feb. 15, 1930) (noting business perceptions of new attitude). Some of the pressure for action came from individuals who believed that prosecution of questionable schemes would create support for revising the law and developing more comprehensive associations. *See, e.g.*, R. Hardy, Memorandum of January 3, 1929 (available at National Archives, Justice Department Records, File 60-126-13); Letter from Felix Levy to William Mitchell (Apr. 4, 1929) (available at National Archives, Justice Department Records, File 60-0, Section 14); Nathan Williams, Memorandum of December 13, 1928 (available at National Archives, BFDC Records, File 712.1); *see also* R. HIMMELBERG, *supra* note 1, at 91-93 (describing pressures applied by National Civic Federation's Committee on Anti-Trust).

114. *See* United States v. Bolt, Nut, and Rivet Mfrs. Ass'n, Equity No. 58-383 (final decree filed Mar. 17, 1931) (available at National Archives, Justice Department Records, File 60-126-13); *see also* Department of Justice Press Release (Mar. 17, 1931) (available at National Archives, Justice Department Records, File 60-126-13) (noting dissolution of association and effect of injunction); Letter from John Lord O'Brian to Charles Graham (Jan. 23, 1930) (available at National Archives, Justice Department Records, File 60-126-13) (notifying association's leader that Justice Department will take legal action); Letter from John Lord O'Brian to William Mitchell (Feb. 28, 1930) (available at National Archives, Justice Department Records, File 60-126-13) (describing efforts of association and FTC officials to alter Justice Department's decision).

115. *See Trade Associations See Warning in Wool Institute Decree*, BUS. WK. 12 (July 9, 1930) (describing case and resulting decree); *see also* R. HIMMELBERG, *supra* note 1, at 95.

116. *See* United States v. Sugar Institute, Inc., Petition in Equity (S.D.N.Y. Mar. 30, 1931) (available at National Archives, Justice Department Records, File 60-104-13; *see also* Letter from James Fly to John Lord O'Brian (Dec. 10, 1929) (available at National Archives, Justice Department Records, File 60-104-13) (suggesting inquiry into sugar reporting system and code of ethics); Letter from John Lord O'Brian to William Mitchell (Jan. 16, 1930) (available at National Archives, Justice Department Records, File 60-126-13) (asking for approval to proceed); Letter from John Lord O'Brian to William Mitchell (Feb. 2, 1931) (available at National Archives, Justice Department Records, File 60-104-13) (recommending legal action against Sugar Institute); J. O'Brian, Memorandum for the Files (Mar. 27, 1931) (available at

Institute,[117] all of which claimed to have previously received "go ahead" signals from government officials.[118]

While undertaking these prosecutions, O'Brian also complained to the Federal Trade Commission about the kind of "self-regulation" that it was promoting through its trade practice conference procedure. The codes of ethical practice, he charged, were being used to establish and maintain illegal restraints of trade.[119] Partly because of his complaints and their implications, partly because of similar charges by congressional and business critics, and partly because a new majority on the FTC was moving FTC policy back toward a more adversarial stance,[120] a decision eventually was made that most of the codes would have to be revised. Announced in April 1930 and made more thoroughgoing in March 1931,[121] the decision led, after repeated delays, to the deletion of questionable rules from a total of eighty codes.[122] In almost all cases, the FTC rejected business pleas to have them reinstated.[123] Only in the case of the marketing code for petroleum

National Archives, Justice Department Records, File 60-104-13) (reporting on conversation with Solicitor William Lamb, who "remonstrated with some emphasis" against Department's insistence that Sugar Institute be dissolved).

117. *See* United States v. Asphalt Shingle & Roofing Inst., Petition in Equity, No. 157-162 (Dec. 30, 1930) (available at National Archives, Justice Department Records, File 60-157-1); *see also* Letter from James Fly to John Lord O'Brian (Feb. 28, 1930) (available at National Archives, Justice Department Records, File 60-157-1) (describing Institute's merchandising plan and code of ethics and concluding that action should be taken against it); Letter from James Fly to John Lord O'Brian (Oct. 31, 1930) (available at National Archives, Justice Department Records, File 60-157-1).

118. These business attitudes are reported in *Trade Associations See Warning in Wool Institute Decree*, Bus. Wk. 12 (July 9, 1930); *Anti-Trust Suit Challenges Trade Association Practices*, Bus. Wk. 12 (Jan. 7, 1931); *Nut and Bolt Decree Draws a Chalk Line for Stabilization*, Bus. Wk. 10 (Mar. 25, 1931).

119. *See* Letter from John Lord O'Brian to Garland Ferguson (Dec. 17, 1930) (available at National Archives, Justice Department Records, File 60-57-32); Letter from John Lord O'Brian to William Mitchell (Jan. 6, 1931) (available at National Archives, Justice Department Records, File 60-57-32). The history of O'Brian's protests and misgivings also is contained in a letter from John Lord O'Brian to Garland Ferguson (unsent) (Dec. 16, 1930) (available at National Archives, Justice Department Records, File 60-57-32). *See also* R. Himmelberg, *supra* note 1, at 96-97 (account of O'Brian's protests).

120. For accounts of these developments, see Herring, *Politics, Personalities, and the Federal Trade Commission, II*, 29 Am. Pol. Sci. Rev. 21, 28-29 (1935); *Trade Practice Codes Debated*, Bus. Wk. 25 (Apr. 16, 1930); *Trade Commission Retreats Behind Ramparts of the Law*, Bus. Wk. 5 (Apr. 30, 1930); *Antitrust Campaign Resumed to Tighten Observance of Law*, N.Y. J. Commerce, Feb. 1, 1930, at 1, col. 1.

121. The FTC's initial announcement is reported in the N.Y. Times, Apr. 6, 1930, § II, at 22, col. 2. A second announcement spelling out the implications for approval of new trade practice rules came on April 18, 1930, § II, at 16, col. 3. The announcement making the revision even more thoroughgoing came on March 30, 1931, and is reported in the N.Y. Times, Mar. 31, 1931, at 46, col. 1. For the principle of revision finally adopted, *i.e.*, rules could only restate the antitrust laws, see Statement of William E. Humphrey (Mar. 7, 1931) (available at Library of Congress, Humphrey Papers, Box 2).

122. The deletion finally was made in June 1931. *See Industries Read Funeral Service over 80 Trade Practice Codes*, Bus. Wk. 10 (June 17, 1931). In 1930 protests from the trade associations led to postponement of revision and a round of hearings held from September 25 to October 25. *See Trade Associations Protest Restrictions on House Cleaning*, Bus. Wk. 13-14 (Oct. 8, 1930); *Trade Practice Code Troubles are Growing Pains, Not Serious*, Bus. Wk. 5 (Apr. 8, 1931); N.Y. Times, Aug. 16, 1931, § II, at 15, col 5.

123. Wooton, *Industries Using Trade Practice Rules Abandon Efforts to Obtain Revisions*, 74 Am.

—one of the natural resource industries that Hoover and other administration leaders were willing to treat as a special case—was the revision rescinded and original code restored.[124]

In the business press, these antitrust actions became the subject of widespread criticism, most of which charged that President Hoover was "reversing" established Republican policy, making the depression worse, and mounting contradictory initiatives that had some agencies promoting "economic self-government" while others acted to block it.[125] Yet even as these charges were made, a number of those advocating Sherman Act revision saw the actions as ultimately working to their advantage. The Hoover Administration's actions would demonstrate to business groups, the revisionists believed, that relief was possible only by amending the law, thus creating broader support for the movement to do so.[126] For a time, the revisionists had hopes that Secretary of Commerce Robert P. Lamont might step forth as a leader in this movement, somewhat as Hoover had done in the revisionist movement of the 1922-1925 period.[127] Some also thought that President Hoover's endorsement and support of their position was not out of the question. Once he understood where antitrust law enforcement was leading and how it worked at cross purposes with his designs for getting an organizational economy to manage itself, he might support the latest efforts to bring an outmoded and hence injurious law into line with the planning and security needs of a modern economic order.[128]

MACHINIST 9666 (JUNE 18, 1931); *Trade Practice Romance is Shattered*, 8 NAT'L SPHERE 25-26 (July 1931).

124. The revisions were announced in Federal Trade Commission, Press Release (Feb. 11, 1931) (available at National Archives, Justice Department Records, File 60-57-32). The restored code was entitled *Trade Practice Conference Rules for the Petroleum Industry as Approved or Accepted by the Federal Trade Commission on June 12, 1931* (available at National Archives, Justice Department Records, File 60-57-32). O'Brian wanted to make a "remonstrance," but Mitchell thought the situation was "delicate" and that a protest would be improper. *See* Letter from John Lord O'Brian to William Mitchell (July 21, 1931) (available at National Archives, Justice Department Records, File 60-57-32); Letter from William Mitchell to John Lord O'Brian (July 21, 1931) (available at National Archives, Justice Department Records, File 60-57-32). For press account of these actions, see *Industries That Had Good Codes Will Now Use Good Lawyers*, BUS. WK. 7 (Feb. 11, 1931); *Trade Commission's Soft Answer Turns Away Oil Industry's Wrath*, BUS. WK. 7 (Apr. 8, 1931); *Trade Board Ruling Viewed as Reversal of Oil Regulations*, N.Y. J. Commerce, Aug. 10, 1931, at 1, col. 6; *see also* R. HIMMELBERG, *supra* note 1, at 98-100.

125. *See Trade Associations under Investigation*, BUS. WK. 22 (Feb. 19, 1930); *Trade Associations See Warning in Wool Institute Decree*, BUS. WK. 12 (July 9, 1930); *Trade Practice Romance is Shattered*, NAT'L SPHERE 25-26 (July 1931).

126. *See* Proceedings of Antitrust Committee, National Civic Federation (NCF) (Dec. 10, 1929, Apr. 11, 1930) (available at New York City Public Library, NCF Papers, Box 134); *see also* R. HIMMELBERG, *supra* note 1, at 91-93 (discussing this view).

127. *See, e.g.*, Letter from W. Bloodgood to Robert Lamont (Nov. 1, 1929) (available at New York City Public Library, NCF Papers, Box 134); Letter from M. Woll to Robert P. Lamont (Nov. 1, 1929) (available at New York City Public Library, NCF Papers, Box 135); Letter from Benjamin A. Javits to Robert P. Lamont (Nov. 4, 1929) (available at Hoover Presidential Library, Presidential Papers, Box 649, Secretary's File—Javits).

128. Association Counsel Louis E. Flye, for example, saw the new push for cooperative market stabilization as an extension of Hoover's earlier efforts "to bring about self-regulation in industry and to raise the standards of commercial conduct" and believed that the President's leadership was now "more necessary than ever before." Letter from Louis E. Flye to George E. Akerson (Sept. 3, 1930) (available at Hoover Presidential Library, Presidential Papers, Box 154, FTC—Correspondence File).

By the second anniversary of Hoover's inaugural, a variety of proposals for allowing previously prohibited business combinations were under discussion. Included were an American counterpart to Germany's Cartel Court (proposed by O'Brian's predecessor as antitrust chief),[129] a business counterpart to the Federal Farm Board,[130] a peacetime counterpart of the War Industries Board, and an expanded Federal Trade Commission empowered to distinguish between good and bad trusts.[131] Yet, much of organized business was still reluctant to mount legislative initiatives, for fear, as one commentator had put it, that Congress would more likely "mess up" than "clean up" the situation.[132] This reluctance, moreover, was enhanced when the revisionists' expectations of administration support failed to materialize. Secretary Lamont kept minimizing the need for revision and the chances of securing it;[133] Attorney General Mitchell refused to accept the notion that there could or should be a "moratorium" on antitrust enforcement because business was not prosperous;[134] and Hoover not only kept his distance from the proposals being made, but rebuffed efforts to enlist his aid in saving the trade practice conference rules previously approved by the FTC. The kind of self-regulation that he had encouraged in 1927, he said, had not involved "consolidations" or "price-fixing";[135] moreover, he had no authority over the FTC and could not interfere in actions that it considered to be in the public interest.[136]

---

129. Donovan, *The Need for a Commerce Court*, 147 ANNALS 138, 143-45 (1930).

130. An agency established in 1929 to stabilize farm markets through the organization of cooperative marketing associations and governmental support.

131. *Industry Gropes for Means to Stop Ruinous Selling*, BUS. WK. 14 (May 7, 1930) (discussing idea of a "Federal Farm Board for industry"); *B.M. Baruch Wants Forum to Cure Overproduction Ills*, BUS. WK. 22 (May 14, 1930) (describing Baruch's call for agency similar to WIB); *Nye Bill to Halt Price Cutting Would Do More Harm Than Good*, BUS. WK. 10 (Jan. 21, 1931) (discussing proposal for expanded FTC). For discussions of similar proposals, see Davis, *Can Business Manage Itself?*, 162 HARPER'S MAGAZINE 385, 389-93 (1931); Donham, *Can American Business Meet the Present Emergency?*, 9 HARV. BUS. REV. 257 (1931); Greer, *A General Staff for Business*, 156 OUTLOOK AND INDEPENDENT 695-97 (1930); Scroggs, *The Anti-Trust Laws Under Fire*, 156 OUTLOOK AND INDEPENDENT 545 (1930).

132. Frederick, *The Influence of Anti-Trust Legislation upon the Technique of Industrial Organization*, 147 ANNALS 95, 102 (1937); *see also Sherman Act Still Is Law, and Likely to Remain So*, BUS. WK. 5-6 (Nov. 26, 1930) (noting business fears that antitrust revision would lead to liberty-destroying regulation).

133. *See* Letter from Robert Lamont to E.E. Hunt (Apr. 26, 1930) (available at National Archives, Robert Lamont Papers, Record Group 40, Box 3); Letter from Robert Lamont to W.M. Ritter (May 5, 1930) (available at National Archives, Robert Lamont Papers, Record Group 40, Box 3).

134. *See* W. Mitchell, Address before the Law School Association of the University of Minnesota (Apr. 15, 1931) (available at Hoover Presidential Library, Presidential Papers, Box 22, Justice Department—Correspondence File) (stating that attorney general "has no authority to declare a moratorium" and suggesting it would be inappropriate to "wink at violations"); *see also Trade Practice Code Troubles are Growing Pains, Not Serious*, BUS. WK. 5 (Apr. 8, 1931) (noting that business had been laboring under misapprehensions now being cleared up; suggesting FTC and Department of Justice cooperation should be fostered).

135. Letter from Herbert Hoover to Abram F. Myers (May 4, 1931) (available at Hoover Presidential Library, Presidential Papers, Box 154, FTC—Correspondence File).

136. *See* Letter from Louis E. Flye to Herbert Hoover (Sept. 12, 1930) (available at Hoover Presidential Library, Presidential Papers, Box 154, FTC—Correspondence File); Letter from Lawrence Richey to Louis E. Flye (Sept. 16, 1930) (available at Hoover Presidential Library, Presidential Papers, Box 154, FTC—Correspondence File).

The most that President Hoover would do was to urge special considerations for natural resource industries, which was probably a factor in saving the petroleum code, and to recommend a congressional inquiry into some aspects of the law's "economic working." These two proposals came in his State of the Union message in December 1930, when, significantly, Hoover coupled the proposals with an assurance that he did not favor "repeal of the Sherman Act." Hoover believed that the "prevention of monopolies" was of "most vital public importance" and that competition was not only "the basis of protection to the consumer," but "the incentive to progress."[137] Of significance, too, was the fact that having made the recommendation, he made little effort to push congressional action on it.[138]

Nor did Hoover change his stance in the face of another wave of proposals that were extensively publicized and discussed in the waning months of 1931. Especially prominent among these were proposals for setting aside the antitrust laws in order to permit recovery planning through government-supported trade associations by Gerard Swope of General Electric and Henry I. Harriman, chairman of a special Chamber of Commerce study group.[139] Hoover's response to both proposals was strongly negative. The Chamber of Commerce, he thought, had embarked on a course that was in neither business's, nor the public's interests,[140] despite the strenuous efforts of his old friend, United States Chamber of Commerce Chairperson Julius H. Barnes, to convince him otherwise.[141] In

---

137. Hoover, *Annual Message to Congress on the State of the Union* (Dec. 2, 1930), 2 PUBLIC PAPERS OF THE PRESIDENTS OF THE UNITED STATES: HERBERT HOOVER 509, 519-20 (1976) [hereinafter PUBLIC PAPERS OF THE PRESIDENTS]; *see* R. HIMMELBERG, *supra* note 1, at 114 (context of message, with commentary).

138. *See Congress Starts to Make Study of Sherman Antitrust Law*, BUS. WK. 30 (Jan. 14, 1931); Williams, *The Reign of Error*, 147 ATLANTIC MONTHLY 787, 787-89 (1931); Letter from John Lord O'Brian to William Mitchell (Dec. 16, 1930) (available at National Archives, Justice Department Records, File 60-0, Section 17).

139. For a discussion of the Swope Plan, see *Trade Association Is Keystone of Swope Stabilization Plan*, BUS. WK. 12 (Sept. 23, 1931); *Friendly Critics of Swope Plan Want to See It Given Fair Trial*, BUS. WK. 15 (Sept. 30, 1931); *Plan for Stabilization of Industry by President of the General Electric Company*, 33 MONTHLY LAB. REV. 1049, 1049-56 (1931). For a discussion of the Harriman Plan, see UNITED STATES CHAMBER OF COMMERCE, REPORT OF THE COMMITTEE ON CONTINUITY OF BUSINESS AND EMPLOYMENT 9 (Oct. 1931) (available at Hoover Presidential Library, Presidential Papers, Box 95, Chamber of Commerce of U.S.—Correspondence File) (report of Harriman's study group); *U.S. Chamber Plan Recognizes New Trend of Business Thought*, BUS. WK. 14 (Dec. 30, 1931). For other proposals made, see *Drive on Sherman Act Gains Impetus Among Business Men*, BUS. WK. 11-12 (Dec. 2, 1931); Letter from Julius H. Barnes to Herbert Hoover (Sept. 17, 1931) (available at Hoover Presidential Library, Presidential Papers, Box 95, Chamber of Commerce of U.S.—Correspondence File) (arguing that antitrust had become "the largest question in business today" and urging a program to halt "destructive price competition"); NATIONAL ECONOMIC PLANNING BOARD, PROPOSALS FOR ECONOMIC PLANNING BOARDS IN THE UNITED STATES 4 (Sept. 1931) (available at Hoover Presidential Library, Presidential Papers, Box 95, Chamber of Commerce of U.S.—Correspondence File) (detailing suggestions by various individuals and including proposal to repeal the Sherman and Clayton Acts).

140. *See* H. HOOVER, *supra* note 12, at 334-35 (citing public statement by Hoover on Oct. 8, 1931).

141. *See* Letter from Julius Barnes to Herbert Hoover (Sept. 17, 1931) (available at Hoover Presidential Library, Presidential Papers, Box 95, Chamber of Commerce of U.S.—Correspondence File); Letter from Julius Barnes to Herbert Hoover (Oct. 5, 1931) (available at

addition, Hoover believed the Swope Plan was in essence a scheme for "price fixing" through the "organization of gigantic trusts." The plan called for "the repeal of the entire Sherman and Clayton Acts and all other restrictions on combination and monopoly," which, in Hoover's opinion, would mean a loss of creativity, the protection of "obsolete plants and inferior managements," and a general "decay of American industry from the day this scheme is born."[142] Hoover expressed these sentiments in a memorandum sent to Solicitor General Thomas D. Thacher and Republican Senator Felix Hebert,[143] both of whom responded as Hoover had hoped. Thacher responded with a pronouncement of the scheme's unconstitutionality,[144] and Senator Hebert responded with a press statement denouncing the plan as monopolistic, bureaucratic, and constitutionally unimplementable.[145] Hoover expected, he said in the letter transmitting the Swope Plan to Thacher, that as President he would have to "meet" the proposal in Congress,[146] and Hoover's statements and actions left little

---

Hoover Presidential Library, Presidential Papers, Box 95, Chamber of Commerce of U.S.—Correspondence File); Letter from Julius Barnes to Herbert Hoover (Oct. 10, 1931) (available at Hoover Presidential Library, Presidential Papers, Box 95, Chamber of Commerce of U.S.—Correspondence File); Letter from Julius Barnes to Herbert Hoover (Nov. 30, 1931) (available at Hoover Presidential Library, Presidential Papers, Box 96, Chamber of Commerce of U.S.—Correspondence File); Letter from Julius Barnes to Herbert Hoover (Dec. 18, 1931) (available at Hoover Presidential Library, Presidential Papers, Box 96, Chamber of Commerce of U.S.—Correspondence File) (reporting adoption of United States Chamber of Commerce recommendations for modifying antitrust laws).

142. H. Hoover, Desk Memorandum on the Swope Plan (cir. Sept. 13, 1931) (available at Hoover Presidential Library, Presidential Papers, Box 92, Business—Stabilization of Industry Plans File) (discussing constitutionality of Swope Plan).

143. *See* Letter from Felix Hebert to Herbert Hoover (Sept. 15, 1931) (available at Hoover Presidential Library, Presidential Papers, Business—Stabilization of Industry Plans File) (indicating reception of materials sent him); Letter from Richey to Thomas D. Thacher (Sept. 15, 1931) (available at Hoover Presidential Library, Presidential Papers, Box 92, Business-—Stabilization of Industry Plans File) (transmitting copy of Hoover's memorandum). Hoover also sent other materials. *See* Letter from Herbert Hoover to Thomas D. Thacher (Sept. 12, 1931) (available at Hoover Presidential Library, Presidential Papers, Box 92, Business—Stabilization of Industry Plans File) (transmitting Swope Plan and suggesting it is "thoroughly unconstitutional"); Letter from Herbert Hoover to Thomas D. Thacher (Sept. 14, 1931) (available at Hoover Presidential Library, Presidential Papers, Box 92, Business—Stabilization of Industry Plans File) (critical memorandum by William Donovan).

144. Letter from Thomas D. Thacher to Herbert Hoover (Oct. 1, 1931) (available at Hoover Presidential Library, Presidential Papers, Box 92, Business—Stabilization of Industry Plans File) (legislation required by Swope Plan not authorized under Commerce Clause).

145. *See* Letter from Felix Hebert to Herbert Hoover (Sept. 18, 1931) (available at Hoover Presidential Library, Presidential Papers, Box 92, Business—Stabilization of Industry Plans File) (enclosing copy of draft statement on stabilization of industry to appear in Providence papers); Hebert, Draft of Proposed Statement of United States Senator Felix Hebert on the Subject of Stabilization of Industry (cir. Sept. 18, 1931) (available at Hoover Presidential Library, Hoover Papers, Presidential Papers, Box 92, Business—Stabilization of Industry Plans File); *see also* Letter from Felix Hebert to Herbert Hoover (Sept. 15, 1931) (available at Hoover Presidential Library, Presidential Papers, Box 92, Business—Stabilization of Industry Plans File) (agreeing with Hoover's opposition to Swope Plan).

146. Letter from Herbert Hoover to Thomas D. Thacher (Sept. 12, 1931) (available at Hoover Presidential Library, Presidential Papers, Box 92, Business—Stabilization of Industry Plans File); H. HOOVER, *supra* note 12, at 334-35.

doubt that he would do all he could to block it. The goals of revisionism, as he perceived them, had now put him actively on the side of the defenders of the Sherman Act.

From late 1931, Hoover clearly saw himself as trying to make his "cooperative system" work while retaining Sherman Act barriers against policies potentially capable of producing the evils of either monopoly or of socialism. While responding negatively to another wave of revisionist proposals in early and mid-1932,[147] sometimes to the point of calling them a "backdoor" to fascism,[148] he sought to woo the trade associations back to an "American Plan" that stressed informational services and cooperative designs for expansion,[149] to erect cooperative machinery for restarting frozen credit and spending flows, and to encourage cooperative solutions

---

147. These included schemes for a National Economic Truce Board to oversee a two-year "truce" on antitrust enforcement, measures to restore and expand a system of trade practice conference rules, and further elaboration of the Chamber of Commerce and American Bar Association plans. To trace the story of the Truce Board proposal, see Letter from Gordon Corbaley to Richey (Jan. 22, 1932) (available at Hoover Presidential Library, Presidential Papers, Box 90, Business File); Statement Submitted to the President by 122 Industrialists (Feb. 11, 1932) (available at Hoover Presidential Library, Presidential Papers, Box 90, Business File); Letter from Herbert Hoover to Malcolm Whitman (Feb. 11, 1932) (available at Hoover Presidential Library, Presidential Papers, Box 90, Business File); Letter from Herbert Hoover to William Mitchell (Mar. 9, 1932) (available at Hoover Presidential Library, Presidential Papers, Box 90, Business File); Letter from Corbaley to Richey (Apr. 7, 1932) (available at Hoover Presidential Library, Presidential Papers, Secretary's File—Corbaley); Letter from Malcolm Whitman to Herbert Hoover (Apr. 12, 1932) (available at Hoover Presidential Library, Presidential Papers, Secretary's File—Whitman); *Little Business Bites the Hand That's Supposed to Feed It*, Bus. Wk. 16-17 (Feb. 24, 1932). For the ABA proposal, see Letter from R. Butler to Herbert Hoover (Sept. 30, 1932) (available at Hoover Presidential Library, Presidential Papers, Box 64, Antitrust Laws File). For proposals similar to Harriman committee proposals, see Atwood, *The Craze for Planning*, 204 SATURDAY EVENING POST 23, 74-77 (Mar. 19, 1932). The bills for restoring trade practice conference rules are discussed in *Congress Warned Not to De-Nye Anti-Trust Law Responsibility*, Bus. Wk. 11-12 (June 1, 1932).

148. E. LYONS, HERBERT HOOVER: A BIOGRAPHY 294 (1964).

149. The effort began with a speech in Indianapolis in June 1931, in which Hoover took note of the proposals for "planning" and argued that both freedom and prosperity could be had through an "American Plan" of "organizing cooperation in the constructive forces of the community." *Address by Hoover to the Indiana Republican Editorial Association at Indianapolis* (June 15, 1931), *reprinted in* 2 PUBLIC PAPERS OF THE PRESIDENTS, *supra* note 137, at 299-301, 305-07; *see also The Hoover "Twenty-Year Plan" for Prosperity*, 109 THE LITERARY DIG. 5-7 (June 27, 1931). Subsequently, Frederick Feiker took charge of a Commerce Department operation designed to stimulate more trade association programs of the "fact finding" or "business stimulation" type, encourage associational "planning boards" to study the needs and prospects of their industries, and then create a nationwide "plan of action" on a "thousand fronts." Letter from Frederick Feiker to Julius Klein (June 30, 1931) (available at National Archives, BFDC records—Feiker Papers, Box 83). For the details of what Feiker had in mind, see F. Feiker, Notes on a Meeting in the Engineers' Club (Sept. 11, 1931) (available at National Archives, BFDC Records— Feiker Papers, Box 81); F. Feiker, Notes Dictated after Division Chiefs Meeting (Sept. 19, 1931) (available at National Archives, BFDC Records—Feiker Papers, Box 81); F. Feiker, An American Economic Plan, address to New York Trade Association Executives (Oct. 30, 1931) (available at National Archives, BFDC Records—Feiker Papers, Box 83); F. Feiker, Address before the American Trade Association Executives on an Ideal Charter for Trade Associations (Apr. 5, 1932) (available at National Archives, BFDC Records—Feiker Papers, Box 94); *see also* Letter from Frederick Feiker to Robert Lamont (Sept. 28, 1931) (available at National Archives, Commerce Department Records—Lamont Papers, Box 1) (reporting on reactions to his proposals at Sept. 24, 1931 convention of American Trade Association Executives).

for industry-specific problems.[150] Hoover's only concessions to the Sherman Act's critics were to renew the recommendation for a congressional study, again without pushing it,[151] and to continue his support for special regulatory mechanisms in the natural resource industries. In the latter category, for example, he tended to look with favor on the efforts of particular business groups and their governmental allies to restrict oil imports, to develop timber production understandings, and to see whether the Supreme Court would expand the "rule of reason" to cover a coal marketing combine.[152]

Hoover's defeat in the presidential election of 1932 did not change his view about the role that antitrust law should play in American economic regulation and development. In the last months of his Administration, some officials in the Commerce and Interior Departments began working more closely with those who hoped to see the Sherman Act modified or repealed.[153] But Hoover believed that the system's major structural defects were in finance, not in production or distribution, and he concentrated on these financial defects as he sought to preserve the national potential for further progress and prevent a potential relapse into "a new form of the Middle Ages."[154] In subsequent years he would strongly criticize the New Deal's efforts to combine a cooperative recovery approach with antitrust relief and government-supported cartelization, as reflected in the code system created under the National Recovery Administration.[155] As he would put it in his memoirs, "[t]he New Deal set up committees of trade

---

150. *See* Robinson & Case, *Economic Recovery Efforts of the Banking and Industrial Committees*, 6 THE WHARTON NEWS 6-7, 18 (Nov. 1932); O. Mills, Confidential History of the National Conference of Banking and Industrial Committees (available at Library of Congress, Mills Papers, Box 59); *see also* W. BARBER, *supra* note 14, at 139-44, 170-84 (discussing cooperative activities to increase lending, spending, and investment via the Reconstruction Finance Corporation).

151. Hoover, *Annual Message to the Congress on the State of the Union* (Dec. 8, 1931), *reprinted in* PUBLIC PAPERS OF THE PRESIDENTS, *supra* note 137, at 430; R. HIMMELBERG, *supra* note 1, at 160-61.

152. R. HIMMELBERG, *supra* note 1, at 102-03, 151-53. The decision in Appalachian Coals, Inc. v. United States, 288 U.S. 344 (1933), eventually resulted in the sanctioning of the marketing combine. *Id.* at 373-78. The case involved a doctrine of "economic self-defense" that had been set forth by former antitrust chief William Donovan (at the time, the coal combine's counsel). *See* Donovan, *Trusts within the Law*, 61 WORLD'S WORK 52, 53-55 (1932).

153. *See, e.g.,* Letter from Frederick Feiker to Roy Chapin (Oct. 3, 1932) (available at National Archives, BFDC Records—Feiker Papers, Box 103); Letter from Rush Butler to Roy Chapin (Oct. 8, 1932) (available at Commerce Department Records, File 82248); Letter from T. Taylor to Roy Chapin (Oct. 7, 1932) (available at Commerce Department Records, File 82248); Letter from T. Taylor to Roy Chapin (Dec. 17, 1932) (available at Commerce Department Records, File 70801); Letter from Roy Chapin to Walter Teagle (Dec. 20, 1932) (available at National Archives, Commerce Department Records—Lamont Papers, Box 19); Letter from Junkin to Roy Chapin (Jan. 20, 1933) (available at National Archives, BFDC Records—Feiker Papers, Box 103); Letter from E. George to Matthews (Jan. 20, 1933) (available at National Archives, BFDC Records—Feiker Papers, Box 103) (containing memorandum on "Antitrust Laws as to National Economic Planning"); Letter from C.J. Junkin to Roy Chapin (Feb. 9, 1933) (available at National Archives, Commerce Department Records, File 82248); Letter from Roy Chapin to C.J. Junkin (Feb. 3, 1933) (available at National Archives, Commerce Department Records—Lamont Papers, Box 19).

154. Letter from Herbert Hoover to Arch Shaw (Feb. 17, 1933) (available at Hoover Presidential Library, Presidential Papers—Secretary's File, Box 847, Shaw File).

155. *See* Hoover, *Effects of the New Deal*, 2 VITAL SPEECHES 444, 448 (1936); H. HOOVER, ADDRESSES UPON THE AMERICAN ROAD, 1933-1938, at 46 (1938).

associations to fix prices and limit production in each trade. It gave sanction to wholesale violations of the Anti-Trust Laws. This was a long step away from free competition and into sheer economic fascism with all its implications."[156]

V.

In the continuing debates over the value of trade associations, Hoover sometimes used an antibigness rhetoric that distinguished between "cooperation" and "consolidation" and depicted "cooperation" as a way to create and preserve viable business units of medium or small size.[157] In these statements, Hoover's position seemed close to Louis Brandeis's view that associational formation could be used as an antitrust weapon.[158] Yet, unlike the Brandeisians, Hoover also saw the "managerialization" of big business as an alternative way to prevent the evils of monopoly. He accepted, in other words, much of the argument concerning the capacity of professionalized managerial power to serve as an instrument of social progress.[159] Having done so, Hoover became an active promoter of some private regulatory structures in which the managerial hierarchies of large business units played key roles. This was the case in his dealings with the rubber, petroleum, motion picture, and radio industries, all areas in which Hoover could be accused of fostering and helping to legitimize the very "consolidations" that he professed to be against. As a consequence, he became at times deeply involved in debates over whether the resulting "regulation" could or should be fitted into what was permitted under the antitrust laws. Anxious to have the social benefits of the "regulation," at times he sided with or even led those seeking to make a place for it. But again, as in the debates over beneficial associational cooperation, he was not willing to remove all antitrust constraints and on occasion gave his support to those seeking to invoke the antitrust laws against the regulatory systems he had helped to promote.

In the case of rubber, for example, Hoover's concerns with British "price fixing" through their rubber cartel led him to advocate an American buying pool administered by the Big Three tire manufacturers, Goodrich, Goodyear, U.S. Rubber, and the organization that they dominated, the Rubber Association of America. This, Hoover argued in 1924, would be particularly effective in an industry in which there were so few primary purchasers. Subsequently, he worked to get such a pool organized and took

---

156. 2 H. HOOVER, *supra* note 12, at 173.

157. *See, e.g.*, H. Hoover, Address before the Annual Meeting of the Chamber of Commerce, Cleveland, Ohio (May 7, 1924) (available at Hoover Presidential Library, Public Statements File, vol. 16, no. 378); H. Hoover, Address before the National Association of Manufacturers, New York, N.Y. on Trade Associations (May 10, 1922) (available at Hoover Presidential Library, Public Statements File, vol. 9, no. 224).

158. *See* T. McCRAW, PROPHETS OF REGULATION 133-34, 146 (1984).

159. *See e.g.*, Hoover, *We Can Cooperate and Yet Compete*, 14 NATION'S BUS. 11, 13 (June 5, 1926); Letter from Herbert Hoover to Harvey Ingham (Sept. 19, 1925) (available at Hoover Presidential Library, Commerce Papers, Box 5, Agric.—Dep't of Agric. & Dep't of Commerce —Propaganda File) (discussing "revolution" wrought by new informational services and separation of ownership from management).

the lead in efforts to extend the antitrust exemptions of the Webb-Pomerene Act[160] to include import combinations engaged in buying materials controlled by foreign monopolies.[161] In the 1928 congressional battle over the amendment—a battle in which congressional "antitrusters" turned back efforts to enact it—Hoover was denounced as a promoter of big business interests and as one who, far from resisting "consolidation," was accepting it as beneficial and inevitable.[162] Yet the proposed amendment would still allow antitrust remedies to be invoked if the import combinations were misused, and throughout the episode Hoover's relations with the Rubber Association were frequently stormy, resembling those with the meat packers during the war. He was particularly perturbed by the Big Three's lack of enthusiasm for developing alternative sources of rubber, their penchant for making deals with the British price fixers, and their attempts to protect rubber stockpiles from needed price declines. On more than one occasion, Hoover turned to the industry's "maverick," Harvey S. Firestone, to bring pressure on the Rubber Association and advance programs on which the Association was anything but cooperative.[163]

Similarly, Hoover's concerns about wastefulness and malfunctioning markets in the petroleum industry led him to advocate regulatory structures in which the major oil companies and the organization that they dominated, the American Petroleum Institute (API), were to play a major role. This was the case, for example, in the schemes developed for oil-related pollution control, for "production planning" through cooperative drilling units and statistically-based demand estimates, for promulgating fair marketing practices, and for regulating oil imports. Again, Hoover not only worked to get such schemes implemented, but to create a place for the schemes within the framework of antitrust law. As noted previously, petroleum was given special treatment in his statements concerning Sherman Act revision, his FTC trade practice codes policy, and his views concerning trade barriers.[164]

---

160. Act of Apr. 10, 1918, ch. 50, 40 Stat. 516 (codified at 15 U.S.C. §§ 61-65 (1982)).

161. Letter from Herbert Hoover to Senator Arthur Capper (Mar. 6, 1924) (available at Hoover Presidential Library, Commerce Papers, Box 208, Foreign Combinations—Correspondence File); Letter from Herbert Hoover to Senator Arthur Capper (Dec. 19, 1925) (available at Hoover Presidential Library, Commerce Papers, Box 208, Foreign Combinations—Correspondence File). Hoover's activities between 1924 and 1928 are detailed in J. BRANDES, HERBERT HOOVER AND ECONOMIC DIPLOMACY 96-102 (1962). Two bills were pushed in the congressional battle: S. 2843, 68th Cong., 1st Sess., 65 CONG. REC. 4230 (1924); S. 1799, 69th Cong., 1st Sess., 67 CONG. REC. 1991 (1925). For Hoover's testimony before congressional committees, see HOUSE COMM. ON INTERSTATE AND FOREIGN COMMERCE, 69TH CONG., 1ST SESS., CRUDE RUBBER, COFFEE, ETC. 3-5, 286, 301 (1926); HOUSE COMM. ON THE JUDICIARY, TO AMEND THE WEBB-POMERENE ACT, 70th Cong., 1st Sess., 20-22 (1928). For a further statement of his goals, see U.S. DEPARTMENT OF COMMERCE, FOREIGN COMBINATIONS TO CONTROL PRICES OF RAW MATERIALS 3-4 (1926).

162. J. BRANDES, *supra* note 161, at 99-102.

163. HOUSE COMM. ON THE JUDICIARY, *supra* note 161, at 21; J. BRANDES, *supra* note 161, at 104; J. Brandes, *Product Diplomacy: Herbert Hoover's Anti-Monopoly Campaign at Home and Abroad*, in HERBERT HOOVER AS SECRETARY OF COMMERCE, 1921-1928: STUDIES IN NEW ERA THOUGHT AND PRACTICE 185, 198-201, 207-08 (E. Hawley ed. 1981).

164. R. HIMMELBERG, *supra* note 1, at 99-103; Pratt, *Letting the Grandchildren Do It: Environmental Planning During the Ascent of Oil as a Major Energy Source*, 2 THE PUBLIC HISTORIAN 28, 36-41, 55-56 (Summer 1980); Pogue, *The Statistical Work of the American Petroleum Institute*,

At the same time, just as in the case of rubber, Hoover was not ready to remove all antitrust constraints and his relations with the major companies were frequently stormy. In 1929, when the API sought governmental endorsement of a scheme to curb temporary overproduction,[165] he lent his support not to those who would help a "great industry" to achieve "self-regulation and general betterment,"[166] but rather to Attorney General Mitchell, who held that the proposal would be subject to antitrust action under existing law.[167] Adopting the API's plan, the President argued at a press conference, would amount to entering a "blind alley that no one would have faith in."[168] Subsequently, he refused to intervene when the Department of Justice took action against a price maintenance scheme in California,[169] a suit that led oil producers to denounce Mitchell as a "modern Savanarola."[170] He refrained as well from endorsing the efforts of some of his associates to secure special legislation under which a new oil conservation board might grant and administer antitrust exemptions.[171]

---

24 PROCEEDINGS OF THE AMERICAN STATISTICAL ASSOCIATION 118-19 (1929); FEDERAL OIL CONSERVATION BOARD, REPORT TO THE PRESIDENT (1929); K. Staggs, Herbert Hoover and the Petroleum Overproduction Problem, 1926-32 (M.A. Thesis, U. of Iowa 1984).

165. *See* Resolutions Passed by API Committee at Houston (Mar. 16, 1929) (available at Hoover Presidential Library, Presidential Papers, Box 216, Oil Matters—Correspondence File) (expressing anxiety about the API scheme); *see also* Letter from Herbert Hoover to Attorney General William Mitchell (Mar. 23, 1923) (responding to press reports that claim API seeking opinion as to legality of proposals) (available at Hoover Presidential Library, Presidential Papers, Box 216, Oil Matters—Correspondence File); Letter from Interior Secretary Ray L. Wilbur to Attorney General William Mitchell (Mar. 20, 1929) (available at Hoover Presidential Library, Presidential Papers, Box 218, Oil Matters—Federal Oil Conservation Board Correspondence File) (soliciting Attorney General's opinion on API's proposals).

166. Letter from Interior Secretary Ray L. Wilbur to Attorney General William Mitchell (Mar. 20, 1929) (available at Hoover Presidential Library, Presidential Papers, Box 218, Oil Matters—Federal Oil Conservation Board Correspondence File). Hoover's opposition to what Wilbur was inclined to support is expressed in Letter from Herbert Hoover to Interior Secretary Ray L. Wilbur (Apr. 8, 1929) (available at Hoover Presidential Library, Presidential Papers, Box 218, Oil Matters—Federal Oil Conservation Board Correspondence File); Letter from Herbert Hoover to Interior Secretary Ray L. Wilbur (Apr. 10, 1929) (available at Hoover Presidential Library, Presidential Papers, Box 216, Oil Matters—Correspondence File).

167. For a discussion of the Attorney General's attitude, see Mitchell, *Little People vs. Big Fellows*, 154 OUTLOOK & INDEPENDENT 404-06 (1930); Letter from Attorney General William Mitchell to Interior Secretary Ray L. Wilbur (Mar. 29, 1929) (available at Hoover Presidential Library, Presidential Papers, Box 218, Oil Matters—Federal Oil Conservation Board Correspondence File).

168. *The President's News Conference* (Apr. 2, 1929), *reprinted in* 2 PUBLIC PAPERS OF THE PRESIDENTS, *supra* note 137, at 55-56.

169. *See* Mitchell, *supra* note 167, at 406; Letter from R. Irvine to R. Hardy (June 10, 1929) (available at National Archives, Justice Department Records, File 60-57-35); Letter from John Lord O'Brian to R. Irvine (June 20, 1929) (available at National Archives, Justice Department Records, File 60-57-35); *see also Order Limits Trade Practices of 19 Western Oil Companies*, U.S. Daily, Sept. 19, 1930, at 11 (reporting United States v. Standard Oil, Equity No. 2542-S (N.D. Cal. Sept. 15, 1930) (consent decree enjoining oil companies from entering agreements to control gas prices)).

170. Mitchell, *supra* note 167, at 406. Herbert R. Macmillan, president of the California Oil and Gas Association, denounced Mitchell. *See* Letter from Herbert R. Macmillan to Attorney General William Mitchell (Aug. 6, 1930) (available at National Archives, Justice Department Records, File 60-57-35).

171. A leading figure in these efforts was Hoover's old friend and war associate, Mark Requa. *See* Letter from Mark Requa to Interior Secretary Ray L. Wilbur (July 23, 1929)

Also, he increasingly came to regard the API as an inappropriate vehicle for concerted industrial action and to look with favor on schemes for a broader and more representative organization able to mobilize support behind an industrial "statesman" and a "statesmanlike" program. He seemed particularly receptive to a proposal under which a prestigious committee chaired by former President Calvin Coolidge would undertake the task of building such an organization and formulating such a program, but this was shelved after Coolidge decided that he did not wish to be involved.[172]

A third industry in which Hoover helped to legitimize a similar form of regulation yet insisted upon retaining antitrust constraints was the motion picture industry. The major motion picture companies had responded to demands for censorship and trust busting by forming the Motion Picture Producers and Distributors of America, hiring Republican politician Will H. Hays as their industrial "czar" and "statesman," and helping the "Hays Office" to develop and enforce an appropriate production and trade practice code.[173] This structure, Hays insisted, was clearly in line with the kind of "self regulation," "government by cooperation," and "progressive associationalism" that Hoover was offering as the answer to the nation's economic and social problems.[174] Hoover appeared to agree with Hays's characterization. He not only gave his blessing at industry functions,[175] but he also worked with Hays to establish a motion picture

(available at Hoover Institution, Wilbur Papers, Box 13); Letter from Interior Secretary Ray L. Wilbur to Richey (Sept. 30, 1929) (available at Hoover Presidential Library, Presidential Papers, Box 217, Oil Matters—Correspondence File); M. Requa, Memorandum on Tentative Plan for Conserving the Oil Resources of the United States To be used as a Basis of Discussion Only (Sept. 1929) (available at Hoover Presidential Library, Presidential Papers, Box 217, Oil Matters— Correspondence File); Letter from Mark Requa to Richey (Sept. 30, 1929) (available at Hoover Presidential Library, Presidential Papers, Box 217, Oil Matters—Correspondence File) (requesting President's comments on Plan for Conserving the Oil Resources of the United States); *see also* Requa, Draft of An Act to Create the Federal Minerals Conservation Board (presented July 25, 1930) (available at Hoover Presidential Library, Presidential Papers, Box 197B, Mines & Mining File) (giving Minerals Conservation Board power to grant antitrust exemptions); M. Requa, Memorandum on Industrial Self-Regulation and Control Supplemented by Cooperation of Government (Sept. 20, 1931) (available at Hoover Presidential Library, Individuals File, Box 1058, Requa File) (urging a Board of Trade to suspend antitrust laws and promote cooperative self-regulation in natural resource industries).

172. Coolidge had thought it might be "agreeable work" when the idea was first discussed in late 1929, but had changed his mind by 1931. *See* Letter from Robert Lamont to J. Lucey (June 29, 1931) (available at National Archives, Commerce Department Records—Lamont Papers, Box 18); Letter from W. Boyd to Robert Lamont (June 25, 1931) (available at National Archives, Commerce Department Records, File 82272, Box 533); Letter from Coolidge to Everett Sanders (Nov. 28, 1929) (available at Library of Congress, Sanders Papers, Box 1); R. Himmelberg, *supra* note 1, at 102-03.

173. Pringle, *Will Hays—Supervisor of Morals*, 148 Outlook 576, 576-78, 583 (1928).

174. W.H. Hays, Address before the Women's City Club of Philadelphia, Pennsylvania, on Motion Pictures and the Public (Apr. 20, 1925) (available at Hoover Presidential Library, Commerce Papers, Box 257, Will H. Hays File); *see also* Hawley, *Three Facets of Hooverian Associationalism: Lumber, Aviation, and Movies*, in Regulation in Perspective 115-19 (T. McCraw ed. 1981).

175. H. Hoover, Address before the Dinner of Motion Picture Producers and Distributors of America (Apr. 2, 1927) (available at Hoover Presidential Library, Commerce Papers, Box 257, Will H. Hays File); *see also* Letter from Herbert Hoover to Julius Barnes (Aug. 14, 1922) (available at Hoover Presidential Library, Commerce Papers, Box 257, Will H. Hays File) (urging Chamber of Commerce involvement in support of Hays's operations); Letter from

unit in the Bureau of Foreign and Domestic Commerce,[176] a unit that in effect functioned as both a government agency and part of the Hays Office. Further, while taking no formal stands, Hoover remained cool toward critics of the Hays organization who proposed to replace its control system with public utility regulation by a federal commission because the organization was a monopolistic and immoral "sellers' cartel."[177] Even though some of the proposals would have put the envisioned regulatory unit in the Department of Commerce,[178] Hoover gave the proponents of these proposals no encouragement and continued to see the Hays apparatus and approach as the "American" solution.

Still, for all of his support of the Hays organization, Hoover was not inclined to back Hays when the Department of Justice decided that the resulting blend of standardization, self-regulation, and binding arbitration of industrial disputes went beyond the Sherman Act's strictures.[179] Hays had hoped for some friendly litigation that would put his operation on a firmer legal foundation.[180] Antitrust Chief John Lord O'Brian, who, in Hays's eyes, was "absolutely impossible," however, refused to cooperate, and as Hays told Hoover in early 1930, O'Brian was "doing more harm to the Administration than half a dozen Walshes or Brookharts or such."[181] Despite Hays's pleas, neither Hoover nor Attorney General Mitchell was willing to go beyond assuring him that there was no desire to "destroy" the

---

Herbert Hoover to Will H. Hays (Apr. 20, 1926) (available at Hoover Presidential Library, Commerce Papers, Box 257, Will H. Hays File) (extending congratulations on success in movie industry).

176. 1926 BUREAU OF FOREIGN AND DOMESTIC COMMERCE, ANN. REP. 46; 1927 BUREAU OF FOREIGN AND DOMESTIC COMMERCE, ANN. REP. 41-42; 1928 BUREAU OF FOREIGN AND DOMESTIC COMMERCE, ANN. REP. 34; 1929 BUREAU OF FOREIGN AND DOMESTIC COMMERCE, ANN. REP. 39.

177. See Letter from F. Rembusch, Secretary of Unaffiliated Independent Motion Picture Exhibitors of America, to Herbert Hoover (June 20, 1929) (available at Hoover Presidential Library, Presidential Papers, Box 63, Antitrust Laws File). For an accumulation of criticism in Hoover's files, see A. Myers, Address before the Trade Practice Conference of Motion Picture Industry, New York, New York, on Fair Methods of Competition in the Motion Picture Industry (Oct. 10, 1927) (available at Hoover Presidential Library, Commerce Papers, Box 420, Motion Pictures File) (Federal Trade Commissioner outlining goals of trade practice conference); Letter from Abram F. Myers, President and General Counsel of Allied States Association of Motion Picture Exhibitors, to Herbert Hoover (Mar. 27, 1929) (available at Hoover Presidential Library, Presidential Papers, Box 198, Motion Pictures—Correspondence File); Letter from Abram F. Myers, President and General Counsel of Allied States Association of Motion Picture Exhibitors, to Herbert Hoover (June 18, 1929) (available at Hoover Presidential Library, Presidential Papers, Box 198, Motion Pictures—Correspondence File); Letter from Abram F. Myers to Richey (Sept. 6, 1929) (available at Hoover Presidential Library, Presidential Papers, Box 198, Motion Pictures—Correspondence File).

178. This was true, for example, of the Seabury Bill being pushed by the Federal Motion Picture Council in America. See Letter from William Chase to Herbert Hoover (with attached memorandum by William Seabury) (May 4, 1929) (available at Hoover Presidential Library, Presidential Papers, Box 198, Motion Pictures—Correspondence File). The Hudson Bill of 1928 would have put the regulatory agency in the Bureau of Education, Department of the Interior. See What the Hudson Bill Provides, 7 CONG. DIG. 312, 312-13 (1928).

179. R. MOLEY, THE HAYS OFFICE 192-201 (1945).

180. Letter from Will H. Hays to Herbert Hoover (Aug. 28, 1929) (available at Hoover Presidential Library, Presidential Papers, Box 63, Antitrust Laws File).

181. Memorandum from Herbert Hoover to Richey (Mar. 17, 1930) (available at Hoover Presidential Library, Presidential Papers, Box 198, Motion Pictures—Correspondence File) (quoting a telephone call from Will Hays).

industry. The antitrust action continued, eventually forcing the abandonment of Hays's standard contract and arbitration system.[182] In 1932 this would be counted as one of the Hoover Administration's major achievements.[183]

Finally, Hoover also assigned regulatory functions in the radio industry to large business units and, yet, insisted that the industry be subject to continuing antimonopoly constraints.[184] Government-encouraged crosslicensing agreements speeded radio development and allowed the new Radio Corporation of America (RCA) to use patents held by General Electric, Westinghouse, and American Telephone and Telegraph. These companies also had played a major role in shaping and operating the regulatory structure that had emerged in the radio industry.[185] This structure initially was a product of Hoover's national radio conferences of the early and mid-1920s, and later it was a product of the legislation he secured in 1927.[186] Owen D. Young of General Electric played the role of industrial "statesman" in these organizational endeavors, and Hoover believed Young to be well-suited to this role. He earlier had characterized Young as the very epitome of what was needed to improve the "institutional quality" of the large corporation and thereby achieve "fundamental" remedies for industrial ills.[187] Yet, as in the motion picture industry, Hoover sided with his Justice Department rather than the industry's "statesman" when the former decided that the crosslicensing arrangements were monopolistic in purpose and effect. In May 1930, in an action that came as a surprise to Young and his associates, the Department filed a successful suit alleging that the arrangements violated the Sherman Act.[188] The resulting consent decree, banning such agreements and severing all corporate connections between RCA and General Electric, also would be counted as one of the Administration's major achievements.[189]

---

182. Martin, *Sherman Act and Motion Picture Contracts for Compulsory Arbitration*, 5 Univ. Cin. L. Rev. 96, 97, 102-03 (1931); McCormick, *Some Legal Problems of the Motion Picture Industry*, 17 A.B.A. J. 316, 320-22, 409 (1931); Comment, *Compulsory Commercial Arbitration and the Sherman Act*, 39 Yale L.J. 884, 885-87 (1930); *see also* United States v. First Nat'l Pictures, 282 U.S. 44 (1930); Paramount Famous Lasky Corp. v. United States, 282 U.S. 30 (1930).

183. *See* Statements on Activities and Accomplishments of the Antitrust Division during the Hoover Administration (Jan. 26, 1933) (available at Hoover Presidential Library, Presidential Papers, Box 1, Justice Department Accomplishments File).

184. P. Rosen, The Modern Stentors: Radio Broadcasters and the Federal Government, 1920-1934, at 24-25, 30-76, 79-91, 101-12, 124-44 (1980); *Organization of RCA*, 52 Electrical World 93 (1920); G. Johnson, Secretary of Commerce Herbert C. Hoover: The First Regulator of American Broadcasting, 1921-28 (Ph.D. Diss., U. of Iowa) (1970).

185. J. Case & E. Case, Owen D. Young and American Enterprise 209-28, 349-60 (1982).

186. Radio Act of 1927, ch. 169, 44 Stat. 1162, *repealed by* Act of June 19, 1934, ch. 652, 48 Stat. 1102.

187. Hoover's description of Young was in a conversation with Atherton Brownell, who quoted him in *The New Dispensation in Industry*, an article that Brownell was preparing (available at Owen Young Archives, Van Hornesville, New York, Young Papers, Business Cycles Materials, Folder 12-17).

188. *See* J. Case & E. Case, *supra* note 185, at 496-501, 591-94; P. Rosen, *supra* note 184, at 150-53; Note, *The R.C.A. Consent Decree*, 1 Geo. Wash. L. Rev. 513, 513-16 (1933).

189. *See* Statements on Activities and Accomplishments of the Antitrust Division during the Hoover Administration, *supra* note 183.

The actions against rubber, petroleum, motion picture, and radio organizations were, to Hoover's critics, evidence of his confusion and vacillation in the face of conflicting or changing political pressures. Yet one can discern in them a pattern that seems best explained by Hoover's continuing adherence to a regulatory design that had become part of his political ideology as early as 1919. Having conceded the necessity of bigness in certain economic sectors and having made further progress dependent on the acquisition of planning and managerial capacity that the government was incompetent to provide, he had embraced the notion of a "private government" rendered effective and responsible through processes that improved the "institutional quality" of its agencies and units. Even as he offered "private government" as a solution, however, Hoover refused to accept the view that antitrust law should be scrapped because it had become outmoded and incompatible with the organizational development needed for further economic progress. Properly interpreted and modified in a few details, the Sherman Act could serve as a check against two tendencies that could close off opportunities for progress, one being the tendency of private regulatory structures to abandon developmental roles and embrace schemes for "protection" or "domination," the other being the tendency of political and governmental agencies to seek tasks that the agencies were incompetent to perform. The Sherman Act was needed to reinforce the improving "institutional quality," which also served as a check against tendencies that could close off progress, and Hoover sought not only to preserve the Act but to use it for these purposes.

VI.

What, then, can one make of Hoover's twelve-year engagement in Sherman Act controversies, an engagement that he later remembered as being among those that perplexed him "daily and in innumerable ways?"[190] On one level, he made contributions to the shaping and defense of the law, most notably to the triumph of the approach adopted in *Maple Flooring* over the approach taken in *Hardwood Lumber* and *Linseed Oil* and to the resistance that delayed the depression-era decision to combine cooperative planning for national recovery with antitrust relief. On another level, he pushed proposals that failed to be adopted, yet did not disappear from the antitrust debate. One notable example was his proposal to broaden exemptions to permit combinations that could meet national informational needs, curb the waste of national resources, and prevent exploitation by foreign trusts and cartels. More interestingly, one can see him as a pioneer in the continuing effort to combine a modern interpretation of the Sherman Act's prescriptions for progress with neo-corporatist notions concerning the capacity of the groups making up an organizational society to devise, establish, and operate the social machinery required to meet its need for planning and management. In this regard, his designs and the efforts to implement them can be seen as forerunners of similar designs and efforts during the Eisenhower period, the Kennedy years, and the recent "stagfla-

---

190. 2 H. HOOVER, *supra* note 12, at 167-68.

tion" and "trade deficit" eras with their debates over "reindustrialization," "industrial policy," and "national competitiveness."[191]

In Hoover's pioneering designs and efforts, moreover, one can find three elements that have remained characteristic of subsequent attempts to reconcile cooperative stabilization and developmental mechanisms with antitrust objectives. The first is the appeal of the idea to technocratic professionals with continuing commitments to liberal and democratic values, especially in periods when they have become disillusioned with or fearful about the continued growth of government. It is among this group that faith in the possibility of a beneficial outcome of such a reconciliation has been strongest. The second characteristic element is the approach's underlying assumption that improvements in the "institutional quality" and "cooperative spirit" of private-sector units and agencies have been and will continue to take place, thus making possible a kind of cooperation and a kind of competition that would complement each other and work together to further national progress. Like Hoover, subsequent champions of the idea have insisted that "we can cooperate and yet compete." The third element is the problematic nature of such an assumption and the difficulty of acting on it in a society whose politics and culture retain much that is hostile or resistant to the attempted reconciliation between the objectives of antitrust and the mechanisms of cooperative stabilization and development.

America, to be sure, was undergoing an organizational revolution in the 1920s and has continued to experience major organizational innovations. But it also retained much of the nineteenth-century state and much of the constitutional order and political culture developed earlier, including a legal code that stressed individual over group rights and a preference for seeking the public good through adversarial proceedings and arm's length bargaining. The resulting group life, moreover, was often not of the kind assumed in the Hooverian formulations or in the similar formulations that followed. The group life was supposed to have or at least to be acquiring the "quality" and "spirit" that would make it the social raw material from which the envisioned rationalizing, stabilizing, and developmental mechanisms could be coaxed and set in operation. But all too frequently, as I have noted elsewhere, those who would do the coaxing had to deal with "a group life geared to the competitive pursuit of narrow and specific interests and with a citizenry that was still capable of being mobilized, at least in part, by anticorporate, populistic, or libertarian symbols and values."[192] This was true of the pioneering Hoover operations, and it has continued to be true of those that have kept trying to implement similar kinds of regulatory designs.

Hoover was clearly a pioneer in a line of thinking and activity that has continued to be offered as the alternative to regulatory and managerial statism. It now seems clear that his twelve-year engagement in Sherman Act

191. Hawley, *supra* note 13, at 63-75; L. Schuppener, *supra* note 2, at 49-57, 170-217; R. Griffith, *Dwight D. Eisenhower and the Corporate Commonwealth*, 87 AMERICAN HISTORICAL REV. 87, 87-116 (1982); Hawley, *Challenges to the Mixed Economy: The State and Private Enterprise*, in AMERICAN CHOICES: SOCIAL DILEMMAS & PUBLIC POLICY SINCE 1960, at 159, 162-64, 172-78 (R. Bremner, G. Reichard & R. Hopkins eds. 1986).

192. Hawley, *supra* note 13, at 72.

controversies was a part of this pioneering. But whether the path along which he would move the United States could lead to the envisioned improvements in American society has remained an unresolved question. Certainly, movement along it proved arduous and problematic in the Hoover era, and it seems to have been equally difficult since.

By *Robert F. Himmelberg*

ASSISTANT PROFESSOR OF HISTORY

FORDHAM UNIVERSITY

Business, Antitrust Policy, and the Industrial Board of the Department of Commerce, 1919

❮ *A mass of rhetoric proclaimed the Industrial Board as a Progressive measure to forestall a post-World War I depression through governmental price manipulation. After a closer look at the personalities and policies involved, Professor Himmelberg argues that the Board was, actually, an effort by organized business groups to force antitrust revision upon the Wilson administration.*

The Industrial Board of the Department of Commerce, though perhaps the shortest-lived of all federal agencies, deserves better than the obscure and drab role assigned to it by historians of America's recent past. The Board, established in February 1919, is usually described, when it is mentioned at all, as simply the Wilson administration's belated response to the grim threat of depression faced by the nation during the winter of 1918–1919. The experience of World War I had left the nation's price structure inflated and distorted; contemporaries blamed the lagging employment and production indices of these winter months upon buyer hesitation induced by the belief that a postwar deflation was imminent. The Industrial Board was officially described in 1919, and has been accepted since, as an attempt to overcome this hesitation and facilitate the readjustment of industry from war to peace. "Through industry-wide agreements," as one modern account states, the Board "was to arrange for maximum price reductions of certain basic commodities," with the goal of accelerating "a return to conditions

Business History Review, Vol. XLII, No. 1 (Spring, 1968). © The President and Fellows of Harvard College.

Editor's note: Two articles in the Winter, 1967 issue of the *Business History Review* deal in additional detail with many of the same agencies and personalities considered by Professor Himmelberg. Readers may wish to consult the following essays for further insights into government-business relationships during the Wilson period: Paul A. C. Koistinen, "The 'Industrial-Military Complex' in Historical Perspective: World War I" (an analysis of the War Industries Board) and Robert D. Cuff, "A 'Dollar-a-Year Man' in Government: George N. Peek and the War Industries Board." Professors Himmelberg, Koistinen, and Cuff came to their subjects and conclusions independently and they were not able to read each other's articles before publication, but their three studies complement each other quite well.

where the law of supply and demand could operate in a 'normal way.'"

Little practical accomplishment can be attributed to the Board. Its operations were impeded and its career shortened when the Railroad Administration, whose support as the largest government purchaser of industrial goods was deemed essential, refused to accept the Board's price recommendations. The only significance accorded the organization's brief existence has come from commentators who, accepting the aims of the Board as they were stated for the public in 1919, have seen the organization as a forerunner of later governmental attempts to stimulate the economy through price manipulation.[1]

A close examination of the Board, in its origins and operations, indicates that this traditional evaluation misunderstands the purposes of the agency and the significance of its existence and activities. The Board, so it will be argued here, was actually another in the long series of efforts by which elements of the American business community have sought to control and reformulate public policy respecting competition. Earlier endeavors in this category have been the object of intensive research. We are well-informed concerning the détente system between the Administration and the Morgan interests during the presidency of Theodore Roosevelt; much is known concerning the attempts made, in 1908 with the Hepburn bill and in 1914 during the writing of the Clayton and Federal Trade Commission acts, to obtain greater security for noncompetitive behavior in return for token governmental supervision. Later efforts, especially those made just before and during the NRA period also have received considerable, though as yet incomplete, illumination.[2]

The Industrial Board scheme, however, has gone unrecognized as part of this series of developments because the underlying aims of

---

[1] Though usually overlooked entirely in surveys, the Board has received brief attention in specialized works such as Joseph Dorfman's, *The Economic Mind in American Civilization,* IV (New York, 1959), 12–13, from which the quotation above is taken, and Gilbert C. Fite's *George N. Peek and the Fight for Farm Parity* (Norman, 1954), 33–36. E. Jay Howenstine, Jr., "The Industrial Board, Precursor of the N.R.A.: The Price Reduction Movement after World War I," *Journal of Political Economy,* LI (June, 1943), 235–50, is the only detailed treatment. Though almost entirely an analysis of the Board's economic theory and technique, the article briefly touches on and anticipates the interpretation of the Board's significance presented here.

[2] Robert H. Wiebe, *Businessmen and Reform: A Study of the Progressive Movement* (Cambridge, Mass., 1963), 45–47, 79–81, 137–41; Arthur M. Johnson, "Theodore Roosevelt and the Bureau of Corporations," *Mississippi Valley Historical Review,* XLV (March, 1959), 571–90; *idem.,* "Antitrust Policy in Transition, 1908: Ideal and Realty," *ibid.,* XLVIII (December, 1961), 424–34; Gabriel Kolko, *The Triumph of Conservatism* (New York, 1963), 65–89, 113–38, 255–78.

For antitrust in the 1930's see Ellis W. Hawley, *The New Deal and the Problem of Monopoly* (Princeton, 1966), esp. chaps. 1–3; and Louis Galambos, *Competition or Cooperation?: The Emergence of a National Trade Association* (Baltimore, 1966), chaps. 7–11.

the agency's promoters and directors had to be and were concealed under a mass of rhetoric which publically advertised the Board's aim as the prevention of a postwar depression. This aim was, in fact, genuine; the members of the Board, from Chairman George N. Peek on down, wanted very much to achieve it. But the methods they used, and the very inspiration for the concept of the Industrial Board, sprang from prior and governing hopes of furthering demands that the business community was making during the winter of 1918–1919 for changes in the government's attitude toward industrial stabilization.

The immediate and urgent goal of this organized business agitation was an emergency suspension of the antitrust laws so as to facilitate the establishment of price agreements against the postwar deflation that most observers expected. But permanent antitrust revision, legislation drastically widening the legal limits of cartelization, was regarded as the fundamental issue. The business movement for antitrust relaxation had begun in November 1918, when many individuals and industries had wanted the War Industries Board to arrange for postwar price protection for business and to use its influence to secure fundamental antitrust revision from Congress. But, though the WIB's chairman, Bernard Baruch, and his associates acknowledged the desirability of these objectives, they had decided not to champion them, for several reasons, and businessmen were thrown back upon their own resources and organizations in seeking antitrust relaxation.[3]

Early in December 1918, the Chamber of Commerce of the United States assumed leadership in mobilizing a showing of business unanimity for antitrust revision; the necessary prelude for an appeal to Congress. At the Chamber's call, a "Reconstruction Congress of American Industry," a meeting of the War Service Committees which had represented the various industries in their relations with the WIB, was held on December 4–6 in Washington. The antitrust question was more discussed than any other at the meeting's sessions, and the Reconstruction Congress' final resolutions called for revision of the Sherman Act so as to permit "reasonable trade agreements," and stressed that "the conditions incident to the period of readjustment render it imperative that all obstacles to reasonable cooperation be immediately removed."[4]

[3] See the present author's "The War Industries Board and the Antitrust Question in November, 1918," *Journal of American History*, LII (June, 1965), 59–74.
[4] "Minutes of the War Emergency and Reconstruction Congress under Auspices of the Chamber of Commerce of the United States of America" (typescript, Chamber of Commerce Library, Washington, D.C.), 229–31.

BUSINESS AND THE INDUSTRIAL BOARD   3

These conclusions paved the way for a referendum which the Chamber held in February and March 1919. By a very large majority, resolutions were approved asking Congress to reconsider the antitrust laws and to formulate "standards of general business conduct to be administered in the first instance by a supervisory body." Shortly afterward, at the Chamber's May 1919 convention, President Harry A. Wheeler presented as a foregone conclusion that regulation of industry was in the offing. Regulation deserved, he advised, "cordial acceptance by organized business" because it would ensure "broad application of the rule of reason wherein agreements between businessmen made in the public interest" would be permitted. The other of the two major business organizations, the National Association of Manufacturers, associated itself with the same revisionist goals at its convention held a few days later.[5]

Events later in 1919 would demonstrate the fallibility of this business assessment of the postwar political situation. No matter how illusory, however, the business presumption of widespread sympathy for its goals was real and encouraged the major business organizations and individual businessmen of standing and influence in government circles to search for a way to obtain antitrust relaxation. By the latter part of December 1918, a number of such individuals, determined not to let an opportune moment slip by, were developing plans for forwarding the business position on antitrust policy.

Secretary of Commerce William C. Redfield represented those who sought to reorient the whole governmental attitude toward industrial cooperation. Though he has received little credit for it, Redfield was a pioneer in establishing the Department of Commerce as a promoter of trade associations and cooperative practices in industry. A businessman himself, onetime president of the American Manufacturers Export Association, Redfield had been a leading Administration spokesman for the view that government should encourage and coordinate, rather than frustrate, industrial cooperation. He had actively supported the Webb-Pomerene bill for the legalization of export cartels and its passage in mid-1918, after years of congressional neglect, had seemed to Redfield a harbinger of similar victories to come.

Immediately after the Armistice, Redfield secured the transfer of

[5] The questions submitted in the referendum are explained in the Chamber's publication, *Referendum No. 26. On the Report of the Federal Trade Committee of the Chamber Regarding Trust Legislation. February 1, 1919.* The results of the voting are given in *Referendum Number Twenty-Six, Special Bulletin,* April 11, 1919. Wheeler, "Foundations for the Future," *Nation's Business,* VII (June, 1919), 17–18; *American Industries,* XIX (January, 1919), 12–15; NAM, *Annual Convention* (1919), 134–56, 285, 324–51.

the WIB's Conservation Division to his department. There, as the Industrial Cooperation Service, it initiated the policy, later extended and broadened (but by no means originated) by Secretary of Commerce Herbert Hoover, of assisting with the development of trade association programs.[6] Early in December 1918, Redfield took a further step in strengthening his relations with business when he established an advisory board for his department composed of former WIB officials. His purpose, he told prospective members, was creation of a new line of communication for "developing helpful relations between the Government and industry to their mutual good." He had in mind, specifically, governmental stimulation of trade association activities. The potential relation was as "broad as industry itself" and he was "not disposed to put limits on the helpful activity that is possible." [7]

Among these "industrial advisors," as Redfield called them, were the figures who would conceive and implement the Industrial Board scheme. These included Samuel P. Bush, an Ohioan, head of a moderately sized steel castings firm and until recently a member of the WIB's Facilities Division; George R. James of Memphis, president of a major southern dry goods concern and chief of the Cotton and Cotton Linters Section of the WIB during the war; William M. Ritter, an Ohio lumber baron and George N. Peek's assistant in the WIB; and Peek himself, a Deere and Company executive who had distinguished himself greatly as the WIB's Commissioner of Finished Products.

Whereas Redfield emphasized the need for encouraging cooperative practices on a long-range basis, Peek, like others among the industrial advisors, laid greatest stress, in December 1918, upon business' urgent need for immediate protection against deflation. When the question of this need had been discussed within the WIB during November, Peek had taken the position that businessmen had learned to cooperate well enough during the war to fend for themselves. By late December, however, the prospective deflation seemed more ominous to him than before. This opinion, and his conversations with Chamber of Commerce officials, had convinced him of the need for "some kind of legislation creating some kind of an Emergency Peace Bureau;" legislation which would let businessmen "have an opportunity to meet and cooperate under Govern-

[6] "Report Covering Activities of the Industrial Cooperation Service, January 1, 1919 to March 15, 1919"; John Cutter (Acting Chief, Industrial Cooperation Service) to Redfield, May 15, 1919; both in file 78253/1, Record Group 40, General Records of the Department of Commerce, National Archives. (Hereafter cited as RG 40.)
[7] Redfield to each of thirteen proposed "industrial advisors," December 3, 1918, file 67009/72, ibid.

mental cooperation" in solving readjustment problems. "I believe it is our duty here," he wrote from Washington, "to see that the Business interests of the country are properly protected after their loyal cooperation with the Government." [8]   But, whether they stressed the urgent and immediate or the more profound reasons for antitrust relaxation, all the individuals in Redfield's circle who would be influential in the development and administration of the Industrial Board supported the postwar business movement for drastic antitrust revision.[9]

By late December, however, nearly all Redfield's advisors had scattered to their homes and their concern with the problem of working out a new business-government relationship would have found no concrete expression had it not been for the ingenuity and energy of William M. Ritter. Though he undoubtedly counted on the support of the industrial advisors at the proper time, Ritter in the latter part of January 1919, independently initiated a proposal for what became the Industrial Board. By this time the economic outlook was genuinely threatening, and Ritter found it easy to interest Secretary of the Interior Franklin K. Lane and Secretary of Labor William B. Wilson in his ideas. Secretary of Commerce Redfield also responded with enthusiasm.[10]

Early in February, Ritter's plan, presented simply as a scheme for readjusting inflated prices and forestalling depression, was discussed at three meetings, the first held on February 3 with Secretary of the Treasury Carter Glass, whose support was deemed especially important. Since buying by government purchasing agents at Board-approved prices was a key element in Ritter's plan for restoring prosperity, Walker D. Hines, head of the largest government consumer of industrial products, the Railroad Administration, was also invited. On February 4, Redfield, now formally the proposal's sponsor, urged its acceptance at a Cabinet meeting. On the 5th, Redfield presented the plan at a meeting of his industrial advisors and other business leaders. The proposal gained more ground at each presentation, and by February 6, by then approved and endorsed on every side, the plan was presented to President

[8] Peek to William Butterworth, December 20, 1918, Peek Papers (Western Historical Manuscripts Collection, University of Missouri).
[9] Ritter to Peek, November 6, 1918, file 21A–A2, Record Group 61, Records of the War Industries Board, National Archives. (Hereafter cited as RG 61,) Peek to Baruch, December 17, 1919, ibid; Bush to Redfield, February 11, 1919, file 67009/72, RG 40; Redfield, "The Letter Killeth –," Nation's Business, VII (June, 1919), 30–31.
[10] Peek gave this account of the Board's origin in remarks during the "Meeting of the United States Industrial Board . . . with Representatives of the Cement Industry," March 4, 1919, Records of the Industrial Board (hereafter cited as RInB), RG 40.

Wilson (who had been in Paris for the Peace Conference since mid-December) in cables sent by Glass and Redfield.[11]

In Redfield's message, the proposal was simply that: [12]

> the Department of Commerce should do all in its power to secure by voluntary action the establishment of a reduced level of prices at which the Railroad Administration and other government agencies would be justified in buying freely. If this reduction were made and announced the public would enter freely upon general purchases and take up new enterprises and new construction. All agree that there is adequate latent buying power which only requires satisfactory prices to become active and effective.

Glass' description of the proposal was nearly identical. He hoped Wilson would approve Redfield's appointment of a committee which would: [13]

> endeavor in voluntary co-operation with business interests to arrive at a level of prices upon which business activities would be more actively resumed; and the Railroad Administration and other spending agencies in the Government would be justified in buying liberally.

On its face, there was only a remote connection between the question of antitrust relaxation, which had been preoccupying the attention of Redfield, Ritter, Peek, and other of the industrial advisors during December and January, and the proposal communicated to Wilson. But, in the light of later developments, the conclusion seems warranted that Ritter and others in the Redfield circle felt that the Industrial Board, once constituted and under their control, could be made to serve both the purposes of which Wilson was informed and also the cause of antitrust relaxation.

The really remarkable feature of the events leading to the plan's approval was that Glass, Hines, and the President himself, should have accepted at face value the proposal as it was agreed to in the February conferences and as it was cabled to Wilson on February 6. At the first conference, on February 3, Ritter had proposed that price reductions should be achieved through "price-fixing by governmental action with the approval of the Attorney-General." Glass and Hines had received this feature of Ritter's plan with hostility; Hines fearing, as he informed a subordinate after the meeting, that "some business men would like to get the Anti-trust Act mixed up in this thing so as to give them a free hand to go

---

[11] For this outline of the February conferences, see Redfield to Wilson, April 15, 1919, Wilson Papers (Library of Congress), and "Conference, February 5, 1919, Office of the Secretary of Commerce," file 78484, RG 40.

[12] Redfield to Wilson, February 6, 1919, RInB, RG 40.

[13] Glass to Wilson, February 6, 1919, *ibid.*

ahead regardless of that Act." Ritter had, therefore, withdrawn his suggestion and it had been agreed that the goal of price reductions could be achieved without any price agreements or price-fixing and without violating the antitrust laws.[14]

The President, too, had some forewarning of the purposes to which the Industrial Board was later put. Baruch, who had accompanied Wilson to Paris in December, was clear-eyed as usual in assessing the plan. "Of course you realize," he told the President, "that although this may be called a stabilization of prices, it is a fixing of minimum prices," and he observed that it might thus be a violation of the Sherman Act. Wilson noted this possibility in his reply of February 13 to the Glass-Redfield overture. "The only possible objection [is] it may be in contravention of [the] Sherman Anti-trust law," he said, but he gave his approval without further comment.[15]

Such apprehensions, in the circumstances in which the Administration found itself in February 1919, were apparently not sufficient ground for firm objections to Ritter's plan. If the proposal offered risks it offered hope, too, of preventing depression and soothing the "restless social situation" which, as Redfield later reminded Wilson, "was the background of thought" in the February discussions of the plan. Only a few weeks previously, on December 4, just before departing for Paris, Wilson had confidently assured Congress that extraordinary methods for returning the economy to its normal condition were unnecessary. Now, though preoccupied with the treaty negotiations, the President realized his mistake. Days before the Industrial Board proposal reached him, Wilson had received a long dispatch from his most trusted advisor in Washington, Joseph Tumulty, who had remained at his White House post to keep Wilson informed of home developments. "It is feared by

[14] What was said and what understandings were reached at the February conferences later became a question hotly contested between the Industrial Board and its enemies, which included Secretary Glass and Hines. Ritter's version of what was said at the February 3 meeting gives no clue that he suggested a definite price-fixing method for carrying out his scheme. But Ritter's description of the conference can be found only in printed form, in the *History of the Industrial Board* that Peek assembled and published privately in 1919 as the parting shot in the controversy between the Board and its critics. The document reproduced in Peek's history is alleged to be a memorandum of the February 3 conference, written by Ritter. The document's reliability is slight; first, because its language is ambiguous and, second, because no verification for its authenticity can be found in the papers of the Industrial Board or in any of the other collections examined in the course of research for this study.
  The statement above that Ritter offered two versions of his plan on February 3, the first of which was sharply rejected, is based on a letter from George O. May, one of the Treasury officials present at the meeting, to Peek of March 26, 1919, in the RInB, RG 40. Hines' comments upon the conference, of which the quote above is a part, support May's remarks, and were written the same day as the conference in a memorandum for T. C. Powell, in file M 23, Record Group 14, Records of the Railroad Administration, National Archives. (Hereafter cited as RG 14.)
  [15] Baruch to Wilson, February 11, 1919 Wilson Papers; Wilson to Redfield, February 13, 1919, RInB, RG 40.

many," Tumulty had written, "that bad conditions cannot be avoided in the early spring and naturally there is a disposition in certain quarters to hold the Administration responsible." Tumulty was not as impressed by the menace of depression as some other Administration figures; he thought, in fact, that the slack period, though serious, would not be protracted. Nonetheless, he urged Wilson to act energetically. The current problems "should be tackled with the same vigor and enterprise that you rushed the war work with." Tumulty's concrete proposals for action were unexciting and hackneyed — the resurrection of Secretary Lane's land reclamation and settlement program and the convening of a Governors' Conference — but his exhortations were impressive.[16] Thus, the Redfield-Ritter proposal reached the President on February 6 with the Cabinet's endorsement; Baruch decided the measure was "a good one;" and gloomy prognoses of the economy's health continued. No wonder Wilson was disposed to accept the Industrial Board idea.[17]

Organization of the Industrial Board proceeded at a deliberate pace. Redfield offered Peek, who was Ritter's nominee, the chairmanship on February 18. By early March, the Board's membership was complete. It included Peek, Ritter, Bush, and James; Thomas Glenn, also a former WIB man and the president of an Atlanta, Georgia, steel fabricating firm; and two men representing non-business interests: Commissioner of Immigration Anthony Caminetti was selected by Secretary of Labor Wilson to represent consumer and labor interests; and T. C. Powell, director of the Capital Expenditures Division of the Railroad Administration, represented the interests of his own agency and other governmental purchasers of industrial supplies.[18]

Endorsements and pledges of cooperation showered down upon the Board as it took shape in late February and early March. These came principally from business organizations, such as the Chamber of Commerce, the NAM, and numerous trade associations, but also from important political agencies, such as the Governors' Confer-

[16] Redfield to Wilson, April 15, 1919, Wilson Papers; Tumulty to Wilson, January 30, 1919, Tumulty Papers (Library of Congress).
[17] Baruch to Wilson, February 11, 1919; Charles M. Schwab to Wilson, February 12, 1919; both in Wilson Papers. Wilson may have been informed, too, by trusted associates, that the Senate Majority leader, Gilbert M. Hitchcock, and other Democratic leaders, warmly supported the plan. See Clarence Wooley to Vance McCormick, February 7, 1919, in "Readjustment, 1919," file in Secretary's File, Record Group 56, General Records of the Treasury, National Archives. (Hereafter cited as RG 56.)
[18] Redfield to Peek, February 18, 1919, file 78484, RG 40. Ritter's argument in favor of Peek as chairman is contained in a long document in the RInB, *ibid.*, titled "Memorandum of Mr. Ritter's Views In Reference . . . to the Work of the Industrial Board." Though undated, its contents show it was written between February 6 and 12, 1919.

ence which met on March 4–5 in Washington, at the President's request, to consider the readjustment problem.[19] Encouraged by these tokens of solid backing, Peek and his associates were emboldened to adopt a set of policies and procedures which placed the Board's practice sharply at variance with its original mandate and which would draw heavy criticism as soon as they were revealed, during the steel conference of March 19–20 (the first and last conference the Board carried to completion).

The policies had been elaborated long before, however; at least as early as March 4, when they become visible in the Board's records in transcripts of preliminary conferences held that day with the brick and cement industries. Briefly summarized, these policies were that the Board's emphasis would be placed upon price stabilization at prevailing levels, though not to the total exclusion of reductions, and that the method of stabilization would be to allow and to endorse, more or less openly, industrial price agreements arrived at in conference with the Industrial Board.[20] The difference between these policies and those contemplated in the February discussions is obvious. The original plan had stressed the importance of price reductions and the rapid restoration of normally functioning markets, and emphasized the necessity for shunning price agreements and price-fixing. The newer policies emphasized the reverse.

It would be mistaken to regard the adoption of these newer policies, the very policies the business community had been calling for, as merely crass opportunism on the Board's part. Though their action partook of this quality, the Board's members undoubtedly felt that the policies they had decided upon represented an honest reconciliation of business interests with the public welfare, and

[19] See William Butterworth (a member of the Chamber's Board of Directors) to Peek, February 27, 1919, Peek Papers; the Chamber's *War Service Bulletin No. 49*, March 10, 1919, and Elliot Goodwin (the Chamber's Executive Secretary) to Peek, March 5, 1919, RInB, RG 40.

The NAM's President, Stephen C. Mason, offered his organization's cooperation in a letter to Redfield of February 27, 1919, *ibid.* The Governors' Conference endorsement came through a resolution offered by Governor Cox of Ohio. See the second volume of the meeting's mimeographed proceedings. *Conference with the President of the United States and the Secretary of Labor by the Governors of the States and Mayors of Cities, ... March 5, 1919*, p. 627ff. An unsigned copy of a letter to Cox of March 6, in the RInB, probably written by Ritter judging from the style, thanks the Governor for securing the Conference's endorsement, but it is not clear whether Cox had acted independently or at Ritter's request.

[20] "Meeting of the . . . Industrial Board . . . with Representatives of the Cement Industry," and "Meeting . . . with Representatives of the Brick Industry," both dated March 4, 1919, RInB, RG 40. The clearest statement of the Board's decision not to press for drastic price reductions was given at the brick conference by Ernest T. Trigg, a member of the executive board of the National Federation of Construction Industries, whom Peek had asked to assist in the Board's contacts with building materials industries and who figured prominently at many of its negotiating sessions. It was the Board's intention, Trigg said, to "establish confidence in the mind of the buying public in existing values of materials. After all, isn't it a fact that the condition of business is almost entirely a question of the condition of men's minds . . . . If the public feels markets are stable, and that, if anything, advances come and not declines, then we usually have good buying."

would serve both equally. Apparently, Peek and his associates felt the theory of the original plan, that price reductions would convince consumers that there would be no further deflation and encourage buying, was entirely wrong. When critics, after the steel conference, charged that the Board had demanded far too small a reduction in prices, the Board defended itself by presenting an ingenious argument against requiring severe reductions. The argument was that prices were not really unduly inflated relative to production costs; that the Board limited its demands to what careful study of cost data showed was appropriate; and that more severe demands would force producers to reduce wages and have other undesired economic effects.[21]

This argument, however, which was elaborately and impressively spun out in argumentation with critics, does not seem to have had much real importance for the Board. Had the Board really taken the argument seriously, it would have conducted its negotiations accordingly. Actually, in only one instance, in the negotiations with the steel industry, did the Board make serious use of cost data. In the several other conferences which the Board held following the steel meeting, the transcripts of meetings and the Board's records do not show that objective criteria were used in discussing a price settlement or that anything other than symbolic concessions was being sought.[22]

The Board, in other words, was not concerned with putting proper limits upon price reductions. Rather, it thought, and probably correctly, that there was a fatal flaw in the prosperity formula of the original plan and that it could not accomplish any positive result, either for business or the public. Price reductions, the Board recognized, could just as likely result in further reductions as in stability. Though the Board might endorse an industry's prices and though government agencies might accept them, there was no guarantee that the ordinary pressures of competition would not stimulate further price-cutting, lead to further deflation, destroy the buyer confidence upon which the whole plan depended, and leave the

[21] Peek to Glass, April 3, 1919, with attached statement of the argument made at a Cabinet meeting the day previous, in *ibid.*

[22] "Meeting of the Industrial Board with Representatives of the Lumber Industry," March 22, 1919; "Meeting . . . with the Representatives of the Cement Manufacturing Industry," March 24, 1919; "Industrial Board . . . Hearing of the Box Board Manufacturers," March 26, 1919; "Meeting . . . with Representatives of the Builders' Hardware Industry," March 26, 1919; "Meeting Between the Industrial Board . . . and Coal Operators," March 26, 1919; and "Meeting . . . with Representatives of the Glass Industry," March 27, 1919, all in *ibid.* Symbolic concessions were strongly desired however; at the cement conference on the 24th the Board went to great lengths, threatening the industry with exposure as uncooperative, in order to extract a trifling reduction, which it accepted, of 5 to 15 cents per barrel.

BUSINESS AND THE INDUSTRIAL BOARD   11

businessmen who had reduced prices in a worse condition than before. Only a definite price-fixing agreement among members of an industry, coupled with the Board's public endorsement of the prices' fairness and with prompt acceptance of the prices by the Railroad Administration, could guarantee the price stability upon which the confidence of buyers and, in turn, prosperity was thought to depend. This reasoning was attractive not only because of its cogency but also because of its conclusion, that price reductions really were not necessary for creating buyer confidence, but that minimum price-fixing was. The rationalization of the public welfare and the interests of business was, thus, complete.[23]

It is possible to admire the virtuosity of the Board's reasoning. It is even possible, perhaps, to admit that Board criticism of the original plan was impressive and that the new policies it adopted, though originating in the desire to help a special interest, were more likely to promote an upswing than the policies of the original plan. It is, however, difficult to judge so generously the propriety of the decision to introduce the new policies. The Board's members ought to have been aware that their policies would arouse opposition, accusation of treachery, and that they might well be initiating a dispute which would paralyze the original effort at readjustment that the Administration had decided to attempt.

Perhaps these considerations were discounted. With respect to one of the elements of policy, the Board's assumption that the Railroad Administration had agreed to accept the Board's price determinations without reservation, Peek and the others do seem to have been simply and honestly mistaken.[24] But with respect to the decisions not to seek significant price reductions and to encourage industrial price-fixing agreements, the members of the Board seem to have felt their position in the Administration was so secure that they could win approval for their own interpretation of the Board's prerogatives.

Shortly before the steel conference, Peek gradually made preparations to bring the Board's intention of encouraging industrial price agreements into the open. He wrote both the individuals responsible

[23] This reconstruction of the justification the Board made to itself of its policies is implied at many points in the statements of Board spokesmen in the transcripts of conferences cited in notes 21 and 23. Perhaps the best indication that the Board's reasoning was such as is outlined in the paragraph above, however, is the discussion recorded in the transcripts of the steel conference of March 19–20. Verbatim minutes survive only for the morning session of March 19 and the afternoon sessions of the 20th and are titled "Meeting . . . with Representatives of the Iron and Steel Industry," March 19, 1919; "Report of Conference of the Industrial Board with Representatives of the Iron and Steel Industry," March 20, 1919, and "Meeting [of March 20] Reconvened at 4:40 P.M. . . ." All transcripts in *ibid.*

[24] Peek's belief that Hines was committed to accept the Board's prices appears utterly genuine in the various statements he made on the subject in February and early March; see, e.g., Peek to Baruch, February 24, 1919, Peek Papers.

for antitrust enforcement: the chairman of the Federal Trade Commission, William B. Colver, on March 10; and Attorney General A. Mitchell Palmer, on the 18th. Both letters requested comment on the Board's proposed methods. While neither letter bluntly stated the Board's policy of informing industrialists they could regard the antitrust laws as suspended relative to price agreements the Board approved (which actually had already been applied during the preliminary conferences of early March), it was clear enough what Peek was driving at. "Every combination in restraint of trade," Peek argued in defense of the Board's intended policy, was not a Sherman Act violation, only "unreasonable" ones; and the fact that the government was party to an agreement demonstrated its reasonableness. Besides, he concluded, the Sherman Act was aimed at private, not governmental, activities "as to pooling and prices." [25]

Before any reply to Peek's queries had reached the Board, the moment arrived when the policy decisions of early March were to be applied for the first time. The Board's conference with the steel industry, scheduled for an earlier date but postponed because of the illness of Elbert H. Gary, chairman of U.S. Steel and regarded as the business community's leading elder statesman, was held on March 19–20. This conference was the central event in the Board's life. From the Board's point of view, a successful negotiation with the steel industry would virtually ensure the success of subsequent negotiations with lesser industries. From a retrospective viewpoint, the importance of the meeting is that its discussions so clearly illuminate the purposes, proximate and ultimate, of the Industrial Board.

As the first session of the conference opened, what seemed the historic character of the event inspired Peek himself to make a declaration of the Board's aspirations: "I feel that this may be an epoch making meeting in the industrial life of this country," he declared. If it could be shown "that there is much merit in real genuine co-operation between Government, industry and labor, so that we may eliminate (and to a large extent preclude) the possibility of the destructive forces, then certainly much good will have been accomplished." He felt that the results of the meeting would "determine the general result in industry for the next few months." If a "constructive" policy were decided upon, other industries would follow suit. "We will demonstrate to the satisfaction of the people of the country that industry should be above suspicion and that

[25] A copy of Peek's letter to Colver of March 10 has not been located, but judging from the references to it in Colver's letter to Peek of March 21, 1919, RInB, RG 40, the text was substantially the same as that of Peek's letter to Palmer of March 18, 1919, *ibid.*

their intentions are entirely honorable and that we may look forward with confidence to a different relationship between Government and industry than has existed in the past."

Gary responded fittingly. The meeting seemed to him a sign "of a growing disposition on the part of the people of this country to establish a basis for the transaction of business which is very much higher than the one heretofore occupied." The meeting was a "great chance . . . to come into close contact with the Government itself, with a view of discussing all the questions which may have a bearing and securing, if possible, the approval of the Government." He and the steel committee started "with the fixed belief . . . that if justice is not done by this Board we had better not try to go before any board; we had better abandon our old idea of advocating cooperation between industry and the Government."[26]

The actual negotiations and decisions made during the conference applied the policies the Board had decided to follow early in March. The steel producers were told that an agreement among them to maintain the prices agreed upon by the conference would enjoy immunity from the antitrust laws. They were told that government purchasers, including the Railroad Administration, would accept whatever prices the Industrial Board approved. Finally, the steelmen were allowed a price list which critics later would condemn as unjustifiably inflated. On this point, the suitability of the prices approved, it must be said that the Board negotiated meaningfully, armed with detailed cost schedules supplied by the FTC, to beat down the prices the steel representatives initially offered. Though the Board's own theory was that establishment of price stability was the critical factor in restoring prosperity, it was plain that the public and the Administration expected significant price reductions to flow from the Board's work. And, an attempt *was* made to achieve lower prices in at least this one case which would be the most closely watched and best publicized of the Board's operations.[27]

Application of its self-asserted powers immediately involved the Industrial Board in a prolonged controversy which soon frustrated its work and finally ended it altogether. The original protagonist

[26] The quotes are from "Meeting with the Iron and Steel Industry," on the morning of March 19, 1919, *ibid.*

[27] *Ibid.*, and the additional transcripts cited in note 24. To sustain the new prices, to make it easier for the industrialists to maintain the price understanding they had reached, Peek agreed, at the late afternoon meeting on the 20th, to include in the Board's announcement approving the prices, the statement that the public should not expect to obtain lower prices within the calendar year. In maintaining the prices, Peek told the steel representatives, the statement would be "the biggest asset" that a steel company could "possibly have. I don't know what I wouldn't have given in times past if in my own business I could say that the government of the United States says this is as low a price as you could get. I think I could get along with half the number of salesmen and less than half the advertising."

in the controversy was the Railroad Administration, which reacted sharply once it learned that government purchasers were expected to accept whatever prices the Board might approve. The rail authority held that it had never been supposed the Board could bind government purchasers, and that if the Board wanted to pledge governmental acceptance of a price, it would have first to secure the consent of the purchasing units. This position was stated repeatedly by RA representatives during the last day of the steel conference, March 20. The next day, when the Board met to draw up a statement announcing and approving the new steel prices, Powell, the rail authority's member on the Board, refused to sign until reference to government purchasers was withdrawn from the formula of recommendation.[28]

At the same time the RA was threatening one of the Industrial Board's policies, the agencies responsible for antitrust enforcement were questioning another and even more vital one. During the steel conference, Peek and Ritter had assured industrialists that the antitrust laws offered no obstacles to a Board-sanctioned agreement on prices. They had no authority to make such assurances, however. Peek had, as yet, received no answer to his inquiry of March 10 to the FTC or that of March 18 to the attorney general.

Intent upon reaching an understanding with the Justice Department before issuing the steel conference statement, Peek and Ritter met with Attorney General Palmer on the morning of the 21st. Palmer's attitude was friendly. He agreed to cooperate with them if possible, but refused to give an opinion, in keeping with the attorney general's traditional practice, until it had been requested by the relevant department head, Secretary Redfield. Assistant Attorney General Todd, present at Palmer's request, struck a discordant note when he complained, with the suggestion of an accusation that Peek and Ritter were to blame, that the press reports of the steel conference had been "rather ostentatiously," and erroneously, stating that Justice Department representatives had been attending and approving its decisions.[29] The total effect of the meeting with the attorney general was, thus, not encouraging, and the letter Peek received the next day, March 22, from the chairman of the FTC was, or ought to have been, downright disturbing. Colver referred Peek to the attorney general since Sherman Act enforcement fell

[28] Memorandum for Hines by Powell, March 19, March 22, March 25, April 2, 1919, file M23, RG 14; Lewis B. Reed to Peek, May 2, 1919, RInB, RG 40; "Meeting of the Industrial Board," March 21 (1:30 p.m.), 1919, *ibid.*
[29] Memorandum for Palmer by Todd, March 24, 1919, file 200515, RG 60; memorandum of a conversation with the Attorney General by a subordinate, identified only by the initials M.C.B., for Hines, March 27, 1919, file M 23; RG 14.

BUSINESS AND THE INDUSTRIAL BOARD   15

within his jurisdiction, but implied plainly that the Board's proce-dures, as described in Peek's letter, conflicted with the antitrust laws. Clearly, the attorney general's opinion, when it was given, might well be an adverse one.[30]

The Board's behavior in the week following these events is best interpreted as proof that Peek and his colleagues genuinely believed they could accomplish what they had set out to do; that is, to create prosperity and publicly demonstrate the benefits of government-industry cooperation. Proof is implied in the way they reacted to the obstacles raised to their policies by the steel conference agree-ment. They seemed unshakably confident in the political strength of their position, certain their methods would survive despite objections the Justice Department or the Railroad Administration might raise to them. These were the marks of men intoxicated by the vision of a dream about to be realized, and not conclusions based upon a sober appraisal or circumstances and history, as events soon would show.

Confidence was demonstrated by the decision to continue with industry conferences already scheduled and to continue the Board's established policies. At these meetings of March 22–27, most of them with building materials industries in keeping with the Board's intention to restrict its dealings to producers of basic commodities, the assurances of the steel conference that the Sherman Act was no barrier to price agreements were repeated. Responding to a direct question on that point at the meeting with coal operators on the 26th, Peek admitted the attorney general had not given an opinion on the legality of the Board's practices as yet, but insisted that "Public sentiment and the sentiment of every branch of the govern-ment would be in favor of doing something," to stimulate business, and utterly discounted the possibility of an adverse opinion. It was not until this same day, March 26, that Secretary Redfield returned from a western tour and the formal application for an opinion which Palmer had suggested could be made.[31]

Expectations regarding Director General Walker Hines' decision as to whether the Railroad Administration would accept the steel price agreement were much less optimistic. Little anxiety was at first evident in the face of the RA's recalcitrance, however, because the Board felt Hines and his lieutenants could be overborne. Re-ceiving no word from Hines after waiting two days, Peek cabled Baruch, asking him to persuade Wilson to "direct" the RA's coop-

[30] Colver to Peek, March 21, 1919 RInB, RG 40.
[31] Citations for transcripts of these meetings are given in note 23. See especially tran-scripts of the coal and box board conferences.

eration.[32] Though confident the RA's resistance could be crushed, the Board soon reached a point where it could not continue its program without actually breaking the deadlock. At the coal meeting on March 26, the industry demanded categorical assurances that the RA would buy at the Board-approved prices if the conference reached an agreement. By the 26th the Board still had no complete certainty of victory over Hines. The wire from Paris remained silent. And when Ritter had paid a visit to Hines on the 25th, he got a sermon upon the Board's mistaken conceptions and had learned only that the steel prices were still under consideration. After hearing the operators' demand, therefore, the Board adjourned the coal conference and made preparations for an immediate showdown with Hines. Leaving Redfield in Washington to contact the President and undercut the RA's position, Peek and Ritter hastily entrained for Chicago where they hoped to find and reason with Hines, who had just headed west on one of the interminable inspection trips his office demanded.[33]

Cables went out on the 27th to Wilson from Redfield and from Fuel Administrator Harry Garfield, who supported the Board. Redfield's message portrayed Hines' refusal to accept the steel prices as a violation of the original understanding concerning the Board, and as springing from the unthinking determination of the railroad men who staffed Hines' agency to beat down coal prices through traditional methods. Pending a reply to the Redfield-Garfield plea to Wilson to compel Hines' surrender, the Board suspended operations.[34]

Had the Industrial Board continued to face only the Railroad Administration's opposition it might well have carried the day. The Board had the advantage in terms of popularity and the personal prestige of its members. Peek's and Ritter's record as WIB administrators gave them an aura of expertise and a superior facility of language in industrial analysis, even if their actual knowledgeability was not superior to that of Hines and his advisors. The RA, staffed as it was by railroad corporation executives and counsel, was highly vulnerable to charges of self-seeking obstructionism. These charges were, of course, not entirely unfounded. Some of Hines' advisors were simply hostile to any form of price-making for railroad supplies except the open market's; and certain of them do seem to have harbored a grudge against their old industrial enemy, the steel in-

[32] Peek to Baruch, March 24, 1919, Peek Papers.
[33] Memorandum for John Skelton Williams, by Hines, March 25, 1919; Hines to Ritter, March 25, 1919, both in file M 23, RG 14. *Iron Age*, CIII, 14 (April 3, 1919), 903–904.
[34] Redfield to Wilson, March 27, 1919; Garfield to Wilson, March 27, 1919, both in Wilson Papers. Powell to Hines, March 28, 1919, file M 23, RG 14.

dustry, and to have believed the steelmen had an unrivaled capacity for fraud and deception.[35]

The RA's resistance to the Board-approved steel prices, however, was based on more reasonable grounds than mere prejudice. The sticking-point was the prices themselves, which seemed entirely too high, especially the price set for rails. In the days immediately following the Board's announcement of the steel prices, Hines was half-disposed to accept them despite this objection. "If the prices give reasonable promise to encourage a general resumption of business, we can undoubtedly help in that direction," he told his subordinates, "by announcing our support of the prices and what we would gain in that way would quickly offset any additional cost which might be involved in paying a slightly higher price than we might get by further trading." Despite these instructions to devise a conciliatory position, if possible, the committee Hines appointed to consider the problem reached an adverse decision on March 26. The prices, the committee told Hines, were not low enough to spark a buying movement. The RA would gain nothing by accepting them and would, instead, needlessly take on a share of responsibility for the Board's extravagant agreement with the steelmen.[36]

At this point, as Hines was deciding he could not accept the steel prices, he was joined by an ally, Secretary of the Treasury Glass, whose entry into the blossoming feud immediately righted the power imbalance between the two original antagonists. What he had learned of the Board's actions in connection with the steel conference had convinced Glass they were tantamount to price-fixing. Hearing of Redfield's request for Presidential intervention in the Board's dispute with the RA, Glass prepared a long cable for Wilson which condemned the Board for exceeding its mandate.[37] He decided to shelve this draft and dispatched in its place merely a request that Wilson withhold any decision in the matter for the time being. But his original message, which he showed to Hines' representatives, defined the issues upon which the war with the Board would be fought out, elevating the controversy from the level of a quibble over the appropriateness of the steel prices to the level of

[35] John Skelton Williams to Hines, March 21, 1919; Memorandum for Hines, by Powell, March 26, 1919, file M 23, RG 14.
[36] The quotation attributed to Hines is taken from a copy of a memorandum in the M 23 file, RG 14, which though unsigned and undated, appears by reason of the documents filed with it and style, to be a memorandum by Hines for an associate, probably Williams, written on about March 25, 1919. See also "Memorandum of Conference in Office of Comptroller Williams . . . March 26, 1919," by Powell; and Williams to Hines, April 2, 1919, both in *ibid.*
[37] Glass to Wilson, March 27, 1919, in "Industrial Board" file, Secretary's File, RG 56.

an argument over the nature and propriety of the Board's policy as a whole.[38]

Wilson, as Glass and others had requested,[39] left Redfield's cable of March 27 unanswered and the disputants felt compelled to make a show of attempting to compose their differences. At a Cabinet meeting at which Peek and Hines appeared on April 2, and at other meetings during the week following, no sign of any disposition to compose differences appeared on either side. Their only result was elaboration and perfection of the opposing positions in preparation for a fresh appeal to Wilson at the proper time.

The case Hines presented against the Board, that it had distorted the original understanding reached in February, had "given immunity from the Anti-Trust laws" to the steel industry, was trying to undermine the government's whole antitrust posture, and had no right to demand the RA to accept its prices, was essentially valid. Hines' assertion that the Board had originally been conceived as a mere "mediator" between government purchasers and industry was, however, an exaggeration. In the original planning, the Board's procedures had not been carefully spelled out, but it is clear that the Board was pictured as possessing an active role, bargaining for price reductions and endorsing them to government purchasers and the public. The RA was correct, however, in holding that it had not been intended to make the Board's endorsement tantamount to a commitment binding all government purchasers. The precise method of the determination and effect of the Board's endorsements had been left ambiguously defined. Hines' terms for a settlement, that the Board would reopen the steel price question and restrict itself thereafter to the position of mere mediator between the RA and industry, implied a complete surrender by the Board of its methods and purposes.[40]

The outlook for the Board's survival grew progressively weaker during the first days of April. Several members of the Cabinet followed Glass' lead and accepted the RA position. But most damaging of all was the opinion Attorney General Palmer gave Secretary of Commerce Redfield on April 1. Though apparently sympathetic to the Board, Palmer was keenly aware of the effect its practices would have upon antitrust administration if they were allowed to stand as precedent. Palmer could, and did, temporarily confine his public

[38] Powell to Hines, March 28, 1919, file M 23, RG 14, for a report of the discussion between Glass and Hines' representatives.
[39] Tumulty to Wilson, March 27, 1919, Wilson Papers.
[40] Hines to Peek, April 4, 1919, enclosing copy of Hines to Glass, April 4, 1919, in RInB. RG 40. New York Journal of Commerce, April 7, 1919. Russell Leffingwell to Glass, April 8, 1919, "Industrial Board" file, Secretary's File, RG 56.

position to a denial that he had approved the Board's operations; but he could hardly refrain from replying formally, and frankly, to Redfield's request. Palmer's opinion characterized the Board's plans in their broader aspects as "in violation of the anti-trust laws" and in their narrowest sense, as a means for arranging prices by agreement solely for government buyers, "unauthorized" by law.[41]

Since, to Peek and his associates, the Board as Hines wanted it would have been useless, both as a depression antidote and as a means for working toward a new antitrust policy, they stubbornly clung to their defenses. Release of the attorney general's opinion would have made the Board's position impossible. But Palmer's neutralism allowed Peek and Redfield to nurse their hope of ultimate vindication by the President. With characteristic boldness, they ignored Palmer's opinion in argumentation with their opponents and rebutted Hines' accusations of illegal practice as best they could. They denied that the Board's practices could be construed as price fixing and argued that, even if the steel agreement was "a combination, . . . the result achieved was certainly a fit field for the application of the rule of reason." They questioned whether it was "good ethics or good politics to allege," as Hines was, "that laws enacted to prohibit voluntary combinations in restraint of trade can be construed to prohibit voluntary combinations in promotion of trade when the government is itself a party and the only binding forces are those of patriotism, facts and sound sense." [42]

The case Hines and Glass had prepared against the Board won out, however, when, after wrangling for two weeks between themselves, the two sides in the dispute turned again to the President for a decision. Hines publicly rejected the Board-approved steel prices on April 11 and both he and Redfield immediately appealed to Wilson. The Board's strategy was to ignore the questions of high policy Hines was raising and stress the practical issues. Redfield argued that the steel prices were in themselves fitting, that they could not have been set at a lower level without precipitating harmful repercussions, and that the Board's program could succeed in its purpose.[43]

Wilson's first impulse was, while cautioning the Board to avoid price fixing, to advise Hines to adopt a more flexible attitude toward

[41] Franz Neilson to Palmer, March 22, 1919; Palmer to Todd, March 24, 1919; Todd to Palmer, March 24, 1919; Palmer to Todd, March 26, 1919, enclosing copy of Palmer to Neilson of same date, file 200515, RG 60. Todd to Palmer, April 15, 1919, file 60/138/0, RG 60. The text of Palmer's opinion was released after the Industrial Board was dissolved and widely published. See, e.g., *Iron Age*, CIII (May 15, 1919), 1304–1306.

[42] Peek to Glass, April 3, 7, 1919; "Memorandum For the Secretary of the Treasury," by Redfield, April 7, 1919, both in RInB, RG 40.

[43] Redfield to Wilson, April 11, 1919, Wilson Papers.

the steel prices and accept them if he could.[44] Scarcely had he cabled these somewhat temporizing instructions to Washington on April 18, however, than Wilson, after reflection, accepted the condemnation of the Board which Glass had sent to Paris on April 14. Peek and the others, Glass argued, had let themselves "be unduly impressed by the steel interests' talk of reduction in wages and fixed prices at rather a high level." They had not honored the original plan but let themselves "be put in the position of sanctioning the practices which were first initiated at the famous Gary dinners and have given Government approval to a minimum price-fixing plan effective for a year." The Board was irredeemably "disposed to persist" in these policies, "unsound economically and politically," and should be dissolved immediately.[45]

Wilson erred badly in failing, at this point, to excise the Industrial Board from his Administration promptly and cleanly. Instead, anxious to avoid the direct involvement in the controversy against which Glass had warned him, the President assumed, wrongly as it turned out, that Glass would see to it that Palmer would kill off the Board by releasing his opinion. His messages to Glass and Redfield of April 21 were weak and inconclusive. Tumulty, through whose hands all cables from the President passed, felt Hines and Redfield should be given more time to compose their feud. Taking advantage of the absence of definite orders in the President's cables, he withheld the message Wilson had sent to Redfield, informing the President that a solution was still possible and advising him to stay his hand.[46]

Tumulty soon regretted his intervention when the dispute wore on, growing increasingly acrimonious and open to public view.[47] Finally, on Tumulty's recommendation, Wilson instructed Hines to end all dealings with the Board. Informed of the President's wish on May 7 by Hines, Redfield announced the resignation of the Board's members on May 8.[48] Already the public recrimination had begun, in which both parties to the dispute freely indulged. Peek had initiated this phase of the controversy on April 29 in a bitter speech before the annual meeting of the Chamber of Commerce in which

[44] Baruch to Wilson, April 15, 1919; Wilson to Tumulty, April 18, 1919, transmitting cables for Hines and Redfield, Wilson Papers.

[45] Glass to Wilson, April 14, 1919, copy in Tumulty Papers.

[46] Wilson to Tumulty, April 21, 1919 (conveying a message for Redfield); Wilson to Glass, April 21, 1919; Tumulty Papers. Tumulty to Wilson, April 22, 1919, Wilson Papers.

[47] Robert P. Lovett to Hines, April 24, 1919; file M 23, RG 14. "Meeting . . . with the Representatives of the Railroad Administration . . . ," April 24, 1919, RInB, RG 40.

[48] Reed to Redfield, April 30, 1919, *ibid.* Tumulty to Wilson, May 1, 1919, Wilson Papers; Tumulty to Leffingwell, May 2, 1919, Carter Glass Papers (University of Virginia Library); Wilson to Tumulty, May 3, 1919, transmitting message for Hines, Tumulty Papers. Hines to Redfield, May 7, 1919, RInB, RG 40.

he had, sensing the Board's imminent defeat, attacked the Wilson Administration as well as Hines and the latter's immediate allies.[49]

Frustrated and vindictive though some of them were, the Board's members believed their efforts had enjoyed success of a kind. The Industrial Board's brief existence. Samuel Bush reflected, had "meant a great deal;" much, he told Redfield, would: [50]

> result from bringing to the front at a very opportune time, the very funda-
> mentals essential to the successful conduct of business and industry in
> time to come, and in the interest of the national welfare. The idea of
> cooperation to save waste and prevent the operation of the destructive
> influences springs from a natural and sound source. It is the expression
> of a natural law and whatever the statutory law may be, it cannot be
> suppressed indefinitely. As you say, man made laws must be made to align
> with natural laws.

George James was also optimistic. He believed that the Board, he told Redfield, had "uncovered certain principles regarding industrial activity which will ultimately prevail and I, therefore, deem it a privilege to have served as a member of your organization." [51]

For the short run, James' and Bush's predictions were inaccurate. In June 1919, the threat of deflation vanished; prices moved upward rapidly and within a few weeks the high cost of living became a pressing issue. Bitterness at business for "profiteering" and conspiring to raise prices replaced the adulatory mood businessmen had thought they detected in the public mind earlier in the year. The Administration concurred with the public in blaming business malpractice for high prices and, through Palmer's Justice Department, started a crusade against hoarding and price-fixing. The times were hardly propitious for the success of the business movement for antitrust revision.[52]

The Industrial Board had, of course, not "uncovered" the "principles" to which James referred. The Board episode does, however, underscore the heightened willingness of businessmen to accept a degree of government regulation in return for industrial stabilization; a willingness which had developed since 1914, as a result, no doubt, of the war mobilization experience. Earlier attempts, including the one of that year, to reshape antitrust policy along these lines had been weakened by the fear among representatives of

[49] Peek, *History of the Industrial Board* (n.p., n.d.), 89–90.
[50] Bush to Redfield, May 5, 1919, file 78484, RG 40.
[51] James to Redfield, May 12, 1919, *ibid.*
[52] The Attorney General's *Annual Report* (1919), 53, and A. Mitchell Palmer's, "A Just and Reasonable Profit," *Nation's Business*, VII (October, 1919), 14–15, reflects the spirit of animosity for business misbehavior prevalent after prices began to rise. See Charles H. Michael, "Trusts Again to the Fore," in the Sunday New York *Times*, October 12, 1919.

smaller business interests that the proposed changes would create a government-big business alliance to their own detriment. In contrast, the Board's policies of 1919, its plans for achieving a new orientation for antitrust policy, accorded perfectly with the expressed wishes of the two major business organizations, the National Association of Manufacturers and the Chamber of Commerce of the United States. Neither of these had supported the 1914 movement aimed at securing much the same objectives.

The Industrial Board's history suggests other points of some significance. The ineptitude of Wilson's leadership in domestic affairs during the "government by cable" period of the winter and spring of 1919, at least in the matter of the Industrial Board, is evident. That the tactics the leaders of the Board used are highly questionable and suggest an undue and unhealthy impatience with the normal policymaking processes of the American democracy, hardly needs to be mentioned. But the main importance of the Board was that it heralded the new, broadly based business concern with stabilization which expressed itself in the succeeding era in an increasingly sophisticated trade association movement and in demands, during the depression of the 1930's, for radical antitrust relaxation.

President Hoover, Organized Business, and the Antitrust Laws: A Study in Hooverian Ideology and Policy

By Robert F. Himmelberg

Hoover as Commerce Secretary under Harding and Coolidge had protected and promoted the trade association movement. Indeed, he had regarded the cooperative activities of businessmen in industrial organizations as the key element in his plans for a better coordinated, stabilized, and more progressive American capitalism. Moreover, as depression president, Hoover relied heavily upon associational business activities to achieve recovery. Yet, Hoover was deeply concerned about the consequences of unchecked cooperative activities and, as President, found the demands of organized business for relaxation of legal barriers to cartelistic activities one of his most pressing and embarrassing political problems. Though paradoxical, in view of his commitment to applying the mechanism of voluntary cooperation to the whole range of economic and social problems, his conviction that intragroup cooperation could easily run to extremes was deep and unalterable.

The source of this conviction lay in Hoover's conceptualization of the American social-economic order. In *American Individualism,* a brief but pithy little book of 1922, Hoover explained how he understood the nature of American life and propounded a political theory which, judging from the consistent and tenacious way in which he rehearsed it in his speeches during the remainder of his public life, was the guide for his actions. Hoover explained that he regarded American society as divided into three functional interest groups: capitalists (including agrarian capitalists), workers, and the general public, represented by the national government. Hoover's concern was for the maintenance of a balance among these groups. Too much power to one would mean fascism, socialism and bureaucratic tyranny, respectively. A fourth contingency was a "syndicalist" situation in which political and economic power would be wielded by a few members of each bloc, the whole constituting a tightly-knit oligarchy. Hoover did not regard these groups as economic collectivities. Rather, he explained, relations between the members of these groups still were and should continue to be regulated by market competition, albeit a competition mitigated somewhat by certain forms of cooperation.[1]

123

An essential point is that Hoover did not fear each of these groups equally as a potential class dictator, or feel that a syndicalist stand-off between all of them was a substantially likely outcome of political evolution.

In the very early twenties, with memories of the excesses of the class rivalries he had witnessed during his war-work in Europe still fresh in mind, Hoover does appear to have wondered whether all interest groups in America might turn into class blocs and destroy the American system. In 1920, speaking of the development of national associations of farmers, workers, and businessmen, Hoover thought the "question of the successful development of our economic system rests upon whether we develop the aspects of these great national associations toward coordination with each other in the solution of national economic problems, or whether they grow into groups for more violent conflict," which could "spell breakdown to our entire national life." [2] The theme received a full statement in *American Individualism*. "If [such groups] develop into warring interests," Hoover wrote, "if they dominate legislators and intimidate public officials, if they are to be a new setting of tyranny, then they will destroy the foundation of individualism. Our Government will then drift into the hands of timorous mediocrities dominated by groups until we shall become a syndicalist nation on a gigantic scale." Even in *American Individualism*, however, and certainly in the speeches of the later 20's and the early 30's, Hoover frankly acknowledged the actual power relations in American society by ignoring organized labor or agrarians as potential class dictators and identifying bureaucracy and business as the two likely sources of political tyranny. That a major preoccupation of Hoover's political thought was a cataclysmic vision of the American system of equality of opportunity, competitiveness and social mobility falling victim to bureaucratic power, is of course precisely what the standard Hoover literature argues. The sheer frequency of Hoover's pronouncements in this vein, especially during the presidential years as he struggled to block one after another Congressional project for expanding government direction of the economy, has however had an unfortunate effect. It has overshadowed and concealed from his interpreters Hoover's equally strong preoccupation with what he thought was an equally dangerous threat to the survival of the American system—business in government.

Though circumstances during the Presidency dictated that Hoover would expend most of his oratorical energy fighting what he thought was a threat of bureaucratic control, it can be shown that in his political thinking the threat of business loomed as large as bureaucratic domination. In *American Individualism* a rhetorical pattern was established that appears in many later expressions of Hoover's political philosophy, especially in the campaign speeches of 1928. Maintaining the proper relation between the state and the

124

business system is defined as the primary problem of modern government. Business is depicted as having threatened the nation, before the reforms around the turn of the century with "a form of autocracy of economic power." The resulting "regulation of public utilities and . . . legislation against restraint of trade" had preserved, and continued to preserve, equality of opportunity, the foundation of the American system. The fight "against economic and political domination" was ceaseless, and the nation sometimes "lag[ged] behind in the correction of that forces that would override liberty, justice and equality of opportunity." But vigilance could prevail; "the principle [of equality of opportunity] is so strong within us that domination of the few will not be tolerated." Over-compensation was, of course, the reciprocal danger. To preserve the "initiative and creative faculties of our people," Hoover wrote, "the Government must keep out of production and distribution of commodities and services. This is the deadline between our system and socialism." [3]

In a number of speeches during the campaign of 1928 and early in his presidency, Hoover endeavored to capsulate his political philosophy. These pronouncements underscored the same enemies of equality of opportunity and individualism that he had defined in *American Individualism*. One of the campaign speeches expressed especially clearly the symmetry of the forces that threatened the American system. First denouncing bureaucratic control of business, Hoover went on to acknowledge that from "bitter experience," the American people had a "rightful fear that great business units might be used to dominate our industrial life and . . . destroy equality of opportunity." He credited the Republican Party with creating the laws that maintained competition and prevented destruction of "the smaller units." "It is just as important," Hoover concluded, "that business keep out of government as that government keep out of business." [4]

References to this appetite of big business for political and economic domination are frequent in the addresses of this period. Hoover's acceptance speech pictured the Sherman Act as upholding Lincoln's conception of the "equal chance" for all Americans; the King's Mountain speech in 1930 assaulted as a "corruptive" influence "any practice of business which would dominate the country by its own selfish interests," and the Valley Forge address in the spring of 1931 warned of the necessity equally to protect individualism from the "deadening restraint of government" and "the encroachments of special privileges and greed or domination by any group or class." [5]

The battles with Congress in 1931 and 1932 and with Roosevelt during the campaign over unemployment and relief, the farm and public power problems, as I have mentioned drove the threat of bureaucratism to the forefront of Hoover's political argumentation. But his tract *Challenge to*

125

Liberty, published in 1934 two years after his defeat at Roosevelt's hands and after a year of the New Deal, returned to the theme of a joint threat to individualism.

Looking backward over the recent past, Hoover sees the "same lack of political cohesion" which had destroyed "Continental Liberalism," the same "growth of indefinite blocs of business, farm, veterans, labor, silver, public works, socialists and what not." Expansion of governmental authority in the economy threatened to entrench these as privileged groups. But the analysis that follows makes clear that the New Deal had enthroned the two most powerful of these. Government intrusion into economic life meant that bureaucrats were exerting increasing control over Congress.

Similarly, the collective control of the economy that the National Recovery Administration was granting to businessmen would soon lead them to exert political control as well.

"Regimentation has already organized some four hundred trades and industries with their officially recognized representatives in the Capitol. These representatives are made effective in influence upon government by the cloak of government agency. Their 1,500,000 different business firms are in every town and village, and each of them has potentially more than one vote. The interests of these regiments run parallel in many directions. Sooner or later their political good-will becomes necessary to every elected person. Thus we have organized invisible government into a smoothly oiled machine."

Congress, he concluded, could not run business, "but business can run Congress—to the bankruptcy of Liberty." [6]

Perhaps it will be thought that, though Hoover's social analysis was somewhat more complex than the anti-statism to which interpreters have generally limited him as an ideologist, the fact had little real importance or concrete effect. The Hoover literature is largely silent as to the existence of policy battles other than those with a Democratic Congress bent upon extending the responsibility of the federal government for aiding the unemployed. Very little has been recorded concerning the Hoover Administration's response to the business community's attempts to seize, through legislation, or to assume, through default of legal administration, that monopolized control of the economy Hoover had rhetorically at least, consistently opposed. The President's response to the business community's efforts through these two means, to achieve a more formal and thorough concentration of economic control, should determine whether Hoover really did see himself during the depression as standing against a future dominated by an organized business bloc.

Hoover's action require inspection at two levels. How did he respond to the pressure businessmen brought to bear to persuade him to support the

126

many plans for abolishing or drastically revising the antitrust policy which assumed an ever-higher place on the agenda of organized business as the depression deepend? Equally, perhaps more important, how did his Administration stand up to the requirement, if the antitrust policy were to survive, that a reasonably adequate enforcement standard be maintained at a time when businessmen attempted to portray every government interference with monopolistic arrangements as a contribution to deflation and unemployment?

The first question is the easier to answer, requiring simply the discovery of Hoover's replies to explicit business requests. However, the background for these requests needs first to be sketched. Well before the depression struck, a very widespread interest in securing relaxation of the federal antitrust policy had appeared within the business community, and several organizations had taken up the cause during the later 1920's.

Antitrust relaxation meant to contemporaries a weakening of the barriers the law proposed to the creation of formalized, workable, cartel agreements. Legal and economic antitrust specialists speak of two basic phases of the policy. One phase has as its object the prevention of monopolization, of the emergence of single-firm domination. The other is aimed against collective control of markets by agreement among competitors against what are called "loose-knit" combinations. Formation of a national policy toward single-firm monopolization had been forged between 1901 and 1920, during the Progressive era. During the 1920's and 1930's the great question in the field of antitrust interpretation and enforcement was how far trade associations and other forms of industrial organization should be allowed to go in strengthening inter-firm cooperation at the expense of competition. Supreme Court decisions in the mid-twenties validated trade associations and their practices in principle; but these decisions and others in the later 20's, especially the Sanitary Pottery decision in 1927, reaffirmed the traditional ban upon cooperative behavior which extended to or tended to result in agreements on prices, production schedules, or allocation of customers. Market competition, the Court made clear, would remain the primary guide for the economy, at least to the degree that the law could influence practice.[7]

Despite the remarkably lax antitrust enforcement policies of the Coolidge era's Justice Department, antitrust revision was already becoming a recognized goal of organized business when the depression began. Of course businessmen's interest in securing leave to form genuine cartels mounted increasingly as the economy swung downward after the fall of 1929. Even an incomplete survey of the attempts business groups made to secure Hoover's backing for revisionist schemes will convey a sense of the number, variety, and intensity of these overtures. Well before the crash in 1929, a group supported by *Forbes* magazine and led by Benjamin A. Javits, a well-known

127

New York trade association attorney, and Manny Straus, an investment banker, began maneuvering to get Administration support for formation of an "Institute for Industrial Coordination." This was to be a grand league of business leaders whose main function, it seems, would have been to lobby for antitrust relaxation with the supposed end of achieving stability of production and employment. Javits, too, once the crash came, was one of the first to urge that Hoover's plan of maintaining investment and employment through the cooperation of the major industries could not be successful unless he sponsored "a revision of the anti-trust laws," thereby making his "industrial co-ordination plan" effective.[8]

The most persistent and, politically, most persuasive group urging Hoover to lead the way on the antitrust question was the Chamber of Commerce of the United States. Led by Julius Barnes, Chairman of the Chamber's Board of Directors between 1929 and early 1932, and Hoover's former associate in the Food Administration during World War I, the organization applied unremitting pressure. This was especially true during 1931 when the Chamber's Committee on Continuity of Business and Employment made its well-known report advocating antitrust relaxation to permit "agreements . . . keeping production related to consumption." Barnes spent much of the fall of 1931 trying to convince Hoover that business sentiment on the issue was too strong to resist. Antitrust revision, he told the President, was "the largest question in business today;" on his trips throughout the country, he insisted, "this question comes up everywhere." [9]

Early in 1932 a large ad hoc body of businessmen representing firms of middling size met in Washington and attempted to impress upon the President the extent of grass-roots support for revisionism. The spokesman for the organization, which styled itself the Industrial Group, tried to impress upon Hoover especially that, as George W. Wickersham put it in a letter the Group solicited from him, "the only chance to get action [on the antitrust question] lies in securing the President's active interest." He alone could persuade "the leaders of both parties" in Congress to act.

Henry I. Harriman, the new President of the Chamber of Commerce, made the same point a little later that year, suggesting that Hoover could, if he wanted, move the House Rules Committee to act on a resolution it had before it authorizing the Judiciary Committee to investigate the revision question. Hoover's laconic reply, referring Harriman to the President's Annual Message of December 1931 in which an investigation had been suggested already to Congress, underscored how remarkably little satisfaction Hoover had given to the revisionists during the depression. Hoover's only public concessions had been given in a speech before the A.F.L. in the fall of 1930 and in the Annual Messages in December of that year and the next one. Hoover had indeed suggested investigation of the antitrust

128

laws, but had insisted substantive change could be considered only in the case of the natural resource industries. Even this limited recommendation was delivered unenthusiastically. And in December 1931 Hoover coupled his repeated suggestion that the natural resource industries might deserve special treatment, with warnings that drastic change in the law's bearing on general industry would "open wide the door to price fixing, monopoly, and destruction of healthy competition." [10]

The revisionists, then, obtained little support from the Administration. Hoover's reply to Harriman in June 1932 was almost insulting. Gordon Corbaley, the originator of the Industrial Group, was infuriated by the fact and, apparently, by the manner of Hoover's refusal to help. "Your Chief," Corbaley wrote Lawrence Richey, the President's secretary, was "the one man" who could give impetus to the revision movement, but it would be "idle to attempt to discuss the subject with him until he can approach it in a very different mind from the one he had when we were in Washington." Indeed, Hoover seems to have come almost to relish what he conceived of as a duty to deflate the various projects businessmen devised for revising or circumventing the antitrust laws. When he learned of the imminent announcement of what became known as the Swope Plan in September, 1931, Hoover hastened to the attack although nothing was asked of him, urging Senator Herbert of Rhode Island to expose the plan as one calculated to establish buisnessmen as a political and economic elite caste.[11]

The acid test for ascertaining the genuineness of these conceptions as a component of Hoover's political ideology is of course not what he said about antitrust enforcement but what he did about it. An investigation of the Hoover Administration's enforcement policy reveals two lines of development. Following the one line creates a strong impression that Hoover's antitrust policy represented a declaration for the survival of antitrust enforcement and the tradition of competitive enterprise. Following the other, however, raises reservations in the observer's mind. Every reader will have to judge the importance of these reservations for himself.

The evidence which suggests that public policy under Hoover represented a revival of a pro-competitive stance is derived from three separate patterns of activity. First there is, simply, the enforcement activity of the Antitrust Division of the Justice Department between 1929 and 1933. Second, there is the clash of 1931 between the Justice Department and the Federal Trade Commission in which the Commission was forced to retreat from sponsorship it had assumed of a large number of "codes of fair competition" that were justly suspected of fostering collusive behavior. Finally, there are the trade-association policies of the Commerce Department. Although the Department had no responsibility for antitrust enforcement, it continued to try to guide the development of industrial cooperation, as it had in the twenties.

129

Its activities therefore help to illuminate the Administration's intentions with respect to the issue of cartelism.

In merely quantitative terms, the record of prosecutions during Hoover's four years against trade associations pursuing cartel-like policies is unimpressive. The number of such engagements were relatively small, totalling only eight. The government's won-lost record was, however, exceptionally good. Of these eight cases, six had been determined by decrees framed on the government's terms at the time when the Hoover Administration ended on March 4, 1933. The remaining two were pending in the lower courts. A skeptic might comment, however, that an impressive won-lost record hardly compensates for what appears to be but a meager number of challenges to trade association conspiracies.[12]

In this context, however, statistics are a poor guide to significance. Though few in number, the impact of the prosecutions was profound. This was true, first because they amounted to a repudiation and reversal of a long period during the Coolidge Administration when the Antitrust Division had actually encouraged trade associations to experiment with cooperative practices that clearly exceeded the guidelines the Supreme Court had provided to govern such behavior. Businessmen received, in other words, a jarring and demoralizing shock when government policy shifted, spoiling their expectation that antitrust enforcement was dwindling to the point of no return. The prosecutions had major significance, in the second place, simply because they raised the probability that any genuine, effective cartel agreements would be hauled into court. And, in a context of declining sales and weak prices, these were the only kind of agreements that were not likely to collapse as soon as they were made.

The Coolidge Administration's antitrust enforcement policies had encouraged trade associations to experiment with the law in two ways. First, by a willingness to tolerate such practices so long as they fell short of plain, overt agreements to fix prices or limit production. In the afterglow of the Coolidge period before the new Administration had made any changes, the threat of antitrust prosecution was so lightly regarded that the *New York Times* business magazine felt that it was appropriate, admiringly and in great detail to describe the Wool Institute's success in holding up prices. Under a normal administration of the antitrust laws, the Institute would gladly have seen the compliment omitted.

But Col. William Donovan, the Antitrust Division's chief during the Coolidge years, had in addition established a special procedure for positively stimulating trade association experimentation with advanced cooperative programs. This had consisted of examining and approving an association's program before its adoption. A liberal approval policy and a willingness to avoid judging too harshly the way the approved program

130

worked out in practice had placed the Justice Department in the potentially embarrassing position of standing behind certain trade associations whose programs were notorious or celebrated, depending on one's point of view, for the liberties they appeared to be taking with the law.[13]

When Hoover assumed the Presidency in 1929, businessmen could, so they thought, look forward to a continuation of those policies. Within a few months, the expectation had been shattered. Almost immediately, the Justice Department reversed Donovan's practice of giving advance approval to trade association plans. Within a year, enforcement policy was challenging certain of the most imposing and precocious of the Coolidge-era experiments, including some that had originally been approved, and the traditional Sherman Act ban on cartel behavior had, in principle at least, been reaffirmed.

It appears doubtful that Hoover was aware of the difficult heritage Donovan and Coolidge had prepared for him, or that the dramatic events just described would be required of his Administration. Hoover certainly knew, long before 1929, of the Justice Department's policy of advising trade associations respecting their plans, but it appears unlikely he was aware how generous the advice had been. He appears to have felt the policy was sound in principle and to have intended it should continue.[14]

Hoover, however, for directly political as well as the more profound reasons we have discussed, was unwilling to countenance such policies. He was extremely sensitive to the criticism that he favored trade combinations and was clearly determined from the outset of his term not to be made the goat for any industry's experiments at the fringes of the law. He demonstrated this in March and April 1929, when the oil industry, through the American Petroleum Institute, prepared a maneuver by which the Administration would be gulled into approving an industry-wide agreement to restrict petroleum production. Upon learning that the oil men had agreed on a limitation scheme, Hoover asked his Attorney General, William D. Mitchell, to investigate; and when a Petroleum Institute delegation came to Washington in April to ask the Federal Oil Conservation Board to approve the plan as a sound conservation measure, Secretary of Interior Wilbur and the Attorney General forcefully rejected the request, suggesting, as one of the oil men put it, that the industry was seeking an "immunity bath" for its scheme.[15]

During the summer of 1929 it was brought home to the Administration that the policies and arrangements inherited from the Coolidge era, if continued, exposed it to serious political embarrassment. The reaction was the same as when the oil men had attempted their maneuver that April. Paradoxically, it was an organization that favored radical liberalization of the antitrust laws, the National Civil Federation, which persuaded the new Administration that antitrust enforcement had been scandalously lax under Coolidge and Donovan. The Federation, a survival from the Progressive

131

era, had become, under the direction of its executive secretary Ralph Easley, heavily committed to anti-radical activity during the 1920's. But the organization still claimed to be, and in some degree was, a meeting ground for capital and labor, and in the late twenties was engaged in lobbying for antitrust revision, arguing, with the support of many prominent industralists and important A.F.L. figures as well, that competition caused industrial instability.

During 1928, the Federation's Committee on Antitrust became convinced that, without stiffer antitrust enforcement, their drive for revision could muster little support. The Bolt, Nut and Rivet Manufacturer's Association, whose program Donovan's office had approved in 1927 but which, the Committee felt, was operating in flagrant violation of the law, particularly attracted the Committee's resentment. When the Justice Department changed hands, the Committee swung into action to obtain prosecution of the Association. It was easy for the Committee to get the Administration's ear. Its Chairman, Wheeler P. Bloodgood, a Milwaukee attorney, was a personal friend of Robert P. Lamont, Hoover's Secretary of Commerce; only a few months previously the two had been partners in a venture known as the Howard Finance Company. Ralph Easley knew Hoover personally. Most important perhaps, the Committee could count on the help of William E. Lamb, one of Bloodgood's legal associates. Lamb had been the Commerce Department's Solicitor during 1921–24 and had worked very closely with Hoover in bringing about the clarification and strengthening of the legal rights of trade associations. Now Lamb penned for the Federation's Committee an analysis which concluded that, under Coolidge, "the apparent policy of the Department of Justice," with respect to encouraging industrial cooperation "was way beyond anything ever advocated by the Department of Commerce" and called for a return to a proper administration of antitrust policy.

In mid-June 1929, Bloodgood began his Committee's attempt to steer the Administration toward a shift in antitrust enforcement when he saw Lamont and warned him that public exposure of past Republican laxity was impending. A well-known trade association lawyer, Felix Levy, from whom the Antitrust Committee had obtained many of its facts, Bloodgood said was threatening to turn his material over to Walter Lippmann, the *New York World's* editor, as a basis for a political attack on the Administration. Lamont took the threat seriously, expressed gratitude when Bloodgood announced he had persuaded Levy to give the new Administration an opportunity to act, and arranged for members of the Antitrust Committee to meet with John Lord O'Brian, who had just been installed as the Antitrust Division's new head. Meanwhile, Lamb's indictment reached Attorney General Mitchell.[16]

132

The Committee's thrusts catalyzed a shift in enforcement policy. O'Brian opened an investigation of the Bolt and Nut Association immediately after he took office on July 1. The Department decided almost immediately to stop approving trade association plans. At the fall meeting of the American Bar Association Mitchell publicly proclaimed the change, repudiating the former approval policy and declaring that the antitrust statutes would be upheld. The message came through clearly to trade association attorneys who visited the Department seeking an indulgence for their plans. "Any extension of trade association activities beyond the limits of the decision in the *Maple Flooring* case," Charles Neagle, the counsel for the National Electrical Manufacturers Association, concluded after his conversation with O'Brian in November, "involved the willingness of those concerned to stand prosecution, either by indictment or by suit in equity." [17]

Neagle's observation fittingly described the principle O'Brian employed as he began to bring a series of court actions in which he sought to limit trade association activities to those which the Supreme Court had validated in the landmark decisions of the 1920's. Associations such as the Bolt, Nut and Rivet Manufacturers Association were employing a variety of cooperative devices that O'Brian regarded as probably illegal in principle and which, he became convinced, were being used to implement price agreements. Despite the ever-worsening depression, three important cases were started during 1930. Those against the Wool Institute and the California petroleum refiners both ended during the same year in decrees meeting the government's terms. During 1931 the Bolt and Nut Association was compelled to sign a consent decree putting an end to the notorious "Graham Plan." Proceedings were initiated during the year also against the Sugar Institute, which Donovan had approved in 1927, and which was nearly as notorious as the Bolt and Nut Institute for its disregard of normal legal limitations. [18]

The Department's successes earned it bitter resentment and criticism from businessmen. The Sugar Institute struck back with a well-funded propaganda attack when it came under fire, claiming treachery since the Department had originally approved its plan of cooperation. The decree against the Bolt Association, its counsel asserted, would "do infinite and unnecessary damage to the entire economic structure of the country, particularly in the presence of the conditions which prevail in the business world." But, insofar as political calculation determined the Administration's antitrust policy, the conclusion seems to have been that public opinion, though it might not be demanding a spectacular trust-busting campaign, nonetheless wanted reassurance that the government was not tolerating blatant price-fixing by organized industry. Both Republican insurgents and Democrats stood ready to exploit any obvious laxity in enforcement that might appear to benefit them politically. It is interesting to note in this connection that Hoover's lieutenants

133

frequently replied to businessmen's pleas for legislative antitrust relaxation with the observation that public opinion would not tolerate it. No doubt they felt the same difficulties inhered in relaxing the law through administrative finagling.[19]

The most striking illustration of the Administration's reluctance to place itself in the position of abetting cartel behavior occurred during 1932 when Col. Donovan asked that it assist him in forming a combination among the soft-coal producers of one of the major mining regions. Donovan, acting as counsel for the mine owners, planned to create a common selling agency arrangement that would apportion output quotas and maintain stable, non-competitive prices. His original request was that O'Brian would simply ignore the prospective combination and allow it to operate. When the reply was that "those promoting this plan ought to proceed on the understanding that they must either obtain legislation permitting it or face litigation to test this plan," Donovan next explained how the Department, if it conducted its case properly, could improve the odds on the Supreme Court's extending the rule of reason to let the agreement stand. O'Brian, first, should stay his hand and withhold court proceedings until the scheme actually was in operation; otherwise a number of important prospective members might hold back. Next, he should agree to try the case on the basis of stipulated facts, to which both parties agreed, placing only the bare legal issues before the Court. O'Brian rejected both requests when they were made initially early in 1932. The Department expected to institute suit in time to prevent the plan "or any part of it from being put into actual operation before its legality has been judicially examined," he said, and could try the case only upon facts developed by the Department's independent investigation. His attitude was not hostile; O'Brian agreed at the outset to expedite the case to the Supreme Court, by the fall term if possible. But he insisted upon leaving the decision to amend the antitrust law entirely to the judiciary.[20]

Between February and August 1932 when the case went to trial, O'Brian softened his position somewhat, and many questions of fact were agreed upon before the trial. Others were contested, however, since, for example, O'Brian felt some degree of coercion had been used to enlist members for the Appalachian Coals organization. As the date for the trial approached there were press intimations that, as Donovan wished were the case, the government sympathized with the mine owners and hoped to draw a liberalization of the law from the Court, but evidence is entirely lacking to support that view. There is good evidence O'Brian was personally convinced that the Supreme Court would follow the established precedents in interpreting the rights of trade associations. O'Brian appeared in court himself and made the chief arguments for the government during the proceedings of August.

134

In his opening statement he expressly denied the government was conducting a "test case" except in the sense any case was such. "This is a straight out, bona fide litigation for which no issues have been framed for this court, and in which both parties are acting in utmost good faith," he insisted. "Counsel for the Government," he asserted, "are in deadly earnest in opposing the legal contentions of defendants." His closing statement was a well-reasoned rebuttal of the argument that the extremely depressed state of the industry warranted extension of the rule of reason to cover the combination it had formed, and persuaded the Court to issue a decree dissolving the Appalachian Coals agreement. The Supreme Court, after reviewing the proceedings, decided to reverse the decision, because it chose to agree with the contentions O'Brian had rebutted and the lower court had rejected. For this famous departure from the traditional rule that overt price and production agreements are illegal per se, a rule to which the Court soon returned, the Hoover Administration can claim no credit, nor incur any blame.[21]

Repudiation of the policies of the Coolidge-era Justice Department was the most important but not the only step O'Brian's Antitrust Division took to reaffirm the traditional antitrust policy. O'Brian soon came into conflict with the Federal Trade Commission which, beginning in about 1928, also had adopted procedures that tended to undermine the Sherman Act. As all the standard works on the Federal Trade Commission point out, the Commission beginning in 1926 approved a large number of trade-practice codes submitted by trade associations. Many of the provisions of these codes represented, as one economist has commented, " 'the substance of things hoped for' by businessmen." In the spring and summer of 1931, following premonitory rumblings in the previous fall, the Commission revised many of the codes, eliminating offensive rules in some instances, qualifying them in others. The Commission's unilateral and wholesale revisions reduced most of the codes to mere statements of the elements of the law of fair competition. Trade associations, recognizing that the Commission's "policy of cooperation with business in order to develop . . . a new era of industrial self-regulation," had ended, realized that only through legislation could the codes again be made effective instruments for reducing the intensity of competition within their industries. It was these disaffected associations that lobbied hardest for passage of the Nye bills of 1932 which were major direct models for the N.I.R.A.[22]

What is not known except very indistinctly is that the Justice Department was directly responsible for the FTC's policy shift. The reason for conflict between the two agencies was the code of the American Petroleum Institute the FTC approved in the summer of 1929. By December of that year, O'Brian and his staff were convinced that the industry was "being led to believe that the Federal Trade Commission has affirmatively approved both

135

price fixing and the allocation of customers." After securing evidence of price fixing and dealer coercion by the West Coast refiners, the Department opened civil proceedings against them in February 1930.[23]

Publicly, the Department minimized the role of the oil code in the conspiracy, although in the decree handed down in September 1930 it secured an explicit mention of one of the offending rules and a statement prohibiting refiners from alleging to their dealer customers that the rule forbade price cutting. Privately, however, O'Brian complained more forcefully. In February 1930 in conference with the entire Commission, he had objected to the rules in the oil code he considered offensive, probably mentioning similar examples in other codes as well. The following June, O'Brian repeated his charges in a "personal talk" with Garland Ferguson, the Commissioner's Chairman. In December 1930 and on several occasions in the spring of 1931, O'Brian continued to press the Commission. In the absence of any other stimulus for the Commission's changed attitude (and none has come to light in the course of this writer's research) it is proper to conclude that O'Brian's representations, together with the involvement, even though tangential, of one of the FTC codes in the West Coast refiners case, were responsible for the policy change that emasculated the trade-practice conference movement.[24]

The third step the Administration took to prevent the growth of attitudes and arrangements that would have helped create a cartelized business system came through the Commerce Department's relations with trade associations. The Department's efforts amounted to a persistent but somewhat pathetic attempt to renew trade association interest in the traditional, relatively innocuous practices that had seemed so important in the 1920's but which the depression had made largely irrelevant. Frederick M. Feiker, a Hoover associate for a time in the early 1920's was made Chief of the Bureau of Foreign and Domestic Commerce in July 1931 and took the leading part in this effort. Before his appointment Feiker had served as managing director of the Associated Business Papers and was a well-known figure in the trade association world. Although Feiker and other Bureau officials took up the contemporary watchword that industries through their trade associations, had to "balance" production and consumption, their recommendations stopped far short of collective controls and amounted to little more than a rehash of ideas from the 1920's. Feiker labored to revitalize faith in these ideas in his speeches before the American Trade Association Executives, in meetings with editors of trade periodicals, and in the Bureau's direct contacts with associations. By the summer of 1932 he acknowledged how hollow the depression made these ideas sound to trade association leaders. "We are entering into a period of the control of production and of prices," he wrote privately, "not on the basis of some of the old slogans or old

136

philosophies, but on the basis (among other policies) of the control of credit (and capital funds) exercised indirectly through the Federal Reserve Board and the Reconstruction Finance Corporation." But Feiker spent his term as the Bureau's director upholding the "slogans" of the Hoover trade association philosophy and had done nothing to bring about the collapse of them he was predicting.[25]

But did Hoover entirely resist the pressure the business community applied so continuously during the depression to make him concede on the issue of antitrust relaxation? There were, in fact, important lapses from the pro-competitive policies I have been describing. Hoover's recovery program depended so largely upon the good will and cooperation of businessmen and their organizations that he could scarcely have escaped concessions upon this issue. Gauging the extent and estimating the significance of these concessions is, however, difficult.

One concession was obvious and above-board and has been mentioned already. In the Annual Messages of December 1930 and 1931, Hoover advocated Congressional investigation of the antitrust laws in relation to the natural resource industries, suggesting that for them enforced competition might be inappropriate. His correspondence with Chamber of Commerce and other business leaders indicates that Hoover anticipated his suggestion would go far to satisfy their demands. In this he was of course mistaken. The scope of the relaxation he proposed was far too limited, and besides, as we have already seen, the Chamber leaders resented the fact that at no time did the President follow his rather lack-luster proposal up with string-pulling efforts to get a Congressional investigation started.

The argument that competitive operations bred inefficiency and waste in the natural resource industries had gained considerable acceptance and was a good deal less controversial than the contention that the antitrust tradition was outmoded altogether. Hoover nevertheless had not wanted to accept the argument. This showed most clearly in his dealings early in his Administration with the petroleum industry, which was clamoring loudly for relief from antitrust prosecution even before the depression began. During this period Hoover invested considerable effort in a campaign to persuade the oil men and the oil producing states that uniform conservation practices, including unitary pool operation, enforced by an interstate compact, was their proper objective. He acknowledged privately that good conservation practices would moderate the pace of petroleum production and help stabilize oil prices. But this would be incidental, and not the main purpose of such programs. The Administration's oil policy, the President told Secretary Wilbur in 1929, should avoid connection with proposals for direct limitation of oil production, whether by the oil men or by a compact among the oil states. "We must put [our policy] on a higher basis than this," he insisted.[26]

137

Heeding perhaps the political power of the oil states, a power of which the oil men and their political representative never tired of reminding the President, Hoover by 1930 was ready to accept oil-state efforts to limit petroleum output through prorationing agreements. But it was the steps the Administration took, in 1931 when the program threatened to break down, that genuinely contradicted the other policies. When the controls asserted by oil-state governors could not continue unless the big Eastern oil companies reduced their imports from Latin America, Hoover, as he publicly announced, permitted the Federal Oil Conservation Board to request each company independently to limit imports.[27]

The Administration's effort went much further than what it publicly announced, however. Secretary Lamont was appointed to negotiate with the companies and worked to initiate and maintain agreement among them. It seems clear that Lamont was effectuating an arrangement that most antitrust lawyers would have held illegal. Overzealous subordinate attorneys in the Antitrust Division, hearing something of these activities from the press, pronounced them illegal and mentioned the matter to their superiors. The Attorney General assured them, however, that they were mistaken, and that the "Federal officials in contact with this are quite aware that it is desirable to keep clear of concerted arrangements." But Lamont's correspondence with Western oil men, in which he explained that continuation of import restrictions depended upon adopting a stiffer proration plan among the states, makes it clear that he was, in fact, the organizer of what can only be regarded as an agreement among the Eastern importers.[28]

At about the same time the Oil Conservation Board initiated a practice that went well beyond mere approval for interstate prorationing agreements and verged upon sponsorship for direct production limitation among petroleum producers. In 1930 the Board had begun to publish periodic reports that made short-run market forecasts and urged industry members to limit their production to a pro-rata share of the market. Initially, the reports emanated from a so-called Voluntary Committee on Petroleum Economics, composed of American Petroleum Institute members, and was published by the Board as its Secretary, E. S. Rochester, explained, "merely as an expression of opinion of gentlemen having no official connection" with it. Beginning in April 1931, however, at the Petroleum Institute's insistence members of the Commerce and other Departments began to sit on the Voluntary Committee and endorse its reports. This made the Board responsible for them, Rochester thought, a conclusion that led him to urge the Board to sever the connection between the government and the Committee. But the relationship persisted, and the reports, estimating petroleum and gasoline requirements and advising all branches of the industry to regulate production accordingly, continued until the very end of the Hoover Administration.[29]

138

The Administration's efforts to maintain a respect for the antitrust laws in the oil industry broke down completely after this, so that not only the petroleum-producing but also the refining and marketing branches of the industry received special treatment. In 1930 the Justice Department had obtained a decree against the California refiners in an action that shook the whole structure of the FTC codes. But in 1931 the Department's policy softened. O'Brian, discovering the 1930 decree was defective, felt additional action was required. But Mitchell in what seems patently a policy move decided by the President, told him to go slowly. Earlier, during the preliminary stages of the government's 1930 prosecution of the California refiners, Mitchell had urged caution upon O'Brian, reminding him that the Administration was working with these companies to bring about oil conservation. While this did not justify lawbreaking, "it does form a reason why we should give careful consideration to any contention by the oil interests that they should be given an opportunity to correct any illegal practices they may have developed." By 1931, apparently even greater consideration seemed justifiable.[30]

Although the Administration maintained a cool attitude toward another major natural-resource industry, the coal industry, and as we have seeen, refused to cooperate with its plan of obtaining judicial antitrust relaxation, the lumbermen received more generous treatment. Early in 1931, the Timber Conservation Board composed of Lamont, Wilbur, Secretary of Agriculture Hyde, and a number of industry representatives, and which Hoover had recently created, began to publish market reports similar to the Oil Conservation Board's. By November the reports had become, in the eyes of the industry, and according to the Secretary of the National Lumber Manufacturers Association, "the focal point around which to secure the balancing of production and consumption."[31]

The members of these favored industries could scarcely have understood these policies as anything less than an invitation to ignore the Sherman Act. Whether this led them to act accordingly is less important than the fact that the Administration, in order to encourage stabilization in the oil and timber industries, was willing to jeopardize the whole effort it was making to maintain the traditional antitrust policy. Executive liberalization of the law in relation to these industries amounted to an admission that the depression had in some measure rendered the traditional policy unworkable and inappropriate, precisely the argument so many attorneys, including those directing the Appalachian Coals scheme, believed they could persuade the Supreme Court to accept with the Administration's support. Moreover, the Administration's selective liberalization jeopardized the credibility of its announced commitment to enforce the antitrust laws.

139

If the Administration had supported cartelism, even in this indirect manner, in nonnatural resource industries, then probably we would have to conclude that Hoover was a devious President indeed, and that while making a show of upholding the antitrust tradition for one constituency, he was nullifying it for another. However, I cannot find much evidence of this. Secretary Lamont did intervene when a price collapse threatened the cement industry in the late fall of 1930, and he appears to have arranged, at least to have been prepared to arrange, and agreement on prices among the producers.[32] But this was an exceptional and, so far as I have been able to discover from the archival and manuscript sources, a unique experiment. Professor Louis Galambos has argued that the support the Administration gave to the Cotton Textile Institute's program for limitation of day-and-night running time to fifty-five and fifty hours, respectively, and for eliminating female and child labor from the night shift constituted an important qualitative change in the government's relations with trade associations. By the criterion employed in the present discussion this does not seem necessarily the case. It is true that limitation of output by agreement had been as unequivocally denounced by the courts as price fixing, and that the CTI program was definitely intended as an effort to limit production. However, the method employed was very indirect and ostensibly served important social purposes. It was these social goals that the CTI magnified in its dealings with the government and the public, and it was possible to represent them as the program's paramount aim. Under the prevailing economic conditions, moreover, the program held little promise of seriously reducing the output of cotton goods. The legality of the program was certainly moot. The Commerce Department's legal authorities, which Lamont consulted before the Administration endorsed the "55–50" plan, "saw nothing out of the way with it." Because the legal issues were ambiguous, and because the CTI plan was not one capable of widespread imitation, it does not appear reasonable to regard the endorsement as lending itself to the erosion of the antitrust laws. The Administration's action can be interpreted as little more than an effort to promote stability by encouraging means that, if unusually vigorous, were not seriously repugnant to the antitrust laws as they had been interpreted by the courts.[33]

The evidence brought forward in the foregoing account supports the conclusion that the Hoover Administration refused to bend to the business community's pressure for administrative antitrust relaxation except selectively, in the area of the natural resource industries where the rationale for control of competition was most persuasive. Even though the Antitrust Division's enforcement activities hardly added up to an antitrust crusade, they were sufficient to maintain the traditional ban upon overt, formalized cartelist agreements. It is doubtful that less formal agreements could have

140

become or remained operational in the context of the depression. The FTC, chastened after its clash with the Justice Department, supported the Antitrust Division's stand; so did the Commerce Department.

Hoover's concern over the threat that a further concentration of economic control posed to the American way, as he defined it, was therefore not merely verbal. This concern was as real as the anti-bureaucratic, anti-centralizing bias that has received so much comment. It seems fair to conclude that we should, as was suggested at the outset of this argument, interpret the presidential Hoover as embattled from two directions, as struggling, in his own understanding of events and in his actions as well, with two, not one, substantial perils to the values he treasured.

References

1. Hoover, *American Individualism* (Garden City: Doubleday, 1922), 41–44, 53–55.
2. Hoover, "Plea for Cooperation," *American Federationist*, XXVIII (January, 1921), 36–37.
3. *American Individualism*, 41–44, 53–55.
4. Hoover, *The New Day, Campaign, Speeches of Herbert Hoover, 1928* (Stanford Calif.: Stanford University Press, 1928), pp. 164–166.
5. Acceptance speech in Hoover, *New Day*, p. 41. Other speeches in *The State Papers and Other Public Writings of Herbert Hoover*, 2 vols., (New York: Doubleday, 1934) vol. 1, pp. 339, 568.
6. Hoover, *Challenge to Liberty* (New York: Charles Scribner's, 1934), pp. 121–129.
7. Few if any major issues involving "close-knit" combinations were before the courts during the period. But many of the major precedents bearing upon "loose-knit" combinations date from the 1920's and 30's. Compare the citations Milton Handler gives in his discussion of the antitrust laws in relation to trade association behavior with those given for the law in relation to mergers and consolidations in U.S. Senate, Temporary National Economic Committee, *Monograph No. 381. A Study of the Construction and Enforcement of the Federal Antitrust Laws* [1941], pp. 9–45, 46–90.
   Since World War II it has been assumed by economists and lawyers in the antitrust field that anti-cartelism was a fixed policy. The major question debated has been whether the law should make greater efforts to break down oligopolistic market structures. See Carl Kaysen and Donald P. Turner, *Antitrust Policy: An Economic and Legal Analysis* (Cambridge: Harvard University Press, 1959).
8. Javits to George Akerson, 25 July 1929; to Hoover, 29 November 1929, in "Unemployment" and "Business" files, respectively, of the Presidential Files, Herbert Hoover Papers, Hoover Presidential Library. All following citations to the Hoover Papers (abbreviated as HHP) are to the Presidential Files.
9. Barnes to Hoover, 10 October and 30 November 1931; 27 May 1932. "Chamber of Commerce" file, HHP.
10. Malcolm Whitman to Lawrence Richey. 17 March 1932 (enclosing a letter, Wickersham to Whitman, 17 March 1932), "Business" file; Harriman to Hoover, 13 June 1932; Hoover to Harriman, 15 June 1932, "Antitrust Laws" file, HHP. *State Papers*, I, 437–438: II, 51–52.

141

11. Gordon G. Corbaley to Richey, 7 April 1932, "Corbaley" file; Hoover to Felix Herbert, 11 September 1932; Herbert to Hoover, 18 September 1932, "Business" file, HHP.

12. The eight organizations against which actions were begun are as follows. (The number before each entry is the number given the case in the *Federal Antitrust Laws: With Summary of Cases Instituted by the United States* (New York: Commerce Clearing House, 1949): (368), Greater New York Live Poultry Chamber of Commerce (February 1930); (369), California oil refiners (February 1930); (375), Wool Institute (June 1930); (377), Asphalt Shingle and Roofing Institute (December 1930); (378), Bolt, Nut and Rivet Manufacturers Association, (March 1931); (379), Sugar Institute (March 1931); (382), Corn Derivatives Institute (April 1932); (383), Appalachian Coals, Inc. (June 1932).

13. Edward S. Mead, "The Wool Institute: A Successful Cooperative Control of an Industry," *Annalist* XXXIV (23 August 1929): 347–348. For Donovan's practices, see especially files 60/104/13 and 60/126/13 for 1927–1928, in Record Group 60 (Records of the Antitrust Division of the Department of Justice), National Archives (cited hereafter as NA).

14. See Thomas Thacher to Hoover, 17 April 1929, "Justice Department" file, HHP.

15. Hoover to Mitchell, 23 March 1929; Mitchell to Hoover, 30 March 1929; "Record of meeting between Federal Oil Conservation Board and Representatives of the American Petroleum Institute," 4 April 1929; Wilbur to R. C. Holmes, 8 April 1929, all in "Oil" file, HHP.

16. The formulation of the policies of the Federation's Committee on Antitrust can be followed in the Committee's "Minutes" of 16 March 1928 and 28 March and 21 May 1929, in boxes 65 and 134 of the National Civic Federation Papers, New York Public Library.

    The maneuvers of the Committee in Washington can be traced in the following letters, all in the General Correspondence files of the NCF: Bloodgood to Lamont, 6 April, 22, 27 June, 5 July, 12 August, 1929; Lamb to Bloodgood, 3 July 1929; Lamont to Bloodgood, 29 June 1929.

17. Undated memorandum (written in mid-August 1929) for Russel Hardy by O'Brian; O'Brian to William J. Donovan, 3 September 1929; both in file 60/10/5, RG 60, NA. Mitchell to George Akerson, 30 October 1929, "Justice Department" file HHP. Executive Committee *Minutes* of the National Electrical Manufacturers Association, 15 November 1929 (in office of the Association, New York City).

18. These cases are summarized in *Federal Antitrust Laws,* as cited in note 13 above. This paragraph is based upon a study, for the 1928–1932 period, of files 60/126/13, 60/104/13, 60/57/32, 35, RG 60, NA.

19. The Institute stated its grievances in a pamphlet, *The Sugar Institute, Inc., Its History, Policies and Achievements,* which frequently turns up in government and business files of the period. See James F. Burke (the Institute's counsel) to O'Brian, 6 May 1930, file 60/126/13, RG 60, NA. For an episode involving a response to critics (in this case Senator King of Utah) see two memoranda, one by George P. Alt for O'Brian, 20 May 1931, one by O'Brian, 22 June 1931, both in file 60/105/5, RG 60, NA.

    Lamont to William M. Ritter, 3 May 1930; to Henry L. Doherty, 19 October 1931, Lamont Papers, RG 40, NA.

20. File memorandum by O'Brian, 7 January, 10 March 1932; O'Brian to Donovan, 26 January, 9 February 1932; O'Brian to Mitchell, 27 January 1932; to Williamson (of the firm of Donovan and Raichle) 27 January 1932; all in file 60/187/67, RG 60, NA.

142

21. A memorandum prepared for Frederick Feiker, Chief of the Bureau of Foreign and Domestic Commerce of the Commerce Department by Jay Judkins, a Bureau official, dated August 1932, relates personal views regarding the future of antitrust law, which O'Brian had stated in a conversation. The memo is in the Feiker Papers, box 7, Record Group 151 (Records of the Bureau of Foreign and Domestic Commerce), NA.
    Transcript of Proceedings, U.S. v. Appalachian Coals, District Court for the Western District of Virginia, in file 60/187/67, RG 60.
22. Myron W. Watkins, *Public Regulation of Competitive Practices in Business Enterprise* (New York: National Industrial Conference Board, 1940), pp. 243–246; John Perry Miller, *Unfair Competition* (Cambridge: Harvard University Press, 1941), pp. 270–178.
23. John H. Amen to O'Brian, 27 December 1929, file 60/57/35, RG 60, NA.
24. Memo for O'Brian by Alber J. Law, 8 December 1930; memo for Mitchell by O'Brian (with draft of proposed letter to Commissioner Ferguson), 16 December 1930; memo for Mitchell by O'Brian, 21 July 1931; in file 60/57/32, RG 60.
25. Feiker to Edward R. Dewey, 15 August 1931: "Notes for use in Asheville Speech, dictated after Division Chiefs Meeting . . . on Trade Association and Stabilization Plans," 19 September 1931; "Notes on a Meeting in the Engineer's Club, New York City, Friday, September 11, [1931] Concerning Relationship of the Department in the Trade Association Movement and the Asheville Convention of the A.T.A.E."; Feiker to E. W. Davidson, 9 May 1932; to Roscoe C. Edlund, 22 September 1932, all in Feiker Papers, RG 151, NA.
26. Hoover, press release, 2 April 1929; Wilbur to R. C. Holmes, 8 April 1929; Hoover to Wilbur, 10 April 1929; E. B. Reeser to Wilbur, 24 April 1929; Wilbur to George H. Dern, 23 April 1929; Wilbur to Hoover, 15 April 1929; E. K. Burlew (with enclosure, statement of Wilbur before Conference on Oil Conservation at Colorado Springs, June 1929) to Theodore Joslin, 17 August 1931. All in "Oil" file HHP.
27. Mark L. Requa to Lawrence Richey, 30 September 1929 (two letters) with enclosure, memo of Santa Fe meeting with oil industry leaders; T. F. Hunter to former Senator Henry J. Allen, 28 February 1931; White House press release, 13 March 1931; Department of Interior press release, 7 August 1931; Requa to Walter Newton, 31 December 1931; all in "Oil" file, HHP.
28. Lamont to Richardson Pratt, 3 February 1931; Walter Tagle to Lamont, 16 June 1931; Lamont to J. F. Lucey, 24, 29 June, 9 July 1931; Lamont Correspondence, RG 40. Lamont to Robert G. Stewart, 20 March 1931; William R. Boyd, Jr., to Lamont, 25 June 1931, file 82272/1, RG 40, NA. Israel B. Oseas to O'Brian, 25 March 1931; undated memo (but written before 31 March 1931) by Attorney General Mitchell, commenting on Oseas memo; both in file 60/01/6, RG 60, NA.
29. Rochester to Secretary Wilbur, 1 April 1932, box 7, Record Group 232 (Records of the Federal Oil Conservation Board), NA.
30. Mitchell to O'Brian, 21 January 1930; O'Brian to Mitchell, 21 July 1931; Mitchell to O'Brian, 21 July 1931; O'Brian to W. B. Watson Snyder, 9 December 1932; in file 60/57/35, NA.
31. "Third Executive Meeting of the Timber Conservation Board," 25 November 1931; in General File, Timber, Timber Conservation Board records, RG 151.
32. William J. Donovan to Lamont, 20, 21 October 1930; Lamont to Theodore Dickinson, 23 October 1930; Dickinson to Lamont, 30 October 1930; Donovan to Lamont [15 November 1930]; Blaine Smith to Lamont, 22, 24 November

143

1930; Lamont, telegrams to a number of cement producers, 1 December 1930; in Lamont Papers, RG 40. Blaine Smith to Lamont, file 82276/21, RG 40, NA.

33. See Louis Galambos, *Competition and Cooperation: The Emergence of a National Trade Association* (Baltimore: Johns Hopkins Press, 1966), Chap. VII, for a different view.

ROBERT F. HIMMELBERG

Born: July 16, 1934.

Education: B.A., Rockhurst College, 1956; M.A., Creighton University, 1958; Ph. D. (hist), Pennsylvania State University, 1963.

Professional Experience: Fordham University—from instructor to associate professor, 1961–1977; chairman, department of history, 1968–71; professor, American History, 1977.

Memberships: American Historical Association and Organization of American Historians.

Publications: Author: The War Industries Board and Antitrust Question in November, 1918, *Journal American History,* 6/65; *The Great Depression and American Capitalism,* Heath, 1968; Business, Antitrust Policy, and the Industrial Board of the Department of Commerce, 1919, *Business History Rev.,* spring 1968.

Contributions: Herbert Hoover and the Crisis of American Capitalism, Schneckman, 1973; The Origins of the National Recovery Administration; *Business,* Government and the Trade Association Issue, 1921–1933, Fordham University, 1976; Herbert Hoover and the Great Depression, In: *Power and the Presidency,* Scribner's, 1976.

The War Industries Board and the Antitrust Question in November 1918

ROBERT F. HIMMELBERG

I N November 1918 the industrial leaders who staffed the War Industries Board believed they had the power to shape in some degree the demobilization and reconstruction policies which would guide the nation from war to peace footing. The response they made to this opportunity provides material for a case study of the businessman cast in the role of public servant and originator of public policy. Not unlike other interest groups one would expect businessmen in politics to pursue their class interests. Placed at the helm of a powerful governmental agency to mobilize industry for either war or postwar recovery, however, American opinion seems to expect from its business leaders not only vigor and consummate skill but disinterestedness as well. The behavior of businessmen of the WIB in November 1918 may help to take tentative measure of the soundness of this expectation.[1]

Disinterestedness was not the hallmark of the WIB's concern over what would be the Wilson administration's postwar policies. The agency's members unhesitatingly supported the reconstruction policies for which the business community was agitating at the end of the war, and tried to find a way to put them into effect. Yet the WIB contained its support of business objectives within moderate limits and backed away from use of feasible but unseemly tactics. The illumination of the considerations placing limits on the WIB's partisanship is both the most interesting and difficult task in putting together the history of the WIB's relationship to business goals at the end of the war.

Mr. Himmelberg is assistant professor of history in Fordham University.

[1] As illustrative of this good opinion of businessmen as emergency administrators, see the judgments upon the WIB in the following, randomly selected, general works: Oscar T. Barck, Jr. and Nelson M. Blake, *Since 1900: A History of the United States in Our Time* (New York, 1959), 226-27; Arthur C. Bining and Thomas C. Cochran, *The Rise of American Economic Life* (New York, 1964), 522; Dexter Perkins and Glyndon G. VanDeusen, *The American Democracy: Its Rise to Power* (New York, 1964), 467.

Two policy goals appeared to be uppermost in the eyes of American industrialists as World War I drew to a close. One of these was a continuation of price protection, and the other—in some ways contradicting the first—was modification of the antitrust policy that prohibited business agreements among competitors. Many industries such as the producers' goods sector of the economy feared their products would suffer a price collapse once war orders fell off. Their fears were well-founded since most of them had expanded their productive facilities during the war and under conditions of declining demand could well anticipate falling prices. It is not surprising that such industries sought some postwar price support mechanism and many of them felt the WIB was the logical candidate for this function. The felt piece-goods manufacturers, for example, as a WIB official described it, looked "to the War Industries Board for assistance and they lean upon us absolutely, and are exceedingly anxious to have us continue during the period of transition from a war to a peace basis. . . ." During the war the WIB had protected the public interest through maximum price-fixing and other means at the expense of profits. Now many industrialists at the war's end failed to understand why those who had asked them "to restrict and restrain" should not now help industry "to get back to peace conditions" by fixing minimum prices for a time at least.[2]

Important as it was to many industries, the mere temporary suspension of free market forces was not the paramount goal which the industrial community hoped was within its grasp in November 1918. Industrial mobilization in 1917-1918 had required the government virtually to abandon the enforcement of the federal antitrust policy and encourage industrial cooperation instead. Every industry had been required to appoint a War Service Committee which linked the industry to its Section, the ultimate administrative unit of the WIB. The Sections in cooperation with their War Service Committees laid down policies which provided for the operation of each industry as a unit rather than as a collection of competing firms.[3] The intent and effect of unitary operation was to subordinate industrial interests to those of the public. This fact had not prevented many industrialists from realizing how powerful an engine of their own welfare cooperation could become when they regained control of their own affairs.

Long before World War I trade associations had been organized in

[2] The quotes are from "Minutes of Conference Held on November 19 [1918]. Felt Section" and "Meeting of the Building Materials Section," Nov. 19, 1918, File 1-C2, Record Group 61, Records of the War Industries Board (National Archives).
[3] The best general description of WIB policies is Grosvenor B. Clarkson, *Industrial America in the World War* (Boston, 1923); see esp. 299-314.

many industries and had introduced a variety of legal cooperative practices such as standardization of products, as well as others, such as price agreements, that were illegal.[4] But the experience of mobilization quickened interest in cooperation throughout the ranks of American industrialists from the representatives of the corporate elite to those of the humblest proprietors. For the first time trade associations developed in many industries and existing ones were strengthened.[5] Their members grew impatient with half-way measures in the art of cooperation, and there was a determination to step up programs of standardization and conservation of materials which in most cases had been legal before the war. Moreover, there arose an even greater determination to sweep aside the prewar antitrust policy so that industry could without hindrance form a genuine cartel system in which the collective will of an industry—not the competitive market—would set prices and production levels. Sympathy for antitrust revision of this character in 1918-1919 was pervasive. Before the war support for it had been limited to larger firms; representatives of smaller concerns were uncommitted or hostile, for they feared that antitrust revision would ultimately benefit the competitive position of the industrial giants more than it would help their own.[6] War experiences apparently erased this distrust, and such organizations as the National Association of Manufacturers (representative of smaller manufacturing concerns) had become, in 1918, enthusiastic for antitrust revision. Well before the end of the war agitation had begun for the suppression of the antitrust policy insofar as it outlawed agreements among competitors. In the winter of 1918-1919 the agitation reached a fevered pitch.[7]

[4] For surveys of trade association practices before 1917 see H. R. Tosdal, "Open Price Associations," *American Economic Review*, VII (June 1917), 331-52, and National Industrial Conference Board, *Trade Associations: Their Economic Significance and Legal Status* (New York, 1925), 7-24.

[5] Available data on the rate of trade association formation indicates a much more rapid growth between 1915 and 1920 than in either the preceding or succeeding five-year periods. See U. S. Temporary National Economic Committee, *Trade Association Survey, Monograph No. 18,* by C. A. Pearce (Washington, 1941), 19, 369, and NICB, *Trade Associations,* 26-27, 319-32.

[6] Hans B. Thorelli, *The Federal Antitrust Policy: Origination of an American Tradition* (Baltimore, 1955), 149, 350-51; Arthur M. Johnson, "Antitrust Policy in Transition, 1908; Ideal and Reality," *Mississippi Valley Historical Review,* XLVIII (Dec. 1961), 432-33; Robert H. Wiebe, "Business Disunity and the Progressive Movement, 1901-1914," *ibid.,* XLIV (March 1958), 680-85.

[7] For the NAM's view by May 1918 that the Sherman Act was an intolerable infringement of the "right of collective economic action in business transactions," see *Proceedings of the Twenty-third Annual Convention of the National Association of Manufacturers . . . May 20, 21, and 22, 1918* (New York, 1918), 107. On industry's determination in the winter of 1918-1919 to break down the anti-cartel side of the antitrust

The WIB was especially sympathetic with the industries which feared a disastrous postwar deflation and gave their plea for governmental price protection the first claim upon its attention. The more general business goal of fundamental and permanent antitrust revision was taken up in its turn.

The simplest way of preventing the collapse of prices after the Armistice would have been to continue the WIB and its powers of industrial regulation. These powers had been used during the war to cope with the problems of an overheated economy. The purpose of price-fixing had been to prevent inflation for the fixed prices had been maximums. Similarly, the WIB had in many cases compelled or approved an agreement among an industry's competitors to restrict production on a pro rata basis when it was necessary to curtail the output of a nonessential industry. It required only the inversion of the purpose of these instruments of control to prevent price declines and excessive production in relation to demand. Thus as the end of the war approached, the War Service Committees of many industries, in conference with their Section administrators or other WIB officials, asked for the continuation of WIB controls if these could be turned to the advantage of the industries. A number of these pleas were relayed to the WIB's ten-man Board.[8] These reports no doubt strengthened the conclusion the Board seems to have reached before any of them came to it, namely that postwar deflation had to be prevented and that the continuation of the WIB would best serve this goal.

According to the WIB's lawyers this continuation could have been obtained merely by the consent of the President. They regarded the President's war powers as very broad, and seem to have felt, in terms of constitutional law, that they resided inherently within the presidential office. Albert C. Ritchie, the Board's counsel, believed these war powers probably extended constitutionally to the signing of the peace treaty. Under them Wilson could simply delegate to the WIB authority for approving industry "pooling and

policy, see the typescript record of the U.S. Chamber of Commerce's "Reconstruction Congress," held in Dec. 1918, library of the Chamber's headquarters, Washington, D.C. See also the Chamber's *Referendum No. 26: On the Report of the Federal Trade Committee of the Chamber Regarding Trust Legislation. February 1, 1919;* and *NAM, Proceedings . . . Annual Convention . . .* (New York, 1919), 134-56, 224-51, 285.

[8] For Sectional and Divisional reports urging a positive WIB attitude toward business pleas for postwar protection, see for example Charles MacDowell (Director, Chemical Division) to Bernard Baruch, Nov. 14, 1918; William A. Ritter (Asst. to Commissioner of Finished Products) to George Peek (Commissioner of Finished Products), Nov. 6, 1918; E. L. Crawford (Asst. to Commissioner of Finished Products) to Baruch, Nov. 9, 1918; W. V. Phillips (Chief, Iron and Steel Scrap Section) to Baruch, Nov. 8, 1918; Charles Edgar (Director, Lumber Section) to Baruch, Nov. 13, 1918, all in File 21A-A2, RG 61.

price fixing agreements . . . without subjecting the parties to prosecution under the Sherman Law." Wilson might object to the plan on policy grounds, Ritchie thought, "but I believe we could get away with it legally."[9]

The rub was, as the Board appears to have known from the outset, that Wilson was likely to object to their plan. Evidence is lacking that Board Chairman Bernard Baruch or any other members contacted Wilson on the subject before the third week of November 1918. But Wilson's attitude during the month or so before the Armistice was one of reticence and apparent lack of interest when presented with ambitious schemes for dealing with the problems of reconstruction, and this must have been known to the Board. The President repeatedly rejected or adopted a cool attitude toward such proposals during October. Early in that month the Republican senators had introduced a bill creating a congressionally controlled reconstruction study commission. When the Democrats promptly countered with a bill for a similar body controlled by the President, Wilson had given it but a lukewarm endorsement when Senator Lee S. Overman asked for it. And thenceforth Wilson ignored the bill, which lay dormant.[10] Similarly, on October 3, when the President of the United States Chamber of Commerce, Harry A. Wheeler, presented Wilson with a proposal for a "Reconstruction Commission," Wilson rejected it. According to Wheeler the proposed commission, to consist of "the social agricultural, commercial and labor interests of the nation," was the Chamber's answer to the danger which "we most fear; i.e. the formulation of class programs to which classes become committed in advance of any general and combined consideration by the proper governmental authority." The Chamber wished "to subordinate the interests of the businessmen as a class to the interests of the

---

[9] See Ritchie to Baruch, Nov. 13, 1918, File 1-A5, RG 61, for Ritchie's argument regarding Wilson's power to suspend the Sherman Act. The source of the WIB's authority is generally regarded by commentators as resting on the Overman Act of May 1918. The Act did not mention the WIB but gave the President the power to use any powers or administrative agencies already created in any way he chose to further the war effort. The Overman Act is usually viewed as a ratification of what Wilson had done in March 1918 —reorganize the war agencies and give the WIB full authority in its field with power to enforce its orders with the weapon of commandeering if necessary.

The point made in the text is that the WIB's Legal Section does not seem to have regarded congressional delegation of extraordinary power as necessary. One important liberty taken by the WIB during the war had been suspension of the antitrust laws, for which there was not a shred of congressional authority. Nevertheless, the Legal Section saw no problem arising from the President's continuing the WIB's authority to suspend the antitrust laws. See Clarkson, *Industrial America*, 94-97, 207, 313, 458.

[10] New York *Times*, Oct. 2, 4, 1918; Wilson to Senator Lee S. Overman (early Oct. 1918), quoted in Ray Stannard Baker, *Woodrow Wilson: Life and Letters* (8 vols., New York, 1927-1939), VIII, 452.

country as a whole," Wheeler said, and hoped to do so through the proposed commission. Perhaps Wilson thought Wheeler was protesting too much.[11] But his uncommunicative rejection of the proposal, like his treatment of the Overman bill, was no doubt to contemporary observers a sign of reluctance on Wilson's part to adopt full-blown schemes for guiding the demobilization economy.

If it can be assumed that the Board felt Wilson would resist proposals for drastic regulation of postwar markets, certain of its activities of early November can be interpreted as a scheme for breaking down this resistance. These activities consisted of a series of predictions by Baruch and other WIB officials that the services of their agency would be required after the Armistice and that the agency would be continued. For example, the New York *Times* on November 12 reported that "War Industries Board officials declared there would be much work for that organization to do [during demobilization]. They foresee no serious industrial dislocation with the Government's grip on all war industries and material held tight. The board retains its authority until peace is formally proclaimed."[12]

The circumstantial evidence argues that in making these public assertions stressing the desirability and necessity of its continuation, the WIB was trying to generate enough public support for that eventuality to encourage Wilson to make it possible. Moreover, there is evidence which indicates that Wilson himself viewed the WIB's propaganda as a campaign designed to involve him in policies he did not intend to pursue. On November 9 Secretary of War Newton D. Baker warned Wilson of the character of a meeting scheduled to take place soon between the WIB and representatives of the State Councils of National Defense. Originally the meeting's purpose was to have been to enlist the aid of the State Councils in keeping the WIB informed on various matters. But with an early armistice a distinct possibility, the WIB had changed the purpose of the meeting. It was now to discuss reconstruction problems. The Cabinet members who composed the Council of National Defense had been invited to the meeting. These members included Baker and Secretary of Agriculture David F. Houston, who wondered whether the meeting ought to be held, since the plans discussed at it would be publicized by the press and might be incorrectly regarded as the plans of the Administration. Baker feared

[11] Harry A. Wheeler to Wilson, Oct. 3, 1918; Wilson to Wheeler, Oct. 5, 1918, Woodrow Wilson Papers (Manuscript Division, Library of Congress).
[12] For accounts of statements to this effect by Baruch and other WIB officials see New York *Times*, Nov. 9, 12, 13, 15, 1918; New York *Commercial*, Nov. 9, 14, 1918; "Chairman Baruch's Statement of Policy," *Iron Age*, CII (Nov. 14, 1918), 1216-17.

especially that the meeting might be confronted with the "suggestion that various emergency instrumentalities are designed to continue under fresh legislation for post-war activity"—a suggestion which Wilson might not decide to take up, but which, if made under the circumstances of the WIB's forthcoming meeting, might cause the President embarrassment. Acting on Baker's advice, Wilson promptly contacted Baruch and instructed him to delete the subject of reconstruction from the meeting's discussions.[13]

If in early November the WIB was mildly insubordinate in arguing its case before the public, it was also behaving somewhat disingenuously. In its public statements the Board argued that profiteering could be expected in certain industries and that the prevention of inflation would be as much its duty as the prevention of price collapses.[14] Actually the Board did not appear to have entertained seriously the notion that it would function as a full-fledged balance wheel to the economy. In all the WIB records of November when the problem of postwar prices was under discussion, one constant theme is sounded—the need for defense against deflation. This was true at all levels. Section chiefs in their recommendations to the Board consistently followed the wishes of their industries in urging protection if the industry expected price declines and release of all controls when the industry expected a favorable postwar market.[15] On several occasions the WIB's Price-Fixing Committee, in meetings with industry representatives, evidenced a disposition to use its powers to hold up a falling market but never intimated that WIB controls would or ought to be used to guard against inflation.[16]

[13] Baker to Wilson, Nov. 9, 1918, Wilson Papers. Wilson's response can be traced in Baker, *Wilson: Life and Letters,* VIII, 576, and in Anne W. Lane and Louise H. Wall, eds., *The Letters of Franklin K. Lane* (Boston, 1922), 299-300.

[14] See esp. the text of Baruch's statement of Nov. 8 in New York *Times,* Nov. 9, 1918, and news stories on the subject in New York *Commercial,* Nov. 8, 9, 1918.

[15] Examples of WIB authorities supporting industrial pleas for protection are given in n. 8 above. For examples of recommendations for release of controls at the behest of the industries involved, see H. C. DuBois (Chief, Abrasives Section), memo, Nov. 19, 1918, File 1-C2; "Automotive Products Section—Minutes of Meeting of Section with Commodity Representatives," Nov. 20, 1918, *ibid.;* C. J. Palmer (Chief, Newspaper Section) to H. B. Swope, Nov. 15, 1918, File 21A-A2, all in RG 61. In only one case surviving in the existing WIB records did it occur to a section chief whose industry expected prosperity that the WIB might have some postwar value as a checkrein on runaway prices and profits. See MacDowell to Baruch, Nov. 14, 1918, *ibid.,* which refers to the views of E. J. Haley, Chief of the Tanning Materials and Natural Dyes Section.

[16] Robert S. Brookings, the committee's chairman, during a "Meeting [of the Price-Fixing Committee] of the WIB with Representatives of the Cotton Fabrics Industry," Nov. 8, 1918, File 4-B1, RG 61, explained that a gradual return to lower price levels was inevitable but that the War Industries Board felt it could "be as helpful probably during the reconstruction period as we have during the war period in stabilizing values."

In spite of the views of the WIB's subordinate administrators, the Board may have been planning to continue maximums on the prices of potentially inflationary industries. There is only one reference in the WIB records showing such an intent and it indicates that maximum price controls would be accompanied by compensating measures advantageous to the industry involved.[17] At best, control of rising markets was decidedly a matter of secondary concern to the Board. Its discussions of postwar price problems revolved around the peril of industries whose prices were threatened. Baruch finally submitted to Wilson the Board's proposal that the WIB should be continued on the legal basis of the President's war power.[18] Wilson disapproved, and by November 20 he had decided that only very limited WIB price-fixing should continue. Three days later he decreed the complete disbanding of the agency by January 1, 1919.[19]

The WIB's reaction was one of acquiescence; no public or private protest was lodged. Baruch and his colleagues briefly considered the possibility of seeking a legislative basis for the WIB's continuation, hopefully with Wilson's support,[20] but this plan was dismissed. Did the prompt surrender to Wilson's wishes reflect a conviction on the part of the WIB's leaders that their duty was simply to execute and not to make policy? Perhaps so edifying a belief was woven into the reasoning, but if so it was not articulated at the time by the men who made the decision. The surrender was based first on the realization that Congress would not be any more sympathetic than the President to extension of the WIB.[21]

Another motive, equally as calculated as the conviction that resistance probably would be futile, probably persuaded Baruch and his colleagues to acquiesce in Wilson's penchant for free markets. When in early November

[17] Transcript of a "Meeting of the Hide, Leather and Leather Goods Section of the War Industries Board with Representatives of the Shoe Manufacturers," Nov. 14, 1918, File 21A-A2, RG 61.

[18] The only evidence this author has been able to locate that Baruch did submit such a proposal is contained in a letter he wrote to Wilson on Feb. 11, 1919, in the Wilson Papers. Baruch refers to having suggested, when chairman of the WIB, a demobilization plan entailing minimum price-fixing together with other practices. The proposal must have been made prior to Nov. 20, the day Wilson decided formally that WIB price-fixing would end immediately.

[19] The decision to discontinue price-fixing was taken at a meeting between Wilson and his "War Cabinet." See Wilson to Brookings, Nov. 26, 1918, filed with the "Minutes of the Price-Fixing Committee," File 4-B1, RG 61, and "Meeting of the War Industries Board," Nov. 21, 1918, File 1-C1, *ibid.* On instructions from Baruch, Peek announced at a "Meeting of Division Heads," Nov. 23, 1918, File 1-C2, *ibid.,* that "everyone is wondering what we are going to have to do with reconstruction and, as a matter of fact, we are going to have nothing."

[20] These matters, including the date of the conference, are described in an undated memo by Ritchie, in File 1-A5, RG 61. A copy of the bill is attached to the memo.

[21] *Ibid.*

the Board began to arrange for the agency's continuation, it seems to have had no reason to believe that any considerable segment of business would oppose its plans. Nearly every report from the lower echelons of the WIB portrayed business sentiment as highly favorable to control of postwar prices, either through WIB regulations or some other means.[22] But in mid-November the tenor of these reports changed as recommendations began to reach the Board from Section Chiefs whose industries, expecting price increases, were eager for the lifting of all restrictions.[23] Perhaps these reports made the Board feel that business opinion was too divided to support a program such as they had planned. The Board in its public statements earlier in November had pictured itself as the agent for preventing both inflation and deflation, depending on the needs of each industry. Although the Board does not seem to have regarded inflationary tendencies either as a serious danger or one it cared to deal with extensively, the industries which were now becoming jealous of their postwar freedom might interpret the WIB's plan as potentially injurious and make it a target of their animosity. The Board had a foretaste of this animosity in mid-November when it proposed to the shoe manufacturers that they accept price regulation for the coming spring season in return for the WIB's preventing the proliferation of styles which would depreciate the standardized stock which manufacturers had in their inventories. In this only recorded case in which the WIB felt compelled to attempt the imposition of maximum prices for the postwar months the reaction of the manufacturers was vitriolic. Baruch was portrayed with wonderful but unintended irony as the tool of the "Administration" which was attempting to impose "paternalism" upon an unsuspecting business community.[24] The division in business sentiment, so vividly illustrated by the shoe men, undoubtedly disposed the Board not to challenge Wilson's desire to dissolve the WIB.

Another more personal reason contributed to the same decision. George Peek, the WIB's Commissioner of Finished Products and its vice chairman in November 1918, was eager to leave government service.[25] This feeling probably was not unique. And perhaps some other members of the Board also agreed with Peek's belief that business would, after all, be able to fend for itself. "The industries of the country have become accustomed to

[22] These reports have been cited in n. 8 above.
[23] See n. 15 above for examples of such reports.
[24] "Meeting of the . . . War Industries Board with . . . Shoe Manufacturers," Nov. 14, 1918, File 21A-A2, RG 61.
[25] George Peek to B. F. Peek, Nov. 21, 1918, Peek Papers (Western Historical Manuscripts Collection, University of Missouri).

working together, under and in cooperation with the Government," he wrote one of his former friends at Deere and Company. "The feeling between competitors in different lines of industry is different than it has been in years past," and business would cope successfully with demobilization problems.[26]

The Board's abandonment during the third week of November of its hope to maintain itself during the postwar months as the protector of the welfare of business did not entirely obviate the possibility that it would act to give a measure of stability to postwar prices. One method for achieving this end was suggested by a number of hard-pressed industries or their Section Chiefs during the two or three weeks following November 23—the date on which Peek informed the subordinate WIB officials of Wilson's decision that the agency be disbanded by January 1, 1919. These industries asked that the WIB approve restrictive market agreements covering prices and/or production for the coming winter. The Board promptly rejected these requests, deciding not to "give approval to agreements of industries for the curtailment of production [or] for pooling in other forms, or for agreements covering prices unless in exceptional cases involving special conditions," and brought to the Board itself for consideration.[27] This rejection was, however, tentative, indicating a reluctance to abandon industry altogether to the vicissitudes of postwar markets. The reasons for rejection proved determinative, however, and by December 11 the Board had finally committed itself irrevocably to this act of abandonment. The date may be fixed by reference to the meeting held that day between the Price-Fixing Committee and representatives of the steel industry. Only a week before this meeting with steel the Committee's chairman had, in turning down tentatively the request of acid manufacturers for aid, held out hope by saying that it was possible—depending on the position taken by certain important industries such as steel—that the WIB might yet work out some scheme for preventing postwar price declines. But when the Committee met with the steel representatives Chairman Robert P. Brookings, forewarned that the Steel Committee's head, Elbert Gary of U.S. Steel, would try to win WIB approval for a schedule of prices upon which the industry had settled, announced that the WIB thenceforward could have absolutely nothing to do with prices.[28]

[26] Peek to H. G. Copp, Nov. 21, 1918, *ibid.* By late Dec. Peek had changed his views and was trying to create an "Emergency Peace Bureau" to provide for price stabilization. See Peek to William Butterworth, Dec. 20, 1918, *ibid.*
[27] "Meeting of the War Industries Board," Dec. 3, 1918, File 1-C1, RG 61.
[28] "Meeting of the Price-Fixing Committee with the Representatives of the Sulphuric and Nitric Acid Industry to consider the Removal of the Present Prices," Dec. 3, 1918;

The reason for the Board's decision not to approve in its dying hour industrial agreements on prices and market shares was altogether different from the ones which had led it to acquiesce in the decision to dissolve the WIB. The continuation of the WIB would have required the approval of the President or Congress, and would not have been feasible without the virtually united support of business. None of these elements was essential for the performance of the maneuver the Board was then considering. Businessmen who had opposed WIB continuation were not likely to object if before expiring the WIB arranged for the stabilization of the prices of threatened industries. Such action required no authority other than that supposed to be invested in the WIB. In short, the Board would ignore both the President and Congress and would proceed to approve private industrial market agreements. The President had delegated the power of such approval to the Board for its wartime activities. The WIB's legal staff believed that until the WIB actually was dissolved this delegated power could be regarded as continuing. If in the final weeks before it ceased to exist the Board approved industrial agreements destined to continue for some time, the federal courts might regard the action as freeing the agreements from the antitrust strictures which otherwise would apply. However, the attitude of the courts was regarded as problematical if the Attorney General challenged the agreements. It was precisely this uncertainty which persuaded the Board to abandon the proposal.

It was not any scruple against bending the law in favor of business which determined the decision. It was rather the fear that if the agreements were invalidated by the courts the whole regulatory record of the agency might be called into question and the validity of its wartime decisions disputed. The WIB took great pride in its war-work, and it was unwilling to see it challenged for the sake of the industries which at the end of the war implored its protection. The pride of the craftsman, to use a Veblenesque figure, triumphed over loyalty to class.[29]

"Meeting of the Price Fixing Committee . . . with the Representatives of the Steel Industry for the Purpose of Considering the Advisability of Discontinuing the Existing Maximum Prices of Steel," Dec. 11, 1918, both in File 4-B1, *ibid.*

[29] This account of the Board's understanding of the legal issues involved in the course it wished to pursue, and of the reason for the Board's decision to follow that course, is taken from a memorandum prepared by the WIB's Legal Section and sent to Ritchie on Nov. 27, 1918. The memorandum dealt specifically with the request of the Non-Ferrous Metals Section for authorization to permit a production agreement among Joplin, Missouri zinc producers, but deals with the principles underlying this individual situation. The analysis of this memo of Nov. 27 was followed by the Board in formulating its decision on Dec. 3 not to sanction such agreements. This fact is stated specifically by Ritchie in a memo of Dec. 3, 1918 to H. M. Channing, the Legal Section's chief. The documents are in File 1-A5, RG 61.

This interpretation of the Board's refusal to sanction agreements which would have been contrary to administration policy and possibly illegal is supported by an examination of the Board's behavior when it considered the possibility of revising the federal antitrust policy. The Board's opportunity to serve business in this area lay in its potential ability to put the case for antitrust revision before Congress with an apparent disinterestedness which business organizations could not hope to simulate. The Board was convinced that revision was a necessity and seriously considered playing the part of lobbyist for the emasculation of the antitrust tradition. In this matter the Board's will was not hamstrung by divisiveness within the industrial community, yet the Board ultimately abstained from action.

The abstention was performed with difficulty. The WIB first took up the question in mid-November when Baruch and Secretary of Commerce William C. Redfield were making arrangements to have the WIB's Conservation Division transferred to Commerce. There it was to continue permanently the work of encouraging standardization and other practices beneficial to industry. Since standardization programs were generally considered legal, the WIB was determined to make at least this contribution to industrial cooperation. In the midst of preparations for turning the Conservation Division over to Secretary Redfield, it occurred to the Division's officers that the transfer would offer an opportune pretext for presenting a bill for antitrust revision to Congress. The bill would be phrased ambiguously; Congress would be asked for "positive legislation . . . to permit manufacturers . . . to cooperate in the adoption of plans for the elimination of needless waste in the public interest," under the supervision of the Federal Trade Commission.[30] The prospects of such a bill for influencing antitrust policy in favor of the industrial community would have depended on the interpretation given it by the FTC and the courts. But this very defect of ambiguity might have been immeasurably helpful in securing its passage. Secretary Redfield was prepared to give the measure his firm support and said that if it "went in with the combined approval of the War Industries Board, the Federal Trade Commission and this Department, I think it would carry."[31] This indirect approach to antitrust revision was, however, thwarted when by executive order the Conservation Division

[30] George K. Burgess (Chief, Bureau of Standards) to Redfield, Nov. 16, 1918, File 67009/72, Record Group 40, General Records of the Commerce Department (National Archives). The letter describes Burgess' conversation of Nov. 15 with Peek, who had suggested the transfer. Baruch to Redfield, Nov. 19, 1918, *ibid.*, encloses a memo by A. W. Shaw, head of the Conservation Division, proposing the bill cited in the text above.
[31] Redfield to Baruch, Nov. 21, 1918, *ibid.*

was transferred to the Commerce Department. There it was known as the Industrial Cooperation Service and restricted itself to the encouragement of definitely lawful cooperative programs.[32]

A second proposal was put forward within the WIB—this one by Edwin B. Parker, the Board's Priorities Commissioner—at about the time the plan of acting in unison with the Commerce Department was receding from prominence. Parker's measure was bluntly phrased and would have allowed a majority of a given industry's firms to set production quotas for all firms in that industry. Sometime in the latter part of November, according to Parker, he discussed his proposal "at length one evening at Mr. Baruch's house with him, Messrs. Peek, Scott[33] and a number of others, and have also discussed it with several other government officials and businessmen, and without exception they have expressed themselves as believing that such a measure would be distinctly in the public interest." Parker evidently hoped after these discussions that the Board would formally support his proposal, and on November 25 he requested Ritchie to have the WIB's Legal Section perfect the draft bill Parker had been circulating. Parker felt that for tactical reasons a new version was necessary: the bill should omit any reference "to the amendment of the existing trust acts," even though it would in effect do just that.[34] Ritchie declined to undertake the task of revision. He pointed out to Parker and Baruch that the bill had "in principle a great deal to commend it," but the measure probably could not pass Congress because it departed too radically from what "wisely or unwisely, has become our fixed policy in dealing with business."[35]

Ritchie's criticism of Parker's proposal seems to have brought an end to the possibility that the WIB would sponsor antitrust legislation. Was it merely the conviction that an overture on antitrust revision would prove unacceptable to Congress that persuaded Baruch and his colleagues to abandon this course? This seems unlikely. As Ritchie, the other members of the Board no doubt recognized the difficulty of obtaining antitrust revi-

[32] See Redfield to Wilson, Nov. 25, 1918; Wilson to Redfield, Nov. 26, 1918; Redfield to Wilson, Dec. 2, 1918, *ibid.* The work of the Industrial Cooperation Service is recorded in "Report Covering Activities of the . . . Service, January 1, 1919 to March 15, 1919," and in John Cutler (Acting Chief of the Service) to Redfield, May 15, 1919, both in File 78253, RG 40. The Service seems to have ended its activities about the middle of May 1919. On at least one occasion a trade association asked the Service to help it arrange a program for output curtailment, but in reaching this definitely illegal objective the Service declined to assist.
[33] Probably John W. Scott, Director of the WIB's Textile Division.
[34] Parker to Ritchie, Nov. 25, 1918, File 1-A5, RG 61.
[35] Ritchie to Parker, Nov. 25, 1918, *ibid.* A copy of this memorandum to Parker was sent to Baruch the next day.

sion. But even after the decision was reached not to throw the WIB's weight behind changes, the members of the Board as individuals continued to express an interest in and plan for it. They evidenced no sense of futility, no belief that opposition to revision was overwhelming. George Peek in mid-December 1918, for example, put the case for antitrust revision to Baruch very matter-of-factly, as though the goals he spoke of were clearly within the limits of the possible. It had been demonstrated, he thought,

that cooperation amount [sic] the members of industry is beneficial, not only to the members of the industry, but to the general public, and the benefits of proper cooperation should not be lost in return to peace time conditions of highly competitive situations brought about by the normal operation of the law of supply and demand. Proper legislation should be enacted to permit cooperation in industry, in order that the lessons we have learned during the way [sic] may be capitalized in the interest of business and the public in peace times. Such questions as conservation to avoid wasteful use of materials, labor and capital: standardization of products and processes, price fixing under certain conditions, etc., should continue with Government cooperation.[36]

Later in December Baruch's actions indicated he did not think revision impossible. Mark Requa, Assistant Administrator of the Fuel Administration, approached Baruch during that month with a proposed bill somewhat similar to the Parker proposal of November. Requa left the bill with Ritchie who discussed its contents with Baruch. Baruch was "very much interested and impressed" with Requa's ideas. However, the proposal had reached him just as he had received his "summons to go abroad," and he could not "give the matter the consideration he would like to give it." He was "sure that he will be glad to take it up more thoroughly upon his return."[37]

It was not Ritchie's arguments against feasibility which persuaded the Board to drop its proposed intervention in favor of revision. The telling argument was Ritchie's expression of his fear of "the cry, which I feel would be made, that Mr. Baruch's last act, before he went back to business, was to try to have the anti-trust laws, to which business has generally been opposed, suspended." In any case, he thought the WIB's official responsibilities did not include recommendations for legislation, and Parker's proposed overture would for that reason bring on criticism. "If the industries of this country want a measure of this kind, then I think they should bring it forward themselves," Ritchie concluded.[38] The Board in deciding to

[36] Peek to Baruch, Dec. 17, 1918, File 21A-A2, RG 61.
[37] Ritchie to Requa, Dec. 26, 1918, File 1-A5, RG 61.
[38] Ritchie to Parker, Nov. 25, 1918, *ibid.*

leave antitrust revision to business organizations as in its decision not to misuse its power in the validation of agreements restraining trade, was exhibiting a jealousy of its reputation for integrity and impartiality, hard won during the war. Thus, when the Board found it impossible to serve both its reputation with the general public and its class, it chose to serve the former.

For most of the members of the Board the choice was probably made with difficulty. In the case of Baruch the choice may have been taken with a sense of relief, for he seems to have been uncertain in November and December 1918 that the antitrust tradition had become obsolete. Many of his colleagues believed that Baruch agreed with their penchant for cartels and no doubt Baruch in conversation gave them reason for their belief. Later during the years of the Great Depression, Baruch would argue for a WIB in reverse—for a "High Court of Commerce" to approve restrictive market agreements since "we have too much to go around with a profit to those who produce."[39] But in November 1918 it appears he was not quite so ready to abandon the tradition of competition the nation had striven to maintain through the antitrust laws. Sentiments he occasionally voiced hinted at a proclivity for the procompetitive stand of the Wilson administration. In mid-November, for example, Baruch horrified Clarence Wooley of the Priorities Board when he denied the need for special attention to business during the demobilization period and asserted he was for letting everyone solve his own readjustment problem independently.[40] And speaking in November before the War Service Committee of the Paint and Varnish Manufacturers, Baruch presented an argument against suspending market forces during reconstruction which reflected reluctance to break with the traditional antitrust policy. "There are limits to what the Government can and ought to do," he said, "and there are some thing[s] which we think we ought to do now perhaps that we wouldn't want to continue and we must weigh them in the balance, whether the commencement might not bring sort of an appetite for the continuance."[41]

Whatever Baruch's inner convictions about the desirability of fundamental change in the antitrust policy may have been, it was only with vast

[39] See for example Baruch's speech before the Ninth Reunion of the WIB on Nov. 11, 1931, a copy of which was enclosed in Baruch to Pat Harrison, Nov. 12, 1931, in File 73A-F9, Tray 109, Record Group 46, Records of the U. S. Senate (National Archives).

[40] Wooley to Joseph Tumulty, Nov. 15, 1918, Clarence Wooley Papers (Manuscript Division, Library of Congress).

[41] "Meeting of the Paint and Pigment Section . . . with the Paint and Varnish Manufacturers for Determining Future Operations of the Industry," Nov. 18, 1918, File 21A-A2, RG 61.

reluctance that he and the Board abandoned the interest of industry to the uncertainties of postwar markets. That the reluctance was overcome, however, is perhaps the most significant aspect of the Board's behavior in November and early December 1918. It was natural that these industrialists in public service should have wished to act in behalf of their peers in the world of business and should have experienced no moral difficulty in reconciling to their own satisfaction business with public interests. To its credit, the Board declined to employ improper methods in furthering pro-business schemes, both in the case of the antitrust question and in other areas of demobilization policy where it found an opportunity to speak up for industrial interests. The Board was opposed, for example, to the War Department's plan, put into effect immediately after the Armistice, for rapid and indiscriminate separation of troops from the army. The Board urged a slower and more selective program, proposing the immediate release of professionals, businessmen, and skilled workers, and the furloughing of an unskilled person only when a former or new employer certified intent to employ him. This hapless wageearner would not be separated until he had actually taken up the employment offered him. This scheme, thought originator Peek, would "prevent dispersion, and tend to reconstruct the non-war industries to their former status," as well as ensure that there would "be no mad scramble for overpaid jobs." Helpful as Peek's plan might have been in the orderly reorganization of the nation's labor force, it was deeply marked by class favoritism.[42]

But the Board took the demobilization scheme no farther than the White House, where it was rejected. Had the Board attempted—in this case or in that of the various proposals it entertained for antitrust suspension or revision—to appeal over the President's head to Congress or the general public, it might merely have overreached itself. On the other hand it might have added significantly to the confusion of the postwar era by heaping still another embarrassment on a President already half-discredited by his failures in the November elections. At the very least, it can be said that the restraint of the WIB's leaders saved them their reputation for impartial and honorable service in the national interest during war. This they coveted and this they do enjoy in the American historical tradition.

[42] The scheme was developed by Peek and supported actively by Baruch and the whole WIB Board. On Nov. 19 Peek presented the plan to Secretary Baker who rejected it. On Nov. 20 Baruch took the proposal up with Wilson and when he proved unsympathetic, the Board simply abandoned it. Peek recounted the affair in a "Memorandum on Demobilization," Nov. 20, 1918, Peek Papers.

MID-AMERICA
An Historical Review

JULY 1969

VOLUME 51   NUMBER 3

Herbert Hoover and the Regulation of Grain Futures

During the 1920's the regulatory function of the federal government generally did not increase. However, the "Farm Bloc" was able to achieve a growth of government regulation in some areas of importance to farmers. One such expansion placed the grain commodity exchanges under the control of a new federal agency. The effort to establish effective regulation of the commodity exchanges was current throughout the 1920's and carried into the New Deal period. Attempts were made in the 1920's, after the passage of the Grain Futures Act, to persuade the Chicago Board of Trade to expand a program of self-regulation and to accept the farm cooperatives in the marketing system. In this effort, Herbert Hoover, as Secretary of Commerce and as President, played a significant role. In addition, his action with regard to the Chicago Board of Trade illuminates his general approach to the relationship between business and government.

The Chicago Board of Trade, the country's major commodity exchange, was organized in 1848 as new transportation and communication links connected Chicago with western producing areas. In the earliest years grain was traded by persons who were buying and selling actual grain as distinct from grain futures. The trading of grain futures, in the beginning merely incidental to the marketing of existing grain, apparently began in the mid-1850's. However, at this time communication was so inadequate that the Chicago Board of Trade did not provide a continuous grain market. Futures contracts were for relatively short periods of time. But, after the Civil War, as communication facilities improved, futures trading began to take on added economic importance while the Board of

155

Trade, itself, gradually became a much more influential economic institution. Futures trading was significantly stimulated in the early 1870's with the adoption of general grain grades by the State of Illinois.[1]

By the late 1880's the Chicago Board of Trade had become highly important in the process of establishing grain prices. Futures trading was well-developed, with professional speculators operating on the market, trading in options to buy or sell specified amounts of grain within a designated period, and engaging in short selling. The increased importance of the exchange caused the Farmers' Alliance, as well as other farm groups, to demand federal regulation of the commodity exchanges. Legislation seeking that goal was introduced in the Populist period, but was not enacted.[2] During the Progressive Era interest in the regulation of future trading continued at a high level, with many bills introduced and with the Democratic Party in 1912 favoring the suppression of "the pernicious practice of gambling in agricultural products by organized exchanges. . . ."[3] By the time of World War I efforts to regulate commodity exchanges had a background of about thirty years. The overwhelming importance of the Chicago Board of Trade in controlling grain prices in the United States compelled attention.

During World War I the federal government effectively stabilized grain prices. However, once wartime controls were removed, price fluctuations developed on the Chicago Board of Trade. This, plus the advent of postwar depression, once again stimulated a desire to regulate the grain exchanges—to eliminate speculative profits and thereby provide fairer and higher prices to grain producers. In response, the "Farm Bloc" pushed through the Grain Futures Act in 1921, which was a general regulatory measure applying to commodity exchanges across the country. Based upon the taxing power of Congress, the bill created the Grain Futures Administration as the supervising agency, and proposed to tax out of existence "puts and calls," which were options to buy grain, and

---

[1] Charles H. Taylor, ed., *History of the Board of Trade of the City of Chicago*, Chicago, 1917, I, 135; Will Payne, "A Reformed Speculator," *Saturday Evening Post*, CCII (Aug. 10, 1929), 8–9.

[2] Legislation was introduced by Benjamin Butterworth of Cincinnati in 1890, but did not emerge from committee. In 1892 an "anti-option" bill regulating the grain exchanges passed the House but died in the Senate. *Cong. Record*, 52 Cong., 1 Sess., 5071–76, June 6, 1892.

[3] See Arthur G. Peterson, "Futures Trading with Particular Reference to Agricultural Commodities," *Agricultural History*, VII (Jan. 1933), 71.

similar practices generally considered to be gambling.   It also would regulate the grain exchanges by requiring the reporting of transactions on the various boards of trade designated as commodity markets by the Secretary of Agriculture.   In one important section (5e) the measure provided that the boards of trade must admit *bona fide* cooperative marketing agencies, which were ineligible for membership under existing rules.   The power to suspend a contract market was given to a commission composed of the Secretary of Commerce, the Attorney General, and the Secretary of Agriculture.[4]   The Grain Futures Act of 1921, however, was invalidated by the Supreme Court as an unconstitutional use of the taxing power.[5]

In the next year the "Farm Bloc" passed a second Grain Futures Act, accomplishing the same regulatory function, but basing its action on the power of Congress to control interstate and foreign commerce.   This time the Supreme Court approved the measure.[6] Immediately after the Supreme Court decision, Chicago Board of Trade officials announced that they would "cheerfully" abide by the regulations of the Grain Futures Administration.   In addition, John J. Stream, president of the Board of Trade, who had opposed the bill, stated that if the law failed "to be the panacea for agricultural ills," it would be the result of the inadequacies of the act itself and not because of any sabotage perpetrated by the Board of Trade.   On the brighter side, Stream subsequently explained that the bill had given the grain exchanges "the stamp of government approval," and "that this action will tend to encourage the grain trade into greater use of the futures trading system."   Moreover, now that the exchanges had met all the demands of the agrarian groups, farmers should cease their agitation against the grain trade.[7]

Within a few days Secretary of Agriculture Henry C. Wallace announced various regulatory measures that the contract markets would be required to observe.   Among other rules, daily reports would be filed by clearing members of the exchanges indicating their total purchases and sales of each kind of grain for each delivery month, the net position of each trader, the aggregate of the "long" and "short" open accounts constituting the net position, receipts and deliveries of grain on future contracts, and the net position of

---

4 *Cong. Record*, 67 Cong., 1 Sess., 1314–17, May 11, 1921; James H. Shideler, *Farm Crisis, 1919–1923*, Berkeley, 1957, 159.
5 *Hill* v. *Wallace*, 259 U. S. 44 (1922) ; *New York Times*, May 16, 1922.
6 *Board of Trade* v. *Olsen*, 262 U. S. 1 (1922).
7 Edward Jerome Dies, "Grain Marketing Under Government Rule," *World's Work*, XLVI (Aug., 1923), 425.

open accounts for customers (i.e., in the case of wheat at Chicago, in accounts totalling 500,000 bushels or more).[8]

Although spokesmen for the Chicago Board of Trade indicated their willingness to cooperate with the GFA, members of the grain trade from the beginning objected most strenuously to what they considered the unwarranted interference of the federal government into the affairs of private businessmen. Complaints were voiced by trade journals and by individuals speaking publicly or privately. Specifically, they feared possible information leaks in the GFA office divulging market operations would drive big speculators off the exchange. Dissatisfaction was particularly present in times of low wheat prices. During such periods trade journals and newspapers carried articles directed to farmers, telling them that the futures regulation was keeping the important speculators off the market, preventing the recovery of prices.[9] The Chicago Board of Trade and other exchanges continued to resist the legislation and were certainly unwilling to go beyond this limited level of control, even in the direction of self-regulation as some were suggesting.

Before long, however, the grain trade began to fear that additional legislation might be forthcoming, and turned its attention to regulating its own activities more effectively. In early 1925 unusual and very erratic fluctuations in wheat futures completely disrupted the grain market. An investigation was undertaken by the GFA, which eventually recommended "some limitation on the size of lines long or short and upon the extent to which an individual speculator may buy or sell within the limits of a trading day...." The GFA also thought it "advisable to place some limitation upon the extent to which prices of grain futures may fluctuate within a single day." However, it noted that these problems could be solved by the exchanges themselves if they wished to avoid additional federal regulation.[10]

Mounting criticism of undue speculation finally caused the Chicago Board of Trade reluctantly to attempt improvements in its methods and thus to brighten its image with government officials. This effort brought Board of Trade officials into closer contact with

---

[8] Department of Agriculture, *Annual Reports of the Department of Agriculture for the Year Ending 1923*, Washington, 1924, 691.

[9] *Senate Docs.*, 70 Cong., 2 Sess., No. 264, "Report by Members of Grain Futures Exchange," 9; Department of Agriculture, *Annual Reports ...for the Year Ending 1923*, 692.

[10] Department of Agriculture, *Speculative Transaction in the 1926 May Wheat Futures*, Dept. Bulletin, No. 179, Washington, 1927, 27.

the new Secretary of Agriculture, William M. Jardine, and also into new relations with Secretary of Commerce Herbert Hoover.

Hoover had been involved with food distribution problems since his days as World War I Food Administrator, and had formed some definite ideas about them.   As an expert on grain marketing he had been called to testify before the House Committee on Agriculture when it considered grain futures legislation in 1921.   Hoover told the Committee that manipulation in grain could and should be ended through agreement among the exchanges to limit the amount of grain that could be handled in speculative trades.   But he also argued for the creation of a "national board of experts" under the Department of Agriculture, "whose essential responsibility would be to improve marketing conditions," but which should also receive some regulatory powers.   The large majority of grain traders, Hoover concluded, "engaged in legitimate business," but a minority harmed the market by depreciating prices.   "A board could control such people by fixing a maximum allowable per trade."[11]   Now, in 1925, Hoover was saying that he disliked the "wholesale gambling" on the Chicago Board of Trade.   After watching the speculative activity of 1925 he wrote a note to Jardine indicating that he believed forces in the Board would be unable to suppress "gambling," and asked him to request the directors of the GFA to suggest constructive proposals for improving the machinery of the Board of Trade.[12]

At the same time Hoover was corresponding directly with the officials of the Chicago Board of Trade, telling them how he, as Secretary of Commerce, viewed their activities.   On August 22, 1925, a letter to a member of the Board indicated that, while Hoover appreciated the improvements that the Board of Trade had made and that he believed hedging was a valuable technique in that it "cheapened the cost between the farmer and consumer by reducing the risk," he still believed that "reward" had been claimed when no "service" had been rendered by those in the grain trade.   Indeed, he knew of "no more glaring exhibit than these millions taken from sheer manipulation of the machinery provided by the Board of Trade. . . ."   At this time Hoover expressed his basic philosophy, describing himself as

---

11 *New York Times*, Jan. 21, 1921.
12 Hoover to Jardine, Aug. 17, 1925, Commerce Department files, I/54, Hoover Papers, Hoover Presidential Library.   All the following citations to the Hoover Papers refer to those located in the Hoover Presidential Library, West Branch, Iowa.

one of those who have hoped and worked that American business might so regulate itself that by commanding the esteem and confidence of the American people it would avoid constant incursion of government into business. I am in hopes that the Board of Trade will soon present such action as will prevent the necessity for further Governmental interference by way of regulation.[13]

The stand Hoover took with regard to the grain trade placed him essentially within the Wilsonian progressive tradition. No conservative of the Coolidge type, he nevertheless believed strongly in individual initiative and in keeping private enterprise free from the restrictions of federal regulation. But Hoover knew that in some circumstances government was obligated to intervene in the private economy for the greater general good. His experience with the Chicago Board of Trade indicates that he preferred to have government work with private business, attempting to point it in the direction of public welfare. Failing this a "national board" would be given the power to take more positive regulatory steps.[14] Thus Herbert Hoover strongly urged the Board of Trade to regulate itself, but knew that if it would not (and he suspected that it would not) the federal government must do so.

The Board of Trade had under consideration at this time a proposal that would establish a modern clearing house. Although apparently the Directors opposed the measure,[15] the clearing house would provide the advantage of a single clearing authority through which the volume of open trades could be observed with greater ease, and thus make apparent when the volume of a single house or group was such that it could have undue influence on prices.[16] The members of the Board of Trade voted to establish the clearing house, a step president Frank Carey claimed indicated the Board's "sincere desire to improve its rules and methods by its own volun-

---

[13] Hoover to Frank J. Delany, Aug. 22, 1925, Commerce Department files, I/54, Hoover Papers.

[14] F. M. Crosby to Theo. D. Hammett, Sept. 15, 1925, and Jardine to Hoover, Aug. 29, 1925, Commerce Department files, I/54, Hoover Papers.

[15] The public-spirited attitude of the Board of Trade may well have been forced upon the Directors by the members. F. M. Crosby, of Gold Medal Products of Minneapolis, wrote to Theodore Hammett, of the Grain and Flour Section, Foodstuffs Division of the Department of Commerce: "Did you know that the Assistant Secretary, who is practically Acting Secretary of the Board of Trade, was working openly against the Clearing House? This clearly indicates the attitude of the Directors of the Board of Trade, as he would certainly not have dared to do so unless agreeable to them." See Crosby to Hammett, Sept. 15, 1925, Commerce Department files, I/54, Hoover Papers.

[16] Julius Barnes to Jardine and Hoover, Sept. 2, 1925, Commerce Department files, I/54, Hoover Papers.

tary action. . . ."[17]   Secretary Jardine hailed the move in his annual report as "progressive" and "far-reaching."[18]

On the other hand, the grain trade generally felt that since it had improved its machinery, some of the restrictions placed upon it in 1923 should now be relaxed. As the Program Committee of the Board of Trade, which had proposed the clearing corporation, reported, the "restoration of so-called privilege trading" would do more than any other single measure to encourage moderate daily fluctuations. The Committee, therefore, recommended that an attempt be made "to secure the full cooperation of the Department of Agriculture" in achieving congressional "removal of the legislative restrictions upon this form of trading."[19] Moreover, the effort to fight the reporting requirement continued. In 1924 members of the Board of Trade had organized an "Association to Restore Free and Unrestricted Grain Markets," with the purpose of securing "such changes in existing statutes as will permit of normal operation with assurance that the necessary speculation and investment trade for carrying the farmers' surplus of grain will not be driven from the market by restrictive laws."[20] The impetus was taken out of the movement, however, when wheat prices on the futures market moved sharply upward, reaching a high of $2.05 7/8 for May futures on January 28, 1925.[21] Traders were making their reports to the GFA with little voiced discontent. But when prices moved downward again in 1926 anti-regulation propaganda re-emerged with increasing volume. Eventually, the principal grain exchanges formally requested the suspension of reporting requirements, a step necessary, it was said, to permit speculative support for a sagging market. The grain trade maintained its pressure on the Department of Agriculture into 1927 and was joined by other organizations such as the United States Chamber of Commerce. Thus, even though some of the officers of the GFA disagreed, the decision was made to bow to the insistent demands, remove the restrictions and test the hypothesis that speculators would move on to the market in the absence of reporting requirements. The rules were suspended for eight months, then reinstituted. The GFA later concluded that

---

[17] Carey to Hoover, Sept. 4, 1925, Commerce Department files, I/54, Hoover Papers.
[18] Department of Agriculture, *Report of the Secretary of Agriculture, 1926*, Washington, 1926, 38.
[19] *Senate Docs.*, 70 Cong., 2 Sess., No. 264, "Report by Members of Grain Futures Exchange," 10–11.
[20] *Ibid.*, 12.
[21] *Ibid.*, 14.

the suspension had not affected the volume traded at all; in fact the volume of wheat and corn traded in the futures markets increased after the rules were reinstated in 1928.[22]

By 1928 pressures were mounting for the enactment of general farm legislation which, when passed in 1929, affected the professional grain trade as significantly as had the regulations established by the Grain Futures Act. During his campaign for President, Hoover promised to devote his attention to improving the well-being of American farmers. Thus in a special session of Congress, called to redeem campaign pledges, the Administration introduced the Agricultural Marketing Act. In the House of Representatives, Congressman Gilbert Haugen described the purposes of the legislation as including more effective marketing of agricultural products, control and stabilization of the marketing of such goods, and the minimization of speculation.[23]

Hoover had long advocated seeking the price stabilization farmers needed through the operation of cooperative marketing associations—opposing the more radical, and he believed socialistic, McNary-Haugen proposal. Farmers working together, aided by the federal government, Hoover suggested, would be able to solve their price problems.[24] The fact that furthering the interest of cooperative marketing agencies would likely be adverse to those of the professional grain trade was not lost upon members of the Chicago Board of Trade. They could see as well that the government now proposed actively to help cooperatives, while still sitting as administrator of the Grain Futures Act, which in part involved relations between the exchanges and the cooperatives. Those associated with the commercial handling of grain, from country elevator operators to members of the Chicago Board of Trade, saw the danger of the Hoover moves to increase the already significant economic strength of the cooperatives. With the organization of the Farmers' National Grain Corporation in October, 1929, an agency designed to coordinate the work of the cooperatives, the threat assumed reality.[25]

From the time the Agricultural Marketing bill was presented until the Federal Farm Board ceased to exist, spokesmen for the

---

[22] *Ibid.*, 16.
[23] *Cong. Record*, 71 Cong., Special Sess., 132, Apr. 18, 1929.
[24] James H. Shideler, "Herbert Hoover and the Federal Farm Board Project," *Mississippi Valley Historical Review*, XLII (Mar. 1956), 712–3; Harrison G. Warren, *Herbert Hoover and the Great Depression*, New York, 1959, 169–70.
[25] Warren, *Herbert Hoover and the Great Depression*, 173.

grain trade vigorously attacked the new plan. The managing editor of the *National Grain Journal,* for example, wrote to President Hoover that he could not understand how one with Hoover's business training and "the great understanding of experience which is the foundation of your learning," would be in favor of cooperative marketing.[26] In an "open letter" to college presidents, the president of the National League of Commission Merchants lamented the thrust of the Agricultural Marketing Act. Indeed, he said that by its support of cooperative marketing, the measure in effect condemned the grain trade "as not quite respectable, not quite honest, and not quite worthy of the protection of the government they support. . . ." Farmers had not developed the grain business, so why should the government now remove individuals and agencies in their favor?[27]

In addition to the basic conflict of economic interest involved, members of the grain trade had other reasons to be unhappy with the Hoover Administration. Having supported the Republican party in the recent Presidential election, they now felt betrayed. E. W. Diercks, vice president of the Winter-Trusdell-Diercks Grain Company, told a friend that "one prominent grain man said to me today, little did he know that when he voted the Republican ticket last Fall that he was voting the Socialist ticket. That is all it means, we are heading direct for Communism." Moreover, grain men would have been considerably happier if Hoover's Federal Farm Board had included a representative of their group. In a conversation with Frederick B. Wells, a prominent grain trader and friend of Hoover's secretary, Walter Newton, Hoover indicated that such an appointment would be made. As Wells later reminded the President, he had been told that it was "an absolute necessity to have an expert grain man of broad experience" on the Board. But the appointment was never made. The grain trade, Diercks argued, deserved better treatment, since it had overwhelmingly supported Hoover in 1928. "All the thanks they have for it," he remarked bitterly, "is a Board apparently intent upon putting grain exchanges and the grain business out of business." Moreover, the grain trade believed that the Administration should have consulted with grain men as plans were being made for the launching of the program

---

[26] J. H. Adams to Hoover, Mar. 23, 1929, White House file, 1-E/160, Hoover Papers.

[27] Robert F. Blair, "Which Way America?" Copy in Records of the Secretary of the Department of Agriculture, Records Group (hereafter R.G.) 16 (National Archives).

after the bill was passed. Indeed, the grain men had not opposed the legislation in the belief that Hoover had told Frederick Wells that no action would be taken that would affect their interests without prior consultation. However, there were no conferences with representatives of the grain exchanges in advance of the meeting held to establish the Farmers' National Grain Corporation, which grain men believed would operate in opposition to their economic interests.[28]

On the other hand, as time passed members of the Hoover Administration were just as resentful toward the grain trade, which they felt was unjustly combating the work of the Farm Board and the Farmers' National Grain Corporation. In April, 1931, James C. Stone, chairman of the Farm Board, complained that "the commission men in Chicago and Minneapolis" had worked to

align the farmers' elevators against the program of the Farmers' National Grain Corporation. Their activities, to a large extent, have tended to confuse the minds of farmers' elevator people in relation to the program of the National and to keep them affiliated with the old commission interests.[29]

A short time later Stone commented that the Board of Trade members "look upon themselves as middlemen, entitled by custom to take a heavy toll from American wheat producers for so-called services, which consist chiefly pocketing by themselves of the largest possible share of the consumer's dollar."[30]

President Hoover, who was deeply involved in fighting the depression, was also becoming aggravated with the way some members of the grain trade were behaving. On July 10, 1931, an irritated President issued a strong statement condemning those who engaged in short selling on the commodity markets. Carefully indicating that he did not refer to "the legitimate grain trade," but believing that short selling had an adverse effect upon the public interest, Hoover roundly censured those whose actions had "but one purpose and that is to depress prices." This, he pointed out, was a primary barrier to a resurgence of public confidence. Such people, he said, attempt "to take a profit from the losses of other people," and certainly deprived "farmers of their rightful income." The President finally directed short sellers to "desist from their manipulations" if they had any concern for the welfare of the country. The

---

28 Ed Diercks to T. G. Winter, Nov. 21, 1929, White House file, 1-E/160, Hoover Papers; Frederick B. Wells to Hoover, Aug. 2, 1929, R. G. 16.
29 James C. Stone to Lawrence Richey, Apr. 4, 1931, White House file, 1-E/161, Hoover Papers.
30 New York Times, May 23, 1932.

overwhelming public support Hoover received as a result of his statement, both in public expression and in letters, indicated that he had struck a popular note indeed.[31]

The struggle between the Administration and the grain trade eventually involved more than charges and countercharges. The Board of Trade had sufficient power to make things very difficult for the Farmers' National Grain Corporation, and thus for the Federal Farm Board. The Farmers' National traded large amounts of grain on the Chicago Board of Trade, of which it was a member. But membership in the clearing corporation was separate from Board of Trade membership. Non-members of the clearing corporation had to pay a clearing fee of ⅛ cent per bushel. Moreover, the Board of Trade had adopted a rule in 1929 barring in the future firms organized as corporations from membership in the clearing corporation, which applied to the Farmers' National. The Farmers' National, however, could acquire clearing-corporation privileges by purchasing a company that had membership in the clearing corporation before the rule was enacted. Therefore, to clear its trades without the extra charge, the Farmers' National quietly acquired the Updike Grain Company in 1931.[32] However, since semi-annual financial statements required of members of the clearing corporation indicated changes in the corporate structure of the Updike Company, the Board of Trade appointed a committee to investigate the Company's affairs. The move against the Updike Company prompted Clarence Huff, president of the Farmers' National, to ask Secretary of Agriculture Arthur Hyde to begin taking steps under the Grain Futures Act that would result in the suspension of the Chicago Board of Trade as a contract market. In addition, the Farmers' National applied to the Board of Trade directors for membership in the clearing corporation, sending along the necessary financial statement and fees.[33] However, the Board of Trade denied the application, president Peter B. Carey reported, because of its Rule 313, mentioned above. This had been enacted, he indicated, because of the limited liability of the officers and stockholders of a corporation.[34] Why this had suddenly become necessary in April 1929, Carey did not say. Clarence Huff then formally petitioned

---

[31] "Short Selling Statement," July 10, 1931, White House file, 1-E/161, Hoover Papers.

[32] "Report on the Hearing before the Secretaries of Agriculture, Commerce, and the Attorney General," July 23, 1932, R.G. 16.

[33] R. W. Dunlap to Peter B. Carey, Apr. 9, 1932, R.G. 16; *New York Times*, May 27, 1932.

[34] *Chicago Tribune*, Apr. 14, 1932.

Secretary Hyde to convene the special commission provided for by the Grain Futures Act, which would consider the charges of the Farmers' National against the Chicago Board of Trade. Specifically, Huff alleged that the Board of Trade acted in violation of Section 5e of the Grain Futures Act in denying a *bona fide* cooperative membership, claiming that the barring of the Farmers' National from a place in the clearing corporation was tantamount to denying it membership in the exchange. Carey immediately responded that according to the legislation involved (the Capper-Volstead Act), in order to be classified as a cooperative an organization must do at least 51 percent of its business with producers. The Farmers' National, he said, did not comply with that provision.[35]

The Board of Trade did not move against the Updike Grain Company until well into May, 1932, when it terminated all rights held by the Company, leaving the Farmers' National without clearing privileges. This action was based on charges that the officers of the Updike Company filed statements on June 1 and December 1, 1931, claiming that they owned stock in the corporation, when in fact, the Board of Trade found, they did not.[36] George Milnor, general manager of the Farmers' National, immediately wired Secretary Hyde that the Board of Trade was causing the Farmers' National "thousands of dollars of irreparable damage," and asked again that the special commission be convened. Hyde answered that a hearing would be set as soon as possible.[37] In fact, Secretary Hyde had already submitted the original request of the Farmers' National for a hearing to Attorney General William Mitchell, asking for a legal opinion. Mitchell replied on May 11 that he believed there was "sufficient reason shown to grant the hearing requested."[38]

Thus a showdown was reached between the Department of Agriculture and the private grain trade. The issue was rather clear. As the *Des Moines Register* explained:

There is no need to recite any of the secondary squabbles. The one main squabble is over the development of marketing cooperatives under govern-

---

[35] *Ibid.*

[36] *New York Times*, May 26, 1932. The officers of the Updike Company retained at least one share of stock each when the Company was sold to the Farmers' National, which would legally qualify the cooperative to its seat on the clearing corporation.

[37] Milnor to Hyde, May 26, 1932 and Hyde to Milnor, May 29, 1932, R.G. 16.

[38] Mitchell to Hyde, May 11, 1932, R.G. 16.

ment sponsorship. No matter what form that development appears in, the grain trade, in its own interest, is bitterly against it. And that is at the bottom of this whole series of attacks by that trade on the marketing act, farm board, stabilization losses and what not."[39]

The Hoover Administration had committed itself to helping farmers through cooperative marketing and was willing to use existing legislation in controlling interests opposed to special benefits for agriculture. The public officials must have realized, as suggested by Alexander Legge, former chairman of the Farm Board, that the members of the Chicago Board of Trade "have set up a little government of their own, in which trials are held like a secret lodge, no lawyer being allowed to represent the client and there being no appeal from their decisions to any court of record."[40] Legge wanted to replace the commodity markets with something better, but Hyde and Hoover were not aiming to rebuild the system. They were simply concerned with turning the existing one more in the direction of helping farmers gain a greater share of the national income.

The circumstances of this crisis put Secretary Hyde in a difficult position—a hot spot, the *Chicago Tribune,* a friend of the Board of Trade, termed it. A supporter of cooperative marketing, Hyde, in whose hands the dispute came to rest, was therefore sympathetic toward the Federal Farm Board, of which he was an ex-officio member. He also had some well-developed ideas about the efficacy of private enterprise, self-reliance, and individual initiative. In addition, action was being threatened under the Grain Futures Act against the Board of Trade at a time when wheat was moving from farms to market and might conceivably disrupt the financing of the crop, i.e., bankers might hesitate to loan money to grain purchasers because of the possibility that futures trading would be suspended on the Chicago market.[41] Still, Hyde knew that steps taken against the Board of Trade by the special commission would most certainly be appealed and thus the case would be tied up in the courts for months. In any case, the commission ordered a hearing for June 8, 1932, directing the Chicago Board of Trade to explain why it had denied clearing-corporation privileges to the Farmers' National. The commission thus brought the Board of Trade's status as a contract market under official review. This was the first time the Grain Futures Act had been used in this significant way.[42]

---

[39] *Des Moines Register,* July 24, 1932.
[40] Legge to Hyde, May 26, 1932, R.G. 16.
[41] *Chicago Tribune,* Apr. 15, 1932.
[42] *New York Times,* May 29, 1932, II, 14; Arthur Hyde, "Press Release —Hearing Called Under the Grain Futures Act," May 28, 1932, R.G. 16.

The Hoover Administration's move against the despised "gamblers" of the Chicago Board of Trade won the approval of most all farmers and others who expressed themselves in letters to the Secretary of Agriculture, to Congressmen, Senators, and editors of newspapers. In March, when the crisis had begun to develop, a farmer from Kansas wrote that "25,000,000 farmers want a padlock put on the Chicago Board of Trade. They have *crooked* the farmer long enough, and we are getting dam [*sic*] sick of it."[43] From Loda, Illinois, a farmer wrote that the Board of Trade had "sucked the very life blood from the producers like so many leeches. They are out now to defeat the farm board if they break up every farmer in the U.S. I plead with you in behalf of agriculture to give no quarter in their dastardly work."[44] A Beaver, Oklahoma, farmer wrote to his Senator that he hoped something could "be done to eliminate Board of Trade control of grain markets. . . ."[45] An official of the Seattle, Washington, "Farmers Exchange, Inc." warned Secretary Hyde to "watch every move these rascals make, for they are the keenest and most versatile financial scoundrels of any country. . . . If you can curb the work of the inmates of this stronghold, you will deserve the thanks of citizens of all civilized lands."[46] Agricultural journals generally joined the chorus of condemnation. *Wallaces' Farmer* commented that the Board of Trade which always "felt itself so pure that it dared not let a farmers' cooperative enter its sacred portals for fear of contamination, is at present screaming with indignation." It had done its best to convince farmers that the Farm Board was of little value, that "long established cooperatives, with only a bare connection with the Farm Board, were also only fit for the ash can. . . ." Editor Henry A. Wallace sarcastically concluded that "the picture of the Chicago Board of Trade as an angel of deliverance, freeing the farmer from the slimy embraces of the Farm Board, will result in nothing except some hearty horse-laughs from the farmers it hopes to fool."[47] Finally, the *Oklahoma Farmer-Stockman* summed up these events by saying: "Thus, the fight goes on to determine whether or not farmers have the right to sell their own products on the 'free and open markets' of the

---

[43] "Farmer" to Hyde, no date. (Kansas City, Mo., postmark, Mar. 26, 1932), R.G. 16.

[44] W. J. West to Hyde, June 4, 1932, R.G. 16.

[45] C. H. V. Earl to Sen. Elmer Thomas, Legislation, Box 24, Thomas Papers, University of Oklahoma Library Archives, Norman, Oklahoma.

[46] James H. Howe to Hyde, July 29, 1932, R.G. 16.

[47] *Wallaces' Farmer*, LII (Sept. 23, 1932), 4.

world. We have always assumed that farmers had this right. It appears that we may have to revise our ideas. . . ."[48]

Defenders of the rights of the Board of Trade were limited to individuals directly involved with the grain trade, newspapers like the *Chicago Tribune,* and trade journals. The *Tribune,* referring to the special commission as "Government by Commissars," lamented the fact that important matters were given to this group for a decision:

Such an administrative board might be impartial, might respect individual rights, might even have a proper knowledge of what private rights are. But such a board of commissars might, with much greater possibility, be expected to act as political expediency and the lust for power dictate.[49]

Similarly the *Chicago Journal of Commerce* completely justified the Board of Trade in its dispute with the Farmers' National and the Federal Farm Board. The Farmers' National, it claimed, was not a "full-fledged co-operative" or the Board of Trade would have given it trading privileges. Since the Farmers' National was based on "wild economic ideas" and dealt in speculative interests, the Board was right in excluding it.

But exclusion was not enough for the price-fixers; they followed a deliberately treacherous tack by purchasing outright the Updike Grain Company, which was a full exchange member, and keeping the purchase secret, thereby benefitting by the facilities offered by the Chicago market while playing against it. Was not this procedure enough to show shady tactics of the grain corporation?[50]

On June 8 the hearing convened in the special conference room of the Department of Agriculture. The counsel for the Chicago Board of Trade, Weymouth Kirkland, argued that the complaint filed by the Farmers' National was premature, in that the Board of Trade was willing to consider the Farmers' National's request for membership in the clearing house but could not because of its refusal to furnish necessary information concerning its financial status. More essentially, Kirkland attempted to show that the Farmers' National was doing more business with non-members of cooperatives than with members, which, under the terms of the Capper-Volstead Act, would deny the Farmers' National classifi-

---

[48] *Oklahoma Farmer-Stockman,* XLV, (Aug. 15, 1932), 8.
[49] *Chicago Tribune,* June 12, 1932.
[50] Reprint from the Chicago *Journal of Commerce,* April 15, 1932 in the William Borah Papers, General, 1931–32, Box 330, Manuscript Division, Library of Congress.

cation as a *bona fide* cooperative. Kirkland's interpretation of Milnor's testimony indicated that in its twenty-one months of existence the Farmers' National handled $104,356,000 worth of grain, and that of this $69,326,000 had been for non-members. This interpretation rested upon classifying business handled for the Grain Stabilization Corporation as non-member business. The counsel for the Farmers' National, Carl Meyer, claimed that business for the Stabilization Corporation could not be non-member business, since it was for a government corporation, and thus not for a private company.[51]

As the Board of Trade expected, the special commission found in favor of the Farmers' National. The commission ruled that clearing privileges had been unjustly denied to the Farmers' National and that the Board had therefore not complied with the Grain Futures Act. Using the power granted by the Act, the commission ordered the suspension of the Chicago Board of Trade as a contract market for a period of sixty days, beginning fifteen days after the date of the order. This meant that no futures trading could occur on the exchange for the sixty-day period. The commission offered to hear an application to mitigate the penalty if the Board of Trade "receded from its position with the respect to the petitioner."[52]

With the *Chicago Tribune* carrying a banner headline proclaiming "U. S. SLAMS BOARD OF TRADE," Peter Carey, Board president, reacted defiantly. "The Board of Trade," he said, "will stay open and it will not compromise by yielding to the commission and admitting representatives of the Farmers' National Grain Corporation to the clearing corporation." Then in a formal statement, Carey said that he was not surprised by the "action of the committee, which is composed of Hoover jobholders. They naturally would decide in favor of the subsidiary of Mr. Hoover's pet Farm Board. . . ." The Board of Trade would appeal to the federal courts as provided by the Grain Futures Act, which would, according to Kirkland, keep the Board of Trade open until a decision was rendered.[53] Naturally, the Board of Trade felt it had been treated unfairly, since it was judged by its protagonist in the feud. There were bound to have been political considerations involved in the decision, members of the Board believed, that would carry no weight in a court. The

51 *Chicago Tribune*, June 12, 1932.
52 "Report on a hearing before the special commission inquiring into the Chicago Board of Trade," July 23, 1932, 28, R.G. 16.
53 *New York Times*, July 24, 1932; *Chicago Tribune*, July 24, 1932.

Tribune reported that many politicians agreed that the action would tend to ingratiate the Hoover Administration with radical farmers in the corn and wheat belt "who under the leadership of [Smith] Brookhart and [George] Norris have waged war on the grain exchanges for years." This would likely counteract the shift of farmers in this region toward Franklin Roosevelt and the Democratic party. The *New York Times* also reported speculation concerning the political implications of the commission's decision. Because of the Hoover Administration's support of the Farm Board, grain men had "leaned away" from Hoover. To counter this, Everett Sanders, a representative of the grain trade, had been appointed Chairman of the Republican National Committee. This, plus the nomination of Roosevelt, had softened the hostility of grain men toward the President. Now, the order of the special commission was likely to reverse the friendlier attitude without really affecting the votes of farmers in the coming election.[54]

On July 30 the Board of Trade filed a petition with the Circuit Court of Appeals asking that the Grain Futures Act of 1922 be declared unconstitutional, pointing out that although the law had been in force for ten years, its most drastic features had not been tested. The Board claimed again that the Farmers' National had not proved itself a legal cooperative, and that the commission was prejudiced against the Board of Trade.[55] On September 27 the Board of Trade filed its brief, basing its argument on the position taken during the original hearing before the commission and its charge that the Grain Futures Act was unconstitutional. Oral arguments were heard on November 11, a few days after the election of 1932. However, with the case pending in the courts, the Administration made other moves intended to satisfy the grain trade.

In early September, representatives of the grain trade had initiated contacts with President Hoover's office and arranged a meeting for several officials of the Board of Trade with the President.[56]

---

54 *New York Times*, July 24, 1932.

55 *Ibid.*, July 27, 1932. On Aug. 8, the day set for the suspension to begin the *Chicago Tribune* reported that the "Pit Celebrates Closing Order by Sharp Rally."

56 R. R. Lamont to Lawrence Richey, Sept. 24, 1932, White House files, 1-E/161, Hoover Papers. The officers of the Farmers' National assumed that its pending legal action was the subject of the discussion between Hoover and the members of the Board of Trade, especially when newspapers carried reports to that effect. On Oct. 13 George Milnor wrote to Hoover noting that the Board of Trade had never suggested a compromise and requesting to be consulted if any compromise was considered. Hoover, knowing nothing of a proposed compromise to the dispute then in

The grain trade, the President was told, still wanted to remove the reporting requirement under the Grain Futures Act. Hoover agreed and later asked Secretary of Agriculture Hyde to consider the "advisability" of lifting the reporting regulations to which the Board of Trade had long objected. In early October Hyde prepared a press release announcing the change in futures regulation. A short time later he went to Chicago and conferred with Board of Trade officials on the change, which was then announced on October 22. Hyde's statement emphasized that grain dealers had claimed that the reporting requirement on trades in excess of 500,000 bushels for wheat had "resulted in narrowing the market, and lowering the price of grain." Hyde hoped that the result of his action would be to increase grain prices, although he had no assurance of it. The relaxation of reporting trades would be in effect until notice was given for reinstatement, or until "undue price fluctuation or price levels occur which indicate manipulation of the market."[57] The Board agreed "to take whatever steps" were necessary "to insure that trading in the market will continue to be properly conducted" and would permit no "harmful short selling."[58]

The meaning of the Administration's action requires explanation, for obviously it was not consistent with its general posture with regard to the grain trade, nor with specific statements such as Hoover's short selling pronouncement of the previous year. Indeed, how could Hoover condemn the grain trade for harboring too many short sellers in one statement and then later release these men from their obligation to report their activities to the GFA? The *Chicago Tribune* suggested that the Administration had at long last changed its mind about the Board of Trade. Although it had once believed that the Board of Trade "was the farmers' enemy and that control of the Board's activities must result therefore in benefit to the farmers," the Administration now had "learned that the assumption was false and the monkeying with the marketing machinery does the farmer far more harm than good."[59] The *Tribune* was rather

---

court, sent the letter to the Attorney General for answer. Attorney General Mitchell replied that the Department of Justice had not proposed a compromise, did not believe one was possible, and intended "to make the best possible presentation of the case against the Board of Trade at the coming hearing in the United States Court at Chicago." See Milnor to Hoover, Oct. 13, 1932 and Mitchell to Lawrence Richey, Oct. 24, 1932, White House files, 1-E/150, Hoover Papers.

[57] *Chicago Tribune*, Oct. 22, 1932 and Oct. 23, 1932, II, 7; "Press Release," Oct. 10, 1932, R.G. 16.

[58] "Dictated over long distance phone from Chicago thru Mr. Newton," Oct. 20, 1932, White House files, 1-E/150, Hoover Papers.

[59] *Chicago Tribune*, Oct. 26, 1932.

far from the truth.   Secretary Hyde and President Hoover still believed that the Board of Trade came within that small group of
economic institutions that needed regulation in order to make the
free enterprise economy of the United States operate properly.   Thus,
within the context of a Presidential election expedient action was
taken in the vain hope of stimulating prices, which would have a
favorable effect upon farmers.   Indeed, during the discussion preceding this move, Frank Knox, publisher of the *Chicago Daily
News* pointed out to Hoover:

If such an announcement could be made by Thursday or Friday that restrictions on grain operations in the interest of the farmers during this
emergency were suspended and this news thoroughly digested by the time
your statement is made Saturday night I believe early next week would see
a dramatic rise in the prices of both wheat and corn.[60]

This would probably influence farm votes more than the current
attempt to force the Farmers' National upon the Board of Trade.
At the same time it would encourage the grain trade to stand by
the Administration.   To believe that Hoover was somehow above
politics, a belief that Hoover fostered, is to misjudge the man.   During this episode, and in others, he proved himself entirely capable
of "political" action.[61]   Although a man of strong principle, Hoover
the politician could sacrifice a belief, just a bit, to secure political
support.

The abiding attitude of the Administration toward the grain
trade had not changed.   This can be seen in the year-end legislative recommendations of the GFA, which proposed to increase
the regulatory power of the GFA by allowing it to control short
selling more effectively, specifically recommending that the GFA
be allowed to impose a limit on the "daily volume of trading and
open commitments of large, professional speculators."[62]

More than a year was required for the Circuit Court of Appeals
to dispose of the case of the Farmers' National Grain Corporation.
On October 31, 1933, it found that the law of 1922 was constitutional, rejecting the Board of Trade's argument that the suspension
of a contract market threatened to cause irreparable property loss
without due process of law, which is prohibited by the Fifth Amend-

---

[60] Knox to Hoover, Oct. 18, 1932, White House files, 1-E/162, Hoover
Papers.   Knox wanted Hoover to state that the President would recommend
that Congress credit 20c for wheat and 10c for corn (per bushel) against
the foreign debt owed to the United States when debtor nations purchased
such commodities in the U.S.

[61] Carl N. Degler, "The Ordeal of Herbert Hoover," *The Yale Review*,
LII (Summer, 1963), 579–80.

[62] *Chicago Tribune*, Dec. 3, 1932.

ment. Citing *Chicago Board of Trade* v. *Olsen* (262 US 1), the Court declared that the Board of Trade operated as a business affected with public interest, and thus was subject to reasonable regulation. The Court also found that the petition of the Farmers' National was not premature in that the Board of Trade was denying trading rights guaranteed under the Grain Futures Act. However, the Court stated that the business conducted for the Grain Stabilization Corporation by the Farmers' National was for a non-member of a cooperative association. The record did not indicate how much of the grain handled by the Stabilization Corporation was for members of cooperatives. Thus the relief sought by the Farmers' National was denied.[63]

By this time the Farmers' National had lost the support of a Federal Farm Board, which was ended by order of President Roosevelt. Thus, within a few months the Chicago Board of Trade, facing new demands in Congress for stronger regulation of commodity exchanges, decided to admit the Farmers' National to the clearing corporation, ending the struggle now two years old.[64] Secretary of Agriculture Henry A. Wallace, nevertheless, carried through with an appeal to the Supreme Court, but the Court, on March 5, 1934, denied a writ of certiorari, allowing the decision of the Circuit Court to stand.

The cause of regulating the business affairs of those who traded grain futures was far from fulfilled at the end of the Hoover Administration in 1933. It was destined to concern Congress in the days of the New Deal and later. To Hoover's credit, he saw the need for regulation and supported the cause. This action was, again, in the tradition of Wilson. Unfortunately Hoover continued to place his trust in the cooperative movement as the answer for the troubles of American farmers long after it became evident that the farmers, within the context of severe depression, needed much more. The conditions of the time rendered the attitudes Hoover formed earlier inadequate to meet the desperate needs of those who still lived on the farms. The tragedy was that Hoover did not realize it. His personal tragedy was in never realizing it.

WILLIAM R. JOHNSON

Texas Tech University

---

[63] *Board of Trade of the City of Chicago* v. *Wallace, Secretary of Agriculture, et al.*, 67 F. 2d 402 (1934).
[64] *New York Times*, Jan. 19, 1934.

Corporate Power and Foreign Policy:
Efforts of American Oil Companies to Influence
United States Relations With Mexico, 1921-1928

N. STEPHEN KANE

INTRODUCTION

The view that large business corporations in the United States dominate the nation's polity and economy has been a persistent theme in social science literature since the end of the nineteenth century.[1] Those who hold this view perceive corporations as virtual empires, deriving their power from economic concentration, which have managed over the past decades to subvert most social institutions to their purposes and to attain a near monopoly over decisions affecting the domestic and foreign policies of the United States. In the field of foreign policy, according to this thesis, the fundamental objectives of the corporations—expansion and profit—have become identical with the national interest. Consequently, the corporations have been able to exert

N. Stephen Kane is Senior Historian in the Office of the Historian, Department of State. He received his doctor's degree at the University of Colorado where he studied under Daniel M. Smith. Articles in his field of interest, United States-Mexican relations in the 1920s, have appeared in *Political Science Quarterly* and *The Business History Review*. He is now at work on a study of business influence on United States foreign policy in Latin America. He acknowledges the helpful criticism of an earlier draft of this article by David F. Trask, Historian of the Department of State, and David W. Mabon of the Office of the Historian. The views expressed herein, however, are solely the author's and do not imply the concurrence of the Office of the Historian, the Department of State, or the United States government.

[1] The literature on this subject is voluminous. To sample a variety of critical views of corporate power from different ideological perspectives, see Adolf A. Berle, Jr. and Gardiner C. Means, *The Modern Corporation and Private Property* (New York, 1932); Adolf A. Berle, Jr., *The 20th Century Capitalist Revolution* (New York, 1954); C. Wright Mills, *The Power Elite* (New York, 1959); Andrew Hacker (ed.), *The Corporation Takeover* (New York, 1964); John K. Galbraith, *The New Industrial State* (New York, 1970); Paul M. Sweezy, *Monopoly Capital: An Essay in the American Economic and Social Order* (New York, 1966); David Horowitz (ed.), *Corporations and the Cold War* (New York, 1969); Morton Mintz and Jerry S. Cohen, *America, Inc.: Who Owns and Operates the United States* (New York, 1971). A response to charges by these and other authors is Neil H. Jacoby's, *Corporate Power and Social Responsibility* (New York, 1973).

effective influence on foreign policy, and to reap substantial private benefits from their intimate relationship with government.

The petroleum industry is frequently cited as an example of effective corporate influence on foreign policy.[2] This is in part the result of the high visibility of this industry, whose operations and products have affected the lives of an increasing number of Americans since the turn of the century. It also reflects the image created by a long series of congressional investigations designed to expose the economic power and political machinations of oil companies. Whatever the validity of these charges, they are considerably easier to assert than to prove. Many of the works purporting to document the influential role of oil companies within the foreign-policy decision-making process often contain little more than unwarranted assumptions and dubious inferences.

This paper presents two case studies as a means of examining the interaction between certain oil companies and the Department of State to determine how effectively they influenced United States policy toward Mexico during the period 1921-1928. The studies involve two pieces of Mexican legislation, the Export Tax Decree of 1921 and the Petroleum Law of 1925, which expressed the government's intention to bring the foreign-dominated petroleum industry under its control—in the first instance by using its taxing power, and in the second by implementing Article 27 of the Constitution of 1917.[3] That article, *inter alia,* declared all subsoil resources the patrimony of the nation, thereby nullifying previous legislation in force since 1883 which regarded petroleum deposits as the exclusive property of the surface owner. The large American oil companies had obtained most of their titles and leases under the old laws. These firms viewed the situation in Mexico with alarm; consequently, they made a vigorous effort to secure aid from the State Department against actions by the Mexican government they regarded as confiscatory.

Several considerations justify this approach. First, the Mexican legislation represented concrete actions which threatened the oil companies rather than abstract intention or idle threats. Moreover, these challenges to American industry occurred during a period in the United States commonly known as the "Republican ascendancy," an era characterized by pro-business bias at the national level of government. Finally, Mexico's initiatives generated the most heated controversies involving the oil companies and the government prior to the nationalization of the petroleum industry in 1938.

---

[2] See, for example, Ida M. Tarbell, *The History of the Standard Oil Company* (2 vols., New York, 1925); Robert Engler, *The Politics of Oil: A Study of Private Power and Democratic Directions* (New York, 1961); Harvey O'Connor, *Empire of Oil* (New York, 1955) and *World Crisis in Oil* (New York, 1962); and Carl Solberg, *Oil Power: The Rise and Imminent Fall of an American Empire* (New York, 1976).

[3] The Pan American Union's *Constitution of the Mexican States, 1917* (Washington, 1957) is a convenient translation of the Mexican Constitution. Mexican mining legislation is surveyed in Marvin D. Bernstein, *The Mexican Mining Industry, 1890-1950: A Study in the Interaction of Politics, Economics, and Technology* (Albany, 1964).

THE ROOTS OF OIL COMPANY POWER

In 1921, the structure of the American petroleum industry was considerably different from what it had been only ten years before. Prior to 1911, the Standard Oil Trust dominated the industry, in spite of the emergence of forces which had begun to erode its marketing position. In that year, however, the Supreme Court handed down a decision declaring Standard Oil in violation of the Sherman Anti-Trust Act, and the Court ordered dissolution of the holding company. The dissolution plan followed a corporate rather than a functional organization, and consequently when the individual firms left the monopoly they were characterized by varying and unequal degrees of vertical integration, size, and financial resources. Standard Oil of New Jersey (SONJ) emerged from the break-up with full vertical integration (producing, refining, transporting, and marketing its own oil), but the other firms immediately began to search for ways they could expand their operations, increase their size, and diversify their products in an effort to achieve greater depth of vertical integration. As a result, the earlier division within the petroleum industry which had pitted the Standard Oil group against independent crude producers, now became a three-way struggle between fully integrated, partially integrated, and non-integrated (the old independent) firms.[4]

Petroleum production in the United States in 1921 was the second largest mineral enterprise in the economy, measured by the value of its products or the expansion of its productive capacity.[5] Increasing consumption, together with a new awareness of the strategic importance of oil as a result of the war, and a growing alarm over the rapid depletion of the nation's reserves, combined to induce close cooperation between the industry and the government during the 1920s. Among other things, this cooperation involved a mutual commitment by the companies, their stockholders, and government officials to engage in a world-wide struggle for the control of petroleum resources in areas previously closed to American penetration. Partly as a result of this aggressive oil policy, and partly in response to market imperatives, American oil companies increased their investments in overseas areas from approximately $400,000,000 to $1,400,000,000 between 1919 and 1929.[6]

---

[4] For additional information on the evolution of the petroleum industry, see Harold F. Williamson et al. *The American Petroleum Industry: The Age of Energy, 1899-1959* (Evanston, 1963), pp. 1-260; and Harold F. Williamson and Ralph L. Andreano, "Competitive Structure of the Petroleum Industry, 1880-1911: A Reappraisal," in *Oil's First Century* (Boston, 1960), pp. 70-84. Mira Wilkins, *The Maturing of Multinational Enterprise: American Business Abroad from 1914 to 1970* (Cambridge, 1974), pp. 146-148, discusses some of the internal organizational changes which the petroleum companies adopted during this period.

[5] Domestic distribution of major refinery products expanded from slightly less than 300,000,000 barrels in 1919 to approximately 857,000,000 barrels in 1929. This increase resulted primarily from the shift in consumer demand from petroleum as an illuminant to a source of energy. Williamson et al. *Age of Energy*, pp. 442-462.

[6] *Ibid.*, pp. 506-532; John A. DeNovo, "The Movement for an Aggressive American

Mexico was one of the most important countries for American petroleum operations during the 1920s. Between 1919 and 1926, that country was the largest producer of crude petroleum outside of the United States. At the time, American capital invested in Mexican oil properties amounted to about $200,000,000, a figure representing the single largest concentration of American investment in foreign oil. This investment was distributed among approximately 150 companies, 10 or 11 of which were fully or partially vertically integrated, and the remainder of which were independent crude producers, owning no pipeline, refining, transportation, or marketing facilities.[7] American firms owned roughly 65 percent of the 193,000,000 barrels of oil produced annually in Mexico by 1921. By the mid-1920s, however, many of the major American firms,[8] deterred by unfavorable Mexican legislation and lured by the prospects of more immediate and larger profits elsewhere in Latin America, curtailed further investment in Mexico and directed their capital instead to Colombia and Venezuela. In spite of these developments, the stake of major American oil companies in Mexico continued to be substantial throughout the decade.[9]

Oil Policy Abroad, 1918-1920," *American Historical Review*, LXI (July, 1956), 854-876; market imperatives are discussed in Raymond Vernon, *Sovereignty at Bay: The Multinational Spread of U.S. Enterprises* (New York, 1971) esp. pp. 27-37, and Wilkins, *The Maturing of Multinational Enterprise*, pp. 138-163.

[7]It is extremely difficult to determine with precision the number of oil companies operating at any given time in Mexico,` or in all cases to trace ownership lines. The following sources are useful, however, in shedding some light on this question: E. Dean Fuller, "The Oil Situation in Mexico in Relation to American Investments: An Argument on Behalf of Various Independent Interests," December 19, 1916, National Archives, Record Group 59, General Records of the Department of State, File number 812.6363/255 (hereafter cited as NA with file number); "List of Oil Companies," prepared by the American Consulate, Tampico, enclosed in Consul James B. Stewart to Secretary of State Charles Evans Hughes, December 3, 1923, NA812.6363/2156; and U.S. Senate, Special Committee Investigating Petroleum Resources, "American Petroleum Interests in Foreign Countries," *Hearings*, 79th Cong., 1st Sess., 1946, *passim.*

[8]The major American petroleum companies and some of their operating affiliates in Mexico during the 1920s include the following: SONJ (Transcontinental Petroleum Company), Standard Oil of California (Richmond Petroleum Company), Atlantic Refining Company (Cía. Petrolera del Agwi), Gulf Oil Company (Mexican Gulf Oil), Texas Oil Company (Texas Oil Company of Mexico), Sinclair Oil Company (Mexican Sinclair Petroleum Corporation), Waters-Pierce Oil Company, Edward L. Doheny interests (Mexican Petroleum Company, Pan American Petroleum and Transport Company, and Huasteca Petroleum Company), John Hays Hammond interests (Continental Mexican Petroleum Company), and Island Oil and Transport Company.

[9]Estimates of American property ownership in Mexico vary, sometimes widely, because different bases of classification are used. The following, however, are helpful for determining the extent of U.S. investment: Chester Lloyd Jones and George Wythe (commercial attachés, Mexico), "Economic Conditions in Mexico, 1927," NA812.50/161, 174; United States Department of Commerce, Bureau of Foreign and Domestic Commerce, "Wealth of Mexico," by William H. Seamon, in *Daily Consular and Trade Reports*, No. 168, III (July 18, 1922), 316; Cleona Lewis, *America's Stake in International Investments* (Washington, D.C., 1938), pp. 220, 589; George S. Gibb and Evelyn H. Knowlton, *The Resurgent Years, 1911-1927*, volume II of *History of Standard Oil Company (New Jersey)* (New York, 1956), pp. 364-365; and Wilkins, *The Maturing*

In view of their stake in Mexico, it is understandable why the oil companies were concerned about the possible application of the provisions of Article 27 to their properties. When they had originally acquired their holdings, in most cases prior to May 1, 1917 (the effective date of the Constitution),[10] they believed that through purchase or lease of the surface, they had obtained "fee simple" ownership and thus a "vested" right to the nonmetallic products of the subsoil. They had little reason at the time to question the legality of the mining legislation then in force, especially when the government in power was legitimate, said that its laws were constitutional, and possessed the power to enforce them. In general, the companies did not challenge the Mexican government's right to assert national ownership of subsoil resources not under private ownership prior to the promulgation of the new constitution. What they wanted, however, was assurance that the government would neither nationalize the privately owned petroleum industry nor confiscate their properties through taxation.

In response to this threat, the petroleum companies formed a voluntary protective association. Organized in late 1918, the Association of Producers of Petroleum in Mexico (APPM) provided a mechanism for facilitating intercompany communication and the collective planning of strategy. It also enabled the companies to pool resources in pursuit of their common objectives. The APPM's primary purpose in Mexico was to represent the industry with a united voice, whereas in the United States its activities were directed toward maintaining contact with government agencies, particularly the Department of State. Although occasionally individual or small groups of oil company executives might appear at the Department to present an appeal, Guy Stevens, who resigned as general counsel of the Texas Oil Company in 1921 to become executive director of the APPM, served as the regular channel for company communications with high-ranking Department officials.[11]

To strengthen their position, the petroleum companies also mobilized other investors in Mexico. Largely through the initiative of the members of

---

of Multinational Enterprise, pp. 31-36, which provides some comparative analysis. Data concerning rates of return on American investment are either too fragmentary or too unreliable to allow for meaningful generalizations.

[10] Statistics vary widely; see Secretary of State Frank B. Kellogg to President Coolidge, February 15, 1927, U.S. Department of State, Papers Relating to the Foreign Relations of the United States, 1927 (3 vols., Washington, D.C. 1942), III, 180 (hereafter cited as FRUS with volume and year).

[11] United States Senate, Investigation of Mexican Affairs; Preliminary Report and Hearings of the Committee on Foreign Relations, Senate Document No. 285, 2 vols., 66th Cong., 2d Sess., I, 290-291, 426-429, 542-543; New York Times, December 10, 12, 1918. The APPM's message is clearly conveyed in Guy Stevens, Current Controversies With Mexico: Addresses and Writings (n.p., n.d.). Membership in the APPM was not limited to American firms. The largest non-American companies, Mexicana de Petroleo "El Aguila", S.A. (Mexican Eagle Oil Company, frequently called El Aguila), an affiliate of the Anglo-Mexican Petroleum Company, and Mexicana Holandesa "La Corona," S.A. (known as La Corona), controlled by Royal Dutch Shell, were members, as well as several smaller British-owned companies.

the APPM, the National Association for the Protection of American Rights in Mexico (NAPARM) was formed in December 1918. Financed to the extent of about $20,000 per month by the oil companies, NAPARM's fundamental objective was to rouse public opinion to support the United States government in taking whatever steps were necessary to secure protection for American lives and properties in Mexico. Under the leadership of executive director Charles Boynton, a former manager of the Associated Press, NAPARM used its own publishing presses to print and disseminate an enormous quantity of literature to American Legion posts, local chambers of commerce, newspaper editors, politicians and other public figures, and business organizations. With headquarters in New York, regional offices in Washington, El Paso, and Los Angeles, a women's division, and a growing national membership of over 2,000 in 1920, the NAPARM was capable of reaching a wide audience and of reinforcing the efforts of the APPM.[12]

The oil companies not only had organizational resources at their disposal to help get their messages across bureaucratic hurdles and into the hands of policy makers, they also could rely for advice and expertise on former high-ranking government officials in their employ during the 1920s. For example, Mark L. Requa, well known director of the United States Fuel Administration's oil division during the war, became a vice-president of Sinclair Oil Company, and Franklin K. Lane, after 21 years of government service resigned as Secretary of the Interior in 1920 to accept a position as vice-president of Edward L. Doheny's Mexican Petroleum and Pan American Petroleum and Transport Company.[13] These men were thoroughly familiar with the federal bureaucracy, and they no doubt retained wide networks of personal and professional contacts within government. Although neither Requa nor Lane were expected to perform services similar to those of Stevens, the companies nevertheless derived at least a marginal benefit from their roles as corporate executives.

An even greater advantage enjoyed by the oil companies was the presence in the State Department of officers who were particularly receptive to company appeals for aid. Men such as Henry P. Fletcher, Matthew E. Hanna, James R. Sheffield, and H. G. Arthur Schoenfeld,[14] predisposed perhaps by

---

[12]Lanier L. Winslow to Leland Harrison, with enclosures, February 15, 1919, Papers of Leland Harrison, Manuscript Division, Library of Congress, Box 6; *Investigation of Mexican Affairs*, I, 291, 403-423; Clifford W. Trow, "Woodrow Wilson and the Mexican Interventionist Movement of 1919," *Journal of American History*, LVIII (June, 1971), 46-72. For samples of NAPARM's publicity materials, see *Plow With Petroleum* (New York, n.d.), *Bread, Bolshevism, Binder Twine* (New York, n.d.), and *What Popular Writers are Saying About Mexico* (New York, n.d.).

[13]DeNovo, "An Aggressive American Oil Policy Abroad," pp. 862-863.

[14]Fletcher served as Ambassador to Mexico (March 1917-February 1920) and Under Secretary of State (March 1921-March 1922); Hanna served as Secretary to the Embassy at Mexico City (February 1917-September 1921) and Chief of the Division of Mexican Affairs (December 1920-March 1924); Sheffield served as Ambassador to Mexico (October 1924-June 1927); Schoenfeld was Counselor of Embassy in Mexico City (March 1924-November 1927). Of the four, all but Sheffield, a wealthy corporation lawyer with limited political experience, were career officers.

background and temperament but most certainly as a result of their field experience in Mexico, were unwavering in their support of the companies and consistent in their recommendations for vigorous protection of American property rights against the "radical" policies of the Mexican government. At no time did they display sympathy for Mexican socio-economic aspirations which might have tempered their hard-line approach. They firmly believed that Mexican petroleum legislation represented an "attack" against the companies, and that if the United States bowed to Mexico in the petroleum controversy, its prestige and influence as a creditor nation would suffer irreparable damage not only in Mexico but elsewhere in the world. A "soft" policy, in their view, would jeopardize American interests in all countries where "nationalistic" upheavals took place.[15]

In short, during the 1920s the petroleum companies were in an excellent position to exert effective influence on the State Department. They possessed adequate organizational and financial resources and they enjoyed the advantage of distinctly favorable environmental conditions. Whether they were successful in converting their power into influence, however, is a much more complex question.[16]

THE OIL COMPANIES AND THE DEPARTMENT OF STATE

The two case studies presented here do not provide an exhaustively detailed account of United States relations with Mexico concerning oil,[17] but

---

[15]Clear indications of the attitude and views of these four men are contained in the following: Memorandum for President Wilson, by Fletcher, August 18, 1919, NA711.1211/187; Fletcher to Secretary of State Robert Lansing, December 11, 1919, and to President Wilson, January 3, 1920, Papers of Henry P. Fletcher, Manuscript Division, Library of Congress, Boxes 7, 8; Fletcher to George T. Summerlin (Chargé, Mexico City), September 9, 1921, NA812.00/25169A; Fletcher to President Harding, November 14, 1921, Warren G. Harding Papers, Ohio State Historical Society, Columbus, Ohio, Box 167; Memoranda for Secretary of State Charles Evans Hughes, by Hanna, April 11, 24, May 10, 1922, NA812.00/25169A, 26097; Hanna to Hughes, May 12, June 19, 1922, NA711.1211/52, 36; Hanna to Fletcher, June 21, 1922, Fletcher Papers, Box 9, Sheffield to Secretary of State Frank B. Kellogg, April 6, 1925, NA812.00/ 27533; Sheffield to Kellogg, April 5, 1926, NA711.12/744; Sheffield to Kellogg, December 24, 1925, January 6, 19, 21, April 15, December 5, 1926, NA812.6363/1628, 1651, 1687, 1795, 1832, 2036; Schoenfeld (Chargé ad interim) to Kellogg, June 15, 1927, NA812.6363/2289.

[16]Social scientists generally agree that influence should be distinguished from power. Power is the potential a particular actor or set of actors has for exerting effective influence; it is the aggregate of resources available for bargaining. Power can be converted into influence, but not automatically. The process of conversion depends on how skillfully power is utilized, and the structure of constraints affecting bargaining relationships. A useful introduction to the subject is Robert A. Dahl, "The Concept of Power, *Behavioral Scientist,* II (July, 1957), 201-215. Arnold M. Rose, *The Power Structure: Political Process in American Society* (New York, 1967) examines power in the domestic political arena; Robert W. Cox and Harold K. Jacobson, *The Anatomy of Influence: Decision-Making in International Organizations* (New Haven, 1973) treat it within the international context.

[17]For extensive narrative studies, see Lorenzo Meyer, *México y Estados Unidos en el*

rather analyze the interaction that took place between oil businessmen and policy makers in the State Department under somewhat different circumstances. In each case, the problem was rooted in Mexican legislation—the Export Tax Decree of 1921 and the Petroleum Law of 1925. The first arose at a time when the United States was withholding recognition from the government of Álvaro Obregón, which came into power in 1920, and the second after normalization of diplomatic relations in 1923. Moreover, the two incidents occurred during different administrations in the United States, those of President Harding (1921-1924) and President Coolidge (1924-1929).

The Export Tax Decree: Taxation as Confiscation

On June 7, 1921, President Obregón issued an executive tax decree establishing an export tax of 10 to 12 percent on petroleum to become effective on July 1.[18] According to Obregón, the tax was necessary as a conservation measure and also to provide a source of income which would permit the government to resume payments on its defaulted external debt, thereby reestablishing its international credit. Obregón's advisers apparently believed that the foreign-controlled petroleum industry, enjoying a rising rate of production and a favorable price structure, could easily absorb a tax that amounted to approximately thirty-five cents per cubic meter, especially in view of the fact that the United States Congress had under discussion a tariff amounting to $1.50 per cubic meter on Mexican petroleum.[19]

In any case, the oil companies vigorously opposed the new tax, labeling it inequitable, illegal, and confiscatory.[20] Their initial strategy in response to it involved appeals to the State Department for protection. Describing the situation as "grave," Harold N. Branch, counsel for the APPM, arranged a meeting between a delegation from the association and Secretary of State Charles Evans Hughes. On June 20, a group of oil producers, led by Doheny, arrived at the Department, and presented a memorandum detailing their case against the Mexican government and requested protection of their interests. Hughes replied that he would consider their complaint, but he offered no further encouragement. Subsequent appeals from the producers for a protest against the tax decree also failed to move the secretary. He was firmly opposed to forceful action on behalf of the oil interests, particularly before they had exhausted local remedies in Mexico and had made a serious effort to negotiate a solution to their problem.[21]

Failing to obtain immediate action from the Department, or even what

---

Conflicto Petrolero (1917-1942) (Mexico City, 1968); and Merrill Rippy, *Oil and the Mexican Revolution* (Leiden, 1972).

[18] A translation of the decree is enclosed in Harold N. Branch (APPM) to Hughes, June 2, 1921, NA600.127/174.

[19] *New York Times,* June 8, 14, 1921.

[20] Statements by Edward L. Doheny (President, Pan American Petroleum and Transport Company) and Walter C. Teagle (President, SONJ), in *New York Times,* June 10, July 2, 3, 1921; and APPM press releases, in *ibid.,* June 25, July 20, 1921.

[21] Hughes to Summerlin, August 6, 1921, *FRUS,* 1921, II, 452; *New York Times,* June 21, 1921.

they could regard as a sympathetic hearing, the companies adopted a more aggressive strategy. On July 1, 1921, the day the tax became effective, Walter C. Teagle, president of Standard Oil of New Jersey, announced that his firm would discontinue all shipments of petroleum from Mexico and withdraw all its tankers from Mexican service, because his firm could not operate profitably under the new tax. Although other company leaders denied that they had agreed on concerted action, all of the members of the APPM participated in the "boycott." They not only ceased shipping, but they also reduced drilling operations and released workers.[22] In this way, the companies sought to intimidate Obregón into rescinding the tax decree or to foment a situation that would result in the collapse of his government and the emergence of a more amenable leader, presumably as a result of intervention by the United States.

The strategy of the companies temporarily threatened to bring about intervention. Claude I. Dawson, American consul at Tampico, kept the Department fully informed about deteriorating economic conditions in the area. He feared large-scale anti-American outbreaks and damage to American-owned wells, and therefore advised reasonable precautions. The secretary's advisors supported Dawson's recommendations, and Hughes requested Secretary of the Navy Edwin Denby to station two warships off Tampico. However, when no hard information about imminent violence at Tampico was forthcoming, Hughes, convinced that the retention of the ships in the area "might tempt some persons to start difficulties with the idea of compelling the United States to intervene, and we might be drawn prematurely into action which might easily be avoided,"[23] asked Denby to have them withdrawn. The secretary had no intention to permit the oil companies to pressure the Department into precipitate acts.

Instead, Hughes' policy was to persuade the companies to discuss a settlement directly with the Mexican government. Early in August, he arranged to have Under Secretary Henry P. Fletcher present a proposal along these lines to Frederic Watriss, legal representative of the Continental Mexican Petroleum Company and the International Petroleum Company and a member of APPM's executive committee. If the companies agreed to negotiate with the Mexican government on the tax issue, the Department would make all the necessary arrangements.[24] Company leaders proved amenable, but they wanted the Department to assume a more active role, and they insisted upon certain conditions as the price of cooperation. The Department accepted these conditions, since none were of material importance,[25] but at

---

[22]Frederick N. Watriss (APPM) to Fletcher, July 7, 1921, *FRUS, 1921*, II, 449; statements by Teagle and Stevens, in *New York Times*, July 2, 7, 1921.

[23]Hughes to Denby, July 1, 1921, and Denby to Hughes, July 2, 1921, NA812.00/25070; Hughes to President Harding, July 2, 1921, NA812.00/25094b; Hughes to Summerlin, July 8, 1921, NA812.00/25080a; Dawson to Hughes, June 30, 1921, *FRUS, 1921*, II, 448.

[24]Fletcher to Watriss, August 3, 1921, *FRUS, 1921*, II, 451.

[25]Watriss to Fletcher, August 5, 1921, Executives Oil Committee to Hughes,

the same time imposed several of its own. Hughes and Fletcher, not wanting to compromise the Department's ban on loans to unrecognized governments, stressed that the oil men were not to discuss loans to Mexico in connection with the tax issue. They were also instructed not to involve the Department in any way in the negotiations, or to refer to the current political situation between the two countries. Beyond these few restrictions, said Fletcher, they could go as far as they wished, acting as businessmen trying to obtain the best possible terms.[26]

Hughes' insistence upon direct negotiations stemmed not only from his view of the proper relationship between business groups and the Department of State, but also from certain practical considerations. He had to take into account, for example, the position of other groups with a stake in Mexico, particularly the American section of the International Committee of Bankers on Mexico (ICBM). The chairman of the ICBM, Thomas W. Lamont of J. P. Morgan Company, was then trying to negotiate a settlement on Mexico's defaulted external debt on behalf of those who held Mexican bonds. Hughes agreed with Lamont that a tax increase on Mexico's most viable and profitable industry had to be an integral part of any bond or debt settlement, because it would provide a reasonably dependable source of income for resumption of payments. From Hughes' perspective, a compromise solution that would permit the companies to continue to operate profitably and enable the Mexican government to siphon increased revenue from the industry, would allow the Department to circumvent altogether the question of the confiscatory nature of the tax decree.[27]

The oil producers also had to view the situation in practical terms. Unable to influence the State Department to issue a formal protest or to undertake more forceful action in defense of their interests, they found it necessary to choose between a private effort to obtain relief in part underwritten by the Department and no attempt at all. The former option implied of course the sanction, if not the vigorous support, of the Department, and it appeared all the more attractive because it imposed no conditions of accountability. Although it meant that the companies would have to reject the leadership of Secretary of the Interior Albert B. Fall, who consistently opposed any attempt by American investors in Mexico to bargain separately with the Mexican government, and the acceptance of Hughes' guidance, it was a

---

August 18, 1921, and Hughes to Summerlin, August 19, 1921, *FRUS*, 1921, II, 452, 453, 456. The companies' conditions included such things as having the Department indicate to the Mexican government that it supported the negotiations and requested the suspension of the tax decree pending a solution to the controversy.

[26]Memorandum of Interview with Under Secretary Fletcher, August 24, 1921, by Harold N. Branch, NA812.6363/1231; Hughes to Teagle; August 20, 1921, *FRUS*, 1921, II, 456-457.

[27]Memorandum of conversation with Mr. Teagle, August 18, 1921, unsigned, Thomas W. Lamont Papers, Baker Library, Harvard University, Box 195; Lamont to Hughes, August 17, 1921, and Hughes to Lamont, August 22, 1921, NA812.51/790; Hughes to Summerlin, August 6, 1921, *FRUS*, 1921, II, 452.

minimal price to pay for the leverage they obtained by association with the Department.[28]

Two series of conversations ensued between representatives of the companies and the Mexican government, before the parties resolved the tax controversy. The first opened in Mexico City on August 29, 1921, and ended on September 3, with the signature of an agreement. Under its provisions, the Mexican government agreed to authorize a temporary suspension of the export tax and to accept payment of all other petroleum taxes in Mexican bonds currently selling at forty percent of par value on the open market. The companies agreed to continue payment of production taxes, to encourage a syndicate of American bankers to enter into an arrangement with the Mexican government for the purchase of Mexican bonds on the open market, and to dismiss all *amparo* (injunction) suits against the government resulting from the decree of June 7.[29] During a second series of discussions in Mexico City between April 24 and May 3, 1922, the two parties reached an accord concerning a new basis for the calculation of tax rates, an optional system whereby the companies could pay petroleum taxes in Mexican bonds or in cash, and a promise by the Mexican government that it would impose no further "special taxes" on the petroleum industry.[30]

The results of the negotiations did not represent an unqualified victory for either the producers or the Mexican government. Minister of Finance Adolfo de la Huerta, who conducted the negotiations for the government, had comparatively less bargaining leverage than the companies. He assumed that the oil men had the full support of the State Department, which his government would have to satisfy in order to obtain recognition,[31] and Thomas W. Lamont had informed him that a resolution of the tax controversy was an essential prerequisite to the financial agreement he desperately wanted.[32] Moreover, the companies had begun to discover salt in their wells.

---

[28]Clifford W. Trow, "Senator Albert B. Fall and Mexican Affairs: 1912-1921," unpublished doctoral dissertation, University of Colorado, 1966, p. 474.

[29]Committee of Oil Executives, "Documents on Conferences and Confidential Report," August-September, 1921, NA812.6363/1231; Teagle to Hughes, August 18, 1921, with enclosure, and "Report of a Meeting of the Committee of Oil Company Executives with their Tampico Managers," September 3, 1921, enclosed in Summerlin to Hughes, September 8, 1921, *FRUS,* 1921, II, 453, 457.

[30]The terms of the agreement are included in the following exchange of letters; de la Huerta to Oil Executives Committee, May 2, 1922, and Oil Executives Committee to de la Huerta, May 3, 1922, in "Dossier of Papers Relating to Conferences Between Secretary de la Huerta and the Committee of Oil Executives," April 24-May 3, 1922, pp. 11-13, enclosed in Teagle to Hughes, May 25, 1922, NA812.512/2873, and "Memorandum for Secretary Hughes," May 29, 1922, from Mexican Division, unsigned, NA812.6363/1234.

[31]Summerlin to Hughes, August 21, 1921, enclosing Mexican Foreign Office to American Embassy, August 20, 1921, *FRUS,* 1921, II, 457.

[32]"Principles Necessary for the Re-establishment of Mexican Government Credit in the Leading Investment Markets of the World," Memorandum by Lamont, enclosed in Lamont to Summerlin, October 10, 1921, enclosed in Summerlin to Hughes, October 11, 1921, NA812.51/663.

The lack of decisive bargaining advantages induced de la Huerta to make concessions; nevertheless, he successfully maintained the principle of both production and export taxes, thus requiring the companies to pay a more reasonable share of their profits as revenue.

The Petroleum Law of 1925: Confirmation of Rights as Confiscation of Rights

A source of even greater concern to the petroleum companies than the taxation issue, one giving rise to more significant international repercussions, was the implementation of the provisions of Article 27 pertaining to the sub-soil. In mid-1925 a mixed commission representing several departments of the Mexican government drafted the bill which became the basis for the petro-leum law in force until 1938. From the perspective of the companies, the most problematic aspect of the Petroleum Law of December 31, 1925,[33] was that it contradicted the "Bucareli understandings"[34] by narrowing the defini-tion of a "positive act" and established a system of "confirmatory con-cessions." Under this system, the government proposed to issue contracts to surface owners of oil lands on which development work (positive acts) had been undertaken prior to May 1, 1917, "confirming" the rights of the owner for a period of fifty years. Owners who claimed pre-constitutional rights in undeveloped lands were given a "preferential right" over third parties to file for thirty-year concessions. Those granted concessions were obligated to com-ply with all federal legislation regulating the petroleum industry. Failure to file for the concessions by January 1, 1927, would result in the forfeiture of all rights.

American oil producers rejected the principle of confirmatory conces-sions on both legal and practical grounds[35] and they devised a three-phase strategy against the petroleum law. While the bill was being debated in the Mexican Congress, APPM and company representatives lobbied at the State Department to persuade Department officials to prevent its passage, or at least to lodge a formal protest against its alleged retroactive provisions.[36]

---

[33]For the text of the law, see *Documents Relating to the Petroleum Law of Mexico of December 26, 1925 with Amendments of January 3, 1928* (Mexico, n.d.).

[34]These were embodied in a set of official minutes signed by representatives of the U.S. and Mexico in Mexico City on August 15, 1923, as a result of conversations con-cerning the controversial agrarian and petroleum issues between the two countries. With respect to the latter, the Mexican commissioners pledged that their government would respect the Mexican Supreme Court decisions declaring that Article 27 of the Constitu-tion of 1917 was inapplicable to American-owned oil properties acquired prior to May 1, 1917, on which some "positive act" of exploitation, broadly defined, had been per-formed. For text of the minutes, see Department of State, *Proceedings of the United States-Mexican Commission Convened in Mexico City, May 14, 1923* (Washington, 1925).

[35]The companies' reaction to the Petroleum Law is evident in Stevens, *Current Controveries With Mexico, passim.*

[36]Memorandum of Conversation with Harold Walker (V.P., Pan American Petroleum and Transport Company, and Executive Board member, APPM), November 27, 1925, by Franklin Mott Gunther (Chief, Division of Mexican Affairs), Memorandum of Conversa-tion with Chester O. Swain (General Counsel, SONJ), presumably by Gunther, Decem-

Secretary of State Frank B. Kellogg and Under Secretary Joseph C. Grew considered several alternative courses, but they were disinclined to risk charges of interference in Mexican domestic affairs. They also believed that protest would not prevent passage of the bill if the government wanted to enact it. Consequently, they opted against "preventive" protest, despite the evaluation of the Solicitor's Office that the bill contained retroactive features. The secretary, however, authorized Ambassador Sheffield to notify the Mexican government informally that the bill appeared to contain provisions that might lead to difficulties between the two countries and unfortunate economic consequences for Mexico.[37]

After the bill became law, the producers made a concerted effort to obtain advice from the Department about how to respond to it.[38] In this way they sought to forge a closer relationship with Department officials, which might pay dividends in increased leverage if they found it necessary to negotiate with the Mexican government, and which would enable them to shift ultimate responsibility for their actions to the Department. Secretary Kellogg, however, refused to sanction an advisory role for the Department, and he specifically instructed Sheffield not to counsel oil company representatives in Mexico concerning confirmatory concessions.[39] When company leaders realized that the Department would not vigorously interpose with Mexican authorities on their behalf, or even advise whether or not they should accept concessions, they finally resorted to local recourse. During January and February, 1926, many of the members of the APPM filed *amparos* against the operation of the law.

Secretary Kellogg had no objections to the companies' decision to file *amparos,* but he believed that the best hope for a solution to the concession controversy lay in direct negotiations between representatives of the companies and the Mexican government. Consequently, he made an effort to persuade the companies to accept the Mexican government's invitation to participate informally in drafting the regulations necessary to administer the law. When the companies proved reluctant, citing their concern that any

ber 1, 1925, Walker to Gunther, December 3, 1925, Memorandum of telephone conversation with Guy Stevens, December 9, 1925, by Gunther, Stevens to Kellogg, December 9, 1925, Swain to Gunther, December 14, 1925, and Walker to Gunther, December 22, 1925, NA812.6363/1611, 1600, 1609, 1627, 1601, 1636, 1637.

[37]The Department's decision was conveyed in Kellogg to Sheffield, October 29, 1925, *FRUS,* 1925, II, 523-525. A legal analysis of the bill is contained in Memorandum by the Solicitor (J. R. Baker), December 7, 1925, NA812.6363/1592. See also Kellogg to Sheffield, November 13, 1925, *FRUS,* 1925, II, 528-529; L. Ethan Ellis, *Frank B. Kellogg and American Foreign Relations, 1925-1929* (New Brunswick, 1961), pp. 29-35.

[38]Stevens to Kellogg, December 29, 1925, Sheffield to Kellogg, January 3, 1926, Swain to Gunther, January 8, 1926, and Stevens to Swain, January 8, 1926, enclosed in Swain to Gunther, January 8, 1926, NA812.6363/1662, 1645, 1675, 1676.

[39]Memorandum of conversation with Mr. Swain, unsigned, December 30, 1925, Kellogg to Sheffield, January 8, 1926, Leland Harrison (Assistant Secretary of State), for the Secretary, to Sheffield, January 9, 1926, Harrison, for the Secretary, to Sheffield, January 13, 1926, and Memorandum by Gunther, January 29, 1926, NA812.6363/1673, 1646, 1640, 1676, 1771.

discussion including reference to their pre-constitutional rights might establish undesirable precedents, Kellogg and Franklin Mott Gunther, Chief of the Division of Mexican Affairs, stressed to company representatives the Department's position that the regulations offered the only feasible solution. Shortly thereafter the producers agreed to authorize their representatives to negotiate in Mexico.[40]

Company representatives engaged in a series of discussions with Mexican officials at Mexico City during February and March. Their primary objective was to persuade the Mexican negotiators to write into the petroleum regulations a modification of the principle of confirmatory concessions, which would explicitly recognize pre-constitutional rights. To increase their leverage, they attempted to maintain a close liaison with the State Department, and by various means to implicate it in the negotiations,[41] but the Department adopted a distinctly arms-length posture. Although the producers presented a draft of petroleum regulations to the government, they made no progress toward achieving their main objective.[42]

The Department's role disturbed the members of the APPM, and they complained to Ambassador Sheffield. Convinced that the Department's failure to provide strong support for the companies placed them at a serious disadvantage, Sheffield consistently urged the Department to adopt a more aggressive policy of "complete protection." Although Sheffield did not admit that he favored some form of intervention as the proper solution to the Mexican problem, by the summer of 1926 he spoke openly about the need to lift the embargo on arms to Mexico. An irritated Kellogg finally summoned him to Washington for consultations. During their subsequent review of the Mexican situation, the secretary stressed that it was inadvisable to lift the embargo, that the United States was not in a position "to serve any ultimatums on Mexico," and that it would be best if the ambassador would concentrate his energies on individual claims cases rather than general policy.[43]

---

[40] Memorandum by Gunther, February 9, 1926, Kellogg to Sheffield, January 26, 1926, NA812.6363/1744, 1709.

[41] The Department refused, for example, to address a series of questions to the Mexican government prepared by the companies, dealing with such matters as how the proposed regulations comported with the Bucareli understandings; nor would it issue a statement requested by the companies criticizing alleged continued violations of American rights under Mexican agrarian legislation. "Memorandum of Proposed Inquiries," February 23, 1926, delivered to the Department by Walker, marked "No action taken" by Gunther, and Sheffield to Kellogg, March 11, 1926, NA812.6363/1783, 1789.

[42] "Regulation of the Petroleum Law of December 31, 1925: Communications Exchanged Between the Secretary of Industry, Commerce, and Labor and the Committee Representing the Petroleum Industry in Mexico, Collaborating in the Work of Preparing the Regulations," enclosed in Sheffield to Kellogg, March 2, 1926, and Sheffield to Kellogg, March 22, 1926, NA812.6373/1781, 1807.

[43] Sheffield to Kellogg, January 19, 1926, Kellogg to Sheffield, January 20, 1926, Sheffield to Kellogg, January 21, April 15, 1926 and Kellogg to President Coolidge, August 26, 1926, NA812.6363/1687, 1696, 1832, 1942a; Sheffield to Kellogg, July 19, 1926, NA812.113/10129. Apparently, the lifting of the embargo was considered by the Department, but rejected. Memorandum to Secretary Kellogg, by Gunther, July 2, 1926, NA812.6363/1929.

Between late December 1926 and the early spring of 1927, the petroleum companies and the Mexican government moved closer to a showdown on the concession problem. At an APPM meeting in New York City on December 30, the producers reaffirmed their agreement reached previously not to accept, apply for, or in any way recognize confirmatory concessions.[44] On January 13, 1927, the Mexican government announced that all companies failing to file for concessions by January 15, would be "consigned" before the Attorney General.[45] On the following day, the producers voted unanimously to institute *amparo* proceedings against the petroleum regulations.[46] The government responded on January 17, by ordering the Department of Industry to transmit to the Department of Justice the names of the companies in violation of the law.[47] Thereupon, the companies reportedly began to release workers in the Tampico oil fields, and they renewed their threats of a total cessation of operations.[48] During February and March, the government tried to induce a split in the companies' ranks by offering "special facilities" to those who would accept concessions.[49] On April 27 the producers decided, against the advice of their local representatives in Mexico, to apply for drilling permits on pre-constitutional lands, and to drill even if the permits were refused.[50] When the government demonstrated its willingness to use troops to prevent this "illegal" drilling, the companies discontinued the practice and once again turned to the State Department.

Claiming that they had exhausted local recourse, the oil producers appealed to the Department during July and August 1927 for "effective protection" to prevent the confiscation of their rights and properties in Mexico.[51] Secretary Kellogg agreed to meet with a committee representing the APPM on August 9 to hear their case. The committee, led by Stevens and General Palmer Pierce of Standard Oil, contended that the Mexican government had confiscated their properties by refusing to grant drilling permits on pre-constitutional lands, cancelling many of those already granted, and forcibly stopping the companies from drilling on their own lands. When the oil men urged vigorous action in their behalf, Kellogg stated flatly that the United States would neither break off diplomatic relations nor consider armed intervention in response to the actions of the Mexican government. The oil men denied that they were seeking intervention, but they also made

---

[44] Report of a Meeting of the APPM, held in New York City, Thursday, 2 p.m., December 30, 1926, NA812.6363/2118.

[45] Sheffield to Kellogg, January 13, 1927, NA812.6363/2123.

[46] Sheffield to Kellogg, January 14, 1927, NA812.6363/2127.

[47] *Diario Oficial,* January 17, 1927.

[48] Sheffield to Kellogg, January 25, 1927, NA812.6363/2148.

[49] Sheffield to Kellogg, April 6, 1927, NA812.6363/2235.

[50] Sheffield to Kellogg, May 11, 1927, Schoenfeld to Kellogg, June 25, August 8, 1927, NA812.6363/2263, 2296, 2339.

[51] Swain to Under Secretary Robert E. Olds, June 28, 1927, George S. Davison (President, Mexican Gulf Oil Company) to Kellogg, July 6, 1927, H. M. McIntosh (President, American International Fuel and Petroleum Company) to Kellogg, August 15, 1927, and Walker to Kellogg, August 27, 1927, NA812.6363/2324, 2327, 2346, 2352.

clear that they had no intention of subjecting the question of their rights to arbitration, which President Plutarco E. Calles had suggested in January 1927, and was supported in the United States Senate.[52] At this point, the secretary left the meeting, and the oil men continued their discussion with J. Reuben Clark, who was also present.[53]

Clark, who served as United States Commissioner on the United States–Mexican claims commissions and advisor on Mexican petroleum matters, was even less sympathetic to the plight of the companies than the secretary. When the oil men, for example, requested protection of their interests as stockholders in petroleum companies incorporated in Mexico, Clark conceded that the Department had followed such practice occasionally in the past, but he added that it could scarcely be defended as a recognized principle of international law. Realizing that the opportunity had arisen to present the companies with a *quid pro quo* in the interests of accountability, Clark offered to advise the secretary not to raise this issue in any future negotiations with the Mexican government, if the companies would furnish the Department with full information about the ownership of their properties in Mexico. The company spokesman agreed, but only after they expressed their firm hope that the Department would deliver strong representations to Mexico whenever a violation of their rights occurred.[54]

The companies' quest for "effective protection" collided with the Department's decision to reformulate its Mexican policy in an effort to break the impasse with Mexico and to obtain a settlement of outstanding questions. By the late summer and early fall of 1927 a consensus had been reached among higher level policy makers that the actions of the Mexican government did not constitute confiscation because the companies were still in physical possession of their properties, that the companies had not exhausted local remedies because there were still many *amparos* pending in the Mexican courts, and that despite their problems the companies were still taking oil out of Mexico. Moreover, they clearly understood that under such circumstances the use of force or even vigorous interference in Mexican domestic affairs would be counterproductive, and that an ideal solution satisfactory to all interested parties was probably unattainable.[55] Thus, by mid-1927, the Department decided to assume a more active role in pursuing a compromise solution of the oil controversy. This decision was in part reflected in the appointment of Dwight W. Morrow, a senior vice-president at

---

[52]Ellis, *Frank B. Kellogg and American Foreign Relations,* pp. 39-41; Robert F. Smith, *The U.S. and Revolutionary Nationalism in Mexico, 1916-1932* (Chicago, 1972) p. 252.

[53]Memorandum by Clark, August 9, 1927, NA812.6363/2384.

[54]*Ibid.*

[55]"Memorandum of the Current Petroleum Controversy with Mexico," by Clark, September 21, 1927, NA812.6363/2382; Memorandum on Mexico by Under Secretary Olds, July 27, 1927, cited in Smith, *The U.S. and Revolutionary Nationalism in Mexico, 1916-1932,* pp. 253-254.

J. P. Morgan Company, as Ambassador to Mexico in September 1927.[56]

By the time Morrow presented his credentials in October, both countries were disposed toward a practical settlement of the oil controversy. The
attitude of the ambassador and Under Secretary Robert E. Olds, who had
assumed full responsibility for Mexican affairs in early 1927, helped to assure
this outcome. Both men were sensitive to some of the major political problems confronting Calles, they opposed armed intervention or the use of force
to resolve political or financial problems, and they perceived Calles and his
colleagues as economic "moderates" who wanted to control rather than to
eliminate foreign enterprise in Mexico. Moreover, Morrow's previous personal
contact with Mexican officials and his close association with Thomas W.
Lamont, apparently convinced him that patience would be far more effective
than pressure in dealing with Mexican representatives. He also agreed with the
Under Secretary that the primary purpose of his mission was to negotiate a
practical compromise which would permit the production of oil to continue
and the government to obtain needed revenues.[57]

On his part, President Calles was no doubt concerned about the possible
adverse impact of a complete rupture between the companies and the government on his domestic reform program. He represented the "national development wing" of the "revolutionary family", which was committed to the
economic development of Mexico. This group wanted to reestablish the
nation's foreign credit and trade position, restore confidence in the monetary
system, revitalize commercial channels, and reconstruct the institutional
machinery of the national economy. At the same time, the Calles administration had to contend with the declining price of silver (one of Mexico's
chief exports), heavy expenditures due to internal disturbances (i.e., suppression of the Cristero rebellion), and overproduction of oil outside of Mexico.
The accomplishment of development objectives and the alleviation of internal
economic distress depended to some extent on an uninterrupted flow of tax
revenue from the petroleum industry, and the attraction of new capital to
Mexico.[58]

---

[56]It is interesting to note that Lamont strongly advised Morrow *against* accepting the
appointment as Ambassador; see Lamont to Morrow, August 5, 1927, and Morrow to
Lamont, September 21, 1927, Lamont Papers, Box 113.

[57]Memorandum by Olds, October 10, 1927, Kellogg to Morrow, November 16,
1927, NA812.6363/2378½, 2421; Morrow to Lamont, November 7, 1927, Lamont
Papers, Box 197; Morrow to Kellogg, November 8, 1927, *FRUS*, III, 187-193; Dwight
Morrow, "Who Buys Foreign Bonds?," *Foreign Affairs*, V (January, 1927), 217-232;
Smith, *The U.S. and Revolutionary Nationalism in Mexico, 1916-1932*, pp. 244-253;
Stanley R. Ross, "Dwight W. Morrow, Ambassador to Mexico," *The Americas*, XIV
(January, 1958), 273-289.

[58]The development program of the Calles group is discussed in Smith, *The United
States and Revolutionary Nationalism in Mexico, 1916-1932*, pp. 229-231, 255-259;
William P. Glade and Charles W. Anderson, *The Political Economy of Mexico: Politics
and Development Banking in Mexico* (Madison, 1963), pp. 112-119; Meyer, *México y
Estados Unidos en el conflicto petrolero (1919-1942)*, pp. 178, 186. For pertinent
comments by two pro-development officials in the Calles administration, see Alberto J.
Pani, *La política hacendaria y la Revolución* (México, 1926), and *Mi contribución al*

The petroleum controversy, however, generated a dangerous split within the Calles administration. Minister of Industry Luis Morones and Minister of Agriculture and Development Luis L. León favored forcing the concession issue, and seizing the recalcitrant companies if they failed to comply. Such action would have enabled Morones to strengthen C.R.O.M.'s political position, and would not have interfered in any significant way with the agrarian program under León's jurisdiction. These men were less concerned about financing national development than individuals such as Minister of Finance Alberto J. Pani; his successor in 1927, Luis Montes de Oca; and Minister of Foreign Affairs Aarón Saénz. By early 1927, the development advocates, who held most of the important positions in the Calles administration, prevailed; they rejected the aggressive policy toward the oil companies urged by Morones, and agreed that a "practical" solution of the petroleum controversy was necessary. Although Calles and his closest supporters had been willing to accept Morones into the administration as a means of consolidating labor support for the government, they were not willing to commit economic suicide by destroying the petroleum industry.[59]

As a result of discussions between President Calles and Ambassador Morrow held in early November, 1927, Calles accepted Morrow's suggestion that a judicial decision in one of the pending *amparo* cases against the Petroleum Law of 1925 affirming the Texas Oil Company decision of 1921, would constitute an important first step toward a solution. Calles promised satisfactory action by the Mexican Supreme Court, and on November 17, the court handed down a decision invalidating those sections of the Petroleum Law which limited oil exploration rights on pre-constitutional lands to fifty years.[60] It also stated that the rights of a surface owner who had performed positive acts could not be restricted, and that confirmation of such rights recognized them. Under the amended Petroleum Law, enacted December 29, surface owners were given an opportunity to accept confirmatory concessions of unlimited duration for lands developed prior to May 1, 1917; applications for which had to be made by January 11, 1929.[61]

nuevo regimen (México, 1936), *passim*; and Aaron Saenz, *La politica internacional de la Revolución: Estudios y documentos* (México, 1961), pp. 141-148.

[59]Information concerning the split in the Calles administration is contained in Ambassador Sheffield to Secretary Kellogg, January 4, 11, 1927, and Chargé Schoenfeld to Secretary Kellogg, September 30, 1927, NA812.6363/2112, 2129, 2372.

[60]It has been alleged that President Calles "dictated" the Supreme Court decision. Ellis, *Kellogg and American Foreign Relations*, p. 51, appears to accept this view, but the evidence is not very clear. In a letter to Under Secretary Olds, dated November 22, 1927, Ambassador Morrow stated that Justice Urbina, a member of the Supreme Court and friend of Calles who had previously served in the Executive Department, told him that all three branches of the Mexican government had desired for some time to make it clear that legitimate property rights would not be confiscated in Mexico. NA812.6363/2437 1/2. See also Meyer, *México y Estados Unidos*, p. 180. In any case, from the point of view of both the State Department and the oil companies, the substance of the decision was far more important than the way it was reached.

[61]A translation of the Court's decision in the Mexican Petroleum Company *amparo*

The Department regarded the Mexican government's action as a substantial adjustment of the concession controversy. Local oil company representatives agreed that a major issue had been settled,[62] but corporate managers in New York were not as enthusiastic. Dismissing the court decision as a "mere gesture," they expressed concern that under the amended law they would receive a new grant of rights subject to new conditions, rather than a confirmation of their original rights, and that by accepting confirmatory concessions they would be compelled to surrender other claimed rights. Morrow was willing to ask Calles to withdraw the amendments, if the producers thought that no legislation was better than what had been enacted, or if they could agree on an alternative. The producers divided on the issue, however, and they refused to commit themselves one way or the other. To still their apprehension, Morrow arranged for an exchange of letters between the Huasteca Petroleum Company and Minister Morones which contained an assurance to the effect that petitions for confirmatory concessions did not imply the renunciation of any pre-constitutional rights, and that they would operate as the recognition of such rights.[63]

When Mexican officials prepared to draft new administrative regulations in pursuance of the amended Petroleum Law, they invited the oil producers to present their views. A committee representing the companies and the APPM conferred with Mexican officials in February, 1928. Morrow remained in the background, taking no part in the proceedings, except to assure both sides that the other was acting in good faith. The oil men, concerned about the status of untagged lands (lands on which no development work had been undertaken), submitted a suggested draft of regulations to Morones, which in effect would have committed the Mexican government to recognize virtually every company claim to underdeveloped oil properties. Morones rejected the producer's suggestions as unacceptable. When he showed his own version to Morrow, however, the ambassador noted that it retained the restricted definition of positive acts which had been written into the Petroleum Law of 1925, and contained other provisions which he perceived as not complying with the Supreme Court decision of 1927.

Consequently, Morrow persuaded Morones to select one of his subordinates to engage in a series of informal conversations with Clark to work out revisions that could be accepted by all sides. In resolving the delicate matter

---

suit is printed in *FRUS*, 1927, III, 197-209; for text of the amendments to the Petroleum Law, see *Documents Relating to the Petroleum Law of Mexico of December 26, 1925, with Amendments of January 3, 1928.*

[62] Memorandum to Olds, by Morrow, November 30, 1927, NA812.6363/2429; Ellis, *Frank B. Kellogg and American Foreign Policy*, p. 51.

[63] The sequence of events described in this and the several succeeding paragraphs is based on the following: Morrow to W. L. Mellon (President, Gulf Oil Company), April 28, 1928, NA812.6363/2557 1/2; Morrow to Kellogg, March 6, 1928, *FRUS*, 1928, III, 298; J. Reuben Clark, "The Oil Settlement with Mexico," *Foreign Affairs*, VI (July, 1928), 600-614; and Stanley R. Ross, "Dwight Morrow and the Mexican Revolution," *Hispanic American Historical Review*, XXXVII (November, 1958), 506-528.

of untagged lands, Morones agreed to include in Article 152 of the amended regulations the exact language of the Bucareli understandings of 1923 concerning what constituted a positive act, while in a supplementary exchange of letters with Morones, Morrow accepted the principle that such acts did not include abstract intentions on the part of the surface owner.[64] On April 3, 1928, Morrow informed Olds that the companies retained whatever rights on untagged lands they had possessed on May 1, 1917, but at the same time he also stated that Clark, after exhaustively investigating the matter, believed that under Mexican law the Department could not successfully assert any claim to rights by surface owners on untagged lands.[65]

On March 27, 1928, the day the Mexican government issued the new petroleum regulations, the Department issued a statement announcing that a "practical conclusion" had been reached to the petroleum controversy.[66] A few of the members of the APPM informed the Department that they intended to apply for confirmatory concessions, but the larger companies continued to insist that they could not accept any solution short of an absolute confirmation of their rights. They criticized the oil settlement as defective because it sanctioned the grant of wide discretionary power contained in the regulations to the Mexican Department of Industry to determine proof of positive acts, abandoned American claimants to the mercy of Mexican courts and administrative agencies, and accepted the legality of the doctrine of positive acts. The nature of their response implied that they would not comply with the new regulations.[67]

A delegation representing the recalcitrant companies called at the Department on May 18, 1928, to discuss the matter with Clark, who had come from Mexico City for this purpose. The producers contended that their acceptance of the regulations would have a serious detrimental effect on their properties in Colombia and Venezuela. Clark replied that they were needlessly concerned, because if a concrete case of injury arose in those countries, the Department would take appropriate action. Assuming the offensive, he claimed that one of the reasons the Department had found it so difficult to resolve the concession controversy was the unwillingness of the companies fully to disclose what property they held in Mexico and how it had been obtained. The oil men asserted that it was extremely difficult in all cases to prove title, and they inquired whether the Department was acquiescing in nationalization by the Mexican government. Clark retorted that the "adoption by other countries of theories of nationalization is not our business; our only concern is with specific cases of injury and violations of legitimate

---

[64]Morrow to Morones, March 27, 1928, *FRUS,* 1928, III, 300.

[65]Draft of Memorandum for the Secretary, prepared by Chief of the Division of Latin American Affairs Stokely W. Morgan, May 29, 1929, NA812.6363/2642 1/2.

[66]The text of the press statement is printed in *FRUS,* 1928, III, 307.

[67]W. L. Mellon to Morrow, April 11, 1928, M. P. Williams (President, Tidal Oil Company) to Kellogg, April 12, 1928, Teagle, Frank Feuille (SOCAL), George O. Davison (President, Mexican Gulf Oil) and R. Burron (Island Oil Company) to Kellogg, April 27, 1928, NA812.6363/2545 1/2, 2546, 2558.

rights." At the conclusion of the meeting, the oil men asked if the Department would request further amendment of the regulations. Clark stated that this would be highly inadvisable, and he forewarned the companies that if they refused to accept the new regulations and file for confirmatory concessions within the allotted time period, they might never again have the opportunity.[58]

The Department adhered to this position throughout the remainder of 1928. All efforts by the producers and the APPM to persuade the Department to change its position were unavailing. By January 1929, those companies unwilling or unable to liquidate filed for confirmatory concessions. Both the United States and Mexico could claim limited victories; the former because it had successfully defended the principle that retroactive legislation was a violation of international law, and the latter because it had successfully maintained its sovereign right to control its own resources. Legally the oil companies stood roughly where they had been in 1923, but strategically their position had been eroded.

THE STRUCTURE OF CONSTRAINTS

In any decisional setting the behavior of policy makers is subject to a variety of constraints. These may be institutional (e.g., budgetary limitations), extra-institutional (e.g., the activity of pressure groups competing for policy preference), or individual (e.g., a particular actor's access to information or level of expertise). The collective impact of such constraints is usually to limit the options available to the policy maker, and to restrict his ability to bargain with other actors.[69] It is appropriate to survey the constraints affecting policy makers responsible for Mexican affairs and their relationship with the oil producers represented in the APPM.

The most important constraints were those deriving from general foreign policies. During the 1920s for instance, the Department made an effort to liquidate previous interventions in Latin America and to develop a policy of non-intervention with respect to the area. Although the policy evolved incrementally, and occasional aberrations occurred, the intent was deliberate. Keenly aware that military or political intervention could easily escalate into war or long-term occupation, and that the costs of such results would far exceed any possible benefits, few policy makers proved willing to support direct intervention in Latin American countries as a means of solving political or economic problems. What they preferred was a commercial policy that would promote legitimate United States interests abroad, without offending Latin American governments or acquiring burdensome and expensive commitments.[70] Whatever the reasons, policy makers accepted non-

[58]Memorandum of Conversation, by Chief of the Division of Latin American Affairs Arthur Bliss Lane, May 19, 1928, NA812.6363/2570 1/2.

[69]For a useful discussion of constraints on foreign policy decision-making, see William I. Bacchus, *Foreign Policy and the Bureaucratic Process: The State Department's Country Director System* (Princeton, 1974), pp. 210-215.

[70]Joseph S. Tulchin, *The Aftermath of War: World War I and U.S. Foreign Policy*

intervention as desirable, and as J. Reuben Clark told the oil producers in August 1927, this circumscribed the options available to the Department.[71]

The United States government's support for the principle of equal commercial opportunity during the 1920s is well known, but what is frequently overlooked is the fact that the Department's concern was for the totality of American interests abroad rather than particular firms or groups of firms. Policy makers understood that the Department could not become the advocate for any interest, in part because simple equity demanded impartiality, and in part because advocacy entailed too many political risks. In 1923, when the Sinclair Oil Company complained about the Department's lack of support for its efforts to obtain an oil concession in Persia, Secretary Hughes took the opportunity to define the Department's relationship with multinational corporations. "Our position," he wrote, "is that we are always ready to give appropriate support to our nationals in seeking opportunities for business enterprise abroad, but we do not undertake to make the government a party to the private interests in order to obtain particular concessions or intervene in favor of one American interest as against another."[72] Four years later, Under Secretary Olds, who worked within these parameters, was sharply critical of the oil producers' inability to understand that "the government is concerned with the protection of property rights as a whole in the international sense, and can not undertake to serve as advisory council [sic] for particular interests."[73]

This concern for the totality of American interests required Department

---

Toward Latin America (New York, 1971); Dana G. Munro, *Intervention and Dollar Diplomacy in the Caribbean, 1900-1921* (Princeton, 1964), and *The United States and the Caribbean Republics, 1921-1933* (Princeton, 1974). Munro and Tulchin agree that political and strategic motives were more important than economic ones in United States policy toward Latin America. Munro concludes that this was the case throughout the period 1900-1933, whereas Tulchin contends that after 1920, economic motives became increasingly important, but in response to bureaucratic and institutional imperatives rather than as the result of conscientiously formulated policy. A contrasting interpretation is offered in Smith, *The U.S. and Revolutionary Nationalism in Mexico, 1916-1932*, who argues that economic motives played a central role. According to his account, the United States sought to use its economic power to control the Mexican Revolution, and to maintain Mexico as a safe preserve for American private investment. He says that policy-makers and businessmen cooperated intimately to accomplish these objectives, but throughout the book he repeatedly concludes that the oil interests and other private investors had no success in influencing the State Department to do their bidding. For stimulating critical comments about the Smith and Tulchin books, see Richard M. Abrams, "United States Intervention Abroad: The First Quarter Century," *The American Historical Review,* LXXIX (February, 1974), pp. 95-102.

[71] Memorandum by Clark, August 9, 1927.

[72] Hughes to President Coolidge, November 8, 1923, *FRUS,* II, 717-718. See also Hughes' interpretation of the "open door policy" in his *Autobiographical Notes,* ed. by David J. Danelski and Joseph S. Tulchin (Cambridge, 1973), pp. 254-257.

[73] Olds to Morrow, May 1, 1928, NA812.6363/2558. Some scholars contend that the concept of impartiality in practice actually favored the larger, more powerful companies. For example, in Persia, according to Michael J. Hogan, "Informal Entente: Public Policy

officers to consider the potential impact of policy decisions on all affected groups. In the case of Mexico, several interests other than oil had to be taken into account. One of the most important was the ICBM. The bankers had a vital stake in Mexico, and thus a clear material incentive to compete for policy preference. During the course of the 1920s they worked out arrangements with the Mexican government to enable it to resume payments on its defaulted external debt, a large portion of which had been floated by United States investment firms. Repayment presupposed political stability in Mexico, and the uninterrupted flow of revenues from the petroleum industry into the Mexican Treasury. Consequently, the bankers firmly opposed armed intervention in Mexico. They also rejected policies which rested on the threat of ultimate force, or direct interference in Mexican domestic affairs, because of possible internal repercussions. They had little regard for the APPM's tactics, and intermittently tried to persuade the oil men to adopt a more flexible, less strident approach. From 1922 on, they stressed the wisdom of a practical compromise of oil controversies, and during the crisis of 1926-1927, they supported either arbitration or a Mexican supreme court decision as the most preferable means of settling the issues.[74] In short, the bankers constituted an effective countervailing weight to the urgent demands of the oil producers, and it is not difficult to understand why, when the Department decided on a compromise settlement, it selected Morrow to succeed Sheffield.

From another vantage point, the role of independent continental

---

and Private Management in Anglo-American Petroleum Affairs, 1918-1924," *The Business History Review*, XLVIII (Summer, 1974), p. 200, the State Department's lack of an even-handed policy favored Standard Oil, and was "undoubtedly a major factor in finally knocking Sinclair out of the Persian competition." Joan Hoff Wilson, *American Business & Foreign Policy 1920-1933* (Lexington, 1971), p. 199, sums up this view as follows: "Inevitably the policy of impartiality favored the largest of those [oil] interests, the ones in the best position to compete abroad for foreign oil fields. Being impartial toward unequals was equivalent as far as oil diplomacy was concerned, to being partial toward the strongest."

What these scholars fail to appreciate, however, is the fact that the concept of impartiality was more a policy orientation than it was a fixed and inflexible principle. The concept was supposed to increase the Department's flexibility in dealing with a widening array of problems generated by the activities of American companies operating abroad. For example, in applying the concept, policy-makers always maintained a distinction between "legitimate" and "reputable" firms on the one hand, and "illegitimate" and "disreputable" firms on the other. The apparent inconsistencies and contradictions which occurred in the pursuit of impartiality were in many cases attributable to forces and/or situations over which the State Department had little or no control: disparities in size and resources between firms, managerial "fatigue" or exceptional aggressiveness in particular firms, bureaucratic rivalries between U.S. executive departments, and unpredictability in host government actions and reactions.

[74] Morrow to Lamont, April 12, 1927, Lamont to Mexican Ambassador Manuel C. Téllez, May 16, 1927, Memorandum for Mr. A. L. Negrete, by Lamont, May 25, 1927, Memorandum for Lamont, by Vernon Munroe (J. P. Morgan Co. executive), enclosed in Munroe to Morrow, December 14, 1927, Lamont to J. P. Morgan, January 16, 1928, Lamont Papers, Boxes 192, 195, 196, 197; N. Stephen Kane, "Bankers and Diplomats: The Diplomacy of the Dollar in Mexico, 1921-1924," *The Business History Review*, XLVII (Autumn, 1973), 335-352.

producers is significant. Although they had no direct stake in Mexico, the independents had a sufficiently substantial material incentive to oppose State Department interference in Mexico on behalf of their multinational rivals. Organized in the Independent American Oil Producers Association, which represented about sixty percent of petroleum production in the United States, they campaigned for a tariff as a means of reducing the privileged status of crude oil imported from Mexico and equalizing a benefit enjoyed exclusively by their competitors. The logical extension of this argument was that any policy benefitting the APPM was a form of unfair "aid." Consequently, between 1920 and 1923, when the multinationals opposed the recognition of Obregón, the independents supported it; in 1926-1927, when the multinationals urged aggressive action as the best solution to Mexican' problems, the independents favored caution and compromise.[75]

Legislative sanction, an important and somewhat underestimated external constraint in foreign policy formulation, also played a role. During the 1920s foreign policy decisions were less frequently the product of executive-legislative bargaining than today; nevertheless, policy makers could scarcely afford to ignore the attitude of Congress. When the controversy over the export tax erupted in 1921, Senator Robert LaFollette, Republican of Wisconsin, introduced a resolution opposing the use of troops in the Mexican oil fields, but the controversy receded before the resolution made much headway. In 1926-1927, however, when it appeared to some observers that intervention in Mexico had become a real possibility, the Senate passed a resolution supporting arbitration of differences between the two countries,[76] and others inquiring about the role of the United States oil companies in Mexico and their relationship with the Department.[77] Moreover, both Houses held hearings which provided further evidence of widespread opposition to aggressive action in Mexico on behalf of the oil companies.[78] Thus, whatever sympathy certain legislators may have had for the plight of the multinationals was effectively offset, and policy makers no doubt discerned that there was no advantage to be gained from provoking either Congress or the public on the issue of Mexico.

In addition to these domestic constraints, American policy makers perceived no real competitive threat from non-American, particularly British-

---

[75] N. Stephen Kane, "American Businessmen and Foreign Policy: The Recognition of Mexico, 1920-1923," *Political Science Quarterly,* XC (Summer, 1975), 304-306; U.S. Senate, Committee on Foreign Relations, *Relations with Mexico: Hearings before a Sub-Committee of the Committee on Foreign Relations,* 69th Cong., 2d Sess. (Washington, 1927), *passim.*

[76] Senate Resolution introduced by Sen. Joseph T. Robinson (Ark.) and adopted in slightly amended form on January 25, 1927, *Cong. Record,* 69th Cong., 2d Sess., vol. 68, (pt. 2), pp. 1843, 2233.

[77] For example, Sen. Resolutions 330 and 367, introduced by Sen. Norris (Neb.) on January 21 and February 24, 1927, respectively, *ibid.*, pt. 3 and 5, pp. 2857-2858, 4642.

[78] U.S. Senate, *Relations with Mexico*; and U.S. House of Representatives, Committee on Foreign Affairs, *Conditions in Nicaragua and Mexico,* 69th Cong., 2d Sess. (Washington, 1927).

owned, petroleum companies in Mexico. Both El Aguila and La Corona joined the APPM when it was organized, and their representatives participated in all of the major negotiations conducted by the association with the Mexican government. Although El Aguila applied for confirmatory concessions on pre-constituional lands in mid-1926, these applications were either withdrawn or forgotten when the company's representatives signed the APPM members' agreement the following December not to apply for, accept, or recognize confirmatory concessions.[79] Thereafter, El Aguila advocated concerted action by APPM members to file *amparos* against the Petroleum Law and its administrative regulations, and it also pressed for the suspension of operations on the grounds that the resultant loss of revenue would compel the Mexican government to compromise.[80]

The role of British-owned firms cannot be separated from that of their home government. Here again, the State Department had little cause for alarm. Early in 1926, the British government officially notified Secretary Kellogg that it was prepared to support the United States position with regard to the Petroleum Law of 1925.[81] On several occasions, British diplomats suggested that as a means of resolving the oil controversy, the United States should request the Mexican government to call a special session of congress to amend the law, or should simply accept Mexico's theoretical claim to ownership of all subsoil deposits, while insisting on immediate confirmation of all pre-constitutional rights.[82] The Department never seriously considered these suggestions, but it did react to reports in 1926 indicating that the British government was encouraging British-owned firms to reach separate agreements with the Mexican government.[83] The Department instructed the United States Ambassador in London, Alanson B. Houghton, to inquire about this matter. He ascertained that the companies had reached

---

[79] Many firms in addition to El Aguila applied for confirmatory concessions during 1926. This was a critical period for the APPM, because the members of the association were unable to agree on how to respond to the Petroleum Law. The companies simply acted on the basis of their individual self-interest; they wanted to hedge against possible contingencies.

Embassy personnel were extremely concerned about this development. Schoenfeld, for example, believed that the companies' actions threatened to break their "hitherto solid ranks" and lead to a "stampede" detrimental to United States policy. Consequently, he "earnestly" requested the Department to urge all petroleum companies operating in Mexico and their home governments "not to yield or compromise" with the principles the U.S. was defending. Chargé Schoenfeld to Secretary Kellogg, October 14, 16, December 5, 1926, NA812.6363/1972, 1980, 2036.

[80] Evidence concerning El Aguila's position is contained in J. A. Assheton (Manager, El Aguila, Mexico) to General Avery D. Andrews (Aguila), January 3, 1927, enclosed in Sheffield to Kellogg, January 4, 1927, and Sheffield to Kellogg, January 26, 1927, NA812.6363/2113, 2142.

[81] British government Aide Mémoire, January 4, 1926, handed to Kellogg by British Ambassador Sir Esme Howard on January 5, 1926, NA812.6363/1662.

[82] Memorandum of Conversation, between Kellogg and Ambassador Howard, April 7, 1926, and Schoenfeld to Kellogg, reporting a conversation with the British Ambassador to Mexico, Ovey, September 18, 1926, NA812.6363/1819, 1949.

[83] Schoenfeld to Kellogg, October 11, 19, 20, 1926, NA812.6363/1975, 1976, 1977.

some kind of an agreement involving unspecified advantages in return for their acceptance of confirmatory concessions, but the embassy was reassured that the companies had committed no act "which would tend to nullify the principles on which the United States is basing its attitude."[84] When El Aguila withdrew its applications for confirmatory concessions in December 1926, the issue receded.

In general, then, the cooperative policies of British petroleum companies and the British government in Mexico relieved United States policy makers from any need to think in terms of special aid to American firms as a means of affording them leverage in a competitive struggle. On the other hand, the British government's strong support for a "practical" solution to the oil imbroglio created pressure that could not be ignored. The British Minister in Mexico, Esmond Ovey, made it clear to Ambassador Sheffield that if the United States succeeded in securing recognition by Mexico of the principles it was defending in the oil controversy, British companies would benefit, but if the United States failed, those companies could not be expected to forego the "advantages to be derived from practical accommodation to the law."[85]

Organization leaders are no less subject to constraints on their behavior than are policy makers. The character of the constraints is considerably different, however, because they relate primarily to organizational maintenance and enhancement.[86] Generally speaking, the structure of the APPM relieved Stevens and his executive committee from the obligation of dealing with some of the fundamental problems which ordinarily occupy the time and energy of organizational leaders. For all practical purposes, the APPM was a single-issue organization with a secure source of funds and a homogeneous membership which perceived the threat posed by Mexican legislation in a similar way. This helped to reduce one common source of organizational strain and internal disagreement, by making it unnecessary for the APPM's leaders to search for effective incentives to attract additional members. Moreover, it enabled the APPM to adopt an unequivocal position and to prosecute it vigorously, because there was no need to generalize in order to accommodate the interests and demands of a diverse membership.

This does not mean that the APPM's activities were always characterized by internal harmony. Common perception of problems and objectives is one thing, agreement concerning tactics is another. The members of the APPM in fact frequently disagreed over how best to respond to the actions of

---

[84] Ambassador Houghton to Kellogg, December 1, 1926, NA812.6363/2038. This reaffirmed the statement made by Sir William Tyrrell, British Permanent Undersecretary for Foreign Affairs, about a month earlier: "British policy in Mexico is to maintain a united front with the United States." Ambassador Houghton to Kellogg, November 12, 1926, NA711.12/788.

[85] Schoenfeld to Kellogg, December 9, 1926, NA812.6363/2047.

[86] The best recent work on the subject of organizations is James Q. Wilson, *Political Organizations* (New York, 1973), esp. pp. 30-56, 78-94, 305-347.

the Mexican government,[87] and no doubt how best to present and to pursue their case with the State Department. Unfortunately, the fragmentary records which are available do not permit an assessment of Stevens' success in brokering these disagreements. It is clear, however, that when the level of discord became sufficiently pronounced, as it did in 1926 during the negotiations between the oil men and Mexican representatives over the petroleum regulations, the result was either a decision to take no action, or an effort to shift responsibility to the State Department. Thus, concern about internal disharmony and the need to eliminate it constituted a significant constraint on the leaders of the APPM, even though it was considerably more homogeneous than many organizations of its kind.

Effective organizational representation usually requires that the group's leaders maintain the credibility of their position with policy makers. The executive committee of the APPM no doubt found this task extremely difficult. From 1917 on, corporate managers of the oil companies claimed that each new piece of legislation enacted by the Mexican government with respect to the petroleum industry confiscated their rights and properties. However, the more they insisted that they were the victims of confiscation, the less they were able to demonstrate persuasively that they had suffered any concrete injury. The discrepancy between their repeated claims and the actualities of Mexican legislation progressively eroded their credibility. In the end, they elevated their position to a matter of inflexible principle, but the State Department was neither ready nor willing to accept it as legitimate.

CONCLUSIONS

Robert A. Dahl has defined influence as a relationship among actors in which "one actor induces other actors to act in some way they would not otherwise act."[88] If this definition is accepted as reasonably accurate, it appears that the oil companies failed to exert effective influence on the foreign policy process. The outcome was largely the result of the structure of the decision-making system. Generally speaking, the wider the system, the more vulnerable it becomes to external pressure. The greater the number of agencies sharing responsibility for the formulation and selection of policy alternatives, the more numerous are the points of access available to those

---

[87]In early 1926, for example, an APPM committee formed to discuss oil matters with representatives of the Mexican government seriously disagreed over whether or not the association should submit to Minister Morones a draft of administrative regulations necessary to implement the Petroleum Law. The chairman of the committee, Swain of Jersey Standard, insisted that no regulations could be drawn up in conformity with the law that could possibly protect the companies' pre-constitutional rights. When the members of the committee voted in favor of submitting a draft, Swain denounced the action as compromising the position of the companies, and he resigned from the committee. Sheffield to Kellogg, March 26, 27, 1926, NA812.6363/1812, 1815. In fact, Sheffield frequently urged vigorous action on behalf of the companies on the grounds that it would help to unify as well as strengthen them viz-à-viz the Mexican government.

[88]Dahl, Modern Political Analysis (Englewood Cliffs, 1963), p. 40.

seeking influence. As the points of access proliferate, so do the opportunities for exerting influence, especially if representatives from one agency or another attempt to utilize input from domestic sources as leverage in the bargaining process. In the two cases analyzed, responsibility for the decisions pertaining to Mexico was confined to the State Department, and within that organization to relatively few individuals who possessed a high degree of decision-making autonomy. At the same time, a variety of constraints sharply circumscribed their ability to select alternatives.

Keeping Dahl's definition in mind, it seems reasonable to conclude that the State Department effectively influenced the oil companies. The available evidence reveals, for example, that the companies were firmly opposed to engaging in direct negotiations with the Mexican government which might involve discussion of the status of their vested rights. The APPM, however, was unable to sustain this position. Given the Department's stress on direct negotiations and the necessity for investors to exhaust local recourse, along with the Mexican government's open willingness to negotiate, the companies had little choice.

What then, explains the fact that the State Department exchanged a series of lengthy notes with the Mexican government concerning the alleged retroactivity of provisions of the Petroleum Law of 1925?[89] These notes reflected the Department's long-standing commitment to the concept of fair treatment of United States citizens and their capital abroad in the fields of trade and investment within the framework of generally accepted principles of international law. The Department would have defended the principle of non-retroactivity, for instance, irrespective of any demands or pressure from the oil companies. Such action was standard operational practice, and cannot be adduced as evidence that the oil companies exerted influence over the policy process.

The setting within which Mexican policy was formulated in the 1920s involved at least four sets of actors: high-level policy makers in the Department, Embassy personnel, corporate managers in New York, and local company representatives in Mexico City. My analysis has revealed a curious inverse relationship among them. Whereas the embassy, with the exception of Morrow and Clark, adopted a harder position toward Mexico than did policy makers in the Department, local company representatives proved more flexible in their approach than the corporate managers. This was probably the result of the way each set of actors perceived its primary objective, and differential exposure to constraints. With respect to the first, the Department's goal was to obtain a settlement of the Mexican problem, but the embassy's was to afford protection to United States nationals and their property; corporate managers wanted to maintain a global profit-making

---

[89]The exchanges between the U.S. and Mexico for the period November 1925 to November 1926 are conveniently collected in *Rights of American Citizens in Certain Oil Lands in Mexico*, Senate Document 96, 69th Cong., 1st Sess., and *Supplement* (Washington, 1926); other relevant notes are printed in the appropriate volumes of *FRUS*.

enterprise, while their local representatives struggled to find specific legal ways for the companies to maneuver. With respect to the second, the structure of constraints affecting policy makers apparently did not have a similar impact on the embassy. Local company representatives, however, were more directly exposed than corporate managers to the political and economic imperatives confronting the Mexican government. Whatever the reasons, the pattern seems clear. Whether it was unique to the cases studied or recurrent in other settings is a question that cannot be answered without additional research.

Decision For Federal Control:
Wilson, McAdoo, and the Railroads, 1917

K. Austin Kerr

AT the end of 1917, almost nine months after the American declaration of war on the Central Powers, President Woodrow Wilson announced to the American public that the federal government was assuming the control and operation of the nation's railroad industry.[1] The President told the nation and Congress that he and his advisers had reached the decision to nationalize this basic industry because, despite its best efforts, private management had failed to provide the efficient railroad operation which the war effort desperately required. In an address to Congress early in 1918, the President had explained the need to unify and coordinate both the operation and financing of the railroad industry. "Unless it be under a single and unified direction," he noted, "the whole process of the nation's action is embarrassed." Wilson assured the Congress that federal control of the industry would protect the interests of all parties concerned, while better serving the interests of the nation in mobilizing for war.[2]

The administration's announcement of federal control of the railroads came as no surprise to informed Americans. It followed in the wake of innumerable reports of failures in the operation of trunkline eastern railroads in moving goods sorely needed both by an economy at war and by the armies at the western front. During the autumn and early winter of 1917, journalists had reported with increasing frequency stories of goods piled high at Atlantic piers awaiting shipment, of loaded freight cars backed up in the countryside along lines radiating from coastal ports, and of war material unloaded on the ground miles from embarkation points. Congestion on eastern trunklines had become so acute, reporters informed their read-

Mr. Kerr is instructor of history in Ohio State University.

[1] For an analysis of this problem in a larger context see K. Austin Kerr, "American Railroad Politics, 1914-1920" (doctoral dissertation, University of Pittsburgh, 1965).

[2] James D. Richardson, ed., *A Compilation of the Messages and Papers of the Presidents* (20 vols. plus 5 unnumbered supplements from 1897-1929, New York, 1909 to 1929), unnumbered supplement for the years 1917-1921, pp. 8418-20.

ers, that rail traffic as far west as Pittsburgh was being impeded.[3] When winter weather appeared and coal shortages developed in some regions, the fuel administration and the mining industry explained that the cause of the problem was not at the mines but in the distribution facilities.[4] In short, by November 1917, operating functions of the railroad industry were in a state of crisis.

Standard accounts of American economic history have noted that this transportation crisis led the Wilson administration to decide upon federal control of the industry. "The inability of the railroads to cope successfully with the exigencies of war needs," one account argues, "and the absolute necessity of subordinating transportation facilities to the one purpose of winning the war, brought about this step."[5] A recent popular introductory text explains that "the snow and freezing weather of December 1917 precipitated a total collapse of internal transportation."[6] There is no doubt that the transportation crisis of 1917 was real and severe and that it helped to create the situation in which the President reached his decision for nationalization; but, the breakdown in railroad operations alone does not fully explain why the Wilson administration chose to nationalize the industry as part of the wartime mobilization effort.

In order to understand the decision to nationalize the industry the historian must appreciate that the crisis in operation occurred in a political and ideological context shaped by developments of the Progressive era. Obviously, the men responsible for the decision brought the preconceptions and assumptions of the prewar years to bear upon their actions during these war months. The Wilson administration not only considered federal control desirable as a potential means of solving the crisis in the routine of railroad operation, but leading officials also saw the nationalization of the industry as an expedient and desirable means of resolving the political and economic conflicts surrounding the industry. In this sense the decision for federal control should be viewed as part of a total conception, as an expression of the efficiency ideology developed more or less clearly during the Progressive era, a conception that American society would be improved if all of its component interests functioned harmoniously together.[7] At the end of

[3] George Rothwell Brown, "Munitions in Danger," Washington *Post*, Nov. 15, 1917; New York *Evening Mail*, Dec. 5, 1917.

[4] National Coal Association, *Daily Digest*, Nov. 26, 1917; U. S. Senate, Subcommittee of the Committee on Manufacturers, *Hearings, Shortage Coal*, 65 Cong., 2 Sess. (Washington, 1918), 41-42.

[5] Harold Underwood Faulkner, *American Economic History* (7th ed., New York, 1954), 591.

[6] John M. Blum and others, *The National Experience* (New York, 1963), 573.

[7] Samuel Haber, *Efficiency and Uplift: Scientific Management in the Progressive Era, 1890-1920* (Chicago, 1964), 74, 119-20.

1917, the men who participated in the process of making decisions in the federal government concerning the railroad industry clearly saw nationalization as a desirable and expedient means of eliminating political conflict between economic interests. Almost instinctively, they believed that with this elimination of conflict a new, efficient industry, working together for the common purpose of winning the war, would emerge. These men, including Wilson and Secretary of the Treasury William G. McAdoo, viewed the transportation crisis as a dual affair which involved both operating problems and seemingly irreconcilable political conflicts. Out of this dual crisis a vision emerged of a nationalized railroad industry, efficiently and harmoniously directed by the federal government.

Immediately upon American entry, the war began to impinge on the political conflict over economic issues which had surrounded the railroad industry throughout the Progressive era. This new factor of the war enhanced uncertainties and brought an element of instability to the politics of railroad transportation. During the Progressive era, political bargaining issues over railroad rates had arisen between economic interests within the business and the agricultural community; chiefly these had involved contests between railroad companies and shippers over general rate levels and arguments among shippers over relative, competitive rate charges. Moreover, by the time the war broke out, organized railroad labor was also actively pursuing its own interests through essentially political means. Naturally, labor's concerns brought a new dimension to the conflict between railroads and shippers.[8] The American entry into the war intensified existing disagreements, both within this segment of the business community and between it and labor, by introducing a new element—the need to mount an effective, economic mobilization effort.

The introduction of the new factor into the conflicting interests surrounding the transportation network came initially in the spring of 1917 when railroad management asked the Interstate Commerce Commission to increase freight rates by an average of fifteen percent. This request, triggering the Fifteen Per Cent Case,[9] followed on the heels of similar management efforts to obtain substantial general increases in freight rates. In 1910

[8] Not only was labor more actively using the strike weapon after 1910 but also in 1916, through threatening a general strike, the rail unions had successfully achieved enactment of the Adamson Eight Hour Act. James W. Kerley, "The Failure of Railway Labor Leadership: A Chapter in Railroad Labor Relations" (doctoral dissertation, Columbia University, 1959), 53-59; Philip Taft, *The A. F. of L. in the Time of Gompers* (New York, 1957), 464. Any gains by labor increased the pressure of the railroads to obtain rate increases; this reinforced the antipathy of shippers toward organized labor.

[9] *Ex Parte 57.* The records of this case are housed in the General Services Administration Warehouse in Franconia, Virginia.

the railroads had asked the ICC for increases averaging ten percent, only to see the Commission dissuaded by a united front of shippers led by Louis Brandeis with his famous arguments for scientific management. In 1913 and 1914 railroad management had again appealed to the ICC for increases in rate payments, increases which the Commission only partly, regionally, and seemingly reluctantly granted.[10] In all of these cases the chief argument of the railroads had been that they needed additional income in order to secure the capitalization necessary to construct modern facilities designed to improve operating efficiency and customer service. After 1914, railroad management was quick to point out that in any time of national emergency the country would need adequate transportation facilities.

Throughout 1917 the railroads continued the rate battles of the Progressive era, using the war to promote the argument that additional funds were essential to improve operating efficiency and service. In March the carriers requested that the ICC quickly approve of a fifteen-percent rate increase. They not only pointed out that the Supreme Court's decision on the Adamson Eight Hour Act would increase their expenses tremendously but also that wartime conditions themselves actually required a rate advance. Opening the case, Samuel Rea, president of the Pennsylvania Railroad, asserted that "the conditions of the railroads today present a menace to the country. . . . It is absolutely essential that the railroads of the country . . . fulfill their duties to meet what we all believe is coming—a crisis in our history. . . ." Under the current rate structure, management's attorneys soon added, the industry could not attain the efficiency so acutely needed in wartime.[11] Rail executives had, in fact, encountered increasing difficulty in obtaining capitalization loans at reasonable interest rates through normal channels.[12] The carriers, therefore, asked the Commission to enable them to fund capital improvements from current income derived from higher rates.

Important shipper organizations, however, vehemently opposed the railroads' plea. Led by agricultural groups and oil shippers who did not enjoy access to pipelines, an *ad hoc* Shippers' National Conference was formed in order to oppose the rate increases. The dominant theme of the shipper

[10] Brief accounts of these cases appear in Robert H. Wiebe, *Businessmen and Reform: A Study of the Progressive Movement* (Cambridge, 1962), 85-88, 141.

[11] *Ex Parte 57*, vol. 1, p. 4; "Petition Before the Interstate Commerce Commission," filed March 23, 1917, *Ex Parte 57*, vol. 1; Interstate Commerce Commission, *31st Annual Report* (Washington, 1917), 55-56. Under a Special Committee on National Defense of the American Railroad Association, popularly known as the Railroads' War Board, the carriers were cooperating with the President's Advisory Commission to the Council of National Defense to coordinate the transportation requirements of mobilization.

[12] Daniel Willard to H. E. Coffin, June 22, 1917, Records of the Council of National Defense, Record Group 62, file 1-T1 (National Archives).

counterargument in the ICC hearings impugned the validity of the railroads' justification for rate increases.[13] Clifford Thorne and Luther M. Walter, representing the Shippers' National Conference, presented the principal argument. Thorne, who had served as chairman of the Iowa Railroad Commission and as president of the National Association of Railway and Utilities Commissioners but who was now in private law practice, insisted that there was no emergency in railroad earnings. The carriers, he pointed out, thought only of expenses exclusive of the increased tonnage resulting from wartime prosperity. Projecting income figures for the first four months of 1917, these shippers contended that the railroad industry anticipated the best profit-year ever, save 1916. Cross-examining E. P. Ripley of the Santa Fe, Walter forced an admission of expected fifteen- or sixteen-percent profits for that line in 1917. Thorne and Walter clearly argued that the railroads were using the war as an excuse to pressure for unneeded and unwarranted private economic gains.[14]

The Commission, announcing its decision in June, denied the full rate increases that the carriers had proposed. The Commission's majority report emphasized the same points which the shippers had used to challenge the railroads' arguments: the facts of economic prosperity did "not suggest a country-wide emergency" or the impending corporate economic doom which the carriers predicted. In order to allow for the increased labor expenses caused by the eight-hour law, the Commission granted the railroads increased rates on hauling coal, coke, and iron ore. These advances, the ICC explained, would provide an additional annual income to the railroads of about $100,000,000. The ICC qualified its June decision, however, by announcing that due to unique uncertainties caused by the war the carriers could at a future date request a reopening of the entire case.[15] This announcement was to have sweeping consequences in less than six months.

Throughout the summer and autumn of 1917, railroad management frequently complained, both publicly and privately, about the Commission's refusal to grant the full rate requests. Management continued to insist that the pressures of financing the war, especially the extraordinary borrowing demands of the federal government, made securing essential credit virtually impossible for the carriers.[16] In addition, the railroads reported that their

---

[13] "Report of the Traffic Committee," Illinois Manufacturers' Association, *Proceedings of the 20th Annual Meeting* (1917), 56-57; "Shippers Need Service More Than Low Rates," *Railway Age Gazette*, LXII (April 20, 1917), 818-19, 838.

[14] "Advanced Rate Case," *Traffic World*, XIX (June 16, 1917), 1336, 1347-51.

[15] ICC, *31st Annual Report*, 56-57.

[16] Press release of Samuel Rea, June 30, 1917, William G. McAdoo Papers (Manuscript Division, Library of Congress).

operating expenses were increasing at a faster pace than revenues. If this trend persisted, Fairfax Harrison of the Southern Railroad wrote to Senator Francis G. Newlands, chairman of the Committee on Interstate Commerce, it would impair operating efficiency and leave no funds available for developing and maintaining service facilities. Harrison told the Senator that this matter was causing rail executives grave concern, for the situation was rapidly passing out of control.[17]

Meanwhile, in the autumn of 1917 the members of railroad brotherhoods were growing restive. They had succeeded in gaining Supreme Court approval of the Adamson Act in the spring, but quick management application of the law had not followed. Most of the men still had to work a six-day week and a ten-hour day.[18] Of more immediate importance to the unions, wartime conditions were rapidly escalating the cost of living. The drop in real wages created enormous pressure from among the ranks of the unions to obtain substantial wage increases at least to meet the inflation.[19] Despite the fact that labor leaders earlier had assured Wilson that there would be no strikes during the war, the feelings of the rank-and-file led to reports in management circles of an imminent demand for twenty-five to fifty-percent wage increases.[20] This threatened management with an added financial burden when executives already considered their fiscal problems critical.

These financial pressures encouraged the railroads to seek a rehearing of the Fifteen Per Cent Case. Following an impressive publicity campaign in which the carriers argued that without a substantial rate increase the transportation demands resulting from the war could not be met, the ICC granted the railroads a reopening of the case.[21] In the testimony which began on November 5, management attempted to verify its public statements. The executives reiterated their now familiar arguments: inflated prices and wages called for an upward adjustment in freight rates lest the financial solvency of the corporations be destroyed; because of the extraordinary borrowing demands of the federal government, railroad loans were unavailable and the sale of stocks impossible; and new income was necessary immediately or the companies would have to forget maintenance

---

[17] Fairfax Harrison to Francis G. Newlands, Sept. 13, 1917, Record Group 62, file 1-A1, 1-T1.
[18] H. D. Wolf, *The Railroad Labor Board* (Chicago, 1927), 32-33.
[19] George J. Stevenson, "The Brotherhood of Locomotive Engineers and Its Leaders, 1865-1920" (doctoral dissertation, Vanderbilt University, 1954), 397.
[20] "A New Movement by the Railroad Brotherhoods," *Railway Age Gazette*, LXIII (Nov. 9, 1917), 832.
[21] George B. McGinty to George Stuart Patterson, Oct. 23, 1917, *Ex Parte 57*, vol. 43.

standards. The only alternative to higher rates, some rail leaders informed the ICC, was more drastic action: either federal subsidy or government ownership.[22]

The most active shipper opposition came from agricultural groups. Initially their spokesmen feared that the Commission would be sympathetic toward the carriers' arguments; but skillful cross-examination by the shippers' counsel, Thorne, helped to prevent a railroad victory. In the hearings, Thorne forced an admission from Rea that the Pennsylvania Railroad enjoyed a good credit rating. Thorne then proceeded to demonstrate that rail earnings as measured by all normal indicators were at an all-time high. Therefore, he concluded, there was no emergency in the rate structure; rather, there was an emergency in the nation's financial markets. Thorne asserted that management's difficulties in obtaining capital were a result of the war, not of poor earnings, and hence were unrelated to rate levels. To demonstrate his contention Thorne pointed out that municipal bonds had declined more in price than those of eastern railroad corporations.[23]

In his closing statement Thorne revealed his solution for the railroads' financial and operational problems: federal operation. This would resolve the political conflict over rates which had plagued the industry constantly since 1910, and there would be no need for repeated requests for general rate increases because the federal government could both command credit and unify the transportation system for maximum operating efficiency.[24]

Thorne's suggestion was strikingly similar to the thinking of certain members of the ICC. In October Chairman Henry C. Hall had criticized the private operators for not achieving maximum efficiency. Then, while testimony was underway, Hall had pointed out that the carriers' operating income per mile of track in 1917 compared very favorably to revenue in past years.[25] Moreover, in November several commissioners, especially Charles C. McChord, had been working with Secretary of the Treasury McAdoo on a plan of federal operation. Therefore, after hearing the arguments, the ICC once again refused to grant the fifteen-percent rate increases. Instead, on December 5, it submitted a special report to Congress

[22] *Ibid.*, vol. 44, pp. 6797, 6302, 6313, 6433-34; *ibid.*, vol. 45, pp. 7601-03; "Railroad Rates and National Defense," *Railway Age Gazette*, LXIII (Nov. 9, 1917), 532.

[23] *Ex Parte 57*, vol. 54, pp. 7654-55, 7378.

[24] Clifford Thorne, *Argument Before the Interstate Commerce Commission in the Fifteen Per Cent Case, Nov. 20, 1917* (n.p.), 4, 17, 25; Clifford Thorne, "Government Operation of American Railroads," *American Cooperative Journal*, XII (Jan. 1918), 205; John Snure, "Washington and the Farmer," *ibid.*, XII (Nov. 1917), 88. Thorne's argument was a logical extension of the shippers' commitment to scientific-management principles begun under Brandeis' leadership in 1910.

[25] Henry C. Hall to Harrison, Nov. 7, 1917, William G. McAdoo Papers; see also Hall's speech to the National Association of Railway and Utilities Commissioners, *Proceedings of the 29th Annual Convention* (1917), 4.

which argued in favor of unified railroad operation.[26] This special report publicly initiated the movement which directly resulted in federal control by the end of December.

Ultimately, President Wilson had to act upon the Commission recommendations. After listening to advice and reacting to pressures from many interests, he reached his decision in favor of federal control and operation. This came after both the food and fuel administrations, no doubt reflecting the sentiments of important sectors of the shipper community, recommended unified rail operation.[27] The military departments also sought radical federal action to end the operating crisis.[28] But perhaps the most important sources of pressure on the President came from progressive confidants. For example, McAdoo, on the day after the ICC's special report, urged Wilson to act "promptly and decisively" in favor of federal control. Believing federal control to be desirable from all points of view, McAdoo was convinced that unified operation would be most efficient. Not only would federal control provide better service, he pointed out, but also it would eliminate the seemingly endless arguments over rate increases. McAdoo was confident that control of the network would save vast sums of money because the government could pay for new capital improvements from the economies of unification, thus improving operation and further reducing costs. No longer would the railroads' publicly aired financial woes disturb Wall Street; therefore, McAdoo argued, federal operation would in general expedite financing the entire war effort. Moreover, he viewed the prospect of federal control as a grand, lasting demonstration of the values of governmental intervention in the public interest.[29]

[26] Interstate Commerce Commission, *32nd Annual Report* (Washington, 1918), 4-9; see also "Unification of Operation," *Traffic World*, XX (Dec. 8, 1917), 1189; "Government Takes Railroad Control," *ibid.* (Dec. 29, 1917), 1382.

[27] *Hearings, Shortage of Coal*, 21; Frank M. Surface, *The Grain Trade During the World War: Being a History of the Food Administration Grain Corporation and the United States Grain Corporation* (New York, 1928), 240-41.

[28] Newton D. Baker to General John Biddle, Nov. 30, 1917, Records of the War Department, General Staff Records, Record Group 165, no. 14424 (National Archives); E. David Cronon, ed., *The Cabinet Diaries of Josephus Daniels* (Lincoln, 1963), 243.

[29] William G. McAdoo to Woodrow Wilson, Dec. 6, 1917, William G. McAdoo Papers. Despite the fact that their general ideas coincided at many points, there is no evidence to suggest that McAdoo and Thorne were engaged in any kind of direct communication with each other. McAdoo, however, did receive advice from progressives. Frederic C. Howe was enthused by the prospects of efficient federal operation. See Howe, "Memorandum for Placing the Transportation Agencies of the Nation in Trust for the Nation and the Security Holders," Wilson-McAdoo series, Dec. 13, 1917 file, William G. McAdoo Papers. Secretary of Commerce William Redfield had suggested a more "affirmative," positive federal regulation of the industry. Redfield to McAdoo, Oct. 25, 1917, Robert W. Wooley Papers (Manuscript Division, Library of Congress). Although at the time of his letter to Wilson, McAdoo apparently had not formulated his ideas precisely in terms of practical application, he was in direct personal contact with members of the ICC. See "Unification of Operation," *Traffic World*, XX (Dec. 8, 1917), 1189.

In December of 1917 it appeared that federal operation indeed would eliminate not only the operating crisis but also the bargaining conflicts surrounding the industry. Most of the major economic groups concerned either openly advocated federal control or could be easily persuaded that it was desirable. The agricultural shippers, led by Thorne, had been the first to call for federal operation. Since 1910, these shippers had been committed to the principle of reforms in efficiency as a device to avoid rate increases; war mobilization offered an obvious chance to see those reforms implemented. Moreover, the coal industry desired firm federal direction if not outright operation of the railroads in order to improve shipping conditions.[30] Among the major shippers, only the Chicago Association of Commerce and the Illinois Manufacturers Association were openly suspicious of federal control, but even they thought unified private operation desirable.[31] The railroad brotherhoods, however, supported government railroad operation. The unions were convinced that a federal response to the crisis provided an opportune time to obtain wage advances and the full implementation of the eight-hour day. The brotherhoods anticipated sympathetic treatment because even before Wilson had called for federal operation he had created a special railroad-wage commission headed by Secretary of the Interior Franklin K. Lane. Clearly, if the federal government were operating the carriers, it would be obligated to accept the Lane Commission's recommendations.[32]

The railroads themselves were the most active of the private groups attempting to influence the President's decision. Railroad management never publicly acknowledged the existence of an operating crisis; its spokesmen reiterated the line that "the American railroad system has not broken down." But privately, railway executives confessed dismay at operating conditions and the possibility of correcting them through private means. Both Daniel Willard of the Baltimore and Ohio, and Rea of the Pennsylvania pinned their hopes for continued private operation on large-scale federal aid.[33] After the announcement of the decision for federal control, Willard wrote that "if I had been in the President's position, I should have done exactly the same as he did under all the circumstances."[34] McAdoo later

---

[30] J. H. Wheelwright, President of the Consolidation Coal Company, to Senator John Walter Smith, Dec. 20, 1917, Records of the United States Railroad Administration, Record Group 14, file 3-0 (National Archives)

[31] *Chicago Commerce*, XIII (Dec. 27, 1917), 4; John M. Glenn to Charles E. Fuller, Dec. 17, 1917, Records of the House of Representatives, Record Group 233, file 65A-H6.10 (National Archives).

[32] "The Railroad Problem," *Traffic World*, XX (Dec. 15, 1917), 1274.

[33] Rea to Willard, Dec. 21, 1917; Willard to Rea, Dec. 23, 1917, Record Group 62, file 1-A1, 1-T1

[34] Willard to Hale Holden, Jan. 3, 1918, Record Group 62, file 1-A1, 1-T1.

reported that railroad management was relieved when the decision for federal control was announced.[35]

In early December, however, railroad management offered the President its own program to relieve the emergency. Politically, the executives appealed to the administration to support rate increases. Furthermore, the corporation leaders sought to use federal credit facilities and to obtain priority production orders for new freight equipment. To solve operating problems they suggested the appointment of a single federal traffic manager to coordinate all war shipments plus a suspension of the antitrust statutes to allow full-scale private pooling. The railroad leaders presented this program in personal conferences with the President and with Senator Newlands. The latter was reported ready to introduce the necessary legislation.[36]

In his discussions with rail executives, however, Wilson, following McAdoo's advice, argued the advantages of federal operation. He reminded the executives that federal, not private, administration could best unify the industry. Federal control offered both a solution to operating problems and to political conflict over rates. Under federal operation, he told management leaders, state regulatory commissions could not impede the implementation of reforms that would effect greater efficiency. Moreover, the federal government could best command the loyalty and cooperation of labor. When the railroad leaders expressed concern over continuation of corporate income, Wilson assured them of federal financial guarantees similar to those used in Great Britain.[37] The President had convinced Willard, at least, that wartime federal control would most fairly guard the rights of private property while subordinating those rights to the public interest of winning the war.[38]

With these arguments Wilson had secured at least the acquiescence of railroad management to his decision for federal control. Thus, by mid-December, the President seemingly had hit upon a solution to the dual crises of operation and political conflict. Federal administration of a unified and coordinated transportation network seemed at the time a desirable means of reforming an important part of the American economic system in order to

[35] William G. McAdoo, *Crowded Years* (Boston, 1931), 461.

[36] Rea to Willard, Dec. 21, 1917; Rea to Board of Directors of the Pennsylvania Railroad, Dec. 18, 1917 (mimeographed); Willard to Rea, Dec. 23, 1917, Record Group 62, file 1-A1, 1-T1; Harrison to Newlands, Dec. 10, 1917, William G. McAdoo Papers; Harrison to Wilson, Dec. 13, 1917, Record Group 62, file 1-A1, 1-T1; Joseph Tumulty to Wilson, Dec. 10, 1917, Joseph Tumulty Papers (Manuscript Division, Library of Congress).

[37] Rea to Board of Directors of the Pennsylvania Railroad, Dec. 18, 1917 (mimeographed); Rea to Willard, Dec. 21, 1917, Record Group 62, file 1-A1, 1-T1. In January the administration's specific proposal for financial guarantees involved averaging each corporation's income for 1916-1917 and paying the result as a "standard return."

[38] Willard to Rea, Dec. 23, 1917, Record Group 62, file 1-A1, 1-T1.

make it efficient. McAdoo, for instance, justified the decision to a congressional committee as an action which, by stabilizing credit and precluding the need for rate increases, would tremendously benefit the entire economy.[39] Social harmony, not political conflict, it seemed to these men in the winter of 1917-1918, would follow almost automatically from federal control. Unfortunately, while solving the operating crisis, the practical decisions of efficiently administering the railroads augmented rather than reduced political conflict. Within six months, most of the nation's shippers would be thoroughly disenchanted with the administration's operation of the carriers, which included large rate increases. By the end of the war, only the appeals of patriotism could enforce the vision of harmony anticipated by Wilson and McAdoo at the end of 1917.

[39] Testimony of McAdoo, U.S. Senate, Committee on Interstate Commerce, *Hearings, Government Control and Operation of Railroads,* 65 Cong., 2 Sess. (Washington, 1918), 814-15.

By Norman Nordhauser

ASSISTANT PROFESSOR OF HISTORY
SOUTHERN ILLINOIS UNIVERSITY

Origins of Federal Oil Regulation in the 1920's*

❡ *The 1920's and early 1930's witnessed the beginnings of federal oil regulation in the United States. Professor Nordhauser argues that oil executives rather than government officials led the way in the movement for regulation and that their dominant goals were the stabilization of prices and profits.*

Since the Great Depression, state commissions and federal agencies have cooperated with oil companies to restrict the market supply of crude oil in the United States. The petroleum corporations have enjoyed the benefits of a system of self-regulation under law that most other industries have experienced only during the NRA period or in wartime. Sometimes justified as conservation of a scarce natural resource, sometimes upheld as a defense measure to insure a steady flow of a strategic material, oil control developed historically as a reaction to short-run threats to capital and profits. This was most clearly demonstrated by the waves of interest in oil production control during the 1920's, the formative years of the program. While the demand for petroleum in the early 1920's grew more rapidly than the supply, most oil investors and lawyers rejected proposals for reform of oil field practices; instead, they relied on unregulated enterprise to guide the oligopolistic industry. But after the simultaneous discovery of several large oil fields depressed oil prices, major corporations in the late 1920's initiated public action to "conserve" the oil supply. Federal and state officials, following the lead of the industry, responded sympathetically to the call from the powerful oil executives for special assistance.

Until 1927, however, limited interest in oil conservation resulted only in a prolonged debate over various strategies for stabilizing oil production. Central to the discussion among industrialists was

Business History Review, Vol. XLVII, No. 1 (Spring, 1973). Copyright © The President and Fellows of Harvard College.

° The author wishes to acknowledge the generous financial assistance by the Newcomen Society of North America during the completion of this essay.

an exchange, begun in 1923, between Henry L. Doherty of Cities Service Corporation and his fellow executives over the merits of government-business cooperation. Major company officials [1] debated with Doherty over such issues as the form which state aid to the industry might take, the role of the federal government in self-regulation of the industry, and even the urgency of the need for governmental assistance. When compared with similar discussions during the early New Deal, the Doherty controversy of the 1920's showed how much the attitude of leading businessmen toward public regulation had been transformed after 1927. Nevertheless, the debate during the 1920's in the oil industry, as in other industries,[2] prepared the way for the modern program of regulation. Most importantly, the debate produced a "scientific" rationale for public regulation of oil fields which, although it was rejected as a wrong theory in the New Era, became a very useful justification for federal and state intervention in the 1930's. To understand this episode, it will be necessary to review certain aspects of the industry's experience in the immediate postwar period, especially with regard to the trade association movement.

THE FAILURE OF POSTWAR COOPERATION

Industrial mobilization in wartime has long been recognized as a stimulus for relaxation of the antitrust laws, cooperation between corporations, and employment of federal power to aid private interests. The experience of the petroleum industry during World War I followed this pattern in American business history.[3] During the brief wartime experiment with new forms of government-business partnership, leading oil executives were brought together in the Petroleum War Service Committee (PWSC) to advise the administration on oil matters. In April 1917, *Oil and Gas Journal*, the industry's foremost trade magazine, applauded President Wood-

[1] "Major" oil companies in the 1920's included the Standard Oil Group, which manufactured 40 per cent of American gasoline, and the dozen or so giant corporations which produced another 24 per cent. The remaining third of U.S. manufacturing was handled by 350 small or "independent" refiners. See Report of the Federal Trade Commission, *Petroleum Industry: Prices, Profits, and Competition* (Washington, D.C., 1928) (hereafter cited as FTC, *Prices, Profits, and Competition*), 76–77.
[2] For example, see Ellis W. Hawley, "Secretary Hoover and the Bituminous Coal Problem, 1921–1928," *Business History Review*, XLII (Autumn, 1968), 247–270.
[3] On mobilization of the petroleum industry, see Harold F. Williamson, *et al.*, *The American Petroleum Industry: The Age of Energy, 1899–1959* (Evanston, Ill., 1959), ch. 8; Gerald D. Nash, *United States Oil Policy: Business and Government in Twentieth Century America* (Pittsburgh, 1968), ch. 3; J. Leonard Bates, *The Origins of Teapot Dome: Progressives, Parties, and Petroleum, 1909–1921* (Urbana, Ill., 1963), ch. 8. Some materials on the war experience were found in Record Group 67 (Records of the U.S. Fuel Administration), National Archives, Washington, D.C. (hereafter cited as RG 67), and in the Mark Requa Papers, Acc. No. 776, Western History Center, University of Wyoming, Laramie.

row Wilson's appointment of "practical oil men" to the PWSC, executives such as Alfred C. Bedford, president of Standard Oil (New Jersey), Harry F. Sinclair, president of Sinclair Oil and Refining, and Edward L. Doheny, president of the Mexican Petroleum Company. "These," said the industry organ, "are men who Know and men who Do. More power to 'em." Recalling the wartime experiment, one oil executive observed that petroleum history could be divided into the era before and the era after the creation of the PWSC. Even the dissolution of the Committee in 1919, he noted, "could not erase the communion in the committee room." [4]

Summarizing the work of the PWSC, the industry's leading journal proclaimed that "trade dissensions and competitions are forgotten and the idea prevailing is one of harmony and practical cooperation." As the end of wartime mobilization approached, major oil company officials frequently spoke out for continued cooperation. "There has been much strife in the old order of things affecting the oil business," noted the *Oil and Gas Journal*, "but the world war has wiped out this antagonism. Why," continued the editor, "should not industrial peace thus created be continuous?" The *Journal* called for a federal oil commission that would carry on the work of the PWSC.

Alfred Bedford of Standard Oil (New Jersey) and chairman of the PWSC, asked the industry in 1917, "if it is so easy for us to work together for our country's sake, I cannot see why, after the war is over, we cannot work together for the good of the industry itself." In December 1918, Bedford called for a permanent body to correspond to the Iron and Steel Institute and other industrial guilds to carry on "the consolidation of the industry." Leaders of the oil industry, upon the conclusion of peace negotiations in Paris, knew that the government would dissolve the PWSC and its sub-

[4] *Oil and Gas Journal* (hereafter cited as *OGJ*), April 19, 1917, 1; *National Petroleum News* (hereafter cited as *NPN*), May, 1917, 7, December 19, 1917, 8, January 2, 1918, 6–8; see also Bernard Baruch, *American Industry in the War* (New York, 1941), 15–29. According to Chairman Bedford, the PWSC's role was to assist the government in filling its orders for petroleum products during the emergency, and "to do so in such a manner as to interfere as little as possible with the industry in its relation to normal business." To insure that war-related industries would receive oil supplies, the PWSC worked with the Oil Division of the U.S. Fuel Administration, headed by California oil man Mark Requa, to establish a priority list for deliveries of fuel oil to key domestic consumers. Otherwise the main interference with business-as-normal was the appeal for gasolineless Sundays. Despite the enormously increased demand for petroleum products, the industry successfully avoided direct price fixing by the government. It was not until May 1918 that Requa, after several advances in the price of crude oil, finally urged the PWSC to restrain inflation voluntarily. In July 1918, the PWSC announced a price schedule that fixed oil prices for the next six months. See *OGJ*, January 3, 1918, 38; Minutes of PWSC meeting for July 13, 1918 and August 9, 1918, Mark Requa Papers; also, PWSC, "The Plan to Stabilize Prices and Maintain Uninterrupted Flow of Crude," New York, August 18, 1918, RG 67, Box 2719.

committees. At Bedford's request, on March 14, 1919, representatives of the foremost oil companies met in an all-day conference at the Biltmore Hotel in New York City to create a national organization, the American Petroleum Institute (API). Emphasizing the recent past, the new trade association announced that its first goal was "to afford a means of cooperation with the Government in all matters of national concern. . . ." The members of the Petroleum War Service Committee became the first board of directors of the American Petroleum Institute.[5]

There was an era of good feelings during the postwar reconstruction, and some oil men suggested that the newly organized Petroleum Institute should attack what they thought was the basic problem of the industry, the periodic instability of petroleum prices created by the discovery and development of new oil fields. A week after the API was founded, *Oil and Gas Journal* correctly predicted that "there will be periods when intensive drilling in the new oil fields — like those of Texas — will become a menace to normal market conditions." The *Journal* reasoned that voluntary regulation might restrict production and thereby protect profits. Experienced oil operators were painfully aware of the scramble for land and production and of the difficulty of convincing landowners and leaseholders of the wisdom of restraining drilling and waiting for better prices. However, the *Journal* believed that working agreement was possible "if oil-producing interests were behind it in good faith, as a matter of self-protection."[6]

In 1919–1920, the move towards industrial cooperation proved to be premature. As in other industries, market conditions deflated the spirit of cooperation.[7] As long as no new American oil fields threatened prices, most oil men preferred to preserve the traditional pattern of unregulated oil exploration and development. An immediate danger perceived by many executives was not an excess of oil, but a shortage because of the accelerating consumption of petroleum products. Rising automobile production and expanding industrial use of fuel oil and lubricants quickened the demand for crude oil. Though imports of crude petroleum increased sharply,

[5] *OGJ*, October 11, 1917, 39, November 22, 1918, 36, December 13, 1918, 44, March 14, 1919, 2, March 21, 1919, 38; *NPN*, June 26, 1919, 16. The PWSC had passed a resolution in August 1918 calling for an investigation of the advisability of creating a petroleum trade association. See PWSC, Minutes of meeting for August 9, 1918, Mark Requa Papers; George Sweet Gibb and Evelyn H. Knowlton, *History of Standard Oil Company (New Jersey); The Resurgent Years 1911–1927* (New York, 1956), 253.

[6] *OGJ*, March 21, 1919, 2.

[7] The steel industry, for example, provided a well documented case of the failure of postwar cooperation. See Melvin I. Urofsky, *Big Steel and the Wilson Administration: A Study in Business-Government Relations* (Columbus, Ohio, 1969), ch. 8.

domestic production in the immediate post-war years did not change significantly. American oil prices climbed to new heights, reaching $3.50 a barrel for Oklahoma crude petroleum in March 1920, a figure unsurpassed in the next forty years. Under such profitable market conditions, the industry's interest in conservation and domestic regulation through cooperative efforts early disappeared.[8]

Federal officials voiced some concern in the postwar period over rising oil prices and an impending oil shortage, but they did nothing (except for the retention of certain public lands as naval oil reserves) to interfere with private development of American oil. In September 1919, Secretary of the Interior Franklin K. Lane instructed Van H. Manning, Director of the Bureau of Mines, to meet with the API and to explain to the oil men that "private enterprise must stand in the forefront in the development of this industry and that what government can do will be supplemental and suggestive . . . ."[9]

As for the new trade association's leadership, president of the API Thomas O'Donnell declared in November 1920 that the public had been unnecessarily alarmed. Not only did he predict that there were many undiscovered oil fields but he forecast that, if the law of supply and demand were not disrupted and if stable property rights remained secured, then the petroleum supply would be adequate for present and future demand. The API president acknowledged a serious shortage of crude oil on the Pacific Coast but blamed "the deplorable situation" on the withdrawal of public lands and the creation of the naval oil reserves. Harry Sinclair, another member of the chorus of executives opposed to government interference, declared in 1921 that there was plenty of oil and always would be. "Exhaustion of the world's supply is a bugaboo," Sinclair snorted. "In my opinion it has no place in practical decisions." Complacency was the order of the day.[10]

In summary, the wartime experience of the industry had advanced

[8] George Soulé, *Prosperity Decade: From War to Depression, 1917–1929* (New York, 1968), 60, 85; FTC, *Prices, Profits, and Competition*, 328, Table 6.
[9] Lane to Manning, September 24, 1919, Record Group 48 (Records of the Office of the Secretary of the Interior), File 1–242, box 425, National Archives, Washington, D.C. (hereafter cited as RG 48). Secretary Lane expressed his unlimited faith in oil executives: "I believe that whatever the body of oil men would agree upon would make for the best use of petroleum and for the protection of this fundamental resource of our industry." On Lane's policies, see Bates, *The Origins of Teapot Dome*, ch. 5. About the effort to secure oil abroad, federal officials were much more bold. See Requa, Manning, and Smith to Harry A. Garfield, February 28, 1919, RG 48, File 1–242, box 424; API, *Bulletin*, October 31, 1920, 2; Nash, *U.S. Oil Policy*, ch. 3; Gibb and Knowlton, *History of Standard Oil*, 278–408; John A. DeNovo, "The Movement for an Aggressive American Oil Policy Abroad, 1918–1920," *American Historical Review*, LXI (July, 1955), 854–876.
[10] API, *Bulletin*, November 19, 1920, 4; December 9, 1921, 3; *NPN*, November 24, 1920, 25–26.

the concept of industrial self-regulation through the evolution of the PWSC into a national trade association. But, as has been indicated, the underlying soundness of the domestic price structure in 1919–1920 led many oil men to discount suggestions that anything was wrong as well as arguments that governmental activity could improve conditions. The *Journal's* warning of 1919 that the oil price structure might crumble with the discovery of new oil fields had been greeted with indifference.

HENRY L. DOHERTY: PIONEER OF OIL CONSERVATION

During the oil shortage of 1919, gasoline had become so scarce in California that it was profitable for mid-continent refiners to ship products by railroad tankcar to the far west.[11] However, the oil drought abruptly ended in late 1920 with the discovery of the Huntington Beach field in the Los Angeles Basin. A tremendous campaign of drilling began, but Huntington Beach had not been fully developed when an even greater strike occurred at Signal Hill in Long Beach. This set off a stampede of drillers, lawyers, promoters, real estate dealers, and other adventurers who raised the population of Long Beach by at least 10,000 in two years. As Signal Hill was exploited, yet another important oil field, Sante Fe Springs, was tapped in southern California. By the end of 1922, two additional, though less significant, fields were opened in the Los Angeles Basin. As a result of these multiple discoveries and the rapid exploitation that followed, California's share of American oil production shot up from 24 per cent to 36 per cent in 1923.[12]

The California oil discoveries coincided with the onset of the postwar depression of 1921, but the full effect of the new fields was not felt in the eastern and mid-continent regions until 1923. Because of high shipping costs from Pacific ports to east coast refineries, Texas and Oklahoma oil producers were temporarily insulated from California competitors during the worst part of the economic slump. In the early months of 1922, prices of Oklahoma crude oil recovered somewhat from the sharp recession. By 1923, however, tank steamers were carrying considerable quantities of California oil through the Panama Canal, a trade which contributed

---

[11] FTC, *Prices, Profits, and Competition*, 206, 311. On purchases of mid-continent crude oil by Standard of California, see *NPN*, February 18, 1920, 115; on shortages of crude oil among independent refiners, see *ibid.*, January 7, 1920, 54. For a thorough study of conditions in California, see Federal Trade Commission, *Report on the Pacific Coast Petroleum Industry* (Washington, D.C., 1921–1922).

[12] John Ise, *The United States Oil Policy* (New Haven, Conn., 1926), ch. 12. While California production soared, new fields, such as El Dorado, were discovered in the mid-continent region. See *NPN*, January 19, 1921, 17–20.

to a 50 per cent decline in prices of mid-continent crude oil. Oklahoma and Texas producers began to protest vehemently against the "unfair" competition from California petroleum at eastern refineries.[13]

Though major refiners enjoyed cheap supplies of raw material in 1923, they lost more than they gained. As crude oil prices declined, so did both gasoline prices and the major oil companies' profits.[14] The pressure of an abundant, cheap supply of crude oil acted as a force for competition throughout the industry. As the California oil discoveries broke the petroleum market, new voices among industry executives called for production control and conservation.

In 1923 Henry L. Doherty became a pioneer in the drive for conservation. Controlling over 200 oil, gas, and electric companies, Doherty was widely acclaimed as "one of the powers of Wall Street."[15] During the postwar oil shortage, Doherty had opposed government intervention to conserve oil. At the second annual meeting of the API in 1920, he acknowledged the scarcity of petroleum but simultaneously voiced the opinion that there would be an abundant supply in the future. In contrast to his later stance, he urged that oil development be carried on as "a non-restricted competitive business," and that any government meddling come to a halt. Freedom, he proclaimed, was absolutely essential to meet the public demand for oil, because in competition "lies the protection of the people."[16]

When discoveries in California transformed a scarcity into a surplus accompanied by declining oil prices, Doherty lost his indifference to conservation and his hostility to all "government meddling." Between 1920 and 1923, his midcontinent oil company, Empire Gas and Fuel, had suffered a 50 per cent decline in profits.[17] In 1923 Doherty, never a man to withhold his opinions, entered

[13] FTC, *Prices, Profits, and Competition*, 206–210, 331–33; Ise, *U.S. Oil Policy*, 107, 111–122; Soulé, *Prosperity Decade*, 96–126.

[14] FTC, *Prices, Profits, and Competition*, 331–32; Gibb and Knowlton, *History of Standard Oil*, 674–75; Ralph Cassady, Jr., *Price Making and Price Behavior in the Petroleum Industry* (New Haven, Conn., 1954), 137, table 13.

[15] *OGJ*, September 21, 1917, 4. See also Glenn Marston, comp., *Principles and Ideas for Doherty Men: Papers, Addresses and Letters by Henry L. Doherty* (Henry L. Doherty & Co., New York, 1923–1924), 6 vols. Total assets of Doherty's company in 1924 were surpassed only by the Standard Oil Group and by Sinclair's Consolidated Oil Corp. See Roy C. Cook, *Control of the Petroleum Industry by Major Oil Companies* (Washington, 1941), 60.

[16] API, *Bulletin*, November 19, 1920, 8; *NPN*, October 16, 1918, 21, December 11, 1918, 28. In 1920, Doherty reported that there would be enough oil "for us and our children and our children's children." Marston, comp., *Principles and Ideas*, V, 198.

[17] *Moody's Manual of Investment* (1923), part 1, 1995, and (1924), 1678; *NPN*, May 30, 1923, 124. In June 1921, Doherty announced that overproduction would not last but Cities Service would have to pay its dividends in scrip. Dividends to common stock declined from $18,000,000 in 1920 to $7,000,000 in 1922. Another writer estimated that in 1921 earnings from the oil division of Cities Service dropped to one-third of what they had been the previous year. Marston, comp., *Principles and Ideas*, V, 234.

into a correspondence, first with his fellow oil executives, and then with federal officials, to publicize the need for government action on oil matters. At the API executive meeting in August 1923, he endorsed what his more conservative critics regarded as drastic modifications of the legal arrangements for oil production. Explaining that the recent wasteful methods exhibited by the industry in the Los Angeles Basin would inevitably produce strong government regulation, Doherty declared: "If we must have some form of government regulation sooner or later, then I am in favor of making our own program and plans and try [sic] to have them forced upon us by some constructive and, if possible, friendly bureau or department of our government." Doherty tried to use the fear of government regulation to stimulate a unity within the industry for *his* plan of government-business cooperation.[18]

Although he was a businessman rather than a geologist, Doherty based his call for government intervention largely on new theories of oil production and technology. Doherty condemned existing oil field practices, especially the low percentage of oil recovered from known underground pools. Failure to raise even 50 per cent of the petroleum in an underground reservoir, Doherty asserted, was the result of the waste of dissolved gas which contained the natural energy to lift most of the oil from the sands. Doherty reasoned that, in order to preserve the gas pressure, scientifically patterned drilling should replace the existing haphazard scramble for wells.

Doherty complained not only about the physical waste of oil but also about the injustices visited upon certain operators in the field by rampant competition. Each land owner, he explained, drilled wells as fast as he could in an attempt to drain as large a portion of the field as possible. If one operator in the field preferred to practice slower and more careful methods of drilling or wished to hold back until the price of oil rose, he risked having the oil under his land drained by his neighbors' wells. Thus, an oil company or land owner could not escape the consequences of the competitive system, nor could it control its own practices; it must produce or suffer losses.[19]

What Doherty criticized was the fundamental rule in drilling and production, the "law of capture." According to that time-honored usage, oil belonged to the land owner who raised it to the surface, regardless of the fact that the oil may have been

[18] Doherty's memorandum, n. d. (probably September 6, 1923), Record Group 70 (Records of the Bureau of Mines), File 651, National Archives, Washington, D.C., (hereafter cited as RG 70).
[19] *Ibid.*

originally underneath someone else's land. The law of capture simply disregarded the migratory nature of oil under pressure. Doherty concluded that the "oil problem" would find no practical solution so long as the ownership of oil and gas was determined by who brought it to the surface.

Cooperative development, or unit drilling of American oil fields was Doherty's idea of a new direction for the industry. State laws should require, Doherty thought, production to be supervised by oil districts staffed by the various land owners in the area. Doherty's plan would have allowed no drilling in a newly discovered field until an oil district had been formed by the majority acreage. Patterned after the irrigation and drainage districts that were handling special water problems in the western states, oil districts would have scientifically planned the location of wells so as to develop a field as a unit with the greatest economy. Under this procedure, royalties from the oil produced in the whole area would have been paid to the land owner(s) and apportioned "on the basis of probable amount of oil under his land before the reservoir was disturbed." [20]

Doherty claimed that unit development would save millions of dollars annually in unnecessary wells. Instead of every land owner, no matter how small his part of the field, sinking a well in his backyard and thereby forcing his neighbors to protect their interest against drainage by sinking an offset well, Doherty proposed that the oil districts limit drilling to the minimum number of necessary wells. Presumably, this would have put an end to oil fields (like the Los Angeles Basin) where the derricks were almost interlocking at the bases.

Doherty's plan reconciled science and law in the interest of efficiency. Under his orderly system of unit operations, major oil companies, wherever they had the majority acreage of an oil field, would have been able to prevent oil from being forced on the market as a result of competitive drilling. Production from new fields could have been marketed gradually, without upsetting the price structure. With oil districts in the hands of the majority of land owners, small maverick parties interested in immediate production could be checked and forced into planned production. In this respect, Doherty's scheme involved not only conservation but, to some extent, the stabilization of investments and profits. [21]

[20] *Ibid.*
[21] While Doherty called for laws to conserve oil, he also pioneered in the development of fuel oil for household heating. Doherty urged the industry to exploit this new market for oil especially because householders could afford to pay more for oil than almost all

FEDERAL OIL REGULATION   61

In the Petroleum Institute, Doherty's ideas received some support from Ernest W. Marland, president of a large oil producing company and future governor of Oklahoma.[22] On September 22, 1923, an API committee headed by the President of Standard Oil (N.J.), Walter C. Teagle, reported that the plan for unit operations and oil districts was worthy of the most careful study. Teagle, however, was opposed to Doherty's solution as impractical and unconstitutional, and he selected to head the API investigation Amos L. Beaty of The Texas Company, who proved to be a major opponent of compulsory unitization.[23] Instead of inquiring further into Doherty's plan, Beaty presented in October 1923 his own plans for changes in the state laws respecting oil production. Beaty's main proposal called for the creation of public commissions in each of the oil-producing states to enforce certain rules "having for their purpose the conservation and economical production of oil and gas." As Beaty indicated, a number of states already had regulatory bodies with limited authority to affect oil production. All that was required to meet current problems in oil production was the creation of such commissions in all oil-producing states and the strengthening of existing agencies. Specifically, Beaty proposed that the state commissions should have the power to approve voluntary agreements between oil companies drilling or producing oil in the same field. Overproduction and waste would be curbed, he argued, by self-regulation under state law. Once approved by state commissions, Beaty concluded, agreements to curtail production would be legally binding on the participants and exempt from antitrust proceedings.[24]

Beaty bluntly refused to respond to Doherty's urgings on the subject of unit operation. "My objections to your plan are so pronounced," Beaty informed Doherty, "that I know you and I cannot agree . . . ." Later, Beaty did explain his presumption that compulsory unitization violated the due process and the obligation of contract clauses of the Constitution. Oil districts such as Doherty had proposed would, according to Beaty, interfere with the contracts between land owners and oil operators which usually called for immediate drilling and would thus deprive the land owner of his royalty without due process. Beaty envisioned thousands of

other customers. See *NPN*, November 28, 1923, 22, December 19, 1923, 33G–J, November 26, 1924, 48–49.
    [22] *Ibid.*, September 19, 1923, 108, October 10, 1923, 25–26.
    [23] Teagle to Board of Directors, September 22, 1923, RG 70, File 651; Gibb and Knowlton, *History of Standard Oil*, 432–33; Henrietta M. Larson and Kenneth Wiggins Porter, *History of Humble Oil and Refining Company: A Study in Industrial Growth* (New York, 1959), 251–53.
    [24] Beaty to Doherty, October 10, 1923, RG 70, File 651.

disgruntled Texans, victims of a scheme to force them to pool their property with that of their neighbors. "It is no answer," he alleged, "to say that the owner would profit in the long run. On that theory, a paternalistic government might order its farmers in a period of overproduction to desist from planting specified crops and console them by the statement that they would profit ultimately. That sort of thing is contrary to the spirit of our institutions; it is vicious in principle." [25] Finally, Beaty maintained that it was a well owner's absolute right to capture oil, even oil that had migrated from someone else's land; as Shakespeare said, "t'was his, 'tis mine, and will be slave to thousands." [26]

Replying to Beaty, Doherty, who had no legal training and who relied on a copy of the Constitution from the *World Almanac*, confidently offered his own interpretation. "Now, a contract may be a very sacred thing under our Constitution," he wrote, "but if it is one which leads to flagrant waste of our most valuable natural resource I am inclined to think the courts would find some way of setting such a contract aside or at least reframing it." [27] Though both men had the same objective of stabilizing production, the conservative lawyer and the untrained pragmatist could not agree on strategy for the fields. From Beaty's vantage point, Doherty was proposing a radical interference with the freedom of businessmen. Worse yet, if Doherty gained acceptance for his larger argument that the public interest was threatened by inefficiency of private practices in oil production, then that same argument might ultimately justify declaring the oil industry a public utility, subject to strict supervision. The specter of public service regulation did not convince Doherty that Beaty's ideas were a better way than his own for controlling production. On the contrary, Doherty thought it much more dangerous for the industry to rely on public commissions selected by the voters than oil districts selected by the majority interest in an oil field. Furthermore, Beaty's plan, thought Doherty, was only a half-hearted attack on the industry's problems since it depended on voluntary agreements between oil men. Coercive state laws for unitization were, to him, the only weapon by which the majority of oil men would safely achieve control of new fields.[28]

[25] Doherty to Beaty, October 12, 1923, and Beaty to Doherty, October 16, 1923, RG 70, File 651.

[26] At one point, Beaty admitted that Doherty's plan "rather appeals to me as something to dream on, but it is another thing to revolutionize the industry." API, *Bulletin*, December 31, 1924, 18–19.

[27] Doherty's memorandum, n. d. (probably September 6, 1923), and Doherty to George Otis Smith, August 23, 1924, RG 70, File 651.

[28] Doherty to Beaty, October 12, 1923, and October 20, 1923, RG 70, File 651.

FEDERAL OIL REGULATION   63

The outcome of the Doherty-Beaty exchange was a stalemate, with no serious action taken on either proposal. Market conditions meanwhile improved as oil production in California leveled off and demand for petroleum products rose. By 1924 the opportunity to use the postwar economic crisis to arouse the industry was lost. Failure to obtain support for his program from his fellow oil men drove Doherty to seek allies in the federal government. On October 20, 1923, he sent to the Director of the U.S. Bureau of Mines, H. Foster Bain, part of his correspondence with Beaty and the API, letters which outlined his unsuccessful attempts to inform the industry of the need for compulsory unitization. "We as an industry now have the matter under consideration," he told Bain, "but we need all the help we can get, and the most natural place to look for advice and assistance is you and your staff." [29]

With the burden of Teapot Dome ever growing, the Coolidge administration was understandably reluctant to respond openly to Doherty's suggestions. After some months of waiting for action, Doherty concluded that federal officials needed further prodding. On August 11, 1924, he wrote a thirteen-page letter to Coolidge describing enormous waste in the petroleum industry and pleading his case for compulsory unitization.[30] In this letter to the President, Doherty also revealed that the federal role in his scheme for production control was now to be larger than he had originally thought. The logic that led him to this conclusion was revealed by Doherty to George Otis Smith, Director of the U.S. Geological Survey. "The difficulty of securing uniform legislation in the various states," he told Smith, "led me to investigate whether the Federal Government had any power in the matter." Doherty had investigated, and now he was indicating to Coolidge a possible course of action. The President could, Doherty suggested, call a conference of governors and request them to secure uniform oil legislation, presumably for unit operation, "and say that unless it is done by a certain date, that you will be compelled to request Congress to pass legislation taking jurisdiction of oil production throughout the United States." Since legal authority over petroleum production was generally thought to reside with the states, justification for federal involve-

[29] Doherty to Bain, Ocotber 20, 1923, RG 70, File 651.
[30] Bain to Doherty, December 10, 1923, and, Doherty to Coolidge, August 11, 1924, RG 70, File 651. See also J. Leonard Bates, "The Teapot Dome Scandal and the Election of 1924," *American Historical Review*, LX (January, 1955), 303–322.

ment had to be found. Doherty discovered the legal excuse for federal action in the preamble to the Constitution — Congress shall "provide for the common defense." To protect the country, Doherty advised the President, the federal government should watch over the oil industry. "A deficiency of oil," he warned, "is not only a serious war handicap to us but an invitation to others to declare war against us . . . ." Such strategic considerations fit neatly with Doherty's call for federal action.[31]

Two events, the reception by Coolidge's administration of a "mandate from the people" in November of 1924 and the disappearance of Teapot Dome from the headlines, enabled federal officials to deal late in 1924 more directly with the issues raised by the oil executives. Doherty had suggested to President Coolidge that the Secretaries of the Navy, Interior, and War Departments, as well as chiefs of the Bureau of Mines and the Geological Survey, were the logical appointments to a new federal agency for the study of oil conservation. In December 1924, Coolidge established a cabinet-level committee of inquiry, the Federal Oil Conservation Board (FOCB) to investigate and report on conditions in the oil industry. Thus Doherty's pioneering efforts for production control in the early 1920's opened a dialogue between oil executives and government officials that would continue through the New Deal.[32]

EARLY WORK OF THE FOCB

Unfortunately for Doherty's purposes, the FOCB conducted its initial research in a period of stable and fairly high prices for crude oil. By 1925 memories of the California boom and the postwar depression years had already faded, while thoughts of Teapot Dome and federal "meddling" were fresh in the minds of most oil men. For its part, the Coolidge administration tried to signal to oil executives that they had nothing to fear from the investigation. From the beginning, the FOCB took the view that the industry

[31] *Ibid.*; Doherty to Smith, August 23, 1924, RG 70, File 651. Doherty's scenario of a governor's conference followed by a request for state legislation and then a proposal for federal legislation, roughly outlines the history of the oil industry during the Hundred Days of 1933.

[32] Bain had advised Doherty in January 1924 to discuss his unit operation idea with Mark Requa and Ralph Arnold, two well-known oil men who helped organize Coolidge's California campaign. After the victory in November, both Arnold and Requa proved to be enthusiastic advocates of government-business cooperation for production control. It was probably the combined counsel of Requa, Bain, Arnold, and a few other Interior Department officials that finally led the Coolidge Administration to take some action in response to Doherty's proposals. See Bain to Doherty, January 17, 1924, RG 70, File 651; *OGJ*, February 26, 1925, 27; Coolidge to the Secretaries of War, Navy, Interior, and Commerce, December 19, 1924, RG 70, File 651.

was the teacher and the government was the pupil.[33] It was the Board's first task to find out how much and what sort of regulation the industry thought necessary. Secretary of the Interior Hubert Work, chairman of the FOCB, therefore sent a questionnaire to the leading oil companies.

Almost all the replies reflected the stable economic conditions of 1925.[34] There was, according to most executives, no possibility of a future shortage, no significant waste in present oil operations, and no need for any laws to alter property rights in oil fields. Walter C. Teagle and Amos Beaty used the FOCB inquiry as another forum from which to attack Doherty's scheme for compulsory unit development. Teagle challenged Doherty's claim that a few scientifically located well sites would result in maximum efficient recovery of oil by announcing his own calculation that "the drilling of a large number of wells in a field results in a larger recovery of oil . . . than would be the case with a smaller number." In other words, the FOCB was instructed that unitization was inexpedient, even from a conservationist's point of view. Beaty echoed Teagle, adding the suggestion that the federal government might legalize agreements between oil companies to restrict output in periods of overproduction.[35]

Industry and agency worked harmoniously from the start of the FOCB inquiry. To help the Conservation Board obtain the honest opinion of the industry, the API appointed a Committee of Eleven to gather data and to report to the FOCB.[36] In May 1925, the API issued the findings as a book, *American Petroleum: Supply and Demand*, which, like the replies to the Board's questionnaires, concluded that there was no urgent need for new laws. The Institute report predicted that there was an oil reserve in the United States sufficient for national defense purposes and other essential uses until the time when science would develop new sources of energy or substitute sources of oil, such as coal, lignite, or shale. Doherty's plan for unit operations was not even mentioned in the report, but, as in Teagle's letter to the FOCB, the opposite theory of production

[33] An influential Bureau of Mines official informed Secretary of the Interior Hubert Work that the "fundamental conception" of the Conservation Board "is that any regulation of the industry that may be found necessary should be maximum from the industry itself and a minimum by Governmental agencies." Memo, F. B. Tough to Work, January 8, 1925, RG 70, File 651.

[34] Replies to the questionnaire are in Record Group 232 (Records of the Federal Oil Conservation Board and Petroleum Administrative Board), National Archives, Washington, D.C., boxes 6, 23, 26–30 (hereafter cited as RG 232). See also Interior Department, Press Release, January 12, 1925, RG 232, box 31.

[35] Teagle to Work, July 15, 1925, and Beaty to Work, February 2, 1925, RG 232, box 27.

[36] See Interior Department, Press Release, January 17, 1925, RG 232, Box 31; API, *Bulletin*, January 24, 1925, 2, 7.

was espoused. Most experts agreed, according to the API study, that rapid, close drilling would bring forth more oil than any other method of extraction. The API study of 1925 clearly established that conservationist sentiment was in short supply among the industry's leadership.[37]

In February 1926, the FOCB conducted public hearings on oil conservation. At this hearing, Doherty was present to fight his battle. "Our most probable territory," he told the Board, had been exhausted; the API's optimism about future discoveries was ill-founded, and there was a possibility of an oil shortage at any point in the near future. Only compulsory unitization would forestall the coming of scarcity. In a crisp exchange with Doherty, E. W. Marland, head of a large mid-continent oil firm, scoffed at the claim of an immediate oil shortage. Doherty's notions he derided as unscientific and unconstitutional, asserting that they were based on nothing more than a quick perusal of the World Almanac. Doherty interrupted to remind the FOCB that, during the California boom, Marland had agreed with him that there was considerable waste of oil. To this Marland lamely replied that his views in 1923 had been biased: "Mr. Secretary, I was then suffering cruelly and stood in need of profit." By 1926, with a dwindling supply and higher prices, Marland was obviously no longer in need of profit.[38]

Having canvassed the opinions of petroleum executives for over a year, the FOCB confronted the difficult task of reporting on national petroleum conditions. Certainly it was nearly impossible to please both Doherty and his opponents. E. S. Rochester, the influential secretary of the Conservation Board, suggested to Work that it might be wise to have two or three oil men review the government's findings before they were published. "The Board cannot afford," Rochester noted, "to take a hasty or false step in a matter so 'explosive.' "[39] Not surprisingly, the first report of the

[37] API, American Petroleum Supply and Demand: A Report to the Board of Directors of the American Petroleum Institute by a Committee of Eleven Members of the Board. (New York, 1925), 3–5, 23–26. The optimism of the API study rested on several predictions, the most important of which was the "billion acre reserve." Geologists acknowledged that there were slightly more than 1,000,000,000 acres of American soil which might possibly contain underground petroleum deposits. Since most of this area was untested, the API report assumed a high number of future discoveries. Besides Doherty, Mark Requa and George Otis Smith questioned these assumptions. See Requa to J. Edgar Pew, November 20, 1925, 1–J/59, Hoover Presidential Papers, Hoover Library, West Branch, Iowa (hereafter cited as Hoover Papers); Smith to Work, August 21, 1925, RG 232, box 23.

[38] FOCB, Complete Record of Public Hearings February 10 and 11, 1926 (Washington, D.C., 1926). In May 1926, Charles Evans Hughes, representing the API, presented a brief to the Conservation Board demonstrating that, under recent Supreme Court interpretations, the federal government lacked the constitutional power to regulate oil production. See FOCB, Public Hearing May 27, 1926 (Washington, D.C., 1926), 3–8, 13–22. For Doherty's reply, see FOCB, Press Release, September 1, 1926, RG 232, box 31.

[39] Rochester to Work, June 14, 1926, RG 232, box 12.

FOCB was an inconclusive document which stated the obvious truth that the total of known and unknown reserves could not be calculated. Instead of dwelling on specific proposals for legislation, the FOCB endorsed the oil executives' request that antitrust obstacles to voluntary agreements should be removed. In its blandness, the report mirrored the sentiment of the majority of the industry's leadership, who could see nothing but danger in government interferences.[40]

THE GREAT REVERSAL

In early 1926, Doherty's efforts to arouse the industry to the pressing need for scientific planning and legal reform seemed hopeless. Unitization had been criticized in the trade association's publication and laughed at by oil men before the FOCB. Yet within one year a dramatic transformation began in the attitude of outspoken oil men toward business-government cooperation and planning. This shift in views was so sharp that Secretary of the Interior Work could observe in August 1927, that the "once great divergence of opinion concerning the necessity for national conservation no longer exists among the leaders of the oil industry . . . ." [41] It was obvious at the time what had caused the fairly sudden reversal — beginning with the discovery of the great Seminole oil fields in Oklahoma, market conditions in the industry had rapidly changed. From 1927 onwards, the growth in known reserves of crude oil had outstripped the rise in demand for oil products. By 1929 oil executives increasingly spoke out for conservation and restrictions on production. The sharp drop in demand after the onset of the Great Depression and the discovery of another enormous field in eastern Texas (1931), accelerated the trend toward regulation.[42]

The newly emerging consensus on the need for production control was based on the very geological theories that the industry had denied when Doherty first presented them to the API and the Conservation Board. After 1927, major oil company executives

[40] FOCB, *Report of the Federal Oil Conservation Board to the President of the United States* (Washington, D.C., 1926). For the failure of industry-wide cooperation in the mid-twenties in other areas, see Louis P. Galambos, *Competition & Cooperation: The Emergence of a National Trade Association* (Baltimore, 1966), and Hawley, "Secretary Hoover and the Bituminous Coal Problem, 1921–1928."

[41] Hubert Work, "Conservation's Need of Legal Advice," address before the American Bar Association, Buffalo, New York, August 30, 1927, RG 232, box 31.

[42] Williamson, *et al.*, *American Petroleum Industry*, 322–25; Carl Coke Rister, *Oil! Titan of the Southwest* (Norman, Okla., 1949), ch. 17. For efforts to control Seminole production, see Minutes of the meeting of the oil executives before the FOCB, May 25, 1927, RG 232, box 9; *OGJ*, May 12, 1927, 29; FTC, *Prices, Profits, and Competition*, 189–193.

never again asserted that uncontrolled close drilling yielded the maximum recovery from oil fields, or that there was little danger of an oil shortage. On the contrary, they applauded almost every effort to hold back oil production as conservation of a scarce material. They loosely applied Doherty's original argument about scientific drilling and oil districts to justify any plan that set limits to the output of oil from a field, region, state, or nation.

While Doherty's belief in conservation through government-business cooperation became the dominant theme in the industry, his specific goal of compulsory unitization was not widely implemented. Instead, Beaty's counterproposal of working with and strengthening the state regulatory commissions became the main avenue to industrial self-regulation under law. In the years after the discoveries at Seminole, oil companies lobbied in the states to increase the power of public commissions over production.[43] E. W. Marland (who had scoffed at Doherty's presentation before the FOCB in 1926), led the legislative battle in 1927 to strengthen the Oklahoma Corporation Commission's rules regarding oil field practices. By 1928, the Oklahoma agency was endorsing statewide agreements between oil producers to check output from Seminole and other fields.[44] In Texas, major company executives who had earlier opposed Doherty's ideas led the fight to increase the power of the Texas Railroad Commission in order that it could be used to restrict Texas wells.[45] Unconvinced by Doherty, they were forced to reconsider the need for conservation after it became clear that there were sizeable reserves in the United States.

In turning increasingly to the federal government for assistance, the major oil companies followed the example set by Doherty. This was hardly the result of changing constitutional views among oil men or of any new strategic importance given to oil in the late

[43] See American Bar Association, *Legal History of Conservation of Oil and Gas* (Chicago, 1939).
[44] On Marland's efforts, see RG 232, box 9; API, *Bulletin*, January 12, 1927, 1; *OGJ*, February 3, 1927, 31, February 10, 1927, 42, March 3, 1927, 32. Mark Requa, oil advisor to Wilson, Coolidge, and Hoover, was impressed by the Marland bill and wrote to financier Bernard Baruch in 1927 that if the bill is passed "it must inevitably stabilize production. This, in turn, means higher prices. . . . This, in turn," he added, "means that there will be an opportunity to make a great deal of money in petroleum shares and petroleum properties if the proposed program is finally brought about." Abandoning the discretion with which presidential advisors are supposedly clothed, Requa ended by urging Baruch to join in setting up a $500,000 organization to buy and deal in oil properties and securities. Requa to Baruch, February 12, 1927, General Correspondence, Baruch Papers, Princeton University Library, Princeton, N.J.
[45] Larson and Porter, *History of Humble Oil and Refining*, 247–263; Robert E. Hardwicke, "Legal History of Conservation of Oil and Gas in Texas," in ABA, *Legal History*, 214–286; *OGJ*, January 31, 1929, 56, February 7, 1929, 32, 58, 60. See also Teagle to Hoover, December 7, 1929, Hoover Papers, box 1-E/203; and Alfred D. Chandler, Jr., *Strategy and Structure: Chapters in the History of American Industrial Enterprise* (Cambridge, Mass., 1969), 208.

1920's. Rather, as Doherty had reasoned in 1923, federal assistance was attractive because it was faster and easier than working for change in all the oil-producing states. Furthermore, in specific areas, such as suspension of the federal antitrust laws and restriction of imports, the state legislatures were powerless. Finally, the federal government was uniquely suited to aid the industry in overcoming the rivalry between oil-producing states by coordinating stabilization in order that the various states would feel that they had a fair share of the national market.

Ironically, the FOCB, which had been formed largely in response to Doherty's call for unitization, became the chief means by which the federal government participated in the industry's efforts to strengthen state regulation. At the behest of oil executives, the FOCB began in 1930 to compute and publish estimates of the national market demand for petroleum for the next six months, and to divide this forecasted demand among the leading oil-producing states.[46] Compiled from data presented to the FOCB by the leading oil refiners, six such forecasts were published between 1930 and 1933. They served as essential guidelines for the states where oil companies and regulatory commissions were working together to limit production. State production control was thus integrated into national forecasted demand; at both levels of government, oil men initiated and guided business-government cooperation.[47]

By 1933 an oil control program was beginning to function, and the New Deal continued that program, improved upon it, and made it permanent. Within industrial circles, the focus of discussion had completely shifted since the 1920's when the majority of oil men had opposed planning and production control. The central issue during the New Deal was to what extent should federal regulation replace state programs in order to make oil control even more effective.[48] Some oil men believed that centralized control, including federal price fixing as well as production quotas, was the only way to insure to the industry higher prices and profits and ef-

[46] See Farish to Rochester, June 22, 1929, RG 232, box 15; Requa to Wilbur, July 23, 1929, Ray Lyman Wilbur Collection, Hoover Institute, Stanford University, Stanford, Calif., box 13. Doherty did not approve of the new conservation program in the late twenties, of "holding back oil by arbitrary proration, in conflict with antitrust laws" instead of applying "scientific plans." See Doherty to Senator George W. Norris, February 22, 1930, C-B/581, Hiram W. Johnson Papers, University of California at Berkeley. Doherty failed to take an active part in the conservation debate between 1927 and 1929 because of serious illness (neuritis and arthritis). See Turner (Director of the Bureau of Mines) to Judge Caster, November 27, 1929, RG 232, box 12.

[47] Committee on Petroleum Economics, Report to FOCB, March 25, 1930, RG 232, box 6; see also J. Elmer Thomas to Smith, March 4, 1930, RG 232, box 7.

[48] Nash, U.S. Oil Policy, ch. 7; Norman E. Nordhauser, "The Quest for Stability: Domestic Oil Policy 1919–1935" (Ph.D. diss., Stanford University, 1969), ch. 7.

fective regulation. During the first Roosevelt administration, Beaty and Marland, oddly enough, were among the leading advocates of increased federal control. The Great Depression and the abundance of oil had changed their geological and constitutional views. Or, perhaps, as Marland had said of his temporary support of Doherty in 1923, they were "suffering cruelly and stood in need of profit." After state and federal regulation restricted oil production in the 1930's, the major oil companies and the API preferred to forget the embarrassing oil debate of the previous decade, except perhaps to acknowledge that Doherty had broken new ground in the conservation movement. Production control was henceforth represented as the inevitable application of scientific methods by rational industrialists to the development of resources.

The experience of the petroleum industry in the 1920's illuminated some of the broader questions about the pattern of government-business relations. Perhaps historians have overemphasized the triumph of technocracy or the march of democracy as factors in the development of regulation and conservation in the New Era.[49] In the case of the oil industry, desires for market control and stabilization were probably the dominant impulses. Doherty's original conservation proposals, and the industry's counterproposals, were directly related to current prices and profits. Historians may also have exaggerated the importance of a neutral federal bureaucracy of experts who pushed conservation upon the industry. On the contrary, the files of the Bureau of Mines and FOCB indicated that every call for conservation by federal authorities was preceded by a corresponding initiative from a major company executive, and was reviewed by organized business operating through the API. By examining the debates over stabilization strategy in other industries, historians may determine if the experience of the oil men was unique, or whether it had counterparts in other sectors of the economy.

[49] Donald C. Swain, *Federal Conservation Policy, 1921–1933* (Berkeley, Calif., 1963), 5–8, 62–66, 70–72; J. Leonard Bates, "Fulfilling American Democracy: The Conservation Movement, 1907 to 1921," *Mississippi Valley Historical Review*, XLIV (June, 1957), 29–57; Samuel P. Hays, *Conservation and the Gospel of Efficiency: The Progressive Conservation Movement, 1890–1920* (Cambridge, Mass., 1963), 2; Erich Zimmermann, *Conservation in the Production of Petroleum: A Study in Industrial Control* (New Haven, Conn., 1957), 2.

CREATING COORDINATION IN THE MODERN PETROLEUM INDUSTRY:
THE AMERICAN PETROLEUM INSTITUTE AND THE EMERGENCE OF SECONDARY ORGANIZATIONS IN OIL

Joseph A. Pratt

ABSTRACT

This article presents a history of the American Petroleum Institute, the largest national trade association for the American oil industry, from its founding in 1919 until the onset of the Great Depression. It illustrates the process by which an important new trade association sought to define its roles in a long divided industry amid the calls for "cooperative competition" in the 1920s. It then examines the evolution of six major functions performed by the API for the petroleum industry: the collection of statistics, public relations, lobbying, fundamental research, the standardization of oil tools, and the establishment of uniform accounting methods.

Research in Economic History, Volume 8, pages 179–215.
Copyright © 1983 by JAI Press Inc.
All rights of reproduction in any form reserved.
ISBN: 0-89232-261-6

I. INTRODUCTION

World War I marks the great divide in the organizational history of the U.S. petroleum industry. Before the war, the rise of vertically integrated firms spurred an organizational revolution that transformed the structure of individual oil companies.[1] During and after the war, a second generation of organizational change began to create institutions capable of forging a working relationship between oil and state and of fostering intraindustry cooperation.[2] The most significant new oil-related institution to emerge in the 1920s was the American Petroleum Institute (API), which was founded in 1919 and quickly became the major trade association for the petroleum industry. In its formative years, the API took a leading role in creating coordination where none had previously existed. It sought to make the petroleum industry more efficient by performing important functions outside the capacities of individual oil companies.

The API took over some tasks that involved primarily the internal workings of the industry and others that dealt with the external relations of the oil industry and other groups and organizations. "Internal affairs" included general concerns of the industry—such as the establishment of a uniform system of accounting—that could be solved only through coordinating efforts of the individual companies. "External affairs" involved attempts to define industrywide adjustments to changes in the industry's relationship to government agencies, labor organizations, and the consuming and voting public. Neither set of concerns had been addressed systematically at the industry level before World War I, yet since that time the ongoing effort to create institutions capable of coordinating these intraindustry matters has been a central development in the organizational history of the American petroleum industry.

In the period from World War I to the onset of the Great Depression, the API sought to define a new institutional order in oil—one that would protect the operating autonomy of individual oil companies while coordinating industrywide responses to a variety of common problems. Although its earliest efforts were not always successful, the API's activities in the 1920s merit serious consideration as the initial attempts to solve important problems of coordination that have continued to plague the political economy of oil in the United States.[3]

II. CREATING COORDINATION:
THE PROCESS OF INSTITUTIONAL INNOVATION

In the years after its founding in 1919, the API had to establish itself as a viable organization by defining its functions. Its general goals were those of most of the trade associations that flourished in the 1920s: to coordinate cooperation within the industry and to serve as a liaison between the industry and government. As a new organization seeking to stake its claim to authority among numerous existing institutions, including private corporations, regional trade associations, and government agencies, the API faced difficult choices. How could its scarce resources best be used to promote the welfare of its members and to convince skeptics in the industry that the API was worthy of their support? It had to achieve several goals: to identify tasks best accomplished at the industry, not the firm, level; to build a consensus for concerted action in the industry; to secure financing and create an administrative structure for the management of its new functions; to coordinate and often augment the ongoing work of individual corporations and government agencies in such areas; and, finally, to gain acceptance from these other organizations and from the industry as a whole for its direction of future efforts. Only then could the API make its newly defined function a permanent fixture within the industry. By following this general pattern in a variety of internal and external affairs of the oil industry, the API created coordination where none had previously existed. In so doing, it also established its own identity as an important part of the modern political economy of oil.

The API's earliest efforts to gain acceptance were aided by the fact that it inherited a functioning organization from the National Petroleum War Service Committee (NPWSC), which advised the Oil Division of the U.S. Fuel Administration during World War I. Under the leadership of A. C. Bedford, then the president of Standard Oil of New Jersey, the NPWSC developed a sophisticated system of advisory committees that included representatives from every region and from every branch of the oil industry. A central committee coordinated the efforts of these advisory committees and worked closely with the fuel administration to assure the production and delivery of essential war products at fair and relatively stable prices. Recognizing the potential benefits of continued cooperation after the war, Bedford and others active in the NPWSC supervised its postwar transformation into the first national trade association for the oil industry. The war fostered an organizational structure for cooperation in an industry long characterized by bitter divisions, and the leaders of the war effort simply appropriated this structure for the API after the armistice. The enforced cooperation of war thus greatly facilitated the creation of the API, which was patterned after the Central Committee of the NPWSC, planned by one of its subcommittees, and staffed by a board of directors and by heads of working committees transferred almost intact from the NPWSC.[4]

After the relatively simple task of creating the API, its members faced much uncertainty about the tasks it would perform. The API's charter, filed in March 1919, contained a vague statement of its general goals open to numerous interpretations.[5] Antitrust laws assured that the API could not continue its primary wartime functions—the balancing of supply and demand for petroleum products. Its choice of tasks was also constrained by a fundamental maxim adopted by its early leadership that "the API never attempts to do for any oil company what that oil company can or ought to do for itself."[6] Within the areas not closed by antitrust laws or by respect for the traditional autonomy of individual companies, the API sought to enhance the efficiency of the industry and to defend it when necessary against outside attacks. Practical decisions on how best to pursue these goals fell to those in charge of the API's daily operations.

As is often the case in the early years of an organization, several leaders dominated the API's formative years, and these men had a far-reaching impact on its subsequent evolution. Much of the responsibility for managing the daily operations of the API fell to Robert Welch, who became its first general secretary after holding a similar position with several of the regional trade associations in the oil industry before World War I. Amid numerous conflicting demands made on the API during its first years of existence, Welch followed the sound advice of Walter Teagle, the president of Standard Oil of New Jersey and one of the API's most active members in the early 1920s: "Select a limited number of things; keep on them; do each of them well—don't try to cover the universe."[7] With strong guidance from Teagle and Bedford and the frequent leadership of such early API presidents as Thomas O'Donnell and J. Edgar Pew,[8] Welch focused the new organization's efforts on several important tasks. By the end of the 1920s, the API had asserted leadership over several activities that helped smooth the internal workings of the industry, such as the sponsorship of fundamental reserach in the interest of the entire industry, the establishment of generally accepted standards for manufacturing, and the definition of uniform accounting procedures. It also had become the primary organization through which the oil industry managed many of its external affairs, including the collection and dissemination of petroleum statistics, the representation of the industry's perspective before a variety of government policymakers, and the performance of public relations work for the entire industry.

A similar process and many similar problems marked the API's assumption of leadership in each of these areas. After pressures from inside the industry, from a prominent member of the API, or from government helped identify a potential area of concern, the API—usually through a special committee composed of members of the board of directors— explored the need to intervene. After deciding on a general course of action, the committee sought the approval of the entire board, which then generally hired a man of proven abilities and national reputation to direct the API's efforts. Under the guidance of experts from within the industry and from government agencies working in related areas, the API coordinated and augmented any preexisting programs of smaller regional oil trade associations, which at times solicited the API's aid in expanding regional programs throughout the nation. In cases where the API's entry into a new area of concern met significant opposition instead of cooperation, it generally reevaluated its plans. Yet on several issues where a determined API leadership encountered strong opposition—in particular, collecting statistics and developing uniform accounting methods—it ultimately persuaded or defeated its opponents using the weight accorded by its high standing in the industry. Even in areas marked by conflict over the proper role of the API, opposition to its initiatives often disappeared after the benefits of its involvement became evident.

III. CONFRONTING THE EXTERNAL ENVIRONMENT OF THE OIL INDUSTRY

For most of its history before World War I, the petroleum industry followed the lead of Standard Oil of New Jersey, which largely avoided taking an active part in areas of concern now generally grouped under the headings of public and governmental affairs.[9] In the new era after the war, however, the industry recognized its need to understand and, if possible, control the impact of changes in its external environment. In an uncertain and at times threatening political climate, many oil men sought to improve the public and political standing of their industry in a systematic manner unprecedented before the war. The API became the primary vehicle for these efforts to manage the industry's external environment, and it sponsored broad industrywide initiatives to explain the industry's views to the government and to the general public in the 1920s.

Robert Welch originally organized the primary external affairs functions undertaken by the API in the Department of Publicity and Statistics, which was created in September 1920. By collecting data about the oil industry and presenting it to the government in easily understood and readily available form, this department laid the foundation on which the API subsequently built its reputation as the central source of information about petroleum. Amid the rapid expansion of such activities in the mid-1920s, the API created a Public Relations Division separate from the Department of Statistics. Through these two units and a Washington-based Governmental Affairs office, the API worked with its members and with other oil and gas trade associations to contain political challenges to the industry's welfare and to foster a more favorable image for an industry long hampered by public mistrust.[10]

The heart of the API's external affairs work was the collecting and disseminating of statistics about the operations of the petroleum industry. Such statistical services were a standard activity for most trade associations in the 1920s, but the API's efforts went beyond those of most other associations. By making the collection of statistics one of its major tasks, the API filled important gaps in the information about oil available to business and to government. The near void of systematic information about petroleum before the creation of the API reflected fundamental changes that had transformed the industry after the turn of the twentieth century. Until 1911, only 8 years before the creation of the API, the industry had been sharply divided into Standard Oil and the "independent" companies, with little exchange of information between the two factions. The dissolution of Standard Oil by the Supreme Court in 1911 further fragmented the industry, breaking up the one institution previously capable of collecting statistics about a large percentage of the oil business. Yet, at the same time, dramatic changes in the volume and the type of petroleum products heightened the need for better information about the supply and demand for petroleum.[11]

The mobilization effort in World War I clearly revealed the inadequacies of existing information about the oil industry. At the beginning of the war, the U.S. Bureau of Mines and the Geological Survey conducted a joint study on the oil industry's ability to meet the growing demands generated by the Allied dependence on American oil. In completing this survey, the government agencies relied primarily on their own previous, less than comprehensive efforts to collect data on oil production and refining. The Geological Survey had long published annual statistics of oil production as part of a series entitled *Mineral Resources of the United States*. The Bureau of Mines was just beginning to collect and publish a monthly summary of refinery statistics. Both sets of figures were compiled from regular reports required by law of individual companies. Although comprehensive in their coverage of refiners and producers, these reports did not cover other important aspects of the oil industry's operations, and they were seldom available soon enough to be of much use in coordinating the operations of the oil industry.[12] To meet its need for quicker access to more detailed information, the U.S. Fuel Administration appointed as chief statistician Frank Silsbee, who had worked for Union Oil of California before the war. In soliciting Silsbee's assistance, the director of the Oil Division urged him to "develop a system that would meet all needs" because "since [the] dissolution of Standard these figures have not been kept."[13] On his arrival at his new job, Silsbee quickly encountered what he later called "the non-existence in Washington of competent and coordinated petroleum statistics," and he turned for assistance to his colleagues in the industry, as organized through the NPWSC. After a bit of arm twisting

to secure the cooperation of several recalcitrant companies, Silsbee succeeded in compiling national figures on petroleum production, refining,
and distribution that were vital to the smooth supply of oil to the bat-
tlefields of Europe. Silsbee set an important precedent that continued
throughout the war by "recognizing the point of the ownership of the
statistics . . . as resting in the hands of the National Petroleum War
Service Committee" and "taking no action that would have the effect
of attaching this work as a permanent feature to any government
agency."[14] While helping the Oil Division coordinate the war effort, he
thus began teaching oil men the utility of detailed statistics about their
industry.

After the war, Robert Welch aggressively pushed the newly organized
API into the void created by the dismantling of the U.S. Fuel Administration's statistical services. Several prominent directors of the API
pushed back. Even amid the enforced cooperation of war, Silsbee had
encountered problems in collecting information about the refining and
pipeline operations of some companies.[15] The end of hostilities further
weakened the cooperative spirit of many companies. Some feared that
the collection of detailed information about the industry would open the
API to antitrust prosecution; other companies feared that such statistics
would inevitably affect the sale of their stock. But the most common
objection was that information supplied to the API might somehow find
its way into the hands of competitors. Welch quieted the first concern
by proclaiming at every opportunity that the API would have absolutely
nothing to do with data on prices. Experience quickly dissipated the
second fear. However, concern about the possible competitive uses of
statistics remained strong enough to hamper Welch's efforts to increase
the quality and quantity of statistics published by the API. The dispute
over the API's proper role in this area climaxed in a public confrontation
between Welch and Robert Stewart, the president of Standard Oil of
Indiana, with the two men almost coming to blows during a meeting of
the API.[16]

Despite such determined opposition from powerful individuals within
the API, Welch did not back away from his commitment to collecting
statistics. Indeed, when the directors named him general secretary, they
assured that this function would be a major undertaking of the API.
Welch's passion for statistical information had been evident before World
War I in his work for two organizations of independent oil men, the
Western Oil Jobbers' Association and the Western Petroleum Refiners'
Association, and during the war in his work on the Statistical Committee
of the NPWSC. He reaffirmed this passion in his first major address to
the API, asserting that "the collection, study, and dissemination of oil
statistics and facts ought to be one of the great objectives of the American

Petroleum Institute."[17] Welch felt that accurate information about the oil industry would dispel a legacy of misunderstanding inherited from the era of Standard Oil's dominance. In addition, he hoped that good data on fundamental conditions of supply and demand would help to break the traditional cycle of boom and bust that had plagued the oil industry. Finally, Welch strongly believed that the API could use statistics to respond to assaults on the oil industry by misguided and misinformed critics:

> I state it as a fundamental principle that no Industry should permit any other agency to give out information concerning the industry itself without the Industry being in a position to check up on the accuracy of the statements, no matter by whom they are made. If a Statistical Department is established by the Institute it should be its purpose to gain a reputation of being so deathly accurate in its work that it would command universal respect and confidence.[18]

Welch's personal quest to gain acceptance for the statistics services of the API ended with his death in 1929, but by that time the API had established its reputation as the most important source of up-to-date information about the U.S. oil industry.

Welch's most persuasive argument in converting skeptics in the industry to join his crusade to develop the API's statistical capacities was his personal pledge that the information submitted to the API would be treated as strictly confidential. Publishing only aggregate figures, the API's staff scrupulously avoided disclosing statistics from individual companies. Welch even used a coding system so that his staff could compile composite data without knowing the name of the company whose figures they were adding into the total. No officer of the API, including the president, had access to the submittals of individual companies. Extreme care in handling this proprietary information paid quick dividends. As experience proved the trustworthiness of the procedures and the staff the API employed to collect statistics, industry cooperation steadily increased.

Welch wanted timely information above all else, and he sought to capitalize on the API's close connections to the oil industry to avoid delays. In collecting figures on production, for example, he made use of a long-standing informal network of information in the oil fields—the "scouts" traditionally employed at an estimated annual cost of $1 million by producers in large fields to collect confidential information on the activities of rivals. Gaining the cooperation of the scouts was not difficult, since they generally provided data about competing firms, not about their own employers. Their weekly telegraphic reports gave the API a dependable and detailed source from which to compile weekly estimates of production in each major oil field that were published in an API

Bulletin and sent to all members within three or four days of the original reports. The accuracy of these figures was checked by comparing the estimates of various scouts active in the same fields and further tested when the Geological Survey published its official figures several months later. As it gained experience in using the scouts' estimates, the API established a reputation for publishing the nation's most current and most accurate estimates of production.[19]

Refinery statistics proved more difficult to collect. In February of 1922 the API *Bulletin* offered the following plea:

> In the near future it is hoped that the refiners of the country will offer to cooperate in such a manner as to enable us to give a reasonable full statistical table showing the condition of the industry from week to week. Do you want this service?[20]

Despite the repetition of such appeals in subsequent *Bulletins,* in Welch's personal correspondence with oil executives, and in several presidential addresses at the API's annual conventions, weekly refining statistics did not appear until 1929. Throughout the 1920s, the API released the most complete information available to it on refining. Monthly statistics on changes in refinery stocks—published only two weeks after the end of the month—appeared regularly in the *Bulletin* after 1922. These figures initially included approximately 55 percent of the national refining capacity. But during the next 5 years, the monthly refinery statistics edged up to approximately 82 percent of the total capacity east of California. Because these figures revealed much about the production and movement of the basic refined products, they could be used by the individual refiner to better understand his position in the market. Indeed, so useful were up-to-date refining statistics that the president of the API hailed the advent of the weekly series in 1929 as "the most valuable thing statistically the Institute has ever done."[21]

Such a statement covered a lot of ground, for by 1929 the API had become involved in the publication of a wide array of information on many aspects of the industry other than production and refining. Drawing from its own sources as well as from statistics gathered by various government agencies, the API regularly published information on the following topics: oil consumption by railroads, vessels, and public utilities; imports and exports of petroleum products; the consumption of gasoline and kerosene by state; drilling activities; and receipts of California oil at Atlantic and Gulf ports. As both a tabulator of some statistics and a clearing house for others, the API fostered a revolution in the availability of information about the petroleum industry. The regular publication of its statistics in tabular form in the API's *Bulletin* and in the oil trade journals fulfilled Welch's desire to "show the fundamental facts relative to the petroleum industry in such a manner as to make it easy to interpret the relationship of the supply and the demand."[22]

Of course, the interpretation of the facts was just as important as their collection, since even the most comprehensive statistics often support different and even contradictory arguments. The API's statistics on conditions within the industry proved useful to individual oil companies, since they allowed each to place its own operations in the context of industrywide trends. They also proved invaluable to the industry as a whole in testifying on fundamental facts about oil before government agencies and Congress. Indeed, by the end of the 1920s, the API's investment in collecting information about the industry had already paid handsome dividends in the form of greatly increased input into the political decision-making process.

In sharp contrast to the decades before the creation of the API, public officials learned to expect expert presentations from oil industry spokesmen in the 1920s. When, for example, the Federal Trade Commission (FTC) launched an investigation of oil prices and profits after World War I, Welch immediately offered the fledgling institute's services. Welch testified at great length about the "fundamental conditions" in the industry. His fact-filled presentation sought to prove that postwar price hikes were reasonable in light of changing conditions in the industry, and this opinion found support in the testimony of several other leading oil men. Welch again gave detailed statistical testimony two years later before the Senate Committee on Manufactures, which Senator Robert LaFollette used to present his case for a renewed antitrust campaign in the oil industry. Subsequent FTC investigations and congressional hearings on water pollution throughout the 1920s also heard well-documented presentations by API spokesmen.[23] Probably the most controversial effort by the API to use statistics drawn from its member companies to influence public policy involved the Federal Oil Conservation Board (FOCB), an interdepartmental agency created in 1924 in response to fears of an impending oil shortage. This board was an advisory body with a mandate to investigate conditions in the oil industry, and the API became one of its major sources of information. The institute's initial response to the creation of the FOCB was to appoint a committee of 11 of its directors to report on the reserves of oil available to the nation. The committee's conclusions that reserves were sufficient to supply America's needs and that the lack of significant waste in the industry made government conservation efforts unnecessary raised a chorus of protests from within the industry, from outside critics, and even from dissenters within the API. To present its conclusions, the API went outside the industry to secure the service of the renowned Charles Evans Hughes, former candidate for president and retired Chief Justice of the U.S. Supreme Court. Despite the protests encouraged by its initial report to the FOCB, the API continued to present forceful and detailed information to the board until its dissolution in 1933. As with its testimony before other agencies, the overall impact of the API submittals to the FOCB is impossible to determine. But the quality of the information available to the API through its members, the API's growing reputation for "deathly accuracy," and the array of authoritative expert witnesses available to the API made it a formidable advocate of the oil industry's position on matters of public policy.[24]

The API undertook sophisticated lobbying more directly through its Washington office. The original charter of the API had called for the establishment of its headquarters in Washington, but New York was subsequently chosen in part because "if located in Washington, the Institute would be misrepresented as an organization intended primarily to influence legislation and to exert pressure on government."[25] Instead, the API created a Governmental Affairs office in Washington and retained as its head Fayette Dow, a former attorney for the Interstate Commerce Commission (ICC), who also represented several other oil trade associations in Washington. Much of Dow's original work was on petroleum freight rate and pipeline rate cases before the ICC and testimony on tax legislation before the House Ways and Means Committee and the Senate Finance Committee. But the steady increase in regulatory activity affecting the oil industry in the 1920s and 1930s expanded the responsibilities of the Washington office, which became, in Dow's words, "sort of an industry clearing house" where government agencies could call for information. Dow saw his function as exposing government officials to the oil industry's perspective on specific issues. He worked hard to establish a reputation for honesty and accuracy so that government agencies would usually accept his information "without question," whether it was presented in the form of written testimony or off-the-record conferences with officials. In short, Dow acted as a modern lobbyist, seeking to influence legislation and regulatory policy through organized and documented presentations of his industry's position to the key officials who decided policy.[26]

The API's ability to present the best available information about the oil industry guaranteed its spokesmen ready access to public officials. Although the API lobbied effectively during the 1920s, its direct access to government policymakers probably peaked between 1933 through 1935, when the API transferred much of its statistical department from New York to Washington to help administer the industry recovery code in the Interior Department.[27] Welch's judgment of the importance of statistics thus proved accurate. As the API organized previously fragmentary information about oil into a systematic, accurate, and comprehensive portrait of conditions in the industry, it greatly enhanced its authority and ultimately its influence over public policy. The API's stated policy from the beginning of its statistical activity was to discontinue collecting any information that became available in timely and accurate form from other sources. In the 1920s, however, the government's under-developed capacities in this area made such a policy largely irrelevant. A tradition of public sector reliance on the API for many petroleum statistics thus began in the 1920s. This arrangement aroused little com-ment until the 1970s, when the oil crisis focused political attention on the government's reliance on industry sources of petroleum information.

In the early 1920s, public relations was the neglected other half of the API's Department of Publicity and Statistics. Robert Welch felt strongly that good statistical work made public relations unnecessary; straight-forward facts, not "PR," would educate the public about the oil industry. Others, notably J. Howard Pew of Sun Oil, disagreed, voicing "no en-thusiasm" for statistical work and urging instead the organization of "a Publicity Committee, whose duties it will be to educate the public, first as to the great benefits to be derived from each of the products manufactured from mineral oils, and second, that the prices at which these products are sold are exceedingly low as compared with other commodities."[28] Such arguments gained increasing favor among the API's directors, who created a temporary Public Relations Committee in 1924 before establishing a permanent division of the API four years later. The early history of this division is an important part of the history of the coming of age of public relations in the oil industry, for the API brought many of the techniques associated with modern public relations to the industry.

The API did not, of course, introduce public relations to the industry. That role is generally accorded to Ivy Lee, who worked for John D. Rockefeller and Standard Oil of New Jersey before World War I. During the war, Lee's firm handled several minor publicity matters for the Fuel Administration and the NPWSC, and A. C. Bedford sought to "transfer" Lee to the API in its early years. After addressing the board "on the subject of publicity as related to the American Petroleum Institute and then the petroleum industry," Lee worked briefly for the API, but Welch proved uncooperative. In an extraordinary demonstration of his strong opposition to public relations, Welch first ignored Lee and then finally fired him, risking the anger of Bedford, who was at once a patron to Lee, to Welch, and to the API itself. After Lee's departure, Welch continued to focus the attentions of the Publicity and Statistics Com-mittee away from public relations, which he considered pap, and toward what he considered essential, the collection of statistics.[29]

There the matter rested until the mid-1920s, when a series of events left the industry reeling. In the first 4 years of the API's existence, the FTC and Senator LaFollette conducted highly publicized and highly critical investigations of the oil industry. Then the Teapot Dome scandal broke, dragging the industry's public standing to new depths—and implicating several prominent directors of the API in criminal activities. Against this backdrop of unfavorable publicity, many within the industry saw the need for a vigorous "education campaign" to improve the public's understanding of the oil industry and to shore up its sagging public—and political—image. A leading trade publication, the *Oil and Gas Journal,* took the lead in defending the industry with the publication in March 1924 of an entire issue presenting "The Oil Industry's Answer" to its critics. Stressing the economic and social benefits generated by the oil industry, the *Journal's* approach foreshadowed that subsequently taken by the API.[30]

Others in the industry followed the lead of the *Oil and Gas Journal.* In the summer of 1924 Standard Oil of New Jersey began a series of "directly educative" advertisements in newspapers throughout its primary marketing regions in the East. These ads drew from "The Oil Industry's Answer" to attempt to explain the functioning of the industry.[31] At the same time, several of the largest regional oil trade associations began to explore ways of conducting a national publicity campaign of a sort never before attempted by the industry. J. Howard Pew and his cousin J. Edgar Pew, who was an active member of both the Mid-Continental Oil and Gas Association and the API, took the lead in deflecting such sentiment toward the API. In pressing the case for API leadership on Robert Welch and A. C. Bedford, J. Edgar Pew argued that "this is not a matter for the Standard Oil to handle."[32] Bedford soon agreed that although "individual companies could do effective work in reaching their own customers," general publicity work had to be done by the industry as a whole.[33] Pew had no doubt that "if the Institute does not take some action, something will be done by one or more of these various organizations (the smaller, regionally based oil trade associations) along these lines, that will not be as advisedly carried out as it should be if the Institute took hold of it."[34] In short, Pew felt that public relations was exactly the kind of industrywide endeavor the API could best coordinate.

While pushing their arguments in meetings with other directors of the API, the Pews also used their influence to help convince the smaller associations that only a national organization active in all phases of the industry—that is, only the API—could successfully coordinate an effective national publicity campaign. The Pews' arguments prevailed, and in early 1924 the API adopted a resolution calling for the creation of a committee to study this issue. W. N. Davis, who was both a director of the institute and the president of the Mid-Continent Oil and Gas Association, took charge of this joint committee of nine API members and eight representatives of the smaller associations. This "Committee on Education" was given 30 days to prepare a public relations plan, complete with budget, for the approval of the API's board.[35]

During this time, a 3-day meeting educated members of the Committee on Education by exposing them to prominent practitioners of public relations. Speakers included public relations men from the Eastern and Southern Railroad, American Telephone and Telegraph (AT&T), the Motion Picture Producers' Association, the National Association of Manufacturers, and the National City Bank of New York, representatives of the consulting firms of Ivy Lee and Bruce Barton, and the director of publicity for Herbert Hoover's relief organizations. The committee seemed especially impressed with the public relations programs of the railroads, and they left the conference eager to sell these modern techniques to the API's board. In exploring the world of public relations for the industry as a whole, the Committee on Education fulfilled an important general function of a trade association; it introduced members of the API to new concepts and developments in related industries and professions.[36]

The board of directors agreed with the committee's recommendations, and in December 1924 it created a Public Relations Committee composed of members from both the API and the smaller associations. The board authorized an annual $100,000-per-year budget for 3 years, with the money to be raised through appeals to the industry. Thus in order to begin its work, the Public Relations Committee had to pass the litmus test for most new activities sponsored by the API: it had to demonstrate its acceptance within the industry by attracting financing. This proved difficult. Despite strong pleas for support from W. N. Davis and J. Edgar Pew, the regional trade associations that had originally petitioned the API to direct a public relations campaign did not back their call for action with dollars. Instead, the committee came to be supported primarily by the contributions of the large companies that were the backbone of the API.[37]

After a reasonable start in securing pledges of financial support, the committee sought a suitable person to direct its efforts. They found no strong candidates within the industry, since most of the advertising men in the individual companies who had been "brought up with the organization" were considered "ineffectual" in planning a broad publicity campaign.[38] The committee chose instead to "employ some outside talent" to guide the industry's attempt to shed its traditional ineptitude in dealing with the public. After considering several of the men who had addressed the three-day meeting, the committee settled on Judson Wel-

liver, an experienced newspaperman who had served on President Warren Harding's White House staff. Welliver proved an excellent choice.
He had good connections within the newspaper business, a working
knowledge of reporting, and a national reputation from his White House
years that gave him a measure of independence from the leadership of
the API.

During 1926 Welliver guided the API's Public Relations Committee
into several "more or less experimental" ventures in reaching the public
with information about oil. Welliver specialized in preparing and widely
distributing general information about the oil industry's role in the economic life of the nation. He did this in subtle and persuasive ways. An
excellent example of his work was a newspaper article with the headline
"A Billion Dollars in Tolls Yearly Provide Modern Highways," which
appeared in an estimated 300 daily papers and 3000 weeklies with a total
circulation of approximately 15 million. This attractive feature story had
been prepared by Welliver's staff, which contacted state highway departments throughout the nation to compile statistics on gasoline taxes
and on road improvements. They then organized this information as if
it had originated in an interview with the Chief of the U.S. Bureau of
Public Roads. After being sent to the chief for his approval, the article
was then made available to newspapers in a finished form that could be
published as received. The end product was an engaging story that summarized for the reader the central role of petroleum in the dawning age
of the automobile, reminded him of the mobility and freedom provided
by the gasoline-powered car, and gently warned of the growing burden
on drivers caused by steadily rising gasoline taxes. All this reached the
reader from the lips of a government official, with no clear indication
of the API's role in preparing the "interview."[39] Similar API releases
featured interviews with an official from the U.S. Bureau of Mines about
the nation's oil supply and a discussion by a retired admiral of the
strategic importance of oil for modern naval warfare. These articles
embodied Welliver's conception of public relations as a long-run effort
to build a more favorable public attitude toward the oil industry.

Welliver's outpouring of publicity for the oil industry did not, however,
generate enthusiastic support within the API. Welch remained unshaken
in his lack of regard for such work. It seems likely that others in the
industry also remained skeptical of Welliver's indirect approach. J. Howard Pew summed up the frustrations of Welliver and those who supported
his work with the bitter comment that "apparently there are a lot of
narrow-minded men in the Institute who are either opposed to or jealous
of Welliver and his achievements."[40] As was to be expected in the early
years of a new organization, disagreements about proper goals and methods hampered the API's efforts to define its role in this new area. Disputes

among strong-willed oil executives accustomed to imposing their views within their own organizations were especially difficult to resolve. One victim of such disputes was Judson Welliver, who resigned his job when the $100,000-per-year budget he had been promised could not be raised from the industry.

In his place, the API appointed Leonard Fanning, an insider with broad experience. Fanning had worked for the *Oil Trade Journal* as financial editor, for the Department of Publicity and Statistics of the API, and for the *Oil and Gas Journal* before joining the API's Public Relations Division in 1928. Under Fanning's direction, the division made a subtle turn from the path marked out by Welliver. Fanning continued to release general information about the industry, but he emphasized enhancing the value of the API's public relations work to its member companies. He began to coordinate his division's work with that of the individual companies by having one man in each supporting company designated as the contact person for the API's work. These individuals, who were often high-level advertising men, served as Fanning's consultants while facilitating the distribution of the API's work within their companies. The establishment of a speakers' bureau; the publication of a handbook to aid speakers from the companies and the API in presenting the oil industry's case; the production of special information pamphlets aimed at filling station customers and at stockholders; the making of a film on the oil industry; the development of materials specifically designed for publication in the house organs of the companies; and the publication in 1928 of the first edition of *Petroleum Facts and Figures,* a comprehensive collection of facts and statistics on the oil industry—all moved the Public Relations Division into more direct contact with the companies. Fanning's work sought to reach more specific "publics"—customers, stockholders, and workers—than had the broader efforts of Welliver to reach and educate "the public."[41]

As was the case with some of the statistical work of the API, another public, the voter, was also targeted for special appeals. In the late 1920s, steadily rising gasoline taxes became the dominant political concern of the API's Public Relations Division. In 1929, the API and representatives of the automobile industry combined to develop a major publicity campaign against rising taxes on gasoline and against the diversion of these taxes to uses other than road building. The campaign featured widely distributed pamphlets pointing out the magnitude of gas taxes and reminding the public of their rapid rise in the 1920s. One such pamphlet showed a cartoon captioned "Where does my mileage go?" with a character labeled "legislature" punching holes in a gas tank to siphon off dollars as another character runs toward him with a bucket labeled "for other uses."[42] As the gas tax and other legislative concerns mounted in the early 1930s, the API created a well-financed, semiautonomous new organization—The American Petroleum Industries Committee (APIC)—"to give persistent and active impetus to the efforts of the industry to reduce taxes, to prevent the diversion of the gasoline tax, to stop evasion (of gasoline taxes by "bootleg" dealers), and to correlate the activities of the industry on all legislative matters, national and state."[43] Using state committees under the direction of a central committee, the APIC sought to "permit pooling of the common resources and strengths of the petroleum industry and permit of united action on wellcoordinated front."[44]

Such activities inevitably raised questions among critics of the oil industry about the fine line between "education" and "lobbying" or "propaganda." The most strenuous objections to the API's efforts to present "the facts as the industry sees them"[45] to the public generally came from those who held a different version of the facts and who did not have the same access to public or political opinion as did the well organized and financed API. Indeed, the institute's numerous organizational advantages over its political opponents gave it one of the most powerful voices in the nation on oil-related matters. This marked a sharp reversal from the situation that had existed before the creation of the API, when critics of the industry enjoyed a near monopoly on the supply of publicity and information about oil to the public. The API's public relations work in the 1920s helped place the petroleum industry's perspective forcefully and systematically before the public for the first time.

Its growing prominence as a spokesman for the industry led some critics to charge that the API was simply a public relations instrument for the large oil companies.[46] In fact, it was that and much more. Welch had misjudged the coming role of public relations, but he had correctly recognized the difference between the two functions originally placed together in the Department of Publicity and Statistics. Statistics were useful in a variety of activities, from coordinating the economic decisions of the individual oil companies, to presenting the industry's point of view in governmental affairs, to more general efforts to alter the climate of public opinion toward the industry. World War I taught that information about the fundamental conditions in the oil industry was essential in a political economy becoming increasingly dependent on petroleum for energy and for national defense. On the other hand, public relations seemed essential to many oil men who feared that unfavorable public opinion might encourage greater government involvement in their industry. The collection and presentation of information about oil in the form of detailed statistics, testimony to government agencies and to

Congress, and public relations campaigns all became permanent functions of the API as it sought to interpret and to respond to changes in the external environment of the oil industry.

IV. COORDINATING THE INTERNAL WORKINGS OF THE OIL INDUSTRY

Of equal importance to the API's external affairs functions in its formative years were its varied efforts to increase the efficiency of the internal operations of the petroleum industry. Large vertically integrated corporations had grown to carry out the production, refining, transportation, and marketing of petroleum, but they could not coordinate many important intraindustry matters. Cooperation among individual firms was needed to address numerous industrywide concerns, but before the creation of the API no means for such cooperation existed. In its early years, the API received a variety of requests from oil companies, regional trade associations, and government agencies for assistance in coordinating intraindustry affairs. It responded by asserting leadership in several important endeavors, including the organization of cooperative, fundamental research on petroleum, the standardization of tools used in the production of petroleum, and the establishment of uniform accounting methods. In each of these areas, the API molded strong cooperative sentiment into practical programs that increased efficiency by reducing duplication of effort within the industry.

Although many associated with the oil industry in the post–World War I era recognized the potential benefits of cooperative research, there was little agreement on the most suitable focus for such research. The lack of agreement among the members of the API's board of directors on the proper scope of cooperative research hampered the institute's initial efforts to organize such work. Amid strong disagreement among its leaders on the best methods for defining, financing, and administering cooperative research, the API made several false starts in launching this program.

These early problems reflected the small scale and the lack of coordination of previous research efforts in the industry. Before World War I, the oil industry generally emphasized a practical engineering approach to the improvement of refining technology, paying little attention to either petroleum chemistry or fundamental research on the nature of petroleum. Not until 1919 did Standard Oil of New Jersey, the historical leader in the industry, create a Development Department (later to become the Standard Oil Development Company). But even this important organizational innovation had as its primary purpose developing existing ideas and inventions, not generating creative research.[47] Other oil companies undertaking organized research in this period also emphasized applied, not fundamental, research.

Outside of the industry, the Bureau of Mines in the U.S. Department of the Interior was the leading center for petroleum-related research. Its petroleum division had been created in 1915, and by the early 1920s it employed numerous highly trained "petroleum technologists" to study the more efficient use of oil and its products. The Bureau of Mines had by this time constructed several experimental stations—at Bartlesville, Oklahoma, and at Pittsburgh, Pennsylvania—for oil-related research. Between the industry and such government laboratories lay the National Research Council (NRC), an official body created in 1916 to further scientific research in general. The NRC specialized in training scientific research workers by sponsoring research in university and government laboratories. As it expanded these activities in the early 1920s, one likely area for expansion was petroleum research, which suffered from a lack of researchers with strong technical backgrounds. Thus in the years after World War I, several institutions in business and government were seeking to increase their participation in petroleum-related research, which seemed destined to become increasingly important in the development of new techniques for producing and refining greater amounts of petroleum products of increasing quality.

The API's early recognition of the potential value of cooperative research was evident in its original charter, which proclaimed the desire "to promote . . . the study of the arts and sciences connected with the petroleum industry."[48] However, this general statement of intent did not address several basic questions: How was the research to be organized? Which "arts and sciences" would be emphasized? How would such work fit in with that being done by individual companies and by the government? The interpretation of this seemingly simple goal proved difficult, and the API spent much of the 1920s developing a plan of action satisfactory to its membership.

The first concrete proposal for cooperative research came from Van Manning, who was the director of the Bureau of Mines for the 5 years preceding his appointment in 1920 as the first director of research for the API. While still at the Bureau of Mines, Manning took a great interest in API work in 1919 and 1920. In preliminary meetings to define the basic functions of the institute, he pressed very hard for the creation of a research bureau. Manning's initial presentation of his ideas before the directors of the institute in August 1919 painted a grandiose vision for cooperative research. The API would coordinate ongoing public and private research projects involving petroleum in addition to undertaking projects of its own design. Another important function of the proposed research division would be "to try out on a commercial scale" the ideas

of investors, with the proceeds from royalties paid on successful inventions to go into a revolving fund controlled by the API in the interest
of the inventors. The price tag seemed small to Manning—approximately
$1 million per year to be raised through levies on the industry.[49]

The response to Manning's proposal was a collective gulp from oil
men. The cost seemed prohibitive, especially at a time when many in
the industry remained skeptical of the benefits to be gained by subscribing
large sums of money to the API, an as yet unproven organization. But
cost was not the primary objection. Even Manning's supporters within
the industry expressed reservations about potential conflicts between his
research division and the laboratories of individual companies. J. Howard
Pew of Sun Oil voiced the sentiments of many others when he stated
that "research work is a function which each refinery should work out
for itself."[50] J. W. Van Dyke of Atlantic Refining Company was less
direct but equally concerned:

> The governing factor in the success or failure of this proposed phase of activity
> depends, I believe, upon the solution of the problem of properly safeguarding the
> priority rights of a manufacturer who is carrying on his own research work on a
> large-scale while attempting to assist in the general research program.[51]

Manning's failure to separate fundamental research on the nature of
petroleum from applied research aimed at the commercial development
of technical advances doomed his initial proposal. Many prominent members of the API feared that their newly created trade association was
trying to move into an area best left to the individual companies.

Despite such opposition, Manning pressed his case within the API.
By November 1919, he reported to Robert Welch that he had

> about gone my limit in my advocacy and publicity of this plan so far as the news-
> papers, technical and trade journals are concerned, and in sending a copy of the
> plan to each member of the Board of Directors of the Institute for their consideration;
> and, in addition, have personally discussed the plan with many members of the
> Board and the Institute.[52]

Almost to the man, researchers in government and in the universities
responded favorably to Manning's plan, their eyes no doubt lighting up
with dollar signs at the prospect of a new source of funding for their
research. Yet the reactions of oil men were much more restrained. In
a letter to Welch, Manning summarized responses by oil-producing companies in their most favorable light by indicating that only 4 of 40 companies responding to Manning's plan were "unfavorable" and only 8
were "non-committal." Yet the tabulation contained a more telling figure. Only 6 of the companies queried by Manning committed themselves

to back their expressions of approval for the program with a subscription for its work.[53]

In June of 1920, Manning won the job as the first director of research of the API without winning his crusade for cooperative research. His letter of resignation from the Bureau of Mines summarized his reasons for leaving as follows: "It is the opportunity of being able to continue in another capacity, the work for the advancement of purposes fostered by the Department that has been the chief factor in determining my decision."[54] Manning's move from government to the API was thus in part an attempt to "capture" some of the resources of the new trade association to further the aims of government research. He hoped that private funds and the technical expertise of specialists in the individual oil companies could be used to carry on amibitious research projects beyond the capacities of the Bureau of Mines.

Manning's expectations proved ill founded. Unable to push through plans for a major cooperative research program, Manning instead spent three and one-half frustrating years directing the API's participation in a variety of relatively small joint research efforts with other organizations. Manning described these activities as "more or less in defense of the industry in cooperation with many other agencies." Included were extensive surveys of water pollution by oil and of the health effects of refinery vapors in cooperation with the Bureau of Mines, motor tests of lubricants produced from California oils, and joint research on motor fuels conducted with the Automobile Chamber of Commerce and the U.S. Bureau of Standards. With an annual budget of approximately $100,000 instead of the $1 million originally requested, Manning continued to push the case for a larger commitment to cooperative research.[55]

In March 1924, he called together a committee of well-known technical experts from universities, from industries other than petroleum, and from several professional societies to formulate a plan for cooperative research acceptable to the API's membership. The absence of researchers from the oil industry on this committee reflected the growing tensions between Manning and his colleagues in the individual companies. According to one of the conference participants, research directors from oil company laboratories were invited but refused to attend the meetings after expressing the opinion "that the whole project reflected adversely upon the company research staffs with the implication that they were not already doing all the research that was needed or justified."[56] The committee sought to ease such tensions and to respond to earlier criticisms by stressing that the API would not become involved in applied research. Instead, the committee focused its efforts on theoretical research on the chemistry and physics of petroleum. Its new plan called for the creation of a research corporation under the joint direction of representatives of the API, the American Chemical Society, and the donors of the $5 million endowment that would be required to operate the program. The corporation, which would thus be organized outside of the existing structure of the API, would administer funds to researchers in university and government laboratories, and it would be run by a well-paid, full-time director—presumably Van Manning.[57]

When support for this revised plan was not forthcoming, Manning resigned his position and took a job with Pan American Petroleum Company. From his perspective, he had been an outsider unsuccessfully attempting to educate the API's members on the benefits of cooperative research by exposing them to the thinking of some of the leading industrial and academic researchers in the nation and by offering a plan for organizing such research in the petroleum industry. He had sought to tie this research into an existing network of government agencies, universities, professional organizations, and industrial laboratories. Despite winning the near universal support of these outside organizations for his plan, however, he had not convinced most oil men that cooperative research could be well coordinated with the ongoing research activities of the individual oil companies. It also must have been clear to Manning—as it is clear from the tone of the correspondence between him and Robert Welch—that he was losing his continuing struggle with Welch over the control of the API's research division. Ever the skeptic regarding Manning's grand plans, Welch used his influence as secretary general to prevent Manning from undermining the API's standing within the industry by embarking on an ambitious, expensive program of cooperative research before first working out the practical details and then gaining the clear support of the industry.

Even after leaving the API, Manning continued to solicit support for his vision of a petroleum research center. His early proposals had attracted the support of Walter Teagle of Standard Oil of New Jersey, and in January 1925, he sent still another version of his plan to Teagle with a plea for its submission to John D. Rockefeller for funding. Manning also sought to gain the backing of Secretary of Commerce Herbert Hoover, whose strong support might rally oil men to the plan. To circumvent the roadblock created by opposition within the API, Manning sought to go outside the institute to finance a research program administered by an independent organization under the direction of a research executive and an advisory committee composed of representatives from a variety of professional organizations.[58]

Teagle objected to the high overhead costs of such an arrangement, arguing instead that every possible cent should be used to fund research, not to administer a research fund. He agreed with Frank Howard, the head of the Standard Oil Development Company, that the API could develop a more efficient administrative arrangement through the NRC, which could substitute for Manning's research corporation in selecting, funding, and overseeing projects. Teagle felt that an advisory committee from the board of directors—with additional guidance from the technical experts in the companies they represented—could help manage the undertaking.[59]

The crucial problem of financing remained. Teagle first looked to the oil industry for funds, which were not forthcoming. He then appealed for support to a patron of the industry, John D. Rockefeller. Manning had suggested soliciting money for research from Rockefeller in 1919 and again in 1925. An editorial in the *Oil and Gas Journal* in 1923 had echoed Manning's idea. In November of 1925, such appeals paid off, as Rockefeller agreed to contribute $250,000 over a 5-year period to the API for the support of fundamental research on petroleum. Rockefeller designated a three-man committee—Walter Teagle, J. C. Donnell of Standard Oil of Ohio, and Robert Welch—to oversee the creation of the research program. In January 1926, the Universal Oil Products Company of Chicago matched the original Rockefeller grant, giving the API a total budget of $500,000 to use in a 5-year program of fundamental research.[60]

These contributions overrode the resistance within the API to cooperative research, and the organization of the program proceeded rapidly. At the API's request, the NRC established a Central Petroleum Committee of nine scientists to solicit and evaluate research proposals, which were quickly forthcoming from researchers in universities and in government agencies. Through a Committee on Research made up of members of its board of directors, the API retained final authority to approve expenditures by the NRC, and three representatives from the API sat as ex officio members of the Central Petroleum Committee. In June of 1926, the committee recommended 21 projects in geology, physics, and chemistry. Four months later, it submitted 14 more proposals to the API, which published decriptions of the projects in its *Bulletin* and asked for comments from its members. After the quick approval of most of the original recommendations, the first projects began before the end of 1926.[61]

After these long delays in setting up the API's research program, once underway it probably proceeded a bit too rapidly for its own good. Seeking to differentiate the API's fundamental research from the applied research of individual oil companies, Rockefeller's three-man committee surrendered too much control to the panel of experts on the Central Petroleum Committee. Early reports from the individual research projects suggested the need for revisions in administrative procedures. The projects were simply too varied and too numerous to be carried out with a $100,000-per-year budget. Another problem reflected the split between the practical-minded researchers in the industry and their more flexible counterparts in academia, who in several cases shifted the emphasis of research in progress away from the concerns described in their original proposals. The sponsors of the research program within the API were already looking ahead to the time when the original grants would expire and they would be forced to turn to the industry for continued support. They knew that concrete results would be required to obtain additional funds. By early 1928, many technical men within the API supported the view "that some definite supervision is urgently needed through an agency connected with the Institute, and representing the more or less 'worldly' interests, and yet capable of a clear conception of the intricacies of many of the problems faced by the research workers."[62] To meet this need, the API created a Committee on Fundamental Research made up of technical specialists from member companies to cooperate with the Central Petroleum Committee in revising the program.[63]

The aforementioned committees of the NRC and the API then held joint meetings to reevaluate previously funded projects. Those judged to hold little promise gradually were discontinued; several of the most successful projects were then expanded. Another wave of cutbacks came with the expiration of the original 5-year grants in 1932, when the impact of the Great Depression made it impossible to raise sufficient funds from the industry to continue the fundamental research program at its original level.

Faced with such financial constraints, the API decided to focus its efforts on two projects of special significance and to finance the work with funds raised by a special canvass of its members. To facilitate interchange between the researchers and experts within the industry, the API established two technical advisory committees, one to deal with projects on the origin and recovery of petroleum and one to advise on projects pertaining to the composition and properties of petroleum. These two general concerns—embodied in long-run commitments to Project 37 on the fundamentals of the retention of oil by sand and Project 6 on the separation of the chemical constituents of petroleum—remained the core of the fundamental research program of the API into the 1960s.[64]

Although the API's cooperative research program never fulfilled the grand vision initially put forward by Van Manning, it nonetheless made significant contributions to the extraordinary advances in petroleum research after the 1920s. The practical benefits in the production and refining of petroleum from the API's fundamental research work more than repaid both the efforts to establish the program and the money committed to it over the years. In addition to the basic knowledge it generated, the program also helped train technical specialists much needed in the modern petroleum industry. For a relatively small investment, the API thus filled in several significant gaps in existing research, and the benefits from its fundamental research gradually and inevitably spread throughout the entire industry.

Unlike the well-publicized fundamental research program, the most important intraindustry function undertaken by the API in its early years went almost unheard of outside the industry. By coordinating an industrywide effort to "standardize" the size, the quality, and the design of manufactured goods used in the production of oil, the API helped save money for suppliers of goods to the oil industry, for individual oil companies, and ultimately for consumers of petroleum products.

In the early days of petroleum development, equipment used in producing and transporting oil had been designed to meet the specifications of each operator. As the industry steadily expanded—both geographically and technologically—the lack of generally accepted designs and sizes for oil equipment began to present problems. The products of separate manufacturers were seldom interchangeable. Repair and replacement costs thus ran higher than would have been the case under a system that allowed for economies of scale in the production and maintenance of oil industry supplies. Distributors were required to carry large inventories to satisfy a variety of customers accustomed to using many different types of materials for the same purposes. The lack of a good "fit" between producers and users—or, more generally, the existence of too many "fits" based on traditions established between specific supply companies and their particular clients in the industry—became increasingly troublesome as the industry grew larger and more diverse.

The obvious need in the oil industry, as in most other large industries, was to "standardize" the basic equipment used in the production of petroleum. In the years during and after World War I, the concept of standardization was making headway throughout the American economy. The word itself came to mean different things in different industries, but a student of the process in the 1920s offered a useful general definition: "Standardization is the selection and adoption, for general use, of materials, methods, processes, equipment, and practices, which experience and economic and scientific research prove to be the most economical."[65] This was not an easy process, for it required cooperation among all segments of an industry in systematically choosing standard products and methods, educating producers and users on the mutual advantages available through adoption of these standards, and then gaining the general use of standardized equipment. Individual operators in an industry had to recognize that temporary inconveniences encountered in standardizing equipment would be far outweighed by longrun benefits.

Such a task was a natural for trade associations, which became active in standardization throughout the economy after World War I. In many industries, the war effort sparked initial enthusiasm for this undertaking, for the work of the Conservation Division of the War Industries Board clearly demonstrated the advantages of reducing the diversity in design among essentially similar products. The wartime experience of the oil industry, however, brought few advances in standardization. Indeed, a major effort to pool the drilling equipment of numerous oil field supply houses to speed the drilling of new wells failed due to differences in the products of each manufacturer. This episode opened the eyes of many oil men to the need for greater uniformity in the production of oil field supplies, thus helping to prepare the way for standardization after the war.[66] With the end of hostilities, the Division of Simplification of the U.S. Department of Commerce took the place of the Conservation Division as the leading government advocate of standardization by assisting industry efforts in this direction. Such efforts were widespread, for standardization was in the air in the 1920s, a decade marked by the pursuit of increased efficiency in industry.

The initial impetus for standardization in the oil industry came from two organizations especially sensitive to the need for such changes. The first was the regional trade association for oil producers in the booming southwestern oil fields, the Mid-Continent Oil and Gas Association. Under the leadership of J. Edgar Pew, who was also an active member of the API, the Texas–Louisiana Division of this association set out in the early 1920s to study the need for standardization of drilling equipment in their region. Their investigation revealed a lack of uniformity of equipment, and it also reported the absence of any regular stock of drilling equipment capable of meeting the demands of the deeper drilling required to locate new deposits of oil in the southwestern oil fields. In the same region, a second organization, the Purchasing Agents Association of Tulsa, also pushed the standardization of oil field equipment. Purchasing agents were responsible for ordering materials for oil companies, and many of them previously had worked with supply firms in the industry. To eliminate the confusion and inefficiency they faced in their jobs, the purchasing agents took the lead in standardizing order catalogs, invoice forms, and, finally, some of the materials used in constructing drilling rigs. Yet the limited progress recorded by both of the organizations active in standardization in the southwestern region only pointed up the need for a more systematic national approach to this problem.[67]

When both organizations turned to the API for assistance, they found a receptive audience. At the third annual meeting of the API in December 1922, standardization dominated discussion. Included on the program were J. Edgar Pew, who reviewed the activities of the Mid-Continent Oil and Gas Association; a representative of the Division of Simplification of the U.S. Department of Commerce, who offered the government's aid in discovering "the true experts in industry itself to bring them together for mutual agreement; to support their findings with the full moral weight of a great Department";[68] and the secretary-treasurer of the Purchasing Agents Association of Tulsa, who summarized his organization's achievements before calling on the API to assert industry-wide leadership over standardization efforts:

> But, gentlemen of the Institute, our Association, with all the cooperation we have had, cannot carry this item of Standardization to a consummation. As purchasers, we are your employees. You, the executives of this industry, must have final say.[69]

These speeches all suggested that the next logical step was a national campaign run by an organization capable of reaching out to all segments of the industry.

The board of directors of the API took up this call, passing a resolution establishing a committee on standardization that included representatives of those organizations already active in the area. Even before the 1922 annual meeting, the API had become engaged in standardization work on a limited scale by sponsoring a meeting of manufacturers of cable tool drilling joints in Pittsburgh in May 1922. This meeting adopted a standard joint, and then appointed a committee "to work out the details" in connection with the adoption of this joint. The meeting included representatives of manufacturers active in both the eastern and the Oklahoma oil fields, and many of them voiced a strong sentiment that the API should adopt more formal procedures for arriving at standards and for securing their adoption. This committee on cable tool joints became one of four standardization committees established by the API at the 1922 annual meeting.[70]

Each of the four committees took responsibility for a general category of equipment, and each had the authority to set up regional subcommittees to help carry out its work. Overseeing the entire operation was a committee on standardization of the API's board of directors. As in most of its work, the API thus created a decentralized administrative structure for the management of its standardization program. This arrangement proved most effective in coordinating the work of hundreds of specialists from companies throughout the nation. Through its committees, the API could reach down into the industry and draw on the expertise of those most directly involved in each branch of the industry in each region. The operating experience of practical oil men and the scientific training of engineers employed by the individual companies could then be brought to bear on the common problem of setting standards. The moving force underlying this administrative arrangement was the voluntary effort of individuals in the industry, and the heaviest burden fell on such leaders as J. Edgar Pew, who made the standardization of oil field supplies a personal crusade.[71]

The procedure followed by the API's committees was simple, though time consuming. First, a likely area for standardization had to be identified. In creating the committees, the API's board of directors took pains to point out that standardization need not be synonymous with regimentation and to assure its members that it would avoid interfering with individual initiative. The API concentrated its efforts in areas where standardization would "meet with the practically unanimous approval of the producers of oil and the manufactures of equipment."[72] In such cases, the API committees coordinated the efforts of all affected in determining proper standards. In practice, this meant a survey of all existing equipment, tests by engineers on the quality of various products and designs, and lengthy discussions among producers and users on the results of these tests. After tentative standards had emerged from such discussions, the API circulated them for discussion throughout the industry. The revised standards were then officially passed by the API's board of directors, and goods produced in accordance with the standards carried an official API seal of approval. "Standard" did not mean static, since the adoption of new products and new methods was not generally delayed by existing standards on similar products. As soon as possible after their widespread adoption, the API standardized new products.[73]

To coordinate the activities of its various committees, the API created a division of standardization with a central office in Dallas, near the Mid-Continent fields. Directing the office was C. A. Young, who had been active in the early efforts to standardize oil field supplies while still an employee of a large oil supply firm. Young's office concentrated on helping the API committees in their work. Its small budget reflected the reliance of the entire API standardization program on the voluntary work of individuals employed in the industry and in government agencies such as the U.S. Bureau of Standards. The Dallas office also organized annual meetings attended by members from all of the various standardization committees and regional subcommittees. These midyear conferences provided a forum in which to define standards, with conflicting views resolved in sessions often lasting well into the night.[74] By the mid-1920s, the results of such meetings were widely available to the industry in numerous issues of the API *Bulletin* and in an API handbook that presented all defined standards in a readily available form.

The definition of standards, however, was only half of the job, for these standards had to be widely adopted by the industry before the benefits of the process could be reaped. The API faced the delicate task of persuading the industry to use standard products whenever possible without raising fears that it was overstepping its authority. The API recognized that the major manufacturers of oil field supplies and their most important customers would determine the early success of its program, and it sought to convince these firms to handle primarily standard products. Little persuasion was required in many cases, for the largest companies had generally taken a leading role in defining standards. The leaders of the various standardization committees furthered the cause with frequent appeals to their colleagues in the industry. J. Edgar Pew, for example, sent letters to the vice-presidents in charge of production of API member companies extolling the merits of the standards adopted for pipe and asking:

> If you could see fit, in placing your orders for new pipe, to make this your practice at the present time, it would help immensely in starting a better condition, I think, and one that will be helpful in your new work as in your old. I wish you would take this up with your Purchasing Department, and let us see if we cannot get this thing started off.[75]

Peer pressure within the industry reenforced such appeals, as those closely involved in establishing standards pressed for their quick adoption by fellow members of the API.

Although progress was often slower than Pew and others preferred, API standards on oil field supplies gradually came into general use. As a permanent and important part of the API's work, standardization proved to be of enduring value. Estimates of the actual savings in costs of materials due to standardization varied widely, but a conservative estimate of about 10 percent of the former cost of various goods seems justifiable. Indeed, J. Edgar Pew—admittedly a biased observer—held that "the standardization work of the Institute is the biggest saving arrangement we have had before the Institute, and this could not have been accomplished in any other manner."[76] Oil men came to recognize another major benefit in addition to reduced costs. The testing that went into the standardization process yielded superior products, such as higher quality drilling equipment which could reach previously unattainable depths. Such benefits probably would have come in time without the API's intervention, but as a national trade association active in all branches of the industry, the API was in an excellent position to hasten the adoption of standards.

Closely akin to the API's work in bringing about greater uniformity in the manufacture of oil tools was its effort to define a uniform system of accounting for the petroleum industry. A great deal of confusion resulted from the lack of standard accounting procedures before and during World War I, as each company kept its own accounts according to its particular traditions or needs: some companies used conservative systems that underestimated profitability; some others that sought to sell large quantities of stock to the public used methods that exaggerated profitability. Investors and tax collectors joined in the call for greater uniformity. The movement to standardize accounting practices in the oil industry thus had several goals: "first, to assist the oil companies in getting the best possible methods of accounting; and, second . . . to suggest a permanent method of accounting so that the public will have a proper yardstick with which to measure the value of the securities of the various companies."[77] In addition, some oil men feared that the government would step in to reform the industry's accounting practices in the absence of initiatives from the industry.

Recognizing a growing concern about existing accounting practices within its membership, the API established a Division of Accounting and Taxation in 1920 and hired an expert from within the industry, M. W. Mattison, to direct what was one of the first divisions of the API. Under Mattison's guidance the movement for standard methods of accounting in the oil industry gained momentum in the mid-1920s. At the annual meeting of the API in 1924, the board of directors authorized the creation of a committee on standardization of accounting methods, and this committee quickly went to work. It was organized along the lines of the other standardization committees, with regional groups coordinated by a central committee which was itself subject to the oversight of representatives from the board of directors. The accounting committees brought together the treasurers, accountants, and controllers from the largest oil companies. In its report on the activities of this committee, the *Oil and Gas Journal* accurately summarized the approach taken by the API to this and other tasks: "The practical accountants in the industry are the men to do the work . . . and the American Petroleum Institute will serve as a forum for their deliberations and will, in addition, give such assistance as it can."[78] After soliciting questions and comments from the industry through the API *Bulletin,* the accounting committee held numerous regional and national meetings to define the best available accounting methods for general use in the industry. The first result was the publication of an approved balance sheet in March 1926. Then came the publication of the committee's consensus on the best methods for keeping operating and income accounts. Before their adoption as API-approved standards, the committee's recommendations were revised after general comments from the industry and then approved by a vote of the API's board of directors.

The API's accounting standards encountered resistance from those segments of the industry that had traditionally attracted investors by using accounting methods that overstated profitability. Possessing no coercive power to force such concerns into line, the API relied on more subtle types of leverage to gain acceptance of its new standards. J. Edgar

Pew, then president of the API, advised Mattison to "push this home at once" after the board of directors approved the initial report of the accounting committee. Pew counseled Mattison to send copies of the approved standards to the Internal Revenue Service, the Federal Trade Commission, and the New York Stock Exchange and then to pay a personal visit to each place to describe their merits. He suggested further that Mattison request any company publishing a statement of its financial position to state that the report was made according to API standards and that the New York Stock Exchange should be persuaded to require a similar statement concerning the reports of all companies that it listed. Such a campaign for acceptance of the standards "would allow you to put the whole matter over with one knock-out punch, and would, if accomplished, serve to discredit forever some of the methods of accounting that are now in practice which are deluding the public."[79]

Mattison's committee clearly carried the early rounds in the fight for uniform accounting methods, primarily by gaining the acceptance of some of the largest oil companies in the late 1920s. The knockout did not come, however, until the intervention of the Security and Exchange Commission in the wake of a stock market crash that did as much to discredit traditional hit-or-miss accounting practices as the API's previous work had done to promote greater uniformity.

V. THE API AND THE CREATION OF COORDINATION

In accounting, as in standardization, fundamental research, the collection of statistics, public relations, and governmental affairs, the API thus took on much of the responsibility for organizing cooperative approaches to problems of industrywide concern. The somewhat awkward phrase "creating coordination" aptly describes the API's activities. After identifying a function best performed at the industry level, the API had to build a consensus for action among its members and then to fashion financial and administrative arrangements capable of addressing problems previously beyond the capacities of either private corporations or government agencies.

In addition to the major concerns discussed above, during its first decade of existence, the API's agenda included cooperative work with the Mid-Continent Oil and Gas Association to secure tax relief for the industry, joint research on motor fuel with the U.S. Bureau of Standards and the Automobile Chamber of Commerce, pathbreaking investigations of petroleum-related water pollution, and a sustained effort to secure low freight rates on petroleum products. In all of these areas, the API was the focal point for oil industry efforts to adjust to an increasingly complex economic and political environment.

The process of adjustment was by no means an easy one, for the API faced constraints from inside and outside the industry. Traditional tensions between the Standard Oil group and "independents" and between vertically integrated companies and those active in a single branch of the industry inevitably surfaced on many issues. The API had to overcome much inertia in convincing some companies that the old ways were not necessarily the best ways. Even when the industry agreed on the need for collective action, the API had to be certain to coordinate its activities with those of several expansive regional trade associations. While charting a course amid conflicting directions from the oil industry, the API's leaders also had to avoid drifting over a vaguely defined line separating legal and illegal cooperation. Prosecution for the violation of antitrust laws was a constant threat, despite the fact that the API avoided any activities that involved pricing. Even in the probusiness climate of the 1920s, the public image of "Big Oil" assured intense scrutiny of all major undertakings of the API. Such difficulties were to be expected when a new organization such as the API sought to define its role among established institutions.

In pursuit of a more efficient and orderly business environment, the early leaders of the API fashioned a versatile institution capable of creating coordination amid a diverse, competitive industry. Their "internal affairs" programs in the 1920s were a logical extension of the first organizational revolution in oil, for the API managed numerous tasks that were beyond the capabilities of the large vertically integrated oil companies that had emerged in the half century before World War I. At the same time, the API laid the foundation for a new generation of organizational change—one concerned primarily with the balancing of the needs of society and the needs of the private oil companies. As one of the first oil-related institutions to attempt to adjust to the changing "external environment" of the industry, the API led the way into areas of concern in business–government relations that have since become increasingly important.

NOTES AND REFERENCES

1. The best general work on the rise of the modern corporation is Alfred D. Chandler, Jr., *The Visible Hand: The Managerial Revolution in America* (Cambridge, Mass., 1977). For an excellent history of this process in the oil industry, see Ralph and Muriel Hidy, *Pioneering in Big Business* (New York, 1955).

2. An overview of this process of organizational change is suggested in Alfred Chandler and Louis Galambos, "The Development of Large-Scale Economic Organizations in Modern America," which originally appeared in the *Journal of American History* (Mar. 1980) and is reprinted in Edwin Perkins (ed.), *Men and Organizations* (New York, 1977), pp. 188–201.

3. Throughout most of the twentieth century, many such problems have gravitated

toward government agencies. The trade association movement in the 1920s, however, represented an effort to deal with many of these concerns through cooperation within industry. Neither the API in particular or trade associations in general have attracted much scholarly attention. For the API, see Leonard Fanning, *The Story of the American Petroleum Institute* (New York, 1959). For a history of one of the oldest trade associations, see Louis Galambos, *Competition and Cooperation: The Emergence of a National Trade Association* (Baltimore, 1966).

4. This summary of the history of the National Petroleum War Service Committee is taken from the records of the Oil Division of the Fuel Administration and from the records of the API. For more specific information, see A. C. Bedford to Mark Requa, letter dated Mar. 13, 1918, File No. 191 (A. C. Bedford), Oil Division—General File, Record Group 67, Records of the Fuel Administration, National Archives, Suitland, Maryland. (These files will be cited hereafter as "Oil Division—General Files.")

5. The goals stated in the charter were as follows:

(a) To afford a means of co-operation with the Government in all matters of national concern, in all lawful ways; and

(b) To foster foreign and domestic trade in American petroleum products; and

(c) To promote in general the interests of the petroleum industry in all its branches; and

(d) To promote the mutual improvement of its members and the study of the arts and sciences connected with the petroleum industry.

For the original charter, see "A.P.I. Board of Directors Minutes," volume 1, 1919–1929, p. 1, Office of the Secretary of the API, Washington, D.C. (These minutes will be cited hereafter as "API Board Minutes.")

6. Minutes of the API Petroleum Research Committee dated March 1, 1924, *Fundamental Research History, 1919–1927*, API Library, Washington, D.C.

7. Leonard Fanning, *The Story of the API*, p. 46.

8. O'Donnell, the first president of the API, was a California oil man who had served as Director of Production of the Fuel Administration. J. Edgar Pew spent much of his career in the Texas and Oklahoma oil fields, and he became a vice president of the Sun Oil Company.

9. For an account of Standard Oil's belated entry into public relations in the years before its dissolution in 1911, see Ralph and Muriel Hidy, *Pioneering and Big Business,* pp. 698–708.

10. The real and imagined abuses of the Standard Oil Trust had created a great deal of uneasiness about the power of "Big Oil," and the API encountered this sentiment in its formative years, when critics called it a tool of the Standard Oil interests.

11. These changes are described in detail in Harold Williamson, et al., *The Age of Energy* (Evanston, 1963).

12. An unpublished history of the U.S. Bureau of Mines is contained in the Records of the Bureau of Mines, Record Group 70, National Archives, Suitland, Maryland. See Box 37.

13. Mark Requa to L. P. St. Clair, telegram dated Feb. 21, 1918, File No. 2664 (F. J. Silsbee—personnel), Oil Division—General Files.

14. F. J. Silsbee to Mark Requa, letter dated July 8, 1918, File No. 2664 (Silsbee, F. J.), Oil Division—General Files.

15. For example, see F. J. Silsbee to Geo. S. Davidson, letter dated May 13, 1918, File No. 694 (Davidson, George), Oil Division—General Files.

16. Leonard Fanning, *The Story of the API*, p. 49.

17. Report of Mr. R. L. Welch to the Board of Directors of the API, Aug. 28, 1919. API Board Minutes, p. 36.

18. Ibid., p. 37.

19. Welch described his methods for assuring the secrecy of information from the member companies to representatives of the Federal Trade Commission in 1927. See, "Minutes of Meeting of API, FTC," dated Jan. 24, 1927, "API, Federal Trade Commission" folder, Box 39, J. Edgar Pew, Vice President files, Sun Oil Collection, Eleutherian Mills Historical Library, Wilmington, Delaware. (This collection will be cited hereafter as Sun Oil Collection.)

20. API *Bulletin,* February 16, 1922, p. 2. A complete set of these bulletins is available at the API Library, Washington, D.C.

21. "What Does the Institute Do?" an address by E. B. Reeser dated December 3, 1929, "American Petroleum Institute—1930" folder, Box 52, Administrative File—General Correspondence, Series 21-A, Sun Oil Collection.

22. API *Bulletin,* March 29, 1922, p. 1.

23. The preparation and presentation of such testimony became a time-consuming job for Welch. Much of his testimony was published in the *Bulletin,* and it is characterized by a tendency toward overkill; Welch's love of statistics expressed itself in detailed and even repetitious use of numbers.

24. For an account of the activities of the Federal Oil Conservation Board, see Gerald Nash, *United States Oil Policy, 1890–1964* (Pittsburgh, 1968), pp. 84–95.

25. API and Its Activities, volume 5, chapter 10, pp. 5 and 6. This study of the API's various activities was made to aid in the reorganizing of the institute in 1930. The Sun Oil Collection contains only a portion of the study. See Box 2, J. Howard Pew, Presidential-Private, Sun Oil Collection.

26. Ibid., p. 6.

27. API and Its Activities, volume 4, chapter 7, p. 6. While in Washington in 1933–1935, the API's statisticians worked with the Planning and Coordination Committee, a committee of oil men that advised the Petroleum Administrative Board on the enforcement of the NRA code in oil. See, for example, Minutes of the Planning and Coordination Committee, October 5, 1933, 10 A.M., Planning and Coordinating Committee Meetings, Records of the National Recovery Administration, Record Group 9, National Archives, Washington, D.C.

28. J. Howard Pew to R. L. Welch, letter dated August 21, 1919, "API . . . Admin. & Organiz. . . . Organization, Organization Policies, and Activities, Circulars & Correspondence, July–Dec. 1919," File 5995, shelf 9A, API Historical Records, API Library, Washington, D.C. For a general history of public relations, see Richard Tedlow, *Keeping the Corporate Image: Public Relations and Business, 1900–1950* (Greenwich, Conn.: JAI Press, 1979).

29. Leonard Fanning, *The Story of the API,* p. 60.

30. *Oil and Gas Journal,* Mar. 20, 1924.

31. L. M. Fanning, "How One Company Is Presenting Facts About Oil to the Public," *Oil and Gas Journal,* Aug. 7, 1924, p. 104.

32. J. Edgar Pew to R. L. Welch, letter dated May 19, 1924, in "Public Relations Committee, API" folder, Box 16, Administrative File—General Correspondence, Series 21-A, Sun Oil Collection.

33. A. C. Bedford to J. Edgar Pew, letter dated May 24, 1924, ibid.

34. J. Edgar Pew to J. Howard Pew, letter dated May 20, 1924, ibid.

35. For the operations of this committee in greater detail, see ibid.

36. The speeches of each expert and the question-and-answer sessions after each speech are printed in a booklet prepared for the committee and contained in the folder cited in note 32.

37. J. Edgar Pew to C. C. Herndon, letter dated April 30, 1925, "API, 1925" folder in Box 20, Administrative File—General Correspondence, Series 21-A, Sun Oil Collection.

38. J. Edgar Pew to J. Howard Pew, letter dated June 3, 1924, in folder cited in note 28.

39. Judson Welliver to J. Howard Pew, letter dated July 28, 1926, "1926 Public Relations Comm." folder in Box 25, Administrative File—General Correspondence, Series 21-A, Sun Oil Collection. Copies of all of the articles discussed in the text can be found in this folder and the one cited in note 32.

40. J. Howard Pew to J. Edgar Pew, letter dated Sept. 7, 1927, "Adm. Gen. API, 1927" folder in Box 25, Administrative File—General Correspondence, Series 21-A, Sun Oil Collection.

41. Leonard Fanning, "Proposed Activities for Division of Public Relations for 1928," undated memorandum, "Adm. Gen., 1928, PR Committee, API" folder in Box 35, Administrative File—General Correspondence, Series 21-A, Sun Oil Collection.

42. "Where Does My Mileage Go?" in "API-Public Relations" folder in Box 42, J. Edgar Pew—Vice Presidential File, Sun Oil Collection.

43. C. B. Ames (president of the API) to J. Howard Pew, letter dated Dec. 16, 1932, "Adm. Gen.-API-1932" folder, Box 65, Administrative File—General Correspondence, A-1932, Series 21-A, Sun Oil Collection.

44. B. H. Markham (director, APIC) to J. Howard Pew, letter dated Jan. 25, 1933, "Adm. General-API, 1933, APIC, 21-A-37" folder, Box 73, Administrative File—General Correspondence, API-1933, Series 21-A, Sun Oil Collection. See also, August Giebelhaus, *Business and Government in the Oil Industry: A Case Study of Sun Oil, 1876–1945* (Greenwich, Conn.: JAI Press, 1980), pp. 119–120.

45. The use of this phrase by the public relations staff at the API can be found in *API and Its Activities*, Chapter IX, pp. 2 and 3. This bound notebook is contained in Box 2, J. Howard Pew—Presidential-Private, Sun Oil Collection.

46. Writing in 1938, for example, one critic asserted that "the American Petroleum Institute early embarked on its practical function as a public relations or propaganda organization." See, William Kimnitzer, *Rebirth of Monopoly* (New York, 1938).

47. For background on the Standard Oil Development Company, see George Gibb and Evelyn Knowlton, *The Resurgent Years* (New York, 1956), pp. 520–531. Also, Henrietta Larson, Evelyn Knowlton, and Charles Popple, *New Horizons* (New York, 1971), pp. 150–153.

48. For a complete listing of the goals in the API's original charter, see note 5, above.

49. A copy of Manning's original proposal dated September 1919 is included in *Fundamental Research History, 1919 to 1927*. This is a bound collection of documents about the API's fundamental research program, and it is located in the API library, Washington, D.C. The document, which is entitled "Plan of Proposed Organization of the Division of Research and Statistics of the API," is over a hundred pages long, but most of these pages are simply letters of support from various people.

50. J. Howard Pew to R. L. Welch, letter dated Aug. 21, 1919 in "API . . . Admin. & Organiz. . . . Organization, Organization Policies, and Activities, Circulars & Correspondence, July–Dec. 1919" File 5995, Shelf 9A, API Historical Records.

51. J. W. Van Dyke to Van Manning, letter dated Nov. 4, 1919, Exhibit W, *Fundamental Research History, 1919 to 1927*.

52. Van Manning to Robert Welch, letter dated Nov. 25, 1919, "API . . . Admin. & Organiz. . . . Organization, Organization Policies, and Activities, Circulars and Correspondence, July–Dec. 1919" folder, File 5995, Shelf 9A, API Historical Records.

53. Van Manning to Robert Welch, letter dated Jan. 7, 1920, "API . . . Admin. & Organiz. . . . Organization, Organization Plans . . . Circulars and Correspondence . . . 1920" folder, File 5995, Shelf 9A, API Historical Records. Numerous replies from individual companies and researchers are also contained in this folder.

54. Van Manning to Woodrow Wilson, letter dated April 26, 1920, file 153.5, General Classified Files (1920), Records of the Bureau of Mines, Record Group 70, National Archives, Suitland, Maryland.

55. "Activities of the Division of Research, API Exhibit D, *Fundamental Research History, 1919–1927*.

56. Benjamin Brooks to Robert E. Wilson, letter dated Jan. 28, 1952, *Fundamental Research History, 1928–1953*. This is the second volume of bound documents on the history of the API's research program. It is located in the API Library, Washington, D.C.

57. For a summary of this research committee's work, see Benjamin Brooks to R. P. Anderson, letter dated Sept. 17, 1924, *Fundamental Research History, 1919–1927*. The same source contains notes from the first meeting of the committee.

58. Van Manning to Walter Teagle, letter dated January 28, 1925, file 022.173, General Classified Files (1925), Records of the U.S. Bureau of Mines. See also, Van Manning to Herbert Hoover, letter dated May 19, 1926, in the same file.

59. Frank Howard to Walter Teagle, letter dated Mar. 27, 1925, *Fundamental Research History, 1919–1927*.

60. The original letter from Rockefeller establishing the grant is included in *Fundamental Research History, 1919–1927*. The exact procedure by which the plan was presented to Rockefeller is difficult to reconstruct from existing sources. In various places, credit for persuading Rockefeller to make the grant is given to J. C. Donnell, Frank Howard, and Walter Teagle. The Universal Oil Products Company was a leader in the development of new techniques to increase the yield of gasoline in the refining process. Its grant apparently was unsolicited and came as a surprise to the leaders of the API.

61. A description of all of the projects is contained in *Fundamental Research History, 1919–1927*. For a general review of the first years of the program, see R. P. Anderson, "Fundamental Research in Petroleum," *Oil and Gas Journal*, Apr. 19, 1928, pp. 154–155.

62. A. E. Pew, Jr. to Members of the Committee on Fundamental Research, letter dated Mar. 16, 1928, *Fundamental Research History, 1928–1953*.

63. The membership of both the Central Petroleum Committee and the API's advisory committee on fundamental research is listed in *Fundamental Research History, 1928–1953*. The same source contains minutes from many of their meetings.

64. Excellent summaries of the histories of Projects 6 and 37 are contained in the *Proceedings of the 32nd Annual Meeting of the API*, Chicago, Nov. 8–13, 1952. See J. Bennett Hill, "25 Years of API Research Project 6," pp. 183–189; Robert E. Wilson and J. K. Roberts, "Honors to API Project 37 Leadership," pp. 190–193. The API Library also contains bound volumes of documents about the operations of most of its research projects, including Nos. 6 and 37.

65. Joseph Henry Foth, *Trade Associations: Their Services to Industry* (New York, 1930), p. 153. Foth's book contains a good summary of the various activities of trade associations in the 1920s.

66. Joseph Foth, *Trade Associations*, pp. 154–155; also Leonard Fanning, *The Story of the API*, pp. 54–55.

67. For a summary of the activities that lead to the API deep involvement in standardization, see "Group Sessions on Standardization of Oil Field Equipment"; *Proceedings of the Third Annual Meeting, American Petroleum Institute*, St. Louis, Dec. 6–8, 1922.

68. William Durgin, "Simplification of Methods and the Value of Cooperation and Coordination by Industries—A Message from Herbert Hoover," *Proceedings of the Third Annual Meeting of the API*, pp. 58–63.

69. O. V. Borden, "What Has Been Done Toward Uniformity of Oil Drilling Methods and Equipment," *Proceedings of the Third Annual Meeting of the API*, pp. 66–69. For a review of the work of the Mid-Continent Oil and Gas Association, see J. Edgar Pew, "Mid-Continent Oil and Gas Association's Activities Regarding Pipe for Deep Well Drilling," *Proceedings of the Third Annual Meeting of the API*, pp. 68–74.

70. For the resolution of the board of directors, see Minutes of the Board of Directors Meeting, Dec. 21, 1922, API Board Minutes, p. 89. For a report on the Pittsburgh meeting, see API *Bulletin*, July 13, 1922, pp. 3 and 4.

71. For a description of this administrative arrangement and a listing of the membership of the committees, see API *Bulletin*, July 9, 1924, pp. 1–8; Oct. 31, 1924, pp. 1 and 2.

72. C. A. Young, "Thirty-Three Years of Standardization—of Oil Field Equipment," *The Drilling Contractor,* June 1951, pp. 55–58.

73. For example, when seamless pipe began to come into wide use in the late 1920s, the API's pipe standardization committee arranged a meeting for the manufacturers of such pipe for the establishment of standards for the new product. This episode and numerous others that reveal the inner workings of the API's standardization process are described in correspondence throughout the papers of J. Edgar Pew. Most of the standardization material is filed in separate folders marked "API" in J. Edgar Pew, Vice Presidential Papers, Sun Oil Collection (May 1976 Addition).

74. For a description of one of these midyear meetings, see *Oil and Gas Journal,* June 25, 1925, pp. 22, 23, and 115. For a lengthy report of the deliberations of the various standardization committees, see API *Bulletin,* Sept. 4, 1925.

75. J. Edgar Pew to W. W. Fondren, letter dated Jan. 5, 1926, "API, Nov 1925–Aug 1926" folder, API 1919–1926, Box 40, J. Edgar Pew, Vice Presidential Papers, Sun Oil Collection. Numerous similar letters can be found in J. Edgar Pew's papers.

76. J. Edgar Pew to J. Howard Pew, letter dated September 17, 1927, "Adm. General, API, 1927" folder, A-1926, Box 25, Administrative File—General Correspondence, Series 21-A, Sun Oil Collection. For a summary of the benefits of standardization, see J. Edgar Pew, "Large Saving from Standardization," *Oil and Gas Journal,* Dec. 1, 1927, p. 152.

77. J. Edgar Pew to E. R. Brown (President—Magnolia Refining Company), letter dated Oct. 24, 1927, "API—Standardization Cte.—Uniform Accounting" folder, API, Box 42, J. Edgar Pew, Vice Presidential Papers, Sun Oil Collection.

78. *Oil and Gas Journal,* Jan. 29, 1925, pp. 144, 146; Mar. 18, 1926, pp. 78, 80, 82; Aug. 11, 1927, pp. 156, 158. For the announcement of the creation of the API's Committee on Uniform Methods of Accounting, see API *Bulletin,* Apr. 15, 1925, pp. 1–2. Also, API *Bulletin,* Oct. 4, 1927, pp. 7–8.

79. Edgar Pew to M. W. Mattison, letter dated Dec. 11, 1926, "API—Standardization Cte.—Uniform Accounting" folder, API, Box 42, J. Edgar Pew, Vice Presidential Papers, Sun Oil Collection.

The Political Economy of Banking Regulation, 1864–1933

The laws and regulations that shaped the structure of the banking industry from the Civil War to the Great Depression were strongly influenced by the banking community. In this period legal constraints on banks were weakened by competition between state and federal regulators trying to increase membership in their banking systems. The elimination of regulation was not completed, however, because the politically most powerful group in the industry, the unit banks, had an interest in preserving some regulations.

N ATIONAL money and capital markets gradually emerged in the United States from the integration of regional markets and the circumvention of regulatory constraints imposed on financial intermediaries.[1] Regulation of the banking industry created a number of impediments to the formation of these markets. Although economic historians have examined the effects of this regulation, they have not given much attention to the economic and political forces that shaped its evolution. Changes in banking regulation were the product of protracted political struggles among different interest groups seeking to influence the structure of the industry. In this paper, the evolution of banking regulation from the Civil War to the Great Depression is analyzed by examining the actions of the three interested parties: the banks, the public, and the government regulators. These were not homogeneous groups but were categorized by divergent economic interests. Influence thus depended on the political coalitions that arose. The most effective political coalition that emerged was formed by the smaller unit banks. The durability of some banking laws and changes in others in this period are largely explained by the considerable influence wielded by these banks.

Journal of Economic History, Vol. XLII, No. 1 (March 1982). © The Economic History Association. All rights reserved. ISSN 0022-0507.

The author is Assistant Professor of Economics, Rutgers University, New Brunswick, New Jersey 08903. Helpful comments on an earlier draft were received from Hugh Rockoff and Richard Keehn.

[1] Studies of the development of American money and capital markets include: Lance Davis, "The Investment Market, 1870–1914: The Evolution of a National Market," this JOURNAL, 25 (Sept. 1965), 355–99; Richard E. Sylla, *The American Capital Market, 1846–1914* (New York, 1975); John A. James, *Money and Capital Markets in Postbellum America* (Princeton, 1978); Richard H. Keehn, "Market Power and Bank Lending: Some Evidence from Wisconsin, 1870–1900," this JOURNAL, 40 (March 1980), 45–52.

THE DUAL BANKING SYSTEM

The point of departure from which opposing interests vied with one another to influence regulation was the establishment of the National Banking System. Created by the National Banking Act of 1864, this system disrupted the existing balance of forces shaping the regulatory environment and restructured the banking industry. The Office of Comptroller of the Currency was established and given authority to charter national banks that were permitted to issue banknotes backed by government bonds. Most banks were induced to join the new system when Congress levied a 10 percent tax on all non-national banknotes. The National Banking Act also regulated the size and activity of national banks by imposing minimum capital and reserve requirements, restricting real estate loans, and prohibiting branching.[2]

These barriers to entry and constraints on banking activity prevented the supply of banking services from keeping pace with the demand as the country grew and expanded westward. The lack of adequate banking facilities was particularly acute in agricultural areas where communities were not large enough to support a minimum size national bank. The unfulfilled demand for more banking services stimulated the public to press for currency and banking reform. Although most agrarian agitation focused on the issue of silver monetization, business emphasized the lack of banking facilities in addition to monetary reform. At the 1897 Indianapolis Monetary Convention, dominated by Midwestern businessmen, it was resolved that the lack of adequate banking facilities should be met by "a diminution of the minimum capital required for banks in places of small population and authority for the establishment of branch banks."[3]

This demand for more bank offices was answered by the states, which began to pass "free banking" laws in the late 1880s and 1890s. These laws permitted new banks to incorporate under general legal provisions instead of requiring them to obtain special charters from the state legislatures. This change made entry into the banking industry much easier.[4] To ensure the attractiveness of the reorganized state systems, the state legislatures required banks to conform to regulations less restrictive than those imposed on national banks. Thus, the Comptroller of the Currency's 1895 survey of state legislation found that all but two states' minimum capital requirements were lower, few imposed any restrictions on their banks' real estate loans, and only sixteen states had reserve requirements.[5] Given this incentive structure, it is not surpris-

---

[2] For a more detailed description of state and federal banking regulations, see Eugene Nelson White, *The Regulation and Reform of American Banking, 1900–1929* (Princeton, forthcoming), Chap. 1.

[3] Quoted in Sylla, *The American Capital Market*, p. 71.

[4] James, *Money and Capital Markets*, pp. 233–34.

[5] *Annual Report of the Comptroller of the Currency* (Washington, D.C., 1895).

ing that national banks grew very slowly from 3,484 in 1890 to 3,731 in 1900, while state-chartered banks increased from 2,534 to 4,405.[6] The federal government had sought to monopolize the regulation of banking, but the short supply of banking services drew the states back into the business of chartering banks, breathing life into the dual banking system.

REGULATORY COMPETITION

Confronted by vigorous competition from state banking authorities chartering new banks and trust companies and faced with strong public pressure, federal officials moved to improve the attractiveness of national bank charters. The Comptrollers of the Currency in the early 1890s were favorably disposed towards legislation that would permit some form of branching to increase banking facilities in rural areas. In 1895, Secretary of the Treasury John Carlisle and President Cleveland both recommended that national banks be allowed to branch.[7] When the unit banks in small towns and rural areas realized that their profitable position and perhaps even their independence was threatened by branching that would allow the larger city banks to reach out into their territory, they rallied to oppose these proposals. Their cause was taken up by Charles Dawes who became Comptroller in 1898. He helped to kill a bill in Congress that would have allowed some branching; in its place, he promoted lower capital requirements to increase the number of rural bank offices.[8] Congress accepted this proposal, and the Gold Standard Act of 1900 allowed national banks with a capital of $25,000 to be established in towns of fewer than 3,000 inhabitants.

The state banking authorities quickly recognized the effect this federal law might have on applications for state charters. By the time of the next survey of state banking laws in 1909, all but one state (Massachusetts) that had minimum capital requirements above the new federal level had reduced their requirements to maintain their advantage.[9] State banking authorities were not anxious to see the number or proportion of institutions under their control decline, the public wanted more bank offices, and the country unit bankers did not want to see the introduction of intrastate branching. This political alignment of interests virtually ensured that reductions in capital requirements would be the predominant legislative response to the insufficient supply of banking services. The result of lower state and federal minimum capital require-

---

[6] Data on the national banks came from the *Annual Report of the Comptroller of the Currency* (Washington, D.C., various years). The series on state banks was obtained from George Barnett, *State Banks and Trust Companies* (Washington, D.C., 1910).

[7] *Annual Report of the Comptroller of the Currency* (Washington, D.C., 1896), pp. 103–04.

[8] Gerald C. Fisher, *American Banking Structure* (New York, 1968), pp. 27–28.

[9] Samuel A. Welldon, *Digest of State Banking Statutes* (Washington, D.C., 1909).

ments and buoyant economic conditions before the First World War was a rapid growth of small banks. The number of national banks rose to 7,518 in 1914 while the number of state banks climbed to 14,512. The anti-branching lobby was further strengthened by these new and often very small financial institutions.

The changes in banking regulation rendered by the Federal Reserve Act of 1913 did not attempt to alter the structure of the banking system; the aim instead was to make membership in the new Federal Reserve System sufficiently attractive to draw in state banks. Reserve requirements were cut, restrictions on real estate loans were reduced, and members could obtain loans from the discount window. The states proved to be obdurate competitors. Many legislatures refused initially to pass legislation enabling state banks to become members of the Federal Reserve, and by 1915 fifteen states had reacted to the reduction of member reserve requirements by lowering their requirements. The Federal Reserve Board criticized the states, but it did not rely on moral suasion alone. In 1921, it secured a further reduction of member reserve requirements. The states reacted to this change; by 1928, 12 states had again reduced their reserve requirements.[10]

The economic theory of regulation provides a general framework for analyzing these regulatory changes. This theory posits that regulation is a good for which there is an active market. Favorable regulation will be supplied to the individuals or groups that have valued it most by voting and lobbying the government.[11] Direct evidence of bankers' influence on legislatures is difficult to find. It does appear, however, that when bankers argued strongly for or against a piece of legislation they could sway the legislature. In New Jersey, the state bankers association had a legislative committee that drew up bills to be presented to the state assembly, and the association tried to organize its members so that they would present a united front at hearings on banking legislation in Trenton. Most legislation proposed by the association was passed with few alterations.[12] The California Bankers Association also had a legislative committee that conferred regularly with the superintendent of banks before each session to discuss possible changes in the Banking Act. The superintendent usually heeded their counsel; the legislature, in turn, was inclined to accept the advice of the superintendent.[13]

The economic theory of regulation typically views regulation as being supplied by a monopoly producer and being demanded by a competing

[10] *Federal Reserve Bulletin* (Washington, D.C., November 1928), pp. 778–805.

[11] George Stigler, "The Theory of Economic Regulation," *Bell Journal of Economics*, 2 (Spring 1971), 3–21; Sam Peltzman, "Toward a More General Theory of Regulation," *Journal of Law and Economics*, 19 (August 1976), 221–40.

[12] Edwin W. Kemmerer, "New Jersey Banking, 1902–1927," *Journal of Industry and Finance* (May 1928), 28–30.

[13] Shirley D. Southworth, *Branch Banking in the United States* (New York, 1928), pp. 36–37.

public. One of the key characteristics of the American banking system, however, has been the absence of such a monopoly regulator. The federal and state governments have instead competed with one another to regulate banks. It has been argued that rivalry between regulators will lead to a dilution and finally an elimination of regulatory constraints.[14] This hypothesis is clearly supported by the gradual weakening in capital and reserve requirements and portfolio restrictions—which most banks favored. But what needs to be explained is why the restrictions on branch banking remained virtually unchanged. The branching issue divided the banking community. The unit bankers, particularly those in small towns and rural areas, were opposed to any changes in the branching laws. They had an important stake in maintaining the existing banking structure and feared that the city banks would penetrate their markets. The unit bankers when threatened were able to exert considerable political pressure. The reform legislation that came out of the Congress clearly reflected the interests of the unit bankers, who formed the largest block in the banking community. There was no new provison for branching, and the decentralized character of the Federal Reserve System was aimed at preventing the "monopolistic interest" from gaining control.

THE BRANCHING ISSUE

At times the regulatory competition led to serious consideration of increased branch banking. The federal authorities wanted to permit branching by national banks to increase the number of bank offices, meet the public's demand for banking services, enlarge existing national banks, and prevent national banks from switching to state charters to obtain limited branching privileges. Support for increased branching also was found in some parts of the banking community. Led by A. P. Giannini of the Bank of America, the larger banks that lobbied hard for more branching believed that it would enhance their position in the industry, increase the efficiency of money markets, and strengthen the banking system. Loopholes for branching by national banks appeared in the National Bank Consolidation Act of 1918 and some of the rulings of the Comptroller of the Currency, but the opportunities for national bank branching nonetheless remained limited.[15]

In the few states in which the law allowed state banks to open additional offices, branching grew rapidly. Nationwide, branch offices as a percentage of all bank offices rose from 5.7 percent in 1920 to 15.7

[14] Jack Hirschleifer, "Comment," *Journal of Law and Economics,* 14 (August 1976), 241–44; and Richard B. McKenzie and Hugh H. Macaulay, "A Bureaucratic Theory of Regulation," *Public Choice,* 35 (1980), 297–313.

[15] Ross M. Robertson, *The Comptroller and Bank Supervision: A Historical Appraisal* (Washington, D.C., 1968), pp. 101–05.

percent in 1930, and the share of branching banks, loans and investments in total loans and investments increased from 18.6 percent to 45.5 percent.[16] These rapid changes prompted the unit bankers to take defensive action by seeking state anti-branching legislation. In 1909, 26 states had no statutory prohibition of branch banking, but when branches began to appear the unit bankers were able to obtain anti-branching laws from state legislatures in all but seven of these states.[17]

In most southern and western states where unit banking was well established, the state bankers associations became the vehicles for the opposition to branching. In Kansas, Illinois, Iowa, Minnesota, Nebraska, and South Dakota, the state bankers associations attacked branching and the bills they sent to their state legislatures to prohibit branching were accepted. In other states such as California where branch banking was already very strong, the unit bankers formed their own separate associations. The California League of Independent Bankers tried to arouse the public to what it perceived as the dangers of branching by playing on their fears of monopoly control. The association's organ, *The Independent Banker*, argued that "the public is more interested in the democratic decentralization of credit control than it is in the progressively concentrative and autocratic control of credit."[18] This populist theme was echoed by the local press. The *San Bernadino Sun* warned that the country customer would become only a numbered account, "a slave, lashed to the chariot of metropolitan control."[19] Although this campaign failed to make any headway in California, it was very successful in areas where branching was unknown or unfamiliar. In a 1924 Illinois referendum the public rejected by a two-to-one vote a law to permit branching, and thereby protected themselves and their local unit banks from the moguls of the big city.[20]

In Congress the unit bankers were able to thwart most efforts of federal officials and the larger banks to obtain legislation allowing full-service branching by national banks. When in 1927 the McFadden Act finally conceded some branching privileges, it was limited to resolving the problem of the inequality between member banks.

Branch banking did expand in the twenties, but only in a few states. No coalition to fight for branching appeared. Compared to the large number of country bankers, there were relatively few bankers in favor of branching, and they were divided among themselves. The largest banks supported nationwide branching while regionally strong banks

[16] Board of Governors of the Federal Reserve System, *Banking and Monetary Statistics, 1914–1941* (Washington, D.C., 1943), p. 297.
[17] Frederick A. Bradford, *The Legal Status of Branch Banking in the United States* (New York, 1940).
[18] Quoted in Southworth, *Branch Banking*, pp. 70–71.
[19] *Ibid.*, pp. 71–72.
[20] *Ibid.*, p. 17.

favored trade-area or statewide branching. Although business and the public bore the costs of a less-than-optimal banking structure, these costs were diffuse. This diffusion of costs impeded the formation of a pro-branching lobby. On the other hand the unit country bankers were keenly aware that they would bear the costs of increased branching. Their perceived common interest made the unit bankers a cohesive group capable of erecting legal barriers to further expansion of branching banks.

THE GREAT DEPRESSION AND BANKING REGULATION

The massive bank failures of the 1930s initially sapped the strength of the unit bankers' lobby by thinning their ranks and discrediting their policies. Several states that previously had forbidden branching altered their laws to enable surviving banks to acquire defunct banks' offices. The Federal Reserve and some influential members of Congress thought that it was an appropriate time to establish a uniform system of banking regulation and to allow freer branching. The first drafts of reform bills would have allowed statewide or trade-area branching; the unit bankers, however, regrouped to fight the federal regulators and the pro-branching bankers in Congressional hearings and behind the scenes. In this struggle, the unit bankers received some support from state regulators who were loath to see the federal authorities assume more control over the chartering and regulation of banks. The unit bankers were successful in their efforts and blocked the more radical changes; the Banking Act of 1933 conceded to Federal Reserve member banks only the same branching privileges as those allowed by state law.[21] The unit bankers, however, were able to achieve this success only because deposit insurance presented a quick, apparently viable alternative that would safeguard the banking system. The small town bankers always had looked favorably upon deposit insurance as a means to protect them from failure, and a few states had experimented with deposit guarantee funds after the panic of 1907.[22] Federal deposit insurance previously had failed to make any headway in Congress because of the intransigent opposition of the city bankers who lobbied vigorously against it, fearing they would end up subsidizing the smaller banks and paying for their mistakes. This impasse was broken after the banking panics when the public was moved to whole-hearted support of deposit insurance. *Vox populi* and the unit bankers formed a formidable political coalition that led Congress to create the Federal Deposit Insurance Corporation, an

[21] Helen M. Burns, *The American Banking Community and New Deal Banking Reforms, 1933–1935* (Westport, Connecticut, 1974), chapters 3 and 4.
[22] Eugene N. White, "State-Sponsored Insurance of Bank Deposits in the United States, 1907–1929," this JOURNAL, 41 (September 1981).

innovation that weakened the previous sense of urgency to modify federal statutes regulating branching.

CONCLUSION

During the Civil War when Congress chose to rely on economic incentives rather than coercion to draw banks into its regulatory system, it unintentionally set the stage for the emergence of competitive state regulators. Although the federal government faced only one regulator in each state, it could not obtain a monopolistic settlement because the number of state banking authorities and legislatures made nationwide cooperation difficult if not impossible.

The competitive reduction of regulations benefited many banks, but the greatest advantage accrued to the unit bankers whose influence was strengthened by the increase in new unit banks. The unit bankers' actions were largely defensive, but what they lacked in terms of leadership or a program they made up in brute political clout. This was not a result of their relative economic importance in the industry. By any conventional measure of banking power their importance was declining at the time they were able to secure many state anti-branching statutes. Their influence may be attributed to their presence in most rural and many urban areas, a presence that gave them a broad political base from which to influence Congress and the state legislatures. Many Americans were intensely suspicious of large banks and thus tended to support local independent banks because they feared the spread of branching into their communities. The unit bankers also found influential allies among state banking authorities who distrusted the aggrandizing tendencies of the federal regulators. The state regulators had an obvious stake in preserving the dual banking system, as did the smaller banks which preferred the looser constraints of the states' banking laws and recognized that these were a product of regulatory rivalry. The elimination of state charters would have left them facing a single federal regulatory agency much more difficult to influence.

From their advantageous political position, the dominant coalition of unit bankers was able to withstand the depression and rapid changes in the banking industry that favored the growth of large branching banks. Rivalry between the state and federal regulators weakened most banking regulations and helped to facilitate the integration of money and capital markets. But the substantial legal impediments to branch banking remained largely unchanged at the behest of the unit bankers. They had the most to lose by drastic changes in regulation and they worked strenuously to influence banking laws. Owing to these efforts the unit bankers largely succeeded in maintaining those regulations they regarded as necessary for their survival.

ACKNOWLEDGMENTS

Beaver, Daniel R. "Newton D. Baker and the Genesis of the War Industries Board, 1917–1918." *Journal of American History* 52 (1965): 43–58. Reprinted with the permission of the *Journal of American History*. Courtesy of Yale University Sterling Memorial Library.

Brandes, Joseph. "Product Diplomacy: Herbert Hoover's Anti-Monopoly Campaign at Home and Abroad." In Ellis W. Hawley, ed., *Herbert Hoover as Secretary of Commerce: Studies in New Era Thought and Practice* (Iowa City, IA: University of Iowa Press, 1981): 185–216. Reprinted with the permission of the University of Iowa Press. Courtesy of Yale University Sterling Memorial Library.

Childs, William R. "Origins of the Texas Railroad Commission's Power to Control Production of Petroleum: Regulatory Strategies in the 1920s." *Journal of Policy History* 2 (1990): 353–87. Copyright 1990 by the Pennsylvania State University. Reproduced by permission of the Pennsylvania State University Press. Courtesy of Yale University Sterling Memorial Library.

Davis, G. Cullom. "The Transformation of the Federal Trade Commission, 1914–1929." *Mississippi Valley Historical Review* 49 (1962): 437–55. Courtesy of Yale University Sterling Memorial Library.

Flint, Sam Hall. "The Great Freight Rate Fight." *Atlanta Historical Journal* 28 (1984): 5–22. Reprinted with the permission of the Atlanta Historical Society. *Atlanta Historical Journal* is now *Atlanta History: A Journal of Georgia and the South*. Courtesy of the Atlanta Historical Society.

Galambos, Louis. "The Trade Association Movement in Cotton Textiles, 1900–1935." *Explorations in Entrepreneurial History* 2 (1964): 31–55. Reprinted with the permission of *Explorations in Entrepreneurial History*. Courtesy of *Explorations in Entrepreneurial History*.

Harper, R. Eugene. "Wilson Progressives vs. DuPont: Controversy in Building the Nitro Plant." *West Virginia History* 48 (1989): 93–107. Reprinted with the permission of the Cultural Center, Department of Education and the Arts, Archives and History. Courtesy of the Cultural Center.

Hawley, Ellis W. "Herbert Hoover and the Sherman Act, 1921–1933: An Early Phase of a Continuing Issue." *Iowa Law Review* 74 (1989): 1067–1103. Reprinted with the permission of the *Iowa Law Review*. Courtesy of Yale University Law Library.

Himmelberg, Robert F. "Business, Antitrust Policy, and the Industrial Board of the Department of Commerce, 1919." *Business History Review* 42 (1968): 1–23. Reprinted with the permission of the Harvard Business School. Courtesy of Yale University Sterling Memorial Library.

Himmelberg, Robert F. "President Hoover, Organized Business, and the Antitrust Laws: A Study in Hooverian Ideology and Policy." In *Herbert Hoover Reassessed: Essays Commemorating the Fiftieth Anniversary of the Inauguration of Our Thirty-First President,* Senate Document No. 96–63 (1981): 123–44. Reprinted with the permission of Schenkman Publishing. Courtesy of Yale University Seeley G. Mudd Library.

Himmelberg, Robert F. "The War Industries Board and the Antitrust Question in November 1918." *Journal of American History* 52 (1965): 59–74. Reprinted with the permission of the *Journal of American History.* Courtesy of Yale University Sterling Memorial Library.

Johnson, William R. "Herbert Hoover and the Regulation of Grain Futures." *Mid-America* 51 (1969): 155–74. Reprinted with the permission of Loyola University. Courtesy of Yale University Sterling Memorial Library.

Kane, N. Stephen. "Corporate Power and Foreign Policy: Efforts of American Oil Companies to Influence United States Relations with Mexico, 1921–1928." *Diplomatic History* 1 (1977): 170–98. Reprinted with the permission of *Diplomatic History.* Courtesy of Yale University Sterling Memorial Library.

Kerr, K. Austin. "Decision for Federal Control: Wilson, McAdoo, and the Railroads, 1917." *Journal of American History* 54 (1967): 550–60. Reprinted with the permission of the *Journal of American History.* Courtesy of Yale University Sterling Memorial Library.

Nordhauser, Norman. "Origins of Federal Oil Regulation in the 1920s." *Business History Review* 47 (1973): 53–71. Reprinted with the permission of the Harvard Business School. Courtesy of Yale University Sterling Memorial Library.

Pratt, Joseph A. "Creating Coordination in the Modern Petroleum Industry: The American Petroleum Institute and the Emergence of Secondary Organizations in Oil." *Research in Economic History* 8 (1982): 179–215. Reprinted with the permission of JAI Press, Inc. Courtesy of Yale University Sterling Memorial Library.

White, Eugene Nelson. "The Political Economy of Banking Regulation, 1864–1933." *Journal of Economic History* 42 (1982): 33–40. Reprinted with the permission of Cambridge University Press. Courtesy of Yale University Sterling Memorial Library.